Indonesian Political Thinking

1945–1965

INDONESIAN POLITICAL THINKING

1945–1965

Edited by HERBERT FEITH
and LANCE CASTLES

CORNELL UNIVERSITY PRESS

ITHACA AND LONDON

This volume was prepared under the auspices of the Asian Literature Program of The Asia Society, New York.

Copyright © 1970 by Cornell University

First published 1970

Standard Book Number 8014–0531–9

Library of Congress Catalog Card Number 69–18357

PRINTED IN THE UNITED STATES OF AMERICA
BY THE COLONIAL PRESS INC.

Preface

The writing of outsiders about contemporary Indonesia often prompts the response: "Yes, but what do Indonesians themselves say?" The objection may be dismissed as naive if the implication is that a single Indonesian view must exist and be somehow the right one. But it is worth taking very seriously if the intended message is that, in the name of academic detachment, "interior" views of political affairs are often taken too lightly, for it is clear that no "exterior" or detached view of a country's political affairs can be satisfactory unless it is based on a great deal of understanding of the "interior" views of the people concerned, actors and audience alike.

The aim of this book is to provide such interior views through a series of vignettes. We would like to show how the flow of events in the first twenty years of Indonesian independence was perceived by those most concerned to explain it, to show how particular controversies looked to those involved in them, and to describe the clusters of ideological orientation in which the different patterns of perception were to be found.

In order to make this volume useful as a documentary record, we have sought to represent the most influential political thinking of the twenty-year period it covers; but we have also tried wherever possible to select political thinking that is impressive for its quality.

Hence there is great variety here. Our material comes from dailies and weeklies, party monthlies and cultural quarterlies, from speeches, lectures, books, pamphlets, and orders of the day. The range is from reflective essays bearing the marks of Fromm or Shils to impassioned manifestoes of rebels writing from mountain hideouts.

It was not easy to combine the two principles of selection. Much of the intellectually powerful political writing of the period had very little influence. Conversely, some of the period's most influential ideas were never presented except in the most hackneyed and sloganistic forms. We were often able to find extracts which struck us as both intellectually impressive and representative of the views of wider groups, but this was not possible in all cases. Thus, some selections have little value other than that of representing a widely held view of a particular problem, whereas others are of intrinsic quality but low on the count of representativeness.

The fact that we have generally been able to find pieces which satisfy us as regards both quality and representativeness is partly a reflection of our own notions of what constitutes quality in political thinking. For us the quality of a set of political ideas is determined in good part by its vividness in a particular cultural context, that is, its capacity to speak meaningfully and evocatively to particular communities and provide their members with clearly comprehensible maps of their political environment. Vividness in this sense is not our only criterion of quality, but it is an important one, alongside such others as scope, penetration, self-consistency, and subtlety.

As we see it, it would be quite inappropriate to judge an Indonesian political thinker—or a political thinker, in this sense of the word, anywhere—by the standards appropriate to the world of scholarship. An Indonesian physicist or biologist should properly be judged by the standards of the international scholarly community and tested for such qualities as originality and analytical power. The same can be said for an Indonesian economist and, indeed, for an Indonesian political scientist, inasmuch as he is writing for an international audience of scholars and is seeking to be detached in relation to value conflicts in his own country. But an Indonesian political thinker, whose work is addressed to fellow members of his own society and whose concern is to set and clarify goals as much as to explain what is happening, must be viewed against measuring sticks of a different kind. One must indeed ask, "How broad, clear, and penetrating is his grasp of the political world about him?"; but one must also ask, "How true is he to the traditions to which he appeals?" and "Do his words have the power to convince and inspire the audience to which they are addressed?" *

---

* Our perspective here, one of looking to the creative aspects of ideological thinking, is partly derived from, and beautifully elaborated in, two very different but equally outstanding essays: Clifford Geertz's "Ideology as a Cultural System," in David E. Apter, ed., *Ideology and Discontent* (Glencoe, Ill.: Free Press, 1963), and Ben Anderson's "The Languages of Indonesian Politics," *Indonesia* (Ithaca, N.Y.), No. 1 (April 1966), pp. 89–116.

In this volume we have reproduced very little detached political writing, though some of what was written in our period, both academic analyses and reflective essays, is of a high standard. The quality material we have been collecting is material intended to persuade, whether at a mass level or at the level of a small intellectual stratum in the cities. Our search has been for political thinking which comprehends and explains the most important aspects of the socio-political environment while it remains intelligible, or at least is easily made intelligible, to large numbers of the politically active (among whom the educated young are of central importance). It had to be neither simplistic in a way which shuts off perception of major facets of political life nor so complex as to be the peculiar preserve of sophisticates. And it had to make sense of a fairly large range of phenomena in the world of modern politics while having the appeal which comes from overt or latent links with traditional explanatory categories and prescriptions.

The search for representativeness brought us up against a variety of problems. How much weight would we give to currents of political thinking which were influential among intellectuals or among the one to four million people who regularly read newspapers but not among the population at large? It seemed important not to weight the volume too heavily in favor of these currents, but we felt we could not take the political sympathies of the population at large as our only measuring stick. A closely related problem was presented by particular ideological groupings whose leaders were far more articulate than those of others; we had to be careful not to overrepresent these. Then, there was the problem of rapid change. Many of the pieces we decided to choose as representative of particular groups present the thinking of those groups at particular points of time rather than over the period as a whole. Here we could do little more than point this out in the notes accompanying particular extracts.

We sought, as far as possible, to include pieces by all the main political thinkers of the period, but this was sometimes difficult to do without including selections which were quite uncharacteristic of these men's thinking. There were the inevitable dilemmas of long extracts versus many short ones and of uninterrupted ones versus excerpts strung together by dots. Moreover, our self-imposed terminal date of October 1, 1965, presented us with problems. Having finished our work on the volume in early 1968, we have been tempted to include material written in the intervening years. We resisted this temptation in all except three instances where special factors seemed to justify our succumbing.

Finally, there were dilemmas to do with the choice between atmosphere and ideas. Our original plan was to put a great deal of emphasis on the atmosphere, style, and flavor of politics. To this end we collected material from novels, short stories, satirical essays, and films, and from the avidly read "corner columns" of the dailies, in which the posturings of political leaders are mercilessly debunked. But we eventually decided that material of this kind would so add to the heterogeneity of the collection as to make it quite unwieldy. So, while we have tried to preserve as much of the original atmosphere as possible in the pieces we have translated, our principal focus has been on political ideas rather than political atmosphere and on the formal and affirmative rather than the casual and cynical expressions of these ideas.

It is not for us to say how representative we have succeeded in making our collection. It would be surprising if our attachment to particular pieces and particular styles of thought and our friendship with particular writers had not affected our choices. Indeed, our attempt to be representative is necessarily based on subjective notions of the relative importance of particular groupings; and subjectivity certainly enters even more fully into our search for quality. In addition, we may well be vulnerable to the charge, which Indonesians often lay against Westerners, of concentrating on the variety and conflict in the Indonesian scene at the expense of the unity. In any case, here are our selections. Let us hope that Indonesian political thinkers will take issue with us on the picture we have presented.

A large number of colleagues and friends have helped us to produce this collection, arguing with us about the organization of the material, going out of their way to find a particular extract they thought we should include, or commenting at length on the book's Introduction or the introductory notes to particular sections. We thank them all, and particularly Soedjatmoko, Onghokham, Ben Anderson, and Jamie Mackie, who provided us with a steady flow of ideas and criticism throughout the project. They have, of course, no responsibility for the final selection. We are also most grateful to those who helped us with translations: L. F. Brakel, Carmel Budiardjo, Glenda Felton, Martha Logsdon, and especially Stuart Graham and Alan Smith. Alan Smith and Buyung Tanisan also did a great deal of research on a variety of small points. Mrs. Bonnie R. Crown of the Asia Society, New York, gave us moral support at every turn and indulgence over a whole series of unkept deadlines. Not least important are the contributions of Mrs. I. M. Evans and Miss Bronwyn Newbold, who had to listen to our talk about deadlines while they typed and retyped our messy manuscripts.

H. F.
L. C.

February 1969

Contents

Contents xv

Indonesian Political Thinking

1945–1965

Introduction

By Herbert Feith

Modern Indonesian political thinking began with the rise of modern nationalism. It began in the 1900's and 1910's, with the coming into being of a small group of young students and intellectuals who saw the modern world as a challenge to their society and themselves as potential leaders of its regeneration. The men and women of this group saw their society as backward, enervated, and exploited, and talked questingly about its possible regeneration. In the 1920's their numbers grew fairly rapidly and so did their alienation from colonial authority; many of them, particularly those studying abroad, came under the influence of various ideologies: socialism, communism, reformist Islam, and the nationalisms of India, China, and Japan. The result was that the earlier rambling discussions of good and bad aspects of the Western impact on Indonesian society gave way to a series of systematically conceived critiques of colonial rule. By the late 1920's the leaders of the movement were talking about Indonesian independence and arguing with one another about how best to achieve it and what content to give to it once it had been achieved. With the publication of the first comprehensive nationalist manifestoes at this time, the adoption of a national flag and anthem, and the decision to make Malay into Bahasa Indonesia, the national language of the state to be born, a large part of the community of the modern-educated committed itself to the gripping new enterprise of Indonesia.*

Leadership of the nationalist movement remained in the hands of

---

* George McT. Kahin, *Nationalism and Revolution in Indonesia* (Ithaca, N.Y.: Cornell University Press, 1952), which provides a political history of the 1945–1950 period, is also a valuable source on the prewar nationalist movement. Of the Indonesian writings of this period there is little available in English. But see R. A. Kartini, *Letters of a Javanese Princess* (New York: Norton, 1964), and S. Sjahrir, *Out of Exile* (New York: John Day, 1949), for insights into the turn-of-the-century and 1930's situations.

small groups of intellectuals throughout the prewar period. This was partly a reflection of traditional values: men of high Western education inherited much of the respect in which literati had been held in earlier periods, particularly in Java. More important, however, was the fact that men of ideas were required for some of the central tasks the movement faced. Leaders of all of the nationalist movements of Asia and Africa have devoted a large part of their energies to persuading their countrymen that their colonial governors had no moral right to rule over them, and no one could lead any of these movements who was not skilled as a formulator and propagator of ideas. But it would seem that ideational work, including agitation and education, played a disproportionately great role in the case of the Indonesian movement. This came about partly because there was little scope in prewar Indonesia for organizational and representational activities—because the Dutch gave the nationalists little opportunity to build parties with grass-roots support and because there was little connection between influence within the nationalist movement and access to the government of the day. And it had to do also with the relatively great importance of ideological disagreements within the movement: between Muslims and Communists in the 1920's, between Muslims and secular nationalists in the early 1930's, and between pro- and anti-Japanese nationalists in the years before 1942.

After the proclamation of independence in August 1945, when the leaders of the nationalist movement became leaders of a government, the range of their activities expanded rapidly. Most of them, however, continued to be intellectually inclined, and, indeed, the situations they faced required them to continue to devote much of their energy to ideas, partly because ideological disagreements were of great immediacy in the years after 1945. Many of the new Republic's military units, which fought the returning Dutch in the ensuing four years, were distinctively ideological—socialist, nationalist, Islamic, and so on—as well as virtually all of its parties; and the Republic had to contend with a Communist revolt and a radical Islamic one while still fighting the effort of the Dutch to reimpose their control.

Even more important, the leaders of the new government came to power in a situation for which their prior experience had not prepared them and for which no obviously relevant models were available. Governing the embattled revolutionary Republic in the years between 1945 and 1949 was a vastly different task from governing either the prewar Dutch colony or the Japanese-occupied territories during the war. It was a matter of working out new roles—new ways of exercising authority and control, new basic policies in many areas, and, above all, effective ways of fighting and negotiating to ward off the Dutch—not merely a matter of Indonesians stepping into roles which had previously been played by Dutchmen and Japanese. For many participants in the revolutionary movement, the 1945–1949 period was one when they had a very clear sense of purpose, as well as a sense of selfless involvement in a common struggle. But as far as the Republic's leadership was concerned, it was a period of sailing uncharted seas, of groping for doctrines, policies, and governmental methods with which to fill the tabula rasa of the new independence. Men who had considered ideas of what choices the country faced, and what their further implications were, were much in demand— as were those with the intellectual agility to apply the ideas of others to new situations. Many of the cabinet and higher civil service positions which had to be filled and a few higher military positions were given to men of this kind.

Thus, both in the prewar nationalist movement and in the period of revolutionary struggle, the connections between the world of political ideas and the world of political power were more than close. The main leaders of the movement were intellectuals—in the sense of men trained in a body of complex ideas and seriously interested in ideas as such—and it is they who were the authors of most of the movement's political thinking.

After December 1949, when the Dutch finally abandoned their claim to sovereignty over the archipelago and the nationalists under Sukarno and Hatta became undisputed rulers of the country, this situation began to change. Men of ideas continued to be in demand for many types of government positions. Some worked on policy formulation, as ministers, civil servants, and brain trusters; others worked on problems of political persuasion, in such departments as Religion, Information, and Education. And many continued to play important roles in political parties. But as government became an increasingly regularized affair and increasingly tied to particular interests, its need for their skills diminished. Furthermore, as the notion of the government as the spearhead of the nationalist movement waned and revolutionary élan gave way to postrevolutionary lassitude, more and more men of ideas came to think of themselves as critics of government actions rather than direct contributors to them.[*]

The Unattached Intellectuals

It was in these circumstances that a distinct group of more or less unattached intellectuals came into being for the first time, a group of men working on the edges of the political arena as writers, journalists, editors, publishers, university lecturers or students who addressed themselves mainly to narrow audiences of highly educated people in the cities or in Djakarta alone. This group was still very small in the early 1950's; most of its members had personal knowledge of most other members, directly or indirectly. And its institutional bases were weak; there were as yet only two major universities in the country, with many of their senior positions held by Dutchmen, and the total circulation of newspapers was only 692,000 in 1955. But its political importance was great. Perhaps a quarter of the authors represented in this volume were unattached intellectuals in this sense.

Being more or less unattached did not mean, however, that they were unconcerned with politics. The very reverse was the case. Much of their talking and writing was in the vein of "If I were making national policy on . . ."; and they usually saw a direct connection between what they were advocating and the fortunes of the several parties in current political controversies. It is true enough that many of them found the political scene increasingly depressing. By the middle 1950's there were many who insisted defiantly that they had given up trying to follow what "the government people and all those politicians" were up to. And the retreat into private life went further in the early 1960's. But a bitter fascination with politics remained even among those who had retreated; they too saw its drama as bewitchingly exciting. And many of them had a strong feeling, particularly when public life had them depressed, that they as intellectuals had a special responsibility to find a way out of the mess. Of the many more or less unattached intellectuals who talked of

[*] The political history of the 1949–1959 period is traced in Herbert Feith, *The Decline of Constitutional Democracy in Indonesia* (Ithaca, N.Y.: Cornell University Press, 1962), which covers 1950–1957; and Daniel S. Lev, *The Transition to Guided Democracy: Indonesian Politics, 1957–59* (Ithaca, N.Y.: Cornell Modern Indonesia Project, Monograph Series, 1966). The 1958–1962 period is discussed, much more sketchily, in Herbert Feith, "Dynamics of Guided Democracy," in Ruth T. McVey, ed., *Indonesia* (New Haven: Yale University and Human Relations Area Files, 1963).

wanting to "get away from politics" and "get on with the job," few thought first and foremost in professional terms; and these few were mostly Chinese-Indonesians. The great majority were at least as much concerned with the setting of goals as they were with the devising of means.

Most of these intellectuals had a strong sense of both stake and responsibility about the Indonesia enterprise. Nationalism and the nationalist revolution had had personal meaning for them in the past and continued as a major element in the moral commitments of many of them. In addition most of them continued to be able to exercise influence in the world of practical politics because of personal connections with the powerful. In terms of social and educational background, they had a great deal in common with the country's top leaders. Their parents, like those of the political elite, were mostly high or low aristocrats who had been drawn into the Dutch civil service, with a small group of professional men thrown in and another small group of village leaders. They themselves had gone to the same handful of secondary schools and colleges. Some of them had been at the apex of power, as cabinet ministers or top officials; and there were few who did not have a close relative or old school friend who was, or had been, at the very top. This was so particularly in the 1950's, when both groups, that of the powerful and that of the more or less unattached intellectuals, were still limited to men who had had at least substantial secondary education before the war and spoke Dutch. It had become much less true by the early 1960's.

A further reason for the intellectuals' fascination with politics can be seen in their vulnerability to it, the way in which their fortunes were tossed about in political storms. Political change was rapid and largely unpredictable throughout our period, and its ramifications extensive, penetrating what in some other societies are intellectuals' islands of autonomy. Thus, a shake of the kaleidoscope of Djakarta politics could raise one author from obscurity to great acclaim and so blacken the name of another that he found it impossible to publish thenceforth. For a university man it could mean that he was provided with a new house and a range of high government positions or that he fell into disgrace, was evicted from his house, and, in much rarer cases, thrown into jail.

Finally, many of the more or less unattached intellectuals were fascinated by politics because their ideas continued to be valued by the powerful. The very weakness of Indonesia's political institutions,

the rapidity of political change, the openness of choices at many
points, the multiplicity of possible models—all these tended to give
intellectuals influential roles to play. Many political leaders, it is true,
felt no need at all for the company of intellectuals. But others, both
government leaders and high civil servants, were often keen to talk
to them, for reassurance and political ammunition if not for advice
and often, too, for the sketching out and clarification of alternatives
and longer-term goals: "What did they do about this problem of the
Muslim extremists in Egypt?" "Do *you* think this means that we are
heading for civil war?" "Is it true that we all ought to read that
book of Rostow's?" "What do *you* think are the really important
things the government should be doing over the next five years?"
"Malaysia *is* an intrinsically artificial thing, don't you think?" "How
would *you* hit back if they argued that a new stadium is perfectly
justified as part of nation building?"

Party Conflict as Ideological Conflict

If the more or less unattached intellectuals were one major group
from which the political thinkers of our period came, a second major
group consisted of those who attached themselves firmly to political
parties. With society and social values changing fast, large numbers
of people, particularly young people with some modern education,
were looking for ideological answers—in part for new beliefs, more
particularly for compelling reasons with which to withstand challenges to the beliefs they had taken over from their families and
communities. And they were finding them for much of our period in
political parties. So, competition between parties was partly competition between systems of ideas. In order to attract members and followers and keep them, and particularly to attract the young, the
parties had to provide answers to ideological problems—to offer men
comprehensible maps of the world around them and compelling up-
to-date restatements of values worth upholding—as well as the more
obvious satisfactions of companionship and collective activity, access
to influential people, and opportunities for personal advancement.
Thus, an important part of political leadership consisted of devising
acceptable ideological formulations, expounding party positions in
ways which related them comprehensively and acceptably to holder
values and perceptions and which served to establish order, confidence, and a sense of direction in men's thinking. The parties had

every reason to value their intellectuals, and on the whole they did.

Party disagreements had been fairly strongly ideological in the prewar nationalist movement, but at that time the parties were not permitted to develop much grass-roots organization. The ideological conflict was thus mainly between intellectual-led groups of urban white-collar people and did not involve large segments of the society. This picture began to change rapidly during the Japanese occupation with the establishment of mass organizations on a specifically Muslim basis and others recruited mainly from the *abangan* (Javanese who are nominally Muslim, but whose actual religious beliefs and practices owe more to Hinduism and to Javanese religion as it existed before the Hindu impact than they do to Islam). And the change was taken a step further in the period of armed struggle against the Dutch after 1945, when various irregular forces were fighting for Islamic, socialist, and nationalist political ideologies as well as for the Republic as such.

The climax of this process of taking ideological cleavages from the white-collar communities of the cities to the mass of the population came in the two years or so of hectic campaigning which preceded the national elections of 1955. This was a period of immensely vigorous organizational activity, in which each of the major contenders built new party branches in small towns and villages throughout the country, held countless rallies and meetings, and enrolled many millions of members. It was also a period of bitter social conflict. If any single issue can be said to have dominated the campaign, it was whether the state should be based on the Pantja Sila (President Sukarno's Five Principles, including The One Divinity), or explicitly on Islam. This issue was highly meaningful to villagers and townsmen alike, but it meant that Muslim communities were pitted against Christian ones, and thorough-going Muslims against secular-minded and *abangan* ones, in ways which strained social cohesion in many local areas and, indeed, in the national community.

Four main parties emerged from the elections head and shoulders above the many others—the PNI or Nationalist party with 22.3 per cent of the total vote, the reformist-led Muslim party Masjumi with 20.9 per cent, the more traditional Muslim party Nahdatul Ulama with 18.4 per cent, and the Communist party, PKI, with 16.4 per cent. The PNI, NU, and PKI each obtained more than 85 per cent of its votes in Java and more than 65 per cent in the ethnic Javanese heartland of East and Central Java; the Masjumi by contrast drew 48.7 per cent of its votes from the less densely populated outer islands and only 25.4 per cent from East and Central Java.

Each of these four successful parties had large numbers of ancillary organizations—worker, peasant, youth and women's organizations, schools, scout groups, and cultural, sporting, and welfare associations of various kinds—extending through small-town society in most parts of the country and into village society as well in many areas. Each had succeeded in making itself the spokesman for a number of pre-existing social and ethnic communities, and in some cases not only a spokesman but a new integrating center.* And each had a *Weltanschauung* of its own, something far wider than a political program or even a set of principles, in effect a modern and more schematic version of the older beliefs of the communities it was representing (and in many areas restructuring and reinvigorating).

In East and Central Java, where the pattern of restructuring and reinvigoration found its fullest expression, the Masjumi had provided a new sense of integration for the *santri* (pious or thorough-going Muslims) of the urban areas, and the Nahdatul Ulama had done the same for the *santri*-minded villagers, whereas the Nationalist and Communist parties had established themselves as representatives and restructurers of somewhat distinct social groupings in the world of the syncretistic *abangan,* the "statistical Muslims" or "Muslims of a sort" (*Muslim-musliman*). Outside Java, relationships between parties and the groups for which they came to speak were generally more accidental and superficial. Party labels had often come to be fixed onto particular ethnic groups, clans, or traditional factions in ways which made little sense in terms of the values of the groups concerned. Thus, one group of princely families in Bali had associated itself with the Socialist Party (later, with fateful results, with the Communists) because a rival group of such families had chosen the Nationalist PNI.

But even in areas like these the links forged in the pre-election period between national parties and particular ethnic, social, and religious communities have proved to be remarkably tenacious. The fourfold patterning of social and cultural infrastructure reflected in

* Clifford Geertz has analyzed this phenomenon in *The Social History of an Indonesian Town* (Cambridge, Mass.: M.I.T. Press, 1965), in *The Religion of Java* (Glencoe, Ill.: Free Press, 1960), and in his "The Javanese Village," in G. W. Skinner, ed., *Local, Ethnic, and National Loyalties in Village Indonesia* (New Haven: Yale University, Southeast Asian Studies, 1959).

the results of the elections has remained an important determinant of political alignments in the country as a whole.

After the 1955 elections the importance of parties in national politics receded, and divisions became less overtly ideological, but the intensity of conflict did not lessen. During the years 1956 to 1958 civilian parliamentary government was under increasingly threatening challenge, in effect from three sides. President Sukarno declared that Western-style "50 per cent plus 1" democracy had failed Indonesia, and offered his alternative, a series of proposals for a "guided democracy" or "democracy with leadership," which obtained the support of the PNI Nationalists and the Communists but were opposed by the reformist Muslim Masjumi and to a lesser extent by the more conservative Islamic Nahdatul Ulama. The central leadership of the army under Major General Nasution gave the President limited support for his proposals and pressed, successfully, for the proclamation of martial law. Thirdly, officer-led movements in several key provinces of Sumatra and Sulawesi (Celebes) took power out of the hands of the Djakarta-appointed civilian governors, asserting demands for more regional autonomy and more funds for their areas, and also for the Sumatra-born and Masjumi-sympathizing Hatta (rather than Sukarno or Nasution) to be brought to the center of the political stage.

By early 1958 the issue was no longer whether predominantly civilian parliamentary government would survive but rather who and what would supersede it—including whether Indonesia would remain a single state. The denouement came in February when several of the regional movements joined forces and established the Revolutionary Government of the Republic of Indonesia, with headquarters in West Sumatra and with the Masjumi leader Sjafruddin Prawiranegara as Prime Minister. Djakarta responded by moving troops against the rebel government and succeeded in crushing it with surprising speed. By the midde of 1958 the rebels had been deprived of their last major town and the civil war was virtually over (though guerrilla fighting went on for three more years).

In Djakarta power passed to a coalition of President Sukarno and the Nasution-led army, and the symbolism of Guided Democracy was triumphant. Of the four parties which had emerged as major in the 1955 elections, three supported "Guided Democracy" (though each with its own apprehensions): the Nationalist PNI, the conservative Islamic NU, and the Communists. The fourth, the reformist

Islamic Masjumi, did not, and neither did the much smaller Socialist Party. But these two had been discredited because some of their leaders had been involved in the rebellion; both of them were banned in 1960.

In July 1959, President Sukarno reintroduced the 1945 constitution by decree, thereby providing his ideas of Guided Democracy with a new institutional framework. At the same time he dissolved the Constituent Assembly, which had long been deadlocked on whether the state should be based on the Pantja Sila or a more explicitly Islamic foundation and ordered an end to this debate.

During the next few years the role of the parties in national politics was relatively small. The Communists certainly played an important role and maintained a high degree of vigor and *élan*. But the PNI, the NU, and the smaller groups were largely paralyzed by the pressure which President Sukarno put on them to praise and acclaim all he said and did. This situation changed around 1963, however, and the 1963–1965 period saw a revival of vigorous party competition in city and village alike. This was partly a response to issues which had arisen from a land reform program, but it can also be traced to the fact that most of the noncommunist parties grew alarmed at the advances of the Communists.

Governments and Their Ideological Activities

The Guided Democracy period after 1958–1959 was one in which the government itself was particularly vigorous about ideological activity. From those years onward President Sukarno's ideas—Guided Democracy, Socialism *à la* Indonesia, Indonesian identity or personality, the unfinished Revolution, unity of Nationalists, Religious People, and Communists, and so on—dominated all public discussion. Formulated as a credal schema and frequently given new twists and new sloganistic forms, these ideas were the theme of all rallies and ceremonies and the subject of indoctrination courses in schools and universities, government departments, and army installations. Ten political parties, including the PNI, the NU, and the Communists, continued to enjoy legal status, but all of them were obliged to express enthusiastic support for the President's ideas on all occasions and to put their own ideas forward in the form of glosses on the President's doctrine. Interparty polemics took the form mainly of accusations that one's enemy was unfaithful to the President and Great Leader of the Revolution and hypocritical in adherence to his doctrines.

The extent to which a single set of ideas was imposed in this third part of our twenty-year period is without precedent in the other two parts. Never before had government leaders insisted on repeated affirmations of support for their ideas as a condition for participation in legal politics.

But there was nothing new about the government's concerning itself intensely with ideological activity. Successive governments had done this since the proclamation of independence, fashioning political goals, devising maps which described the right and wrong paths to those goals, and propagating all these ideas widely. Many of the extracts we have reproduced here, from the 1945–1949 and 1949–1958 periods as well as the 1958–1965 one, are the product of this concern.

President Sukarno's speeches were of enormous importance in the years of armed struggle against the Dutch, rallying support for the revolutionary movement, firing its members with enthusiasm and a sense of clear purpose, and establishing a minimal consensus between the various political groups included in it. Other government leaders, such as Hatta and General Sudirman, devised their own formulations of government ideology; and numerous civil servants, soldiers, and guerrillas devoted their energies to spreading the ideas of all of these. In the "Liberal" period after 1949 the attempt to gain support for more or less consensual political ideas was signally unsuccessful—because there was no external enemy helping the government to fashion unity among the diverse groups, and because all of the political parties enjoyed a high degree of freedom in propagating their ideas. But the attempt was sustained, in the speeches of President Sukarno and Vice-President Hatta and various leaders of the army and in the activities of the Departments of Education, Information, and Religion.

In all three periods government ideological activity was partly a product of the need to devise frameworks of consensus. Successive governments were obliged to develop and inculcate overarching ideological formulas which would serve as connecting tissue between the various more or less ideological parties (or those of them which were legally tolerated at a particular time) enabling them to cooperate with each other. In addition, ideological activity served to legitimize governments and regimes, creating voluntary or quasi-voluntary support for their purposes and a degree of trust in their political machinery and so reducing the need for governments to use coercion and repression.

Thirdly, government ideological formulations competed with those of the parties. Just as the several parties felt compelled to provide their followers with clear and explicit maps of the social and political world about them and with guides to action in this world, so successive governments felt the need to provide such maps for their agents, the members of the civil service and the armed forces; for many if not most of these people were members or sympathizers of parties, and it was highly important for a government that its officials' actions should be dictated at least as much by its own ideological perspectives as by those of the parties of which they happened to be members. In addition, there is an important sense in which governments competed with the parties for the loyalties of the population at large, seeking to mold the political orientations of the young and especially of young people entering the group of the political public (roughly coincidental with the one to four million people who regularly read newspapers).

Finally, government ideological activity was often an attempt to deal with cynicism, shame, and despair. Perceiving disenchantment and pessimism among government employees and in the political public in general at various times, successive governments responded with symbolic and ideological activities intended to regenerate hope, morale, and a sense of momentum. This response had its roots in traditional perspectives, reflecting faith in the effectiveness of exhortation and a belief that any task can be accomplished if one approaches it in the right state of mind (and none if one's mind is not properly attuned). It must also have reflected the traditional notion that kings should symbolically create order in the universe. And it probably drew much of its importance from the untraditional notion that the state should be the spearhead of progress.

Five Streams of Political Thinking

As a glance at the Contents will show, we have divided our material in three different ways, according to time periods, streams of political thinking, and particular controversies. The argument that the twenty-year period should be divided into three parts—the period of armed revolution from August 1945 to December 1949, the "Liberal" period lasting until 1958–1959, and the period of Guided Democracy until the coup and counter-coup of October 1, 1965—is unlikely to be contested; it is the commonest of the periodizations used by Indonesians. But there may well be vigorous disagreement with our notion of a five-fold division in relation to the streams of political thinking: Radical Nationalism, Javanese Traditionalism, Islam, Democratic Socialism, and Communism.

In the late colonial period and the early years of independence Indonesians generally thought there were three kinds of political thinking. Sukarno, in 1926, wrote of Nationalism, Islam, and Marxism as the three main ideological families into which all Indonesian political organizations fitted. The various government compendia on parties and parliament issued by the Ministry of Information between 1950 and 1955 used a slightly different tripartite division, considering all parties as fitting into either the Marxist, the Nationalist, or the Religious group. Their religious category included the small but active Protestant and Catholic parties as well as the Muslim ones. The Marxist parties in this categorization included the orthodox Indonesian Communist party, PKI, as well as the PSI or Socialist party, which stood in the social-democratic tradition, and the Murba party or Party of the Masses, originally formed around the radically nationalist and eclectically Marxist ex-Comintern agent, Tan Malaka. The Nationalist group included the radically nationalistic PNI, the more aristocratic PIR or Greater Indonesia party, and a range of minor parties whose orientation followed one or the other of these two.

The main difficulty with this particular form of tripartite classification is that each category is too heterogeneous. There were very big contrasts between the thinking of the Communists and that of the Socialists, to take the clearest example. In addition, important trends are left out of consideration.

Under Guided Democracy the threefold classification was given official status in a new form. The progovernment coalition of parties was called *Nasakom,* an acronym standing for Nationalists, Religious People, and Communists. But the way in which this acronym was used informally implied that a fourth major ideological tendency existed, namely, that of the "banned parties," the Muslim party, Masjumi, and the Socialist party, opponents of Guided Democracy.

The fact that four ideologically distinctive parties emerged as major in the 1955 elections, receiving far more votes than any of the other contenders, has led many to think of Indonesia's ideological scene in terms of a fourfold division. We ourselves are impressed by the importance of this division; but the correspondence between major parties and distinctive streams of political thinking was not complete. One or two parties, most clearly the PNI, were influenced by more than one such stream. One, the Nahdatul Ulama, developed no distinctive body of ideas related to modern politics, with the result that its leaders tended to borrow from the Masjumi for these despite the contrasts in life-style between the leaders of the two parties and their often acrimonious hostility in actual politics. Finally, there were two important streams of thinking, Javanese traditionalism and democratic socialism, which were not characteristically embedded in any one of the four major parties though each of them exercised some influence within several.

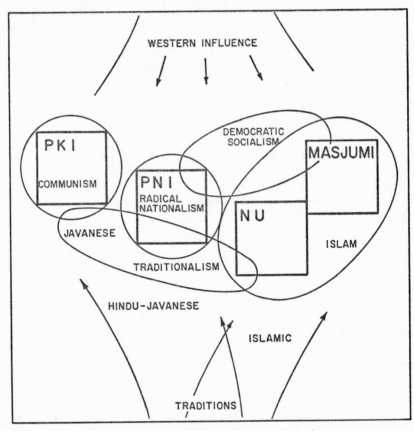

Political parties and streams of political thinking.

For our purposes, then, we have chosen to distinguish five streams of thinking whose relationships with one another and with the four big parties are graphically presented in the accompanying diagram.

It shows these streams in relation to the tension between particular traditional heritages (at the bottom) and in relation to the modern— chiefly Western—world and its ideas (at the top). The diagram emphasizes the duality of Indonesia's traditional heritages, the fact that the older Hindu- and Buddhist-laced tradition of Java has remained distinct from Islam (despite the fact that almost all Javanese have been nominally Islamic and a minority much more thoroughly so for four centuries). On the other hand it makes no sharp distinctions among the ideological influences taken over from the West. The most important of these influences was Marxism, which came powerfully in both its Leninist and social democratic forms. Liberal democratic influences were much weaker, and conservative brands of Western political thought were mostly rejected a priori, though some of them left their mark, not least on the important group of lawyers.

We have located the PKI higher in the diagram than any of the other three large parties because it seems to us that the Communists went further than any other major party in breaking with the past and taking their concepts directly or indirectly from the West, though they also worked with traditional *abangan* and similar appeals. The democratic socialism of the Indonesian Socialist Party (PSI) was similarly modern in its central ideas but far less successful in establishing itself among the mass of the people. The PSI was very influential in capital-city politics, especially in the late 1940's and early 1950's, but fared badly in the elections of 1955, obtaining only 2 per cent of the vote. However, as we have sought to show in the diagram, democratic socialism influenced important leaders of other parties as well, particularly those of the Masjumi and the PNI.

Indonesia's Islam was divided by opposition between a reformist-led denominational-cum-political group centered in the Masjumi party and a conservative-led one centered in the Nahdatul Ulama. The reformist-led group had both modernist and fundamentalist streams within it and was particularly strong in West Java and the outer islands, drawing support there from many traditionally minded segments of the Islamic community as well as from the reform-inclined. The conservative or traditional group, historically a product of the reaction against reformism, was particularly strong in East and Central Java. Between 1945 and 1952 various reformist religious, social, and educational organization were joined with the conservative (and more Javanese) Nahdatul Ulama in the federatively organized Islamic political party, Masjumi. But in 1952 the Nahdatul

Ulama left the federation and constituted itself as a political party in its own right. Our diagram is based on the situation between 1952 and the banning of the Masjumi in 1960. As the diagram suggests, the NU was the most traditional of the large parties. The chief non-Islamic influence on the Masjumi was democratic socialism, whereas the non-Islamic affinities of the NU were with radical nationalism and, especially, Javanese traditionalism.

Perhaps the most controversial element in our classification is the depiction of Javanese traditionalism as a stream of thinking in its own right. No outstanding figure has emerged as the Sukarno, Sjahrir, Natsir, or Aidit of Javanese traditionalism, and its ideas have never been set forth in a systematic fashion. But they are certainly distinctive, and their influence was considerable in our period. It is true that no mass party emerged to uphold them. The organization which most closely reflected them (the Greater Indonesia Party, PIR) was even less successful in the 1955 elections than was democratic socialism's PSI. But, just as democratic socialist thought influenced many nationalists, Muslims, Christians, army officers, and nonparty intellectuals, so Javanese traditionalism powerfully permeated the PNI, the NU, and, most of all perhaps, the armed forces and police and the *pamong pradja* or territorial administrative corps.

Finally, we come to radical nationalism, of which the PNI has been the main organizational vehicle. The PNI occupies most of what middle ground there is in Indonesia's multi-directionally segmented political arena. Our diagram shows its affinities with Javanese traditionalism, with Communism, and with democratic socialism. The notion of nationalism as the highest common factor which could unite the people has been with the radical nationalist ideologists since Sukarno's 1926 essay on "Nationalism, Islam, and Marxism" (see XIIa). A latter-day exponent claimed in 1963 that any Indonesian—whether Protestant, Catholic, Muslim, Socialist, or Communist—could say, "Supposing my party did not exist, most of its members would join yours [the PNI]." *

This fivefold classification—Communism, Radical Nationalism, Javanese Traditionalism, Islam, and Democratic Socialism—seems to us to break up the ideological cacophony of our period into meaningful clusters of blendable voices and with some historical accuracy to

* Sajuti Melik, *Pembinaan Djiwa Marhaenisme* (Fostering the Spirit of Marhaenism) (Djakarta: Pantjaka, 1963), p. 43.

suggest who has felt himself ideologically akin to whom in Indonesian politics. In addition, there may be value in picturing the conflict between Left and Right—using these terms here solely with reference to the criterion of sympathy and antipathy with Communism—in juxtaposition to the tensions between the modern-minded and the tradition-minded of the two main traditions. It should be noted, however, that the congruence between the Javanese tradition and procommunism on the one hand, and between Islam and anticommunism on the other, though a real fact of Indonesian politics in our period, has never been complete; nor is it inherently necessary as the diagram might suggest.

Moreover, although the diagram describes the relationship between our five streams of political thinking and the four main political parties as they emerged in the 1955 elections, it fails to mention other important political forces including President Sukarno, the army, the *pamong pradja* corps, and the minor parties. This shortcoming could be overcome in certain respects—at the expense of cluttering up the diagram. One might, for instance, locate President Sukarno in the center of the radical nationalist circle. The Indonesian Socialist Party could be pictured as a small box in the center of the democratic socialist circle and the Greater Indonesia Party (PIR) as a small box in the center of the Javanese traditionalist circle. The *pamong pradja* corps could be conceived of as a long thin rectangle extending diagonally from the Javanese traditionalist circle through the radical nationalist circle to the democratic socialist one; and one could even locate several of the major regional and ethnic groupings at different points. But there seems to be no clear way of accommodating the "national-communist" Murba party, or the Christian parties, or such important figures as Hatta and Nasution.

The army presents a particularly knotty problem. Almost the full range of ideological orientations has been represented within it. But membership of a single institution has tended to mute ideological conflict, and the army has often acted as a single more or less unified political force. Indeed, it has tended to develop a distinct ideological character of its own. We thought for a time of treating army thinking as a sixth ideological tendency but eventually rejected this idea because we became convinced that, outside a relatively narrow range of questions connected with the army's own position, army thinking was not distinctive in our period.

Distinctively Indonesian Thinking?

How much of what is reproduced here is distinctively Indonesian? In drawing attention, as we have, to the ideological character of Indonesian political thinking and to the social and political functions of ideology, we have left this question out of account. But it demands consideration, if only because readers of what we have assembled will be struck by what *seem* to be characteristically Indonesian features, distinctive values, and, particularly, distinctive conceptual categories and formulations of questions, as well as distinctive similes, metaphors, and styles of expression.

Any generalization we can make about the distinctive characteristics of the political thinking we have selected is necessarily broad and contestable. But we shall attempt three generalizations: From our perspective the political thinking of our period is diffusely moral; it is characterized by a tendency to see society as undifferentiated; and it is optimistic.

In saying that we see it as diffusely moral, we mean to draw attention to the fact that few political thinkers seemed to regard any aspect of politics as belonging to a zone of moral neutrality. Politics was rarely thought of as an area in which paradox and irony frequently prevail. And it was rarely described as being like a machine, characterized by a distinctive set of processes, with individuals more or less limited to acting out particular roles. Nor was it thought of as consisting of particular institutions of which one might ask whether they functioned well or not. The tendency was to look to the moral strengths and weaknesses of the leading actors. Were they nobly intentioned or hungry for power? Brave or cowardly? Wise or foolish? Patriots or men out for themselves?

We would not want to exaggerate this point. There was, indeed, a widespread notion that the political arrangements of a particular time formed a system or regime; this fitted well with the tendency to see recent Indonesian history as a set of distinct time periods, each with its characteristic features. And particular facts of political life were often explained predominantly by reference to such system or institutional factors as multi-partyism or the overcentralization of power. But even the writers who gave institutional analysis of this kind an important role tended to introduce a diffuse moralism into their analysis at some point, relating a particular impersonal pattern or trend to the nobility and courage or the greed, cowardice, and selfishness of individuals.

In general one can say that normative concerns so dominated the political thinking of this period that utilitarian ones were left largely out of account. The question of *what* is to be done absorbed men's attention almost to the point of exclusiveness; few political thinkers devoted themselves to questions of *how,* to considering what were effective ways of tackling particular tasks—and this not because we have *defined* political thinking to exclude consideration of means.

Secondly, Indonesian political thinkers tended not to think of their society as divided into a variety of groups with differing interests. One division was highlighted, the complementary one between "the leaders" and "the people," and a great deal was said about the qualities leaders should have, the heavy responsibilities they bore—both to be "close to the people" and to elevate them and free them from the bonds of ignorance—and the scope they had to transform the environment in which they worked. But relationships of conflict were given far scantier attention. Some attention was given to conflict between parties and ideological groups and to conflict between generations but very little to conflict between ethnic groups and virtually none to class conflict, except among the Communists. In general, divisions were described as less important than underlying unities or explained away in terms of the shortcomings of particular leaders, the failure of particular political arrangements, the legacy of colonial strategies of divide and rule, or the interference of foreigners.

"The people" were commonly thought of as a whole, with leaders being duty bound to represent the interests of this whole—if represent is, indeed, the word, for there was often little concern for the actual views and feelings of the mass of villagers. A leader who was thought to be working for his own group rather than for the people as a whole was often regarded as merely selfish, for there was little conception of segmental groups having legitimate interests. Nor was much concern expressed for the individual, in the sense which that word has in the West. This holistic perspective showed itself, also, in a marked preference for collectivist forms of social organization, a dislike of the profit motive and *enrichissez-vous,* and a notion of the ideal state as one which was organic and a source of personal meaning to its members.

Thirdly, Indonesian political thinking was generally optimistic. Some Muslims and some Christians spoke of man as the likely debaser of his own highest schemes, but this was a minority emphasis. And there was virtually no equivalent of the Western constitutionalist's concern with civility, *mesure,* and checks and balances. Moreover, one has the general impression that most of our authors were confident about their country's future, more so than Western observers of the Indonesian scene. And it is certainly true that few of them concerned themselves with such depressing subjects as population and agrarian poverty in Java, the growing gap between the have and have-not nations of the world, and the possibilities of nuclear holocaust.

The fact that we have concentrated on relatively formal and affirmative presentations in making our selections for this volume and have not included extracts from gossip columns or from short stories or film scripts should make us hesitate before going too far in generalizations about optimism. As we have noted earlier, much of the ideological activity of governments was an attempt to stave off disenchantment and demoralization. And it was not only government ideologists who felt impelled to attempt this but also party ideologists and many of our more or less unattached intellectuals. Much of the optimism in the writing of our period should, therefore, be seen as the optimism of "cheerers up," men who sought to shake their followers out of the inactivity which comes from cynicism, disillusion, and the feeling that things have been going very badly. But the impression remains that this was a basically honest cheering up, that most of those engaged in it had a sense that things would indeed become much better before too long.

One form of optimism was voluntarism, the notion that all things could be achieved if men approached them in the right frame of mind, with good motives, determination, and fraternal solidarity with each other. This notion was often expressed in the assumption, or conviction, that Indonesia's problems would be easily solved if one could only recapture the spirit of a particular past period, most frequently the spirit of 1945.

A second form, seemingly contradictory but often found in the same men, was progressivism, in which the current stage of history was seen as one of predetermined ascent. This, too, was very common, and, indeed, many writers expressing intense dissatisfaction with the state of affairs they were writing about nevertheless saw current history as the unfolding of a sequence from lower to higher stages, from an old, fossilized and static society to an emerging, dynamic one. Faith in education and faith in youth were common to voluntarists and progressivists alike.

These generalizations about Indonesian political thinking are preliminary, and readers have every right to take issue with them. Anyone looking at what is reproduced here with comparisons other than contemporary Western ones in mind is most likely to arrive at different conclusions. But suppose that our generalizations are accepted. What then of the problem of explanation? How is one to account for these particular features? And in what sense are they distinctively Indonesian? These questions raise the whole problem of the relationship between sociological and political perspectives and those of the history of ideas. We shall not attempt any answer here but shall confine ourselves to a quick survey of alternative hypotheses.

One way of looking at the features which seem distinctive is to see them as elements of traditional Indonesian thinking, elements which were so firmly ingrained that they determined the choice between modern ideologies, survived the triumph of these ideologies, and were absorbed into them. Variants of this perspective focus on the Islamic tradition, the Javanese tradition, and the traditions of other ethnic communities. Other variants extend the focus to see particular formulations as characteristic not only of Java or Islam or all of Indonesia but of "Eastern" thought in general.

It is impossible here to attempt any systematic comparison between the three characteristics we have highlighted and particular Indonesian traditions; but the parallels are clearly great. What we have described as a tendency to see society as undifferentiated is clearly related to the centrality of harmony in the Javanese tradition (see Va and Vb) and the traditions of most of the ethnic communities of the archipelago. It is also related to religious syncretism and mysticism, both highly important aspects of old Javanese thinking and both pointing to the ultimate unity of what appear outwardly as contrasting and contradictory phenomena. And it can be seen as a reflection of the traditional vantage point of political thinking in old Indonesia, that of the court poet or court philosopher, the courtier of a king with god-king claims—a vantage very different from that of the ecclesiastically anchored prophet who sees it as his task to "speak truth to power."

Similarly, one could interpret the optimism of contemporary political thinking as a reflection of the old Indonesian view that men could become attuned to the rhythm of the cosmos, could achieve insight into the character of the supernatural forces shaping their lives and affect these by magico-mystical means. Indeed, this same old notion has been said to be part of the explanation for the appeal of pro-gressivism to Indonesians of our period; for being attuned to the rhythm of the cosmos implied mentally keeping up with changes in the external environment. And one could cite numerous other paral-lels, all of them fascinating if one's concern is with tracing the proc-esses of sifting and transmogrification which occurred as the Indo-nesians of the last one hundred years attempted to use traditional categories and classifications to comprehend the ideas and facts of modern political and social life.

But it is equally true that these three features can be found in political thinking in other parts of the non-Western world, including areas well outside the ambit of "Eastern" thought. This suggests that a number of formulations which seem at first distinctively Indonesian or Eastern should be seen in relation to the interests of particular groups and to particular types and phases of socio-political transi-tion as well as being regarded as residues of traditional values and perspectives. First and most clearly, holism, the tendency to look away from social conflict, is characteristic of ruling and privileged groups in general, and it is from these groups that most of our au-thors come. In addition, both holism and progressivism can be seen as manifestations of what Albert O. Hirschman has called the "group-focused image of change," an image which he sees as widespread in countries where rapid economic and social change has come relatively recently into a society hostile to individual self-improvement (be-cause in the old society individual improvement could take place only at the expense of other members of the group, the total product hav-ing long been stationary). In this "image," widespread in nineteenth-century Russia as well as in many parts of Asia, Africa, and Latin America today, a dynamic, progressive society is thought of as an ideal, but the dynamism is one which leaves individuals in their previous places in relation to the group.*

One sociological explanation of the tendency to see politics in diffusely moral terms relates this to the fact that an autonomous

* Albert O. Hirschman, *The Strategy of Economic Development* (New Haven: Yale University Press, 1961), pp. 11ff.

politics often comes into existence before men have developed a distinct cultural model in terms of which to understand it. It is argued that diffuse moralism is the cultural model characteristic of traditional agrarian societies where the sphere of politics is seen as barely distinct from that of morality and religion, and that men in the contemporary non-West tend to fall back on this older model in situations where they have known an autonomous politics for too short a time or in too confusing circumstances to have developed widely accepted explanations of how it works. In the Indonesian case there was little development of representative institutions under colonial rule and a tendency for nationalists to reject such development as there was in this direction, then a traumatically convulsive Japanese occupation. All this did little to provide frameworks through which men might comprehend the workings of the national state politics which emerged after 1945, and so, it is argued, post-1945 political thinkers who wanted to be widely understood had to talk the older language of all-pervasive morality.

Thirdly, voluntaristic perceptions of politics have been related to various patterns of socio-political and mental change. Some writers regard voluntarism as a characteristic product of impatience, arising in situations where the gap between the ideal and the actual is so immense that demoralization would result from any frank attempt to deal with the difficulties of bridging it. Others have argued that it is a characteristic form of the mental processes which take place when fatalism is assaulted. Lucian Pye has advanced the hypothesis that "People who have just learned that they should be able to push aside the concept of fate . . . may find it peculiarly difficult to accept as just and right a new sense of fate as the work of scientific laws defined by statistics and probabilities . . . to leave a world filled with unpredictable but realistic spirits and enter a probabilistic world based upon new laws of chance." *

In the last instance all one can say is that those who seek explanations of particular features of Indonesian thinking must keep both historical-cultural and contemporary-sociological spectacles close at hand, must look both at long-established casts of thought and at the processes of change which have borne in on these and transformed them. If this seems at first sight as a belittling of what is distinctive

* Lucian W. Pye, *Politics, Personality, and Nation-Building* (New Haven: Yale University Press, 1962), p. 294.

about Indonesian political thinking, the impression is mistaken. For the creativity of the Indonesian political thinkers of today is manifest at least as much in their grappling with tumultuous change as it is in their maintenance of a sense of continuity with the perspectives of their forefathers.

PART ONE

CENTRAL THEMES

I
The Common Struggle

The following eight extracts are chosen to illustrate two overlapping subjects: the shared goals of the men who led Indonesia's Revolution of 1945–1949, and the ideas thrown up by the actual course of this Revolution.

The goal of an independent Indonesian nation state was first formulated in the late 1920's and early 1930's, a halcyon period in which the nationalist movement attained a new maturity and before it lost its main leaders as a result of the increasingly severe Dutch repression of the middle and late 1930's. We have not gone into the ideas of this period in this volume, but the first two selections here hark back to it. Sukarno's introductory statement comes from a speech of 1930; some may want to read it in conjunction with his restatement of these ideas in 1957 (IVa). The complementary piece from Hatta which follows it dates from 1956, but it too is an exposition of the ideas of the nationalist movement as they were hammered out twenty-five years earlier. Characteristically, Sukarno speaks of unity and greatness, Hatta of prosperity and democracy, but the two views have a great deal in common.

The next major period of goal formulation came on the eve of the proclamation of independence in 1945. From early 1945 onward the Japanese rulers of Indonesia gave more and more concessions to the Indonesian nationalists working with them and in March they proclaimed the establishment of an Investigating Committee for the Preparation of Independence, in which a large group of leading nationalists debated the ideological and constitutional principles on which the projected independent state would be founded. In this debate, Sukarno presented his *Pantja Sila** or Five Principles; we

* Unfamiliar terms are explained in Appendix II.

have taken sections of his celebrated exposition as our third extract.

Independence was eventually proclaimed on August 17, 1945, two days after the Japanese surrender, and so the Republic of Indonesia came into existence. On the following day a constitution was adopted, a modified, somewhat democratized version of one prepared by the Preparatory Committee. Its Preamble is included as a further classic statement of principles and aspirations.

Unrecognized by either the Netherlands or its Western allies, the newly proclaimed Republic faced difficult strategic choices as British troops and then Dutch ones arrived on the scene. Sukarno's wartime associations with the Japanese were clearly a liability and, partly because of this, power passed in October and November to Sutan Sjahrir, who had headed an underground contact organization during the war. Sjahrir as Prime Minister and Hatta as Vice-President sought to save the new Republic by forcing Holland to negotiate with it and by appealing to the victorious Allies, particularly the United States, to take their principles of democracy seriously. This strategy of appealing to the West and its "new order after the war" ideals is expressed in the Political Manifesto of November 1, from which our fourth extract is taken. It is also argued for in XVc (Sjahrir), and opposed in XVd (Tan Malaka).

But the process by which independence was safeguarded was by no means one of negotiation only. It involved four years of guerrilla fighting in Java, Sumatra and parts of Kalimantan (Borneo) and Sulawesi (Celebes); it involved the violent overthrow of a number of Indonesian princely and aristocratic groups which had buttressed Dutch power; and it generated a great deal of the atmosphere characteristic of the great revolutions of history—treachery and denunciation, passionate dedication, and the sense of a new dawn. Some of these revolutionary aspects are brought out in the sixth and seventh extracts here, and there is something of them also in IIb, XIIc, XIVa, and XIVb.

Like the leadership of the prewar nationalist movement before it, the leadership of the revolutionary Republic lacked organizational unity. In August 1945 the attempt was made under Sukarno's auspices to introduce a single-party system, but this was soon abandoned, and in November 1945 the Sjahrir–Hatta leadership encouraged the free growth of parties, thus allowing a latent pluralism to become manifest. Subsequently, instability was acute and for several years cabinets rose and fell with great speed, thanks in part to the unpopularity into which each of them fell as a result of the concessions it felt obliged to give to the Dutch. Moreover, at one point before and during the Madiun Communist revolt of September 1948, *ideological* conflict was intense and pervasive—see XIIb and XIIc.

But the 1945–1949 period has nevertheless been thought of nostalgically ever since as one of unity and common endeavor. And while it is true that there is an element of historical myth-making here, it is also undeniable that the *feeling* of unity was powerful at the time —despite the multiplicity of parties, the compromise-or-no-compromise, fight-or-negotiate arguments, the ideological disagreements, and the frequently falling cabinets—thanks principally to common hostility to the Dutch. Consensual formulations of political ideas had great appeal, considerably greater than in our two later "eras"—which is part of our justification for considering the period of Revolution together with the shared ideas of the nationalist leadership. As an example of this consensual thinking, we have chosen as final extract in this section Sukarno's discussion of leadership as a calling.

Ia

Sukarno The Promise of a Brightly Beckoning Future* (1930)

This classic statement of nationalist fundamentals comes from Indonesie Klaagt Aan (*Indonesia Accuses*),† *the long speech which Sukarno made in his own defense when on trial before the Bandung District Court in 1930. He was charged with "deliberately expressing [himself] in words wherein the disturbance of public order and the overthrow of the established Netherlands Indies Authority were recommended" and eventually was sentenced to four years' imprisonment.*

The PNI . . . knows that in the consciousness of nationality, in nationalism, lies the strength which can pave the way to future happiness. For this reason, the PNI has strengthened and nurtured nationalism from something which scarcely breathed to a living nationalism, from an instinctive nationalism to a conscious nationalism,

---

* The titles of extracts used in this book are not necessarily those of the authors. Most of them have been chosen by the editors to describe or paraphrase the content.
† *Indonesia Menggugat* (Djakarta: Ministry of Information, 1960).

from a static nationalism to a dynamic nationalism—in short, from a
negative nationalism to a positive nationalism. It had to be a positive
nationalism, Your Honors, because a nationalism that is simply a
feeling of protest or of resentment towards imperialism would not
help us. Our nationalism must be a positive nationalism, a creative
nationalism, a nationalism which builds, creates, and sacrifices. . . .

This nationalism makes our people see the future as a sunrise bright
and glimmering and fills their hearts with rising expectations. No
longer does the future seem like a pitch-black night, and no longer
are their hearts filled with suspicion and resentment. Such a nationalism will make our people willing and happy to undergo any sacrifice
to secure that beautiful future which has raised our desires. In short,
with this nationalism our people will have a soul, will live, will no
longer be like corpses as they are now! . . .

And how do we strengthen that nationalism? How do we bring
it to life? There are three steps: first, we show the people that the
life they led long ago was a good life; second, we intensify the
people's realization that their life today is a dismal one; third, we
turn their gaze to the bright and shining rays of a future day and
show them how to reach that future full of promise.

In other words, the PNI arouses and brings to life the people's
awareness of their "glorious past," their "dark ages," and the "promise of a brightly beckoning future." The PNI knows that only consciousness of this trinity of ideas can make the flower of victory open
and revive the withered nationalism of our people.

We had a glorious past; we had a period of brilliance! Your Honors,
can there be one Indonesian whose heart does not sigh as he hears
the story of those beautiful times? Who does not feel the loss of
that greatness? Is there one Indonesian whose national spirit does
not come alive as he hears the history of the might of the kingdoms
of Melaju and Sriwidjaja, of the greatness of the first Mataram
period, of the greatness of the ages of Sindok and Erlangga, Kediri
and Singasari, Madjapahit and Padjadjaran, of the grandeur of Bintara and Banten and of the second Mataram period under Sultan
Agung? Where is the Indonesian who does not sigh as he remembers
the flag of bygone days, seen and honored as far afield as Madagas-
car, Persia, and China? And conversely, can there be one man who
does not hope and believe that a people who achieved such greatness in the past must have the strength to attain a glorious future,
must have the capacity to rise again to their former grandeur? Who

does not feel new life and new strength in him when he reads the history of our past? So, too, through knowing of this past greatness, a national spirit has been brought to life among our people, kindling anew the fires of hope in their hearts and regaining for them a new soul and new strength.

Of course, former times were feudal times, and this is the modern age. Our intention is not to recapture those feudal times. We never discuss the conditions of feudalism; nor do we have any regard for them. We are aware of the evils they brought the people. We only point out to our own people that the feudalism of the past was alive; it was a feudalism without disease. It was a healthy feudalism, not a sickness. It was a feudalism filled with possibilities for growth, and if its life had not been interrupted by foreign imperialism it could without a doubt have run its own course and settled its own evolution. In other words, it, too, could have conceived and given birth to a healthy modern society.

In contrast, what about our present-day society? That is not healthy. Neither is it full of possibilities for growth. It is sick, empty. We spoke earlier of the lot of Indonesians today, when we described how imperialism's methods are ruining our society, and this will have given you some idea of present conditions. Because our time is limited, that will suffice; it is unnecessary to elaborate further. However, it is crucial that we emphasize here that what most brings the national spirit of our people alive is their awareness of the misery of their lives at present.

The real discontent has not been of our making; the genuine and original discontent is the work of imperialism itself!

Respected Judges, I have described the first and second steps of the PNI's effort to promote a national spirit, steps aimed at awakening consciousness of the past and of the present. About the third step —the pointing to the beauties of tomorrow and to ways of achieving it—it is not necessary, time being short, to say much, since the entire effort of the PNI toward the organization of power, its every action internally and externally, its every movement, yes, its very body and soul are all ways of working toward and realizing the promise of the future. And the Indonesian people's ability to get there? For the PNI this is no longer in question. Although they are now almost as lifeless as a corpse, the Indonesian people who flourished and were so exceedingly great in the past must have sufficient strength and ability to rebuild this greatness in the future, must be able to rise again to the heights they achieved before, and indeed to surpass them.

But what about the future? What form will it take?

No man can accurately foretell the future. Nobody can determine in advance, according to his desires, the way tomorrow will be. No man can foresee history. All we can do is to establish the targets and to study the trends. Not even the Marxists, for example, were able to predict the exact form which a socialist society would take; they could only know its broad outline and disposition. Only the faint glow of Indonesia's future is discernible today, like the beautiful rays of dawn. We can just hear the promises it holds, like the melody of a distant *gamelan* on a moonlit night. As in the *wajang* story, before the coming of Prince Danadjaja,* we become aware of the glow that surrounds him and hear the song of the birds that accompany him, so, too, has the beautiful future that is coming already been foretold to us who wait with hopeful heart. We already hear a promise that millions worth of income will not be taken away to another country. We hear the promise of a life for our people that will be happy and secure, of social welfare which will meet and fulfill our needs, of an open and democratic organization of our political life, of unfettered artistic, scientific, and cultural progress. We hear the promise of the future United Republic of Indonesia living in friendship and mutual respect with other nations, of an Indonesian national flag adorning the Eastern sky, of a nation strong and healthy internally and externally. . . .

Ib

Mohammad Hatta Colonial Society and the Ideals of Social Democracy (1956)

This extract comes from Past and Future,† *an address which Hatta gave when receiving an honorary doctorate from Gadjah Mada University. It was delivered on November 27, 1956, four days before his retirement from the Vice-Presidency.*

From the viewpoint of the capitalist economy which invaded this country, Indonesia was a huge estate, the exploitation of which was based on two highly profitable factors, a rich soil and a supply of

---

* Another name for Ardjuna, third of the Pandawa brothers.

† Ithaca, N.Y.: Cornell Modern Indonesia Project, 1960; reprinted by permission.

cheap labor, which strengthened its international competitive position. Production was not carried out in order to supply the domestic needs of the country itself but was completely geared to the world market, thereby ensuring the highest possible profit. As an outlet for industrial goods from the Netherlands, Indonesia was not yet very important. Its primary economic function was exclusively that of a producing country. This is why the economy of the Netherlands Indies could be characterized as an "export economy."

As to its political structure, the Netherlands Indies was a police state, a type of state organization in conformity with the purpose of the colonizing power to exercise complete political, economic, and social control. Under these conditions there was no room for democracy. Everything was organized hierarchically: the executive corps (*pangreh pradja*); the police; the army. Fundamental to the system was the position of the rationalized organization named *Inlands Bestuur* [Native Administration], culminating in the *bupati* or regent. Over and above this regent a powerful system of *Europees Bestuur* [European Adminstration] had been established, which issued all the orders and had supervision over the officials of the *Inlands Bestuur*. In such a setup it was not the competent and idealistic native officials who were appreciated but rather those who were proficient in carrying out orders.

This is the reason why the Indonesian community, oppressed as it was, could not develop properly. The deeper capitalism penetrated into the Indonesian community, the worse became the living conditions of the people, who had no more powers of resistance left. The foundations of the community were destroyed by three types of exploitation that were perpetrated successively over three centuries; the system of the Oost-Indische Compagnie [East India Company], the so-called "cultivation system," and the system of private initiative. And in all these extortions the colonial government acted wherever necessary as "the natural guardian of colonial capitalism," to use the words of J. E. Stokvis.

Listen also to how aptly Dr. J. H. Boeke describes the social destruction caused by colonial capitalism in Indonesia:

Individualizing liberal principles and capitalist penetration have destroyed social foundations and driven the economically weak into a merciless social struggle in Indonesia, perhaps to an even greater extent than in Europe. We all know that the capitalist system in its full growth has invaded Indonesia like a foreign conqueror and succeeded in conquering it in a few decades. Even more drastic than in Europe has been the disintegrating effect in the colonial territory of a policy that was based on the interests of those who were well equipped, knowledgeable, and always ready to fight. The economic policy which opened up Indonesia to tough-minded capitalists, the communications policy which shortened distances and abolished isolation, the system of free trade which intensified competition in internal commerce, the taxation system with its increasing emphasis on money and individual assessment, the western legislation and administration of justice, the educational policy—all these have exercised a disintegrating influence on the native community and its social organs, to which the weak force of the numerous people was not equal. All these have broken down the existing social organization without molding a new one, creating misery without generating new strength, and the result has been a degradation of the human spirit.

This is not the pronouncement of an Indonesian revolutionary, but the result of a scientific analysis by a colonial economist, a man of deep human feelings.

It was this knowledge, together with the facts of daily experience in racial and individual life, that gave substance to the ideal of a future Free Indonesia. And the cognizance of the Dutch colonial aims, in which there was no place whatsoever for aspirations toward Indonesian self-government, reinforced the national spirit. "A Free Indonesia, one and indivisible" and "Struggle on the basis of our own strength" became the slogans of the national movement. Statements by Dutch leaders, such as H. Colijn, who said that it should be made clear to Indonesian nationalists that Dutch authority over Indonesia was established as firmly as Mont Blanc on the Alps, only served to add fuel to the fires of Indonesian nationalism, which were already aflame. To smother them was no longer possible!

In this way our prewar freedom movement gave birth to four of the five principles on which our present State is based: Humanity, the Unity of Indonesia, the Sovereignty of the People, and Social Justice. These were ideals for the future—a reaction to the bitter reality of the people's misery, constant humiliations, national extortion, and suffering under a colonial and autocratic power.

Free Indonesia had to become a national state, one and indivisible, free from foreign colonial domination in whatever form, political or ideological. The principles of humanity had to be carried out in all segments of life, in the intercourse between individuals, between employers and workers, between the different groups of the population. Although generated by the struggle against colonialism, these humanitarian ideals had not only an anti-colonial and anti-imperialistic character, but were also directed toward the freeing of man from all oppression. Community relationships were to be characterized by an atmosphere of family and fraternity. The socialist literature which found many readers, and the labor movement of the West which could be observed from afar and nearby, confirmed these ideals and made them into firm convictions.

This feeling, with which the spirit of the national movement was deeply embued, was later incorporated as a basic principle in the Preamble to the Constitution of the Republic of Indonesia, in the following words: "Independence being in truth the right of all peoples, colonialism, which does not accord with humanity and justice, must be abolished throughout the world."

The "Universal Declaration of Human Rights," consisting of thirty articles, was adopted by the United Nations Organization on December 10, 1948, during its meeting in Paris. When Indonesian leaders, who in their younger days had been fighting as pioneers, heard the declaration in article I that "all human beings are born free and equal in dignity and rights," it was as if they heard themselves speaking. It gave them the feeling that people wanted to realize their own long-held ideals in international society. When it was already considered fitting to carry out these ideals internationally, should these ideals be neglected in the national sphere?

There was yet another fundamental question to be solved. Once Indonesia achieved independence, what form of state organization would be best? Experience with the colonial autocratic government in the form of a police state had given rise to the ideal of a democratic constitutional state in the minds of the younger generation of Indonesia. The state, it was believed, should have the form of a Republic based on the sovereignty of the people. The sovereignty of the people, however, as envisaged and propagated in the circles of our national movement, was at variance with Rousseau's concepts which were characterized by individualism. Sovereignty of the people in Indonesia had to be rooted in its own society, which is collectivist in character. Whatever its other sources, Indonesian democracy should also evolve from indigenous Indonesian democracy. Moreover, the national spirit which had developed as a natural reaction to

Western imperialism and capitalism intensified the desire to look in our own society for foundations on which to build a national state. Western democracy was rejected a priori.

When we study the French Revolution of 1789, which is known as the source of Western democracy, we find that the slogan "Liberty, Equality, and Fraternity" was not carried into practice. This is not surprising, because the French Revolution broke out as a revolution of individuals, aiming to liberate persons as individuals from the ties of feudalism. The liberty of the individual was given first consideration. When this liberty had been gained, its connection with equality and fraternity was forgotten.

Although the French Revolution aimed at carrying out the ideal of complete equality—which is why, besides liberty for the individual, equality and fraternity were also stressed—the democracy which it practiced brought only political equality.

Politically, every individual was accorded equal rights. Rich and poor, men and women, had the same right to vote and to be elected as members of parliament. Beyond these rights, however, there was no equality. As a matter of fact, when the spirit of individualism kindled by the French Revolution flared up, capitalism thrived increasingly. Class strife became aggravated, oppression of the economically weak by the economically strong became more severe. Wherever there are strongly conflicting interests, wherever there are oppressors and oppressed, fraternity is hard to find. The system of individual economic responsibility resulted in a worker's livelihood being secure only as long as he was strong and able to work. He was dismissed and neglected once he became old and sickly and lost his ability to work.

Clearly, democracy of this type was not in conformity with the ideals of the Indonesian struggle for independence, which aimed at realization of the principles of humanity and social justice. Political democracy alone cannot bring about equality and fraternity. Political democracy must go hand in hand with economic democracy, otherwise man will not yet be free, and there will not be equality or fraternity. Therefore, social democracy covering all phases of life which constituted human existence was the ideal of Indonesian democracy. The ideal of social justice was made into a program to be carried out in our future national life.

It was really from three sources that these ideals of social democracy came to life in the minds of the Indonesian leaders at that time.

First, Western socialist thinking attracted attention because it advocated and strove toward the principles of humanity. Second, there were the teachings of Islam which demand honesty and divine justice in human society and fraternity among people as creatures of the Lord in accordance with the essential qualities of Allah, the Merciful and the Benevolent. Third, there was the knowledge that Indonesian society is based on collectivism. These three considerations only served to strengthen the conviction that the democratic structure that was to become the basis of the future government of Independent Indonesia should be derived from the indigenous democracy prevalent in the Indonesian village.

The old Indonesian states were feudal states, ruled by autocratic kings. Nevertheless, in the villages a democratic system remained in force and lived a healthy life as part and parcel of *adat-istiadat,* old usage and traditional custom. This fact provided sufficient evidence for the conviction that indigenous Indonesian democracy would have strong powers of endurance, live healthily, and be "neither cracked by the sun nor rotted by the rain." This is also why indigenous democracy was idealized to such an extent in the national movement. Many were the leaders who felt it to be sufficiently complete to become the basis of the government of a modern state. "Take away the feudalism and capitalism which are suppressing it," they said, "and it is bound to blossom forth and live healthily on a solid foundation!"

Social analysis shows that the indigenous Indonesian democracy was able to maintain itself under feudalism because the soil, the most important factor of production, was the communal property of the village people. It did not belong to the king. And the social history of the Western world shows that in the feudal era the ownership of land constituted the basis of liberty and power. Whoever lost the title to his land, lost his freedom and became dependent on others; he became the servant of the landlord. Whoever was the owner of a great deal of landed property had power, and the extent of his power was in proportion to the amount of land he owned.

Because landed property in the old Indonesia belonged to the village community, village democracy could not be eliminated, regardless of efforts by the feudal power to suppress it. On the basis of the common ownership of the soil, each individual, in carrying out his economic activities, felt that he had to act in accordance with common consent. Consequently, one finds that all heavy work that could not be done by one individual person, was performed by the system of *gotong rojong*, mutual assistance. Not only were matters which according to the Western judicial system were within the area of public law taken care of in this way, but so also were private matters such as building a house, working the rice fields, accompanying the dead to the graveyard, and so on. This way of life, based on common ownership of the soil, had created the custom of mutual consultation. All decisions concerning matters of common interest were taken by mutual consent, or in the words of a Minangkabau saying: "Water becomes one by passing through a bamboo pipe; words become one by mutual agreement." The custom of taking decisions by way of mutual consultation created the custom of holding general meetings in a regular meeting place, which were presided over by the head of the village. All adult and indigenous members of the village community had the right to attend these meetings.

We have not yet mentioned all the democratic elements in the original Indonesian village. There are two further elements: the right to make joint protest against regulations issued by the king or prince that are felt to be unjust; and the right of the people to leave the territory over which the king has authority when they feel that they do not want to live there any longer. Rightly or not, these last two rights have often been thought of as the right of individuals to decide their own fate. As is well known, the right to make an ordinary joint protest has been resorted to up to the present time. When it happens that the people strongly disapprove of a regulation issued by the *bupati* [regent], the *wedana* [district chief], or some other authority, one sees a great many people congregating at the particular town or village square, where they will sit quietly for a certain length of time, without doing anything. In the old days it was not very often that the Indonesian people, who are by nature patient and complying, acted like this, but when they did, it made the authorities consider whether they had not better revoke or modify their orders.

These five indigenous elements of democracy—the general meeting, mutual consultation, *gotong rojong* or mutual assistance, the right to make joint protests, and the right to remove oneself from the king's or prince's authority—were esteemed within our national movement as solid principles for the social democracy that was to become the basis for the future government of Free Indonesia.

Subsequent analysis, made quietly and free from the desire to idealize everything that is indigenous with us, has shown that the good points of our village democracy cannot all be applied indiscriminately at the level of the state. The system of consultation as it is practiced in the villages means that decisions are taken unanimously, with everyone agreeing, after the matter has been discussed thoroughly. No decision can be taken before unanimity has been reached, and the matter remains a subject for discussion both within and outside the general meeting. It would be impossible to reach such unanimous decisions in a parliament with all its different parties and political antagonisms. In this matter, whether one likes it or not, one has to accept the system of Western democracy whereby decisions are taken by a majority of votes.

On the other hand, "agreement" such as is usually imposed in totalitarian countries, is not at all in harmony with the notion of Indonesian democracy, because real agreement can only be arrived at by mutual consultation. Without consultation, where everyone has the right to advance his opinion, there cannot be any agreement. However, in a democratic collective society such as Indonesia's, the mentality of individual persons is different from that in an individualistic society. In all their actions and in the voicing of their opinions, Indonesians are primarily guided by the common interest. Their own interests are completely bound up in the common interest. Therefore, it is naturally easier for them to reach agreement. But, although the individual in his way of thinking and acting is guided by the ideals of the common good, he is not a mere object of the collective entity, such as is the case in totalitarian countries. He remains a subject with his own will, able to move about freely and make his own special contacts and to practice differentiation. Socially speaking, he maintains his own ideals and devotes his thoughts to his own or the common welfare.

This was the kind of society in the minds of those who were doing their best to create an appropriate democratic system for the future Free Indonesia. In no case did they want to relinquish the ideals of social democracy that were more or less fundamental to social organization in our original community. In the political field a system of popular representation with consultation was designed, based on the general interest of the community. Extensive autonomy, reflecting the idea of "government by those governed," would have to be carried into effect. In the economic sector, the national economy would have to be organized on a cooperative basis, and the government would have to have the duty of controlling or supervising those branches of production important to the State and those which vitally affect the life of the people. In the social sector, the development of man's individuality would have to be safeguarded. The State would direct its efforts toward the happiness, well-being, and moral worth of man.

Ic

Sukarno   The Pantja Sila (1945)

This piece comes from The Birth of Pantja Sila,* *a speech delivered extempore on June 1, 1945, before the Investigating Committee for the Preparation of Independence, the establishment of which had been proclaimed by the Japanese in March. The Pantja Sila, or Five Principles, first set out in this speech, were subsequently written into the Preamble to the Constitution and accepted as the philosophical foundations of the Indonesian state. One of Sukarno's major concerns at the time was to combat the proposal for an Islamic state (see IVc, Ve, VId, and the introduction to Section VI).*

We will establish an Indonesian national state. I ask Ki Bagus Hadikusumo and others of the Islamic group to excuse my using the word "Nationalism." I, too, am a man of Islam. But I ask that you do not misunderstand when I say that the first basis for Indonesia is the basis of nationalism. That does not mean nationalism in a narrow sense, for I desire a national state such as I spoke about in the meeting in Taman Raden Saleh several days ago. An Indonesian National State does not mean a state in a narrow sense. As Ki Bagus Hadikusumo said yesterday, he is an Indonesian, his parents are Indonesians, his grandparents were Indonesians, his ancestors were Indonesians. It is upon Indonesian nationalism in the sense meant by Ki Bagus Hadikusumo that we shall base the Indonesian state.

A National State! This matter needs clarifying first, even though I have already said something about it in the mass meeting at Taman Raden Saleh. Let me elaborate and spend a little more time upon the question: what is it that is called a nation? What are the requirements for a nation?

According to Renan, the requirement for a nation is the desire to be united. The people feel themselves united and want to be united.

* *Lahirnja Pantja Sila* (Djakarta: Ministry of Information, 1960).

Ernest Renan said that the requirement for a nation is *le désir d'être ensemble*, the desire to be united. According to Ernest Renan's definition, it follows that what becomes a nation is a group of people who want to be united, who feel themselves united.

Let us look at a definition by another person, namely, that of Otto Bauer in his book *Die Nationalitätenfrage*, where the question is raised "Was ist eine Nation?" and the answer is given: "Eine Nation ist eine aus Schicksalgemeinschaft erwachsene Charaktergemeinschaft" [A nation is a community of character which has grown out of a community of shared experience]. This, according to Otto Bauer, is a nation.

But yesterday when—if I'm not mistaken—Professor Supomo quoted Ernest Renan, Mr. Yamin said: "Out-of-date." Indeed, gentlemen, Ernest Renan's definition is out-of-date. Otto Bauer's definition, too, is already out-of-date. For at the time when Ernest Renan formulated his definition, at the time when Otto Bauer formulated his definition, there had not yet emerged the new science called geopolitics.

Yesterday, Ki Bagus Hadikusumo if I'm not mistaken—or Mr. Munandar—spoke about "unity between men and place." Unity between men and place, gentlemen, unity between human beings and where they live! Men cannot be separated from place—impossible to separate people from the earth under their feet.

Ernest Renan and Otto Bauer only looked at men alone. They thought only about the *Gemeinschaft* and the feeling of men, *l'âme et le désir*. They were only thinking of character, not thinking of the earth, the earth inhabited by those people, the place. What is the "place"? That place is a country. That country is one unity.

God Almighty made the map of the world, created the map of the world. If we look at the map of the world, we can point to where the "unities" are.

Even a child if he looks at a map of the world, can point out that the Indonesian archipelago forms one unity. On the map there can be shown a unity of the group of islands between two great oceans, the Pacific Ocean and the Indian Ocean, and between two continents, the continent of Asia and the continent of Australia. Even a child can tell that the islands of Java, Sumatra, Borneo, Celebes, Halmahera, the Lesser Sunda Islands, the Moluccas, and the other islands in between are one unity.

Similarly, any child can see on the map of the world that the islands of Japan, stretching on the eastern brink of the continent of Asia as a breakwater for the Pacific Ocean, are one unity. Even a little child can see that in South Asia the land of India is a single unity, bordered by the extensive Indian Ocean and the Himalaya Mountains. Even a child can tell that the British Isles are one unity. Greece can be shown to be a unity, also; it was placed that way by God Almighty: not Sparta alone, not Athens alone, not Macedonia alone, but Sparta plus Athens plus Macedonia plus the other regions of Greece—all the Greek islands comprise a single unity.

And so what is it that is called our native land, our country? According to geopolitics, Indonesia is our country. Indonesia as a whole, neither Java alone, nor Sumatra alone, nor Borneo alone, nor Celebes alone, nor Ambon alone, nor the Moluccas alone, but the whole archipelago ordained by God Almighty to be a single unity between two continents and two oceans—that is our country.

Therefore, if I recall that there is a relationship between people and place, between men and their lands, then the definitions given by Ernest Renan and Otto Bauer are inadequate. *Le désir d'être ensemble* is inadequate. Otto Bauer's definition, "aus Schicksalgemeinschaft erwachsene Charaktergemeinschaft," is also inadequate.

If you will excuse me, I will take Minangkabau as an example. Among the people of Indonesia who have the greatest *désir d'être ensemble* are those of Minangkabau, numbering approximately two and a half millions. These people feel themselves to be one family. But Minangkabau is not a unity, it is only just a small part of a unity. The inhabitants of Jogja also feel *le désir d'être ensemble*, but Jogja also is only a small part of a unity. In West Java the people of Pasundan deeply feel *le désir d'être ensemble*, but Pasundan, too, is only just a small part of a unity.

Briefly, the Indonesian Nation is not merely a group of individuals who, having *le désir d'être ensemble*, live in a small area like Minangkabau or Madura or Jogja or the Sunda region or the Bugis region, but the Indonesian Nation is the totality of all the human beings who, according to geopolitics ordained by God Almighty, live throughout the unity of the entire Indonesian archipelago from the northern tip of Sumatra to Irian. All of them, throughout the islands! Because amongst these seventy million human beings *le désir d'être ensemble* already exists; there is already *Charaktergemeinschaft*. The Indonesian Nation, the Indonesian People, the people of Indonesia total seventy million persons, but seventy million who have already become one, one, once again one!

This is what we must all aim at: the setting up of one National State upon the unity of one Indonesian land from the tip of Sumatra right to Irian! I am confident that there is not one group amongst you, neither the Islamic group nor the group called the nationalist group, which does not agree. This is what all of us must aim at.

Let no one think that every independent country is a national state. Neither Prussia nor Bavaria nor Saxony is a national state, but the whole of Germany is one national state. It is not the small areas, neither Venice nor Lombardy, but the whole of Italy, the entire peninsula in the Mediterranean bounded to the north by the Alps, which is the national state. It is not Bengal nor the Punjab, nor Bihar and Orissa, but the entire triangle of India which must become a national state.

Similarly, not all the states of our country which were independent in the past were national states. Only twice have we experienced a national state, namely, in the time of Sriwidjaja and in the time of Madjapahit. Outside these we have never experienced a national state.

I say with the fullest respect for our former rajahs, I say with a thousand respects for Sultan Agung Hanjokrokusumo, that Mataram although independent was not a national state. With respect for Prabu Siliwangi of Padjadjaran, I say that his kingdom was not a national state. With respect for Prabu Sultan Agung Tirtajasa, I say that his kingdom in Banten, although independent, was not a national state. With respect for Sultan Hasanuddin in Sulawesi where he set up the Bugis kingdom, I say that the independent land of Bugis was no national state.

The national state is only Indonesia in its entirety, which existed in the time of Sriwidjaja and Madjapahit, and which now, too, we must set up together. Therefore, if you gentlemen accept this, let us take as the first basis of our state: Indonesian Nationalism. Indonesian Nationalism in the fullest sense. Neither Javanese nationalism, nor Sumatran nationalism, nor the nationalism of Borneo, nor of Sulawesi, Bali, or any other; but Indonesian Nationalism of all of them together, becomes the basis of one national state. . . .

But, but—undoubtedly there is a danger involved in this principle of nationalism. The danger is that men will possibly sharpen nationalism until it becomes chauvinism and think of "Indonesia über

Alles." This is the danger. We love one country, we feel ourselves one nation, we have one language. But our country, Indonesia, is only just a small part of the world. Please remember this!

Gandhi said: "I am a nationalist, but my nationalism is humanity."

The nationalism we advocate is not the nationalism of isolation, not chauvinism as blazoned by people in Europe who say "Deutschland über Alles," who say that there is none so great as Germany, whose people, they say, are supermen, corn-haired and blue-eyed "Aryans," whom they consider the greatest in the world while other nations are worthless. Do not let us hold by such principles, gentlemen; do not let us say that the Indonesian nation is the most perfect and the noblest whilst we belittle other peoples. We must proceed towards the unity of the world, the brotherhood of the world. We have not only to establish the state of Indonesia Merdeka, but we also have to proceed toward the familyhood of nations.

It is precisely this ideal which comprises my second principle. This is the second philosophical principle which I propose to you, gentlemen, which I may call "internationalism." But when I say internationalism, I do not mean cosmopolitanism, which does not grant the existence of nationalism, which says there is no Indonesia, there is no Japan, there is no Burma, there is no England, there is no America, and so on. Internationalism cannot flourish if it is not rooted in the soil of nationalism. Nationalism cannot flourish if it does not grow in the flower garden of internationalism. Thus, these two principles, which I propose first of all to you, are closely linked one with the other.

And now, what is the third principle? It is the principle of *mufakat*, unanimity, the principle of *perwakilan*, representation, the principle of *permusjawaratan*, deliberation among representatives. The Indonesian state shall not be a state for one individual, shall not be a state for one group although that group be the wealthy. But we shall set up a state of "all for all," "one for all, all for one." I am convinced that an absolute condition for the strength of the Indonesian state is *permusjawaratan-perwakilan*.

For the Islamic group, this is the best way to safeguard religion. We are Muslims, myself included. Do excuse me, my Islam is far from perfect. But if you open up my breast and look at my heart, you will find it none but a Muslim heart; and this Muslim heart of Bung Karno's wishes to defend Islam in *mufakat*, in *permusjawaratan*. By means of *mufakat* we shall improve everything including the safety of religion, that is, by means of discussions or deliberations in the people's representative body. Whatever is not yet satisfactory, we shall talk over in a *permusjawaratan*. The Representative Body—this is our place for bringing forward the demands of Islam! It is here that we shall propose to the leaders of the people whatever we feel is needed for improvement.

If we really are a Muslim people, let us work as hard as possible so that most of the seats in the people's representative body which we will create, are occupied by Muslim delegates. If the Indonesian people really are a people who are for the greater part Muslim, and if it is true that Islam here is a religion which is alive in the hearts of the masses, let us leaders move every one of the people to mobilize as many Muslim delegates as possible for this representative body. For example, if the people's representative body has one hundred members, let us work, work as hard as possible, so that sixty, seventy, eighty, ninety delegates sitting in this people's representative body will be Muslims, prominent Muslims. Then, automatically, laws issuing from this people's representative body will be Islamic, also.

I am even convinced that only if this has actually happened may it be said that the religion of Islam truly lives in the souls of the people, so that 60 per cent, 70 per cent, 80 per cent, 90 per cent of the delegates are Muslims, prominent Muslims, learned Muslims. Therefore, I say that only when that has happened, will Islam be alive in Indonesia, and not merely lip service to Islam. We assert that 90 per cent of us profess the religion of Islam, but see in this gathering how many per cent give their votes to Islam? Forgive me for raising this question. For me, this is proof that Islam is not yet truly alive among the people.

Therefore, I ask you all, both those who are not Muslims as well as those who are, and especially those who are Muslims, please accept this third principle, that is, the principle of *permusjawaratan-perwakilan,* unanimity arising out of deliberation amongst representatives.

In the representative body there will be the greatest possible struggle. A state is not truly alive if it is not as though the cauldron of *Tjondrodimuko** burned and boiled in its representative body, if there is no struggle of convictions in it. Both in an Islamic state and also in a Christian state, there is always a struggle. Accept Principle

---

* Tjondrodimuko is the name of the deepest and most dreadful level of hell; to emerge from this level is to have passed the supreme test.

Number 3, the principle of *mufakat*, the principle of representation of the people!

Within the people's representative body, Muslims and Christians will work as hard as possible. If, for instance, Christians desire every letter of the regulations of the Indonesian state to conform with the Bible, then let them work themselves to death in order that the greater part of the delegates who enter the Indonesian representative body are Christians. That is just—fair play! There is no state that can be called a living state if there is no internal struggle. Do not think that there is no struggle in Turkey. Do not think that in the Japanese state there is no clash of minds. God Almighty gave us minds so that in our social life from day to day we might constantly rub against each other, just like the pounding and husking of paddy to obtain rice which in turn becomes the best Indonesian food. Accept, then, Principle Number 3, the principle of *permusjawaratan*.

I will now propose Principle Number 4. During these three days I have not heard of this principle yet, the principle of well-being, the principle which asserts that there shall be no poverty in Indonesia Merdeka. . . .

Do not imagine that if the people's representative body were already in existence, we should automatically have achieved this well-being. We have seen that in European states there are representative bodies, there is parliamentary democracy; but is it not precisely in Europe that the people are at the mercy of the capitalists? In America there is a representative body of the people, but are not people in America at the mercy of the capitalists? Are not people at the mercy of the capitalists throughout the whole Western world?

This is due to one thing, the fact that the people's representative bodies which have been set up there, have merely followed the recipe of the French Revolution. What is called democracy there is nothing but mere political democracy alone; there is no social justice at all, there is no economic democracy at all.

I remember the words of a French leader, Jean Jaurès, who described political democracy. "In parliamentary democracy," said Jean Jaurès, "in parliamentary democracy every man has equal rights —equal political rights; every man can vote, every man may enter parliament. But is there social justice, is there evidence of well-being amongst the masses?" Furthermore, Jean Jaurès said also: "In parliament, a worker's representative who possesses that political right can bring about the fall of a minister. He is like a king! But in his place of work, in the factory—today he can bring about the fall of a minister, tomorrow he can be thrown onto the street, made unemployed, with nothing at all to eat."

Do we want conditions like that?

Friends, I suggest: if we are looking for democracy, it must not be Western democracy, but *permusjawaratan* which brings life, that is politico-economic democracy which is capable of bringing social prosperity.

The people of Indonesia have long spoken of this matter. What is meant by *Ratu Adil?* What is meant by the idea of *Ratu Adil* is social justice. The people want to live in comfort. The people, who have felt that they lacked enough to eat, enough to wear, created a new world under the leadership of *Ratu Adil,* in which justice did prevail.

Therefore, if we truly understand, remember, and love the people of Indonesia, let us accept this principle of social justice. That is, not just political equality, for we must create equality in the economic field, too, which means the best possible well-being. The *permusjawaratan* body we shall establish must not be a deliberative body for political democracy alone, but a body which, together with the community, will be able to give effect to two principles: political justice and social justice. We shall discuss these matters together, brothers and sisters, in the body for *permusjawaratan.* . . .

The fifth principle should be: To build Indonesia Merdeka in awe of the One, Supreme God!

The principle of Belief in God! Not only should the Indonesian people believe in God, but every Indonesian should believe in his own God. The Christian should worship God according to the teachings of Jesus Christ, Muslims according to the teachings of the Prophet Mohammed; Buddhists should perform their religious ceremonies in accordance with the books they have. But let us all believe in God. The Indonesian State shall be a state where every person can worship his God as he likes. The whole of the people should worship God in a cultured way, that is, without religious egoism. And the state of Indonesia should be a state which has belief in God!

Let us observe, let us practice religion, both Islam and Christianity, in a civilized way. What is that civilized way? It is with mutual respect for one another.

The Prophet Mohammed gave sufficient proofs of tolerance, of respect for other religions; Jesus Christ also showed that tolerance.

Let us, within the Indonesia Merdeka which we are going to build, declare in keeping with that: the fifth principle of our state is belief in God in a cultured way, belief in God with noble behavior, belief in God with mutual respect for one another.

My heart will rejoice if you agree that the state of Indonesia Merdeka shall be based upon belief in the One, Supreme God.

Here, then, in the lap of this fifth principle, all the religions to be found in Indonesia today will obtain the best possible place. And our State shall have belief in God, also. Remember the third principle of *mufakat*, of representation—there is the place for each of us to propagandize our ideals in a manner that is not intolerant, that is, in a cultured way!

Brothers and sisters: I have already proposed the "Principles of the State." There are five. Are these *Pantja Dharma*, the Five *Dharma*? No! The name *Pantja Dharma* is not suitable here: *Dharma* means duty, whereas we are speaking of principles. I like symbolism, the symbolism of numbers, also. The fundamental obligations of Islam are five in number; our fingers are five on each hand; we have five senses, *Pantja Indera*; what else is five in number? [One of those present: "The five *Pandawa*."] The *Pandawa* also are five persons. And now the number of principles: nationalism, internationalism, *mufakat*, well-being, and belief in God—also five in number. The name is not *Pantja Dharma*, but I named it with the advice of a linguist friend *Pantja Sila*. *Sila* means basis or principle. And it is upon those five principles that we shall build Indonesia Merdeka, enduring and agelong.

Or perhaps some of you do not like that number of five? I can compress this number until there are only three. You ask me what are the three products of that compressing?

For decades past I have been thinking about this, that is, the principles of Indonesia Merdeka, our *Weltanschauung*. The first two principles, nationalism and internationalism, nationalism and humanity, I compress into one, which I call socio-nationalism. And democracy, which is not the democracy of the West, but together with well-being, I also compress into one; this is what I call socio-democracy. Belief in God with respect for one another is the one principle left.

And so, what originally was five has become three: socio-nationalism, socio-democracy, and belief in God. If you prefer the symbolism of three, then take these three.

But perhaps not all of you like this *tri-sila* and ask for one, one principle alone? All right, I shall make them one, gather them up again to become one. What is that one?

As I said a while ago, we are establishing an Indonesian state which all of us must support. All for all. Not the Christians for Indonesia, not the Islamic group for Indonesia, not Hadikusumo for Indonesia, not Van Eck for Indonesia, not rich Nitisemito for Indonesia, but Indonesians for Indonesia—all for all! If I compress what was five into three, and what was three into one, then I have a genuine Indonesian term, *gotong rojong,* mutual cooperation. The state of Indonesia which we are to establish must be a *gotong rojong* state. Is that not something marvelous: a *Gotong Rojong* state!

Gotong rojong is a dynamic concept, more dynamic than the family principle, friends. The family principle is a static concept, but *gotong rojong* portrays one endeavour, one act of service, one task, what was called by Mr. Sukardjo one *karyo,* one *gawé.* Let us complete this *karyo,* this *gawé,* this task, this act of service, together. *Gotong rojong* means toiling hard together, sweating hard together, a joint struggle to help one another. Acts of service by all for the interest of all. *Ho-lopis-kuntul-baris*— One, two, three, heave! for the common interest. That is *gotong rojong!*

The principle of *gotong rojong* between the rich and the poor, between the Muslim and the Christian, between non-Indonesians and those of foreign descent who became Indonesians. This, brothers and sisters, is what I propose to you.

Id
Preamble to the 1945 Constitution

The constitution which begins with these words was adopted on August 18, 1945, the day after the Republic of Indonesia was proclaimed. The Pantja Sila, or Five Principles, are incorporated in its final paragraph. It has been published many times, for instance in The Indonesian Revolution: Basic Documents and the Idea of Guided Democracy (Djakarta: Department of Information, 1960), pp. 59–83. *This translation is our own.*

Independence being in truth the right of all peoples, colonialism, which does not accord with humanity and justice, must be abolished throughout the world.

The struggle of the Indonesian independence movement has reached the happy stage at which the Indonesian people have been escorted safely to the threshold of an independent Indonesian State which is free, united, sovereign, just, and prosperous.

By the Mercy of Almighty God, and moved by the noble desire to live as a free nation, the Indonesian people hereby proclaim their independence.

Further, to establish a Government for the Indonesian state which will protect the whole Indonesian people and fatherland, to promote the public welfare, improve the livelihood of the people, and join in establishing a world order based on freedom, everlasting peace, and social justice, the Independence of the Indonesian People shall be ordered in a Constitution of the Indonesian State, in the form of a Republic of Indonesia which is based on the sovereignty of the people and on the pillars of the One Deity, just and civilized Humanity, Indonesian Unity, and People's rule guided wisely through consultation and representation, in order to achieve Social Justice for the whole Indonesian people.

Ie

Political Manifesto of November 1945

The following is a shortened version of a Political Manifesto which was prepared by several government leaders of the new Republic, endorsed by the Working Body of its Central National Committee or Parliament, and published on November 1, 1945, over the signature of Vice-President Hatta. Its appearance was one expression of a major political transformation, in which cabinet leadership passed from President Sukarno to Soetan Sjahrir, theretofore chairman of the Working Body of Parliament, who assumed the new position of Prime Minister. The full text of the Manifesto in English translation is included in Illustrations of the Indonesian Revolution *(Djakarta: Ministry of Information, 1953).*

It is two months now since we made clear in every possible way our desire to live as a free people. Today we are entering a new phase in our fight for freedom, and we are conscious that the eyes of the world are on us, with a view to ascertaining what our views and objectives are. It is therefore incumbent on us to afford the world every facility to study us and to realize that not only is our cause grounded on truth, justice, and humanism, but also on common sense and sane thinking. . . .

On March 9, 1942, the Dutch Government in Indonesia surrendered to the Japanese in Bandung without offering much resistance to the invaders. As a result of that Dutch defection, the unarmed Indonesian people were delivered to the tyrannical excesses of the Japanese militarists; and for a full three and a half years the Japanese worked their will on the population, subjecting the people to a type of pressure and oppression unknown in the last few decades of Dutch rule here. The Japanese looked upon Indonesians as mere cattle. Not a few Indonesians were sacrificed by them in the interests of Japanese aggression. Forced labor was imposed on the common people, while peasants were intimidated into handing over to the Japanese the fruits of their toil. The intelligentsia was bludgeoned into lying to and deceiving the people, and the entire population was obliged to conform to Japanese military discipline; it was made to drill and carry out orders with soldier-like precision. The Japanese are gone, but the little military knowledge they infused into us remains, especially among our youth.

The Dutch must accept responsibility for what has happened. After centuries of so-called "training," on March 9, 1942, the Dutch handed over seventy million people to the Japanese in a condition of military unpreparedness and intellectual backwardness. Indonesians lacked the wherewithal to stand up to Japanese might and oppression and fell easy victims to Japanese propaganda. Not trusting us, the Dutch deliberately refrained from giving us military training; bent on keeping us ignorant, the Dutch denied education to the masses.

As they groaned under Japanese excesses, our people began to take stock of the Dutch and the consequences of Dutch rule. With sharper insight they were able to perceive how ineffective and valueless the Dutch administration had been. From that moment Indonesians awakened to the true state of affairs, and there was a sudden upsurge of nationalism far stronger and deeper than ever before. And that nationalism was heightened by Japanese propaganda directed towards Asianism. Tyrannical Japanese rule could neither curb nor stamp out the growth of Indonesian nationalism; in fact, it was instrumental in fostering the growth of self-respect and patriotism among the masses, and in arousing the desire to be rid of Japanese as well as all other forms of foreign domination.

Millions of our peoples died while countless other millions bore every manner of suffering under the three and a half years of Japanese rule; for this the Japanese are responsible, but so, too, are the Dutch for having denied us the mental and material strength needed to stand up to the Japanese. Yet, there is one point that must not be overlooked. Although the administration of Indonesia and the management of her industries were nominally Japanese, it was really the Indonesians who—because of the glaring inefficiency of the Japanese —carried out all the functions previously in Dutch hands. This factor is important because it gave us valuable training and self-confidence.

After having handed us bound hand and foot to the Japanese, the Dutch have not even a shadow of moral right to take the virtuous stand that we cooperated with the Japanese; the less so because, generally speaking, the Japanese obtained a greater measure of cooperation from Dutch men and women in their employ than from the Indonesians. The Dutch willfully ignore the anti-Japanese aspect of Indonesian nationalism. Overtly and covertly the Indonesians resisted the Japanese, by means of sabotage, uprisings, and other forms of opposition. Thousands of nationalists fought for this with their lives. Others underwent tortures. Yet others lived like hunted animals. Witness what happened at Blitar, Tasikmalaja, and Indramaju, in Sumatra, in West Borneo, and in many other places. Other nationalists who worked in the open along constitutional lines in order to strengthen national consciousness were forced into working with the Japanese. They had no option but to march and to goose-step and to shout out war cries in the approved Japanese manner, because they served in regiments raised by the Japanese for their own purposes.

The nationalists who worked with the Japanese never for a minute, in spite of their enforced presence in the totalitarian camp, forsook the nationalistic ideals which had for years been their guide. This is evidenced by the Constitution they framed for the Republic of Indonesia; although it was worked out during the time of the Japanese occupation, the entire document is entirely democratic in form and spirit. On the seventeenth of August 1945 the Republic of Indonesia was proclaimed, and it marked the culmination of the political desire of the Indonesian people to attain sovereignty for their nation. Like an irresistible tidal wave, it carried every Indonesian along with it.

Meanwhile, the Japanese had begun negotiations for their surrender to the Allies. The world at large, especially those who had helped bring the United Nations into being at San Francisco, was faced with the question of Indonesian sovereignty vis-à-vis the

Dutch, whom the United Nations recognized as vested with sovereignty over Indonesia. Whenever they appeared at international conferences, the Dutch claimed that they had never looked upon Indonesia as a colony and that, consequently, the Indonesians had nothing but love and affection for the Dutch Government. But for two months now the world has seen how determined the Indonesians are to have nothing to do with Dutch imperialism. In every possible way the Indonesians have manifested their desire to remain a sovereign people. The Dutch want to reimpose their rule on Indonesia; the foisting of Dutch imperialism on us will be nothing but a deliberate violation of the Atlantic Charter and the United Nations Charter; and it will result in endless bloodshed and sacrifice of life, for only by force and force alone can the Dutch try to pull down the government which we have set up.

Nor have the Dutch any moral right to walk into Indonesia to resume their old imperialistic policies, on the assumption that they bear no blame for their past sins or for their surrender, which resulted in seventy million Indonesians being delivered to the tender mercies of Japanese militarism. Justice denies the Dutch any say in our affairs, and any sanctioning of their imperialistic aspirations will mean violation of the principles of justice and humanity.

The San Francisco Charter places responsibility for the welfare of dependent peoples on certain nations, but these nations themselves are not empowered to violate the basic principles of that Charter.

There can be no doubt that the Dutch have no logical or reasonable answer to offer for the difficulties they are faced with, and this makes their position all the more untenable. Up to now there has been no sign of the Dutch having other intentions than restoring the old colonial system, despite their proclamation of a statement made by Queen Wilhelmina in 1942. The Dutch know that they are unequal to the task of imposing their domination on us, but they are buoyed up by the hope of being able to utilize the Allied forces, which are here to disarm the Japanese, to crush the determination of the Indonesians to maintain their sovereignty, and thereby make it possible for the Dutch to colonize all over again. Whatever they try, the Dutch will never be able to make us give up the type of government we have chosen for ourselves because the burning flame of our patriotism will render null and void all Dutch designs on us. So long as the world can see no other way out of the present impasse except that of supporting the Dutch claim on Indonesia and so long as such action leads to deprivation of the right of Indonesians to decide their own destiny, so long will Indonesia be unable to contribute her material wealth to the enrichment of the world. . . .

The political burden we have shouldered lays upon us the responsibility for the well-being of our country as well as an obligation to satisfy the world family of nations that we are discharging our duties in an efficient and just manner. We entertain no hatred for the Dutch or for any other foreign people, and certainly none at all towards the Eurasians who are flesh of our flesh and blood of our blood. The logic of circumstances alone should make that evident, because we know and realize that the needs of our country and of our people call for technical, financial, and educational assistance— just to mention three forms of help we shall require from outside sources for many years to come. In this connection the Dutch enjoy a distinct advantage over others—they have been here and are familiar with conditions in Indonesia. Indonesian independence will necessarily entail a complete reorientation of political relations between us and the Dutch, but it will not affect Dutch capital or Dutch lives.

The incredible richness of our land gives ample promise of better living standards for our people in common with the rest of the world, if only this great latent wealth of ours is properly exploited. In that task the peoples of all nations—most of all of the United States, Australia, and the Philippines—will find ample opportunity to help us with their money and skill.

However, both Indonesia and the world will be denied this chance of cooperation for our mutual benefit if opposition from the Dutch withholds recognition of our country or of the form of government we have chosen for ourselves. In such an event not only will we and the Dutch be losers, but also the world at large, which is eagerly hoping for material and spiritual contributions from Indonesia towards the satisfying of world needs.

When the Republic of Indonesia is formally recognized, we will accordingly take appropriate action regarding a number of important matters. All debts incurred by the Dutch East Indies government previous to the Japanese surrender and fairly chargeable to us we will unhesitatingly take over. All property of foreigners will be handed over to them, with one exception—we reserve the right to acquire at fair prices such property as shall be deemed necessary for the welfare of the country. In concert with our immediate neighbors and the rest of the world we intend to take our place in the Council of the United Nations to further and implement the ideals contained in the San Francisco Charter.

Our internal policy will be based on the sovereignty of the people, and we will put into practice all steps necessary to bring home to and to evoke in the breasts of Eurasian and European residents of our country the highest feeling of patriotism and democracy.

In a short while we intend to demonstrate our adherence to democratic ideals by calling a general election, in accordance with the constitutional principles laid down for our country. There is always the possibility that such an election may result in far-reaching changes in the composition of the government. Also the elected representatives of the people may call for far-reaching constitutional changes.

Citizens and residents of Indonesia will be the beneficiaries of the reconstruction program we plan to put into operation. Such a scheme calls for large credits as well as manufactured goods from the United States, Australia, and other countries having trade relations with our country. All groups of the population, provided they do not commit breaches of regulations, will be guaranteed the opportunity to engage in any legitimate form of work they may desire.

The Dutch government and the Dutch people have now reached a point where they must make up their minds regarding Indonesia. Do they intend to follow blindly the lead given them by a small band of capitalists and imperialists, selfish and self-seeking, who are bent on sacrificing the youth of Holland in the risky venture of trying to subjugate Indonesia anew? Or have they the vision and the ability to adjust themselves to changed conditions and, by means of peaceful discussions, secure for themselves and their descendants in this country the predominant place they hold in trade and industry, thereby also making it possible for themselves to live here and earn their livelihood in peace and security?

If

Masjumi of North Sumatra Welcoming the Social Revolution (1946)

This statement was issued by the North Sumatra Division of the Masjumi party on March 12, 1946, at the end of one of the episodes

of the 1945–1949 period in which violence was directed principally
at fellow Indonesians. This was the so-called East Sumatran Social
Revolution of early 1946, in which the several petty sultans of this
region were overthrown and many members of their families killed.
The translation is from Osman Raliby, Documenta Historica (Djakarta: Bulan-Bintang, 1953), I, 274–275.

The current of social revolution which has swept through the
principalities of East Sumatra is not only bringing in political changes
and changes in the structure of government, but is also bringing
benefits in the form of new ideas and progress in the Islamic religion.

The Islamic Political Party Masjumi, as a party of the Muslim people which has as its goal the defense and advancement of the Republic of Indonesia, views this social revolution as a second step toward full realization of the principle of the sovereignty of the people
interpreted as broadly as possible. As a result of the changes it has
brought, every piece of land which is part of the Indonesian State has
automatically come under the direct control of its government, control which is to be exercised according to the principles of democracy. Thus, an end is put to an anomaly which has long been a puzzle
to experts in constitutional matters, namely, monarchical forms
within a Republican state.

As a political party with a religious basis and religious ideals the
Masjumi also views these changes as the sweeping away of a barrier
which has stood in the way of the Islamic reform movement. The
principalities have long been strongholds of traditionalism in the
religious sphere. The people of the principalities were shackled in
their religious views and unable to oppose the ideas of the kings
and princes who called themselves and considered themselves *Ulil-
Amri.** Islamic movements with progressive ideas were deliberately
prevented from extending influence into these territories. Prior permission had to be received from the ruler before Islamic associations could be established.

The funds which they were required by religious teaching to use
for the advancement of religion were, in fact, not in evidence. If
there were bodies which were so bold as to collect *zakat* [obligatory
alms] for distribution among the poor and indigent so that the rights
of the poor might not continue to be violated by a section of greedy

* Literally, those in authority; freely translated as "defenders of the faith."

and grasping *ulama,* such action was obstructed. It once happened that the chairman of an Islamic organization in Sungai Rempah was sentenced to a month in jail by a principality tribunal because he had dared to set up a place for Friday prayers alongside the place which the principality had established for Friday prayers. A section of *ulama* and mosque officials were required to pray for the long life of the ruler. A thousand and one instances could be provided of former rulers hampering the Islamic reform movement.

It is not surprising, therefore, that the development of the religious movement has been uneven in East Sumatra. In the principalities religious teachings were directed toward lulling men to sleep, so that there arose the belief among people who did not look for an explanation of this situation that the religion of Islam concerns itself only with the hereafter.

Thanks be to God! With the destruction of the principalities, the course of religious activity can be made uniform throughout the region of East Sumatra.

The Islamic Political Party Masjumi is aware of the heavy responsibility it now bears, namely, to bring the spirit of Islamic reformism into what were the principalities and to carry political awareness into the mosques, religious schools, and so on, so that the places where the One God is being worshipped will ring with the sounds of the struggle to defend and develop the fatherland. Merdeka!

Ig
T. B. Simatupang[*] The Nation and the Regions in the People's War (1949)

This fragment is taken from Laporan dari Banaran (*Report from Banaran*), *a volume of memoirs which General Simatupang published in 1960 (Djakarta: P. T. Pembangunan). Banaran is a village near Jogjakarta, which served as a guerrilla headquarters after the second Dutch attack ("police action") of December 1948.*

I am not a Javanese; I am an Indonesian born in Tapanuli. Yet never in my wanderings through Java during this war of independence have I felt foreign the slightest bit. Sjafruddin, the son of West Java who is leading the people's struggles in the Minangkabau mountains, doubtless does not feel himself foreign there. So it is, too,

[*] For biographical information on the authors, see Appendix I.

with Hidajat, the son of West Java who is commanding the people's fight in all Sumatra; with Simbolon, born in Tapanuli but commanding in South Sumatra; with Kawilarang, the Minahasan who leads the people in Tapanuli and East Sumatra; with Nasution born in Tapanuli but now Commander for Java; with Sadikin from Banjumas who commands in West Java; with Gatot Subroto from Banjumas who leads the people's fight in Solo; and with Sungkono, another child of Banjumas who leads the independence fight in East Java. Is there any more positive proof that this people's war is a national war, although in view of circumstances it is organized on a regional basis?

But this people's war also obviously has its regional aspects. A region that carries on a war on the basis of its own resources—even though within a broader context—inevitably increases its self-respect. Each such region gives birth to its own tales of heroism which become sources of regional pride. This war is certainly strengthening the bonds between the military leaders, the regional administration and the local notables, who feel they are all in it together. Moreover, to attract the mass of people, full use is made of the heroic traditions of each region: the story of Diponegoro's struggle has in my experience been a living reality in this district around Banaran, while in Central and East Java generally many people see our struggle in the light of their belief in the prophesies of Djojobojo.*

In other regions, naturally, other symbols serve as bonds. Java fights its war independently of Sumatra, although both islands acknowledge the leadership of the Emergency Government of the Republic of Indonesia and of the Commander-in-Chief, and in both islands each district, large or small, fights the people's war practically from its own resources.

Perhaps we may say that as a result of this people's war our consciousness and self-respect as a nation will increase, while the means by which the war is fought will also apparently strengthen, in each region that carries on the war, the consciousness of its own value, strength, and personality.

The forces which have been awakened during this war may be likened to a river in time of flood. The question arises: when the war ends—as in time it will—what will happen to these forces? Can we use the gigantic potential of this river to generate electric power? Can we use this abundant water to bring fertility to the fields and

* A twelfth-century East Javanese king, reputed in Javanese tradition to have prophesied the downfall of his country and its subsequent rise to greatness.

plantations of our people? Or will the great force of its swirling torrent bring suffering and distress to our people when its present target, Dutch power, has disappeared?

We are going to need social "engineers" who can put to work the mighty forces which this war has stirred up, that they may bring happiness and prosperity to our people and not endless misery and destitution.

Such were my thoughts as we returned "home" to Banaran after wandering forty days from village to village and from mountain to mountain in the region of Jogjakarta and Surakarta, where the heart of Java has beaten since the dawn of our history.

Ih

Sukarno The Work of a Leader (1951)

This extract is translated from Spirit, Will, and Deed, *an address which the President gave at Jogjakarta on September 17, 1951, after having an honorary doctorate conferred upon him by Gadjah Mada University. The Indonesian version was published as* Ilmu dan Amal (Geest-Wil-Daad) *in Jogjakarta (Ministry of Information, 1951).*

I am called a political leader. What, then, is my task? My task, like that of all political leaders, is not to waste time with merely theoretical meditations, but to activate people to deeds. A leader's task is to bring the group he leads to act, to bring the class he leads to act, to bring the nation he leads to act. Why does a man become a leader if not to bring men to act? But an act is an effect, the effect of desire, the effect of will. There is no action without desire, there is no action without will. Therefore "to bring men to act" implies that the will must first be activated. And if this truth is related to questions concerning the life of a nation or a society, then it means that the leader must above all activate the collective will, must shake, awaken, move, intensify the collective will. For what? To give birth to collective action, to bring about a collective deed. That is the pattern of everything I have done since my youth until now. That is the meaning of the trilogy I enunciated in 1932, National spirit, National will, and National deed. Other people contribute science, or discuss, analyze, and develop theories. I am happy if I am able to carry out the task allotted to me, that is, to awaken men to action, to activate men to deeds! Let me say it again in order to

bring men to act; I try to activate the will, the collective will. I try
to awaken the collective will, to make it more determined, to set
it aflame!

There are people who lack understanding of the significance of
will in historical processes. There are many Marxists who, because
they have read that Marx did not recognize free will but, on the contrary, always propounded the principle of necessity in the development of society, conclude that human will is without significance in
historical processes. But what is the reality? The reality is that we
have to distinguish clearly between will and free will. Both the idealistic and the historical-materialist (Marxist) philosophies state that
the human will is very significant in historical processes. It is true
that Marx denied the existence of free will, but he never denied the
significance of the will as such. Moreover, he never denied the
significance of personality, and he once spoke of "die Riesenrolle der
menschlichen Persönlichkeit" [the gigantic role of the human per-
sonality]. . . .

So I see in the human will the driving force of all economic and
all historical processes. It is the origin, it is the internal source, of
all events in society; it gives force to everything that happens in a
community.

What is known as economic necessity or historical necessity or any
kind of necessity at all in the process of human life does not mean
that there is no human will, does not mean "absence of free will."
Decidedly not! "Economic necessity" or "historical necessity" has its
source in the necessity of every man to will-to-live, and—as a consequence of that—in the necessity of man to make use of existing
circumstances in order that he be able to live.

On these grounds, according to my opinion, it is the duty of every
Indonesian leader to activate the will of Indonesians and to activate
the Indonesian national will to the highest endeavour. Without the
will of individuals there can be no national will, and without national will there can be no national action. . . .

The leader must activate the will of the masses to struggle. That
has been the only ambition in the depth of my heart since my youth:
to activate the will of the masses to struggle. There is only one undying fire in my heart: to activate the national will to struggle, yes,
to shake the national feeling for the struggle in order that national
deeds may be born, for, indeed, national deeds are the only key to
the gate to happiness.

Thus, the question now is this: can the will to struggle be activated? Can the fighting spirit be activated? Can the will-to-struggle of a nation be called up so that it is prepared to move, to toil, to labor, and to wrestle, to sacrifice, to suffer, to be ready to spring into a sea of fire in order to achieve its objective? The history of the world has proved that such things are possible. World history is not void of ardent national movements, which did, it is true, arise on the basis of objective factors, yet in which the will of the masses had clearly been activated by competent leadership.

On what does the strength or weakness of the masses' will to struggle depend? It depends on three factors: first, on whether the aim or ideals which call the masses to struggle are attractive or not; second, on the feeling of capability, of competency or ability among the masses; and third, on the power which in fact exists among the masses. Thus, in the first place, on what is called the prize; in the second place, on the feeling of strength; in the third place, on actual strength. The able leader should thus picture to the people what is the value of the prize of the struggle; the able leader must enlarge the feeling of capacity among the masses to obtain the prize of the struggle; and the able leader must build up the power of the masses in a real way in order to win the prize of the struggle. Such a leader could activate the masses' will to struggle. . . .

Here, again, I am attempting to bring the element of struggle to the fore. Our nation has a character reflecting Pantja Sila, but that does not mean that the Pantja Sila has already assumed concrete form in every part and every corner of our society, that it has already been realized in all fields of the life of our society! There are people who say: "Of what use is Panja Sila while there is still much poverty among the people? Of what use is Pantja Sila while people still too often contravene the principle of humanity?" Brothers and sisters, is it Christianity which is at fault if there are still many people who are not Christlike? Is it Islam that is to blame if not all its injunctions are as yet being followed? Is it a defect in Pantja Sila if there are still Indonesians without religious convictions, if there are still conflicts and provincialism, if there are still people who act harshly toward their fellowmen or are national-chauvinists; if sovereignty of the people has not been effected completely; if there is still poverty and hardship?

No, the defect is that we ourselves, also in the matter of Pantja Sila, forget the element of struggle. As regards Pantja Sila, too, people must think in terms of spirit-will-deed! The Indonesian people must continue to struggle, to struggle in the widest sense of the word; in the first place, in the sense of building up the country—building it up both materially and morally—in order that the Pantja Sila is truly made manifest in all fields of life.

For, just as every individual exists in a network of circumstances which influence and limit his material life, so a nation exists in a network of circumstances influencing and circumscribing its life. The individual's struggle is a struggle to use and conquer circumstances, in order that his whole being may grow and develop. Similarly, the national struggle should be a struggle to use and conquer existing circumstances so that the soul and being of the nation may grow and develop in its internal as well as its external aspects.

II

Parliamentary Democracy
and Its Critics

In 1949 the Dutch finally abandoned their attempt to reestablish control over Indonesia. At the Round Table Conference held at The Hague between August and November of that year they agreed to give up their claim to sovereignty over all except West New Guinea or West Irian and to support the establishment of the Republic of the United States of Indonesia (RUSI), a federation of which fifteen small Dutch-built states would be members but where preponderant power would lie with the sixteenth member state, the Republic of Indonesia. The RUSI came into existence on December 27, 1949. The next few months, however, saw the quick collapse of the Dutch-established states (see Xa), and so by August 17, 1950, RUSI had been transformed into a new unitary state, the second Republic of Indonesia.

The seven or eight years after 1949 were a period of parliamentary democracy. Parliament was a nominated body until 1955, but it was a central institution throughout the period. Cabinets fell when they could no longer command a majority in it, and, indeed, they fell frequently. Parties were very powerful, the army and President Sukarno relatively weak, and civil liberties rarely denied.

In the first three and a half years after 1949 governmental leadership was in the hands of Hatta and a group of moderate, business-like, and "pro-Western" leaders around him, who tended to see the revolution as a thing of the past. These men concerned themselves intensively with reconstruction and economic development, tasks which they saw as requiring not only administrative normalization but also a policy of protecting the powerful position of Dutch and other foreign capital, at least for some years. They had little time for nationalist militancy or the messianic expectations which had been generated in the period of the revolution. An extreme version of this view is presented in XIIIc. A more moderate and more characteristic version, in which consolidation and economics-first are justified in terms congruent with the mood of revolution, is presented in the first extract of this section; and this is paralleled by VIId. Our second extract here presents a more complete rejection of the consolidationist position.

In the third and fourth extracts two of the most influential thinkers of the day discuss the loss of élan which characterized this period, the mood of disappointment, rudderlessness, and frustration which led men to make adverse comparisons with the atmosphere which had characterized the years of revolution.

The sense of disappointment as well as the political ferment remained intense throughout the parliamentary period, and eventually the system of parliamentary democracy itself became one of its targets. Apprehensions about competitive party politics grew after 1953, when campaigning started in earnest for the expected parliamentary elections, eventually held in 1955; for it soon became clear that campaigning would be strongly ideological, much of it centering on whether the state should be based on the Pantja Sila with its inclusive principle of The One Deity or on Islam. Fear that this could destroy national unity is expressed in our fifth extract here.

For a time there was great hope that the 1955 elections would serve to regenerate Indonesia's democracy, but, as things turned out, governmental weakness and instability was as great after the elections as before. So, the next two years saw the emergence of several new challenges to the existing framework of political institutions.

One group of leaders demanded a greater role for the army—see XIVb and XIVc. Another group demanded greater autonomy for the regions, especially those outside Java—see Xb and IIh. But what finally proved to be the strongest challenge came from President Sukarno himself, with his ideas of Guided Democracy. Two expositions of these form our sixth and seventh extracts here. They should be read in conjunction with one or another of the general antiliberal statements reproduced in this volume—Vd, Vf, Vg, and XIVb. And they should be read together with the Communist statement in IIIf, especially as there is an important sense in which this debate marks the entry of the Communists onto the central political stage.

On the whole, parliamentary democracy was accepted with little discussion of what it involved and later rejected with few men coming to its defense. But some defenses there were, and excerpts from two of these make up our final items in this section. They are perhaps best considered alongside the more detached analysis of General Simatupang in XIVd.

IIa
Staff of the Armed Forces   Widening the Meaning of Heroism (1951)

This message was issued on Heroes' Day, November 10, 1951, the sixth anniversary of the Battle of Surabaja against the British. It appeared in the Djakarta weekly, Mimbar Indonesia, *of the same date. Authorship of it is attributed to Major General T. B. Simatupang.*

Each year on the tenth of November all Indonesia remembers and honors its heroes.

On this day, Indonesians visit the heroes' cemeteries where they observe one minute's silence and lay flowers on the graves of those who gave their lives for the freedom and happiness of their nation.

This tradition, which started during the struggle for independence, of setting aside one day in which the people of Indonesia remember their heroes is one which needs to be preserved. Remembering those who gave their lives either in the struggle for independence or during the campaign to restore security throughout the country serves to deepen our understanding of how great was the price we have paid to gain our independence and to protect our nation in the face of internal threats.

This understanding provides our nation with something we can cling to and believe in in the midst of the difficulties we now face; this understanding provides the stimulus to work with greater devotion.

The freedom achieved by the spilling of so much blood and so many tears cannot be trifled with; it is our obligation to the heroes we remember and honor each Heroes' Day to utilize our freedom in the best possible way so as to abolish poverty, ignorance, hunger, and fear from among our millions of people. Our heroes died convinced that they were sacrificing their lives in the cause of achieving an independent, prosperous, strong, and just Indonesia. When we remember them, we realize that the ideals for which they gave their lives are still far from being realized.

Indonesia possesses all the essentials necessary to become a just, strong, and prosperous state; she is endowed with sufficient natural wealth, enough inhabitants, and the struggle for independence has already proven that she is prepared to fight and work to realize the ideals she has embraced.

The Indonesian nation still needs to increase its skill and experience in all fields, but it certainly possesses the ability to accomplish this task. Increasing skill and experience is a matter of time and of working according to a plan. We have all the resources required to become a strong and prosperous nation; whether or not these resources can be utilized depends upon the capacities of the groups providing the leadership for the development of our nation. Up to now these groups have not always shown themselves to be fully devoted to this task. It is to be hoped that the remembrance of the heroes of our nation serves to increase their dedication. The meaning accorded to "Hero" so far has been that of a fighter killed in action fighting for his homeland. This is understandable, because until the transfer of sovereignty our primary task was to struggle for our independence, and, under the prevailing conditions, to be prepared to sacrifice our lives was the only course open to us.

Under these circumstances it was natural that "heroism" was identified solely with the sacrifice of one's life in the cause of achieving independence. That this usage has persisted is also easily understood.

However, the time has come for a widening of the meaning of heroism so as to include the performance of all actions which are of great benefit to the homeland, all actions which display extraordinary ability, probity, dedication, and tenacity.

Many of the difficulties which we now face are the result of reluctance to direct our thoughts, which for years have been slanted toward heroism on the battlefield, toward heroism in other fields of no less importance to the welfare of the nation.

We must continue to accord the highest respect to those who have sacrificed their lives for the independence and welfare of the nation. We must continue to preserve our people's willingness to sacrifice their lives whenever it is necessary to do so in order to defend our independence, because independence once gained may not last forever. It must be continuously defended and will be lost if we neglect its defense for even one moment. But willingness to fight by itself is not sufficient to produce a great nation. National Independence can be achieved and defended by heroes of the battlefield, but national greatness can only be achieved when a nation produces heroes in science, industry, shipping, education, and development.

The heroes of Indonesian independence were the youth. It was they who provided the dynamic for the Proclamation of Independence; it was they who formed the armed forces after the proclamation; it was they who provided the strength needed to defend independence; it was they who gave their blood for freedom.

The old structure in Indonesia was changed mainly because it was no longer acceptable to the younger generation. The generation which provided the support and leadership in the struggle for independence has not yet succeeded in providing support and leadership in the drive for development since recognition of our independence. In comparison with the situation at the beginning of the struggle for independence, the youth of today appear as if inhibited in our state and society. There are several reasons for this.

First and most important: the youth poured all its energy and activity into the struggle during the revolutionary period. This is especially true in comparison with other groups.

Second: the youth were indeed in the frontline so long as fighting-spirit and courage were the foremost considerations. However, in times when skill and experience are required, other groups gradually take over the leadership.

Third: many groups which had deliberately remained a little to the rear during the struggle for independence have reappeared and are utilizing their experience so as to compete successfully for the positions they want.

The above factors make clear why we can now say that our nation and society is "older" than it was at the commencement of the revolution; the tempo of working, the freshness of thinking, and the measures used have certainly changed because of these factors. All these things have the effect of producing fatigue, yes, sometimes even cynicism and indifference among many of the youth.

Heroes' Day is Youth Day. Indonesia will not overcome her present difficulties and progress rapidly toward prosperity and greatness if the generation which led and supported the struggle for independence does not overcome its weaknesses and shortcomings so as to provide leadership and impetus in the development of the new Indonesia.

IIb

Nugroho Notosusanto   A New Generation (1952)

This extract comes from the Djakarta student magazine Kompas
*of May 15, 1952. The author, then a twenty-one-year-old student, had
written an article opposing the teaching of Dutch in secondary
schools which had drawn a reply from Jef Last, a Dutch writer and
long-time supporter of Indonesian independence who was then
living in Indonesia. Believing that he had known Nugroho before
the war, Last expressed surprise at what he saw as the unreason-
able nationalism in the position he was now taking. Nugroho replied
that he was not the Noegroho whom Last knew but another and a
member of a very different generation. His reply speaks for the young
intellectuals whose political orientations had been formed by their
participation in the Student Army during the Revolution.*

I am glad to have made your acquaintance, Mr. Last, be it only
by chance and by letter, because you are a Dutchman different from
the Dutch against whom we fought to the limit of our resources
during the armed conflict. I have heard quite a bit about you and
about the way in which you espoused our Fight for Freedom.

My reaction to your letter and to your point of view will, of
course, be different from the one you expected from ——, the other
Noegroho! I am not of the same generation as Noegroho but belong
to a younger generation which grew up amid fighting, struggle, and
combat. I am of that group of young people who three years ago were
described as the Indonesian *pemudas,* who were chased from place to
place, ambushed, and literally slaughtered by General Spoor's men,
whom your Government Information Service described as terrorists
and extremists—whereas Noegroho's generation were the "level-
headed," peace-loving people of "broad vision."

In writing all this to you, Mr. Last, I am not motivated by hatred
or rancor, not in the least. I only want to make it clear that I am
different from the young people of the Indonesian generation with
which you are acquainted. We look at the situation of our people
in a different way from that of the Noegroho generation, let alone
that of the generation of Takdir Alisjahbana with its high-flown
theories.

Your introduction to me is at the same time an introduction to a
still newer generation of Indonesian young people which has al-

ready gained its position in the community even though it has not yet completely voiced its ideas. Three or four years ago we were known as the Student Army. That was the name which our society came to give to all the secondary school and university students who freely left their desks for interests greater than personal ones to join in a life-and-death struggle to save our people from drowning in the mud of history.*

I hope you do not feel that I am digressing: I am purposely starting with a long introduction to throw as much light as I can on the sources of my view of the problems of our People in this period and of what I called "The Problem of the Dutch Language." I hope you will judge me with the measuring stick of my own generation, not with that of the previous generation which frolicked to its heart's delight in splendid theories. Permit me now then, Mr. Last, to start my reply to your letter:

First of all, I want to say that you are wrong—it may be perhaps a misunderstanding—in thinking that I wanted to replace the Dutch language with English. That was not my intention. I wanted to say that Dutch had to be replaced by Indonesian. Only in the transitional period would English books replace such Dutch books as had not yet been translated into Indonesian. That the teaching of English at secondary schools has been very unsatisfactory is something I pointed to in my previous article, and, of course, this has to be improved, and much is already being done to this effect. . . .

Prerevolutionary standards cannot be used in the present times. I have already touched on the question of teaching personnel. But, of course, one cannot argue for the teaching of Dutch simply on the grounds that the teaching of English has not yet reached the required standard because of a lack of competent teachers. This would be more or less the same as arguing for Dutch "guidance" of the Indonesian people on the grounds simply that at the most 10 per cent of us can read or write, an argument which is clearly absurd, as you would agree. Only recently, during the revolution, have our people thrown off laziness, indolence, and sluggishness. They are conscious of their own strength, although in many respects they have still not learned well enough how to work themselves and not to depend on the charity of foreigners for everything. The shortage of teachers,

* *Tentara Peladjar* or Students' Army was the popular name given one unit of the TNI, the Seventeenth Brigade, which consisted entirely of secondary school and university students.

too, is something which we will have to overcome ourselves by making a supreme effort. This shortage in every field must lash us into extraordinary activity. It must not come to the point, where Indonesia again slips down into the abyss of laziness and inferiority complexes. It is not only the teachers of English in this country whose qualities are insufficient when you measure them according to the famous criterion of the "international standard," but also our public servants, officers, and entrepreneurs, and even our farmers who do not know about mechanization, kolkozes, *sovkozes,* and so on! And tell me, did we at the time we took up arms in the various parts of our country against General Spoor's army ever worry whether our army's combat value had reached the international standard? As a matter of fact, our *bapaks,* who are now giving themselves to so much theorizing, were trembling in fear and were counseling us on the need to start negotiations. We had better negotiate and keep on negotiating, without building up as much support as we could. They were full of deference to the "international standard" whereas we were struggling against mountains of difficulties. And when these mountains had been dug away, it was so easy for them to pat their *pemudas* on the back and give them fulsome praise, which stuck like syrup. . . .

As you can see, "patriotic feelings" come through in the tone of my letter—to use one of your expressions—a fact which I do not at all want to hide. Indeed, my generation is one which still has patriotic feelings, in contrast to the previous generation which calls it "broad-minded," universalist, and supranational to receive pats on the back from their elder brothers overseas. Perhaps you can suppress your patriotic feelings easily because your people's "Eighty Years' War" has been molding for so long in the pages of the book of history. It is different with us, who have only recently completed our "eight years' war"—counting the Japanese period—whose purpose it was to bring into being our State, the manifestation of our desire to form one People with an Honor and a Pride of its own, a war whose scars are still fresh among the new generation which experienced it in all its intensity. . . .

I have heard the following comparison made in connection with the problem of the Dutch language: "Good, but why throw out your old boots before you have been able to get new ones?" As a result of the revolution we find ourselves in a situation where our boots were discarded long ago, whereas the new ones are still pinching, giving us blisters on our feet. Do we have to put on Abu Kasim's boots again, purely because our new boots do not yet quite fit? Would we not be far better off to do something about these new boots of ours than to keep on walking in those old patched-up ones? . . .

What you say about "half-intellectuals" could be true, but we are more in need of such so-called "half-intellectuals" who are giving 100 per cent of their efforts to help their people to make progress by a supreme effort than of "full intellectuals" who only think of themselves, because they do not love their People wholeheartedly. What I have seen in Djakarta, Bandung, and other cities confirms my suspicion about the existence of such a tendency among groups of students who are living in a Netherlandophilic atmosphere. (I am of course generalizing very broadly here.) I recall the arguments of some of my comrades when we went off to the battlefield, as for example, "If all students started defending the country and left their desks, the People would have to pay for the damage, because this would create a shortage of intellectuals." With such arguments they contented themselves while continuing their studies, although deep in their hearts they felt a stab of pain when they saw their fellows voluntarily abandoning their pleasant student lives in order to defend Freedom. I am drawing attention to this to show that there always have been people who indulge in nice theories in order to camouflage their fear of difficulties.

The difficulties which are confronting us now after the end of war are in my view greater than those which existed when the war was still being waged, especially as our élan has started to dwindle.

I am not concerned with hollow slogans, though you may think I am. I simply want to present the idealism of youth set over against crooked cynicism.

IIc

Mohammad Natsir Lassitude and the Display of False Glitter (1951)

Natsir gave this speech as a Masjumi party leader on Independence Day, 1951, the cabinet he led having fallen four months previously. The full text is published in M. Natsir, Capita Selecta, II (Djakarta: Pustaka Pendis, 1957), pp. 53–57.

Six years have gone by. For almost two years our Fatherland has

been a completely sovereign state. The enemy in the form of colonialism has been banished from our land. Our people have achieved the
status of an independent nation and have joined the ranks of other
independent peoples. Indonesia has been admitted to membership
in the United Nations. The withdrawal of Dutch troops from our
Fatherland has been completed. It could be expected that our people
would be more joyful than in the past. That is indeed how it should
be!

But what is the situation we see before us? When we look around,
we see very few joyful expressions. It is as if the Independence we
have obtained had brought but few benefits. It would seem that expectations have not been fulfilled. The gain is like a loss.

This is all in contrast with the attitude prevailing at the beginning
of the revolution. All sorts of complaints are heard now. There is
disappointment, ideals have been lost sight of. Everywhere there
prevails a feeling of dissatisfaction, a feeling of frustration, a feeling of hopelessness. This is the situation that confronts us after nearly
two years of independence and sovereignty. Formerly, a joyful enthusiasm prevailed, even with the loss of wealth, even with the loss
of home and belongings, even with the loss of sons on the field of
battle. But now the people are dispirited and disappointed, although
the independence of their Fatherland is achieved, the fulfillment
of their ideals and aspirations for decades, even centuries.

Why has this change come about? We cannot answer this question
in one or two words. The whole issue requires a survey of what has
happened in the structure of our society. We can only instance some
of the more apparent factors evident at present. There is a general
tendency now to assess the sacrifices made and to insist on the
recognition of the worth of these sacrifices. Deliberately, attention
is drawn to all that was sacrificed, and it is demanded that public
recognition be accorded for all these sacrifices. Formerly, sacrifices
were made for the sake of the people, and now it is expected that
an appropriate reward should be given in return. Of course, every
one of our countrymen had a share in our revolutionary struggle as
far as sacrifice is concerned. As has been mentioned, wealth, effort,
and family were given up for the struggle. Then, there was compas-
sion and sympathy, but now there has emerged the malady of cupidity; sweat is grudged, time is grudged, and selfish thoughts are upper-
most. No one has his heart in his work. Effort is avoided, even for
the carrying out of personal duties and obligations. All imperfections

and shortcomings are allowed to remain. There is no will and no desire to bring about improvement. Selfish personal advantage is sought rather than fulfillment of ideals of service to others. The lamp of idealism shines no longer; its oil is consumed; the gleam has gone; and no one knows what to do next.

We ask the Muslim community: Is this the situation aspired to in the ideals of the Muslim community? Was it for this that Muslim fathers and Muslim mothers willingly let their children fight? Is this state of affairs acceptable to the Muslim community? The answer will be "No." And if the answer is "No," it is an indication that the struggle is not yet completed. Indeed, it means that the struggle has just begun. It means that the enemy has not disappeared. He has merely changed form and position. Previously there was an external enemy who could be confronted forthrightly. Now, the enemy is within, disintegrating the strength of the people.

Have you been infected by the malady of indifference and become unconcerned at what you see happening around you? Have you, too, been infected by the malady of cupidity and become unwilling to roll up your sleeves and unwilling to lose some sweat? Have you, too, lost all sense of distinction between right and wrong? Have you, too, become obsessed in self-seeking, calculating all things in terms of advantage and profit? Have you, too, become dispirited, no longer aware of the ideals that impulsed your thoughts and actions, making you dynamic and bursting with initiative? Have you come to think: "My task is finished and now is the time to divide the profits produced by the struggle of the past"?

If so, then you are of those who secure gains but feel as if they had had losses. You are in the middle of the current, but you feel as if you were at the edge of the stream, and for that reason you have stopped paddling; the swift flowing current will carry you drifting away again even though you may loudly complain and try to place the blame on others. The current will carry you drifting away to a place where you did not wish to go.

You would do well to remember the commandment of God given in sura An-Nur, verse 39: "Their deeds are as a mirage in a desert. The thirsty one supposeth it to be water till he cometh unto it and findeth it naught." You are like the traveler in the scorching desert and you will not find your longings satisfied. Instead, you will find the punishment of God inflicted for deeds carried out on a wrong basis and without a plan.

Do you want to get free of the clutch of that current? To get free you must paddle, and to do this you must be prepared to sweat, you must be prepared to step onto the battlefield that stretches before you into the distance.

The poverty of the people in the midst of the God-bestowed wealth of nature, the lassitude and dispiritedness, the disregard for moral standards and high ideals, the display of false glitter, the danger of disintegration and confusion stirred up by a hidden hand—all this constitutes a field of struggle demanding resoluteness and daring. This struggle can only be waged if there is flourishing enthusiasm, readiness to accept self-effacement, and the capacity to open up new roads in a planned manner.

IId

Sukarno   The Crisis of Authority (1952)

This excerpt comes from the President's Independence Day address, August 17, 1952. The full text was published as Harapan dan Kenjataan *(Hope and Facts)* *(Djakarta: Ministry of Information, 1952).*

A paradox exists in Indonesia today. For decades we have longed for authority. For decades we have longed for an authority of our own. And now that we have our own authority, we do not respect it. Awareness of having our own government is something that is missing among part of our people. It is indeed true that whenever an armed revolution is brought to an end, there will be groups that cannot adjust themselves to its ending. That is true of every revolution. For what is a revolution? A revolution is a clash between two groups of forces colliding with each other. That was the case with the Indonesian revolution. We represented one group and the Dutch, the other. One could compare us to one factory and the Dutch to another factory and say that one factory tried to outdo the other. The Indonesian factory was up against the Dutch factory; the factory of independence contended with the factory of colonial rule.

Each of these factories has flywheels, and although the factories have come to a stop, their flywheels keep on turning still. They keep on turning in spite of the fact that the armed revolution has come to an end. The Round Table Conference succeeded in stopping the activities of the Indonesian and Dutch factories, but certain flywheels in these factories could not immediately be brought to a stop. Andi Azis, Soumokil, Westerling, Bosch and Schmidt, Abdul Hamid,* and extremists on our own side who are opposed to our Republic—all these are flywheels which should have stopped but are still turning and thereby damaging and destroying things in the factory. And because the flywheels are out of coordination with the factory, they fly to the right and to the left, and so it comes about that the extremes sometimes meet.

I am giving you this picture to show that at the end of any armed revolution there will always be individuals or groups which cannot adjust themselves to the political conditions produced by it. But in Indonesia it is not merely this that has happened. As I said previously, we are now plagued by another calamity, the disease of not respecting authority, the disease of denying authority. I have said on other occasions that we are the victims of four kinds of crisis. First of all, there is a political crisis because many persons do not believe in democracy any more. Second, there is a crisis in the apparatus for the maintenance of law and order. Third, there is a crisis in our way of thinking and analyzing. Fourth, there is a moral crisis. But in point of fact we are suffering from yet another crisis, the crisis of authority.

Because people do not respect Authority, a crisis of Authority comes into being, and because there is a crisis over Authority, people do not respect Authority. One bites the other, and the other hits back. This is a vicious circle. How shall we break through it? The sole way to do so is to restore Authority to its throne. The authorities should be bold enough to reestablish the instinctive and natural respect for Authority. The authorities should act determinedly to make Authority effective once more.

Apart from Authority with a capital A, there is authority with a small a. That, also, is experiencing crisis. That, too, is being bitten and smacked. Those who are answerable in this respect are not those who are in authority, but those who are not. Those who are in responsible positions do not have Authority, and those who have authority are irresponsible. The crisis surrounding authority— the one with the small *a*—is a twin brother to the crisis surrounding Authority with a capital A. The two are children of the same mother

* All of these were involved in coups and rebel movements against the authority of the new central government in the period immediately following December 1949.

and represent a wayward mentality. No outsider, not even the gods from Olympus, can heal us of this ill; only the Indonesian people can heal themselves, and they should do it soon as possible.

Love of loot, love of plundering, love of arson, love of treachery to one's fellow man, love of killing, love of toting guns—all these result from a peculiar way of thinking. And this way of thinking is strengthened by the existence of the crisis surrounding Authority and normally arises when there is a vacuum in authority. The mental crisis itself produces an authority crisis, that is true, but the authority crisis adds to the mentality crisis. There is more of this biting and being bitten in turn; they both cause a crisis and result in a crisis. Plainly, the way to deliver our people from this vicious circle is to give authority real Authority once more. Authority should free itself from the coils of this vicious circle and be bold enough to act with real and instinctive Authority. Right is right, right must be protected and strengthened, right must be put into action irrespective of persons.

Do not place the emphasis on a relative truth, namely, that disturbances of the peace are due to shortcomings in our present economy. Look at what happened during the Japanese occupation. Has there been any time in our recent history when our economy was more disturbed, more chaotic, more knocked about than during the Japanese occupation? Thousands of people died of starvation, hundreds of thousands of people were victims of semistarvation, and millions were badly hit economically. But we had none of the marauding and robber gangs we find now. Why? Because at that time there was Authority, and the instinctive and natural respect for Authority.

At that time the Authority was fascistic, but that is merely a matter of the nature of that Authority. That does not alter the fact that Authority existed and that it was an instinctive and natural Authority. . . .

The difference between our hopes on August 17, 1945, and our achievements by August 17, 1952, is big. As the reports of the various ministries show, we have progressed in many matters of detail, but the aspirations we dreamed of have not yet materialized, and we are still far from them. Politically, in economics and in social matters we have not achieved what we aspired to. Why?

Is it because seven years is too short a time? Possibly, especially when we reflect that it is only during this past two and a half years that we have been able to devote ourselves to constructive activities.

Indeed, construction is much more difficult than destruction. The constructive facet of any revolution calls for more time than the destructive facet. Although we know this, it is often forgotten by certain sections of our society who lack patience and, instead of placing the emphasis on work, just keep on asking for this and that.

Or is it that the time has not been too short but rather that our hopes were pitched too high? Were our ideals too noble? Were our aims too lofty? Are our ideals too noble? Is it too noble an ideal to want a republic, strong internally and externally, embracing the whole of the former Dutch East Indies? Are our hopes pitched too high if we wish for an Indonesia which is economically self-sufficient, if we know that our country is rich in metals, crops, resources, and manpower? Are our aims too lofty if we seek social betterment, if we want the whole state to live as one big family, in prosperity and justice, free from poverty—knowing that Indonesia has always believed in a system of co-operation on all levels of society and that our country has been famous for its ability to feed and clothe its people? I believe not, and there are many other nations that share our ideals.

I return to the question: Why is there this big difference between hope and achievement, between ideals and reality, although it is but fair to admit that seven years are but a second in the history of a people? Willy-nilly, my mind goes back to a point in time when we were still at the beginning of our revolution. What did we not do then? In the space of a few days we succeeded in pulling down the colonial fortress that had been so strongly built during the course of three and a half centuries. In a matter of weeks we brought back into being again on August 18 a big army that had been disarmed by the Japanese. In a few days we overcame grave situations that often descended upon us like the sudden onrush of an ogre. We accomplished a great deal in those few days because we did not count in terms of years, or months, or weeks—but in terms of days.

And now? Now we see lassitude all around. All around we see dissatisfaction which produces no dynamic or positive response. It would almost seem that we had no idealism left. It would almost seem that we had lost the ability to struggle in a big way. It would seem that the enchanting goddess of "self-interest" had beckoned us in her direction.

Why are we like this now when our stature was so great at the beginning of our revolution? The correct answer is: At the beginning of the revolution our hearts were full of the spirit of the Proclamation of August 17, 1945, which burnt in our breasts like a bright and glowing flame.

Will it be possible for us to recapture the spirit of the Proclamation? To do so we must first have the spirit of national freedom which refuses to succumb to even the slightest trace of colonialism. Second, we must have a sincere spirit, forgetting the word "I" and knowing only the word "we." Third, we must have the spirit of unity—real national unity and not merely loyalty to one's family or group. Fourth, we must have the constructive spirit that knows no tiring and builds up the state and its people from scratch.

Only by recapturing that spirit and placing the accent all the time on constructive activities will we be able to run along with seven league boots or fly with the vest that gives wings to its wearer. Only thus will we be able to bridge the gap between our hopes and reality. For, imbued with such a spirit, we shall shed all inertia, forgetting tiredness, exhaustion, and lassitude. We shall become a dynamic people, a people free from the evil of envy, and our country will be the embodiment of the hopes of the living and the dreams of our friends who are dead. Indonesia will become prosperous, for its people will know that only work and action will bring prosperity to all.

IIe

Sukarno *Electioneering and National Unity* (1954)

This piece is taken from the address of August 17, 1954. The election campaign had been in full swing for more than a year at the time of this speech, although it was not until September 1955 that the elections were actually held. The full text was published as Berirama dengan Kodrat (*In Tune with the Cosmos*) (*Djakarta: Ministry of Information, 1954*).

We are midway on the road toward perfecting our democratic life. We are in the thick of activities preparing for the general elections.

Indeed, democracy still needs to be perfected in our country. For nine years we have endeavored ceaselessly to improve it. We have always made use of democratic institutions, however imperfect they may be, to solve all kinds of problems, big and small. Never have we abandoned the democratic principles which, from time immemorial, indeed, have been alive in our society as a legacy from our ancestors.

The Constitution of our State, which has known several alterations since the Independence Proclamation, has always provided in its Preamble that our Independence should be organized on the basis of Pantja Sila, which include the principles of Democracy and Social Justice. These principles, Democracy and Social Justice, were primary elements in our National Revolution. They were the fire that kindled our Revolution, that set it ablaze. These two are demands made by as well as to our Revolution! . . .

Piles of difficulties and deficiencies bar our road. Yet, shall we allow these difficulties and deficiencies to deter us from carrying out the general elections? No, we shall not. Once again, we shall not! Difficulties and shortcomings are inherent in any new kind of work. The point is how to get it done *in spite of* all the difficulties and short-comings!

We *must*— I repeat, we *must* carry out the elections, in order to realize the ideals of our National Revolution and to accomplish the demands that this National Revolution has made of itself.

Indeed, the elections must be held! This is a national duty! Not only the Indonesian people look forward to their being held; the whole world is watching and taking keen interest in the first general elections to be held in Indonesia. There are people who doubt our ability to carry out the elections, and also people who hope that the elections will fail because they dislike the idea that political stability should come to Indonesia. There are even people who do more than take an interest; they have certain hopes regarding the outcome of these elections and have been surreptitiously active in efforts to realize these hopes.

Therefore, in all seriousness I remind the entire Indonesian nation —who will exercise their voting power presently—and all leaders who enjoy the confidence of the people: Be careful! Be careful! Be on your guard against anything that may harm our national interest. Fix your attention on our national interest. We must never forget, not even for one small moment, that it is the Indonesian nation itself and no one else which can vouch for the right of Indonesia to determine its own fate.

And—as I have stated again and again—do not allow the elections to develop into an arena for political conflicts in a way which will jeopardize the wholeness of our national unity. Symptoms of aggravating controversies do exist. Symptoms of a breakdown of the spirit of tolerance have emerged. Are we not aware that democracy will be wrecked in the absence of tolerance, that democracy is the very manifestation of tolerance? Do you want to raise dangerous ghosts during the election campaign, ghosts of Hatred and Envy? Raise them, and you will see that democracy will be devoured bones and all by its own devilish offspring. The democracy you have in mind will then vanish from existence; our national strength will vanish; the glory of our National Revolution will fade away. Terror and anarchy, disorder and bloodshed will remain—much to the vociferous delight of the enemy who will see his hopes come true.

As I said some time ago, Democracy is a vehicle toward the attainment of a perfectly just and prosperous society. General elections constitute a vehicle for the perfecting of that democracy. Thus, general elections are simply an instrument for the perfecting of a vehicle. If the spirits of Hatred and Envy should be allowed to emerge and run berserk during the general elections, if the wholeness of our nation should be torn to pieces as a consequence of these elections, if the nation's strength should be shattered as a consequence of them, then my warning when I spoke of medicine that is worse than the disease it is to cure, will have come true.

Why is it that people are so quick to lose their heads and let their passions run high while putting forward their convictions in the course of electioneering? It is because a great many people lose sight of the real object of elections.

What is the real object? It is to elect a Constituent Assembly (and a House of Representatives) which is to draw up the final Constitution of the State we proclaimed on August 17, 1945—no more, no less. I repeat: of the State we proclaimed on August 17, 1945—not of another state and not of a new State either. By means of these elections, by means of this Constituent Assembly, we want to draw up a final Constitution to bring our present provisional Constitution to perfection, while remaining true to the ideals of our National Revolution. Once again, *while remaining true to the ideals of our National Revolution,* for which thousands of our youth have given their lives, for which millions of common people have made their sacrifices, for which the Indonesian people have fought for decades. The forthcoming elections are only a democratic means of continuing our activities toward realizing the ideals of our National Revolution—no less, no more. He who deviates from the original ideals of our National Revolution in the course of the general elections is disloyal to and acting contrary to the National Revolution.

IIf

Sukarno   Let Us Bury the Parties (1956)

The following two fragments are from speeches which the President gave on October 28, 1956, to a meeting of youth delegates from all parties and on October 30, 1956, to a teachers' union congress. At these two meetings the President first suggested that the way out of the country's current instability and demoralization should be sought through "guided democracy." The full texts are in Indonesia, Pilihlah Demokrasimu jang sedjati (*Indonesia, Choose Your True Democracy*) (*Djakarta: Ministry of Information, 1956*)

We are always telling outsiders (the nations of Asia and Africa on the one hand, America and China on the other) to be united, united, united, and indeed to be active in the cause of unity, to unify actively. Is this not paradoxical, when we look at ourselves? Here in our own country we are wrangling with one another. In this, we are faced with a paradox. The paradox concerns the Youth Pledge. The Youth Pledge of October 28, 1928, called upon us to be one people undivided. As Wilhelm Tell said, "Wir wollen sein ein einziges Volk von Brüdern" [We want to be a united people of brothers].

That thought constitutes the core of the Youth Pledge of October 28, 1928. But now, in contrast to what that pledge called for, we are divided, and divided not only by ethnic and regional feelings. There is a disease that is sometimes even worse than ethnic and regional feeling! What is this disease, you ask? It is the disease of parties, brothers and sisters! Yes, I will be frank: the disease of parties.

In November 1945—let us be quite frank—we made a most serious mistake. We suggested the establishment of parties, parties, parties. That was one of the mistakes of November 1945. Now it is taking its toll.

Just look at the situation. Quite apart from the disease of ethnic and regional loyalties, we are afflicted by the disease of parties which, alas, alas, makes us forever work against one another!

In Shanghai I told of a dream I had had. In a speech there I spoke of my dream of a nonaggression pact, a Pacific nonaggression pact. Tonight, I am dreaming again. And do you know what I am dreaming of tonight? What is my dream as I face young men and women whose eyes shine like the eternal stars in the sky?

Do you know, young men and women, what I am dreaming of as I speak before you? I am dreaming, *lha bok ja* as the Javanese say, at a crucial moment, that the leaders of these parties will meet at a crucial moment, *musjawarah* among themselves and take a joint decision: Let us act together now to bury all the parties!

Some people are ridiculing Bung Karno's dreaming. Dreams, dreams, dreams, daydreams, they say. Well, if you don't like the word dream, if you do not like my speaking of daydreaming, I had better change the word: I am not dreaming, I am not daydreaming. I am suggesting that the leaders should hold a *musjawarah* and take a joint decision to bury the parties!

People ask, what is all this about, what does Bung Karno want, does he want to become a director–proprietor of society? . . . I do not want to become a dictator. That would be against my spirit, brothers and sisters. I am a democrat, I am really a democrat. But my democracy is not the democracy of liberalism, is not liberal democracy, absolutely not.

I have said several times that the democracy I crave for Indonesia is not a liberal democracy such as exists for Western Europe. No! What I want for Indonesia is a guided democracy, a democracy with leadership. A guided democracy, a guided democracy, something which is guided but still democracy . . . .

Our situation with respect to the party system is one of complete disruption. It is not healthy; it must be transformed entirely. Especially, if we want to build as people have in other countries I have seen, for example, in the Chinese People's Republic, we must transform the party system completely. At the very least we must rationalize it and make it healthy.

As you know, in one of my Independence Day speeches made more than a year ago, I said I hoped the general elections would be able to restore our party system to health. Remember, at that time I said that I hoped the elections would be able to reduce the number of our parties, which at that time stood at thirty, so that there would be just a few parties. That is what I was hoping! I even said to the people at that time: "You, the people, use the rights you have in the elections! You must be the judge." But, look what happened! After the elections there were even more parties than before, even more. So now I say, what can we do? What are we to do with all these parties? What shall we do to forge unity among them, to make them into a single association, into a unity of revolutionary forces. . . .

You ask, why should the parties be buried? Is that not burying democracy? No, brothers and sisters! If we bury the parties and, having done that, do nothing, and then if there arises an individual who governs by himself, and particularly if he rules by the whip—yes, in that case democracy is dead.

But my aim, brothers and sisters, is to make our society healthy. Whatever anyone says, there is not a single person who can justify the existence of forty parties in our country. You cannot justify that, you cannot justify it, you cannot. None of us can justify a situation like this. There is not a single person who can justify the existence of so many parties. This must be rationalized, must be rationalized, must be put on a sound basis. How? At least, at the very least, the number of parties must be reduced.

If one wants to reduce the number of parties, which party is to be buried? One party will say: Why should I be buried? Why not you?

That is logical, it is logical. No one wants to have his own party buried while another party is left alone. You cannot do things that way. Therefore, I propose that we bury them all together, without favors to anyone. Let us bury them, bury them, bury them!

And what should be done then? That depends on the leaders. Bung Karno has certainly a view of his own, but Bung Karno is not a director–proprietor or a dictator. Let us leave it to the leaders whether to establish just one party, or not to have any party but to form a single mass movement, or to establish several parties on a rational basis. Let us leave all that to the leaders. It is not up to me! Of course, I have a concept of my own, and if I am asked, I will, God willing, set it forth.

IIg
Sukarno Saving the Republic
of the Proclamation (1957)

This extract comes from a speech of February 21, 1957. In this speech the President presented the "concept" to which he had referred on October 30, 1956 (see IIf), that is, his own proposal on

how to realize "guided democracy." The full Indonesian text is in
Kepada Bangsaku (*n.p.: Panitya Pembinaan Djiwa Revolusi, n.d.*),
pp. 435–448.

In the history of the Republic of Indonesia, now more than
eleven years old, we have never achieved stability in government.
Every government has had to face difficulties: difficulties because of
what is called lack of authority, difficulties because of what is called
the omnipresence of a strong opposition.

Every cabinet in the course of these eleven years has had to en-
counter the same difficulties; each has lacked authority and each has
had to face strong opposition, so that no cabinet has been able to
survive for any reasonable length of time; each has finally crumbled,
and the country has had to go through a cabinet crisis until, eventually, a new cabinet was formed.

For eleven years we have tried to overcome these difficulties in
all sincerity, in all honesty. However, everytime we have met with
the same experience.

And so I thought about why this situation exists. At long last, I
came to the conviction that we had used a wrong system, the wrong
style of government, that is, the style which we call Western democracy.

Ever since we initiated the national movement—and the more so
since we proclaimed our independence on August 17, 1945—we
have been enthralled by democracy and have wanted to put democracy into practice, for, indeed, democracy is the animating principle
of our soul, and the inspirer of all our acts. However, the experiences of these eleven years have convinced me that the democracy
we adopted, the democracy we have been using, is a democracy
which is not in harmony with the soul of the Indonesian nation. It
is what I call Western democracy or, if you like, parliamentary democracy. It has become clear to me that the democracy we have
practised for eleven years is an imported democracy, a democracy
which is not Indonesian. And since this democracy is an imported
democracy, not an Indonesian one, not a democracy which is in
harmony with our spirit, we have experienced all the excesses which
result from effectuating an imported idea as well as all the excesses
ensuing from implementation of a democracy which is not in harmony with our personality.

In this Western democracy, in this Western parliamentary democracy, we find the idea of the opposition, and it is this idea of the opposition which has made us go through hardships for eleven years, because we have interpreted this idea of opposition in a way which does not accord with the Indonesian spirit.

I once talked to a leader, an opposition party leader. Let me make plain that it was not a man of the current opposition. I said to him: "The measures taken by the present government are good. Why don't you frankly admit that they are good?" The opposition man's reply was: "It is not the opposition's job to say that the government is doing well."

This, then, is how the idea of opposition is interpreted. Opposition is interpreted as outright condemnation of the Government, *coûte que coûte!* Opposition is interpreted as an endeavor to overturn the existing government whenever possible and to replace it by a government composed of the opposition itself. This is why I now want to invite the whole Indonesian nation to reconsider our system of government and to consider and endorse—that is, if you approve of it —the Concept I shall now set before you.

What, then, is my Concept? My Concept consists of two points. The first concerns the Cabinet, the second concerns a Council which I call the National Council.

What about the Cabinet? As to that, brothers, let us form a *Gotong Rojong* [Mutual Assistance] Cabinet. I expressly use the term *gotong rojong* because this is an authentic Indonesian term which provides us with the purest likeness of the Indonesian spirit. The cabinet should include all political parties and groups represented in parliament which have obtained a certain quotient of votes in the election.

At present we have a cabinet which includes a part of the political parties and groups. Let us now try to form one which comprises all political parties and groups.

It will be abundantly clear from my statement that I do not propose any violation of the position of parliament. There were initially people who thought I would propose dissolving or freezing parliament. This is not true! Parliament shall go on. The present parliament is indeed the product of general elections, the product of elections in which all the people of Indonesia have taken part. However, the cabinet to be formed should not be an old-style one, after the pattern of the cabinets we have had these eleven years. It should be a new-style cabinet, whose ministers are persons from all parties and groups in parliament which have obtained the electoral quotient.

It is clear, brothers and sisters, from the above, that I do not take sides, that I do not discriminate in the matter of which parties should take part in the cabinet. All parties and all groups should take part in it. That's why I call it a *Gotong Rojong* Cabinet. In a foreign tongue I say: "Alle leden van de familie aan tafel, alle leden van de familie aan de eettafel en aan de werktafel" [All members of the family at table; all members of the family at the eating table and at the working table]—without any exception. This is a manifestation of Indonesian *gotong rojong,* a manifestation of the Indonesian identity. . . .

How, then, should the *Gotong Rojong* Cabinet I propose be set up? I have just said that we should not discriminate, that we should no longer ask: Are you Masjumi, are you PKI, are you Nahdatul Ulama, are you Protestant, are you Catholic? No, we should not. All parties in parliament should be given the right to participate in the cabinet. So many members in parliament, so many ministers in the cabinet. This is just, just because it does not discriminate, just because we simply regard ourselves as Indonesians—no more and no less. No matter what political party an Indonesian may adhere to, he remains —when all is said and done—an Indonesian. And, as I have just said: All members of the family at table, at the eating table, at the working table.

I have not spoken of how one should determine the electoral quotient as this is merely a matter of implementation. What I have set out for you is the principle, the family principle, the *gotong rojong* principle. If this principle is implemented, the opposition, as we have interpreted it for eleven years, will be done away with; deliberation, *musjawarah,* will go hand in hand with the family principle and work in an atmosphere of *gotong rojong;* the opposition, as we have interpreted it for eleven years, will disappear. It is true that there will always be differences of opinion. In fact, these very differences of opinion will bring us to progress. *Du choc des opinions jaillit la vérité,* as the French saying goes. This French saying is true and to the point. Differences of opinion do not mean, should not automatically mean, that one opposes *coûte que coûte,* that one tries to topple the Cabinet *coûte que coûte.*

I do not know, brothers and sisters, how large the electoral quotient will be. It may be ten, it may be twelve. I leave the number to the implementation stage. And, besides the large electoral quotient, there should be a small electoral quotient. A smaller electoral quotient should be introduced for the smaller parties, so that they, too, will also have the opportunity of participating in the cabinet, even though they are allotted only vice-ministerial seats. If such a cabinet can be formed, it will be more secure than its predecessors.

Next to the *Gotong Rojong* Cabinet I propose that a Council be established, a Council which I wanted at first to call a "Revolutionary Council." In the end, however, I plumped for the name "National Council," because national means the whole body of the nation, in all its length and breadth.

I call it a National Council, because I want this Council to be so composed that it includes the entire Indonesian nation, irrespective of grouping. This National Council should include, first of all, representatives of or people from functional groups in our society. As outlined in my Concept, the National Council shall include a representative of or a person from labor circles, because labor is a functional group of tremendous importance; a representative of or a person from the peasants, as the peasants also constitute a functional group of very great importance; from the intelligentsia, as the work of development cannot make headway without the assistance and activity of the intelligentsia; a representative of or a person from the group of national entrepreneurs, as national enterprise also holds a most important position in our society; a representative of or a person from the Protestant group; a representative of or a person from the Catholic group; two representatives of the *Alim Ulama*;* a representative of or a person from the women's group; a representative of or a person from the youth; a representative of or a person from the 1945 Generation; a representative of or a person from the group which can express or set forth the problems of the regions. And beside these, my brethren, I want this National Council to include the Chief of Staff of the Army, the Chief of Staff of the Navy, the Chief of Staff of the Air Force, the Chief of the State Police, the Attorney General, and several Ministers who hold important portfolios. And, God willing, I myself will lead this National Council.

Why, brothers, do I propose a National Council, and what is to be its function? The function of the National Council will be to assist the Cabinet with advice, whether such advice is requested or not, because the National Council is composed of representatives of or persons from functional groups in our society. Therefore, I regard the

* Muslim religious scholars.

Council as a reflection of our society, while the Cabinet would be a reflection of Parliament.

On the one hand we may liken the cabinet to a compressed form of parliament; on the other hand, the National Council may be likened to a compressed form of the living society, the bustling society, the dynamic and active society. The National Council and the cabinet shall stand side by side. . . .

I know, brothers, that several among you or several groups object to the PKI's taking part in the cabinet. I ask in all sincerity, brothers and sisters: Can we continue to ignore a group which obtained six million votes in the general elections?

In all seriousness, I do not take sides. I only want national peace. I want to introduce a system of *gotong rojong* government without siding with any one party.

Again I ask: Don't we want development in as big a way as possible? And if we want development in as big a way as possible, brothers, do we not need all the energy that is to be found in our society, so that all of it can be devoted to the work of development? And is it not a fact, brothers and sisters, that the Indonesian Communist Party has many followers among the workers?

Let me say it once again: I am not taking sides. I am only expressing what is in the heart of hearts of our society, what was in the heart of hearts of our youth when, on October 28, 1928, they took the pledge of "One Nation, One Country, One Language"; what was in the heart of hearts of us all when we made the Proclamation of August 17, 1945. At those times, there was no split, there was no split—once again, there was no split in the inner self of the Indonesian Nation. Only afterward did a split occur and grow bigger, my brothers, as if we were to be torn apart. Let us return to our former ideals, to our original ideals. It has been said that Bung Karno is putting forward this Concept to turn the cabinet to the left. No, brothers and sisters, for me, there is no left or right. I merely wish that the Indonesian Nation may become whole again, that the State may become whole again. I do not discriminate, brothers and sisters. It is I who have often quoted a great foreign leader: A nation divided against itself cannot stand. Do we want to become a nation divided against itself? Do we want to crumble and collapse?

Therefore, brethren, let us surmount all those splits. Once again I say: I do not take sides, I want to propose something that is in harmony with the Indonesian spirit, the real spirit of the Indonesian Nation, that is: the spirit of family life. Therefore, I call this Cabinet a *Gotong Rojong* Cabinet. Therefore, I call this Council a National Council. A *Gotong Rojong* Cabinet which works hand in hand with the National Council will constitute an immense and strong bridge connecting the Government with the living forces in our society.

IIh
Mohammad Natsir Restoring Confidence in Democracy (1956)

This piece comprises part of an address given by Natsir as chairman of the Masjumi party on the occasion of its eleventh anniversary, November 7, 1956, thus within two weeks of President Sukarno's first calls for a "guided democracy" (see IIf). This section of the address follows the one reproduced as VIc. The whole piece was published in the Djakarta daily Abadi *on November 9, 10, and 12, 1956.*

Since 1950 the Masjumi has made every effort to become a stabilizing factor ensuring Indonesia's safe progress through this period of transition fraught with dangers external and internal. Since 1950 the havoc and destruction wrought in the struggle of the preceding years and the weaknesses resulting from centuries of colonial rule have posed grave problems never before confronted by the Indonesian people and their leaders.

There is the problem of defining the structure of the Indonesian state comprising thousands of islands and hundreds of different ethnic groups.

There is the problem of organizing the rehabilitation and resettlement of veterans, each of whom must be given, without delay, the opportunity to play whatever part he is best fitted for in the reconstruction and development of the country.

There is the problem of raising the living standard of the people, that under colonial rule was reduced to existence on a few cents a day, and of awakening and developing the capacities of the people to achieve a better living standard.

There is the problem of restoring security, a problem whose solution is prerequisite for all moral and material progress.

There is the problem of defining the role of the Indonesian Republic in international affairs as a member of the family of nations.

There is the problem of eliminating illiteracy and developing the population's general knowledge—both urgent problems, for literacy and general knowledge are essential to the functioning of democracy.

There is the problem of training experts capable of ensuring the efficient functioning of government administration and the country's economy.

There is the problem of so defining the basis for democratic government by elected representatives of the people that the Indonesian Republic will be governed by the people for the people in accordance with the will of the people.

Over the last six years the various political parties in Indonesia, the Masjumi included, have sought to solve these problems. What is the balance of achievement after six years?

It must be admitted that—although threats to the very existence of the Indonesian Republic in 1949 and at the beginning of 1950 and periodic serious crises arising since 1950 were surmounted, and although a parliament has been elected in conformity with the requirements of democratic government—those essential problems directly and immediately concerning the spiritual and material well-being of the Indonesian people have not yet been solved.

So far, we have not yet been able to free millions of our people from the bonds of poverty. Yet, with the spectacle of want and misery on every hand, we see the odious contrast of a few living in carefree luxury.

So far, we have not been able to provide protection of life and property in those regions where the population lives in constant fear, day and night.

So far, we have not been able to devise effective, efficient means of exploiting the natural wealth of the land and seas of our country.

So far, we have not been able to utilize the available manpower effectively for the task of reconstruction and development; nor have we been able to inspire the people with enthusiasm to work for a better future.

So far, we have not been able to organize a sound, efficient state apparatus in which appointments are made solely according to knowledge and experience.

Because there are so many urgent problems unsolved, the situation produces incompetence and confusion in every sphere, in the administration of the state and in all sectors of our economy, with the result that there is everywhere gross wastage of manpower, money, and time. Intrigue is rampant and self-interest is the primary consideration.

The final result is that dissatisfaction becomes general and all sense of social responsibility is disregarded. Little else is heard but recrimination and abuse, and objective appraisal is an exception. Unless this situation is changed radically and quickly, discontent will mount to desperation, with all the consequences that implies.

Among some sections of the population there is an attitude of resignation coupled with blind hope for the coming of a *Ratu Adil*, a powerful leader whose wisdom would right all wrongs.

There are those, too, who propose destruction of the system we have built up and installation of a kind of modern *Ratu Adil* of some supreme authority, vested with unrestricted powers, which could be expected to bring an immediate solution to all our difficulties.

Some sections of the population are now beginning to ask themselves whether our present democratic system should not be replaced with a dictatorship. It is argued that the existence of numerous political parties is the source of all the ills besetting our country, and, if a solution is to be reached, this multi-party system should be abolished and replaced by either a one-man dictatorship or a one-party dictatorship.

Such thinking must not be allowed to pass unchallenged. Let us examine the problem more closely. In the first place this idea of a dictatorship is completely at variance with the concepts set down in the teachings of Islam. The ideology of a dictatorship is an ideology uncompromisingly rejected by the Muslim community.

There is also another factor which must be considered: the geographical distribution of Indonesian territory and the ethnic diversity of the Indonesian population. The Republic of Indonesia comprises thousands of islands, a territory that extends over an area greater than that of Western Europe. The population distributed over these islands includes hundreds of different ethnic groups with different cultures and different languages.

What is it then that has united these islands that form the Republic of Indonesia? Has this unity been achieved by compulsion, by force of arms?

No, it was not coercion. It was not compulsion imposed by some dictatorial power that united the thousands of islands of Indonesia. It was not force or fear that forged the bond of Indonesian unity. It was the esteem, the loyalty, the affection of all the Indonesian people for the central government they had all played a part in creating.

The central government is seen as a protecting power safeguarding the interests of every Indonesian citizen, as a body of men whose human mistakes can be called to account by representatives of the people. The conduct of the country's affairs is seen as government by the people, for the people, in accordance with the will of the people. It is the attachment of the Indonesian people to their government, their confidence in their government, that has formed the bond of Indonesian unity.

Without this loyalty, without this affection—and it is only with a democratic system that these feelings can be preserved—the state would inevitably collapse. The suppression of democracy and the installation of a dictatorship ruling by force and intimidation would spell the disintegration of the Indonesian state.

It is impossible that a dictator, exercising power only by destroying all liberty, could impose his individual will at bayonet point throughout the thousands of islands of Indonesia, on the entire eighty million inhabitants of Indonesia with their diverse cultures and traditions.

The last six years have shown all too clearly the complete failure of force to bring back to the fold of the Republic those who have taken up arms.

Yet it is possible that there could emerge not one dictatorship, not the domination of a single dictatorial regime, but a dozen, a hundred dictatorships, each pursuing its own way. Should it ever happen that democracy is destroyed in Indonesia, it would mean the end of the Indonesian State. May God protect us from such a catastrophe.

It is no exaggeration to say that the Indonesian people stand today at the crossroads. If we accept the fact that only a democratic system of government can preserve the Republic of Indonesia, then there is posed the crucial question: Are the democrats of this generation in Indonesia able to restore full confidence in democratic institutions? Are those who cherish democratic ideals prepared to prove beyond all doubt that our problems can be solved by democratic means?

The answer to this question is the answer to the question whether the Indonesian Republic will stand or fall.

Let us realize that a system of democratic government is far more complex in its functioning than any other system. It is for us to face up to these complexities with all determination, for without constant vigilance, democracy can degenerate into anarchy.

To emphasize this point I would like to recall the words that Sjafruddin Prawiranegara wrote some five years ago in an article entitled "Indonesia at the Crossroads."

If the leaders of the people are not prepared to work for the interests of the people, if appointment to office is thought to be an end and not a means, then the danger arises that democratic government will gradually give way to anarchy, and in conditions of anarchy power will be seized by armed groups or by those controlling armed groups.

Here is traced the course of events that would lead to the installation of a dictatorship, and it is precisely this calamity that we must prevent.

All our strength, all our efforts must be given to preventing such a catastrophe. All partisans of democracy in positions of responsibility in the government administration and the armed forces, and the leaders of political parties must realize that our problems will not be solved by hurling sanctimonious accusations at opponents. The exchange of abuse, of accusation and counteraccusation will lead us nowhere.

Let us, all of us, ask ourselves honestly whether our own individual actions have always served the cause of democracy, whether we are so free of failings, whether the accusations we level so readily at others might not be made against ourselves. If we are, all of us, prepared to submit ourselves to the searching light of honest self-criticism, if we are prepared to put behind us the faults we have committed in the past and to work on a new, forthright approach, then there is hope for the future.

Fundamentally, the difficulties we are faced with stem from three causes: first, lack of idealism and the resultant attachment to base materialist values; second, failure to distinguish clearly between right and wrong and the consequent brazen disregard of all standards of probity; and third, complete lack of realism in the assessment of current problems and in the allocation of responsibility. These are the factors which have produced the spectacle of dislocation and inefficiency with which we are now faced.

These shortcomings are not confined to what might be called the executive élite; in every section of the population these same disquieting symptoms are in evidence.

With a democratic system of government it does sometimes happen that objectives can only be attained rather slowly—in contrast to the functioning of a totalitarian regime where all obstruction is ruthlessly eliminated. That does not mean, however, that a democratic regime cannot function efficaciously, that consultation and agreement freely entered into are obstacles to efficient government.

It is our decided conviction that the institutions of democracy in Indonesia are established firmly enough to be able to overcome existing weaknesses. It is certain that democracy in Indonesia can provide the solution to our problems, providing that the political parties are prepared to observe their responsibilities. There is potential enough among the Indonesian people—within the political parties and outside the political parties—which, realistically applied, can accomplish all that is needed to restore full confidence in democracy.

IIi

Mohammad Hatta A Revolution Should Not Last Too Long (1956)

This extract, * *like Ib, is taken from Hatta's November 27, 1956, address at Gadjah Mada University, delivered a few days before his resignation as Vice-President. This part of the address is a carefully considered presentation of his fundamental disagreements with President Sukarno. In this respect it may be coupled with the Hatta extract reproduced as XIId.*

Will our nation suffer the same fate as befell the French Revolution of 1789, which started out with the slogans "Liberty, Equality, and Fraternity," but which in actual practice afterward brought only freedom to oppress, inequality and strife, and the freedom to live in poverty and wretchedness? What we see around us daily in Indonesia makes it seem that nothing but lip service is given to the Pantja Sila, that it is not being used as a light by which to organize a new society. Every group is competing with every other in a scramble for profits. One's own group comes first; the community as a whole is forgotten. In theory we profess collectivism, but in fact and by our actions we are strengthening individualism. In theory we support social democracy, but in fact and by our actions we are promoting the spirit of liberal democracy.

* Reprinted, by permission, from *Past and Future* (Ithaca, N.Y.: Cornell Modern Indonesia Project, 1960).

Political parties, which in reality are a means of organizing public opinion in order that the people may learn to feel responsibility as citizens of the state and members of society, have been made into an end in themselves, the state becoming their tool. In this way it is being forgotten that promoting the interest of a political party at the expense of the people is immoral and incompatible with the Pantja Sila, particularly as regards the principle of Belief in the One God.

Also, membership in a political party is often the criterion for appointing civil servants to posts, both here and abroad, rather than the principle of "the right man in the right place." Public servants who are not members of any political party or who belong to an opposition party feel that they no longer have standards to go by and become disillusioned. This destroys their peace of mind and their zeal for work and is apt to lead to improper practices and mental corruption. Instead of strengthening the character of the officials, party politics makes for the opposite and weakens their character. Finally, they join a party not out of political conviction but merely because they want security.

When one looks at recent developments in our country and society, one gets the impression that after the independence of Indonesia had been achieved, with no small sacrifice, our idealistic leaders and freedom fighters were pushed back, while political and economic profiteers came to the foreground. Such profiteers have used the national movement and its slogans for their own ends and have ridden on the backs of political parties for these same private ends. This situation has inevitably resulted in political and economic anarchy followed by corruption and demoralization.

Such is the face Indonesia presents today, after having been independent for this number of years. Clearly, this is not the kind of Free Indonesia that was visualized by our freedom fighters of earlier days.

Everywhere today one finds a feeling of dissatisfaction. It is felt that the reconstruction of our country is not going as it should, that the situation is still far from what we had hoped for, and the value of our money is progressively declining. The gap between the actual state of affairs and our expectations is so great that in disgust people are apt to overlook the constructive things that have actually been accomplished. Just think of our achievements in the fields of education and training programs and in agriculture! All these achievements are overshadowed, however, by the many unfinished and neglected projects, which because of their very nonaccomplishment are doing untold damage to the state and the livelihood of the people. The depreciation and destruction of capital goods everywhere is even more apparent to the eye. Just look at the deterioration of our roads, of our irrigation system and our harbors, look at the spreading of erosion, and all the rest.

The growth of democracy is also being stunted by constant political squabbles. The just Indonesia we are all waiting for is still far away. Establishment of the autonomy of the various territories of Indonesia, on a basis which ensures them their own finances and proper financial arrangements with the central government has yet to be carried out, in spite of the fact that it is now eleven years since this most important duty of government was incorporated into the Constitution. . . .

My purpose in presenting this picture, which highlights the tremendous gap between yesterday's ideals and today's realities, is not to spread a feeling of pessimism. I firmly believe in the power of the regenerative process in our community. The demoralization which is rife in all phases of life today may retard this process, but it cannot stop it altogether. Our nation is now undergoing a period of trial for freedom and its responsibility for its own destiny. We are conscious of our freedom, but we do not yet feel our responsibility. In the long run it will be realized that there can be no lasting freedom without self-restraint, without a sense of responsibility to the community to which one belongs.

A thoroughgoing social analysis would show that all our rebellions and our splits, our political anarchy and adventurism, and all the steps taken in the economic field which have created chaos result from the fact that our national revolution was not dammed up at the appropriate time. Those who say that our national revolution is not yet completed are wrong indeed. A revolution is a sudden explosion of society which brings with it an "Umwertung aller Werte" [a transvaluation of all values]. A revolution shakes the floor and the foundations; it loosens all hinges and boards. Therefore, a revolution should not last too long, not more than a few weeks or a few months. It should then be checked; the time will then have arrived for a consolidation which will realize the results produced by the revolution. What is left unfinished is not the revolution itself, but the efforts to carry its ideals into effect over a period of time after the foundations have been laid. The revolution itself takes only a short time; the revolutionary period of consolidation may take quite a long time, even up to several decades. Thus it was with the French Revolution, with the Russian Revolution, with the Kemalist Revolution in Turkey, and so on.

It is not possible for a revolution to go on for too long, because if it is not checked in time, all the hinges and boards that have come loose will become a jumble, and, in time, new elements will come in and take advantage of the chaotic situation. It will no longer be clear where freedom ends and anarchy begins.

In point of fact our national revolution, having continued for several years, ought to be checked. Its energies should be guided in an orderly fashion so as to teach the mass of the people to become conscious of their responsibilities in democracy. Democracy cannot possibly live without a sense of responsibility. Therefore our people, who have never known democracy at the level of the state, must first be trained in democracy.

But, although we had had no prior training or teaching of responsibility under the sponsorship of a government with authority, we wanted in a great hurry to set up a parliamentary democratic government. We wanted to run a parliamentary democracy without democracy and without a parliament! This resulted in the political anarchy which we have gone through during the last few years. This is why the government has lost its authority. The authority of the government has further declined because party politics introduced and maintained the peculiar custom that power is, in fact, not vested with the responsible government, but with the party councils which are not responsible. In this way the standing of the government has become that of messenger boy to the political parties. A further effect of this is the fact that the most prominent party leaders are not members of the cabinet. Those who are appointed as cabinet ministers are not too prominent; sometimes they are second- or third-rate persons who have no special knowledge of the tasks entrusted to them. This is the reality we now have to contend with as a result of a false interpretation of the course a revolution should follow and of the limit of a revolutionary period, and also as a result of a party system which robs the government of the power it should hold in its hands.

III
Guided Democracy
and Its Critics

The period of parliamentary democracy may be said to have come to an end in March 1958, when fighting began in earnest between the central government and the Sumatran leaders who had established the PRRI—Revolutionary Government of the Republic of Indonesia —in the previous month. The PRRI challenge is variously prefigured in IIh, Xb, and XIVd and denounced in Xc. Its quick defeat, coming on top of the "takeover" of all Dutch properties in December 1957, ushered in a new political order, one in which government was far more authoritarian and parties and parliament much weaker, and in which President Sukarno and the leaders of the Army played greatly enhanced roles.

The symbol of Guided Democracy was predominant from mid-1958 onward, and its only vigorous opponents, the Masjumi and Socialist parties, were reduced to speaking in soft voices. But a great deal of argument continued regarding the constitutional form in which the idea of Guided Democracy should be set. In February 1959 the government decided to press for a return to the constitution of 1945, but the Constituent Assembly refused to give this proposal the necessary two-thirds majority. Eventually on July 5, 1959, President Sukarno dissolved the Assembly and reintroduced the old revolutionary constitution by decree, following this with a fast series of political changes, which were all justified as part of "Returning to the Rails of the Revolution," the theme of his August 17 Independence Day address of that year. Excerpts from this speech and from the Supreme Advisory Council's supplementary document which presented its ideas more schematically, form the first two extracts of this section.

The next three pieces have been selected to show the development of the President's thinking in the years after 1959. They should be read together with XIIe on *Nasakom* unity and the dangers of Communistphobia and XVi on the doctrine of the New Emerging Forces.

The ideology of Guided Democracy rang in all ears throughout this period and the number of its official and semiofficial interpreters was large, but we have not included their work here, largely because President Sukarno said the same things and said them better. We are including, however, as our sixth and seventh extracts, pieces which expressed support for important features of the current political order on grounds which were very distinct from the official ones.

For those who opposed the central features of Guided Democracy it was difficult to find a safe way to express their point of view. The eighth extract here discusses this problem in relation to freedom of the press, and the ninth is an example of the way in which protest was expressed in indirect and muted forms. The tenth, by Hatta, is markedly more open in its hostility to the established order; Hatta's unique prestige enabled him to make trenchant criticisms with relative impunity. The eleventh selection, an outright denunciation of Sukarno and his works, was written and published in exile. And the last is included as an example of post-1965 attitudes toward the years of Sukarno's ascendancy.

IIIa
Sukarno Returning to the Rails of the Revolution (1959)

This piece is taken from the speech of August 17, 1959, a speech which may be seen as the ideological counterpart of the constitutional change effected on July 5 of that year, when President Sukarno dissolved the Constituent Assembly and decreed the reintroduction of the constitution of 1945. The speech was subsequently declared the Political Manifesto (Manipol)* of the state and its formulations remained the central criteria of loyalty until about 1964.

The Constituent Assembly proved to be incapable of settling the questions which faced it. The Constituent Assembly proved incapable of becoming the savior of the Revolution. So, because of that failure of the Constituent Assembly, for the sake of the interests of

* *Manifesto Politik Republik Indonesia* (Djakarta: Department of Information, 1959).

the Country and People and to safeguard the Revolution, I issued a decree on July 5 which runs as follows:

With the Blessing of the One Supreme God,

WE, THE PRESIDENT OF THE REPUBLIC OF INDONESIA,

AND SUPREME COMMANDER OF THE ARMED FORCES,

State in all duty:

That the recommendation of the President and the Government to return to the 1945 Constitution, which was conveyed to all the People of Indonesia in the President's Address of Counsel on April 22, 1959, did not result in a decision by the Constituent Assembly on the basis stipulated in the Provisional Constitution;*

That in connection with the statement of the majority of members of the Constitution-making Body to the effect that they would not attend sittings again, it is no longer possible for the Constituent Assembly to conclude the task entrusted to it by the People;

That such circumstances give rise to conditions in the institutions of the state which endanger the unity and the safety of the State, the Country, and the People, as well as obstructing over-all construction and development to achieve a just and prosperous society;

That we are forced, acting with the support of the majority of the People of Indonesia, and impelled by our own conviction, to follow the one and only way of saving the State of the Proclamation;

That we are convinced that the 1945 Constitution is infused with the spirit of the Djakarta Charter of June 22, 1945, and that the Djakarta Charter is part, with that Constitution, of a single chain of unity;

On this basis, therefore,

WE, THE PRESIDENT OF THE REPUBLIC OF INDONESIA,

AND SUPREME COMMANDER OF THE ARMED FORCES,

Decree the dissolution of the Constituent Assembly; Decree that the 1945 Constitution shall be in force again for the whole of the Indonesian People and the entire country of Indonesia as from the date of this decree, and that the Provisional Constitution shall no longer be in force.

The establishment of the Provisional People's Consultative Assembly (which shall be composed of the members of the People's Representative Council augmented by delegates from the regions and from groups) and of the Provisional Supreme Advisory Council will be effected in the shortest possible time.

Decreed at Djakarta,

July 5, 1959.

In the Name of the People of Indonesia,

* The proposal had obtained the support of a simple majority in the Assembly but not of the required two-thirds.

PRESIDENT OF THE REPUBLIC OF INDONESIA,
SUPREME COMMANDER OF THE ARMED FORCES,
SUKARNO.

Yes, brothers and sisters, after passing through the "Year of Decision" and the "Year of Challenge," * we have now come back to the original basis of our struggle. We have now arrived at the "Rediscovery of our Revolution."

What is the meaning of this?

Does this mean merely the replacement of the 1950 Constitution with the 1945 Constitution? No!

Does this mean only that we should "step up our spirit" or "strengthen our will?" No!

Does this mean merely that we are looking for technical perfection and technical efficiency in our work and all our efforts? No! . . . We are looking for changes more profound than those. We are looking for a realization of the deepest possible kind—a realization which penetrates into the bones, into the marrow, into the mind, into the feeling, into the soul, and into the spirit—the realization that we have deviated from the principles and goals of our struggle. We are looking for the deepest possible realization of the fact that the basic characteristics of our Revolution cannot be any other than the principles and objectives which we proclaimed on August 17, 1945.

Inner changes, becoming aware of having deviated in this way, will automatically bring about changes and improvements as regards physical and material affairs.

People of Indonesia, awaken again now! Rise up again with the spirit of the Proclamation in your hearts! Abandon the past! But do not complain. Complaints are the signs of a weak soul. Yes indeed, the past has been wrong. We see that past now as ten years of wasted time. But do not complain. Be proud and happy that we are now aware of this, and march on!

If we study the revolutions of other nations, we always find deviations. Some deviations are temporary, others continuing. The temporary deviations were corrected; the continuing ones resulted in decadence.

It is the continuing deviation which is dangerous. It sometimes results in the total failure and death of the Revolution or it creates

---

* These are the titles of President Sukarno's Independence Day addresses of 1957 and 1958, respectively.

decadence lasting for decades and resulting in the breaking out of another revolution. The French Revolution really failed and came to its death because of continuing deviation. The Sun Yat-sen Revolution, continuously sidetracked by the Kuo-min-tang, developed ultimately into a counterrevolution.

What about our own deviation? We thank God with all our hearts that this deviation of ours has not yet degenerated into decadence. At the right moment we were startled into consciousness and corrected ourselves. At the critical moment we started to think and rethink, to become aware of this deviation, to fight against it, to slam the steering wheel around and take to the right road again. At the critical time the common people sounded the gong. At the critical time Marhaen and Sarinah, Dadap and Waru cried out: "You leaders! You are deviating, you are off the track!" As I said the other day, the social consciousness and political consciousness of the Indonesian people, if compared to that of other nations, is really something to be proud of. Their social and political consciousness is not to be bettered in many other nations. And, indeed, our Revolution is a People's Revolution. Our Revolution is not a palace revolution—it is not what one foreign writer calls "a revolution which is the prelude of the prerevolutionary days."

It is well that this reminder should be heard by the people who call themselves leaders. If they are leaders, then let them keep this in mind, that those they lead are not a flock of goats or ducks or dwarfs, that they are a people whose social and political consciousness is already high!

It is thanks to this high social and political consciousness of our People that the deviation has not lasted too long. Only two or three years after we began to feel that development and progress were not going smoothly, the common people were sounding the alarm. Two or three years of stagnation and we were able to find the causes and roots of that stagnation, to pull out those roots, to make the necessary corrections, even radical and fundamental corrections.

So, don't complain. March forward, without stopping or hesitating, on the original rails of our Revolution!

Let none among us doubt that truth of "the rails" of our Revolution. Let none among us say that the principles and objectives of our Revolution may change, too.

There are indeed people who are always in doubt, there are indeed defeatists, who call themselves "philosophers," and who, using the proposition that nothing is permanent and unchangeable—*panta rei* is their proposition—ask the question whether the principles and objectives of our Revolution may not also or cannot also change? Can't we haggle a bit about the goal of social justice? Can't the struggle against colonialism be modified here and there? Can't we make changes in what we set out to achieve on August 17, 1945?

Questions like this are themselves deviations! Indeed, they are very serious deviations, being the result of a spirit of compromise.

In the life of man in this world there are several truths which are eternal and unchangeable. Such cannot be subjected to compromise, they cannot be modified or amended without changing them into falsehoods. These truths cannot be abandoned without depriving man of what guides him.

Take for instance the essence of the American Declaration of Independence, and the Communist Manifesto, two documents which, according to Bertrand Russell, have divided the world of man into two groups which are cut off, the one from the other.

Both the Declaration of Independence and the Communist Manifesto contain several truths, which remain truths and remain valid eternally. Who—if he really be Man, and not a being without direction—who would dare to try to amend the truth of the sentence in the Declaration of Independence which says that "All Men are created equal, that they are endowed by their Creator with certain inalienable Rights, that among these are Life, Liberty, and the Pursuit of Happiness"?

Who—if he really be Man, and not a being without direction— would dare to contradict the truth of the red thread which runs through the Communist Manifesto, that the greater part of mankind is oppressed, oppressed and exploited by the other part, so that "Workers of the World, you have nothing to lose but your chains; you have a world to gain. Workers of the World, unite!"

These sentences or basic thoughts contain truths which may not be doubted or amended. The basic spirit is the Conscience of Man. They both concern the entire field of relationships between man and man. They are not like a charter which is concerned with one nation alone, for instance the Magna Charta of the British. They are not like a pact between several powerful countries, like, for instance, the Atlantic Charter. They are not a basis for the formation of a Pax of some country, like the Pax Britannica, or the Pax Romana, or Pax Americana, or Pax Sovietica. No! They are a basis for the formation of a Pax encompassing the whole of humanity, a Pax Humanica, a Pax of all the human creatures who inhabit this earth.

In Washington three years ago I argued for a Pax Humanica on the basis of the Declaration of Independence. In Moscow I argued for the Pax Humanica on the basis of several sentences in the Communist Manifesto.

Human beings are the same everywhere, "Mankind is one." That is what I say everywhere when I travel the world, whether in the West or in the East, in the North or in the South, in all the eight parts of the world. The Social Conscience of Man permeates the souls of all human beings in the whole world. And this Social Conscience does not change, it does not want to be amended, nor does it want to be modified.

The principles and objective of the Indonesian Revolution are congruent with that Social Conscience of Man! Social Justice, individual Freedom, national Freedom, and so on are all manifestations of that Social Conscience of Man. Social Justice and Freedom are universal demands of the conscience of Man. Therefore, let there be none among us who seek to amend or modify the principles and objectives of our Revolution!

I have already visited the greater part of the world. Before that, I had long been convinced that the social consciousness of all people on the face of this earth is the same, wherever they may be. And this conviction of mine has been strengthened by what I have seen on my trips abroad, including the Latin American countries.

What did I see there? People everywhere under the dome of the sky do not want to be oppressed by other nations, do not want to be exploited by any group whatever, even if that group is from their own people.

People everywhere under the dome of the sky demand freedom from want and freedom from fear, whether these are caused by threats from within the country or threats from abroad.

People everywhere under the dome of the sky demand freedom to organize their social activities in a constructive way in order to heighten individual happiness and the happiness of the community.

People everywhere under the dome of the sky demand freedom to express their opinions, that is, they demand those rights which are usually called democracy.

That has been my conviction from former times, and that is also what I saw everywhere. These demands have emerged like an explosion during the twentieth century, but, actually, they have been in the heart of man for centuries, because these demands are at bottom nothing but manifestations of the Conscience of Man.

For centuries this Conscience of Man has been latent, submerged; for centuries it has been submerged in man's soul, like fire covered over by chaff. Ultimately, it explodes in a revolutionary way, ultimately it explodes in a historically revolutionary way. All at once it bursts out concurrently as a massive demand; all at once it became a simultaneous demand. It can no longer be dealt with as though by the liter or the kilo. It cannot possibly be met by reformist means, it cannot possibly be handled piecemeal. Its simultaneous demands, which burst forth in a historically revolutionary way, must be dealt with by revolutionary means.

The demands of the Indonesian People are also like that! Its demands for social justice, for independence and freedom, for democracy and so on have burst forth in a revolutionary way in our generation, having smouldered for decades in our hearts like fire buried under chaff—and these demands of the Indonesian People must be met in an overwhelmingly revolutionary manner. They cannot possibly be dealt with liter by liter, or kilo by kilo. Reformist means are impossible, piecemeal methods are impossible, compromise is impossible. And in order to deal with these demands in an overwhelmingly revolutionary way, we ourselves must have a revolutionary spirit. That, indeed, is one of the reasons why we have returned to the Constitution of the Proclamation. . . .

What are our short-term objectives and what are our long-term objectives?

The short-term objective which I have presented to you is the very simple program of the Working Cabinet—food and clothing for the people, security, and continuance of the struggle against imperialism —and also maintenance of our identity amidst the pulls to the right and left which we are now experiencing in the turbulence of the world as it advances towards a new balance.

And our long-term objective is: A just and prosperous society, the elimination of imperialism everywhere, and laying the foundations of a durable and eternal world peace.

To overcome all the problems involved in these short-term and long-term objectives, we clearly cannot use the systems and tools of the past. We must throw out the system of liberalism completely and replace it with guided democracy and guided economy. We must dismantle the old apparatus which was clearly inefficient, replace it by a new apparatus. We must establish a new order, a new reordering, to see that guided democracy and guided economy can function. This is the meaning and content of the term "retooling for the future," which I used in the People's Representative Council recently.

Retooling of all the instruments of struggle! And the consolidation of all these instruments of struggle once they have been retooled!

Retooling of the executive body, that is, the Government, the civil servants, and so on, vertically and horizontally.

Retooling of the legislative body, that is, the People's Representative Council.

Retooling of the instruments of power of the State—the Army, the Navy, the Air Force, and Police.

Retooling of the instruments of production and distribution.

Retooling of the organizations in society—political parties, social bodies, and economic bodies.

Yes, be on your guard, everything will be retooled, everything will be ordered and reordered. Indeed, some organs are already being retooled.

Retooling is now being carried out in the executive field. I hope it will be carried out in the legislative field, as well: Whoever does not take the oath of loyalty to the 1945 Constitution will be thrown out of the People's Representative Council. Whoever is involved in a rebellion will be dismissed from it and sentenced. Whoever does not understand the meaning of "Returning to the 1945 Constitution"— it would be better if he simply left the Council!

The People's Representative Council should become a new kind of parliament. It should not only follow the spirit of the 1945 Constitution. It should now become a body which assists the Government and is assisted by the Government. (The Council cannot overthrow the Government; the body that can overthrow the Government is the People's Consultative Congress.) And this is not all, for I hope that in the spirit of returning to the 1945 Constitution, in the spirit of Guided Democracy, in the spirit of building a just and prosperous society, that the People's Representative building will no longer be just a place for futile, endless talk or just a place where votes are taken. It should be, above all, a place where ideas and concepts which are historically useful for the people are born. Only with such a self-retooling can the People's Representative Council become an instrument of development, an instrument of struggle, an instrument of Revolution.

The other instruments of power of the State, the Armed Forces and the Police, must also be retooled. In the past, liberalism has had many disastrous consequences for these instruments. *Bapakism,** provincialism, separate territorial policies, playing with councils, the PRRI, the Permesta, and the other similar boils and sores—all these really had their origin in liberalism, which allows each man to act as he likes, and were in addition fanned and helped by foreign subversion. Put a stop to this situation! The instruments of State power must be completely weaned from liberalism, now that they are in the shade of the flag of the 1945 Constitution. They must now become instruments of the Revolution again.

The same is true in respect to the instruments of production and distribution. All of them must be retooled! All of them must be reorganized, must have their steering wheel turned towards realization of Article 33 of the 1945 Constitution,† using the rails of guided democracy. For instance, the State set up several bodies in charge of organizing and expanding various fields of production and distribution, but what happened? Not that production and distribution were properly organized and expanded; rather those bodies became the nest of people who filled their own pockets till they bulged, people who became wealthy, people who became millionaires.

There must be an end to this! This situation must be changed! Not only must these bodies be retooled, but also all instruments vital to production and all instruments vital to distribution must be under the control of, or at least supervised by, the Government. It cannot be allowed to happen again that because these vital instruments are not under the control of or supervised by the Government, a few speculators or profiteers can bring turbulence to our whole national economy and throw the means of meeting the people's needs into chaos.

Organizations, too, must be retooled. Political parties must be re-

* The obeying of a particular leader or commander wholly, to the extent of unconcern with laws and general rules.
† This is the same as Article 38 of the 1950 Constitution, which is cited in IVb. See also the discussion in XIIIa and XIIIb.

tooled, social bodies must be retooled, and economic bodies must
be retooled. I shall proceed with the efforts of the *Karya* Cabinet*
to simplify the political party system and make a new election law.
Simplifying the party system and holding elections on a new basis—
this is retooling, too.

I would like to repeat some of what I said on July 24 in the People's Representative Council: "I have already effected retooling in
the executive field, and, as I said a while ago, we must continue
that retooling in all fields, in the economy, in politics, and in society."

Once again: retooling in all fields! And what does retooling mean?
Retooling means replacing the instruments, changing the tools and
the apparatus which do not accord with the thinking of guided
democracy, and replacing them by new tools, new equipment, and
new apparatus which are more in accord with the new outlook. Retooling also means economically using all of the tools which still can
be used, as long as they can be repaired and resharpened.

Retooling in the social field is in the most fundamental sense the
gathering together of all energies, all sources of strength and all
tools, both those which are now being used and those which are not,
legal and official sources of strength, semi-official ones and completely nonofficial ones. Retooling means total mobilization, the total
gathering together of material strength, the total gathering together
of spiritual strength, and the shaping of these strengths to make them
ready for the struggle, to make them ready for the struggle to fulfill
the task which is the responsibility of the Working Cabinet, which is
really a program for the entire Indonesian people. . . .

Brothers and sisters! I am approaching the end of my address.
Now listen very carefully to what I say here:

We have now returned once more to the fold of the 1945 Constitution. Let me emphasize here that the 1945 Constitution has never
fallen in this Revolution of ours, has never died, so that its reactivation is only a formal statement called a "Presidential Decree." The
1945 Constitution never died; on the contrary it was forced to lie
down and keep quiet on the waves of Renville, the waves of Linggadjati, the waves of the Round Table Conference, the waves of
the Constitution of the Republic of the United States of Indonesia
and the 1950 Constitution, the waves of the Indonesian-Dutch Union

* The cabinet of Ir. Djuanda (April 1957–July 1959) which was replaced by
a Sukarno Cabinet at the time of the return to the 1945 Constitution.

—all of which have completely disappeared, thanks to the patriotic spirit of the Indonesian Nation and the fighting spirit of the People of Indonesia.

Similarly, liberal democracy, which was born as the foam of the waves of that evil compromise and which dammed up and caused confusion in the Indonesian Revolution, has now been blown clear away by the patriotic spirit and the fighting spirit of the People of Indonesia; and now the flag of Guided Democracy begins to be flown, a flag which is an original possession of the Indonesian Nation.

I give thanks to God, the God Who commands all of nature, that the course of the Indonesian Revolution has been like this. Although it lost its way for a while, it finally found its way back to its own true rails.

IIIb

Supreme Advisory Council The Political Manifesto as a General Program of the Revolution (1959)

After President Sukarno had given his celebrated "Returning to the Rails of the Revolution" speech of August 17, 1959 (see the previous extract), the Supreme Advisory Council, under its Vice-Chairman Roeslan Abdulgani, expounded the significance of this speech as the Political Manifesto and set forth its principal tenets in a schematized form. A fragment of the Council's text is reproduced here. The full text is in Manifesto Politik Republik Indonesia *(Djakarta: Department of Information, 1959).*

The Political Manifesto as pronounced by the President/Supreme Commander in his address on August 17, 1959, cannot be separated from the decree of the President/Supreme Commander of July 5, 1959; said Political Manifesto is in fact an official elucidation of the decree of the President/Supreme Commander of July 5, 1959.

Therefore, the Political Manifesto is of the utmost importance to the struggle of the Indonesian people in completing its revolution which has a national and democratic character. With the existence of this Political Manifesto, the Republic of Indonesia for the first time in its fourteen years of life, has broadcast through its Head of State a historic document which clarifies the basic problems and the general program of the Revolution which covers all fields.

Briefly, the Political Manifesto contains two things which are urgently needed in smoothening the way of the Indonesian Revolution:

First, the Basic Problems of the Indonesian Revolution;

Second, the General Program of the Indonesian Revolution (main efforts).

With the existence of the Political Manifesto which contains these two things, the Republic of Indonesia possesses a broad outline of State Policy and the people of Indonesia possess an official guide in their struggle to complete the Indonesian Revolution. On the basis of understanding of the basic problems of the Indonesian Revolution and relying on the Program of the Revolution, it will be easier to keep the Indonesian people one in thought and action.

The basic problems of the Indonesian Revolution must be understood by every citizen from the time he enters school and the more so after he has come of age. There must be large scale instruction concerning the basic problems of the Indonesian Revolution in the schools as well as outside of the schools. The Indonesian people must be one in thought concerning their own revolution because only if there is unity in thought can the Indonesian people unite themselves in will and action.

The Program of the Revolution must become the program of the Government, the program of the national front, the program of all political parties, all mass organizations and all citizens of the Republic of Indonesia.

Certainly, each party, organization, and individual may have their respective political outlook, may have their own program, but what has already been decided as the Program of the Revolution must also be their program, and they must participate in carrying out this program.

After clarification of the basic problems of the Indonesian Revolution and after clarification of the program of the Revolution thanks to the existence of the Political Manifesto, it will be possible to draw a line between the Revolution and the counterrevolution, and between friends and enemies of the Indonesian Revolution. In this way a subjective decision about who is a friend and who is an enemy of the revolution can be avoided, and unnecessary conflicts among the people can also be prevented. On the other hand, what will emerge and come to the fore are only the conflicts between revolutionary and imperialist forces, and these conflicts must be concluded with the victory of the revolutionary forces.

IIIc

Sukarno   The Dynamism of Revolution (1960)

This extract is translated from the August 17 speech of 1960, which was published as Laksana Malaekat Jang Menjerbu dari Langit Djalannja Revolusi Kita (*Like an Angel Which Strikes from the Sky: The March of Our Revolution*) (*Djakarta: Department of Information, 1960*).

When I speak about the last few years, the sound of the falling stones of the house of liberalism in Indonesia thunders in my ears, and I hear the rhythmic boom of the mallet of construction upon the foundations of the new building, the House of the People, the House of Indonesian Socialism, of which those investments are the foundations. And I can also hear squeals of convulsion from the inhabitants of the old house who still want to preserve that old building: the unofficial councils, the "PRRI," the "Permesta," the "RPI," the "Manguni," this League, that League, this newspaper, that newspaper, this document, that document! They squeal in consternation!

Yes! Without hiding anything, I certainly admit it: we make radical changes, but we also build! We build, and for that we make radical changes. We break down, we pull out, we uproot! All in order to be able to build. Revolution is uprooting and building up. Constructing and uprooting. Revolution is to "build tomorrow and to reject yesterday." Revolution is to "construct tomorrow, pull down yesterday." Let no one say that I am static. I want to go on being in time with the waves of the Revolution. Revolution is like the waves of the ocean which roll perpetually, like a typhoon which blows forever. Do you remember the revolutionary slogan I gave you some time ago: *"Mandek-amblek, mundur-hantjur"* ["To stop is to collapse, to retreat is to perish"]?

The American Revolution, the French Revolution, the Russian Revolution, the Chinese Revolution, all of them have in their own way uprooted and constructed. That uprooting and constructing is like the huge surge of the waves of a mighty ocean. No man can withstand those waves, for to do so is to withstand the ocean itself. Whoever tries to withstand the waves of the ocean, and thus the ocean itself, will be swept away by the terrible power of that ocean.

Yes, I repeat, I want to go on being in time with the waves of the Revolution. That is why I do not try to withstand the waves. On the contrary, I try, as President, to steer the ship of state in the same direction as the waves of the Revolution. And that direction is the Policy of the State as clearly expounded in the Political Manifesto.

It is the reactionaries whom I mentioned above who try to withstand those waves. Their fate is already written on their brows. At present they are still making every attempt to brake the Juggernaut of the Revolution, but soon they will be crushed beneath its wheels!

Indeed they are unconscionable people! In their endeavors to bend the Revolution toward their own interests they say that the Indonesian Revolution has failed. Do you still remember what Kartosuwirjo said? To provide a grounds for the proclamation of his "NII"* he said that the Indonesian Revolution had failed! Just exactly the same as what is being said by those in the new fashion, who squeal in convulsions. They, too, say the Indonesian Revolution has failed!

What has failed? The Indonesian Revolution has not failed and is not going to fail so long as the People of Indonesia are loyal to the objectives of the Revolution and loyal to the Message of the Suffering of the People. The Indonesian Revolution has not failed, for we are still striving in order to implement the ideals of the Revolution of August 1945, that is, a fully independent Indonesia clean of imperialism, a democratic Indonesia clean of the remnants of feudalism, an Indonesia with Indonesian Socialism and free of l'exploitation de l'homme par l'homme.

Once again: the Indonesian Revolution has not failed! What has failed are those people who do not recognize the objectives of the Revolution, the people who do not recognize the Message of the Suffering of the People, who go as far as wanting to obstruct the implementation of the Message of the Suffering of the People. It is they who have failed—the reactionaries, the cynics, the hyper-intellectuals, those whose wealth is "made," those of "vested interests," those who squeal and whose eyes roll in convulsions because every stronghold of their interests and every stronghold of the defenses they once had is crumbling and falling. Their political parties which have no real roots in society are crumbling and falling; their alliances made in a reactionary spirit and with foreign adventurers and the

* Negara Islam Indonesia: Islamic State of Indonesia.

PRRI-Permesta-RPI are crumbling and falling; their business firms, which fatten their stomachs by plundering the wealth of the People, are crumbling and falling; their institutions for learning and for the press which are filled with "Dutch-isms" and textbook thinking are crumbling and falling. All these are crumbling and falling, in scattered ruins, because they have been crushed beneath the wheels of the Juggernaut of the Revolution, crushed by the Revolutionary People, crushed by the People who are inspired by the spirit of the Political Manifesto and of *USDEK.*

It is only for those who want to build up capitalism and feudalism in Indonesia that the Revolution has failed! For us, for the common People of Indonesia, the Revolution has not yet ended, and for that reason we march forward in order to implement the ideals of the Proclamation. Our Revolution could fail if we did not wholeheartedly implement the ideals of the Proclamation, if we did not wholeheartedly implement the Political Manifesto, if we did not wholeheartedly implement the Message of the Suffering of the People! For that reason it is ridiculous for people to talk at present about the failure or otherwise of the Revolution!

There are those who rejoin: But our Revolution has been going for fifteen years. Is fifteen years not long enough to make an evaluation?

Brothers and sisters! In the life struggle of a given nation, in its growth and its consolidation, fifteen years is, in fact, only a beginning. I have often said that Revolution is not to be measured by days or years. Revolution is to be measured by decades or multiples of decades. Fifteen years is only a first phase—at the most it constitutes the end of the first phase, at most, "the end of the beginning" —which must be followed by other phases no less great and tremendous.

On and on go the strivings of that Revolution, on and on one phase is followed by another. As I have said: "For a fighting nation there is no journey's end."

This is what some time ago I called the dynamic of Revolution. And for anyone who understands the course of Revolution, for anyone who participates actively in its mighty current, for anyone who positively and constructively contributes to it—does not oppose it, does not hold it up or desperately turn it upside down, as do the reactionaries—for those who join in that mighty current of the Revolution, the dynamic of the Revolution becomes a Romanticism arousing a passionate spirit—drawing, binding with spiritual longing, inspiring, fascinating.

Frankly, I tell you: I belong to the group of people who are bound in spiritual longing by the Romanticism of Revolution. I am inspired by it, I am fascinated by it, I am completely absorbed by it, I am crazed, I am obsessed by the Romanticism of Revolution. And for this I utter thanks to God Who commands all nature!

There are people who do not understand Revolutionary logic. Those are the people who say in the midst of a journey, "The Revolution is over," whereas in fact the Revolution is not yet completed and still goes on, on, and again on. This is Revolutionary logic: once we start a Revolution, we must continue that Revolution until all its ideals have been implemented. This constitutes an absolute Law of Revolution, which cannot be denied, which cannot be argued about any more! Therefore, do not say, "The Revolution is over," while the Revolution is still on the march; and do not attempt to dam up or slow down a particular phase of the Revolution, which is itself but a consequence of earlier phases.

There are also people who, oh yes, understand and agree on all the phases. But they ask: "Do we need to be always inflaming the spirit of Revolution? Is it necessary for everything to be done in a Revolutionary way? Could it not be done more patiently, could it not be done by means of *alon-alon asal kelakon* [slow but sure]"?

Good heavens! "Slow but sure"? That is impossible! That is not possible, unless we want to be crushed by the People! Last year I declared: Let there be none among us who seek to amend or modify the principles and the objective of our Revolution. Now I will make another declaration: Let there be none among us who seek to change or moderate the Revolutionary Spirit! Although we have been in a state of revolution for fifteen years already—yes, although in future we may have been twenty-five or thirty-five or forty-five years in a state of revolution—I say: Let there be none among us who seek to change or moderate the Revolutionary Spirit! I repeat over again what I said last year, that the social consciousness of the People everywhere, all over the face of the earth, is the same and is very highly developed. Do not be mistaken about this, let there be no slip on this! It is this consciousness of the People which demands, which demands urgently, that all conditions or comparisons which are unjust must be wiped out and that something fitting must quickly be put in their place—in a speedy way, in a revolutionary way. If those conditions and comparisons are not wiped out and replaced quickly, this New Consciousness will explode like dynamite, will explode like Krakatau in 1883 and will flare up into a mighty movement, which in this twentieth century could threaten peace and equilibrium throughout the world.

Look at events in East Asia! Look at events in Latin America! Look at events on the continent of Africa, whose people, it was thought but a while back, still had no consciousness at all! How wrong that was!

In the address of August 17, 1959, I said that the People everywhere want to free themselves in a revolutionary way from all the chains of colonialism; that the People everywhere want to lay down in a revolutionary way the material basis for a more just well-being; that the People everywhere want to wipe out in a revolutionary way all social contradictions caused by feudalism and capitalism; that the People everywhere want in a revolutionary way to develop their national identity; that the People everywhere want in a revolutionary way to obliterate every danger or threat to world peace—that they are opposed to atomic bomb tests, opposed to war pacts, opposed to Menderes, opposed to Syngman Rhee.

The world today is a tinderbox of Revolution. This world today holds revolutionary electric power. This world today is "loaded with revolution." Three-quarters of all of mankind on the face of this earth, I said in my address last year, are in a revolutionary spirit. It has never before happened that the history of man has gone through such a revolution as this present one—so strong and so tremendous, so wide-sweeping and universal, a Revolution of Humanity which surges, flashes and thunders simultaneously in almost every corner of the earth.

And we want to creep like snails, to crawl like tortoises? We want to go "slow but sure," to sit back, sipping hot, sweet tea, clicking our fingers at the doves to encourage them to coo, in the greatest possible enjoyment, as people do who hold a cooing contest between doves?

Wake up, you people who suffer from revolution phobia! We are now in the midst of a Revolution, and not just a small Revolution, but a Revolution greater than the past American Revolution or the past French Revolution, or the present Soviet Revolution. A year ago, I explained that this Revolution of ours is at the same time a National Revolution, a political Revolution, a social Revolution, a cultural

Revolution, and a Revolution in Man. Our Revolution, I said, is a five-faceted Revolution, a multi-complex Revolution, a Revolution which is "a summing up of many revolutions in one generation." I said a year ago that we must therefore move fast, we must run like the obsessed, we must be dynamically revolutionary, we must incessantly and relentlessly extract every idea, every ounce of fighting energy, every grain of creative power, every atom of sweat in our bodies, in order that the outcome of our Revolution can match the dynamic of social consciousness which surges in the breast of society as a whole.

All the more so if we fully understand that this Indonesian Revolution is a part of the Great Revolution which inspires three-quarters of the human race! All the more so if we see the red glow of fires reflected in the Eastern skies, the red glow of fires reflected in the Western skies, the red glow of fires reflected in the Northern skies, if we see that all the skies around us are glowing with the fire of Revolution. Seeing all this, it is forbidden for us to creep like snails, to crawl like tortoises, forbidden for us to go "slow but sure," forbidden for us to nurture revolution phobia!

Look and take heed: A state which does not grow in a revolutionary way will not only be crushed by its own People. It will also soon be swept aside by the Typhoon of Universal Revolution which is the most important phenomenon in the world at the present time. This does not concern Indonesia alone, it does not concern only the nations which are at present in a period of transition and development. It concerns all nations. The states and nations which are already old, and the states and nations which feel that they are already "settled," will also eventually be shaken by that Typhoon of Universal Revolution—that is, if they do not adjust themselves to the changes and upheavals which are leading to the formation of a New World, free from colonialism, free from exploitation, free from color discrimination, free from spying on each other with atom bombs and thermonuclear weapons in their hands.

IIId

Sukarno A Nation That People Respect and Admire (1962)

This is part of Sukarno's 1962 annual Independence Day address —the last occasion, perhaps, on which he had a convincing success to lay before the people. The full English text is in Sukarno, Indonesia's Political Manifesto, 1959–64 (*Djakarta: Prapantja, 1964?*), *pp. 187–226.*

Now that the security question has been solved and the West Irian question brought to an end, our assets for solving the problem of the economy have been greatly increased. For the restoration of security alone, as I have said before, we had to devote 50 per cent of our entire national resources, and later, with the addition of the tasks of the Threefold Command of the People,* this amount became yet greater. We have devoted nearly three-quarters of our national effort to re-establishing security and implementing the Threefold Command of the People. We have thrown in more than 70 per cent of our national resources for these two purposes! Listen carefully once more: More than 70 per cent! Do you understand that this is one of the biggest causes of difficulties in our economic life? Do you understand why, with more than 70 per cent of national resources committed in this way, the food and clothing program has not as yet been implemented satisfactorily?

I know of the sufferings which exist here and there and I bow my head before those who suffer. I say "Go ahead, please go ahead, be angry with me! Go ahead, point your finger at me! Go ahead, pour your wrath upon me—and I will accept it all calmly." Let me just add that it is indeed true that I gave priority to the settlement of the problems of security and of West Irian, despite the fact that I realized that nearly three-quarters of our national resources would have to be tied down as a result.

Was that policy of mine right? Or were those acts of mine wrong? History will bring down the final verdict. Security had to be restored this year, had to be, once more, had to be restored within this year, and could not wait until next year. And West Irian had to be freed this year, had to, had to—three times—had to be brought under the authority of the Republic this year, before the cock crows on January 1, 1963. This had to be if we did not want the matter of West Irian to be postponed indefinitely again, if we did not want to be fooled by such smooth tricks as the "State of Papua." In keeping with timing strategy, 1962 was the right year to give the rebel gangs the *coup de grâce,* and the people themselves could suffer the dis-

* This Command was contained in President Sukarno's speech of December 19, 1961, and propelled the campaign for the liberation of West Irian into its final and most intensive stage.

turbances to security no longer. And again in keeping with timing strategy in connection with the international situation, 1962 was the right time to strike the *coup de grâce* at Dutch imperialism in West Irian. Objectively speaking, 1962 was the decisive year for us in the matter of smashing that imperialism to pieces. Another year, another opportunity, would not come again immediately.

It was the same in another instance. August 1945, right after World War II had ended, was the moment which, in keeping with timing strategy, was objectively the one and only moment to make the Proclamation of Indonesia's Independence. In 1929 I had stated: "At the end of the world war which is coming, at the end of the Pacific war, at that time Indonesia will become independent." And because of these words of mine, the Dutch threw me into prison for years!

Well, that is how matters stood: Security and West Irian could not wait a single day longer, whereas it would be possible for us to solve the problem of food and clothing as we went along. And solving it would become easier, for the resources we had used to restore security and secure the return of West Irian would be able to be used to deal with the economic problems. Apart from this, the food and clothing situation can be said to be still reasonable. Can it not, considering that we have been throwing nearly three-quarters of our national potential into the problems of security and West Irian? Considering that we are living under semiwar conditions? Considering that vital development projects are being built, involving the expenditure of thousands of millions? Considering that we were stricken last year by a most terrible drought and by a new plant disease called *gandjur?* Are there any Indonesians dying of starvation? Are there any Indonesians going naked from lack of clothes?

On the other hand, is there any Indonesian who does not feel proud that he is an Indonesian when he sees the successes we have had, in the political field and as regards development of every kind? Who is not proud that this Republic is his? Who is not proud that he is a member of a nation that is no longer the laughingstock of the world but a nation that people respect and admire? Who is not proud of this, despite the fact that we still have our shortcomings? And more: Who is not proud that he is a member of a nation that is not stagnant, of a nation that is moving, moving, moving on swiftly towards the building of a great state, whole and strong, that stretches from Sabang to Merauke, a great state that moves forward fast toward a life that is noble and respected, just and prosperous, that is a beacon to others, that has no *exploitation de l'homme par l'homme*, and that is rapidly becoming one of the champions of the new emerging forces, a nation that is moving to realize socialism based on its own national identity? Who is not proud of this?

IIIe

Sukarno   The Revolution Goes On (1965)

This piece comes from the Independence Day speech of 1965 and so from one of the President's last speeches before the coup of October 1965. The speech was published as Reach to the Stars: A Year of Self-Reliance *(Djakarta: Department of Information, 1965). By this time Sukarno's relations with the Communist Party had become very cordial and his relations with the main body of leaders of the army much cooler than in earlier years.*

We should not apply the wrong standards in measuring our revolution. A revolution can only be measured by revolutionary standards! A revolution cannot be measured by the standards of textbooks, even ones written by bald-headed professors from Oxford or Cornell University, or anywhere else. It seems that I still need to stress this point because there are still people who regard imperialist textbooks as a standard for impeccable ideas, as something sacrosanct which may not be challenged or disturbed. Are the imperialists' *mission sacrée* and "white man's burden" divine laws? Are they? Open your eyes, you who have gone astray!

How do we measure a revolution by revolutionary standards? Everything must be scrutinized: is it for the public well-being or is it not? *Pro bono publico,* this is our slogan. For the well-being of the public! Even though some personal losses may result, even though there may be some whose businesses earn fewer profits, if something is *pro bono publico,* they must accept it. On the other hand, if some people get more cars, more bungalows, more refrigerators, more air conditioners, if some can send their children to school in Europe or in Outer Space, for that matter—if that is not *pro bono publico,* then it must be rejected. Unless—unless, I say—we are dealing with someone who has become a foreigner in his own country or a citizen of some foreign country! Yes, unless we are dealing with someone who has violated, or sinned against, or betrayed the revolution!

Look at the workers and the farmers, the main pillars of our revolution! They are indeed worthy of this designation; it is correct for me to call them the main pillars of the revolution. They work, they produce, without complaints and without fuss. They have their demands, of course, but these are usually reasonable. If a worker wants his wages increased a little in order to buy schoolbooks for his children, does this not make sense? If a farmer wants to have land, a small piece of land, does that not make sense? It reminds me of the *ludruk Marhaen** artists who say: "If you have a hoe without a piece of land, where are you going to use it!" But there are those among us who want to play the nobleman, who want to play the boss, who consider themselves owner of the revolution or president-director of the Republic, who then do not want to make sacrifices for the Republic themselves but want the Republic to make sacrifices for them. Such people—parvenus, charlatans, profiteers of this kind—should be "promoted" to the status of inhabitants of the prison on Nusakambangan Island!

I have always said that the class struggle should be subordinated to the national struggle. And I am glad that this appeal of mine has been understood by the overwhelming majority of the people. But I should like to issue a warning: if the corruptors and swindlers of state wealth continue with their truly anti-Republic and anti-people's "operations," then do not be startled if the struggle between groups flares up one day and consumes the luxurious living of these corruptors and swindlers!

Our revolution is no longer at the stage of trials, no longer at the experimental stage. We have no more need to make experiments or trials. The revolutionary spirit and the revolutionary laws have been formed. Like a football team, we must not bring out players who are not yet "formed," who are not yet mature. Our revolution has found its form, and this stage has laid new requirements upon us, new demands, new standards.

Those who were progressive yesterday are possibly reactionary and anti-progressive today. Those who were revolutionary yesterday

---

* *Ludruk* is an East Javanese form of popular theater, semicomic and usually having a contemporary background. PNI-sponsored *ludruk* groups are called *ludruk Marhaen*.

are possibly counterrevolutionary today. Those who were radical yesterday are possibly soft and incapable of resistance today. Therefore, let none of us pride himself on the basis simply of past services. I am disgusted with all that old rubbish! It makes me sick! Even if you were a baldheaded general in 1945, if you are a splitter of revolutionary national unity today, if you are creating disorder in the Nasakom front today, if you are an enemy of the main pillars of the revolution today, then you have become a force of reaction! On the other hand, if you were nothing before and are nothing now but are faithful to the revolution, then you are a revolutionary force! These are the forces—men or women, old or young, high or low—it is such revolutionary forces as these which I shall bind together, all without exception, which I shall draw together into one force, to make into a gigantic power "resembling a typhoon which sweeps the oceans." . . .

Since the Political Manifesto, Pantja Sila and *Nasakom* have become more and more firmly implanted, and as it has become more and more difficult for the reactionaries to oppose all this openly, a symptom which has recently become very conspicuous is the increasing number of hypocrites, impostors, sweet-of-tongue-evil-at-heart people. All of them claim to accept the Political Manifesto, all of them claim to adhere to the Pantja Sila, all of them claim that they agree with *Nasakom*. This being the case, heed my words when I say that the main criterion for a revolutionary is oneness between word and deed. Assess your leaders, assess people, assess everyone first and foremost by their deeds. Judge your leaders, judge people, judge individuals first and foremost by their deeds! If their deeds diverge, kick them out of our midst!

Let us also judge the organs of state, the mass organizations, the political parties and other bodies according to whether there is oneness between their words and their deeds. I should like to call upon the political parties in particular to compete with each other in intensifying their role in the present Manipolist offensive. Revolutionary political parties are very effective instruments for encouraging and activating the masses to take part in the Revolution. There can be no doubt of this; to doubt it would be to doubt the truth of the Political Manifesto. However, I will stress once more that I am speaking of *revolutionary* political parties. Those that are not revolutionary, worse still those that are antirevolutionary, will no longer have the right to exist in Indonesia. The action suspending the Murba party proves that the Government will not hesitate to act against

political parties if they deviate, if they split our unity. I call on the
Manipolist political parties to purge themselves and keep on purging
themselves of hypocritical elements, "BPS" elements, right-wing socialist elements, elements with a *Nasakom* phobia, spineless individuals, hypocrites and the like, and to keep on competing as Mani-
polists in serving the Message of the People's Sufferings and in taking the offensive, armed with the "Five Talismans."

I call upon the organs of state to unite themselves truly with the
People. One can never serve the People enough, still less too much.
Do not be like members of the colonial civil service who saw the
People as a specter. The People are your point of origin, the People
are your strength. You must pay all tribute to the People. The People
are your source!

I call upon the entire People to use all ways and means to fortify
revolutionary national unity. Root out any principle-ism which rejects cooperation and unity, ostensibly on grounds of principle,
grounds of ideology, of religion, and so on. Last March, the Provisional Madjelis Permusjawaratan Rakjat decided to prohibit anti-
Nationalist propaganda, anti-Religious propaganda and anti-Communist propaganda. This is a very good decision and it proves that
the supreme legislative organ in our country understands its responsibilities. Implant this decision by the Madjelis in your minds
and carry it out with the greatest possible tolerance!

IIIf
Sakirman   The Positive Aspects
of Guided Democracy (1960)

This selection has been translated from the May–June and July–
August 1960 issues of the PKI's theoretical monthly, Bintang Merah
(Red Star). *A member of the Politburo, Ir. Sakirman may be taken*
as speaking for the party leadership as a whole or at least for its
dominant group.

It is certainly not easy to gain a correct understanding of the political line the Party has pursued in the recent past, especially since the
party adopted its attitude of approving the return to the 1945 Constitution.

The difficulty which some comrades have in understanding this
political line of the Party is due in the first place to the fact that the

disease of subjectivism is still sometimes present, even in our own circles, hence a particular political problem is often seen in only one of its aspects and from a one-sided point of view. There are some among us who only see the shortcomings of the Party Leadership and not the fruits of the great and heroic struggle of the Indonesian People under the leadership of the Party. They see only the short-comings in particular clauses of the Constitution of the Republic of Indonesia and in the practical implementation of these clauses and do not want to see the positive aspects of what we have experienced in practice with the 1945 Constitution. They see the negative aspects of a *Gotong Rojong* Parliament and not the positive aspects, and on the other hand they want to see only the positive aspects of the elected Parliament, not the negative aspects. They see only the failure of the August revolution, not the results achieved by it. . . .

In his book *Two Tactics of Social Democracy in the Democratic Revolution,* Lenin clearly analyzed the problem of the connection between the bourgeois-democratic revolution and the Socialist revolution. According to Lenin the stage of the bourgeois-democratic revolution and the stage of the Socialist revolution are not only closely linked but mutually influencing and even mutually determining. The first stage should lay the foundations for the birth of the second and, on the other hand, the second should determine the character of and provide direction of development for the first.

According to Lenin, the two stages have both common characteristics and differences. The bourgeois-democratic and the Socialist revolutions have in common the fact that both must occur under the leadership of the proletariat as a necessary condition, as a *conditio sine qua non,* of their success. Unless there is proletarian leadership of the course of the revolution in this period of imperialism, the bourgeois-democratic revolution will stall and so lose its proper direction, toward Socialism. And with this loss of direction, the bourgeois-democratic revolution will slowly or rapidly become a counterrevolution, which will mean it will have met with total failure.

The differences between the two stages of revolution are to be found in the matter of targets, in the determination of tactics and program, and in their respective tasks.

The feudal-monarchical power of the Tsar and his lackeys was the principal target of the democratic revolution in Russia, and to destroy this target the Russian proletariat had to unite with the peasants, including the middle peasants, to neutralize the wavering groups and to isolate the kulaks.

In the socialist Revolution in Russia, the principal target was the power of the Mensheviks, who had betrayed the revolution and were cooperating with the imperialists. In order to destroy the power of the Mensheviks completely, the proletariat, which ought to have complete hegemony both formally and in fact, united with the poor peasants and peasant laborers, isolated the wavering elements, and smashed the remnants of the kulaks.

In connection with the problem of the similarities and differences between bourgeois-democratic and Socialist revolutions, it needs to be pointed out that the "heroes" of the Second International, the right-wing socialists who have made deviations of principle from the revolutionary line of Marxism-Leninism, believe that the bourgeois-democratic revolution should be led by the bourgeoisie as a condition for the fullest possible development of capitalism. In their opinion the Socialist revolution can only be born after the peasants and the half-proletarian poor throughout the world have been boiled in the belly of capitalism, to become a proletariat which will be the "vanguard" of the Socialist revolution.

So, according to the "logic" of the right socialists, who are well enough represented in Indonesia, the new Socialist revolution can only be born after the whole world has developed monopoly capitalism, after the areas called "backward" have been plundered and looted by the imperialists. But it is obvious that their concept of the leadership of the Socialist revolution is only a mask to conceal their evil intentions, namely, to give the imperialist states "historic rights" to colonize those other countries which are said to be still backward.

Experience in the Soviet Union, in the Chinese People's Republic, and in the other Socialist countries of Eastern Europe has shown that Lenin's theory about the problem of leadership of the bourgeois-democratic revolution is completely supported by the facts, that is, that no wall exists dividing the stage of bourgeois-democratic revolution from the stage of Socialist revolution, and that the hegemony of the proletariat is a principal condition for guaranteeing the success of the first stage, which is success in proceeding to the second stage. . . .

Is it true that the practices of the 1945 Constitution which is in operation at present are really not guided democracy but a political and economic system which is semifascist, which is more evil than liberal democracy? Is it true that the agitation about the bankruptcy of liberal democracy was really only intended to influence the public to pass judgment on liberal democracy, so that this could be replaced by a system which is even more bankrupt than liberal democracy?

It is true, as Comrade Aidit explained in his report to the Seventh Plenary Session of the Central Committee of the Party, that liberal democracy and the practices of the 1950 provisional constitution in general contributed a lot within certain limits, in bringing down the reactionary Sukiman Cabinet, in defeating the attempted coup of October 17, 1952, and so on. But as well as these we also had experiences under it which were not so pleasant, because it was impossible to prevent the growth of undesirable excesses such as corruption and smuggling, to solve the basic problems facing the People, and so on.

The Party's attitude and view toward Guided Democracy was fully discussed and decided upon by the Seventh Plenary Session of the Central Committee of the Party, in November 1958, thus long before Indonesia returned to the 1945 Constitution.

In his report to that Plenary Session Comrade Aidit declared:

There are things which can weaken the idea of Guided Democracy and sincere efforts must be made by all lovers of Guided Democracy to prevent these. For example, the idea will possibly be turned upside down by political adventurers and speculators, by parties, groups, and individuals who did not gain the confidence of the People in the elections.* Thus, the impression could arise that Guided Democracy was established for those who could not possibly succeed through democratic procedures. So Guided Democracy would seem to have been created not according to the desire of President Sukarno, but merely to fulfil the immediate ambitions of a few people who are politically bankrupt. Such an impression must be avoided.

The value of the idea of Guided Democracy will be reduced if there are people who intend to use it as a channel or a springboard to dissolve the parties† and kill the political life of the People which has been developing since 1908. In this way the impression could arise that Guided Democracy was only preparation for a military dictatorship or personal dictatorship. This impression must also be avoided. In order that the idea

* This probably refers mainly to the national-communist Murba party, the Socialist party, and the army-connected IPKI (League of Upholders of Indonesian Independence).

† These included some high army officers as well as some Murba party leaders.

of Guided Democracy should remain strong and not give rise to the least doubt among the Indonesian People, the following conditions need to be fulfilled.

First, Guided Democracy must be aimed at guaranteeing a democratic and healthy political life for the Indonesian masses and at uniting the Indonesian People on as broad as possible a basis. In other words, Guided Democracy must mean, politically, the 100 per cent realization of the President's Concept, especially the formation of a *Gotong Rojong* Cabinet based on proportional representation, as a faithful reflection of the unity of all the anti-imperialist forces in our country. Economically, Guided Democracy must mean giving first priority to the state sector of the economy to enable it to lead in the development of the entire economy of the country and to destroy the power of foreign monopoly capital.

Second, leadership in the implementation of the idea of Guided Democracy must be in the hands of President Sukarno, as initiator of the idea of Guided Democracy and the President's Concept, and as a democrat whose courage was tested when he refused to be made a dictator by the military at the time of the affair of October 17, 1952. As a consequence of this stand, President Sukarno must be given the special right to fill a part of the membership of parliament,* following democratic and legal procedures and choosing patriots who hold the confidence of the People.

Guided Democracy and the President's Concept are weapons of the Indonesian People with which to strengthen their unity in the fight against imperialism. To strengthen national unity, democracy must be broadened for the People and narrowed for the enemies of the People. If this is carried out, an important leap will have been taken in the efforts of the Indonesian People to settle its contradiction with imperialism completely.

We have known President Sukarno as a patriot, as an anticolonial democrat with a great deal of political experience in external as well as internal affairs. We know Bung Karno as a big-hearted leader who can generally place the interests of the People and state above his personal interests.

As a big-hearted democratic and patriotic leader with much experience and knowledge concerning the problems of society, Bung Karno, of course, bases his viewpoint and political attitude on the strength of the mass of the People. . . .

One specific aspect of the problem of relations with the middle group in Indonesia is that they hold state power and do not all

* This is a reference to the establishment of the wholly nominated *Gotong Rojong* Parliament.

refuse the Communists a place in the government or other bodies of state power. This also gives rise to new aspects which have not been encountered in the history of the struggle of the People overseas in the past or the present, except perhaps in one or two areas. It is easy to see how difficult it is to solve the problem of relations with groups or individuals who are not only stronger in their formal positions but who are also "more valued and more respected" in the eyes of the People whose political and ideological consciousness is still not at a high level.

Some comrades have grown anxious, fearing that the deteriorating economic situation will make it difficult for the Party to maintain and strengthen links with the groups in power, because there is the possibility that the People will consider that groups which generally support their power must also share responsibility for the dilapidated condition of the economy. This anxiety is inappropriate, because the People know that until a *Gotong Rojong* Cabinet is formed, the Communists cannot be blamed for a situation which will possibly continue to deteriorate. And even if a *Gotong Rojong* Cabinet is formed, and it becomes clear that this cabinet is incapable of bringing about any radical improvement in the situation, it will not be possible to put all the blame on the Communists.

IIIg
Selosoemardjan Guided Democracy and Our Cultural Traditions (1961)

This extract* comes from a paper which was originally written in 1961 and presented to the Pacific Science Congress held in Hawaii in September of that year. It was subsequently published in the January 1963 issue of the Review of Politics *(Vol. XXV) under the title "Some Social and Cultural Implications of Indonesia's Unplanned and Planned Development."*

A remarkable social change in the political field has resulted from the President's measures for social reintegration; the political parties, previously functioning as powerful nuclei of influence on the political, economic, and social sectors of the nation's development, have been reduced to a relatively weak voice in defining the destiny of the country. As a consequence of the law on the simplification of the

* Reprinted by permission of the *Review of Politics.*

party system, most political organizations either lost their legal existence or the autonomy of defining for themselves their political goals and the basic ideologies which formerly imbued their activities. The ten political parties that secured the required presidential recognition are still free to engage in political activities, but they are subject to military control in the areas under martial law and to preventive police regulations in the areas under civilian administration. Political activities in the context of Indonesian democracy can be freely exercised insofar as they are not at variance with the Political Manifesto. Any political action beyond the legally set limitations may end up in the withdrawal of presidential recognition.

The strict rules on political parties have had not only a quieting effect on the political level: they have also swept away a great many of the disorganizing influences on the population in general, particularly in the rural areas where people used to follow the orders of political leaders without knowledge of their significance and real meaning. The administration on village and higher levels, which in the past had to spend considerable time and energy coping with unrestricted extraparliamentary actions of opposition parties, has now regained its stable position and official prestige in dealing with a more or less politically homogeneous society.

Within the organization of the administration itself, the personnel is no longer divided into overt factions which in the past were responsible for much of the administrative inefficiency because of intergroup conflicts, mutual suspicions, and political favoritism in the distribution of key positions and financially profitable jobs. So far no one has been punished under the rules directed against senior government officials having relations with political parties. Nevertheless, this regulation has by and large produced the desired effect; overt party influence is effectively banned from the administrative personnel, and only covert and weak party preferences can be distinguished in offices where formerly a particular party had been able to control a majority of the personnel. The political party is no longer the chief channel for vertical mobility in the administration of the country. As political party leaders cannot use issues and courses of action to rally their followers in mass organizations, they have lost much of their social prestige. Only those whose prominence was the consequence of outstanding personal qualities have retained their prestige both within and without the party.

The focus of political life has shifted to the administration itself.

Political parties no longer decide legislative and executive issues; the decisive powers are now entirely in the hands of the administrative officers, the President on the national level, and the Governor, the *bupati*, and the village headman, each for his own area of jurisdiction.

In the past, political parties served as sources of conflicting political norms. A party's norms were the norms of its members and influenced both political life and social relations. The new situation, with all parties, moreover, obliged to endorse the same Political Manifesto as directed to the attainment of one common national goal, the planned establishment of an Indonesian socialist society, has meant that there is only one source of political norms: the President. The possibilities of political conflicts, which may arise from the differences of interest among the leaders of the ten recognized parties, are now reduced to differences about means of implementing the eight-year plan. . . .

The move from liberal to guided democracy meant a change to a one-man administration in Djakarta, as well as all the way down to the lowest level of jurisdiction, working with an advisory body and a representative council of appointive membership. This change was effected without any observable resistance. The smoothness of the change, however, is not simply to be explained by popular weariness with party conflicts and by the sense of powerlessness of the political parties with their vested interests in confronting the President and the support of the armed forces. The facility of the change may in some measure be attributed to the fact that the centralized and personality-centered type of administration was generally felt to be more consistent with the institutionalized authoritarian structure of Indonesian society at large.

The history of Indonesia is replete with kings, sultans, rajahs, and other absolute rulers whom society regarded as the mediators between this world and the cosmological powers that control the life of man and society. Thus, society entrusted to them all powers— social, religious, and political—and expected that the powers would be applied for the welfare of the society. Encroachment on the rulers' powers appeared to be an offense against the cosmological powers and would invariably incur a social punishment or disaster.

This belief system is, in a slightly different form, honored in the relations between the traditionally elected village headman and the village community in Java. Since the village communities acquired control over land and all members of the community could share on an equal basis in the use of it, the *primus inter pares* had to be elected from among the landholders as chief of the community. Election is for life, and it is a general phenomenon in each village community that the election of a village headman is guided not by determining the skills or formal education of the candidates, but by their honesty, helpfulness, reliability, and wisdom. Once elected, the village headman is expected to act as a father to the whole community, rewarding its good members and punishing deviations from the traditional social norms, but always acting as a *sesepuh*, a wise elder, who is constantly trying to promote the happiness and prosperity of his community and harmony between his village and the unseen spiritual forces that live in and around it.

In the cultural context of this belief system it was hard for the less sophisticated and non-Western-educated groups of Indonesian society to adjust to the Western democratic system of collective government, which imposed upon them a cabinet or an executive council composed of members representing political parties alien to the indigenous population. The process of adjustment was the less successful when the parties developed into sources of never ending conflicts. As a consequence, the deculturation of the collective system of government, followed by a planned reculturation of the personality-centered type of administration, encountered a smooth path among the people.

IIIh

Rosihan Anwar   Neither Quixotism nor Surrender (1961)

This discussion of the problem of press freedom under Guided Democracy is taken from a letter written by the former editor of the Djakarta Socialist daily, Pedoman, *to the Executive Board of the International Press Institute and published in this institute's journal,* IPI Report (Vol. IX) *of March 1961.* Late in 1960 Rosihan Anwar had acceded to a demand of the Indonesian government that he sign a nineteen-point undertaking, pledging his support for the Political Manifesto and a number of other current formulations of*

* Reprinted by permission of *IPI Report.*

state policy. He had thereupon been suspended from membership in the International Press Institute by a decision taken at the request of the one-time chairman of the Indonesian national committee of the IPI, Mochtar Lubis, a former editor who had been under arrest for four years for expressing opposition to President Sukarno's ideas and actions. Rosihan Anwar wrote the letter from which this piece comes to protest against the suspension of his membership. Ironically, the government had forced his paper to close down before the letter was written.

The last few years have in many of these new states seen the collapse of the institutions usually connected with a functioning democracy, together with the emergence of a trend toward authoritarianism and in some countries even a gravitation of power toward the military. One may regret this retrogression. This shift clearly reflects some inherent weaknesses in the body politic of these nations. However, it has also uncovered the bedrock of political life in these nations. It has shown more clearly than ever the basic forces at work and the basic problems with which these nations are confronted, even before the question of democratic government is raised.

This step backwards has forced us to reflect anew upon the problems of democracy in these new states and has made many of us realize the necessity of having, first, to create the conditions under which democratic institutions could properly function in these new states. At the same time many of us are convinced that the possibilities for a development toward democracy are not lost, although we have become aware that a much longer and tougher struggle is required and that a sufficiently strong power base as well as a sufficient degree of political maturity are essential conditions for democratic institutions to function properly.

The problem, therefore, is not how to maintain the democratic institutions provided for in the democratically worded formal constitutions of these new states, but rather how to create the conditions in which such could function properly. Now, several of these countries have made the step backward, but to those of us who have not lost their belief in the possibilities of the realization of democracy in these countries, this bedrock is not the point of ultimate decline but is our new point of departure from which to work for the realization of our goals.

And so it is from this bedrock then that those who are moved by their belief in democratic principles will have to work toward the creation of democratic principles and to help build the power structure on which the edifice of democracy could rest.

All this has, unavoidably, also affected the position of the press and the position from which the democratic journalist has to work.

It has been brought home to him that democracy does in the final analysis not rest on the guarantees embodied in the Constitution, but in the awareness of the people of their rights and on their willingness to fight for them.

Restated against the background of the changes in the past few years his task then is to help increase and nurture the awareness of human rights, the rights of the people, and to help foster their willingness to work and fight for them.

Seen in this light, the task of the democratic journalist is, given the conditions under which he has to work, to carefully nurture these feelings and convictions among the public as well as among the people who work in the various agencies of government. It is to try carefully to push back the area of government arbitrariness and abuse of power and to build up that kind of a relationship with his public which will enable him to widen his sphere of influence and effectiveness.

In doing so he has to be careful not to lose touch with the very forces in which he sees hope for democratic development. For the time being he has to accept the historically conditioned reluctance of the people to fight for what they think is their right. Having only the experience of autocratic government behind them, of their feudal rulers and of a colonial government, this is understandable. But it does limit the scope for his own fight and affects the tempo with which he can reasonably expect the fuller development of such democratic awareness and militancy on the part of the people.

It also affects his place in the order of things. The only place for the democratic journalist is in defence of these human and democratic rights of the people. Even under a government with honest democratic institutions, the pressures for keeping power centralized in many of these new states will be so great that it will be impossible for the democratic journalist to associate and identify with such a regime, for his primary concern is not orderly and effective government, but the defence within the limits of the possible, of the fundamental rights of man.

He has to wage this struggle from whatever area of operation is consigned to him by the regime of the day. The main thing is that he keeps fighting. Given the prospect that the period of more or less authoritarian rule is going to be a rather prolonged one, irrespective of the democratic or nondemocratic orientation of the government in power, the position in which all this puts the democratic journalist is not an easy one.

The trend and gravitation of power towards the army, the trend towards autocratic government, is not the work of a single power-hungry man or group. It is the result of pressures which operate in these new states on the social fabric and on the cohesion of the body politic. These pressures will still be there when those under whose aegis this process of concentration of power was consummated will have left the historical scene, disappeared from the political scene.

It is the duty of the democratically minded press and the journalist devoted to the ideals of freedom of the press to keep the flickering flame of democratic aspirations alive in the face of governmental pressure, and to kindle it by strengthening the belief of the people in their rights and their willingness to fight for them.

It is this which in the final analysis determines the position of the democratic journalist in these countries and the scope of his struggle. If he goes beyond it, he loses his touch with his public and stands out in isolation—a Don Quixote, at best.

On the other extreme is abject surrender to the official doctrine of the government in power, in which he, again, is isolated from his public.

In such a situation, then, his task, so it seems to me, is clear. He has to remain in close contact with those elements and forces among the public and in the governmental apparatus which hold out the best hope and possibilities for widening the area of public participation and judgment. He has to try to keep alive their spirit and their belief and faith in the ultimate superiority of democracy. He has constantly to try to push back the barriers behind which the press has been zoned in by governmental regulations.

But in order to do this, he has first to be there, to exist, even if existence is only possible on the basis of the restricted area to which the press has been consigned.

It would be wrong to look at these restrictions as the final word in this respect. We should look at them as a temporary arena.

There is not the slightest chance in Indonesia of the establishment of a monolithic power structure exercising effective control over the whole of Indonesia and in all areas of human activity.

The social pressures, the conflicts of interests even within the limited circle of the political elite in power are too great. Each of these conflicting interests at one time or another will need the press, whatever press there is. And in this fluidity and diversity inherent in the situation, there lies the possibility for the press to gradually build its own position of strength. It is the task of the democratic journalist to work on this, to strengthen his position in relation to his public, to show that even within the restricted situation the fight for democracy is not hopeless.

We should not overlook another thing. Apart from the pressures tending toward concentration of power, we should not forget that the nationalist struggle is rooted in a desire for more freedom and more rights for the people, that whatever may happen in terms of concentration of power at the top, there is and always will remain a strong strain of democratic potential.

Should the democratic journalist abandon these forces and let them fend for themselves, only because he cannot operate under ideal conditions of freedom? Should he in order to keep his hands clean and his reputation unblemished like an old maid, close down his paper and sit back with an attitude of self-righteousness? This it seems to me is a betrayal of our obligation to the ideal of democracy, and a cowardly act.

Again, if the matter were simply the overthrow of an usurper, the closing down of a paper or the jailing of journalists would serve the concrete purpose of precipitating a crisis.

Issuing an open challenge to governmental curbing of the press would then be an act of valid heroism.

As I myself see it, the press will, for quite some time to come, have to operate within the limits set by an authoritarian government. These limits constitute the journalist's battlefield, his jumping-off point. And as long as he is convinced that even within these limits he can extend his voice however guarded, however veiled beyond these limits, and be heard beyond these limits, it is his duty to carry on. Likewise, as soon as he sees that this is not possible any longer, it is his duty to cease his activities as a journalist.

The criterion, then, by which a journalist in such a situation should be judged in terms of his devotion to the ideals of freedom of the press and democracy is not to what extent he is victorious, but by the question of whether he has associated himself with the powers that be or not. He cannot and should not be held responsible for the conditions under which he has to wage his struggle.

We may very well have to accept the inevitability of a prolonged period of authoritarian or more or less authoritarian government in many of these new states. Should the democratic journalist just wait for this period to pass and only become active when a really free press is possible? Isn't it rather his duty, as long as the press has not become a government monopoly, to keep alive, open, the few channels to reach his public, to keep alive the faith in human rights and freedom, and a mental climate, in which are pockets of mental resistance and independent judgment?

I will not further indulge here in a treatise about the pressures which operate in these new states and which are the underlying cause for the general drift towards authoritarianism and autocratic government. It has only been gradually, and as the result of many disillusionments that now this phenomenon is better understood, not only by us who are living here under those conditions, but also by Western scholars and observers. For those interested in these general problems I refer to the increasing number of publications on this subject, by Edward Shils, Raymond Aron, Monroe Berger, Arthur Schlesinger, Jr., etc.

This then is where I stand. I have taken this position not without a great deal of soul-searching and self-examination as to my basic motivations. I have done so as honestly as I could. Though the problem has ceased to exist, because of the closing down of my paper by government order, on January 7, 1961, I have no regrets.

IIIi

Kalimantan Evangelical Church The Church and the Indonesian Revolution (1962)

This excerpt comes from a Statement of the General Synod of the Kalimantan Evangelical Church issued in October 1962 in stenciled form. A church in the reformed tradition, it is one of the many regional churches which are members of the Council of Churches in Indonesia. Its membership numbered 31,500 in 1958.

THE GENERAL SYNOD OF THE KALIMANTAN EVANGELICAL CHURCH, bearing in mind the urgent need for Christian thinking about and evaluation of the Indonesian Revolution and the appeal of His Excellency, President Sukarno, "to create or give birth to new ideas and new conceptions, precisely because our Revolution cannot be brought to a conclusion by using the old outdated textbooks," has thus formulated the views, positions, and calling of the Church in the Indonesian Revolution:

A. *Views*

1. The Kalimantan Evangelical Church holds the conviction and the faith that God is working in and has a hidden purpose in this Indonesian Revolution and, because of this, that this Indonesian Revolution will continue to stand under the judgment and mercy of God.

2. As a church open to discussion and new facts she dares to justify and welcome all the changes brought about by the Indonesian Revolution which bring the possibility of a proper improvement in human life.

B. *Positions*

1. The General Synod sees the Indonesian Revolution as that which destroys and builds, builds and destroys, . . . which in the words of *Djarek* [President Sukarno's Independence Day address, 1960; see IIIc] "constructs tomorrow and pulls down yesterday" in the clear light of *metanoia*, of the radical atonement which destroys and discards what is old, and accepts, and is made new in and by, Christ.

2. It evaluates the "Three-Fold Aim" of the Indonesian Revolution —justice and prosperity in society, the elimination of imperialism, and the foundation of world peace—as being in the province of God's Kingdom. It sees it in the light of the abundant life and perfect peace which has come as a result of the suffering, death, and resurrection of Christ, through Whom God has reconciled all to Himself.

3. The Revolution can serve as a bridge to the well-being of the country. If power is appropriately controlled, by a system of checks and balances, it can serve to distribute wealth fairly and provide men with a decent livelihood. But we know with certainty that the last word and the highest power lies with God Himself, that sinful men acting as the completers of this Revolution and acting without the forgiveness and constant renewal which comes from the love

and mercy of God, can so twist the ideals of humanity, justice, and prosperity that a new oppression and exploitation arises *in the name* of the Revolution.

C. *Calling*

Starting from and standing upon its Faith in Jesus Christ, the Church is called to carry out its duty within the Indonesian Revolution in the three dimensions of the Church's own calling, those of Unity, Witness, and Christian Service, . . . in the following fields:

1. The Mental Field: In which all Christians and the Church have a great opportunity to destroy the remnants of the mentality imposed by colonialism and to replace it with that of Pantja Sila, developing the mentality of the people and the community on a healthy, dynamic, and responsible basis.

2. The Cultural Field: In the current phase of development of Indonesian culture, when what is being pushed forward strongly is the value of Indonesian man in the setting of the Revolution which is leading towards Indonesian Socialism with all its characteristics of mutual aid, the Church is called upon to make this value more complete by throwing on it the light of the "new man" in Christ. In the efforts being made to realize a national Indonesian culture, what should be sought is an appropriate synthesis between the various elements which can be termed our "common cultural goods," and also with what is universal in culture.

3. The Socio-Economic Field: The Church is aware that economic prosperity and social justice are absolute conditions for a worthy, decent, and good life. We are called to see this in the right perspective. The striving for material security and economic justice which has constituted a strong impetus to the revolutionary tempest, can be a manifestation of the abundant life promised by God. But if it is inspired by wrong motives it can become a curse to mankind. . . .

4. The Political Field: The Church is deeply aware that no system of government can be free from sin. Therefore, the Church, the whole Christian people, together with all the people of Indonesia, is called upon and has an obligation to scrutinize government power and balance the sovereignty of the people against it. In this period of the Indonesian Revolution the system of Guided Democracy, which is dynamic and indigenous, can act as midwife to a stable and strong government, but it must fully serve national integration and

national development and be fully responsible to the people. For the stable progress of the nation within this framework of Guided Democracy a healthy ethos is necessary, and it is demanded, too, that the state be responsive to the Mandate of the Suffering of the People and be called firmly, justly, and with deliberate wisdom to become the prime promoter of the people's welfare and the development of national consciousness. In this regard, all Christians and the whole people are obliged to accept the authority of the state and to evaluate all the measures of government in a positive and critical spirit according to whether they will serve to realize a just and prosperous society.

IIIj

Mohammad Hatta   A Dictatorship Supported by Certain Groups (1960)

The article from which this is taken, entitled "Our Democracy," was published in the May 1, 1960, issue of the Djakarta weekly Pandji Masjarakat *and banned soon afterward. In publishing it, Hatta broke a long silence. The article was republished in large editions in 1966.*

The history of Indonesia in the last ten years shows a great chasm between idealism and reality. The idealism has been striving for the establishment of a just government which would carry democracy into effect in the best possible way and with as much prosperity as possible for the people. The reality is that of a system of government whose development is taking it further and further away from real democracy.

During the last two or three years in particular there have very clearly been government actions which have violated the constitution. The President, who according to the 1950 Constitution was not responsible and beyond criticism, appointed himself to form a cabinet. In doing this he carried out a responsible act of government without bearing responsibility for it. The government formed in this peculiar way was simply accepted by parliament without any objection of principle being advanced. Indeed there were people who defended the President's action on the argument that it was a "situation of emergency."

Later, President Sukarno dissolved the Constituent Assembly which had been chosen by the people before its work of producing a new constitution was finished and promulgated a return to the 1945 Constitution by decree.

According to that 1945 Constitution the President of the Republic of Indonesia was the chief executive. The parliament, which existed under the 1950 Constitution, having been established on the basis of the elections of 1955, was confirmed as a temporary parliament to remain in existence until a new one could be formed on the basis of the 1945 Constitution. Although this action of the President violated the constitution and represented a coup d'état, it was approved by a majority of parties and by a majority in the parliament. A minority group saw it as a violation, but the members of this group reconciled themselves to the facts of the new situation. By taking a position of this kind the parliament abandoned its birthright.

Not long after that President Sukarno took a further step. After getting into a disagreement with the parliament over the budget, he decreed that it should be dissolved and reconstituted on the basis of a concept of his own. This new parliament has 261 members, half of whom are members of parties and the other half from what are called functional groups, that is workers, peasants, the youth, women, religious leaders, intellectuals, the army, and the police. All of these members have been appointed by the President. The 130 members of political parties have been chosen mainly by the parties themselves, from among their members in the parliament which has been in existence up to the present time, but members from the opposition group have been eliminated completely.

President Sukarno based all these actions on his view that the Indonesian revolution, which aims at establishing justice and prosperity, is still unfinished. The revolution will go on until a just and prosperous Indonesia is realized, and so all forms and structures are of an interim character. He is not against democracy, he says. On the contrary, his aim is to realize a true democracy, a *gotong rojong* democracy like that of Indonesian society as it originally existed. He condemns Western-style democracy, the free-fight democracy of everyone bashing at everyone else which has so far been practised in Indonesia. As he says, this free-fight democracy has broken up national unity and led to the work of development being neglected.

This liberal democracy was to be replaced by what he called guided democracy. The guided democracy he had in mind was a means of implementing a planned development program by vigorous action under a single leadership. This ideal was to be supported by close co-operation amongst the four large groups influential in society: the nationalists, the Muslims, the Communists, and the army. The center of gravity of government and legislation would no longer rest in Parliament, but rather in two new bodies, that is, in the National Council, which has now been changed to become the Supreme Advisory Council, and in the National Planning Council.

Within this system the only task of parliament is to provide a legal basis for decisions which have already been taken by the government on the basis of considerations or proposals from these two bodies. In this way, according to Sukarno, all deliberation would be quick and there would not be all the useless talk in which people had indulged in parliament up to that time. The Supreme Advisory Council and National Planning Council, having been established on a basis set down by President Sukarno himself, would be able to constitute a "pressure group," a group pressing for action.

But with this change in the parliament which makes all members appointees of the President, the last remnants of democracy have disappeared. Sukarno's guided democracy has become a dictatorship supported by certain groups. . . .

So we have seen a set of political developments ending in chaos, a democracy ending in anarchy and so opening the way to its enemy, dictatorship. As we have warned, this is an iron law of world history. But world history also shows that a dictatorship which depends on a single man's authority does not last long. And so the system to which Sukarno has given birth will last no longer than Sukarno himself. No man can live for ever. When Sukarno is alive no longer, his system will collapse of its own accord like a house of cards. There is no man in his team of associates with the caliber and the authority to keep the system going. Nor is there any indication in society that the system is popular.

If we examine the groups within the *Gotong Rojong* Parliament which are to support Sukarno's system, it is clear that they are not homogeneous. Indeed, they consist of a number of mutually antagonistic political currents which are disposed to check and obstruct each other. They are able to cooperate with each other on the basis of *musjawarah*, because Sukarno is the one who makes the decisions and because they do what he says.

In a situation like this, the democratic forces in society are forced to wait patiently to see what will come of this conception of Sukarno's. As long as his policy is supported by the largest political currents and by the groups which are in power, all in a totalitarian spirit, the forces of democracy will not be able to do anything. The totalitarian spirit is strong at the moment as a result of rebellion in several regions.

As for me, I have argued with Sukarno for a long time about the form and organization of government needed for efficiency. It seems good to me that Sukarno should be given a fair chance within a reasonable time to see if his system will succeed or fail. I have taken this position ever since our unsuccessful negotiations about two years ago.

There are objective criteria which will be decisive in this matter. Has his system brought prosperity for the people or not? Has it brought the prosperity whose image Sukarno himself has created with all the richness of his fantasy? Is he capable of arresting the decline in the living standards of the masses within a short time? Can he stop the continuing inflation within a not too long span of time, this inflation which leads men to despair? These are the appropriate criteria by which his concept must be judged!

That Sukarno is a patriot who loves his country and wants to see Indonesia just and prosperous as soon as possible cannot be denied. And this is, perhaps, the principal motive leading him to take these unusual steps, which he has taken entirely on his own responsibility. The only trouble is that, his character and gifts being what they are, he always sees only the broad outlines of anything he is creating. He does not consider anything to do with the details, though these may be relevant and indeed decisive when it comes to the matter of implementation. And so he often achieves the opposite of what he intends.

IIIk
Sumitro Djojohadikusumo The Failings of Sukarno (1959)

This extract comes from Searchlight on Indonesia, *a mimeographed booklet written in December 1959 and published by the group of PRRI—Permesta exiles living in Malaya, Singapore, Hongkong, and other places, of which Dr. Sumitro was a principal leader. The view it expresses was then characteristic of many Socialist party intellectuals inside Indonesia as well as outside it, but those inside the country were unable to express it until after October 1, 1965.*

We are at the close of the first decade since Indonesia gained recognition as an independent and sovereign Nation-State, after five years of armed struggle in defence of its freedom proclaimed on August 17, 1945. It is with distress that we set out at this juncture to appraise the general state of affairs in our country.

Important parts of the world can look back on 1959 as "the year of prosperity" and are looking forward to the future with abounding optimism. The industrially advanced countries are moving toward an unknown level of progress and prosperity to ever higher standards of living. Despite balance of payments irritations the United States has reached new peaks of production and wealth. The Soviet Union has held the world's attention by its incredible and spectacular feats in the field of science; its economic progress has reached a stage where the country and its leaders have now a direct stake in a detente of the cold war. Western Europe has doubled its gross national product in ten years, i.e., an annual rate of increase of 10 per cent.

Astonishing was Japan's recovery from dejection and defeat to a creditor country and to a formidable competitor, meeting the highly industrialized countries on their own grounds with quality goods. Japan's national product has increased in this period at an average of 12 per cent per annum! Even in the surrounding countries of Southeast Asia governments and people are determined to come to grips with basic economic and social problems in order to grind through the process of "take-off" into development and further growth.

In this setting and by contrast Indonesia, Southeast Asia's richest country in resources, endowment, and manpower potential, has come to be regarded as the sick man of the region, lying in the sequelae of a disease brought about by a regime that is as depraved as it is incompetent. It is a cause of grievous injury to the national pride and the self-respect of Indonesian patriots. The appalling degree of economic stagnation and regression, social deterioration, political disintegration and confusion, and the people's daily struggle for mere physical survival have come about as the cumulative result of policies pursued under Sukarno's rule. There is no prospect for improvement so long as the conduct of public policies remains in the hands of Sukarno and his cliques. . . .

The consecutive stages of developments that have led our country to the present state of affairs can be viewed as the failure of a social leadership that has abused and depraved its political power.

On this count Sukarno must take the brunt of the responsibility, if for no other reason, because he has deliberately and persistently undermined those groups or alignments that had the serious will to devote their energies and competence to the practical realization of ideals and promises given to the people. Instead, motivated mainly by his fear of loss of personal status, he has chosen to favor a kind of political elite that in their approach to concrete and basic social issues are imbued with the prevalence of emotion and of intangible sentiments, who are diffuse in their thinking, and who are frequently led by mystical symbolism. Worse, they consist of people who lack fundamental integrity and who allow their private interests and inclinations to prevail over national dedication to the country and the people.

Sukarno, as the national hero who has led Indonesia's struggle towards freedom and independence and as the public personality wielding at one time the greatest influence among all layers of society, has forfeited the trust that was placed in him by history and destiny, by a contemptuous neglect of his responsibilities and of his duties as a statesman and as a nation builder in the true sense of the word. His pervert behavior as political leader and statesman has done immense damage to the standards of public conduct and to the mores of public service. It has deprived the country's social and political vanguard of the drive and power to tackle the fundamental problems that must be solved if the objectives of stability and development are to be attained and if the many promises to our people are to be even half-way met.

Sukarno's example of political tactics and methods of playing one group against the other for the sake of his own survival has inevitably had its harmful effect on the rules, the mores, as well as on the scale of values adhered to by the group of politicos that together with Sukarno has gradually risen to the upper strata of political leadership within the sphere of the Djakarta regime. Consequently, instead of the dynamic leadership much needed to inspire the country and the people towards economic advancement and social progress, a system of spoils has become the accepted code for the clique of political toadies who regard concepts of devotion to duty and integrity in the discharge of public service with contemptuous cynicism.

Under such circumstances, therefore, the problems that are of real and vital importance to the masses have seldom been seriously tackled. True, our people have been made to swallow dose after dose of high-sounding formulae that may have served as opiates but that have contributed next to nothing to the actual alleviation of the burdens of daily life. As long as general formulae, concepts, terms and terminologies, words and wordings are not clearly defined in terms of accepted standards and of the values that those standards represent, everything remains meaningless and devoid of operational significance. This is particularly true when they cannot be assessed against criteria appropriate to concrete efforts in the realities of the social process and becomes even more dramatically obvious when in a given situation the confrontation with the realities demonstrates actions and behavior that are in flagrant contravention of the self-righteous formulae and concepts wielded by the ruling cliques. It then dangerously aggravates the confused and diffuse thinking on social and political problems of vital importance and gives rise to a Babylonian interpretation of verbose semantics.

Or, as has happened under Sukarno's rule, the point comes where only those interpretations are considered as "right" and "correct" that suit the tempers and the capricious whims of the powers that be. There is a complete disregard of the fact that, under the particular conditions of social change in a newly emerging nation where the cultural values are going through a process of "Umwertung aller Werte" (transvaluation of all values), a prime task of the social and political leadership is the establishment of a climate conducive to the application of generally accepted standards.

In this context and in the absence of institutions with established traditions, there should be at least a purposeful attempt to ensure that public conduct is guided by self-imposed mores that apply to every member of the community without bias or discrimination. In view of the existing social fabric of the newly developing and independent countries of Southeast Asia and elsewhere, it is mainly through the conscientious efforts of the leadership that we can ever hope for the prevalence of the rule of law, rooted in the canons of morality. Only then can we give meaning to our often expressed intent to strive for "a prosperous society" that will also be "a just society."

Are we, in saying these things, indulging in idealistic wishful thinking, or even in masochism? Are we passing beyond the boundaries of practical politics? Are we better advised to leave these matters to the moralists or to the political thinkers who from their lofty ivory towers can view them with the necessary detachment—a detachment we do not possess and do not even care to possess? We do not believe so.

We have stressed the above aspects of the political dilemmas on the basis of the hard-won and often bitter—though enriching—experiences of two decades as an active participant in the arena of successive political tussles as well as on the basis of close observation of the social and political events in contemporary Asia. We emphasize them, knowing and realizing full well that in the context of the hard realities of political life in some Southeast Asian countries today, public conduct conforming to mores, criteria, and scales of values that give substance and meaning to worded formulae is practically nonexistent. This is so for the simple reason that no adequate, scrupulous, and honest effort has been made in this direction by the social leadership. But in the social-cultural framework of the countries concerned the growth and acceptance of values and rules of social and political conduct concomitant with the emergence of new social and political institutions are contingent on a sustained endeavor by the leadership—an endeavor that large sections of the community must be made conscious of.

It is exactly the virtual absence of accepted mores and of institutionalized rules of political conduct and of constitutional behavior that make it mandatory for responsible leadership to foster the growth of such rules and values and to consider this as an essential element of their task. It also calls for a preparedness to subject themselves to the rules and restraints that apply to others' behavior—to identify themselves with the problems of the masses.

This is not reasoning in the abstract; it involves the very elements of practical politics—and of power politics, for that matter, if power is to be the necessary vehicle on the road to development and progress. For it is only in these conditions that an inspired and joint attempt of social forces can be undertaken in a task that of necessity entails current sacrifices—or at least the forgoing of immediate rewards—for the sake of future benefits.

We deeply feel, and it is borne out by contemporary political history in our part of the world, that when those fundamentals that we have touched upon are set aside, political leadership inevitably decays and degenerates. It will ultimately be able to do no more than to mouth the worst possible sloganisms of the kind that, although initially meant as propaganda, become perverted into convenient cloaks of, as well as instruments for, the morbid propensities of the ruling groups. At some stage this policy of sloganism will boomerang, carried by the volatile forces of bitter frustrations and unfulfilled dreams.

III 1

Suharto Ending Three Deviations (1966)

What follows is part of the opening address which General Suharto, then Deputy Prime Minister ad interim, gave on April 24, 1966, to the Extraordinary Unity and Reconciliation Congress of the PNI. President Sukarno had vested General Suharto with executive powers six weeks earlier in what was in effect the second stage in the major shift of power which followed the unsuccessful coup of the "September 30 Movement" on October 1, 1965.

Recent history records that the deviation of the September 30 Movement–PKI, whoever supported it, overtly or covertly, with whatever strength and by whatever means, from outside the country or within it, has been destroyed by the people together with the Armed Forces.

Brothers and sisters, there have indeed been many deviations, both in the prologue to the September 30 Movement–PKI affair and in its epilogue. Many among us, especially those who are so quick to call themselves "leaders of the people," must answer for these deviations.

So great have these deviations been that the people, led by the younger generation in co-operation with the Armed Forces, must act as correctors, must bring the country back into line with the spirit of the 1945 Constitution and the Mandate of the Suffering of the People, must return it to the rails of the Indonesian People's Revolution.

In the epilogue of the September 30 Movement–PKI affair, three sorts of deviations are to be found intertwined.

They are: first, the extreme left radicalism of the PKI which, using slander and terror, wants to monopolize the fruits of the revolution and to foist class struggle upon Indonesia under the guise of such grand-sounding slogans as "progressive-revolutionary," "radical," "for the people," "communist-phobia," and so on. There cannot be any monopolizing of the revolution in Indonesia, and there cannot be class struggle in Indonesia, because these are not wanted by the people;

indeed, the Indonesian people are not familiar with classes and do not have them.

Second, there is political opportunism motivated by personal ambition, led on and used by the puppetmasters of the BPI,* the political opportunism whose practitioners are determined to keep going with their *Durna*† practices without heeding the wishes of the people or having their support, but by slander and other such disgusting methods.

Third, there is economic adventurism, whose practitioners immorally and antisocially create chaos in the people's economy and the finances of the state for their own personal ends, thereby causing suffering to the people.

In the view of the people, and also in my own view, these three forms of deviation endangered security and order and the stability of the course of the government and the revolution, threatening the personal safety and authority of the President–Supreme Commander–Great Leader of the Revolution–Bearer of the Mandate of the MPRS, threatening the unity of the people and the state of Indonesia and constituting a deviation from the teachings of the Great Leader of the Revolution.

This means that, in order to execute the Instruction given me by the President–Supreme Commander–Great Leader of the Revolution–Bearer of the Mandate of the MPRS, on March 11, 1966, I must take firm action against these three forms of deviation.

As I have repeatedly stressed, implementing that Instruction and eliminating all forms of deviation is not something that I am doing by myself or could do by myself. It must be implemented in full awareness and full responsibility by the Armed Forces and the progressive-revolutionary masses, which includes the PNI and Marhaenist Front.‡

Brothers and sisters of the PNI and the Marhaenist Front, allow me finally to put to this gathering some hopes, messages and convictions.

If the PNI and Marhaenist Front of the future is to be truly rooted in the hearts of the people, if it is really to become the vanguard of

* The Central Intelligence Body, headed by Dr. Subandrio.

† The *wajang* figure *Durna,* a teacher and royal advisor, has become a symbol of amoral and Machiavellian behavior.

‡ The Marhaenist Front is the cluster of workers', peasant, women's, youth, students', and other organizations under PNI leadership.

the *marhaen* people's struggle, it must be free from the three deviations I have mentioned. So the body of the PNI must be cleansed not only of persons who were involved in or secretly supported the September 30 Movement–PKI but also of political opportunists and economic adventurers. The unity of the PNI and the Marhaenist Front cannot have any basis other than the Pantja Sila and the teachings of the Great Leader of the Revolution, Bung Karno. Therefore, the political line of the PNI and Marhaenist Front must accord with and strengthen the compact alliance of the People, the Great Leader of the Revolution, and the Armed Forces. The PNI and Marhaenist Front must be capable of becoming a vehicle for the struggle of the progressive-revolutionary nationalists who are religious and whose spirit is socialist, must join with other progressive-revolutionary forces of the Indonesian people to realise the Three Demands of the People* as an essential requirement of the completion of our revolution.

In forging unity and holding fast to the principles I have put forward, all participants in this congress will, I hope, first, forswear slander, intimidation, provocation, and baseless accusation and, second, consult in a spirit of generosity in order to arrive at a consensus. Third, victory must go to our revolution, to our Pantja Sila, to our people, to our *marhaen* masses, and under no circumstances to individuals or groups within the body of the PNI and Marhaenist Front. And what is required for that is good faith, a spirit of honesty, and common sense.

* To dissolve the PKI, to bring down prices, and to oust incompetent ministers. These demands were put forward initially in January to March 1966, by the student action front, KAMI.

PART TWO

STREAMS OF THOUGHT

IV

Radical Nationalism

If any of our five ideological streams can claim a central position in Indonesian political life, it is radical nationalism. If any can claim to have exercised a pervasive influence on all the others, it is similarly radical nationalism. Indeed, if a single phrase were required to sum up the mood of Indonesia's public affairs in the period of this collection, 'radical nationalism' would serve fairly well.

Radical nationalism has its roots in the "nationalism pure and simple" of those Indonesians of colonial days whose central political concern was the attainment of independence and whose involvement in nationalism was not part of a broader commitment to Islam or socialism. Not all "nationalists pure and simple" have been radical nationalists, but radical nationalism has always had very strong influence among them, and in the post-independence period radical nationalism alone has maintained itself as a distinctive ideological tendency. "Nationalism pure and simple" has largely disappeared, with moderate nationalists tending to become less distinctively nationalist in outlook and better characterized as under democratic socialist or Javanese traditionalist influence.

A group of Indonesian students at universities and colleges in Holland and Indonesia in the 1920's, seeing the sharp conflicts between Muslims and Communists in Indonesia's anticolonial movement, became convinced that neither religious nor Marxist–Leninist appeals could unite the Indonesian people against Dutch rule. In 1927 their conviction found expression in the establishment of the Indonesian Nationalist Party (PNI) under the chairmanship of the young engineering graduate Sukarno, a party which put itself forward as the vanguard of the whole Indonesian nation, of Indonesians of all creeds.

As IVa suggests, this party was radical in its nationalism from the beginning. Its leaders, many of them strongly influenced by Marxism and all sharply alienated from Netherlands Indies colonial society, sought to work for Indonesian independence by what they called "revolutionary mass action," in practice by holding mass rallies and practicing noncooperation with the Dutch (boycotting Dutch-established representative councils and refusing to enter the civil service).

Sukarno's PNI of 1927 was outlawed within three years, and its successor organizations, operating in an environment of greater repression, were more moderate, fragmented, and small. Radical nationalism was, in fact, rarely in view in the decade before the Japanese invasion. Its influence, however, was enormously strengthened during the period of Japanese rule, both by the anti-Western propaganda of the Japanese and by the important roles which Sukarno and other Indonesian leaders of radical nationalist persuasion were able to play.

A second PNI, intended as a state party, was established a few days after the proclamation of independence in August 1945, but this was then dissolved ten days later. In November 1945 a new PNI came into existence as one of a number of new parties, appealing, in effect, to those who preferred nationalism as a central point of ideological orientation to Islam, socialism, Christianity, or any of their variants. Significantly, President Sukarno did not join this party, but as founder of its predecessor of the same name he held a position of especially high prestige among its leaders and members.

Once the Dutch had been forced to withdraw from political control of Indonesia, the PNI and other, smaller, nationalist parties found it necessary to redefine their roles. Of the PNI's leaders a minority accepted the fact that their party represented no more than a section of the population. These were mostly men with sympathies for democratic socialism, with a fairly strong commitment to parliamentary democracy and a pragmatic concern for economic stabilization and development.

But the radical nationalists among the PNI leaders were unwilling to accept such a major restructuring of their political outlook. As IVb and IVd suggest, for them the PNI's task remained that of making itself the vanguard of the nation as a whole, or of that 95 per cent of it who belonged to the masses (in PNI terminology, the Marhaen masses). Hand in hand with this position went a concern with mobilization and leadership rather than representation, together with a concentrating on the struggle against imperialism, against the continuing Dutch presence in West Irian, against the great power of Dutch and of other western businesses, against Hollywood's "cultural imperialism," and so on. Hand in hand with it also went strategies of alliance with the Communists and active support for President Sukarno's proposal for a Guided Democracy. Indeed, when Guided Democracy was established as a set of political arrangements, radical nationalism provided the dominant ideological themes.

If Sukarno's stature among Indonesia's ideologists of the 1945–1965 period is high, his stature among the radical nationalists of this period is overtowering.* In fact, most of the other radical nationalist thinkers were little more than expositors of his ideas, not only because of Sukarno's great political power but also because they failed to present the case as compellingly as he. Indeed, many of the extracts by Sukarno in other sections of this volume could be considered as supplementary to the radical nationalism section, particularly Ia, IIIa, XIIa, XIIIe, and XVf.

But Sukarno's ideological formulations are in some respects more individual than those of Sjahrir, Natsir, and Aidit who were all tied to their parties. With respect to his pro-Communism during the last years of Guided Democracy (IIId, XIIe) and to the Jacobin fascination with revolution which characterized his thinking throughout the whole Guided Democracy period (IIIc), it would seem that he imposed a cast of thought rather than expressed ideas which were a commonly accepted part of radical nationalist thinking.

One other radical nationalist of importance, Muhammad Yamin, is represented in XVa, and radical nationalist formulations are also contained in IXb, XIVa, and XVd, XVg, and XVh.

As our final extract of this section we have included a fragment of Marhaenist apologetics in which radical nationalism is thoroughly transmuted into the categories of Javanese thought. It should perhaps be read after the items in the Javanese traditionalism section.

* Similarly we are unable to refer to any further literature on radical nationalism other than studies of Sukarno's ideology: Bernhard Dahm's book, in English translation, *Sukarno and the Struggle for Indonesian Independence* (Ithaca, N.Y.: Cornell University Press, 1969), and Donald E. Weatherbee's *Ideology in Indonesia: Sukarno's Indonesian Revolution* (New Haven: Yale University, Southeast Asia Studies, 1966). The general cast of Sukarno's thinking emerges very clearly from *The Autobiography of President Sukarno as Told to Cindy Adams* (Indianapolis: Bobbs Merrill, 1965).

IVa

Sukarno   Marhaen, a Symbol of the Power
of the Indonesian People (1957)

This extract is taken from Marhaen and Proletarian, *a speech which the Indonesian President delivered to a PNI gathering on July 3, 1957, the thirtieth anniversary of the party's establishment, and which was published in English translation by the Cornell Modern Indonesia Project.**

Permit me, Brothers and Sisters, to depict for you the motives and reasons why I and several friends set up the Indonesian Nationalist Party on July 4, 1927. . . .

First, the aim: An aim which may not be changed—which may not be changed today, which may not be changed in the days ahead. And what is that aim? It is no more and no less than a society which in today's terminology is called a just and prosperous society, and which, in the terminology of 1927, was called a society of *sama rasa sama rata*. This aim must remain fixed and may not be changed.

Second, the Indonesian Nationalist Party from 1927 onward insisted that an absolute condition (described as the most important condition in 1927, but in fact an absolute condition) for achieving this objective, was national independence. *Indonesia Merdeka*, Independent Indonesia, was even called for by the Indonesian Nationalist Party in the words "Independent Indonesia Now, Now, Now." Three times now!

Third, as is already clear, the aim is a just and prosperous society, or an egalitarian society, or, in words better known by the whole world, a socialist society, in the pure sense.

To attain a socialist society, or an egalitarian society, or a just and prosperous society, we had to cross a golden bridge, named *Indonesia Merdeka*, Indonesian Independence. There arose the question, how to achieve Indonesian Independence. And it was the Indonesian Nationalist Party that gave to this a firm answer: through revolutionary mass action.

There were those, especially at that time, who said we could attain national independence without revolutionary mass action, that it could be won through education, through negotiations with the

* Ithaca, N.Y., 1960; reprinted by permission.

Dutch, through playing parliament in the Volksraad. As you know the Dutch, as a result of pressure from their parliament in the month of November 1918, had given their well-known November Promises. There were people who supposed that independence or, at the very least, extension of political rights could be attained merely by requests, by petitions.

In newspapers, in meetings, in the Volksraad, or in other councils, it was later stated that independence or extension of political rights might be given as a gesture, out of goodness of heart.

I remember, how, when I was only seventeen years old, I heard of the November Promises in which the Dutch promised the People of Indonesia an expansion of political rights. I can still remember how many leaders rejoiced, thinking: Ah, now we will certainly get an extension of rights which will ultimately bring us to an Independent Indonesia. At that time I, as a youth of seventeen years, had already begun to shake my head. No! Independence would not be attained this way. I said outright at that time to the late Hadji Oemar Said Tjokroaminoto that I did not believe that the November Promises would be fulfilled.

And in fact, Brothers and Sisters, those November Promises were not fulfilled. What was the reason? The reason was that the November 1918 promises were given by the Dutch at a time when the Netherlands was in great danger. The First World War was then raging at its worst. Communications between the Netherlands and Indonesia may be said to have been entirely cut and, added to this, there was in the Netherlands a strong movement amongst the workers—a movement intent even on overthrowing the Netherlands royal dynasty. It was under these conditions that the November Promises were made. On the one hand, requests from the People of Indonesia for extension of rights; on the other hand, pressure from workers in Holland itself, pressure to overthrow the dynasty; and disruption of communications between the Netherlands and Indonesia caused by the First World War.

It was under those circumstances, then, that the November Promises were made. But when the war was over, when relations between the Netherlands and her colony could be restored, when conditions considered normal at that time became normal again, when the workers' movement in Holland had subsided, the promises of November 1918 were completely forgotten. . . .

But, in spite of these experiences of 1918, there were still many among the leaders of Indonesia who thought that National Independence could be attained by asking, by petitioning, even by begging. But the Indonesian Nationalist Party in 1927 asserted that National Independence could not be attained by such methods, but must be won by means of revolutionary mass action.

These were the three fundamental points: the aim—a just and prosperous society; the conditions to attain it—via the golden bridge; and the only means by which the golden bridge could be won— revolutionary mass action. These were the three fundamentals of the Indonesian Nationalist Party.

And now it may be asked, what is it that is called "mass"? What is this mass action which is revolutionary—revolutionary mass action? What is said to be the mass, what is called "the masses"? It is here, Brothers and Sisters, that there arises the idea of Marhaen, the concept of Marhaen.

What Mr. Soewirjo said a moment ago: that the people of Indonesia, the Indonesian masses, are primarily workers and peasants, is true. I ask that stress be put upon the word "primarily," because what I meant by the term "masses" in 1927 was not solely workers and peasants (even though primarily they *are* workers and peasants), for, apart from the workers' and peasants' groups there are many other groups who are neither workers nor peasants.

For example, Brothers and Sisters, the *tukang roda** are not workers and not peasants; to what group do they belong? The street vendors who put up the wayside stalls, they are not workers nor peasants; what group includes them? In 1926 there was a term well known in Indonesia, the term "proletariat"; the meaning of this term was often not understood. The term proletariat was used in 1926 to describe the whole of the poor, the common people; but they are far from being all proletarians.

"I am a proletarian," people used to say, but those saying this were often not proletarians at all. There was a farmer from Tjidjerokaso who said "I am a proletarian," but he was not a proletarian. There was the keeper of a small food stall at the Idjan Crossroads who said "I am a proletarian," but he was not a proletarian at all. To whom then does the term proletariat apply? In 1927 in my lecture courses, especially those for the cadres, I said that a member of the proletariat is a person who sells his labor power to another, without himself owning the means of production. The proletariat are the

* Roadside tire menders.

workers who do not participate in ownership of the means of production. But our nation includes tens of millions of people who are not covered by the term proletariat. There are great numbers indeed who are not laborers, very many who do not sell their labor power to others.

I have explained before to my comrades, my old friends, how I came to use the term "Marhaen." It was for no other reason but that on a certain day I was walking in the rice fields to the south of Tjigereleng and came across a man hoeing a field. I asked him: "Brother, who owns this field?" "I do," he said. And so he participated in ownership of the means of production, owning that rice field. "And the hoe, who owns that?" "I do." "These tools, who owns these?" "I do." "But, Brother, you live in poverty?" "That's right, I live poorly." And I thought to myself then, this man is clearly and certainly not a member of the proletariat. He is a pauper, he is poor, he suffers a great deal, he has not enough to live on. But he is not a member of the proletariat, for he does not sell his labor power to another without participating in ownership of the means of production. His rice field is his own, his hoe is his own, his sickle is his own, his rake is his own. Everything is his own property; the crop of his rice field is for his own use. But still he is a pauper, he is poor. Nevertheless, he is not one of the proletariat; he is a small farmer, a very poor farmer, barely making a living, a "chicken flea farmer" as I said at that time. He is not one of the proletariat. Then, Brothers and Sisters, I asked him "What is your name?" "Marhaen," he said. He said that his name was Marhaen. I had an inspiration: Now, this name I will hold to; I will use this name to describe the destitute People of Indonesia.

And of poor Indonesians there are not one million, not two million, or three, but almost all of the Indonesian People. Almost all of the People of Indonesia are Marhaen! They are the poor, common people; yes, the poor worker; yes, the poor peasant; yes, the poor fisherman; yes, the poor clerk; yes, the poor stall vendor; yes, the poor cart driver; yes, the poor chauffeur—all of these are embraced by the one term, Marhaen.

Why are almost all of the people of Indonesia poor? That is something I explained in my lectures at that time. I explained that Dutch imperialism, which had been operating in Indonesia for decades, even for hundreds of years, had a different character, a different nature from, for instance, British imperialism. At that time I told members of the Indonesian Nationalist Party: British imperialism, for example, which operated in India, had the character of a mercantile imperialism—a trade imperialism, in order to sell British-made goods in India. And in order that the People of India should be able to buy those British-made goods, British imperialism in India at that time did not impoverish the People of India too much. It still took care that some purchasing power should exist among the Indian people; for a population which is completely pauperized is not able to buy goods. It was because of this, as I said in 1927, 1928, and 1929, that British imperialism provided education for the People of India quite early. Schools were established in India, even colleges and universities were set up in India, just in order to maintain some purchasing power among the Indian people. And, therefore, the Indian people were not made too poor.

As a reaction to British imperialism in India—and of course there was a reaction, for all people eventually desire independence, . . . as I said in 1927: even the worm will turn, let alone man, when trodden upon over and over again, he will certainly revolt eventually —as a reaction to this imperialism, the People of India began a movement known as the Swadeshi movement. In order to counteract the imports from Britain, the Indian people declared that they would not buy British goods: The People of India started the Swadeshi movement, made their own goods, wove their own cloth, spun their own thread, even set up their own factories. This Swadeshi movement was a logical consequence of the nature of British imperialism which was "trade-capitalistic."

But what was the nature of Dutch imperialism in Indonesia, Brothers and Sisters? Dutch imperialism in Indonesia was not, I said, first and foremost a merchant imperialism (though it had some aspects of trade, Brothers and Sisters, and of no mean dimensions— it was still, however, not primarily mercantile imperialism). The Dutch imperialism which operated in Indonesia was primarily of the kind that Hilferding called "finance capital." The Dutch brought money to Indonesia, not to give to the Indonesian people—"Here's some money for you. . . ."—Oh, no! Rather money to invest in Indonesia, in the form of factories, in the form of estates, in order to squeeze out, to dig up, to scratch up all the kinds of riches there are in Indonesia. Capital, investment capital, was introduced into Indonesia, was made to work in Indonesia like an all-powerful giant, I used to say. This money worked in Indonesia, digging out Indonesia's wealth to be taken to Holland and to be sold in Europe, to gain profits in Europe which were brought again to Indonesia to be planted in Indonesia, in order to dig out Indonesia's wealth once more. And that wealth was taken again to Europe, was sold in Europe, and bore profit in Europe. And that money became finance capital again, was once more brought to Indonesia, planted in Indonesia, used in business in Indonesia. Round and round in this fashion for decades, indeed, for centuries.

Now the consequences of investment capital are different from those of trade imperialism. What does investment capital seek? You want to set up a sugar refinery, for example, so you need land on which to plant sugar cane; and it is desirable that the rent for the land should not be too high. People who are clever, people who know the score, people who understand their own interests, ask high rents for land. And, therefore, the People of Indonesia were not taught; a knowledge of their own interests and their possible advancement was withheld from them, in order that land rents might remain low. What does a sugar refinery need? A sugar refinery needs workers, workers to work in the refinery, workers to work in the cane fields. In order that they might not demand higher wages, these workers were not provided with skills. Their wants and necessities were suppressed.

So, the main tendency was a different one. Whereas trade imperialism gave some small heed to the purchasing power of a people—I do not say that trade capitalism makes a people free and independent, not at all, but merely that it somewhat maintains the purchasing power of a people—whereas trade imperialism acted thus, the imperialism of investment capital suppressed the needs and skills of the people. It needed cheap rents; it needed cheap labor. Therefore, a process took place in Indonesia called pauperization, the pauperization of the Indonesian people. So that—as I explained in my defense speech in the Landraad court in Bandung, later printed as a book, *Indonesia Menggugat* [*Indonesia Accuses*]—Indonesia came to be "small" in style; everything became small-styled. For example, no assistance was given to increasing needs. Everything was constantly pauperized. Everything came to have the stamp of smallness: the small worker—a pauper; the small farmer—a pauper; the small fisherman—a pauper; the small cart-and-horse owner—a pauper; the small employee—a pauper. Everything was small. And this applied not only to the proletariat alone (that is, the workers who sold their labor power without participating in ownership of the means of production); it applied to the whole of society.

It was in this connection, Brothers and Sisters, that I said that the whole of society suffered pauperization, and I needed a name for all those who were pauperized. A name for the worker and the peasant, for the fisherman and the carter, for the low-ranking policeman and the children of the troops of the former Indies army, as well as for the reporter and the stall-keeper, yes, for every kind of all these small people.

It was lucky, praised be the Lord, that one day I had an inspiration when I was talking to Marhaen south of Tjigereleng. He seemed to become a symbol of the small man of Indonesia. A symbol of the power of the Indonesian people. A symbol of the explosive force, the explosive material for achieving *Indonesia Merdeka*.

I said a moment ago that British imperialism, the trade imperialism in India, could eventually be beaten by the movement led by Mahatma Gandhi, characterized by Swadeshi and Satyagraha—that is, civil disobedience; as the people of Central Java say: *hambalela* [rebel]—*swadeshi, satyagraha*. Swadeshi especially constituted strong competition by the Indian people themselves capable of counteracting imports from Britain. It was by such means that the people of India eventually won India's independence.

But we, the Indonesian People, could not achieve Indonesia's independence by means of Swadeshi. No—because we did not have the material with which to build a great movement capable of beating imperialism here. We could not overcome a strong investment-capital system merely by a Swadeshi movement—no! And for that reason the Indonesian Nationalist Party stated emphatically in 1927: The only power which can throw off Dutch imperialism in Indonesia is revolutionary action by the masses, mass action by all of Indonesia's Marhaens, who are tens of millions strong. And this, Brothers and Sisters, is what happened after August 17, 1945, when all of Indonesia's Marhaens, young people, workers, and peasants, rose and acted.

IVb

PNI   The Aims of the Party (1952)

This excerpt is taken from the statement of party principles adopted by the PNI in December 1952. The statement is included in

Kepartaian dan Parlementaria Indonesia (*Indonesian Party and Parliamentary Affairs*) (*Djakarta: Ministry of Information, 1954, pp. 26–42*). *Many of its formulations have their origins in the writings of the party's theorist Sarmidi Mangunsarkoro.*

The movement of the Marhaen masses aims at the creation of a Marhaenist society. This Marhaenist society is one of equal feeling and equal happiness in which no person may oppress another and no group oppress another group.

In a Marhaenist society, people always cooperate with each other and consciously help each other. Everyone has the right to take part in determining state matters of every kind in a lawful and orderly way and, at the same time, has duties corresponding to his strength, and shoulders responsibilities according to his talents and abilities. The state is led by a Government of the People, that is, one which reflects the wishes of all the people, in particular of the Marhaen masses.

Everyone is free in respect to choice of a religion and adherence to it. Everyone can achieve a maximum of self-development in accordance with his talents and feel the wisdom and blessings of the cultural life of the people.

Everyone lives prosperously because everyone has the opportunity to work conscientiously.

All large industries and enterprises are controlled by the state so that their profits accrue to all citizens.

Capital and private enterprise are so regulated that it is not possible for them to become a means of exploitation. On this basis, a happy life is guaranteed to everyone who works, and happiness is assured for the society as a whole. . . .

Studies show there are at present in Indonesian society feudal traditions and groups, seeds of national capitalism, giant foreign enterprises, and people who are still ignorant. All these things greatly hinder the growth of a Marhaenist society.

We must fight all of them or change them to conform with the necessities of a Marhaenist society.

Among the new seeds we must plant, there is first and foremost the seed of democracy in all fields, political, economic, and social.

Political democracy involves the right of every person, man or woman, to choose or be chosen as a representative of the people, in the central assembly or in a regional one. This representation by the people means we can determine whatever happens in the state.

Economic democracy involves, for example, the establishment throughout the state of people's cooperatives which make it possible for our people, poor as they are, to help each other in their own joint interests in conducting economic enterprises as well as they can, so that they can stand up to pressure from capitalistic firms whose only goal is self-interest. Apart from that all large and vital enterprises must become government-owned as quickly as possible or jointly owned by government and private enterprises so that the government can control them in the interests of all the people.

Social democracy means, for example, compulsory and free education for every child from elementary school to university. It also means a massive fight against illiteracy.

This democracy which we are planting must be practised consistently and carried into every sphere of social life, into the home, the office, the factory and everywhere else. Democracy implemented consistently means there is equality in everything, but in a well-ordered way. Only a well-ordered egalitarian social structure can create a state of affairs in which welfare and happiness are shared equally by all.

Because that social well-being can, in fact, only be achieved if there is prosperity and progress, the Marhaenist society must bring a basic attitude which accords with this necessity. . . .

The problem now is how power should be exercised in society. What is needed, fundamentally, is the establishment of a Marhaenist government, that is, a government whose ideology and endeavors are always in accordance with the interests of the great majority of the people who are poor and, because of that accord, can guarantee the well-being of the people as a whole.

The apparatus of society and the state must be organized so as to serve the interests of the Marhaen masses. For this to be achieved the majority of members of every representative body of the people must be Marhaenists, that is, defenders of the common people and soldier-fighters for a Marhaenist society. So the Marhaenist movement must fight to win in general elections.

Besides representative bodies of the people which are political, there must also be economic councils consisting of workers' representatives, executives of enterprises, and representatives of the government agencies charged with regulating and supervising the production and distribution of goods necessary to the lives of the people. Such councils would be concerned in particular with labor relations and the production and distribution of essential commodities for the people.

In capitalist society the dominant power of private property is the source of crime and exploitation. Seeing this, we must strive to put limits on private property, in particular as regards ownership of land and means of production of vital materials. These two things must be supervised by the government and regulated so that they can be used in accordance with the interests of all the people. (The right of ownership is a social function.)

Marhaenists consistently carry out Article 38 of the Provisional Constitution of the Republic of Indonesia,* which reads as follows:

1. The economy shall be ordered as a common endeavor on the basis of the principle of family relationship.
2. Branches of production which are important for the state and which control the livelihood of many people shall be controlled by the state.
3. Earth, water, and the natural riches in them shall be controlled by the state and exploited to give the people maximum prosperity.

The use of land and capital being regulated by the state in the interests of the people, competition between enterprises will disappear, and it will be possible to determine with accuracy what quantity of goods needs to be produced in order to meet the real needs of the people. In the same way it will be possible to determine the number of hours which workers must work in order to satisfy the necessities of production, in a way which still leaves them free time for cultural activities.

Also, workers' wages will no longer be determined under pressure of competition between workers. What a worker earns will depend on what he needs to live as a civilized human being. For this purpose, a definite measure of living costs will be established and wages regulated so that they are no lower than this minimum. In this way a fair and equal division will be achieved.

Moreover, if this system could be extended throughout the world, there would no longer be the economic crises which now always arise as the result of uncontrolled production. Unemployment would be unknown. Men would be obliged to work, and working relations within an enterprise would be regulated in such a way that everyone would feel happy in his work.

Housing and health must be regarded as of prime importance.

* This article is discussed in XIIIa and XIIIb.

Provisions must be made for every person's security in old age and every person's lot in times of trouble.

In a Marhaenist society, every citizen can achieve a level of progress which makes him aware of being both a human being and a citizen. To make this possible, there must be compulsory education for every child. The opportunity to learn must be given as widely as possible; education must be free; and there must be scholarships for the gifted. In this way every young person, provided he has ability, will be able to advance himself as far as his foundation allows.

There must be equal opportunity to progress, so that the child of a rich man is no longer the only one able to go to high school or university. In this way the possibility for society to advance, both economically and culturally, will be guaranteed.

IVc

Sukarno   The National State and
the Ideals of Islam (1953)

This passage comes from an address of the same title which President Sukarno gave at the University of Indonesia in Djakarta on May 7, 1953. A number of things the President had said in the preceding months had drawn fire from the Islamic side, particularly a speech at Amuntai in South Kalimantan in which he was reported as saying that "The state we want is a national state consisting of all Indonesia. If we establish a state based on Islam, many areas whose population is not Islamic, such as the Moluccas, Bali, Flores, Timor, the Kei Islands, and Sulawesi, will secede. And West Irian which has not yet become part of the territory of Indonesia, will not want to be part of the Republic." Subsequently, A. Dahlan Ranuwihardjo, Chairman of the Muslim students' association HMI, wrote to President Sukarno asking for clarification of the relationship between a national state and an Islamic state and between the Pantja Sila ideology and the ideology of Islam. The speech excerpted here was Sukarno's reply. The Indonesian version is Negara Nasional dan Tjita-tjita Islam *(Djakarta: Endang, 1954).*

There is misunderstanding among my Muslim brothers about the word "nationalism," just as there is misunderstanding in nationalist circles about the ideals of Islam. What is the misunderstanding among the Muslims about the word "national" and its meaning? This misunderstanding is not of recent origin but has existed for decades. It should therefore be rooted out of the soil of Indonesia at the earliest possible moment.

More than twenty-five years ago, in 1926–1927, this misunderstanding was highlighted in that there was serious conflict among Muslim brethren on the question whether nationalism is allowed in Islam or not. The disagreement over whether nationalism is allowed in Islam or not did not exist only between the nationalists and the Muslim groups. There were two camps among the Muslim groups themselves, and the differences between them were very sharp.

I remember the time. I was in Bandung then and was propounding the national unity of Indonesia. I suggested to the people that they fill their hearts with a burning feeling of nationalism. But I also said with a warning that our nationalism should not be chauvinistic, that it should be a nationalism that regards the nation as an inseparable part of humanity as a whole.

At that time there was beginning to arise within our national movement the stream of revolutionary nationalism which later manifested itself in the form of the Partai Nasional Indonesia [Indonesian Nationalist Party], the Pendidikan Nasional Indonesia [Indonesian National Education Association], the Partindo [Indonesia Party], and so on. In Islamic circles there was strong disagreement. One camp asserted that what Bung Karno was doing to further nationalism, the feeling of nationhood and nationality, was not against the teaching of Islam. The other camp said it was wrong because Islam did not acknowledge nationality.

The Permi [Indonesian Muslim Association] in particular proclaimed: Islam acknowledges nationality and nationhood, and what Bung Karno is putting forward is right. Bung Karno is right, too, when he says, "Beware of chauvinistic nationalism; Islam, too, does not countenance chauvinism!" What he is referring to in Islam is opposition to *asjabijah* [intolerance]. *Asjabijah* is forbidden by Islam. So it is right that Bung Karno should say, "Oh, you Indonesians, burn with the feeling of nationalism, love this country of yours, love this nation of yours, live in the spirit of national life." We say Bung Karno is right and is not contradicting Islam.

This was the Permi party's opinion, especially as it was voiced by the late Mochtar Luthfi. There was the other, opposing group which asserted "Bung Karno is wrong. . . ." This group was mainly

concentrated in Bandung under the leadership of Brother A. Hasan.
. . . He established a group in Bandung called Persatuan Islam
[Muslim Association] or Persis.

And so the Permi Muslims opposed the Persis Muslims. Over
what? Over the question of "nationalism" and "national." This conflict over the idea of national and nationalism has filtered down to
the present time so that even now there are still misunderstandings
among Muslims as regards the meaning of the words national and
nationalism.

And as I have already stated, there are also misunderstandings,
grave misunderstandings, in nationalist circles regarding Islamic aspirations. So there are comparable misunderstandings. We should
get rid of them. In my opinion Islam is not really opposed to nationalism. Islam does not prohibit us from forming a national state.
People always think erroneously that being a nationalist means worshipping your country. No! In loving my country I do not worship
it. . . .

Because of these circumstances [modern imperialism], especially
economic exploitation, political frustration, and loss of cultural identity, it was inevitable that nations on both sides of the life line of
imperialism would become conscious, desire freedom, desire their
individuality, desire to return to possession of their own identity.
This is what is called nationalism. And it has nothing to do with anti-
Islam, anti-communism, anti– any ideology. It is above all the feeling of desire, the desire to go back to one's own identity, the desire
for freedom, the desire to smash the chains binding one's hands, the
desire to be in control of one's own affairs, the desire to shape one's
own cultural identity—this is nationalism, Brothers and Sisters. . . .

Except, perhaps, for the Chinese People's Republic which is already a national state, this process of forming national states is still
going on and is still not complete. Egypt has obtained independence,
but it is Egypt without the Sudan. There is an Independent Indonesia but, in fact, without West Irian. Other independent states have
been established, but they do not yet embrace in their territory
all of their respective peoples.

And, therefore, we are now seeing efforts being made by nationalist and religious groups in Tunisia, Algeria, and Morocco to establish
the national state of El Maghribi. Egypt wants to join with the
Sudan to become a national state of Greater Egypt. We wish to
have an Indonesian national state in our hands. This process of

forming national states is still going on. As you can see Laos, Cambodia, Annam, and Cochin China are today in violent turmoil. What for? To form a national state, the name of which I do not know. This process is still going on, whereas in Europe it has been completed. . . .

What is the historical paradox which exists in the world today? In Europe people want to abolish national borders; they want to establish a pan-European state. Here, people want to establish national borders. Here is Indonesia; outside this is not Indonesia. This is Indo-China; outside it is not Indo-China. This is Greater Egypt; outside is not Greater Egypt. This is Maghribi; outside is not Maghribi. Here the process of forming national states and establishing boundaries is still going on. But there is the historical paradox that the other part of the world now wants to abolish and remove the boundaries which have been established.

Be that as it may, I ask the entire Indonesian people—not only the nationalists, but the Muslims, the Christians, the Buddhists and those without any religion—to be fully aware of the period in which we are now living. I do not want to limit the basic human right of men to propagate their respective ideologies, of the Muslims to propagate their Islam or the Communists to propagate their communism. I merely want to urge and emphasize, to remind people, to emphasize the period we are now in.

We are in the throes of a national process. In history there are what one historian has called "historical processes and historical hastes". . . .

I do not know whether you have read in Jean Jaurès' book *La Grande Revolution* of the historical haste which led Babeuf to attempt a social revolution in the process of developing parliamentary democracy and the national state. Babeuf's attempt clearly found little resonance among the people, because the spirit of the people at the time was not one of social revolution. We have experienced something like this, too; the Madiun affair is an example of historical haste. Those people wanted to have a communist society immediately based on equality and fraternity. They thought we were ready for that. They thought the time had come for a social revolution. They forgot that we are still living in a national phase, a national revolution.

As you know, the response of the people was not as they had hoped. Why? Because objectively and subjectively the people were still living in the national phase. And therefore I suggest to you, the youth, the students, the leaders—again without detracting from the right of every group to propagate its ideology—have a real understanding of the period, the phase of our national life at the present time. Live in this phase. Complete our national revolution. Do we not all say that our revolution is a national revolution?

Not only the nationalists, but the socialists, the communists, as well as the Muslims and Christians, all of them say: This is the national revolution. And what is the task of a national revolution? It is no more and no less than the establishment of a national state. Finish this first. Put the emphasis there. Finish this first. Emphasize this.

Why did we make our August 17, 1945, proclamation? Was not the proclamation hailed by the entire Indonesian population, all eighty millions? There was not a single exception then, was there? Because the proclamation was based on facts completely in accordance, in harmony, with the time. It was based on nationalism, on Pantja Sila, on democracy. At that time we were as one. Everyone hailed the proclamation with joy. Consequently everyone was prepared to sacrifice his life and property in the cause of the proclamation, because there was resonance between our action and the time.

Now that we are back to this, you will realise that I have come to the point of my address. Mr. Ranuwihardjo has asked what is the relation between the Panta Sila and Islam.

I want you to understand that this Pantja Sila is already a compromise, the making of which has involved blood and tears. Anyone who opens our history, especially for July 1945, a month before the proclamation of Indonesia resounded through the heavens, anyone who consults the records of our discussions, our debates, our quarrels with one another—for at that time we were close to hating each other—will understand that the Pantja Sila is a compromise.

In the sessions held then by the Investigating Committee for Indonesian Independence, Muslim leaders were sitting together with nationalist leaders and socialist leaders. In the beginning our talks were calm, but later they became very heated. Our national unity was almost shattered then, and if it had been shattered the August 17 proclamation would not have been possible. At the time there was myself; there were Kijaji Mansjur and Ki Bagus Hadikusumo; there were the other Muslim leaders; there was Abdur Kahar Muzakir; there was Chaerul Saleh; there was Muhammad Yamin. Leaders from all over Indonesia were gathered together to discuss the basis of the state to be proclaimed.

How dangerous that situation was! But God the Almighty inspired us, gave divine guidance for our unity. He gave us a basis on which all of us could agree, namely the Pantja Sila, which has remained in each of the three constitutions of the Republic of Indonesia. The Constitution of the Republic of Indonesia at Jogjakarta, the Constitution of the Republic of the United States of Indonesia, and the present Provisional Constitution of the Republic of Indonesia, all these firmly embrace the Pantja Sila because it is a compromise which is able to unite all these groups.

For that reason you should be aware of the grave situation which existed in July 1945. Let us not experience a situation like that again. Let us not destroy our unity. And if I say "destroy our unity," if I say that, I mean destroy, kill, explode, annihilate the state for which we have struggled together with so much suffering and sacrifice. Return to unity! As I have repeatedly said, I am not prohibiting any person from propagating his ideology. But remember, absolute unity, absolute unity, absolute unity, put the emphasis on unity. Do not throw it into jeopardy.

I am thinking of the Christians, the Christian group. Not one, not three, nor a hundred, but thousands of Christians died in the struggle to defend freedom. What is to happen to the hopes of the Christians? Should we not value their sacrifices, too? Their hope is to be with all of us members of a united and free Indonesian people. Do not use the term "minority," no! The Christians do not want to be called a minority. We have not fought to be called minorities. The Christians say: "We have not sacrificed our sons to be called a minority." Is that what you want? What everyone wants is to become a member citizen of one free state, the united Republic of Indonesia. It is the same with me, with the *ulamas,* the youth, the officials, everyone without exception: everyone wants to be a citizen of the Republic of Indonesia, everyone, without any minorities or majorities.

Does not Islam, as a matter of fact, put the emphasis in this matter on *musjawarah.* I am answering the question put forward by Dahlan Ranuwihardjo. How does it accord with democracy? In return I ask the help of the *ulama.* I have never found the word "democracy" in the Islamic vocabulary. I have only found *musjawarah.* Moreover, I have never found the term "voting" in the vocabulary of Islam. What Islam urges is *musjawarah,* discussion. There is no suggestion of voting, so that one side can say: "My party has the larger numbers, so I must win." No.

Democracy, what we really mean by democracy, is not just "half plus one are always right." Democracy for us is *musjawarah.* We have established democracy to show clearly to the outside world, and to convince ourselves completely, that we do not want autocracy. And that we do not want theocracy. I repeat, Islam knows no theocracy; it does not accept one favored group's dominating the others.

That is the sense in which we are using the word democracy. Not half plus one are always right; not half plus one always win; no, not at all. Islam prescribes *musjawarah—musjawarah* in an atmosphere of wisdom. Democracy is not a goal. Democracy is merely an instrument, an instrument of wisdom, a way to use wisdom to achieve an object in the affairs of society and the state. One way, and a way we all want, is our own "democracy," which is, as I have often said, a democracy with leadership, a democracy with wisdom, and not just voting. If it was just a matter of voting, then why hold *musjawarahs,* why hold debates? It would be better to just assemble. Assemble! Ready? And now an issue, for instance, the issue of Islam or not? Vote! Result: half plus one are always right. Now the issue of communism, vote! No more discussion, just vote.

But, Brothers, that is not what we want, and it is not what Islam wants. Islam wants *musjawarah; musjawarah* among brothers, *musjawarah* to achieve what we all want in a way as wise as possible and a way which is able to satisfy all sides.

IVd

Roeslan Abdulgani   Our Nationalism Is Based
on Democracy and Social Justice (1957)

This is part of an address delivered in the Constituent Assembly on December 3, 1957. The full Indonesian text appears in Tentang Dasar Negara Republik Indonesia Dalam Konstituante (*Discussions of the Basis of the State of the Republic of Indonesia in the Constituent Assembly*) (*n.p., 1958*), *III, 348–382.*

Amidst the profusion of theories on nationalism, we understand nationalism as that kind of nationalism which is in harmony with the requirements of modern times. Modern times have no room for theories on nationalism which base their unifying bond on a community of culture, religion, or race alone. Modern times confront us with a historical necessity, the necessity of having a unifying bond in the form of a desire and a will to live together, of the existence of a great sense of solidarity to be welded further day by day, which comes into existence because of a common historic destiny, a common historic suffering, a common historic victory, in short, a common historic sharing of joys and sorrows.

And, such a sense of nationalism does exist in our hearts. We suffered together in the past, and we brought our ideals into existence while we were in the agony of our sufferings. We suffered as a nation; we nurtured our ideals as a nation.

I consider it necessary to explain the concept of nationalism because the Honorable Member Hamka, though admitting during this session that nationalism was necessary as a basis of the state, doubted whether all our people really know what we mean by it. He doubted this the more because of his encounters with our people in the hinterlands of Sulawesi, Kalimantan, and so on.

In this connection we should never lose sight of the meaning and the function of the group of leaders in a society, of the group to which we all belong. In Indonesia, as anywhere else, there are always the conscious few, the minority which is conscious of that which the inarticulate masses feel impulsively or intuitively.

To argue the dubiousness of the word nationalism because the masses have not yet grasped the sense of that word is tantamount to placing ourselves in the train of thought of the colonial rulers in the past. The latter denied the existence of an Indonesian nation because, they said, the Indonesian people were split up and grouped in ethnic units which differed one from the other and even clashed with one another.

A close study of our own history will show us that Dutch colonialism, with the subsequent support of international capitalism and imperialism, destroyed the entire house of our nation. What was worse, the pyramidal structure of the Indonesian society was completely disarranged sociographically. Two hundred thousand Dutchmen succeeded in holding political power in the colonial state of the Netherlands Indies, a state which was used as a tool to exploit tens of millions of Indonesians. They held sway on top of the Indonesian social pyramid, after the commercial capital of the [Dutch] United East Indies Companies and subsequently the industrial and banking capital of the world had utterly destroyed the Indonesian middle class. The

late H. O. S. Tjokroaminoto described this middle class in his book
Islam dan Sosialisme [*Islam and Socialism*] as "independent artisans
and independent farmers who led a comfortable existence by their
work but were afterwards reduced to a multitude of destitute wageworkers." Those two hundred thousand Dutchmen then filled the
middle layer of Indonesian society with the remnants of the native
feudal group who were used as the administrative tools of the Netherlands Indies colonial government. They also filled that layer with, or
suffered it to be filled by, two million Chinese and tens of thousands
of Arabs who acted as their economic instruments. This middle layer,
which was filled with the remnants of feudalism and more than two
million Foreign Orientals, acted as a buffer, as an instrument to
check the advancement of the Indonesian People.

Oppressed by these two layers, which held the political and the
macroeconomic power in their hands, our people lived in microeco-
nomic bitterness. This was a macroeconomy to foreigners, for it implied macro income for them, with micro work; but it was a microeconomy in the sense that the Indonesian people got micro income
for macro work!

A microeconomy of this kind only gave our people scope to earn
their living from small-scale shipping, retail trading, and, especially,
small-scale farming. Thus, they shared the fate of millions of Asians
in the basins of the Indus, the Ganges, the Irrawaddy, the Yangtse
Kiang, and the Hoang Ho whom Professor Wertheim described as
"the teeming millions of farmers of forty centuries." Politically, they
were subject to the orders of an authoritarian foreign government;
economically, they were bled white by foreign nations.

In such bitter social-economic conditions, ideals were born which
were diametrically opposed to the political systems of authoritarianism
and feudalism, and which were also diametrically opposed to the
economic system of exploitation. In such circumstances, the ideals of
democracy and social justice inevitably came into being.

Is it any wonder that in such circumstances our nation was destined
by history to acquire a sense of nationalism which was at once characterized by a commitment to democracy and social justice?

Is it any wonder that its democratic character, or its feature of
sovereignty of the people, is inherent in the history of its struggle for
independence? Is it any wonder that its commitment to collectivism
and socialism—in other words to social justice—is inherent in its
sense of nationalism?

Therefore, in the circumstances which were decreed by history, Indonesian nationalism had to go hand in hand with democracy and social justice. This is in the nature of history; this is the identity of the Indonesian nation!

In advancing the principle of nationalism as the starting point of my discussion, I am fully cognizant of the well-intended cautionary remarks which have frequently been made with regard to the concept of nationalism. These cautionary remarks call for self-restraint, lest the Indonesian concept of nationalism become chauvinistic, narrow-minded, aggressive, jingoistic; and lest it manifest itself as xenophobia.

We accept these cautionary remarks in all calmness. However, if they are based on the common characteristics of the nationalism of the Europeans, we cannot accept them unreservedly. It is not right to place Asian nationalism or Indonesian nationalism, in particular, in the same category as Western European nationalism, which has been attended by such excesses as chauvinism, militarism, and Nazism. This is historically wrong.

In Western Europe the concept of nationalism was born roughly two centuries ago, in the period of transition from an agrarian to an industrial society. In the course of that transitional period, the upper and middle classes were born; they monopolized the label of nationalism. The birth of Indonesian nationalism and of Asian nationalism in general came as a reaction to Western European colonialism.

Thus, since colonialism involves political domination, economic exploitation, and cultural penetration, our nationalism has three aspects:

First: a political aspect which involves overthrowing the political domination of foreign nations and replacing it with a democratic system of government;

Second: a socio-economic aspect which involves efforts to put an end to foreign economic exploitation and to build a new society which is free from poverty and misery; and

Third: a cultural aspect which involves reviving its identity and attuning it to the exigencies of the times.

Objectively these three aspects constitute one indivisible whole. Indonesian nationalism, as part of Asian nationalism, is not a "historical category of the period of emerging capitalism," as Stalin wrote in his book *Marxism and the National Problem.* Indonesian nationalism is a historical category of the collapse of colonialism and imperialism on the Asian and African continents.

Therefore, as soon as we decided to base our state on the principle of nationalism, the principles of democracy and social justice appeared as inevitable concomitants. Viewed objectively, this kind of nationalism cannot possibly turn aggressive or chauvinistic. We may conclude that the allegations which sometimes reach our ears to the effect that nationalism is outmoded and contains the seeds of the destruction of mankind are tales told by colonial Europeans to lull the fighting spirit of the Asian and African nations and put them to sleep.

IVe

Sajuti Melik   Marhaenism as the Science of Our Struggle (1963)

This passage is translated from Pembinaan Djiwa Marhaenisme *(Fostering the Spirit of Marhaenism)* *(Djakarta: Pantjaka, 1963), a collection of articles from the Djakarta PNI daily* Suluh Indonesia. *In translating the Indonesian word* ilmu, *we have consistently used the English term "science," but readers should be aware of the other sense of this word, which corresponds roughly to "mystical knowledge."*

The Indonesian nation was formed thousands of years ago. Let us consider it as dating back simply to the Kingdom of Sriwidjaja, that is, to the seventh century. So the struggle of the Indonesian nation has also existed since the days of Sriwidjaja. That kingdom was formed as a result of a national struggle. So it is inaccurate if people say that the Indonesian national struggle began only with the establishment of Budi Utomo on May 20, 1908.

Every struggle has its science. And so the "struggle-science" of the Indonesian nation has existed since the days of Sriwidjaja, though, like other sciences, it has undergone changes. The struggle-science of the Indonesian nation in the Madjapahit period was different from that during Sriwidjaja. The struggle-science which existed after the destruction of Madjapahit was different from that which existed during Madjapahit. And the struggle-science of colonial days, since the sixteenth century, was different from that of the pre-colonial struggle.

Even during colonial times there were different kinds of struggle. Here we can distinguish two levels: the struggle which was aristo-cratic-theocratic in nature, and the struggle which was democratic. And both of these are included in the national struggle.

Now, the establishment of Budi Utomo in 1908 brought a new type of struggle to the Indonesian nation, the type that is of the people. Before 1908 the struggle of the Indonesian nation was a struggle of aristocrats and religious elite; after the establishment of Budi Utomo, it was a popular one. Popular does not mean only that the struggle was now concerned with the interests of the people, but also, and primarily, that it was based on the strength of the politically con-scious people and the mass organizations.

Why, then, has the struggle of the Indonesian nation been a popu-lar one since the beginning of the twentieth century? An explanation anywhere near complete would need a treatise of its own, but the main point is because modern imperialism, which dominated Indone-sia since the 1870's, aroused the people to consciousness. This popular consciousness then changed the character of the struggle of the Indo-nesian nation. This means that it also changed the character of Indo-nesian nationalism. It changed it from an aristocratic nationalism to a popular nationalism.

Thus, popular nationalism, or the national struggle of the people which sprang up after the beginning of the twentieth century, pro-gressed further and further. And the science of this struggle pro-gressed further and further, too! That progress resulted from experi-ence and from the increasing awareness of the people.

After Budi Utomo in 1908, several other popular organizations were established in the following years. Those of a political nature and not regionalistic were: the Islamic Traders' Association [Sarikat Dagang Islam, 1911] which later became the Islamic Association [Sarikat Islam]; the Indies Party [Indische Partij]; the Communist Party of Indonesia [Partai Komunis Indonesia, 1920]; the Republic of Indonesia Party [Partai Republik Indonesia or PARI, 1926]; and still others.

Bung Karno has grouped the people's organizations which have existed since 1908 into several "generations" according to the level of their struggle. Or, we may say, according to the level of their awareness. They are: "the Pioneer Generation," "the Resolute Genera-tion," "the Experimental Generation," "the Breakthrough Generation," and "the Implementing Generation." The late Professor Yamin has set down the years of these "Generations" as follows: the period of the Pioneers, 1908–1927; the period of the Resolute, 1927–1938; the period of Experiment, 1938–1942; the period of the Breakthrough, 1942–1950; the period of Implementation, 1950–(?). This fivefold division can be condensed into a threefold one—the period of the Pioneers, the period of the Resolute, and the period of the Implementers.

From the years given by Professor Yamin it can be seen that the term "Pioneer Generation" refers to the mass organizations of the period from 1908 to 1927, covering the five political parties mentioned above—Budi Utomo, Sarikat Islam, Nationaal Indische Partij, Partai Komunis Indonesia, and Partai Republik Indonesia—whereas the term "Resolute Generation" covers the organizations which are based on Marhaenism, especially the Partai Nasional Indonesia and the Partai Indonesia, both of which were led by Bung Karno himself.

Marhaenism, then, is the resolute affirmation of the struggle-science of the Indonesian people or the struggle-science of the Indonesian nation which has been made more resolute. So Marhaenism cannot be separated from the science of the struggle of the Indonesian nation in general, whether this be the science of the struggle before the birth of Marhaenism or the science of the struggle after the birth of Marhaenism.

That which was born before Marhaenism prepared the way for the birth of Marhaenism, whereas that which was born after Marhaenism was the implementation of Marhaenism. According to the declaration of Bung Karno at the PNI Congress at Solo in 1960, it is an emanation or manifestation of Marhaenism. So it is true to say that Marhaenism is the struggle-science of the Indonesian nation. It is our resolute and mature science of struggle.

This struggle-science was able to be born because it had been pioneered by earlier parties and organizations, in particular by BU, SI, PKI, and PARI. We can say that Marhaenism would not have been born in 1927 if, for example, those parties had not existed earlier.

Furthermore, because anything born of Marhaenism is an emanation of it, we can contend that the Proclamation of Independence would not have occurred on August 17, 1945, if, for example, Marhaenism had not been born in 1927.

Marhaenism is the continuation and completion of the earlier Indonesian struggle-sciences, that is, of the struggle-sciences of organizations, especially parties which existed before the birth of Marhaenism. These sciences, together with the experience of the earlier parties, are parties, the material out of which the theory of Marhaenism was created. Hence, we can say that Marhaenism encompasses all appropriate theories from the sciences and parties which preceded it.

All the parties formed before the birth of Marhaenism had merit, and all of them contributed theory and experience of struggle to the formation or discovery of Marhaenism, so that it is as if Marhaenism is a blend or synthesis of the sciences of the struggles which preceded it.

V

Javanese Traditionalism

The traditional political forms and concepts of the Indonesian peoples are not part of the subject of this book.* As in other societies faced with disruptive exogenous change, however, there has been a tendency deliberately to utilize elements of the indigenous traditions in ideologies designed to face the new situation. Where the traditional element in such ideologies is strong, they may be called traditionalistic.

Many of the Indonesians who turn to the past for guidance find it in Islam; VIa is an example of Islamic traditionalism. But in this section we are concerned rather with those who turn to the non-Islamic elements of tradition. We have chosen to confine our attention to those looking primarily at the Javanese traditions, because only the Javanese are so numerous (comprising about half the population), and their non-Islamic traditions so developed that their traditionalism is an important ideological force on the national level. Balinese traditionalism and Minangkabau traditionalism (for instance) do exist, but they have no more than local importance.

We begin with two passages from traditional Javanese literature. Selection Va, describing a happy kingdom, is the conventional opening of performances of the Javanese *wajang* or shadow play; in this or a similar form, it is recited before countless audiences throughout the island every night. The following passage, from the *Nitisastra*, describes the conditions of the Kali Age, the final, worst age of the

* Javanese traditional political ideas and institutions are described by Soemarsaid Moertono, *State and Statecraft in Old Java* (Ithaca, N.Y.: Cornell Modern Indonesia Project, Monograph Series, 1968), while their relevance to recent politics has been pointed out by Ann Ruth Willner, *The Neotraditional Accommodation to Political Independence: The Case of Indonesia* (Princeton, N.J.: Princeton University, Center of International Studies, 1966).

Hindu cycle. Many traditionally minded Javanese look upon the period covered by this book as such a topsy-turvy age. In the words of a popular song:

> We have lived to see a time without order
> In which everyone is confused in his mind.
> One cannot bear to join in the madness
> But if he does not do so,
> He will not share in the spoils.

In the third passage we pass from traditional literature to traditionalist ideology. Here, in a piece originally written not in Javanese but in Dutch, a Javanese aristocrat is consciously facing and rejecting the egalitarian and individualistic West. We had to go well back into the past to find the anti-egalitarianism of the Javanese tradition expressed as forthrightly as it is here; this element has been abandoned or hidden from public view since 1945.

In Vd the process of change from traditional writing to traditionalistic ideology is taken a step further. Professor Supomo is using Western political theory, as well as the Japanese model, to devise an ideal which will harmonize with indigenous traditions and values.

The influence of Javanese traditionalism on the political discourse of independent Indonesia has been somewhat patchy. Forced to operate within an environment of liberal democracy or revolutionary nationalism, it has adopted a protective coloring, finding direct public expression only on subjects where its themes harmonize with elements of stronger ideologies. In Ve, for instance, the representative of a small traditionalist party is expressing the fear of orthodox Islam which is a vital part of the Javanese traditionalist view of Indonesian politics, but which is shared, too, by radical nationalists and Communists.

In no segment of the Indonesian polity was Javanese traditionalism more powerfully represented than in the *pamong pradja,* the corps of territorial administrators who carried an aristocratic ethos through the Dutch and Japanese periods to be gradually modified and dissipated in free Indonesia. So it is perhaps fitting that our last two extracts should come from a *pamong pradja* conference.

The paucity of Javanese traditionalist representation in the third part of this book concerned with debates over controversial issues may be due partly to faulty selection, but it also reflects the failure of this ideological tendency to develop a distinctive approach on many national questions. Significantly it is in the national identity section that its influence is most clearly evident—in IXb, IXd, and IXh—but here, too, its influence is far from exclusive.

Javanese traditionalist influences can also be seen in much of the thinking of President Sukarno reproduced here, particularly perhaps in Ic, Ih, and IId, and to some extent in the thinking of other radical nationalists. Indeed, odd as it may seen, it is often difficult to draw the line between Javanese traditionalism and radical nationalism. The two streams share the same eclecticism, reverence for the unitary state and its leader, and rejection of individualism and capitalism. Sociologically this has much to do with the fact that the Javanese aristocracy have been a salary-earning rather than a property-owning class. Thus, the angry nationalist lawyer or journalist is often the son —and the dutiful son—of the aristocratic district officer or school-inspector. It has been at times of the greatest ascendancy of Sukarno and his generation of nationalists (as in August–October 1945 or after 1959) that the subtle influence of Javanese traditionalism—for instance, in titles and forms of address—has seemed most pervasive.

The distinction remains, however. Even the unrivaled Javanese talent for syncretism cannot entirely reconcile the traditionalist yearning for order, hierarchy, and tranquility with the revolutionary romanticism of Sukarno.

Va

Ki Reditanaja   A Happy Kingdom

This version of the prologue which usually precedes performances of the Javanese shadow-play wajang *is taken from* Kartawijoga, *published in 1951 in an Indonesian translation by R. Hardjowirogo, and attributed to Ki Reditanaja,* dalang [puppeteer] *to the court of Surakarta.*

Once upon a time there was a country of great renown. Although there are many communities on this sky-enclosed and ocean-bound earth, and many which are great and free, there is no other like the kingdom of Mandraka. Our story begins in this country because among a hundred countries it had no peer, and among a thousand countries not ten would equal it. This kingdom was on everyone's lips, for it was of high rank, with mountains behind it, rice fields on its right, a river on its left, and a great harbor before it. Everything planted there flourished; everything could be bought cheaply. Throughout its territories there was peace, as was proved by the traders who traveled night and day in complete safety along its highways. Peace was also evident from the way the people lived crowded together, their houses touching each other. The farmers in the villages had no need to pen or tie their buffaloes, cows, ducks, or chickens, and during the day all these animals were free to wander over the pastures, returning at dusk quite alone, as there were no thieves. Peace was guaranteed because the country was free from attacks by enemies and none of the king's followers were evil. The king's authority was respected and harmony prevailed. Mandraka was honored by other countries, for, truly, she was a powerful kingdom whose light shone brilliantly and radiated afar, so that she was famous in far distant places. Not only the states of Java, but even many beyond the sea paid homage to her, so that at certain times princesses were sent to her as gestures of deference, and goods were offered her in tribute.

The name of the king was Narasoma, which means a king who is patient with his subjects. He was also called Salja, a man of wisdom; Madradipa, a man of fame; Madrakeswara, a man of great repute; and Somadenta, an honest man with the soul of a priest. And there were many countries which yielded to him without fighting, for no other reason than that they were dazzled by the power of this wise king who was always giving alms, who gave clothes to the naked, food to the hungry, comfort to the bereaved, and a stick to help those walking in slippery places. None could deny the generosity of the king in Mandraka. Such was the excellence and generosity of His Majesty that this whole night would not suffice to tell it, so here we will stop.

Vb
The Old Javanese Nitisastra   The Time of Trouble

This fragment is a translation of verses 7 to 12 of Canto 4 of the Old Javanese Nitisastra, *a work of moral precepts which is believed to date back to the late Madjapahit period and is based on the Indian* Nitisastra. *We have made this translation from the Dutch translation*

of R. Ng. Poerbatjaraka (Bandung: Bibliotheca Javanica, 1933) and
the Indonesian translation of the government publishing house Balai
Pustaka (Djakarta, 1951).

Truly, when the Kali* time comes at the end of the age, only
riches are valued. The virtuous, the brave, the pious, and the learned
are all subordinate to the rich. The esoteric teachings of the priests
are forgotten; the good families and the rulers are reduced to poverty.
Children deceive and disobey their parents, and members of the
lower castes become merchants, warriors and scholars.

The earth shakes and is covered with darkness; rulers no longer
bestow gifts but receive them from the rich. Clowns go into the forest
to meditate ascetically and in accordance with the Kali time. The
lower castes insult the merchants and the merchants no longer respect
the kings who, indeed, are no longer worthy of respect. The kings
despise the Brahmins, and the Brahmins no longer fulfil their religious tasks.

The earth loses its sanctity and medicinal herbs their potency.
Brahmins, warriors, merchants, and common people mix promiscu-
ously, and all consider themselves worthy to be priests, and, having
arrogated these rights, they hold in contempt the sacred books, in-
vocations, and spiritual exercises. They are so puffed up that they
equate their own bodies with the ultimate truth.

The influence of the Kali time makes people wild and quarrelsome
for high positions. They do not know their own station; they fight
their own kinsmen and seek refuge with their foes. The sacred places
and their furniture are damaged; those forbidden to enter defile them
with their presence. The temples are left desolate. Curses lose their
force and acknowledged rights their validity, through the actions of
the uncivilized masses.

Those who give alms become poor, and the mean become fabu-
lously rich. The wicked live long, but the good are denied their
proper span of life. Contemptible actions are considered noble, and
stupidity is called wisdom; the base are called honorable—truly a
strange attitude! The King becomes a creature of his ministers, and
those with authority misuse it.

The tjempaka tree, the mango, the sandalwood, the bougainvillea,
the fragrant bakula and the naga flower tree are cut down to make
fences around useless plants. Geese, peacocks, and nightingales are

---

* In the Hindu cyclical conception, the last of the stages of history.

slaughtered to make a place for crows and herons. The kept dogs fare abundantly; they are sated on the blood and flesh of beautiful maidens.

Vc
R. M. S. Soeriokoesoemo The Right of the Wise (1920)

This extract comes from "Sabdo Pandito Ratoe" ["The Word of the Wise Prince"], an article written in Dutch in April 1920 and published as a brochure (Weltevreden: Indonesische Drukkerij, 1920).

On the grounds of their divine origin all men are equal. In this respect democracy is perfectly right. There is a single Source and a single Life.

But this one Life expresses itself in the world of manifestations in an endless variety of forms, all obeying their own laws to be true to their own natural character.

Glass, for instance, is broken more easily than steel. That is a law in the world of metals. It is easily observed. If you chop off a branch of a *waru* tree and casually put it into the ground somewhere else, it will grow into a tree. A branch of another tree will not do the same. The capacity of the *waru* to grow is just greater than that of other trees. One does not ask why. Nature alone knows the answer. And the sensible villager is careful not to grow his precious fruit trees in the immediate proximity of the *waru*. Free competition between *waru* and fruit trees? No, indeed! The fruit trees would certainly lose out.

Free competition among such unequal kinds of elements is out of the question. The farmer does not allow free competition in his field. Similarly, a well-organized state should protect the weak. The strong should not be favored still further by efforts to secure a more favorable and advantageous position for them. Anyone who allows free competition between the weak and the strong is acting unwisely and therefore unjustly.

The inequality which exists in the world of plants has been shown in this example. This inequality means that there are no equal rights. Peanuts are planted after the rice harvest. Why should rice come first? Why do the peanuts not have the right to benefit first from the abundance of nutriments in the soil, and why must they content themselves with what remains, with what the rice deems fit to leave?

Why should quinine and tea plants grow in cold regions? By what right do these plants acquire lordship over those areas of delightful climate?

For the sweet potato a small quantity of water is enough; it makes no demands of the rice, which is provided with water in abundance. That is, at least, wise, wiser than many a group of civil servants who put the State in a difficult position by their high salary demands and so force money out of the little man's pocket—because, of course, people do not dare to seize Capital by the collar and wave a fist before its sly, dividend-seeking eyes! . . .

If men had equal rights, there would be no duties to be performed; each individual would be on his own, insisting on his rights. No society would then be possible. The child would be left to its own devices, because it would insist that its rights be respected. There would be no unity but only diversity; no order, only disorder. The right of the father, the right of the mother, the right of the child, the right of the prince, the right of the people, and the right of the wise man—none of these would exist. All would be merged in that one right of the democrat. . . .

Democracy has invented a system in which equal rights are granted to every one: the wise man and the idiot, the man who does intellectual work and the laborer, the man of high moral stature and the debauched. It wants to give effect to equal rights and to throw them as a sheet over all places of unequal height. But this sheet will lie crookedly, resting only on the protruding points. The deep thinkers who remain in the hollows will not be helping to hold it up and so they will be deprived of all rights. This is the first injustice of democracy.

If democracy is victorious, the right of the strong will be at its side. There is nothing to be said against this as such, provided that this right is used to enable the higher faculties of man to speak and not the animal in him. In this way the weak will always be served. And in a democratic State the wise and intelligent are the weaker party. It is this party which democracy must serve; if it fails to do so, it is committing a second injustice.

The path democracy chooses is uneven. At each side of it the beast is lying in wait, just waiting for the chance to waylay its human prey. Woe to the democrat who in an unguarded moment forgets the rugged spots of his path; he will stumble and fall into the abyss, a prey for the beast.

Why do people choose this dangerous path? Is there really no other way which leads to the goal? Is nature really so poor that there is nothing more for us to learn from her? Look at the complete family: the father and mother with their children, sons and daughters, big and small. Is this not a State in the small?

Here the father takes charge of statecraft, while the mother and wife is given economic management as her special task. The children do all of their work on the orders of the parents. Father sees to it that the youngest child is charged with the easiest work. Father and mother talk together pleasurably about their affairs and the children take part in the conversation and enjoy the companionable atmosphere. If times are bad, the children immediately notice it from the worried look on mother's face and the seriousness of father. Then they keep quiet and wait patiently for whatever father will ask them to do. The duties which father asks his wife and children to carry out are happily accepted, and there is no grumbling. What father says is right, because father is wise!

That is the ideal of the family—and also of the State. By contrast, a capitalist state may be compared with a family in which the father is henpecked and the mother cares mainly for finery and neglects her duties toward the children. Then there is no peace; quarrels are an everyday occurrence; and the children are always grumbling and expressing their discontent. If mother persists in neglecting her duties, a clash will become unavoidable.

And if a clash comes, the children will emerge on top and have their turn at running things in the family. The father and mother will have to do what they are told; the roles will be reversed. That is the picture of the democratic state. The children act as the head of the family. Things may go well in the beginning, but soon the children will clash with each other because everyone insists that he will not lose out on anything as far as his rights are concerned. In such a family duties are not recognized, everyone demands his rights first. Rights first, duties to be accepted later—perhaps! The picture is clear and it is not favorable to democracy.

In fact, the [Netherlands] Indies present us with the same picture —only with the difference that the children do not have their own parents any more. A foreign couple have been put in as guardians. The man, who is good-natured, is dominated by his wife. And the wife cares only for gold. Like the wife we discussed earlier, she loves finery. She wastes her money in foreign countries and thoroughly neglects the children. But some of these children realize that if the housekeeping is done in this way, things will eventually go wrong. They start telling the others that they are entitled to better care. Then they talk about the democratic feast at which many wonderful dishes are offered. When the other children begin to believe this, they immediately demand of the woman that she should prepare all these dishes. The woman refuses to do this, because it would mean restraining her desire for money to waste in foreign countries. The reason she gives is that these dishes are only for grown-ups. But this does not satisfy the children, and so they start screaming loudly. The good-natured old man shakes his head doubtfully.

Prambanan is in danger! * Seeing the danger with which Prambanan is faced, some of the children meet to discuss what to do. "Let us go to Borobudur," one of them says, "and find out there what our own father wants. His will will be law for us. Let us warn our brothers now that democracy without wisdom spells disaster for us all! . . ."

Equality and brotherhood—the wise man preaches these, too. But he does not teach the equality of democracy, where what is proclaimed is equality of rights—rather the equality of the family, in which the eldest son who bears a greater share of the duties and obligations, has also more rights than his younger brother, who is still at the playing stage. In a family like this there is no equality of rights, yet equality and brotherhood in the fullest sense prevail among the children.

The slogan of brotherhood should be understood in this spirit. The present writer is often demanding equality and equal rights for his compatriots, but one need not dwell on the fact that the notion of equal rights here has a completely different meaning from that on which the idea of democracy is built.

In this struggle against democracy it is fundamental truth which is at stake. The idea of equal rights can only be based on a belief in life as a once-over affair. If man lives and dies only once, then justice requires that all men should have the same rights, notwithstanding the bad example of Nature, which just never does endow two persons with the same rights, that is, capacities.

Happily, we have seen that man does not live once only and does

* Prambanan and Borobudur, moments of eight- and ninth-century Java, are apparently used here as symbols of the Javanese past.

not just die, and so we do not have to act against Nature. Man lives eternally and his agony of death is ultimately only imaginary. What dies has always been dead and what lives will live on eternally. What is usually meant by death is the death of illusion; it is its ending that is called death (*patine roso**). . . .

The Wise man to whom rights are due and who disposes of power will not use the right of the strong to serve his own interests as an animal would. So this right is only safe in the hands of the Wise man, the bearer of the wisdom of God. Anyone who distributes equal rights to people of unequal development, who believes that the word of the unenlightened villager is of the same value as that of the Wise man, is neither sensible nor just.

But where are we to find the Wise man, to whom right is due and who will divide rights among people? The *Nitisastra*† says, "Do not pride yourself on your wisdom until you have proved yourself superior to a thousand wise among the wise." This amounts to the conclusion that it is practically impossible to find such a Wise man. But this does not detract from the case, as long as the principle is accepted: respect for one's superior, without simply falling into servility, should set the basic tone of society. There must be acknowledgement of the divine right due to the Wise man, not a denial of this or a disputing of it on the grounds that men being of divine origin are therefore equal. All men may have a common Source, but it must be accepted that the bearer of God's wisdom is also the bearer of right.

Statecraft should be based on this principle. Wise men should be at the head of the State and should be chosen by the Wise and not by the people. Those who owe obedience may also enjoy the first fruits of social welfare. So the people, who have to show obedience at all times, will be served first. The Wise one will enjoy the least of the world and also the last. This has always been the view of the great Indies [Indonesian] princes, whose deeds are honoured right down to the present day, though it is now perhaps no more than a formality.

In times of rice shortage, the prince will abstain from food. Fasting when the time of sowing is approaching has been the rule. Let those who are about to be put into the highest positions, who will hold the reins of government in their hands and the weal and woe of the

---

* Literally, death of feeling.
† See the introduction to Vb.

country, earn least of all. Then we will see whether those who thirst after wisdom will not be sifted out from among those who thirst after money.

Ruling should not be made attractive in terms of gold. If it is, it will become impossible to stop place-hunting in government, place-hunting by all means, legal and illegal.

The power of money must be checked by not attaching value to money. This is the only solution, and in this the government must set an example for us.

In earlier times the Prince sought to associate with the Wise, who were above all simple and had finally overcome their thirst for money. Money had no value then, except exclusively as a medium of exchange. The richest merchant never came near to the Prince. In this way the people more or less learned to eschew money as something unworthy. Nobody would deny that this phenomenon, in one or other form, was still to be observed in Javanese society until very recently. The Javanese cares more for titles than for money, because in his eyes every title brings him closer to the Prince. . . .

Vd

Supomo   An Integralistic State (1945)

This passage is translated from Professor Supomo's address to the Investigating Committee for the Preparation of Independence of May 31, 1945. The Committee functioned under Japanese auspices, but members enjoyed a high degree of freedom in expressing their views. The full Indonesian text is in Muhammad Yamin, ed., Naskah Persiapan Undang-undang Dasar 1945 *(Drafting the 1945 Constitution)* *(n.p.: Jajasan Prapantja, 1959), I, 109–121.*

The basis and the structural form of a state are closely connected with the legal norms which have grown out of its history and with its social structure. What is good and just for one state is therefore not necessarily good and just for another, because the situations of the two are not the same.

Every state has its own peculiarities connected with the history and characteristics of its society. Therefore policy for the development of a State of Indonesia must be made to accord with Indonesian social structure as it exists at the present time and to agree with the demands of the time, for example, the aspiration of Indonesia within the environment of Greater East Asia.

With this in mind, let us look at some examples of other states. The basis of Western European constitutional structure is individualism and liberalism. This quality of individualism which affects all fields of life—economic legislation, the arts, and so on—separates man as an individual from his society, sees him as cut off from those with whom he associates. Individualist man and the state regarded as an individual—these invariably give rise to imperialism and exploitation, producing chaos and disruption in the world, physically and spiritually.

You know that we must shun these qualities in the work of building the State of Indonesia. Indeed, Europe itself is now experiencing a very deep spiritual crisis because the people have become tired of the greed which stems from this spirit of individualism.

The basis of state structure in Soviet Russia at the present time is the dictatorship of the proletariat. Such a basis may agree with the particular characteristics of the social situation in Russia, but it is in conflict with the character of indigenous Indonesian society.

Another type of state is that of national-socialist Germany prior to its surrender in the present war. That state was based on the philosophy of the totalitarian state, on the idea of the political unity of the people, or integralistic theory. Among its principles was the principle of leadership as a core idea—*ein totaler Führerstaat* or state totally under leadership—and that of the sharing of one blood and one soil as between the leaders and the people [*Blut und Boden Theorie*].

Of these national socialist ideas, the principle of the unity of leaders and people and the principle of the oneness of the entire state fit in with the thought of the East.

Let us now look at an Asian state, at the philosophical foundations of the state of Japan. The Japanese state is based on the eternal physical and spiritual unity among His Majesty the Emperor, the state, and the entire Japanese people. The Emperor is the spiritual center of the entire people. The state is founded on the idea of family. The Imperial family is called "Koshitu," that is, the supreme family.

This basis of unity and family is very much in agreement with the nature of Indonesian society.

Having examined briefly some examples of the nature of other states, I will now say a few words about what does and what does not fit in with the social structure of indigenous Indonesia. As you are no doubt aware, the indigenous social structure of Indonesia is the creation of Indonesian culture, the fruit of the Philosophy or inner spirit of the Indonesian people. The inner spirit and spiritual structure of the Indonesian people is characterized by the ideal of the unity of life, the unity *kawulo-gusti,** that is, of the outer and the inner world, of the macrocosmos and the microcosmos, of the people and their leaders. All men as individuals, every group or grouping of men in a society, and every society in the life of the entire world— each of these is considered to have its own place and its own obligations [*dharma*] according to the law of nature, the whole being aimed at achieving spiritual and physical balance. Man as an individual is not separated from other individuals or the outside world. Men, groups of men, and, indeed, all groups of creatures, all are interacting and interrelated and all have influence on each other. This is the totalitarian idea, the integralistic idea of the Indonesian people which is embodied in its indigenous form of government.

In the indigenous Indonesian system of government, which can be seen right up to the present period in the villages, both in Java and in Sumatra and other parts of the Indonesian archipelago, officials are leaders who are one with the people and are always obliged to maintain the unity and harmony of their society.

The task of the village head or leader of the people is to give effect to the people's sense of justice. He must always give form to the people's feeling for justice and to their ideals. Therefore he "holds firmly to the *adat*," in the words of a Minangkabau proverb, concerning himself with every new development in the society and for that purpose always consulting with people or with the heads of families in the village, in such a way that the spiritual bond between the leader and the whole people is always maintained. This unity between the people and their leaders, and between the various groups of the people, is characterized by a pervasive spirit of *gotong rojong* [mutual assistance] and of family.

So it is clear that if we want to establish an Indonesian state in accordance with the characteristic features of Indonesian society, it must be based on an integralistic state philosophy, on the idea of a state which is united with all its people, which transcends all groups in every field. According to this philosophy, the head of state and government bodies must have the attributes of real leadership, must point the way to the noble ideals and aspirations of the people. The state must be of the nature of an executive body, a creator of laws arising from within the hearts of the entire people. According to this theory, as I interpret it—and it is a theory which is in agreement with the indigenous Indonesian spirit—the state is nothing but the entire society or entire people of Indonesia, as an ordered, structured unity.

On this interpretation, the attitudes and actions of the state are not like those of an all-powerful individual, cut off from the individual men of the area and having its own interests distinct from those of the citizens as individuals; this is the individualistic idea. According to the integralistic view of the state as a nation in its ordered aspect, as a united people in its structured aspect, there is basically no dualism of state and individual, no conflict between the state organization on the one hand and the legal order of individuals on the other, no dualism of state and society-without-state [*Staat und staatsfreie Gesellschaft*]. There is no need to guarantee the fundamental rights and liberties [*Grund und Freiheitsrechte*] of the individual against the state, because the individual is an organic part of the state, with his own position and an obligation to help realize the state's greatness, and also because the state is not a power center or political giant standing outside the environment of the individual man's freedom.

The English philosopher Jeremy Bentham (in the late eighteenth century) thought that the goal of the state was "the greatest happiness of the greatest number," but this idea is based on individualism. According to the view of the state which I regard as being in conformity with the spirit of indigenous Indonesia, the state does not identify itself with the largest group in society, nor with the most powerful group politically or economically, but rather transcends all groups and individuals, identifying itself with the whole people in all its layers.

Let me not be misunderstood: The theory of the integralistic state or totalitarian state does not mean that the state pays no heed to the existence of groups as such or to man as an individual. No, that is not the intention. This philosophy is concrete and real; it does not turn everything into abstractions, as does the theory of individualism. The state recognises the existence of real groups in society and respects them. But all individuals and all groups must be aware of their position as organic parts of the state as a whole, must be aware of their obligation to strengthen unity and harmony among all of the parts.

Ve

Atmodarminto   The *Abangan* Case against an Islamic State (1957)

This piece comes from a speech made in the Constituent Assembly on November 12, 1957. By speaking frankly as a representative of the abangan *Muslims, the syncretistically minded who have persistently rejected the absolute claims of Islam, Atmodarminto drew the anger of the Muslim parties and the delighted approval of the PNI and PKI, whose speakers had not wanted to refer so openly to cleavage among self-confessed Muslims. Gerinda, the small Javanese traditionalist party which Atmodarminto represented in the Assembly, had been brought into alliance with the Communists as a result of the Islamic state issue. The full Indonesian text appears in* Tentang Dasar Negara Republik Indonesia Dalam Konstituante (*Discussions of the Basis of the State of the Republic of Indonesia in the Constituent Assembly*) (n.p., 1958), I, 63–78.*

Generally speaking, our society is not, as yet, an Islamic society. Beliefs, customs, and traditions inherited from our ancestors still form the basis of our society—witness the belief in the ghosts of ancestors and a variety of other ubiquitous spirits believed to bring happiness. Evidence of this is provided by the smell of incense, found everywhere on nights regarded as holy, and by the large number of people who make pilgrimages to places believed to harbor friendly spirits and who go to graveyards on certain days to offer flowers to the dead.

On ceremonial occasions such as births, engagements, weddings, or funerals, the great part of the population are sure to prepare vari-colored food-offerings (according to local custom) to provide nourishment for the spirits of their locality and their ancestors in order to obtain their blessing. On such occasions, too, they do not fail to offer specially prepared rice and chicken to our Prophet Mohammed (may God's peace be on him!).

It is true that, according to Indonesian history, a number of Islamic kingdoms were established both in and outside of Java, the rulers of which called themselves Sultans, Shahs, or, even, in some cases, Caliphs.

However, the establishment of these kingdoms was not the result of the existence and expansion of an Islamic society in Indonesia, nor was it due to most of the subjects of these kingdoms embracing Islam. These kingdoms were founded because of the desires of the rulers and a few of their influential followers. It is because of this fact that, right up until now, the Muslim religion has not come to dominate the spirit of Indonesian society.

One need only look at the history of the establishment of the Islamic kingdoms of Java—such as Demak, Padjang, and Mataram, Tjirebon and Banten—which in 1579 attacked the Hindu-Javanese kingdom of Padjadjaran, thus making all West Java part of an Islamic kingdom. Despite this, nearly all that remains from these Islamic kingdoms, apart from mosques, are krises, spears, shields, and royal carriages, all showing strong Hindu-Javanese cultural influence. Thus, history shows the Islamic religion has never been able to dominate the souls of most Indonesians. Of the people throughout Indonesia who regard themselves as Muslims, most in fact embrace *abangan* Islam—that is, an Islam still permeated with old beliefs. Ever since the time of the *walis*, there have been to my knowledge conflicts in Java between Islamic doctrines, between the *abangan* and orthodox Muslims. There are times when this conflict heightens and times when it subsides. Often when it has increased in intensity, wars have occurred, resulting in the removal of the capital from one place to another. The removal of the capital from Demak to Padjang, and from Padjang to Mataram—both of which were accompanied by wars—resulted from heightened conflict between orthodox and *abangan* Islam, or between Islam and old Java.

Of course, in each instance, power-seeking leaders were able to provoke or exacerbate the conflict. It is to be hoped now that Indonesia is independent that this cannot happen again. . . .

As everybody knows, there is a variety of religions in Indonesia, four of which are recognized by the government: Islam, Catholicism, Protestant Christianity, and Balinese Hinduism. Furthermore, among the Muslims there are orthodox Muslims and *abangan* Muslims. Thus, I believe that of the recognized religious groups three can hardly subscribe to the second proposal * and that these three will be reinforced by the strongly nationalistic *abangan* Muslim group. Disagreement with the second proposal will probably also be expressed by mystical groups which are many and have a significant number of

* That Islam be the basis of the state.

followers; by religious groups which are not yet recognized by the government, such as Buddhism and Confucianism; and by adherents of several political and economic ideologies. . . .

Since our national revolution began with the proclamation of August 17, 1945, the philosophical basis of the Republic of Indonesia has remained unchanged, so there is no historical precedent for any other basis—Islam included. Therefore, that Islam become the basis for our state is a new idea, and one which I regard as highly unrealistic and speculative. Its implementation would perhaps involve excessive dangers and would certainly provoke divisions among us which might intensify to the point of civil war. To make Islam the basis of the state would mean that the Muslims would reap the entire benefit of our national revolution and that other groups, including the mystical groups, would be regarded as dispensible. . . .

Even though it has been explained that Islam as the basis of the State is good and will not harm other groups, actually all the arguments put forward are only promises. Will those promises be enough to satisfy other groups? That is up to them. Personally, I am still very uncertain and suspicious of these promises. My uncertainty and suspicion are not based merely on prejudice and imagination, but on the facts of history—whether it be the history of the expansion of other religions outside Indonesia or of the early expansion of Islam in Java—and the facts of the period of independence.

The entry of Islam into Java approximately coincided with the rise of the empire of Madjapahit and its Prime Minister Gadjah Mada, and its expansion coincided with the decline and fall of Madjapahit. When the Islamic movement, guided by the *walis,* first began to expand, it strove only to assert the freedom of men to embrace a religion and live according to its rules. About 1460, Javanese Muslims were permitted by the ruler of Madjapahit to establish a Muslim province at Demak, which became a kingdom in 1578, after the collapse of Madjapahit. But after the Muslims had established a fully sovereign kingdom, they quickly changed their policy; whereas at first they sought freedom for all beliefs, once they had established their authority, they no longer tolerated other religions in their territories. In East Java, the Tenggerese people were driven into the region of Mount Bromo, and in West Java the Badui were forced to flee to the remote region of Tjibeo.

This harsh and cruel attitude of the Islamic kingdom of Demak was expressed not only toward people of other religions but also toward

Muslims of deviant opinions. A *wali* called Pangeran Panggung was condemned to be burnt to death because of a doctrinal difference. Another *wali*, Pangeran Siti Djenar, was condemned to death by decapitation, and his body replaced by that of a dog in full view of the crowd. A religious teacher, Kijaji Ageng Pengging, was condemned to be killed by having his hands cut off.

Likewise in the period since independence, the Muslim parties have not kept the promises—promises made not only to the populace in general, but also to their own Muslim supporters—which were written into their constitutions and platforms and which clearly aimed at achieving prosperity for the people. After the Republic of the United States of Indonesia was replaced by the unitary Republic of Indonesia, the Islamic parties three times formed the nucleus of, and held the Prime Ministership in, coalition cabinets. Yet, in all that time the people did not become prosperous because the leaders of the Islamic parties, once in power, either broke or forgot their promises. They quickly changed their goal to looking after their own interests and those of their group.

On the basis of this historical survey, it is hard to believe the promises offered in defense of Islam as the basis of the state. It is certain that if Islam were made the basis of the state, there would be discrimination between Muslim and non-Muslim citizens. For example, only Muslims could be chosen President or Cabinet Minister, and only Muslims could be appointed as Secretary-Generals and department heads. Once Islam became the basis of the state, the state would automatically be regarded as "Dar-ul-Islam" * and the powers of the Caliphate would be vested in the Islamic group, as explained by a leader of an Islamic party at Makassar. Certainly, if a state is based on Islam, the only citizens with full rights are the Muslims, and the rights of non-Muslims must be diminished. It is also possible that full rights would be denied to my group, that is the *abangan* Muslims, because a Muslim politician once drew a line of demarcation between his group and the *abangan*, deriding the latter as "two-headed snakes." It is also possible that mystical associations would be banned, as has often been urged on the government (the Ministry of Religion) by several Islamic politicians. However, what is certain is that the

* Islamic political theory divides the world into the Dar-ul-Islam, the territory ruled according to the divine principles of Islam, and the Dar-ul-Harb, or territory of disorder. There is no direct reference here to the Darul Islam movement then in rebellion against the government in several provinces, though there is probably an insinuation.

Communist Party would be forbidden to exist. Indeed, if the Palembang Congress of Islamic Scholars were in power, Islamic burial would be denied to Communists, and their marriages annulled.

Vf

Sawarno Djaksonagoro   The Spirit a Leader Must Have (1959)

This comes from a paper given to a conference of the pamong pradja, *the members of the territorial administrative corps, in Solo in late 1959, soon after the promulgation of Presidential Decision No. 6 of that year. This Decision, issued in the wake of the repromulgation of the 1945 Constitution, greatly enhanced the powers of territorial administrators, particularly the heads of provinces and regencies (*kabupaten*). The paper has not, as far as we know, been published.*

In what spirit should regional government according to the Presidential Decision No. 6 be carried out? It should certainly be guided by the essential spiritual qualities of the people affected by it. Because the Presidential Decision is a legal enactment of the government, it follows that the heads or leaders of the regions whose actions are regulated by it are men of great importance. The success or otherwise of the Presidential Decision depends in large part on them. Their character must accord with the spirit of the common people. They must be men who can feel with the common people and understand their desires.

Among the common people no one is more honored than the man who is like the wise knight [*satrio pandita*], a man with the character of a noble knight who acts with wisdom and discretion and lives the simple life of the man of holiness, one whose qualities of leadership are like those pictured in the *Hastha Brata*.*

The particular specifications of regional government law can be changed as situations require. What remains constant is the spirit needed in men guiding the affairs of government, the qualities of the *satrio pandita* which must inspire those who have the honor of participating in tasks of government. As the *pamong pradja* corps was created to provide leadership in governmental affairs, its members should be aware of what their position means and be guided and permeated by the character of the *satrio pandita*, which would then

---

* The eight attributes of the *satrio pandita*, derived from the epic *Ramayana*.

automatically also infuse the implementation of Presidential Decision No. 6.

Where a leader has a *satrio pandita* character, he acts impersonally with the result that his leadership is not felt as restrictive but constitutes a bond between himself and those he leads. In that situation there is almost no difference between leader and led because the leader does not feel that he is leading and the led do not feel that they are being led.

If one may illustrate all this with figures from the *wajang* literature, the example could be suggested of the relationship between Ardjuna, who is well known as the wild buffalo of the Pandawas, the symbol of all strength, and Semar, who was born to be Ardjuna's guide. Ardjuna, famous as *lanang ing djagad,** can do nothing unless he is guided by the wisdom of Kijaji Lurah Semar, who is really an incarnation of Bathara Ismaja.†

Krishna could not play an important role in the *wajang* stories if it were not that the spirit of his teacher, Bagawan Padmonobo, had materialised in his person when he was young and was known as Raden [prince] Nojorono. As a symbol of the bond between leader [Bagawan Padmonobo] and led [Raden Nojorono], Krishna called himself Prabu [king] Padmonobo. This should be the spirit which moves those who implement Presidential Decision No. 6. This spirit should give life to the Presidential Decision as the basis for relations between leaders and led, just as Bagawan Padmonobo gave life to Raden Nojorono.

The essence of being a leader in our culture is always to act anonymously or impersonally or, as the Javanese saying has it, "Tut wuri handajani." This means that followers should not be seen by their leader but should be able to feel his authority, which should envelop his person as a flower is enveloped by its fragrance.

These notes are intended as a contribution to the Public Service Association of the Ministry of the Interior, in the hope that the *pamong pradja* corps will be able to act as its duty and calling requires and help to guide the common people safely out of the *gara-gara ing mangsa kartika,*‡ out of the tempest which now rages in our society.

In all-night *wajang kulit* performances, during the *gara-gara* or tempest, the *satrio* appears with his three servants, Semar, Gareng,

* The quintessence of masculinity.
† A god.
‡ The tempest of the month of Kartika, the beginning of the rainy season.

and Petruk, and the accompanying *gamelan* music changes from the *pathet* 6 to the *pathet* 9.* May the *pamong pradja* corps be the *satrio pandita* who arrives with his three servants Semar, Gareng, and Petruk to introduce the *pathet* 9 atmosphere in the history of the nation's struggle!

Vg

Sawarno Djaksonagoro   The Village as a Model (1959)

This extract, like the one before it, is taken from a paper given before the pamong pradja *conference held in Solo in 1959. This paper too has apparently remained unpublished.*

What is the political structure our people should use to reflect their inner will? The best would be one which accords well with their personality and culture. Does an example of a structure fulfilling these conditions still exist? Yes, in village society. You cannot understand village society if you do not understand the personality of the Indonesian people.

The quality which our ancestors saw as characteristic of the highest nobility of spirit was not showing off or pushing oneself forward. This stands in contrast to what is characteristic of the West, with its extreme individualism. Avoiding self-assertion is very much in agreement with our culture in the real sense, which is characteristically anonymous and enduring.

Thus, it is not surprising that no one knows who built what have survived as the cultural relics of our ancestors, though these constitute a cultural heritage of the highest value. No one knows who created these, not even any of the Western scholars. Who, for instance were the architects of such monuments as Borobodur, Prambanan, Panataran, and so on? The answer is: no one knows. If you are fortunate, you may have heard that these monuments were the work of what the Westerners call the Hindu-Javanese, which is another way of saying they do not know.

If we look carefully and with an open mind at life in the village, it becomes obvious that the inhabitants of the village have a feeling of being one with their village. In their eyes their *lurah* [village head] is not only the executive head of their small territory, but their father

---

* The *wajang* performance has three time periods, each with its appropriate and markedly distinct musical mode (*pathet*).

and helper. We in Indonesia used the term *bapak* [father] for *lurahs* before we ever used it as a general term of respect for those we honor. . . .

The lesson to be learned from this is that it is just this quality of anonymity, of not pushing oneself forward, which characterizes all authority which is obeyed by people in Asia in general. If the bearer of authority abandons this quality and asserts himself directly and openly, the aura of authority will fall away from him, and his influence will disappear. This is how it is with the position of the *lurah* in the life and activity of the village. He is prominent without pushing himself forward.

One can see this quality of anonymity not only in the position of the *lurah*, but also in the way in which the villagers discuss and carry out action in the village. They treat meetings of the people's representative council of their village as just village gatherings. At these meetings, which are attended by the *lurah* and the inhabitants of the village, old and young, men and women, discussions are held with an intentional lack of formal procedure. Discussion is like that in a family; it is like a family head discussing a problem with members of his family.

The anonymous character of discussions is such that the meeting does not sense the *lurah*'s leadership because he intentionally desists from exerting it. He does not know who will put forward proposals or who will find ways of solving problems. The atmosphere is pervaded by a feeling of calm and quiet, because the Western-imported notions of ruling party and opposition have not penetrated the village. Discussion does not follow formal procedures, with first and second readings and so on. In brief, the sense of harmony is such that there is no real consciousness of being in a meeting.

But the miracle is that every problem is solved. And when the village people leave the meeting place no one feels proud or that he has emerged victorious because his suggestion was accepted. And on the other hand, no one feels disappointed or unhappy because his proposal was rejected. There is no division between movers of motions and others who are obliged to accept these motions. What the members feel and take home with them is the memory of having reached a decision together.

Anyone of them who violates such a decision faces sanctions heavier than those of the criminal law. Such a person will be ostracized by village society and will feel his isolation as a very severe penalty. So here the functions of judge and prosecutor become unnecessary. The disapproval of the entire village community accomplishes the tasks of judge and prosecutor alike.

When the Dutch set foot in Indonesia, they immediately understood the effectiveness of the *lurah*'s influence in village society. They then began to give this a clearer form with their *Inlandsch Gemeente-Ordonnantie* [Native Community Ordinance], taking the village as an autonomous body. But because they saw the village in ways which were strongly influenced by Western conceptions of autonomy, the Ordinance, intentionally or not, bore the stamp of Western views of Eastern society. Thus, the picture one obtains from reading this Ordinance is a mere caricature, a distortion of the activities of village society.

Moreover, their view of the village, apart from being heavily influenced by Western notions of autonomy, was related to their own interests. In the field of revenue-raising, for instance, the *lurah* as father-helper was degraded to become a collector of land tax and other taxes. In the economic field he was made an agent to find fertile irrigated fields on which foreign firms could plant sugar and tobacco. As far as his police powers were concerned, he became an instrument to safeguard the lives of the giant capitalists, making them free to ride roughshod over others in satisfying their greed. And the foreign Asians used him as a cover to conceal all their dishonest dealings.

Originally a symbol of continuity in village life and a link with the original founders of the village, the *lurah* was pushed out of this position by the Native Community Ordinance and given the very saddening position just described.

In the development of society in Indonesia, it is the villages which have the oldest form. Their form of social organization is the most original and genuine the Indonesian people possess and the one which most fully meets their needs in the sense of according with their personality. So, despite the fact that the Dutch distorted village society, its spirit remains fixed and unchanged and constitutes a source of life and an inspiration for the common people outside the towns.

VI
Islam

About 90 per cent of the people of Indonesia are Muslims. A number of the rebellions launched against Dutch rule in previous centuries were fought under the banner of Islam. And in the twentieth century, too, the first organization to obtain a mass following was the Sarikat Islam, founded in 1912.

Nevertheless, the appeal of Islam in the politics of independent Indonesia has been sectional rather than national. The Islamic parties have found favor among the indigenous trading classes and among the peasants of the more orthodox regions—West Java, Madura, and a number of areas of the outer islands—but large sections of the Javanese peasantry and of the aristocratic and educated sections of most ethnic groups have preferred nationalist or socialist ideologies.

Nor has Islam enjoyed organizational unity. After the decline of the highly political Sarikat Islam in the 1920's two denominational and less distinctively political groups competed for the support of the Islamic masses. The Muhammadijah, founded in 1912, pressed for renewal and purification of Islam along the lines advocated by Mohammed Abduh and his followers in Egypt; this organization was strong particularly in urban commercial communities and among the better educated. The Nahdatul Ulama, established in 1926 by a group of more conservative religious scholars and teachers, mainly from Islamic schools in rural East and Central Java, set out to defend traditional forms of religious belief and practice against the Muhammadijah attack.[*] There were other reformist organizations as well—

* For a discussion of the issues on which reformist-conservative disagreements were centered, see Clifford Geertz, *The Religion of Java* (Glencoe, Ill.: Free Press, 1960), pp. 148–161. Most of the literature on Islam in post-colonial Indonesia is by anthropologists and illuminates the background rather than the substance of Islamic politics. Apart from the works of Geertz, see Robert R. Jay, *Religion and*

for instance the militant and puritanical Persis led by A. Hassan in Bandung—and other conservative organizations, such as Perti and Al Wasjlijah in Sumatra. And in the field of political parties there was the much reduced remnant of Sarikat Islam (renamed PSII) and several smaller organizations which had split off from it. But the principal conflict remained between the Muhammadijah and the Nahdatul Ulama.

These two were, however, moving toward closer cooperation on the eve of the Japanese invasion, and under Japanese auspices they and several small organizations were merged into a new body called Masjumi (Consultative Council of Indonesian Muslims). In 1945 the Masjumi was reorganized and then quickly became one of the strongest parties in Indonesian politics. Passage If from the Masjumi of North Sumatra reflects one aspect of Islamic politics in this period, participation in revolutionary change.

But the Republic proclaimed in 1945 took Pantja Sila, not Islam, as its ideological foundation (see Ic and IVc). Thereafter, at least until 1959, the creation of an Islamic state was the major goal of the Muslim groups, though there were much vagueness and disagreement about what this involved and sometimes hesitation to use the phrase "Islamic state." Only a small minority took the extreme position of armed rebellion on behalf of their ideal. The first to do so was the Darul Islam movement in West Java, led by a former PSII leader, S. M. Kartosuwirjo. In 1953 Tengku Mohammad Daud Beureueh, the principal Muslim leader of the Atjeh region of North Sumatra, followed suit, and VIb expresses straightforwardly the Islamic justification of his rebellion.

The great majority of Muslims continued to work through constitutional channels, hoping for victory in the Constituent Assembly that was to be elected. But the organizational unity they had achieved in the forties was not to last. From 1949 on the Masjumi came increasingly under the control of a group of reformists led by the Sumatran Mohammad Natsir, and in 1952 the predominantly Javanese-led Nahdatul Ulama seceded from it to establish itself as a party in its own right. The result was to split the Muslim vote in the 1955 elections, and

---

Politics in Rural Central Java (New Haven: Yale University, Southeast Asia Studies, 1964); James T. Siegel, *The Rope of God* (Berkeley: University of California Press, 1969); and C. A. O. van Nieuwenhuijze, *Aspects of Islam in Post-colonial Indonesia: Five Essays* (The Hague and Bandung: W. van Hoeve, 1958).

the Masjumi, which had previously been thought capable of securing an absolute majority or large plurality, won only one-fifth of the votes, fewer than the PNI. The Nahdatul Ulama obtained another 18 per cent, but even in combination and with a few much smaller groups the Muslim parties were short of a majority.

Despite broad similarities of outlook between Masjumi and NU members, the two parties played markedly different roles from 1952 onward. The Nahdatul Ulama generally cooperated with the radical nationalist elements (who in their turn were often in alliance with the Communists) and was thus able to participate in all governments after 1953. The Masjumi attempted to stem the Sukarno tide and was gradually bent down by it. Discredited for its association with the regional rebellion of 1958, it was officially banned two years later and thereby forced to accept drastic limitations on its activities.

As an ideology addressing itself to contemporary political affairs, Indonesian Islam has been dominated by the ideas of the reformists, and reformism has been typified by the thinking of the former Masjumi chairman, Mohammad Natsir. A disciple of the fundamentalist A. Hassan but also strongly influenced by Western liberal and socialist thought, Natsir appears characteristically in these pages as an advocate of progress (IIc), stability (VIc), and tolerance (VId). The extreme poles of his political ideology appear in IIh, a plea to cherish parliamentary democracy, and VId, an attack on secularism in the tradition of Hassan.

In their emphasis on stability and economic development, the reformists around Natsir have always stood close to the democratic socialists. This emphasis is expressed here not only by Natsir but by Sjafruddin Prawiranegara, the Masjumi's leading authority on economics (XIIIc).

The Nahdatul Ulama, though of major importance as a political party, is poorly represented here, largely because its leaders have not as yet produced a distinctive political ideology. The NU's statements of goals are usually traditional and scholastic, as in VIa, and almost unrelated to its political strategies. At other times they are mere restatements of positions formulated by the reformists. Its policies of cooperation with the Left, particularly, were not provided with an ideological rationale, a fact which made for persistent tension between the party's central and local leaders and left it vulnerable to charges of opportunism.

Anti-communism has always been a major concern of political Islam

in Indonesia, though it was not always openly expressed. We have included one fairly extreme presentation of Islamic views of communism in XIIg. The violence of expression in this passage is not
unusual for Indonesian Muslim publicists, especially in moments of
crisis. This should be particularly noted in view of the moderate tone
of most of the selections in this section.

The final passage of this section is at once individual and consensual.
By R. A. A. Wiranata Koesoema, a Sundanese aristocrat without strong
ties to any Islamic organization, it expresses an outlook which is
shared by Indonesian Muslims of diverse political views, including
many in secular parties. It also exemplifies the apologetic stance
found in much contemporary Muslim writing, particularly that of the
innumerable reformists we have chosen to ignore for the sake of
presenting a rounded picture of the thought of Mohammad Natsir.

VIa

Nahdatul Ulama God's Law and Its
Interpretation (1954)

*This extract comes from the "Interpretation of the Principles of the
Party," adopted by the Nahdatul Ulama party at its Congress of September 1954. The full text can be found in* Risalah Politik *(Political
Chronicle), 3–4 (Djakarta: Pengurus Besar Nahdatul Ulama, 1955),
pp. 1–18. The argument presented in the final part of the extract
for the importance of adherence to* madzhabs *or schools of interpretation in Islam is distinctive of the Nahdatul Ulama and contrasts with
the Muhammadijah (and general reformist) view of most Masjumi
leaders that a Muslim may adhere to a particular* madzhab *but that
this is not required.*

If the history of human events is subjected to analysis, it will be
seen to consist of two elements—the spiritual and the physical. A
level of happiness can be achieved if these two elements proceed
and are fostered in accordance with their origins and characteristics.
Medical science has determined ways in which man's body—its
conditions, characteristics, welfare, and the way it should be cared
for—can be measured. If the rules of hygiene are violated, for example, if people live in water, eat rocks, drink poison, do not breathe,
and so forth, this human physical structure will be destroyed.

If the body must be treated thus, then clearly the spirit as well must always live in accordance with the rules which govern its development and welfare. If these rules are violated or replaced by other rules which deviate from the obligatory ones, the spirit will be destroyed. Thus does the religion of Islam define the Way of Humanism.

The mind of man is already jaded and exhausted from its attempts to organize world prosperity and peace, and yet the world continues to be in utter confusion. It has been in unstable motion throughout the centuries and right up to this moment because all the charters, treaties, and laws that have existed have been designed solely to regulate outward activity. And this situation will continue to exist as long as the driving force behind it exists, that is, inner corruption and irresponsibility, producing moral waywardness which resides in each human soul. In this matter Islam possesses a guide in these words attributed to the Prophet Mohammed (may his soul be in peace!): "Know you that there is a lump of flesh in the human body, and if it is good, then the whole body will be good, while if it is corrupt then the whole body will be corrupted. Know you that this lump of flesh is the spirit, the soul."

Thus the material world is only capable of organizing human physical activity and has no sanctions whatever other than material ones. Therefore, it is not surprising that slogans of freedom, equality, justice, welfare, mutual assistance, peace, and the like, whether in the political field or the economic or social are all empty resounding phrases. Nor is it surprising that coining pretty slogans and designing constitutions and charters couched in well-chosen and formally correct words should, in fact, make no net contribution to the essence of humanity and civilization. Herein lies the glorious function of Islam in relation to international laws for ensuring a lasting welfare and peace.

If, on the ground that they want to be classed as progressive, against all that is out-dated, and pursuing absolute free thought, people shed the ties of religion, whether in their private lives or in international relations—because they are of the opinion that religion restrains and fetters freedom of thought and action and limits the exercise of basic human rights—they are trapping themselves into becoming utterly out-dated ultra-conservatives. For this tendency is nothing new in human history; it was pioneered by the Aad and Tsamud and their ilk thousands of years before Christ.

People who look around and conclude that religion is a symbol of immobility and conservatism and set themselves to imitate the Western Renaissance, finding this to be more dynamic and progressive, are sorely mistaken. For if they are honest and fair, they must acknowledge that all laws prevailing in the West have their source in Roman law, the development of which was intimately connected with religion (Judaic and Christian) and with further elements which were taken here and there from the Muslim Arabs in the Middle Ages, when Islam flourished in Spain and other parts of Europe.

It is clear, then, that history has never witnessed, in any country, a system of law which did not have its origin in religious teachings. Another conclusion is that all laws and ordinances are based on heavenly law, that is, on religion.

From this religious trunk, people make derivations like branches and twigs, according to their strengths and capabilities, and with an eye to their needs in the light of time and place and long experience of trial and error. Thus, one group borrows from another and each nation takes others as its models, adding or subtracting as is appropriate after mature consideration with the aim of achieving a body of law which best serves the one goal—the common good.

In this respect we submit Islam as a firm and living religion, a religion intended for all mankind from ancient times, which has not changed or altered its principles since the times of the prophets Adam, Noah, Abraham, Moses, and Jesus (that is, in things pertaining to faith in Almighty God and in the unseen). What has changed is only the details of regulating human society to guarantee the common welfare in each age and place.

Furthermore, Islam functions as a religion which has revised and perfected the previous religious teachings, which had suffered change at the hands of man, and restored them to their original holiness and validity.

According to Islamic doctrine, everything has to be based on achieving bliss and averting disaster in the next world and must be valid for all times and places. No action will be prescribed by Islam unless it brings happiness and utility for both the individual and the community. When something is forbidden by Islam, it is certainly because it involves injury or danger for the individual and the community. All this derives from the Guide of Islam as expressed in God's word in the Koran, sura 21:107: "We sent thee not save as a mercy for the peoples."

Why not adopt the laws of Islam, considering that they firmly lay down equality in the relations of man with man, so that all are to be treated the same in rights and obligations, male and female, rich and poor, ruler and ruled, high and low? Why reject Islam, when it takes no account of rank, except as measured by service? Why not accept Islam, which abolishes and forbids narrow and fanatical national pride or chauvinism and pride in race or skin color on the ground that these are not properly things in which to take pride, considering that they cannot be changed by the hand of man? What determines a man's glory or shame is the strength or weakness of the faith that burns in his breast. Why do people object to receiving Islam as a basis for all law, despite the fact that there is no discrimination in Islam between converts and old believers? . . .

Thus does the religion of Islam express the principles of a general charter covering the good, happy, and peaceful life for all civilised people, whose practicability is demonstrated by the fact that the banner of Islam which was planted firmly in the Arabian peninsula fluttered from Spain to China, from the time Islam was first proclaimed by our Great Prophet Mohammed (may his soul be in peace!) as the charter of a civilised state down to the time of his successors from generation to generation.

The basic foundation of the law of Islam is the Koran. But, since it only lays things down in broad outlines, with an elevated style and grammatical quality which allows variations of meaning, it is not admissible that just anyone should interpret it according to his own wish.

Our Great Leader, the Prophet Mohammed (may his soul be in peace!), was the first to explain the inner meaning of the Koran. So all the Sunnah [traditions] which cover his words and deeds form a general commentary on the Glorious Koran, as decreed by God in the Koran: "And we have revealed unto thee the Remembrance that thou mayst explain to mankind that which hath been revealed for them" (16:44); "Verily in the messenger of God ye have a good example" (33:21); "Say, [O Mohammed, to mankind]: if ye love God, follow me; God will love you" (3:31).

Thus the Koran and Sunnah comprise the basic legislation of Islam, the source from which all laws needed by the Muslim people in all ages and places are derived.

In the age of the beginning of Islam, the application of this law presented no problem, because the Koran was in the midst of a people who spoke its own language—namely the Arabs—while the Prophet Mohammed (may his soul be in peace!) was among them to explain it. . . .

After the death of the Prophet Mohammed (may his soul be in peace!), many of his Companions scattered from Medina where they had been with him to Syria, Iraq, Egypt, Yemen, and so on. Many problems arose in that period of rapid expansion of the Muslim community. Many people came to the Companions to ask their opinions and judgments on various problems. The Companions, in their various corners of the earth, gave their opinions and judgments in accordance with the Koran and Sunnah as they had observed their application in similar cases in the days when the Prophet was alive.

From that time differences of opinion began to arise among the Companions. These differences arose over law or jurisprudence for such reasons as this: One Companion had witnessed himself, or heard the Prophet's words on some question, but another Companion had happened not to be present on that occasion. Now this latter Companion, who had not heard those words of the Prophet might "interpret" the law on this subject (that is: apply all his powers of thought and knowledge to reach a decision which would not contradict the text of the Koran and Sunnah). Having given this interpretation, he might later cancel it after receiving information about a conflicting tradition [hadith or Sunnah], or he might maintain it on the ground that the hadith was in his opinion not strong.

This matter required very deep investigation, both on the point of how far the sense was consistent with the existing text, and on the point of how reliable the person who had reported the hadith was. Sometimes when the Companions observed an action of the Prophet, they did not know why he did it, so that there was a difference of opinion as to whether the action was obligatory or merely permissible. Sometimes they disagreed about the reasons for a rule, for instance, the rule about standing when a body is being carried past for burial. Half of the Companions thought that we stand to pay respect to the angel who accompanies the body, so that we ought to stand only for the body of a Muslim. Other Companions held that this standing was on account of the horror of death, so that we should stand for everyone, Muslim or not. Yet others thought that the standing owed its origin to an occasion when the Prophet stood up when the body of a Jew was being borne past in order that his glorious head be not lower than the Jew's corpse, concluding therefore, that

the rule about standing applies exclusively to the corpses of unbe-
lievers.

Then came the third period, that of the *Tabi'in,* of the generation
of Muslims who came when all the Companions of the Prophet had
died. The problem faced now was still greater, as the community had
so grown and the range of Islamic power spread so far that the
Muslim people no longer consisted only of Arabs but included other
peoples, so that to understand the Koran and Sunnah required study
of Arabic and its grammar.

In this and the succeeding age (that of the *Tabi'ut-Tabi'in*) the
explanations and judgments of the Companions were so valued as to
determine the course of legal decisions and jurisprudence alongside
the Koran and Sunnah. In these periods the needs of men for a complete system of law and jurisprudence on various problems of worship
and secular transactions increased in accordance with the expansive
and dynamic character of the society, and, except for the principles
and broad outlines, not all the answers to these problems were found
within the Koran and Sunnah. And yet Islam as a religion, living
and complete in its legal structure and suitable to every age and
generation, had to be ready and able to deal with these problems.

The history of legislation and jurisprudence in Islam knows what
is called *idjtihad,* that is, interpretation such as was effected by the
Companions, the *Tabi'in,* and the *Tabi'ut-Tabi'in. Idjtihad* is the full
application of all powers of thought and knowledge to arrive at a
firm decision on a problem which is not immediately clear in the
Koran and Sunnah. This effort of determining a matter, using the
principles of comparison [*qijas*] and interpretation [*idjma*], may
under no circumstances conflict with the basic principles set down
in the Koran and Sunnah.

Effecting *idjtihad* is not easy, for merely to understand the Koran
requires knowledge of many categories relevant to the Koran, such
as the distinctions between the common and the special, the absolute
and the conditional, the general and the detailed, the abrogating
and the abrogated, and so on . . . and considering that (as we
know) the quality of the grammar in the Koran is so high, that a very
deep knowledge of the Arabic language is necessary.

So it is with learning about the Sunnah, which involves delving
into hundreds of thousands of hadiths—Imam Buchari alone collected 600,000 hadiths. On the hadiths, knowledge is required to
evaluate their quality—for instance, which are *mutawatir* [undis-

rupted], which are *mursal* [imperfect], which are *muttasil* [un-broken], which are *ahad* [insufficiently attested], which are *hasan* [sound], and so on—as well as knowledge of the life history of the person who reported the hadith (the *rawi*), covering who he is and of what character and whether his exact wording may be accepted. . . .

One who effects *idjtihad* must have knowledge of which opinions of the Prophet's Companions and the later scholars have become a matter of consensus [*mudjma'alaih*] and which are a matter of dispute [*chilaf*] and why this is so, and he must be able to conclude, with good reasons, which opinions of the Companions and scholars are closer to the basic principles of the Koran and Sunnah so that they may be accepted. To effect *idjtihad* also requires facility in the science of analogy [*qijas*], that is, to reach by analogy a decision on a matter which is as yet obscure but can be compared with another matter on which the law is already defined. And this work of comparison requires knowledge of what is "clear analogy" [*qijas djali*], "balanced analogy" [*qijas musawi*], and "unbalanced analogy" [*qijas adnawi*], so that a decision may be reached which is in harmony with the basic law.

Thus, briefly, is the matter of *idjtihad*. Those who effect it are called *mudj'tahid*, of which there are various kinds. Those called *mudj'tahid mutlaq* are not limited by the rules laid down by other *mudj'tahid*. Among these are Imam Abu Hanifah, Imam Malik, Imam Muhammad bin Idris ash-Shafi'i and Imam Achmad bin Hanbal. The fruits of their interpretation in the form of complete collections of Islamic laws are called *madzhabs* or schools, that is, the Hanafi, Maliki, Shafi'i and Hanbali *madzhabs*. Through these *madzhabs* a legal basis can be provided to regulate all the needs of man in daily life and in worship. And there is nothing in any *madzhab* which is in contradiction with the Koran and Sunnah. Because these two form the basis of Islamic jurisprudence, it is not possible that the results can conflict with the Koran and the traditions [Sunnah].

Thus, only the *madzhabs* constitute the sure, obligatory, and automatic way which everyone must travel who wishes to implement the religion of Islam in human society, whether in matters of worship or in daily life, in all its branches, individual and social. From ages past right to the present the people of Islam throughout the world have known, acknowledged, and upheld these four *madzhabs* (Hanafi, Maliki, Shafi'i, and Hanbali).

In line with the liberty of thought in Islam, no one is forbidden to "interpret," provided he satisfies the conditions required of a *mudj̆-tahid*. The Muslim people are not worried that the existence of these *madzhabs* will give rise to differences of opinion which cause splits and enmity. This is not to be expected since the variations in essence do nothing more than demonstrate the breadth of Islamic law [*Shari'at*]. So they are considered a blessing. . . .

The constant efforts of mankind throughout its history to create order, prosperity, and lasting peace have always ended in failure. The very mortals who want to free the world from fear and arbitrariness in practice make the world fearful of themselves. They seek sympathy, but their deeds win them hostility. Such is the tragedy of the materialistic world, which worships things because it denies God and religion! What was meant to create peace on earth gives birth to strife and upheaval! The world of materialism, under whatever name or system, is now holding a dagger to its own throat, a tragic spectacle unequaled in human history. And in the future the world will see the fact that the victory belongs not to the laws of materialism but to those of Islam, because Islam maintains the balance between matter and spirit, between this world and the world to come!

VIb
Manifesto of the Atjeh Rebels (1953)

On September 21, 1953, Daud Beureueh "in the name of the Muslim people of the Atjeh region" proclaimed Atjeh part of the Islamic State of Indonesia headed by Kartosuwirjo, so initiating a rebellion which was to continue desultorily for eight years. This is part of the statement issued in justification of the rebellion, originating probably from the group of young Muslim intellectuals around Daud Beureueh. Part of it, expressing regional rather than religious grievances, is not reproduced here. For the Atjehnese, who consider their country "the doorstep of Mecca" and whose prolonged resistance to Dutch colonialism was inspired by Islamic fervor, regionalism is bound up with Islam. The full statement appears in Alibasjah Talsya, Sedjarah dan Dokumen-dokumen Pemberontakan di Atjeh (*Djakarta: Penerbit Kesuma, n.d.*).

In the name of ALLAH, we the people of Atjeh have made new history for we wish to set up an Islamic State here on our native soil.

We are tired of watching developments in the State of the Republic of Indonesia. And no wonder! For many long years we have been hoping and yearning for a state based upon Islam, but, far from these dreams of ours being realised, it has become increasingly evident with each passing day that some Indonesian leaders are trying to steer us onto the wrong path.

We are conscious that the basic principles of the Republican State do not guarantee freedom of religion, freedom to have a religion in the real sense of the word. To put it plainly, the Islamic religion which makes the life of society complete cannot be split up. For us, the mention of the principle of Belief in One God in the Constitution of the State of the Republic of Indonesia represents nothing more than a political maneuver. Belief in the One God is for us the very source of social life, and every single one of its directives must apply here on Indonesian soil. It is not possible for only some of these directives to apply while others do not, be this in criminal or civil affairs, in the question of religious worship, or in matters of everyday life.

If the Law of God does not apply, this means that we are deviating from Belief in the One God.

If the Constitution of the Republic of Indonesia guaranteed freedom of religion, that is to say, Islam, religious law would long have been able to operate in Atjeh, whose people are 100 per cent Muslim.

In fact, the Attorney General's Office has even attempted to introduce a prohibition against sermons containing any politics in mosques and other places they called religious places. But for us, politics is part of the religion we believe in. If we may be permitted to say so, the Attorney General's Office was the first official agency to strive to obstruct us in the practice of our religion. It should be called to account for this before the Constitution of the State and also before God, if officials of the Attorney General's Office are religious beings and believe in God.

It was with bitterness that we heard the remarks of Sukarno, President of the Republic of Indonesia, calling in essence for the establishment of a State based solely on nationalism. Sukarno declared he is afraid that if the State is based upon religion, those who do not want religion to be the basis of the State will secede from it.* Very well: then we shall therefore be the ones to secede from a state that is based upon nationalism. We understand the meaning of national-

* See IVc.

ism and religion. Some people may think that religious people have no sense of devotion to the Indonesian nation and motherland. Such thoughts are only possible among people who do not understand the meaning of the Islamic religion.

These feelings of bitterness and dissatisfaction have nurtured our desire to set up an Islamic State. Some people may blame us for this, but the blame should in the first place be placed on the shoulders of Sukarno himself.

Our God has said: "Any one who does not practise the laws established by God is an infidel." . . .

If we now establish a State, this does not mean that we shall be setting up a state within a state, because in our hearts and souls we have always regarded the State of the Republic of Indonesia as but a golden bridge leading to the creation of the state for which we have long been yearning. But this golden bridge no longer appears as a means of getting where we want but as an obstacle, especially since our sense of loyalty to a Republic based upon nationalism no longer exists. Yet loyalty is the very pillar of a state; and moreover our unity within the Republic of Indonesia is not bound by any universally valid law. Their State experts believe that the laws in force in the Republic should be the laws of the state itself, laws enacted according to certain processes, even though these laws may differ from the laws of our religion; but in our opinion it is the laws of Islam that should apply.

If some people maintain that the establishment of an Islamic State in Atjeh is a violation of the law and will bring chaos in its train, then our answer is that what we do is the natural result of chaotic laws or of chaos in legal affairs. Chaos which results from chaotic laws cannot be remedied unless we first correct the basic cause.

We regard action to set up an Islamic state as being better than living under chaotic laws, and if the Republican Government understands this, it will appreciate that the only way to solve the problem is by improving the basic principles of the state and its policies. The path of violence will be quite useless for we can well imagine how many victims would fall in the armed conflict. This is why we urge the Indonesian Government not to use arms in dealing with our problem. If they do, then we shall certainly resist with whatever arms we have.

VIc
Mohammad Natsir   The Aims of the Masjumi (1956)

This passage comes from the address which Natsir gave on Novem-
ber 7, 1956, when the Masjumi was celebrating its eleventh anniver-
sary. This section of the address is followed by the one reproduced
as IIh. The full address appears in the Djakarta daily Abadi, *Novem-*
ber 9, 10, 12, 1956.

The Masjumi was founded on November 7, 1945, when the struggle
was raging against the onslaught of the Dutch colonial army. The
Masjumi came into being as an expression of the will of the Muslim
community of Indonesia, represented by leaders from every region
of the Indonesian archipelago who had assembled on that day in
Jogjakarta, then the capital of the Republic. The Masjumi became
the embodiment of the ideals of Islam that have for hundreds of
years inspired the Indonesian people, the ideals cherished by tens
of millions of our countrymen, the noble aspirations which, for
centuries, have been defended with devotion and courage.

What is sought in striving for the fulfilment of these ideals? What
is the aim that is aspired to?

It is the aim of liberating man from the toils of superstition, of
banishing from the minds of men all fear except fear of God the
Creator, of upholding the Word of God so that true spiritual freedom
will prevail.

It is the abolition of all tyranny, the ending of exploitation of man
by man, the eradication of poverty that is sought in striving for the
fulfilment of these ideals. To serve these ideals is to strive to abolish
human want and human misery, the scourges that are the source of
irreligion and unbelief. To strive for the fulfilment of these ideals
is to combat the false ideas of chauvinism that are the root of intolerance and enmity between peoples. To be true to these aims is
to strive to build a society in which the dignity of man is accorded
full recognition, a society in which each member extends a helping
hand to his neighbor, a society that rejects the idea of the survival of
the fittest.

Time and time again the history of our fatherland has shown the
determination of the Muslims of Indonesia to defend these ideals
without thought of worldly wealth or even of life itself. The un-

yielding struggle of the Muslims of Indonesia in upholding the Word of God is known to us all here. It is a struggle that has been maintained through the centuries, and the military campaigns of Imam Bondjol, Teungku Tjik Di Tiro, Diponegoro, Hasanuddin, and others must be seen as expressions of the will of the Muslim community to defend the ideals of Islam.

Certainly the nature of the struggle depends on the circumstances and the time. Yet, if the intensity is sometimes less, the devotion of each successive generation of Indonesian Muslims is as a brightly burning torch that can never be extinguished.

The representatives of the Muslim community who assembled in Jogjakarta on November 7, 1945, were fully conscious of the responsibilities they bore as custodians of the heritage of Islam in our fatherland, and they understood, too, the tasks that faced them in adapting the form of struggle to the requirements of the situation then prevailing. In founding the political organization that is the Masjumi they created an instrument of struggle dedicated to serve the Muslim community of Indonesia in upholding the teachings of Islam as the guiding principles in all aspects of private life, in all aspects of social relationships, and in the conduct of affairs of state.

VId
Mohammad Natsir The Dangers of Secularism (1957)

This section comes from a speech which the Masjumi chairman made on November 12, 1957, in the Constituent Assembly, in which the relationship of Islam to the state was the main issue of controversy. For examples of the viewpoint Natsir was opposing, see IVc and Ve. The full Indonesian text appears in Tentang Dasar Negara Republik Indonesia Dalam Konstituante (*Discussions of the Basis of the State of the Republic of Indonesia in the Constituent Assembly*) (*n.p., 1958), III, 429–442.*

Secularism is a way of life, the opinions, aims, and characteristics of which are limited by the boundaries of worldly existence. Nothing in the lives of secularists has objectives beyond the limits of this world, such as the hereafter, God, and so forth.

Although they may at times acknowledge the existence of God, in their day-to-day life as individuals secularists do not recognize the necessity for a relationship between the human soul and God, whether such a relationship be expressed in everyday attitudes, behavior, and actions or in prayer and worship. . . .

Mr. Chairman, to depict the nature of secularism more clearly, let us take as an example a marriage bringing together secularism and religion, as where a religious woman is married to a secular man. For this woman her marriage ceremony in the church is of deep significance. She feels that the union is blessed by God, and she regards it with reverence. For the husband, the ceremony is a meaningless formality, like buying a train ticket. He feels neither reverence nor any other emotion and obeys the rules merely because most people do. When they have children, this is for the wife not merely the fulfilment of her femininity, but also the creation of a new human being, a new member of society, to serve mankind in accordance with God's command. For the husband, having children is no more than a custom to satisfy the instinct to possess descendants. . . .

Secularism, Mr. Chairman, separates the sciences from moral and cultural values. It teaches that ethics should be divorced from science. The view emerges that economics should be divorced from ethics. Social science should be separated from moral, cultural, and religious norms. So, also, should psychology, philosophy, law, and so on.

For the sake of objectivity, ethics may usefully be separated from science, but there are limits to the extent to which the two can be separated. Technological progress has made possible the production of the atom bomb. Should the scientists who contributed their energies to the construction of this bomb share responsibility for its use? For those who divorce ethics from science, it is easy to deny responsibility for the use of the bomb. Here we can see the extent of the influence of secularism. Science has been made an end in itself, "science for the sake of science."

Neither in individual nor social life does secularism provide firm guidelines. The standards used by secularists are of many types. Some condemn co-habitation by an unmarried couple as violating morality; others do not. It is important for a state to decide upon a definite attitude on this matter. Secularism cannot provide a firm viewpoint here; religion can.

The property rights of the individual, the respective rights of workers and employers, the meaning of the phrase "just and prosperous society" are all defined by our faith. Secularism is not prepared to accept Divinity as the basis for solving such problems. So, one is driven to see the sole source of our opinions and values in the evolution of society, which for centuries has gone wherever it has been pushed by secularism. This will not provide a firm set of beliefs. Thousands of societies have given rise to a great variety of values. Consider, for example, the question of suicide. Some societies sanction it; others forbid it. Which attitude is to be adopted? It is important that a state define its general attitude on this matter because this attitude will influence its decisions on relevant legal questions. Here again, secularism cannot provide a positive view.

Whenever the question "What is the meaning of life?" arises, secularism cannot answer it and does not feel that an answer is required. People for whom life has lost its meaning will experience spiritual degeneration. It is not surprising that secularism is conducive to neuroses in individuals. People need a set of beliefs, the basis of which does not change. If this is lost, they are liable to experience a spiritual upheaval. Such are the consequences of secularism for human relations. The connection between religion and mental health is acknowledged by modern psychology. In the secular state, economic, legal, educational, social, and other matters are decided according to material interests, and if attention is sometimes paid to spiritual concerns, this does not go beyond man-made boundaries.

There is one influence of secularism the consequences of which are even more dangerous than the consequences I have already mentioned, and that is that secularism, as we have already explained, degrades the source of the principles governing the lives of men from the Divine to the human level. Such teachings as "do not kill" and "love your neighbor" have their origin, according to secularists, not in Divine Revelation, but solely in what is called social existence.

For example, at some time in the ancient past our ancestors realized that to live in peace and to cooperate would be advantageous to all, and from this realization, it is said, originated the laws forbidding murder and enmity. We will see how dangerous are the consequences of this view. Primarily, by degrading beliefs and civilised standards to the level of a product of a changing human society, men's regard for these principles is lowered. Man feels himself superior to these standards. Instead of regarding them as something to be revered, he regards them solely as tools, since they are his own creation.

Indeed, Mr. Chairman, the secularist regards concepts of God and religion as mere human creations, which are determined, according to him, by social conditions, not by revealed truth. For him religion and doctrines about the existence of God are relative, changing arbitrarily in response to human invention. . . .

Of course, nobody denies that there are good ideas in the Pantja Sila. But the explanations given by the supporters of Pantja Sila indicate that they themselves cannot decide what are its true contents, its proper sequence, its source, its nucleus, and the interdependence of its components. Because these are not clear, difficulties will gradually increase. Since the basis of our state needs to be clear and distinct so as not to confuse the nation, it is difficult for our group to accept something which is vague.

The Pantja Sila itself is responsible for this vague quality. Pantja Sila is an abstraction, a "pure concept" which in reality cannot stand alone. We can compare it with the numbers we use. For example, the number 5 cannot really stand alone. In practice, we can only meet with 5 horses, for example, or 5 chairs, 5 people, 5 boats, and so on. The numeral 5 is always connected with something substantial. Similarly Pantja Sila, being a "pure concept," must, if it is to become a reality, be united inseparably with norms and positive relationships which can give it substance. Left by itself, it is not real; it has no definite existence.

But, Mr. Chairman, Pantja Sila does not want to seek definite substance or root itself in any existing ideology. It wants to continue to stand alone. Because if it acquires roots, it will come to assume a particular ideological form. I do not know whether this form would be Islamic or Communist, but it is just this choosing of a definite form and content that Pantja Sila rejects.

Pantja Sila wants to remain neutral. Indeed the raison d'être of Pantja Sila, the justification of its existence, is remaining neutral. Pantja Sila wants to adopt a neutral stance, above all existing ideologies, a neutral stance, so high above it all, above the emotional turmoil of Indonesian humanity, that it will not acquire any roots whatever in the hearts of the people.

Pantja Sila desires to remain neutral, colorless. If it were to assume a color, an ideology, it would acquire a definite form, it would no longer be neutral; its raison d'être as a common denominator would be lost; it would no longer be Pantja Sila. For this reason Pantja Sila will always want to cling to its neutrality, to reject a positive content. For this reason it will always want to stand alone as a "pure concept." And as a pure concept standing alone it lacks any reality in the positive world. For this reason it can have no substantial existence.

Evidently, Mr. Chairman, provided it survives as Pantja Sila, it does not matter that it has no substantial existence. This is the tragedy confronting a secular and neutral Pantja Sila. If this is the case, Mr. Chairman, how can Pantja Sila be used as the foundation of the state? . . .

Pantja Sila as a state philosophy is for us obscure and has nothing to say to the soul of the Muslim community which already possesses a definite, clear, and complete ideology, one which burns in the hearts of the Indonesian people as a living inspiration and source of strength, namely Islam. To exchange the Islamic ideology for Pantja Sila is, for Muslims, like leaping from the solid earth into empty space, into a vacuum.

VIe

Mohammad Natsir Islamic Tolerance (1954)

This extract comes from an article on "Keragaman Hidup Antar-Agama" (Interreligious Harmony), first published in the Masjumi magazine Hikmah (Djakarta), VII (February 1954), and reproduced in M. Natsir, Capita Selecta, II (Djakarta: Pustaka Pendis, 1957) pp. 225–229.

When the terms of the present provisional Constitution were being discussed in Parliament, it was quite apparent that representatives of the Christian community found the terms of Article 18 guaranteeing "freedom of religious belief, conscience, and thought" to be an inadequate safeguard for religious liberty.

There was a noticeable measure of confusion on the part of numerous members of Parliament regarding the Muslim standpoint on the question of religious freedom. Fortunately, these uncertainties among the parliamentary deputies were dispelled by the statement, made at a special session by the chairman of the Masjumi group, outlining the Muslim viewpoint in respect to this article of the Constitution.

Symptoms of disquiet disappeared from the parliamentary scene, but this disappearance did not at all signify that there were no longer any misgivings or even fears regarding the Muslim standpoint among those sections of the population practising other religious beliefs. Such misgivings are still very much in evidence, and as long as this situation continues it is our duty to make every effort to remove the doubts creating this attitude of fear. . . .

The tenets of Islam uphold a principle which can serve as a means of solving the problem; the ideals of our faith teach us to respect the diverse cultural patterns in Indonesia where various religious beliefs have been followed for centuries.

In affirming the Muslim standpoint there are several points which should be emphasized. First, it must be stressed that the attainment of belief in the Oneness of God is, in effect, a spiritual revolution liberating man from the bonds of superstitious fears. With the attainment of belief in the Oneness of God man is brought to an awareness of the Being of God to whom he has surrendered his spirit. But man must come to an awareness of the Being of God without compulsion of any sort. In the teachings of Islam it is insisted that genuine acceptance of religious faith cannot be acquired under constraint.

Second, it is the Muslim view that only a faith held in the way that conforms to the teachings of Islam can be considered as a true religious faith. When the profession of religious belief represents merely a conventional expediency and is not based on a sense of deep-rooted spiritual conviction, there is no question of true religious faith. Again, it may be pointed out that the tenets of Islam specifically reject any forced imposition of religious belief. In the Koran we read, "There is no compulsion in religion." This statement comprises the basis of the Muslim attitude to religious faith.

Third, awareness of the Being of God is a favor conferred by Divine grace, a favor that is to be acquired only through proper teaching, through careful guidance, and through calm and reasoned discussion. The followers of Islam observe the injunction given in the Koran: "Call unto the way of thy Lord with wisdom and fair exhortation, and reason with them in the better way." Muslims are commanded to exhort, to persuade with reasoned argument, but to abjure the use of force in seeking to spread the teachings of the Prophet.

Fourth, confronted with the differences of views and the divergences of belief that are encountered in the course of everyday existence, the Muslim must neither remain indifferent nor give way to despair. Rather must every Muslim seek some common feature in the various religious beliefs. It is the duty of every Muslim to promote understanding between the congregations of different faiths by putting into practice the teaching of the Koran: "Say: O People of the Scripture! Come to an agreement between us and you: that we shall worship none but Allah, and that we shall ascribe no partner unto Him and that none of us shall take others for lords besides Allah."

Fifth, every Muslim must have an unfailing capacity for self-restraint, never giving way to impulses of passion, in endeavoring to foster better understanding with the followers of different faiths. With an unshakeable conviction in the truth of his creed, and strong in the awareness that Allah is the God of all mankind, the Muslim must personify the spirit of tolerance. . . .

Sixth, the attitude of tolerance emphasized in the teachings of Islam is an attitude of positive action. It is an attitude that calls for a preparedness to seek a basis of conciliation between diverse beliefs. But more than that—freedom of religious belief is for a Muslim dearer than life itself. It is the obligation of every Muslim not only to succor those of other faiths who are victims of religious persecution and to provide those who have been deprived of religious freedom with the facilities for worshipping God in their own way, but also, should the need arise, to defend with his life the right of others to liberty of religious belief. The teachings of the Koran require that a Muslim defend those who are driven from their homes for having worshipped God. It is required that a Muslim should defend monasteries, churches, places of prayer, and mosques wherein the name of Allah is spoken.

This is the attitude toward other religions that is enjoined in the Koran and the hadith, and it is this attitude that the entire Muslim community in Indonesia must uphold, inspired by the desire to serve God.

If religious liberty is to be really safeguarded, if, in the interests of national unity, real understanding is to be fostered among the various religious communities in Indonesia, obviously, no effort must be spared to inspire the entire Indonesian people with the attitude of tolerance and mutual respect described above.

VIf

R. A. A. Wiranata Koesoema Islam and Democracy (1948)

This extract comes from a booklet, Islamietische Democratie in Theorie en Praktijk (*Bandung: Pusaka, 1948*).

The Islamic community in its real essence is democratic. It affirms the parliamentary principle and gives equal social and civil rights to everyone, irrespective of nationality and religion.

The Caliph, the spiritual and temporal head of the Muslims, was not a dictator who took decisions himself and forced the people to do his bidding, denying them any right to participate in deciding issues which had the closest connection with their well-being. No, that would cry to Heaven as a violation of what is due to any man by virtue of his birth, be he rich or poor, of high or low birth: freedom of expression in the best sense of the word, equality of rights and opportunities, and comradeship.

Quite the contrary: the democratic spirit of equality, liberty, and community responsibility was so deeply rooted in the hearts of Muslims that any tyranny was out of the question from the beginning.

The Caliphs considered themselves responsible to the people and could be called to account for their acts of government. In his speech on the occasion of his election as Caliph, Abu Bakr (632–634) expressed this point of view in this way:

> Oh my people, I have been elected as your leader, although I am not the best among you. Therefore, help me when I am acting rightly, and bring me back to the right path when I deviate from it and do wrong. The weak among you shall be strong in my eyes, until I have defended their true right, and the strong among you shall be weak in my eyes until I have made them observe the duties which are binding upon them. . . . No people ever gives up the fight on God's road, but God destroys it. Obey me, as long as I obey God and His Prophet [Mohammed]. If I do not obey God and His Prophet, I have no claim to your obedience.

This statement by the first Caliph shows that the Caliph, unlike a dictator, was only the steward of the Islamic State and was this in the name of the people, which was itself bound by the law, even as the Caliph was. Of course, he had to see to it that the law was obeyed. Therefore, acts of the Caliph could be reasonably discussed and faulted, for, as Abu Bakr himself wished it, anybody had a right to show him the right path if it happened that he had been led astray. In other words, the people controlled the leadership and had a voice in the government of the land.

In Islamic democracy it is out of the question that the Caliph should have to be obeyed blindly in every respect and that no one should have a right to challenge his authority. To invest a mere mortal with unchallengeable authority would lay the axe at the root of Islamic doctrine. Is spiritual liberation not the most important message of Islam and the most beneficent blessing it has brought to humanity?

For that reason those who follow others blindly are compared in the Holy Book of the Muslims, the Koran, with "dumb, driven cattle." No, they are even lower than that (7:179). When non-Muslims objected that they could not embrace Islam because their forefathers had followed a different path, the Koran answered them with the question "Even if their forefathers were foolish?" (2:170; 5:104).

The only mortals, after the Holy Prophet Mohammed, whose authority calls for the greatest respect are our parents. Here too, however, the Koran emphasizes: "But do not obey them when they insist that you identify with Me [that is, God] that of which you have no knowledge" (31:14, 15); in other words, when they insist that you accept as your masters, apart from God, objects or human beings; that you ascribe to them the same characteristics as to God; that you adore them and obey them blindly (3:63); or that you give in to your own base passions (25:43). A similar restriction applies also to the authority of the Caliph, for the Koran emphasizes: "Help each other in goodness and godliness and do not help each other in sin and aggression" (5:2). In other words, the Caliph cannot demand of his subjects to follow him in what they consider evil. . . .

The foundation of Islamic democracy is the liberty of the individual spirit. No one has a divine right to govern; no one has been chosen by God as a special instrument to express His will, so that he is free from error or mistake. That would amount to deification of man, which is the gravest sin man can commit (31:13; 4:48), because one of the consequences of such a deification of man is that the Leader is relieved from all responsibility for his acts of government, and all public control ceases.

The opportunity to compete for the office of Caliph is given to everyone, and only he can attain this office who fulfils the Koranic requirement: "The most distinguished among you is he who best attends to his duty [in respect of God and His creatures]" (49:13). Neither riches nor the numerousness of his offspring brings a man closer to God, but faithfulness and good works (34:37). For anyone having the required qualifications Islam opens the opportunity to be on the highest rung of the social ladder to which his achievements entitle him.

It is of the greatest importance for the State who and what sort of man the Caliph is. For that reason the Prophet was not succeeded after his death by any of his descendants, but in succession by *elected* Caliphs, Abu Bakr, 'Umar, and 'Uthman (644–656), while after these three notables one of the Prophet's nephews, 'Ali, was elected Caliph (656–661). For that reason, too, Islamic history records many examples of slaves who climbed to this highest position. . . .

According to Islam, all peoples and all races are equally God's chosen peoples. All peoples equally enjoy God's blessings. All are endowed with gifts of head and heart; all are fitted with equal means for the development of body and soul. The applicaton of these gifts and endowments and the proper use of these means bring rewards. And this applies to all parts of humanity, without distinction of race, blood, or nationality.

Doesn't the sun shine equally on all? Don't they all breathe His air equally? Doesn't God's earth give equal means to sustain life for all? Doesn't history show that those who are considered backward people today, once occupied the pinnacle of civilization? Does the world have any one country, one nation, or one race, which can rightly boast to be the only creator of civilization and can proclaim from the rooftops that it owes none of its culture to that of neighboring countries or peoples? Aren't the various civilizations continuations or, at best, transformations and combinations of various elements of several other cultures? Has any culture ever existed as an isolated self-contained unit? Doesn't all this prove that humanity forms a single family, which inherits and bequeaths the same inheritance of important goods?

And further, didn't God send a Prophet to every people to bring it to a higher moral and spiritual level (10:47; 13:7; 22:67; 5:48)? It is for that reason that the Koran teaches us that all prophets form a single community (21:92; 23:51, 52), that all of mankind are one people (2:213; 4:1; 20:22), and that all Muslims are under an obligation to believe in and honor all prophets of the world (2:4; 2: 136; 4:152). Mohammed tried in this way to create a general fraternity of mankind.

This idea of the brotherhood of man has made such a deep impression on Muslims, that one of their greatest poets wrote a poem, which comes down to this, that the several parts of the human race relate to each other as the members of one body, to such an extent that when one of them is hurt the other members feel the pain, too. . . .

What we mean by democracy in Islam is not only universal suffrage or government of the people, by the people, and for the people. Nor is it just that we are inspired by the conviction that we humans are equal in our quality as spiritual beings and that the individual can only develop himself by entering into the service of his fellowman. There is far more to it than just that.

The principle of human equality which is preached by all true religions is without doubt ennobling, as is the idea of the human fraternity or social community which transcends geographical, racial, and national borders. But it is, at best, a theory, an ideal awaiting realisation. If it is not carried into practice, it remains a pious wish or a hollow phrase, fit for hanging on the wall as an ornament.

Let us not forget that our outward conduct is only a mirror of our inner nature and that our social habits and relationships are determined by the condition of our feelings and emotions.

We must also not forget that matter is by nature unequal. With all the goodwill in the world we cannot remove this inequality or diversity from the realm of matter or destroy it, however hard we may try. Leaving aside the other things of the created world, we cannot make two human beings look alike, feel alike, think alike, or act alike. It is, therefore, futile to try to bring about equality or unity by stopping this diversity in its existence.

Actually, the striving for unity, equality, and fraternity does not belong to the realm of matter. It is an inner spiritual longing, although it tries to express itself in material surroundings. So the Koranic program of action begins with spiritual training, the disciplining and the ennoblement of the human spirit.

What, then, does Islam do to see to it that the ideals of human unity, equality, and fraternity play a significant part in the life of Muslims? What does it do to see that there is no contradiction between theory and practice, between ideal and reality?

Like all other true revealed religions, it creates a suitable frame of mind among its faithful by impressing human unity, equality, and fraternity upon them deeply, by repeated instruction. By doing away with the priesthood and with hereditary kingship, it makes man completely free and raises him to full mastery of his own material as well as spiritual destiny. The value of the soul and the dignity of the individual are placed prominently in the foreground (79:40; 91:9, 10; 17:70; 95:4, 5). It regards spiritual greatness, godliness, and righteousness, which find expression in good works, as the only grounds for human respect, and so destroys all distinctions of race, color and position. It declares further that rich and poor, high and low, are equal with God, as they have proceeded from one and the same being (6:99). Poverty and inferiority are two different things in Islam. There is enough real equality in Islam to undo the greatest of inequalities.

Apart from and in addition to this theoretical aspect, Islam also has its laws on production and distribution, its agrarian and commercial laws, the purpose of all of which is the establishment of an ideal socialistic world.

But it begins, as I have said, with the regulation, the disciplining and ennobling of the spiritual impulses and instincts. This is done by spiritual means, all of which aim at effectively socializing man's emotions, for instance, by the communal prayers five times per day, in a mosque or an open field, at which there is not the slightest discrimination between high and low, rich and poor; by the annual thirty days of fasting which make the rich experience bodily to some extent the fate of the poor and the indigent; the *zakat* or taxation for charity; and, finally, the yearly meeting of Muslims of all nationalities, races, colors, and countries of the whole world at Mecca, where the Islamic principle of equality and fraternity is strictly observed, and where the faithful are required, all without exception, from the richest to the poorest, from king to lowliest subject, to be on a footing of absolute economic equality. On that occasion all are required to do away with the last vestige of distinction, their clothing. Dressed in only two seamless sheets of linen, they assemble around the Holy Dwelling, the Kaaba, and while walking in procession around it, they call out as if by one mouth, *Labbaika-llahumma, labbaika!* "Here I am, all at your service, O Lord. Here I am, all at your service!"

So the Muslims have a view of life which is unequaled in its breadth and universality, and the methods to put this universal view into practice, which make them the only spiritually democratic people in the world.

VII
Democratic Socialism

Socialism and democracy enjoyed the almost universal approbation of the political public in our period, and few spokesmen of any political tendency would have failed to declare themselves both democrats and socialists. The compound "democratic socialism," however, is here applied to the thinking of Soetan Sjahrir and his followers, which owed much to European social-democracy and found organizational form in the Indonesian Socialist Party (PSI).* "Democratic" as a qualifying term is not entirely appropriate, for the men of this persuasion had scant success among the mass of the people. The PSI's membership was largely limited to urban people of higher modern education, and the considerable influence it enjoyed came through channels other than the ballot box or mass rally. Where they differ from other Indonesian socialists is in their concern for individual freedom, their openness to world intellectual currents, and their rejection of obscurantism, chauvinism, and the "personality cult." "Liberal socialism" might be a better label, were it not that "liberalism" in Indonesian political language is closely linked with unbridled capitalism.

Organizationally, democratic socialism had its beginnings in 1932 when Sjahrir and Hatta returned from their studies in Holland and established the Nationalist Educational Association (Pendidikan Nasional Indonesia or "New PNI"). This body devoted itself to a strategy of building up cadres of politically mature, self-reliant members who would be able to keep nationalist activity going even if their top leaders were put away. The contingency for which this strategy was

* For a discussion of the PSI see Jeanne S. Mintz, *Mohammed, Marx, and Marhaen: The Roots of Indonesian Socialism* (London: Pall Mall Press, 1965); and the Introduction by B. R. O'G. Anderson to S. Sjahrir, *Our Struggle* (Ithaca, N.Y.: Cornell Modern Indonesia Project, Translation Series, 1968).

devised was not long in coming. In 1934 Hatta and Sjahrir were both arrested and sent into exile in East Indonesia, to be released only on the eve of the Japanese invasion.

During the Japanese occupation Hatta went along with Sukarno in cooperating with the country's new rulers, but Sjahrir led a small underground contact organization against them. After independence was proclaimed, a reaction set in against the collaborationist leaders; and this, combined with the advantages which were expected to accrue if negotiations with the Allies were handled by a man untainted by collaboration with the Japanese, soon brought Sjahrir to the Prime Ministership. He held this post between November 1945 and June 1947.

The first passage in this section comes from this early postwar period, as do the extracts from Sjahrir's pamphlet *Our Struggle* (XIa and XVc) and the young Republic's Political Manifesto (Ie).

In 1945–1947 one of the strongest parties in Indonesia was the Socialist Party led by Sjahrir and Amir Sjarifuddin, which sought to combat the authoritarian legacies of the Japanese period as well as to prevent the re-establishment of colonial rule. As in other countries the struggle against fascism had blurred for a time the distinction between Communism and Social-democracy. But in February 1948 the Communist-sympathizing Amir Sjarifuddin took a majority group of the Socialist Party into a Communist-controlled People's Democratic Front (FDR), and this led Sjahrir and the group of young intellectuals around him to leave the Socialist Party and establish a new Indonesian Socialist Party (PSI).

The PSI remained a major political force in the early 1950's, also enjoying considerable prestige outside Indonesia. Our second passage in this section, a part of Sjahrir's address to an Asian socialist conference, comes from this period.

But the party's influence within Indonesia was waning. It had greater attraction for intellectuals than any other party and a pivotal role in much of the country's political debate. Moreover, its sympathizers included prominent leaders of other parties and others highly placed in the army and civil service. But its xenophilia became more and more of a political liability and in the middle and late 1950's it was frequently criticized, in a way which found wide resonance, for being "cut off from the people." Examples of this criticism can be seen in IIIa, IIIc, and IXb. Its lack of mass appeal was shown very clearly by its poor performance in the 1955 elections.

President Sukarno's actions to establish Guided Democracy created great dilemmas for the PSI. A few of its leaders joined the 1958 rebellion in Sumatra and Sulawesi and denounced Sukarno's government in uncompromising terms. Most preferred to make a minimal accommodation to the new order, sailing perilously between the Scylla of sacrifice of principle and the Charybdis of police repression and retaining a limited influence as muted critics of the regime. This contrast is well expressed in the statements of Sumitro Djojohadikusumo and Rosihan Anwar (IIIk, IIIh).

The outstanding representative of later democratic socialist thought and of the majority view in the division which developed in attitudes to Guided Democracy was Sjahrir's brother-in-law, the author and publisher Soedjatmoko who provides the last two excerpts of this section as well as IXc and XIIId.

One of the most striking characteristics of the democratic socialists, their openness to the culture of the outside world, is beautifully expressed in the artists' manifesto reproduced as our third extract in this section, while their radical commitment to modernization is illustrated in IXe. Many passages in other sections of this book reflect democratic-socialist viewpoints, even when the authors are not members of the PSI. Among them are Ib, IIa, IIi, IXe, XIIIb, and XIIIf.

VIIa
"S" Our Nationalism and Its Substance (1946)

This extract comes from an article first published in Dutch and then in English in the Djakarta journal The Voice of Free Indonesia *of April 27, May 4, and May 18, 1946. Its title there is "Our Nationalism and Its Substance: Freedom, Social Justice, and Human Dignity." Its authorship is sometimes attributed to Sumitro Djojohadikusumo.*

The phenomenon of Indonesian nationalism can only be understood in relation to the other movements for freedom to be found in all Asian countries. These began in the form of a reactionary resistance to living in servility and submission to the Western countries which exerted political, military, and economic power in the countries concerned. In their search for a way of being able to determine their own destiny and to protect themselves in life, the people in these Eastern countries first tried to master the technical and organizational methods through which Western domination was outwardly manifested. . . .

However, in their search for Western knowledge and mastery of

Western technique, most of these people maintained an inner cultural seclusion. While they wanted to master Western knowledge and power, they were indifferent with regard to the origin from which that knowledge and technique had ultimately sprung, namely, the culture and mind of the West. This phenomenon caused a situation of inner uncertainty in life; people often did not feel the necessity of binding cultural norms, a situation which must again be explained by the strong anti-Western tendency which could be observed in every Asian movement at a particular stage. It can be explained psychologically by the irresolution and indecision which surrounded the mental atmosphere of our movement in that stage. There was inner seclusion on the one hand and suffering on the other, due to the realization that one needed the technical, organizing means of the West if one wanted to play a part in world events. This irresolution caused a resentment and aversion against all that had the slightest Western trace, and as a result of it the struggle for freedom ran the risk of being caught in the contradiction between East and West. Japan, for instance, has never been able to go beyond this phase.

But, as the process of maturation developed, clear signs could be observed of a later stage. The movements for freedom in India and Indonesia, for instance, have broken the contradiction between East and West, with the result of a widening of the mental horizon which makes it possible for the struggle to be fought against the background of universal values. In penetrating deeper and being receptive to the overwhelming riches of the Western mind, the leaders of this later stage found their inner certainty again. They allowed themselves to be influenced by those elements of culture which could be fertilizing and developing and could help build free and harmonious personalities. And at the same time they realized that it was required of the West that it should conform to the standards of truth, beauty, and kindness —standards which have been proclaimed for ages by the prophetic figures of the East though differently formulated and applied.

The West itself has been in a process of self-examination and reform for a long time. The realization has grown in the West that the application of knowledge and technique can have fatal results if moral values and standards are trampled upon and denied. The chaotic collision of world powers, with all the potentialities this contains—annihilation by atomic energy—is seen there as man suffering at his own hands because of a lack of inner, moral resistance.

The essential task for modern man today, whether he comes from the West or the East, is to rescue himself from the abyss by re-establishing his proper position in relation to the cosmos. In all this he must be led by the standards of truth, beauty, and kindness which together constitute the elements of human dignity.

This universal concern is today no monopoly of either East or West; it is the task of man as man, whether he considers it as an injunction of the Almighty or considers man as a being who finds his center in himself, but considers it his primary duty, if he is to be inwardly distinguished, to live by noble standards.

But the realization and maintenance of human dignity is not possible in a situation of servility and submission of one people to another. There can be no human dignity without freedom to determine one's own fate. We have experienced all too painfully that in a system of domination human dignity with all its components of truth, beauty, and kindness are trampled upon and violated.

Hence, there is fierce resistance to all that hampers and frustrates freedom and a strong will to determine ourselves the form of the new society we seek to build. This is not resistance driven primarily by feelings of hatred, resentment, and aversion toward foreigners. It has arisen because we consider freedom as a condition, as an essential condition without which it is impossible for us to be ourselves, to form ourselves and our community.

Freedom is a condition for human dignity. But freedom and human dignity are ideas which remain sterile if they do not find concrete application in the society in which we live. . . .

Under the system of capitalism and imperialism the functional distribution of the social product is left to the free working of social forces. Defenders of liberal economic policy such as Lionel Robbins and Friedrich Hayek base their reasoning on the assumption that only under a system of free marketing and free pricing would the functional imputation to the several social forces be sufficiently guaranteed. According to these theorists, a free market means that there would in the long run be no chance of under-payment or over-payment. . . .

But, and this is too easily forgotten by the defenders of the liberal economy, the element of power plays an important and often decisive role in the totality of factors on the side of demand and supply, respectively. And this element of power needs to be considered in a broad sense, involving the organization of the parties involved, in-equalities of income on the side of the demanders and suppliers respectively, and so on. . . .

As regards Indonesia and other colonial countries the disadvantage is obviously on the side of the ruled. On the one side there is an over-supply of unorganised and illiterate laborers, a complete lack of social legislation, and small landholders who lack money and have found it difficult to adapt themselves in their contacts with Western organiza-tions. On the other hand there is the strong and well-organized capital-ist power of these Western firms and organizations. . . .

Because of these circumstances the economic problem in colonial countries should be looked upon as a special and acute case of the general problem of a just distribution of the social product. A specially acute case because under a colonial system economic power can make itself felt in such an unlimited way. The economic policies of Western governments were far too greatly influenced by powerful economic groups.

It is, therefore, obvious that the political liquidation of the colonial system should be accompanied by a change in social and economic conditions. The distribution of the social product should no longer be left to the forces of a free market.

The organization of economic life we have in mind is a planned economy guided by socialist ideas. A just distribution of the social product, such as would meet the demands of human dignity, is only conceivable within the framework of socialism.

VIIb

Sjahrir   Nationalism and Internationalism (1953)

This extract comes from an address of the same title which was given to the first Asian Socialist Conference, held in Rangoon in Janu-ary 1953. The address was published by the Asian Socialist Confer-ence in the same city and same year. We have made minor verbal changes.

Among peoples struggling for their freedom the drive to express their individuality is not only understandable and just but necessary. The drive for more pronounced self-esteem and self-assertion is necessary. These constitute the main parts of the urge for emancipa-tion from slavery and aggression. But among peoples who are independent and free, this urge for differentiation often degenerates into arrogance and excessive pride. Then the drive to excel turns into ambition and lust for power and into the psychology of imperialism. . . .

Nobody can any longer deny that the multi-nation system in Western Europe has become something irrational. Each country persists with its own regulations, tariffs, and so on and intends to maintain its own separate administration in the face of much bigger problems involving them all, such as common defense, the scarcity of raw materials, and the question of markets and, indeed of such problems as the need for a common policy regarding the continuation of Western European culture, which, despite its diversities, is characterized by a basic community of spirit. In facing the rest of the world, Western Europe has had a single history in the last few centuries, even though this was a history of internecine warfare. One can speak of one tradition and one spiritual heritage, namely Western culture and Western democracy. Nationalism in the various countries of Western Europe continues to obstruct the rapid realisation of an idea which has long been accepted as necessary, namely, the creation of a United States of Europe.

This same nationalism in the respective countries of Europe makes it difficult for the countries which possess colonies to give these up and seek a new relationship with ex-colonial peoples on the basis of equality. National prestige, national egotism, makes such an attitude impossible. For this reason, even the moderate nationalism of the democracies of Western Europe is known in the colonies as aggressive, militant, and tyrannical. For the same reason this nationalism, which is tolerant and moderate at home, wages wars in the colonies, thereby keeping the world in tension and danger of war, although the majority of the people in the home country have no notion of the consequences of this nationalism of theirs for colonial peoples longing for freedom, or of its repercussions for the world situation in general. It is clear enough that even this tolerant and democratic nationalism still contains sufficiently objectionable and even dangerous aspects.

The nationalism of colonial peoples aspiring toward an independent national existence is completely different, however. It wages its struggle against the aggressive, expansionist, and imperialistic nationalism which regards the backward countries as no more than prey and booty to be possessed or, at best, to be divided among themselves. It also wages a struggle against the ambiguous nationalism of the democratic

West in so far as it tolerates and perpetuates colonial conditions. It wages a struggle against this ambiguity and demands that the same norms of democracy be applied to it which the West applies to itself. It demands the right of self-determination, strives for freedom from oppression and exploitation.

This nationalism is a source of new life and strength for backward peoples. It is capable of instilling greater energies into them. It arouses enthusiasm in them, faith in their capacity to create a better life and in their ability to catch up with the more advanced countries. This nationalism is able to strengthen men's will for the progress of mankind. It stands under the sign of progress and justice. Inasmuch as it really expresses the aspirations of the people, it is progressive.

But as soon as freedom has been achieved, this nationalism is exposed to the dangers of the nationalism of independent nations. Then we are confronted with the problem of adapting this nationalism to the needs of mankind for peace, progress, and prosperity. If this fails, then this nationalism will become a negative factor, a factor of conservatism and reaction. Then it will become egocentric and degenerate into intolerance and self-glorification. This kind of nationalism will then not contribute to the lessening of world tensions. On the contrary, it will increase international tension and unrest. As long as the struggle is directed against the old rulers, for instance to the achievement of economic freedom after political freedom has been won, this danger will not be so great. But even during this struggle the point may be reached at which the feeling of self-importance and self-assertion has risen so high that people believe that the life of other peoples, which have not yet advanced as far as they themselves, should be subordinated to their own country's growth and progress.

A world order aimed at the maintenance of peace and the regulation of relationships between peoples comes into conflict with the egotism of those nations which are not farsighted enough to realise that world peace and order are a common interest of all nations. It is impossible, indeed unthinkable, that one nation could impose its will on the rest of the world. Thus, nationalism can never eliminate antagonisms. Nationalism should make people conscious of the necessity of international cooperation in the interest of the people themselves and should prevent the continuous clash of wills, tensions, struggle, and war between the nations.

This is not all. The fact is that nations depend on each other for their continued existence. There is a world economy; a world division of labor and of production has developed outside the conscious will of men. There are countries which cannot continue to exist if the greater part of their needs in food for their peoples is not imported. There are countries which will never be able to catch up in their economic development unless they establish a much more intensive intellectual intercourse with countries more advanced technically; these countries cannot hope to continue in existence if there is no improvement in their techniques of production. There are countries which are overpopulated, countries which cannot hope for progress as regards their prosperity or their standards of living, or even to maintain these standards even with improvements in their productive apparatus and organization because their rate of population increase is greater than their rate of increase of production and national income. Besides, there are still many areas in the world which are practically unpopulated. There are heavily industrialized countries where agriculture does not produce enough food for the population. There are agrarian and underdeveloped countries which have to import all the modern industrial goods which make for the amenities of life from abroad. There are relatively fertile and sparsely populated areas where the standard of living is low and where there is poverty only because techniques of production are primitive, because the rates of increase of population and production are not equal. These are all problems which can only be solved rationally and on an international basis.

There is an extreme kind of nationalism which is only out for its own immediate interests and which tries to get and keep everything for itself, thereby inviting countermeasures from other countries. If this is allowed to go on, the world will consist of watertight compartments called nations which will finally strangle each other or cause explosions, and, possibly, one big explosion or world war. Nationalism in this extreme form is irrational and will lead to disaster. It can provide no solution for the problems arising out of the community of peoples and nations in this world.

Internationalism, on the contrary, is rational; it is based on dispassionate reason; it is also based on the trends of the actual development of mankind. . . .

However one particular kind of internationalism, that of orthodox Marxism, is open to criticism. . . . Marx and Engels envisaged an internationalism without nations, a unity and common march of the workers or proletariat united in a way which would transcend all national boundaries, in the face of the capitalist class which was also united throughout the world and across all national boundaries. This internationalism was to be able to establish world government, a world dictatorship of the proletariat, after the world revolution. The internationalism of Marx and Engels was not conceived in terms of the cooperation and organization of all nations, but as a unity of all the workers and the proletariat, ignoring the position of the nation. This was the internationalism of the class struggle as conceived by Marx and Engels. At the beginning of the Soviet Revolution, Lenin was still thinking in the framework of this concept of internationalism, but soon afterwards he gave it up and began with the idea of building socialism in one country. Trotsky, on the other hand, clung to the old idea much longer.

As we have pointed out before, there is nothing left of this kind of internationalism in Stalin's Russia today. The Russian state and nation have acquired an all-embracing importance in the thinking of the Russian communists. The proletarian internationalism which is still being presented as the new version of the class internationalism of Marx and Engels and of the *Communist Manifesto* is no more than a misleading label for Russian nationalism and for the endeavor to make the workers and the nationalist movements in the colonies and the backward countries subservient to Russian nationalism.

Internationalism, as we understand it, proceeds from the existence of nations which are component units in the society of the nations. These units have come into being because of several circumstances— a common tradition, common origins, a common language, a common fate and shared ideals such as the ideal of freedom of the oppressed peoples, and so on. The existence of nations is manifest and asserts itself daily among all groups and classes of a particular nation. It is not only the bourgeoisie which is nationally conscious but also the worker and the peasant. Nations are existing realities. So one cannot conceive of internationalism without acknowledging the existence of these nations as a basis. Nationalism is the soul of each nation. It is that from which the individuality and personality of that nation stems.

The problem of internationalism today is to achieve concerted co-operation among nations on the basis of recognition of the reality of these nations and their nationalism. The problem is also to prevent nationalism from leading to constant conflicts and chaos in the life of the people. To this end the nations must realise more and more the necessity for internationalism. . . .

There is ample grounds for criticizing the United Nations. But it appears that the U.N. has more chance than the League of Nations to develop into a real world organization aiming at the establishment of a world order where war will be impossible and where the licentiousness of national sovereignties will be restrained and checked by a collective body, an organization of all nations concerned to control relations between peoples and nations.

In the long run it may perhaps be possible for such an organization to undertake an even more positive task, the elimination of some of the basic causes of discontent among nations. It could do this by abolishing inequality and injustice in the distribution of the world's production, by abolishing the exploitation of nations by other nations so that there will no longer be discord among them, by granting all nations and peoples an equal position before the law, by eliminating all colonies and granting independence and freedom to all peoples who can then become members of that organization of the nations, and by putting an end to all the tensions and antagonisms caused by the unequal development of the world's peoples, by raising the so-called underdeveloped countries and peoples to the level of the developed countries. In short, such an organization would have the positive task of working to achieve justice and security in the life of the nations and peoples. . . .

The road for us, democratic-socialists, is clear. So is the direction we have to take. Our position with regard to nationalism and internationalism is now also clear. We are internationalists with a correct understanding of nationalism.

VIIc
Gelanggang   Heirs of the Culture
of the Whole World (1950)

This "Statement of Faith," dated February 18, 1950, was composed by a group of writers associated with the cultural journal Gelanggang. *The writer Asrul Sani is believed to have played a major role in drafting it. This translation, by A. H. Johns, was published in* Meanjin *(Melbourne), XIX (December 1960), 387.*

We are the legitimate heirs of the culture of the whole world, a culture which is ours to extend and develop in our own way. We are

* Reprinted by permission of *Meanjin Quarterly.*

born of the common people; and for us this term implies the inchoate mass from which new and healthy worlds of thought and expression may be born.

It is not so much our brown skin, black hair, and slanting cheek bones that make us Indonesian, but rather what is revealed by our character and way of thinking.

We do not wish to limit by a name this Indonesian culture of ours. On the other hand we do not understand it as the refurbishing of something old to be a source of self-satisfaction; we envisage it as something vigorous and new. For this Indonesian culture will be determined by the manifold responses made on our part to stimuli from every corner of the globe, each one of them true to its own nature. And we will oppose any attempt to restrict or impede a re-examination of our scale of values.

For us, our revolution implies the discarding of old and outmoded values, fit only for obloquy, and their replacement by new ones. Until this is done, our revolution is not complete. Our results may not always be original, but our fundamental quest is humanity, and in our study, analyses, and quality of vision, we have our own characteristics: further our attitude to the community in which we live is that of men who are aware of the mutual interaction between artist and society.

VIId
Soedjatmoko   The Need for Creative Adaptation (1954)

This fragment* is taken from an editorial in the first issue (July–August 1954) of the cultural journal Konfrontasi.

The condition of our society is as if it were no longer in motion. Such movement as still exists is movement backwards. It is as if we were regressing in search for the peace of the old days and were afraid of everything new unless it presents itself in an old and recognized mask. This backward movement is the product of a fear of the spirit, a fear of the new and the unknown. Its roots lie in our sterility, in our lack of confidence in our creative capacity. Withdrawing in this way cannot be put on a par with traditional attitudes which, whatever else can be said of them, had vitality and vigor. It can only, in fact, be described as cultural isolationism. . . .

* Reprinted, by permission, from *Economic Development as a Cultural Problem* (Ithaca, N.Y.: Cornell Modern Indonesia Project, 1958).

Even at the briefest look, one cannot but see that our lives have become shallower and more superficial in these last few years. It is as if a large part of our society, and in particular of our group of leaders, have lost their feeling for values. There is practically no effort to fight for values, either in the sense of defending old values or of breaking through these and advancing new ones. There is almost no exchange of ideas or national debate, that is, debate involving the whole of society about basic problems whose resolution will shape our future, except occasionally where someone sees that political advantage can be gained from it. Furthermore, there are no new ideas, no new school or current of thought. All we have is "tendencies."

The social changes which have appeared in our society since the revolution have manifested themselves and, indeed, continue to do so in differing views, differing traditions, differing customs, and different values. But most of these changes have not impinged on the consciousness of the political and cultural elite. So the members of the elite lack the awareness which would lead them to ask how far these changes foreshadow solutions to our problems. As one would expect, the result is sterility in our cultural life. The picture of our society is one of weakness and rottenness at every point. Self-confidence, self-reliance, and the revolutionary élan born of these, have all disappeared. Gone, too, is the sense of total commitment to the struggle. What is left is a halfheartedness of character and action, a cynicism born of lack of faith, and the smallness of mind which is characteristic of men who are incapable of lifting themselves up, breaking through their personal limitations, and growing in the course of abandoning themselves to a larger cause.

The political crisis our people are experiencing is something very similar to what one can see in the cultural and literary fields. The symptoms are the same: confusion, weakness, a loss of confidence, and the disappearance of values. The "political life" of the capital does not have the slightest connection with the forces at work in society. Because of this divorce between political maneuverings on the one hand and the interests of the people on the other, popular movements have become paralyzed. Our national energies are spent in quarrels among ourselves. Neglect of the regions has caused the emergence of various problems, visible in the cultural field, too, which threaten to undermine the unity of Indonesia even further. The total picture is one of halted national development, of stagnation, splits, and social disintegration. . . .

The causes of this crisis of ours are certainly not to be found in any lack of vitality in our people. The strength of our nationalism alone shows that. And so does the active demand of the people, particularly those outside the large cities, for change and a broadening of their lives; this demand exists even in this present situation where we are shackled by national crisis. The crisis is clearly one of leadership. Its cause is to be found in the inability of our national leaders to adapt themselves to the new situation we have been facing since the achievement of independence. It lies in their incapacity to understand that the world in which we have taken our rightful place is different from the world which we saw from a limited nationalist vantage point in the period of our struggle against the Dutch and that it is different in the demands it makes of us. We can only meet these demands if we are willing to look at the interests of the people and the state in terms of political, economic, and social development, if we are willing and able to see these interests in terms of the growth of national strength and in terms of the broadening of life for every member of society and every family.

This means that we must reformulate our national goals for the second revolution. We must come to a new determination of our aims in the light of our needs in our present situation in the world and in terms of the economic, social, and cultural changes which have occurred in our society since the revolution. These aims must be formulated in such a way that they can revive our confidence, our capacity, and our idealism, enabling us to work for a better life. And, in addition, they must be realistic. That means they must be formulated with a recognition of the limits of our capacities and our means.

Here lies the failure of our old leaders. They deserve our gratitude for guiding us to the threshold of independence. But, unfortunately, they cannot free themselves from the attitude and cast of mind which they had in the first stage—and, indeed, had to have, for it was a source of strength to them. What is needed for the second stage of the struggle is something completely different. The first stage of the struggle was political and was carried on within narrow limits. Being directed against Dutch domination it was primarily antithetical. The demands of today are ones which call for creative strength. Here is the source of our crisis.

VIIe

Soedjatmoko Toward a Strategy
of Modernization (1963)

*In the following pages we are reproducing the greater part of a
"Memorandum on Scope and Purpose of Seminar" which was circulated in advance of a seminar on "Cultural Motivations to Progress in
South and Southeast Asia" by Soedjatmoko as the Seminar's director.
The Seminar, sponsored by the Congress for Cultural Freedom and
the University of the Philippines, was held in Manila in June 1963.
Its proceedings, edited by Robert N. Bellah, were published two years
later as* Religion and Progress in Modern Asia *(New York: Free Press,
1965), and the text below is taken from this volume.* *

In the course of the fifteen years in which the modernizing elite in
the new states in South and Southeast Asia has had to deal with the
question of economic and social development, it has become quite
clear that the traditional value systems operating in this area pose a
much more important problem in the modernization process than had
been anticipated by most of these modernizers. If it was thought at
first that the bonds of tradition impeding social and economic development could be broken in a frontal attack against tradition and as the
result of the secularization accompanying the process of education,
urbanization, and industrialization, the realization has come that the
relationship between tradition and the modernization process is a
much more complex one, requiring a clearer understanding and a more
vigorous analysis. Especially in the field of economics a beginning has
been made with such studies, and some cultural factors impinging
upon economic behavior and upon the process of economic development have been identified. These studies, however, generally leave
unanswered the questions that confront the modernizers—those who
have dedicated themselves to the deliberate manipulation of political,
economic, and social factors for the purpose of effectuating rapid
progress and development.

It seems, therefore, that the time has come to face up to the general
problem posed by the unsuspected strength and ubiquitous influence
of traditional value systems in the modernization process, in order to
see how the impetus for progress can be strengthened and sustained.

The welding together of disintegrating, smaller, and more primitive

* By permission of the Macmillan Company.

forms of social organization into larger, new, cohesive, and viable
political units capable of effectuating economic development, which
has been the main task of the political leadership in the new nations
in South and Southeast Asia, has forced that elite, in varying degrees,
to take into account and to harness traditional forces for that purpose,
at least in those states that are unable or that prefer not to use force
or totalitarian methods. The problem faced by the modernizers among
the political elite has been how to utilize these forces without being
captivated by them and without losing the impetus for rapid social
change.

Also, the existence of more than one concept of modernization
among the modernizers themselves made a political struggle between them inevitable, leading the adherents of various concepts of
modernization to secure some degree of political support from the
traditional forces. The recent history of some of these new nations has
shown that those modernizers who were unwilling to make such com-
promises with the more traditional forces soon found themselves on
the sidelines of the political arena. The mobilization of the political
strength of traditionalism in this way has become an important power
factor, adding to the already formidable weight of social and mental
inertia that keeps large parts of the population of these countries im-
mobilized. Moreover, in the countries with Western parliamentary
systems, as well as in those countries that are in the process of building new political structures in South and Southeast Asia, these modernizers have been compelled, for the sake of welding sufficient political
power, to come to terms, though in varying degrees and forms with
traditionalism; and this, too, has strengthened traditionalist forces considerably more than many modernizers had anticipated—except, of
course, in those instances where the modernizers are committed to the
forcible destruction of traditionalism and its underlying social organization, with a view to releasing dynamic new social forces.

At the same time, the uncertainty and anxiety accompanying the
breakdown of traditional values and social structures without their
immediate replacement by new ones have, in several of these countries,
led to militant and fundamentalist reassertions on the part of the
various traditionalist forces, endangering the possibilities for com-
paratively smooth transition toward modernization.

These three factors, the requirements for political integration, the
power struggle among the modernizing elite, and the fundamentalist

reaction of traditionalism, make it a matter of great importance for the modernizing elite to prevent further hardening of the resistance against modernization and make the question of how to link up at least some elements of the traditional value system to the modernization process an extremely important one.

In the economically more developed nations, economic growth is a self-sustaining process of continuous innovation, change, and development. It is predicated on a particular view regarding the significance of life on this earth, on the acceptance of the idea of progress, that is, of a present better than the past and a future potentially better than the present. It assumes the perfectibility of man and society as a continuous possibility; it assumes man's ability to control and improve his natural environment, as well as the legitimacy of man's desire to do so. The question now is whether or not such views and attitudes are totally alien to the traditional value systems in South and Southeast Asia. Are there elements or variants of these value systems that could be harnessed for the modernization process; are there, on the other hand, elements that inherently constitute impediments to modernization? And is secularization the only way to overcome these impediments to progress?

Essentially, the problem is, how elements of the traditional value systems and the new values of progress can be integrated on the basis of the present general desire for a better life.

Very little is known about these questions; very little is known of the relationship between these traditional value systems and social action in general; and even less is known about this relationship in connection with the needs and desire for economic and social development. In fact, a clearer definition of these traditional value systems in relation to the concept of progress is very much in order.

At the same time, a closer look at the modernization process in general, as a historical phenomenon, is indicated, as is an attempt to relate the generalizations that can be made regarding this process with the specific value systems operating in South and Southeast Asia. A clearer understanding of the function of ideologies, old or new, with their particular perspectives on the future and their impacts on the will and determination of a people, in this process of political integration and social transformation, is also much needed. An inquiry into the traditional value systems might also shed some light on the relative receptivity for particular modern concepts of progress as embedded, for instance, in the liberal and in the Marxist outlooks, in the open or closed concepts of the future. The views on history and the historical process in traditional cultures are relevant in this connection.

Briefly, then, the questions these modernizers face—and for which they have had so far to find their answers by dint of their political instinct—are the following: What are the keys to the traditional and modern mainsprings of creative social action that could sustain the modernizing process? Should traditionalism be treated simply as an enemy? Is it possible to fight it in open battle without being crushed by it? Or without being isolated and reduced to political impotence? Is it possible to undermine traditionalism by an indirect approach? Is it possible to activate and mobilize those elements in traditional culture that would lend themselves to support for progress without encouraging at the same time other elements in traditional culture that would tend to impede progress?

VIII
Communism

Of all the ideological tendencies we are considering, communism is the easiest to relate to organizational facts; if we ignore the rarely and perfunctorily advanced claims of some Murba party leaders that theirs is the true communist organization, communism is the ideological stream associated with the Indonesian Communist Party (PKI). It is also the most self-consistent of these five streams, and we have found it the easiest to present here, though this is in good part because of our decision to leave out communist writings of the pre-1951 phase and to concentrate on the period of the Aidit leadership.

Founded in 1920 (when the Indies Social Democratic Federation abandoned that name), the PKI is the oldest Communist party in Asia. It is also the oldest of the major parties in the Indonesia of our period, although it virtually ceased to function after the suppression of its revolt of 1926–1927, becoming fully organized again only in 1945. After 1945, however, it quickly became a party of great strength, evidently building on support it had organized in the early 1920's, mainly among *abangan* Javanese, in both villages and towns. And following the suppression which it suffered after a further abortive rebellion, the "Madiun Affair" of September 1948, it regained its strength fairly quickly once more after Aidit, Lukman, and Njoto assumed leadership of it in 1951. By 1956 Aidit was speaking "in the name of one million Indonesian Communists." By 1965 the PKI's claimed the membership figure had risen to three million. It was the largest Communist party outside the Sino-Soviet world for some years before its suppression in 1965–1966 and played a role of considerable importance in the world communist movement. To complete our list of superlatives, it is the most intensively studied of Indonesia's parties.[*]

[*] See particularly Ruth T. McVey, *The Rise of Indonesian Communism*

As far as ideological formulation was concerned, the Indonesian Communist leaders had a much easier task than those who fashioned the thinking of the other four streams. Granted the comprehensive and highly schematic character of what they took from overseas, the range of questions to which they had to find answers was fairly narrow. Thus, little of what is to be found in the following pages will be strange to students of communist writings. The PKI leaders of our period were thoroughly schooled Communists and they rarely allowed themselves to venture into heterodoxy.

But their very orthodoxy and the fact that so many questions were answered—or ruled out—for them a priori made it possible for them to innovate in certain areas. They often spoke of their "creative application" of Marxism–Leninism and of its "Indonesianization," and the vigor and freshness which comes through in their writing suggests that this claim is worth examining seriously.

Although there is occasional evidence of this freshness in the five extracts which follow, there is rather more in some of the other sections. Thus, one sees something of the thinking which gained the PKI a reputation for strategic inventiveness in Ir. Sakirman's writing on Guided Democracy (IIIf). One sees something of the thinking which gained the party a reputation for a concern with concrete practical problems in Aidit's treatment of the problems of mismanagement and corruption (XIIIg). And one sees something of the approach which gained it a reputation for flexibility and reasonableness in Aidit's discussion of "nativeness" (IXg) and Lukman's of ethnicity (Xf).

Finally, it may be worth drawing attention to IXf by the Communist-sympathizing Mrs. Utami Suryadarma. The fusion of communist and radical nationalist thinking in this piece reflects the climate of opinion in the last years of Guided Democracy. And it throws light on the hope on which the Aidit leadership's whole strategy was based, that it might be possible for the Communists to come to power relatively peacefully through an alliance with other anti-imperialist groups, and particularly with the radical nationalists.

This hope was drowned in blood in the months following the Untung coup. We have trespassed our time limit to include one ex-

---

(Ithaca, N.Y.: Cornell University Press, 1965), Donald Hindley, *The Communist Party of Indonesia, 1951–1963* (Berkeley: University of California Press, 1964); and J. M. Van der Kroef, *The Communist Party of Indonesia: Its History, Program and Tactics* (Vancouver, B.C.: Publications Center, University of British Columbia, 1965).

ample (VIIIe) of the rethinking this disaster has provoked among the surviving Indonesian Communists. In condemning the previous strategy from a Maoist viewpoint, the author is, of course, writing with the benefit of hindsight, but (as a careful reading of IIIf will suggest) many of his ideas were probably expressed as grumbles behind the scenes during the years of the Aidit ascendancy.

VIIIa
D. N. Aidit A Semifeudal and Semicolonial Society (1957)

This extract comes from Indonesian Society and the Indonesian Revolution, *one of Aidit's major theoretical statements, which was approved by a plenary session of the PKI's Central Committee in July 1957 as a manual for use in party schools. The full text is in Aidit's* Problems of the Indonesian Revolution (*Bandung: Demos, 1963*), *pp. 5–61.*

In modern Indonesia, the power of the autocratic kings had been overthrown but this did not mean that the feudalists did not still play a role in the colonial regime. The feudalists, that is, the nobles and the landlords, were an important weapon in the hands of the imperialists, enabling them to continue with their economic exploitation and political suppression of the people. Colonial power is the dictatorship of the big foreign bourgeoisie and the domestic feudal class. By means of such dictatorship, the foreign bourgeoisie not only controlled Indonesia's financial and economic sectors but also the military and political situation in Indonesia. . . .

The exploitation by imperialism and feudalism during the time the Dutch were in power, and particularly during the Japanese regime, impoverished the Indonesian people more and more deeply, especially the peasants, pressing them into a state of bankruptcy, of starvation, and of never being able to enjoy decent housing and sufficient clothing.

The basic contradiction in Indonesian society in the modern era, the contradiction between imperialism and the Indonesian nation, reached one of its climaxes with the outbreak in August 1945 of the national revolution in Indonesia. As a result, the Indonesian nation took independence into their own hands. During this revolution, the Indonesian people fought a heroic struggle against the most basic enemy, imperialism. But another basic enemy, the feudal landlord class which was the most important social basis for the forces of imperialism, was not overthrown. This means that the basic force in the Indonesian revolution, the peasants, were not sufficiently aroused and drawn into the revolution. The separation made in the implementation of the two basic tasks, that is, the anti-imperialist task of national revolution and the antifeudal task of democratic revolution, was the main reason why the August Revolution failed.

The PKI Program states among other things: "The tasks of national emancipation and democratic change have not yet been carried out in Indonesia. The yearnings of the Indonesian people for complete national independence, for democratic liberties, and for an improvement in their living conditions have not yet been realized."

The PKI Program goes on to say that "the Round Table Conference Agreement signed by the Hatta Government and the Dutch Government on November 2, 1949, fixed Indonesia's status as semicolonial. The so-called transfer of sovereignty that took place on December 27, 1949, in accordance with the above agreement, was aimed at creating the illusion among the Indonesian people that Indonesia had been granted complete independence and that this 'transfer of sovereignty' was irrevocable, complete, and unconditional." The actual state of affairs was that with the signing of the RTC Agreement, the Hatta Government restored Dutch imperialist power over Indonesia's economy.

By means of the RTC Agreement, the Indonesian reactionaries, who had completely capitulated to the imperialists, strove to hold back and suppress the national independence movement and the democratic movement of the Indonesian people. But the result was quite the reverse! Under the strong and widespread pressure of the masses of the people, the RTC Agreement was abrogated unilaterally in April 1956 and later, all the "debts" to Holland were unilaterally repudiated by the Indonesian Government. Although these were important political steps and were in keeping with the rising anti-imperialist spirit of the people, they did not bring about any important changes in Indonesian society.

The abrogation of the RTC Agreement meant basically that the Indonesian people had obtained political independence in 80 per cent of the territory of their country, though in West Irian, the other 20 per cent, there was yet no political independence for the people. West Irian is still completely under Dutch domination. The political independence which the Indonesian people now possess is not full and stable political independence but is only half and is under the constant threat of the reactionaries. Domestic reactionaries working in collaboration with the Dutch, American, and other imperialists are doing all they can to restrict and destroy political independence for the people, and besides this, the national bourgeoisie are trying to limit the political independence of the working class and other progressive people.

Extremely clear evidence that Indonesian society is still semicolonial is the fact that Indonesia is as yet not independent in the economic field. The imperialists (the big foreign capitalists) still dominate in the economic field in Indonesia. Utilizing their dominant position in the sphere of the economy, and by means of their mercenaries, the imperialists also participate in determining political developments in Indonesia. Imperialist companies such as Shell, Caltex, and Stanvac control our country's oil reserves. Foreign estate companies still control the estate lands, and an important part of sea transport is in the hands of the KPM.* Import and export trade and internal trade are still controlled by what are usually referred to as the "Big Five": the Internatio, Borsumy, Jacobson van den Berg, Lindeteves-Stokvis, and Geo. Wehry companies. Important trade facilities such as transport are in part or wholly in the hands of big foreign capitalists. The big banks which dominate Indonesia's economy, such as the Factorij, the Handelsbank, the Escompto, the Chartered Bank, the Great Eastern Bank, and others are all owned by Dutch colonialists or other imperialists.

The policy of the imperialists in the field of economic affairs is not in principle different from what it was at the time Indonesia was fully colonized. They have continued to run their old enterprises and have opened up some new ones. This means that they can directly make use of Indonesia's raw materials, extract Indonesia's natural deposited wealth, and utilize cheap Indonesian labour power. They are economically bearing down upon our national industry, both that run by the State and that run by the national bourgeoisie. The result is that the big foreign capitalists stand in the way of developing the productive forces in our country. It is this imperialist control of banking, finance, and commodities which plays such a decisive role in the economic life of our country in the present period.

In order to safeguard their capital and facilitate their exploitation of the broad masses of the peasants and other groups of the people, the imperialists utilize compradores [agents] and usurers to throw out wide nets of exploitation extending from the busy commercial harbors on the coasts and from the towns right out to the remotest villages.

* The Dutch-owned interisland shipping company.

The compradore class is the creation of the imperialists, their assistants in exploiting the broad masses of the people. The compradores not only serve the interests of one imperialism, but each of them serves the interests of a particular group of imperialists.

In order to obtain political power, the imperialists have placed their compradores in the bourgeois parties which they have turned into parties that faithfully serve their interests. By utilizing the bourgeois parties and masking their activities as being in the interests of "religion" and "ideology," they have made use of the executive and legislative bodies as well as the bureaucratic apparatus of the government to serve the interests of the imperialists whose servants they are, doing all this so as to split the unity of the people and obstruct the growth of the progressive forces under the leadership of the Communist party.

Besides the economic power of the imperialists, important and heavy remnants of feudalism still hold sway in Indonesia. These include the following:

(1) the right of the big landlords to monopolize the ownership of land worked by the peasants, the majority of whom cannot own land and are therefore forced to rent land from landowners on terms fixed by the landlords;

(2) the payment of rent to the landlords in the form of goods which account for an important part of the crops produced by the peasants, all of this resulting in impoverishment for the vast majority of the peasants;

(3) the system of rent-payment in the form of work on the landlords' land, which places the peasants in the position of slaves;

(4) and, finally, the accumulation of debts which are shackles around the necks of the majority of the peasants and place them in a position of slavery vis-à-vis the landowners.

Continued prevalence of these feudal remnants has led to backwardness in farming techniques, to impoverishment of the vast majority of the peasants, to the shrinking of the domestic market, and to the inability of the country to carry out industrialization.

The double oppression of imperialism and feudalism has resulted in broad masses of the people, particularly the peasants, becoming more and more destitute, and to some of them going bankrupt, living in conditions of slavery and seminakedness. The double oppression of imperialism and feudalism has also led to national industry and national culture being very heavily suppressed.

In modern Indonesian society, the contradictions between imperialism and the Indonesian nation and the contradictions between feudalism and the broad masses of the people, above all the peasants, are the basic contradictions. There are, of course, other contradictions such as those between the bourgeoisie and the proletariat, between the reactionary classes themselves, and between one and another imperialism. But, however that may be, the contradiction between imperialism and the Indonesian nation is the most basic of all contradictions. The struggles which arise out of these contradictions and the ever-deepening contradictions within a semicolonial and semifeudal society will undoubtedly lead to the further development of the revolutionary movement. The Indonesian Revolution has emerged and grown out of the contradictions existing in Indonesian society which are daily becoming more intense.

These are the conclusions that we can draw from the characteristics of a semicolonial and semifeudal society. These characteristics are not essentially different from the characteristics of Indonesian society before the August 1945 Revolution. This is because the August Revolution did not complete the implementation of the two basic tasks of the revolution at once, that is, the task of the anti-imperialist national revolution and the task of the democratic antifeudal revolution.

The fact that these two basic tasks of the revolution have not been completed means that the August Revolution has not yet been completed in its entirety. Up to today, imperialism still holds sway in Indonesia whilst the most important social basis of imperialist power, the landlord class, has not yet been overthrown.

VIIIb

D. N. Aidit   Indonesia's Class Structure (1957)

This statement, like the preceding one, is taken from Indonesian Society and the Indonesian Revolution *of July 1957, and appears in Aidit's* Problems of the Indonesian Revolution *(Bandung: Demos, 1963), pp. 5–61.*

In Indonesian society today there is a landlord class and a bourgeois class: the upper strata of the landlord class and the upper strata of the bourgeois class are the classes that govern. The governed are the proletarian class, the peasants, and besides them all kinds of petty bourgeois groups; all these make up by far the largest group in society. Thus, it can be said that the way out of Indonesia's semicolonial and semifeudal conditions is by changing the balance of forces between the classes that govern on the one hand and the classes that are being governed on the other.

The attitudes and positions of all classes, those that govern and those being governed, are completely determined by their social and economic position. Thus, the character of Indonesian society not only determines the targets and tasks of the revolution but also determines the forces pushing the revolution forward. Which classes can be included within the forces pushing the Indonesian revolution forward? In order to know this, we need to make an analysis of the classes within Indonesian society.

The landlord class which exploits and suppresses the peasants and does more to oppose the political, economic, and cultural development of Indonesian society than to play a progressive role, is not a force pushing the revolution forward but is a target of the revolution.

The bourgeois class is composed of the compradores and the national bourgeoisie. The big bourgeoisie that is compradore in character directly serves the interests of big foreign capitalists and is thus fattened up by them. In the Indonesian revolution, the compradore bourgeoisie is not a driving force but an obstacle, and therefore a target.

The national bourgeoisie displays two features, however. As a class that is suppressed by imperialism and whose development is also stifled by feudalism, this class is anti-imperialist and antifeudal, and in this respect it is one of the revolutionary forces. But on the other hand it fundamentally lacks the courage to fight imperialism and feudalism because it is economically and politically weak and has class ties with imperialism and feudalism.

This dual character of the national bourgeoisie explains why we have had two sets of experiences with them. Within certain limits this class can take part in the revolution against imperialism, against the compradores, and against the landlords, as they did during the August Revolution* for example, but at other periods they trail behind the compradore bourgeoisie and become their allies in the coun-

* This is the PKI's term for the Revolution which began in August 1945.

terrevolutionary camp (for example, during the "Madiun Affair" in 1948 and during the mass arrests of August 1951). . . .

In facing the wavering character of the Indonesian national bourgeoisie attention should be paid to the fact that it is precisely because it is politically and economically weak that it is not very difficult to pull this class to the left, to make it stand firmly on the side of the revolution, so long as the progressive forces are large and the tactics of the Communist party correct. This means that the wavering nature of this class is not fatal; it is not insurmountable. But on the other hand, if the progressive forces are not large and the tactics of the Communist party not correct, then this economically and politically weak national bourgeoisie can easily run to the right and become hostile to the revolution.

The petty bourgeoisie besides the peasants, that is the urban poor, the intellectuals, the small traders, the handicraft workers, the fishermen, the independent workers, and so on, have a status which is almost the same as that of the middle peasants. They also suffer from the oppression of imperialism, feudalism, and the big bourgeoisie and are every day pressed further and further toward bankruptcy and ruin. This is why they are one of the forces pushing the revolution forward and are a reliable ally of the proletariat. They can only attain their freedom under the leadership of the proletariat. The intellectuals and the student youth are not a class in society but their class position is determined by family origin, by their conditions of living, and by their political outlook. The small traders in general have stalls and small shops and either employ just a few assistants or none at all; they live under the constant threat of bankruptcy because of exploitation by imperialists, the big bourgeoisie, and the moneylenders. The handicraftsmen and fishermen possess their own means of production; they do not employ any workers or perhaps employ only one or two. The independent workers are persons in various spheres of work, such as private doctors and lawyers; they work on their own; they do not exploit others or exploit others only very slightly. All the petty bourgeoisie besides the peasants can generally support the revolution and are good allies of the proletariat. Their weakness is that some of them easily come under the influence of the bourgeoisie, and this is why special attention must be devoted to carrying out propaganda and undertaking revolutionary organizational activities among them.

The peasants account for 60 to 70 per cent of the population of Indonesia; they make up the biggest group and together with their families number tens of millions of people. The peasants are basically divided into the rich peasants, the middle peasants, and the poor peasants. There are, indeed, some persons among the rich peasants that lease out a part of their land, carry out moneylending, and brutally exploit the peasant-laborers, and they are by nature semi-feudal; but besides this they themselves generally participate in labor, and in this sense they make up a part of the peasantry. Their productive activities will continue to be utilized for a certain period to come, and they can also help the struggle against imperialism. They are capable of adopting an attitude of neutrality in the revolutionary struggle against the landlords. This is why we cannot consider them as part of the landlords.

The middle peasants are independent economically; they generally do not exploit others and do not earn interest on money; on the contrary, they suffer from the exploitation of the imperialists, the landlords, and the bourgeoisie. Some of them have too little land to live on. The middle peasants can not only become part of the anti-imperialist revolution and the agrarian revolution, but they can also accept Socialism. This is why they are one of the important forces pushing the revolution forward and a reliable ally of the proletariat. Their attitude toward the revolution is a decisive factor for victory or defeat because the middle peasants will constitute a majority in the countryside after the agrarian revolution.

The poor peasants together with the agricultural laborers comprise the majority in the villages in our country, prior to the agrarian revolution. The poor peasants have no land or not enough to live on; they are the village semiproletariat; they are the largest force pushing the revolution forward. It is natural for them to be the most reliable of the allies of the proletariat and a basic part of the forces of the Indonesian revolution.

The poor peasants and the middle peasants can only attain emancipation under leadership of the proletariat, and the proletariat can only give leadership to the revolution if it has made a firm alliance with the poor and middle peasants. What we mean when we use the term "peasants" is mainly the poor and middle peasants that make up the majority of the inhabitants of the villages. In leading the people's struggle in the countryside, the Party must always strive to be able to draw in and mobilize 90 per cent of the village inhabitants and must firmly base itself on the poor peasants and the peasant laborers as well as make an alliance with the middle peasants.

The Indonesian proletariat consist of about 500,000 workers in modern industry, transport worfers, factory-workers, repair-shop workers, mine-workers, and so on. The workers in small industry and the handicrafts in the towns number more than two million. The agricultural and forestry proletariat and other groups of workers make up a very large number. All this amounts to about six million or, together with their families, some twenty million, which is about 25 per cent of the entire population of Indonesia. Besides this town and village proletariat, there are also in the villages of Indonesia millions of peasant laborers, those village inhabitants who generally own no land and agricultural implements and who make a livelihood out of selling their labor power in the villages. The peasant laborers are the group which suffers most in the villages and their position in the peasant movement is just as important as that of the poor peasants.

Like the proletariat in other countries, the Indonesian proletariat has very fine qualities. Their work makes them unite in the most advanced economic forms; it gives them a strong understanding of organization and discipline, and, because they do not own any means of production, they are not individualistic in character. Furthermore, since the Indonesian proletariat has been the victim of three forms of brutal exploitation, that is, imperialism, capitalism, and feudalism, they have become more firm and more thoroughgoing in the revolutionary struggle than the other classes. Unlike Europe, Indonesia is not fertile soil for social-reformism and so the whole proletariat is very revolutionary indeed, with the exception, of course, of a small number who have become the scum. Because the Indonesian proletariat has been led by its revolutionary political party, the Communist Party of Indonesia, ever since it appeared in the arena of revolutionary struggle, it is the most politically conscious class in Indonesian society. And as a large part of the Indonesian proletariat consists of bankrupt peasants, it has natural bonds with the broad masses of the peasants, a fact which facilitates their alliance.

Although the Indonesian proletariat has certain unavoidable weaknesses, such as, for example, its numerical weakness by comparison with the peasants, its youth by comparison with the proletariat in capitalist countries, and the low level of its culture by comparison with the bourgeoisie, it is, nevertheless, the basic force pushing the

Indonesian revolution forward. The Indonesian revolution will not succeed unless it is under the leadership of the Indonesian proletariat. To take a recent example, the August Revolution was successful in the beginning because the proletariat more or less consciously took an important part in it, but later on, the revolution suffered defeat because the role of the proletariat was pushed into the background and the upper strata of the bourgeoisie betrayed the alliance with the proletariat (the "Madiun Affair"), and also because of the fact that the Indonesian proletariat and its political Party had not yet gained enough revolutionary experience. Without the proletariat's taking an active part, nothing will ever run properly in Indonesian society. This has already been proved and will continue to be proved by history and experience.

It must be understood that although the Indonesian proletariat is the class which has the highest political consciousness and organizational understanding, the victory of the revolution can never be achieved without revolutionary unity under all circumstances with all other revolutionary classes and groups. The proletariat must build up a revolutionary front. Of the classes in society, the peasants are the firmest and most reliable ally of the working class, the urban petty bourgeoisie is a reliable ally, and the national bourgeoisie is an ally under certain circumstances and within certain limits: this is the fundamental law which has already been and is being proven by Indonesia's modern history.

Loiterers and vagrants are among the products of a semicolonial and semifeudal society, of the fact that this society has given rise to unemployed in the villages and towns, that these unemployed then live a life of vagrancy without any idea of what to do and are eventually dragged down into criminality, living and working as thieves, robbers, gangsters, beggars, prostitutes, and in other such abnormal ways. This group is wavering in character; some of them can be bought up by the reactionaries, others can be brought into the revolution. In the event of their entering the revolution they can become the ideological source of roaming destructive elements and of anarchism within the ranks. They can easily be made to waver, both by material bribes and by incitement to hatred and to the smashing of anything constructive. They can easily be swayed by loud and fiery speeches. They can easily be told by the counter-revolutionaries to mouth revolutionary phrases so as to oppose and destroy the Party of the working class, the workers' movement, and the revolutionary movement in general. This is why we must be skilful in changing their characteristics, especially their destructive nature.

Based on the above analysis of the classes in Indonesian society, it is clear which classes and groups are the pillars of imperialism and feudalism, that is, the landlords and the compradores. They are obstacles standing in the way of the revolution and that is why they are the enemies of the people. The above analysis also makes it clear which classes and groups are the basic driving force of the revolution, that is, the working class, the peasants, and the petty bourgeoisie. It makes clear, too, which class can take part in the revolution, that is, the national bourgeois class. This is why the workers, the peasants, the petty bourgeoisie, and the national bourgeoisie are the People and make up the forces of the revolution, the forces of the united national front.

VIIIc

D. N. *Aidit* The Three Political Forces (1959)

This extract is taken from "For Democracy and a Gotong Rojong Cabinet," Aidit's General Report to the Sixth National Congress of the PKI, held in September 1959. The PKI had gained greatly from the events of 1958, particularly from the discrediting of its archenemies, the Masjumi and Socialist parties, several of whose leaders had become involved in the PRRI—Permesta rebellion in Sumatra and Sulawesi. But in 1959 it was facing active hostility from the side of the army, which had succeeded in having its Congress delayed and was embarrassing the party by its restrictive measures against Chinese petty traders in rural areas. Aidit's term "progressive forces" may be taken to refer to the PKI itself, "middle-of-the-road forces" referring principally to President Sukarno, the PNI, and the Nahdatul Ulama (in roughly that left-to-right order) and "diehard forces" principally to the Masjumi and Socialists. The full text is in Aidit's Problems of the Indonesian Revolution *(Bandung: Demos, 1963), pp. 279–438.*

Following the holding of the first parliamentary elections in our country, the Fourth Plenum of the Central Committee of the Party made an analysis and drew the conclusion that there are three political forces that are almost balanced in size: the diehard forces, the progressive forces, and the middle-of-the-road forces, each of which have their own concept of how to complete the August 1945 Revolution.

Thus, there are contradictions in our country between these three forces, some of which are sharper than others, some of which are not basic contradictions and others of which are. The contradiction between the progressive forces and the middle-of-the-road forces is not a basic contradiction; it is a contradiction among the people. But the contradiction between the people and the diehards is a basic contradiction because the diehards represent the interests of the imperialists who are the enemies of the people.

What is the situation today of each of these forces? And what sort of balance exists between these three forces? We can state the following in this connection:

Because of their excessively reactionary, extremely antinational and antipeople policy, the prestige of the diehard forces has fallen greatly, and they have "lost all perspectives"; they no longer have any hopes of getting back into leadership and control of the central government by parliamentary means. This is why they have tried to force their concept on the nation via extra-parliamentary means of terror, and they have even gone to the extent of organising a rebellion to get the reins of government back into their hands. They have taken the road of fascism. Their basic force no longer lies in the confidence placed in them by a section of the Indonesian people who are politically the most backward, but in assistance in the form of money, arms, and other military equipment from the United States and Dutch imperialists and the Kuomintang; it lies in the support of a few corrupt military personages, in terrorist organizations, in sabotage in military and economic affairs, in smuggling and illegal barter trade. Basically, their strength lies in help from the imperialists.

More and more, the followers of the counterrevolutionaries are abandoning them, but at the same time their ties with the imperialists who direct all their activities, especially the United States imperialists, are getting closer. If they did not get any assistance from abroad, these diehard forces would no longer have any role.

Even so, we must not make light of the diehard forces because there are still factors in their favor. The first and the most basic is the fact that Indonesia today is still in essence a semicolonial and semifeudal country. As long as our country is still a semicolonial country it means that imperialist domination still prevails in our country, and it means, too, that there is still a basis of existence in our country for reactionary forces, for the diehard forces. As long as our country is still semifeudal, the domination of the counterrevolutionary landlords will still prevail. Feudalism is the social basis of imperialism. Feudal survivals, still dominant in economic life, social life, and cultural life will always be a source of life for the diehards.

Thus, even though the diehards have already sustained heavy political blows, even though their antinational character has been more and more exposed, even though they have been more and more exposed as using religion as a mask and misusing *sukubangsa* sentiments, even though it has become clearer that they are hostile to the people, nevertheless as long as our country is a semicolonial and semifeudal country, the diehard forces will continue to represent a force which we must unceasingly expose and oppose with all our might.

As regards the middle-of-the-road forces, we have had a number of experiences. Our Party has drawn the conclusion that the middle-of-the-road forces on the one hand vacillate in their resistance to imperialism and feudalism because of their economic ties with the imperialists and the feudalists that have not yet been completely severed, and because they too are part of the exploiting class. But on the other hand, they are revolutionary because they must, in the interest of preserving themselves and safeguarding their livelihood, get rid of imperialist and landlord obstructions. If the progressive forces are great and the Party's program is one which benefits the middle-of-the-road forces, if the Party's style of work is good and if the progressive forces are able to deal heavy and well-aimed blows against the diehards, there is the possibility that the middle-of-the-road forces will, for a long period of time, remain loyal to the anti-imperialist and antifeudal struggle.

The conclusion has also been drawn that if these middle-of-the-road forces are no longer loyal to the policy of anti-imperialism, if they abandon their class interests and prostitute themselves before the diehards, they can, together with the diehard forces, aim blows against the progressive forces so as, for a certain period of time, to obstruct the development of the democratic movement. But several major experiences that we have had prove that the alliance between the middle-of-the-road forces and the diehards, such as during the time of the Hatta and Sukiman Cabinets, are not at all to the advantage of the middle-of-the-road forces; on the contrary, their economic interests are being pressed more and more by the foreign monopolists and compradores, and their political prestige falls because they are condemned by the people for participating in the game of selling out the Republic of Indonesia and its people.

The Indonesian national bourgeoisie are in general a commercial bourgeoisie. Their excessively weak position in economic affairs makes them very dependent upon export and import trade, with the stress upon import, and this means that they are dependent upon the imperialists who dominate these two spheres. If their position as a commercial bourgeoisie is so weak, then even more striking is their weakness in the sphere of industry.

If the Indonesian national bourgeoisie had a strong position in the sphere of industry, they would stand up to the foreign monopolists more courageously as competitors; they would defend their right to exist as industrialists and would oppose the imperialists. As industrialists, they would also put up greater opposition to the survivals of feudalism because they would be in need of a secure home market. In this resistance against imperialism and the survivals of feudalism, they would come together with and march side by side with the masses of the people who are also anti-imperialist and antifeudal.

But in their position as a commercial bourgeoisie almost all their efforts are dependent upon the imperialists. They must bring themselves into conformity with the conditions fixed by the imperialists. Even if they had the intention of putting up resistance, they would not be strong enough. These circumstances are the reason for the very uncertain and very inconsistent features of the Indonesian bourgeoisie, and these circumstances have made our country fertile soil for the growth of compradores and bureaucrat capitalists. But on the other hand, the weak economic position of the national bourgeoisie does not provide a strong material basis for sharp contradictions between the national bourgeoisie and the working class in general. To a certain extent, this fact helps in the building of the national front.

But what has been stated above does not mean that the Indonesian national bourgeoisie is not an important political factor. They exert a significant ideological and political influence among the intellectuals and within the State's apparatus. This is why the question of building unity between the progressive forces and the middle-of-the-road forces is still an important matter, side by side with striving to prevent the middle-of-the-road forces from capitulating to the diehard forces and the imperialists.

Since they do not have sufficient strength and courage to oppose the imperialists in economic affairs, certain groups of the national bourgeoisie, in line with imperialist policy, sharpen the antagonisms between the Indonesian capitalists themselves, between the so-called "indigenous" and "nonindigenous" businessmen, and together with this, spread the poison of chauvinism among the people. This means protecting the big foreign enemy and beating one's own colleagues; the foreign enemy becomes stronger and more dangerous while one's own colleagues get beaten to pulp. This is a policy of "destroying one's own house to let the burglar in." That they indeed let the burglar in is evident from their attitude toward big foreign capital investments. They not only do not oppose these but have actually created an Act on Foreign Investments for this purpose.

If they were genuinely against foreign capital, their foremost task would be to reject big foreign capital investments and to undermine the position of existing foreign investments. If they fail to reject big foreign capital investments while making the foreign proprietors of small shops and stalls the target of their opposition, this is not a truly national policy; it is a policy of the domestic landlords and money-lenders who are making use of chauvinism in order to intensify their own exploitation of the working people. And yet in actual fact, their historic task is to unite Indonesian capital as far as is possible, to oppose the big foreign capitalists and to participate in the work of industrialising the country, or, in other words, to pursue a policy of "strengthening one's own house and throwing out the burglar."

Following the stride forward taken in the anticolonial struggle when the enterprises of the Dutch colonialists were taken over, the egoistic character of a part of the middle-of-the-roaders became very clear indeed. After the workers, at great risk and in complete disregard for their own interests, had taken over the Dutch enterprises, the egoistic middle-of-the-roaders, by making use of their power in the government, tried to get these enterprises shifted over into their own hands. It was here that there was a meeting place between the interests of the middle-of-the-road forces and the reactionary forces which could provide a platform for their joint reactionary policy. This is an important factor behind the hucksters' agreements between the diehard bourgeoisie and right-wing nationalist elements under the slogan of "containing Communism." They believe that if they take over this imperialist slogan, there will be people ready to excuse their antinational deeds.

The middle-of-the-roaders wavered at the time the workers, in a spirit of noble patriotism and at great risk, took over the Dutch colonialist enterprises. But as soon as the opportunity provided itself, they came forward to "safeguard" the achievements of the workers' struggle; they strove to prohibit the activities of the trade unions and get themselves into the positions previously occupied by the Dutch colonialists. But fortunately, it was in the main possible to frustrate this policy of turning these taken-over Dutch enterprises into private concerns, thanks to the strong resistance of the Indonesian people and President Sukarno. But the reactionaries are still making strong efforts in this direction, and there is even evidence that they have made some progress. A new danger is that some of the managers of these enterprises are misusing their positions to enrich themselves and their clique and to hamper production so as to prove that "the government and the workers are incompetent," while at the same time proclaiming that the private businessmen are more "competent."

In view of the fact that the "prestige" of the diehards has fallen, the American imperialists cannot for the time being effectively pursue their policy in Indonesia via the diehard forces headed by the leaders of the Masjumi and the Indonesian Socialist party. Therefore, the imperialists badly need new compradores from among the middle-of-the-road forces, both civil and military, while at the same time trying to restore the position of the Indonesian diehard forces. This is the background to the attitude being taken by the rightist wing of the middle-of-the-road forces who are trying to get the entire middle-of-the-road forces to quit the policy of co-operation with the progressive forces.

But within the middle-of-the-road forces there are also left and center wings as well as the rightist wing. The center group in the middle-of-the-road forces is usually not a strong group, but it is in a position to "link up" the left wing with the right wing, and it has a strong tendency to come down on the side of the stronger of the wings within the middle-of-the-road forces. This is why the victory of the left wing within the middle-of-the-road forces is a magnet which can succeed in winning the center wing over to the left and thus prevent the middle-of-the-road forces from shifting to the right.

The left wing in the middle-of-the-road forces opposes the policy of selling out to imperialism and the domestic reactionaries. The policy of the left wing in the middle-of-the-road forces within certain limits reflects the feelings and hopes of the mass of the followers of the middle-of-the-road forces which to a large extent consists of the petty bourgeoisie. The left wing in the middle-of-the-road forces displays a more resolute anti-imperialist standpoint and cannot easily be drawn into the clutches of the imperialists. They also do not agree with the hucksters' agreements reached between the right nationalist group and the diehards, because these are not in harmony with the interests of the mass followers of the middle-of-the-road forces, especially the petty bourgeoisie. They also oppose the Foreign Investment Law because this law will mean commission earnings and other profits for only a small handful of the leaders of the middle-of-the-road forces, to the detriment of the mass of followers of these forces themselves. These internal contradictions within the middle-of-the-road forces can, if they do not get too sharp, be solved quietly. But if they become too sharp, if the consciousness of the left wing becomes high enough and the right wing continues to adopt a diehard attitude, this must lead to a split.

In connection with completing the demands of the August 1945 Revolution, the conclusion can be drawn that at the present stage, the left-wing of the middle-of-the-road forces no longer have any confidence in the ability and honesty of the upper layer of the national bourgeoisie to carry this out. They also witness the growth of the forces of the Indonesia proletariat and are beginning to be conscious of the fact that the working class is occupying a more and more important position in the national independence movement in leading the completion of the demands of the August Revolution. But this does not mean that the left group of the middle-of-the-road forces has already accepted and recognised the leadership of the proletariat. In order for this to happen the proletariat must even further strengthen itself and show that it has a greater ability to defend the interests of the entire people. . . .

As regards both the take-over of the Dutch enterprises and in the question of smashing the counterrevolutionary rebels it was proven that the Indonesian proletariat is more and more able to take its place and has begun to be recognized as the vanguard in the national struggle at the present stage, as the vanguard in the struggle of the Indonesian people to complete the demands of the August 1945 Revolution. The Indonesian people have displayed in the course of the three general elections so far* that they have no little confidence in the PKI and in the progressive forces in general. The birth of the concept of President Sukarno, which is aimed at the formation of a *Gotong Rojong* Cabinet based on proportional representation, or in other

* This refers to the parliamentary elections of September 1955, the Constituent Assembly elections of December 1955, and the provincial and regency (*kabupaten*) elections held in most provinces in 1957 and 1958.

words the participation of Communists in the Central Government, was a correct reflection of the hopes of the entire working people. Such great support for the establishment of a *Gotong Rojong* Cabinet would not have been possible had the people not had great confidence in the PKI. This confidence has become even greater since the people have had direct and good experience in regions where Communists are directing the government, where the people have seen for themselves the unity between what Communists say and what they do, where the people have for the first time got the feeling that they are participating in deciding the course of government and participating in deciding the course of development of society in their region.

But it is not easy for the progressive forces to develop themselves. The left-wing of the middle-of-the-road forces aims, besides striking a blow at the diehards, at utilizing and restricting the progressive forces. The right-wing of the middle-of-the-road forces strives to hold back the development of the progressive forces with its policy of "striking to both the left and the right," but because of jealousy, anxiety, and a terrible fear of the development of the progressive forces, it is striking more blows to the left than to the right. In the interests of its rightist policy, it is prepared within certain limits to make a compromise with the diehard forces. The diehard forces are striving with might and main not only to hold back the development of the progressive forces but also to "smash" these forces.

In addition to the efforts being made by the right nationalists to hold back the progressive forces, the efforts by the diehard forces to strike at and eventually smash by means of force the progressive forces and the continuous encouragement to smash the Communist movement that is coming from the imperialists, the Trotskyites* also feel that they would be committing a great sin if they did not take part in this campaign of "hunting down" the Communists.

It is clear what difficulties are being faced by the progressive forces in developing themselves. The Communists must not feel self-satisfied with the successes they have achieved in developing the progressive forces; on the contrary, they must always raise their vigilance and tirelessly continue to strengthen and expand their links with all sections of the people. There are still important shortcomings in our Party's work of building the national front. Among Party cadres, there is still haziness about the nonbasic and the basic contradictions in Indonesian society today, and there is insufficient understanding that,

* This presumably refers to the Murba Party and its sympathizers.

under certain circumstances, antagonistic contradictions can turn into nonantagonistic contradictions, while nonantagonistic contradictions can turn into antagonistic contradictions. Because of this haziness and lack of understanding, we are insufficiently able in time to make use of all situations to strengthen the national front. By studying more theory and by gaining more experiences, as well as by not forgetting to draw conclusions from the experiences that we have already gained, we shall gradually be able to overcome these weaknesses.

The entire development since the time of the Fifth National Party Congress (March 1954) bears out the correctness of the analysis concerning the "three forces and the three concepts of completing the August 1945 Revolution." It is also a fact that these three forces are undergoing constant shifts and up to the present these shifts have been to the left. From the point of view of its following, the PKI has not only become a national Party covering the entire country and all nationalities, but it has also become the largest party in our country.

How is the balance of forces today, after the struggle against Dutch imperialism went forward a stage with the taking-over of the Dutch enterprises, after the PRRI-Permesta rebellion has basically been defeated and after their failure to prevent the return to the 1945 Constitution? It can be said with certainty that the position of the diehard forces has seriously deteriorated, and, together with that, the progressive forces have become greater, while the middle-of-the-road forces have remained basically the same. Even though the reputation of the leadership of the middle-of-the-road forces has fallen because they vacillated too much in the struggle against the counterrevolution and because of the hucksters' agreements with the diehards reached by the rightist wing of their leadership, the position of the middle-of-the-road forces has been helped by the fact that the left-wing of these forces has remained anti-imperialist, and in view, too, of the fact that a part of the masses of the diehard forces have shifted to the center. The PKI's political line towards these three forces is unchanged, namely, develop the progressive forces, unite with the middle-of-the-road forces, and isolate the diehard forces. This means carrying out the slogan, "Improve the national front work, further isolate the diehard forces!"

VIIId
D. N. *Aidit*   The Struggle of the Peoples of
Asia, Africa, and Latin America (1963)

*This extract is taken from Aidit's Political Report to the Plenary
Meeting of the PKI's Central Committee which was presented December 23–26, 1963, at the end of a year in which the party had
moved from neutrality in the Moscow-Peking conflict to alignment
with Peking. This text is taken, with minor changes, from D. N. Aidit,
Set Afire the Banteng Spirit! Ever Forward, No Retreat (Peking:
Foreign Languages Press, 1964).*

At the present time there are two mighty currents of contradiction
on a world scale, the contradiction between Socialism and imperialism (monopoly capitalism) and the contradiction between the oppressed nations and imperialism. These two mighty currents unite in
one great current of revolution against imperialism. These two contradictions are the main or principal contradictions in the world today.

We cannot say that the contradiction between Socialism and imperialism is not a main contradiction because some of the Socialist
countries are waging a bitter struggle in all fields against imperialism.
It is quite true that the final objective of U.S. imperialism is to destroy the most powerful Socialist country, the one which possesses
nuclear weapons, that is the Soviet Union. The U.S. imperialists will
never like having another large nuclear country besides themselves.
But we cannot close our eyes to the fact that there are Socialist countries whose state leaders are striving to eradicate or at least gloss
over the contradiction between Socialism and imperialism, by speaking fine words about U.S. imperialism, by praising the leaders of
this foremost imperialist state, and in other ways. They say, for
example, that world problems can be solved if there is cooperation
between the two great powers, between a certain Socialist country
and the U.S.A.; they say that Eisenhower is peace-loving, and even
worse, they proclaimed Kennedy a hero of peace after his death,
mourned deeply over his death, and shed bitter tears. And now they
consider Johnson as the continuer of Kennedy's so-called peace-loving
policy.

We are compelled to talk about this because the policy of speaking fine words about the U.S. imperialists, including praising the leaders of that imperialist state, now being pursued by the leaders of certain Communist Parties in other countries, has led to a difference of opinion between our Party and the leaders of these Communist Parties. We Indonesian Communists, and together with us all the Communist Parties in Southeast Asia as well as many more Communist Parties and other revolutionaries in Asia, Africa, and Latin America, are facing U.S. aggression, intervention, and subversion at every moment, in direct or indirect forms .The U.S. imperialists have never ceased to perpetuate murder of human beings, incuding children and old people, in various countries. In such a situation, the leaders of some Communist Parties in other countries are saying that the leaders of the state responsible for these murders are "reasonable" and "peace-loving." We can understand it if, for the sake of political decency, statesmen sent congratulatory messages when Kennedy became President of the U.S.A. and messages of condolence when he died, but it is quite incomprehensible to us if there are Communists who regard the leader of a state that is the gendarme of international reaction as "reasonable" and "peace-loving."

How can the leaders of a state that, since the moment the Second World War ended, has not for a moment stopped waging aggression, intervention, and subversion against other countries he regarded as "reasonable" and "peace-loving"? The politically conscious working people of Indonesia would spit on us Indonesian Communists if we were to speak like that. Goodness only knows what the working people in South Vietnam, Venezuela, Angola, Portuguese Guinea, and other countries would do if the Communists or revolutionaries in these countries were to speak like that, for these people are bearing arms in their hands. The humanitarian sentiments of a Communist are borne in his condemnation of imperialism and imperialist leaders, in particular of U.S. imperialist leaders, and in his inexhaustible sympathy for the oppressed nations that are opposing the imperialists, particularly for those who are everyday experiencing the threat of aggression and murder at the hands of these imperialists. Hollow is the humanitarianism of those who praise the leaders of U.S. imperialism and thereby weaken their class consciousness. Humanism is never "universal"—humanism is always class humanism. . . .

Since there is now a revolutionary situation that is continually surging forward and ripening in Asia, Africa, and Latin America, the most principal of the two main or principal contradictions at the present time is the contradiction between the oppressed nations and imperialism. The struggle of the peoples of these three continents is shaking imperialism to its foundations and seriously weakening it.

There could also be a main contradiction in Europe and America if a mighty wave of revolution were to surge forth in these countries. Today this is not yet the case, both because imperialism is still powerful in its own place of origin and because of the influence of social-democracy and modern revisionism on the working-class movement in these regions. Some people are of the opinion that the main contradiction today is in capitalist Europe because it is in this part of the world that the proletarian revolution is most likely to break out. This is a manifestation of "Europe-centrism," a variation of the dogmatic view of the proletarian revolution with which the opportunist parties of the Second International were afflicted. It was Lenin himself, creatively developing Marxism in the era of imperialism, who proved both theoretically and by the practice of the Great October Revolution that the revolution need not break out first in the most advanced capitalist countries but could occur in the country where the chain of imperialism was weakest. The Great October Socialist Revolution of 1917 proved that the dogmatists were wrong. The Socialist revolutions in China, Korea, and Vietnam, which are agrarian countries, took place before the Socialist revolution in advanced capitalist Europe. The same applies to Cuba too. All this proves that Lenin is correct and that the dogmatists are wrong.

At the present time, the weakest link in the chain of imperialism is not in Europe or in North America or in Australia, but in Asia, Africa, and Latin America. This is why the proletariat throughout the world must center its attention on the revolution on these three continents. This is why, in order to consolidate the Socialist system, the most important task of all Socialist countries is to support the struggle of the peoples on these three continents. . . .

In connection with the struggle for national independence, there are some people who incessantly proclaim that this struggle cannot be successful without the help of the Socialist countries. Their purpose in doing this is to ensure that the Communists who are fighting for national independence should not dare express any opinion that differs from the official standpoint of a certain Socialist country, for, were they to dare to do this, they would not get any help and thus not be victorious. In view of this form of political blackmail our Party needs to stress more strongly than ever a point whose truth is established by dialectical materialism and which has already been proved by Lenin. We must stress that it is the internal factor that causes a qualitative change to take place in anything, whereas the role of the external factor is only supplementary. The outbreak of the Indonesian revolution in August 1945 was not caused in the first place by assistance or stimulus from without but first and foremost because the internal factors were already ripe, namely, the revolutionary struggle of the Indonesian people. . . .

Our Party always stresses, in keeping with the teachings of Lenin, that the revolutionary struggle for national independence is inseparable from the revolutionary struggle throughout the whole world against imperialism and capitalism. But at the same time, our Party also stresses that the factor which is decisive for the victory of the national independence struggle is the forces of the people in each of the countries where a struggle for emancipation is being waged. This is the reason why our Party educates its members and the Indonesian people to have the courage to stand on their own feet, to have confidence in their own strength, and to possess the "ever forward, no retreat" resolve. This is why it educates the people in the spirit of the red *banteng*. . . .

Southeast Asia is one of the central points in the region of the world's main contradiction. Objective as well as subjective conditions are excellent in this area. In order to win victory for the struggle of the oppressed nations in Southeast Asia, in order to break down the imperialist fortress which is already in very poor shape and very shaky, the struggle of one oppressed nation must have close links with that of the others. Revolutionary solidarity between these nations must be strengthened.

Indonesia's role is very important indeed in the struggle for national independence in Southeast Asia. This should be realized and understood because it places a very great responsibility on the shoulders of every Indonesian revolutionary, and particularly of the Communists. In Indonesia today there is no armed struggle, as there is for instance in South Vietnam. But it is a mistake to think that this means that Indonesia's role in Southeast Asia is not very important. In Indonesia it is not only the people but also the government that is waging a struggle against imperialism, and if necessary with arms. This latter is proven by the struggle that was waged against the counterrevolutionaries of the "PRRI-Permesta," the struggle to stamp out the counterrevolutionaries of the Darul Islam-TII, the struggle for the liberation of West Irian from Dutch imperialism, and, today, the struggle to crush "Malaysia."

With the upsurge in the wave of revolution in Southeast Asia, it is impossible to prevent the total destruction of imperialism in Southeast Asia headed by the U.S.A. The movement for national independence in this region will definitely achieve victories and will definitely develop into a mass struggle against capitalism. The collapse of the imperialist fortress in this region will generate a mighty tidal wave overwhelming imperialism. It will be a great help to the development of the world Socialist revolution.

The Communist parties in Southeast Asia that are still waging a struggle for national liberation have the same basic tasks: (1) to draw over the broadest possible mass of the people and to organize them in a united national front; (2) to penetrate as far as possible into the villages to build an alliance of workers and peasants; (3) to strengthen the Party's leadership of the broad masses of the people and be skilful at making use of all forms of struggle; and (4) to strengthen cooperation between the peoples and Communist parties of Southeast Asia. These are the *four amulets* with which to overthrow the *four demons* in Southeast Asia: imperialism, feudalism, compradore capitalism, and bureaucratic capitalism.

The victory of the Indonesian revolution will signify a mighty breakthrough against the fortress of imperialism, it will signify a great stride forward in the anti-imperialist struggle, and its rays will shine afar, even beyond the borders of Southeast Asia. This is the reason why the imperialists, in particular the U.S.A., devote such great attention to developments in Indonesia and make it the main target of their intervention and subversion in Southeast Asia.

VIIIe
A PKI Self-Criticism (1966)

This is part of a statement appearing in the Indonesian Tribune, *Tirana (Albania), Year 1, No. 2, January 1967, under the title "Build the PKI along the Marxist-Leninist Line to Lead the People's Democratic Revolution in Indonesia." It was purportedly written in Central Java in September 1966 by the Politburo of the Central Committee of the PKI, and authorship of it is often attributed to Sudisman, one of the five main leaders of the PKI under Aidit, who was arrested in December 1966, tried, and shot in October 1968. The English has*

been corrected with the aid of an Indonesian typescript. A compara-
ble document produced by the pro-Soviet "Marxist-Leninist Group
of the PKI" can be found in Information Bulletin, *No. 18 (Prague:*
Peace and Socialism Publishers, 1967).

The only possible sources of the serious weaknesses and mistakes of
the Party in the period after 1951 are the petty-bourgeois class origin
and lack of knowledge of Marxism-Leninism of the Party leadership.
Lenin has taught us that without a revolutionary theory there can be
no revolutionary movement and that the role of vanguard fighter can
be fulfilled only by a party that is guided by the most advanced theory
(V. I. Lenin, *What is to be done?*). The experience of the Indonesian
Communists fully testifies to the truth of Lenin's teaching. The PKI
was unable to fulfill its role as the vanguard of the Indonesian working class not only because of the Party leadership's failure to integrate
revolutionary theories with the concrete practice of the Indonesian
revolution, but also because it chose a road which was divorced from
the guidance of the most advanced theories. This experience shows
that the PKI had not succeeded in establishing a core of leadership
that was composed of proletarian elements, which really had a correct
understanding of Marxism-Leninism, an understanding that was systematic and not fragmentary, practical and not abstract.

The ideological weaknesses of our Party have a long historical root,
namely, subjectivism. The social basis of subjectivist ideology is the
petty-bourgeois class with its multiplicity of small enterprises, in
particular, individual farms. Our Party is surrounded by a very large
petty-bourgeois class, and many Party members originate from this
class. Inevitably, petty-bourgeois ideas and habits are brought into
the Party. The petty-bourgeois method of thinking in analyzing problems is subjective and one-sided. It proceeds not from facts, from the
objective balance of forces among classes, but from subjective wishes,
subjective feelings, and subjective imagination. This subjectivism is
the ideological root of the errors of dogmatism and empiricism in the
theoretical field, of Right or Left opportunism in the political field,
and of liberalism or sectarianism in the organizational field, that have
afflicted our Party. . . .

Right opportunism in the political field reveals itself first and foremost in the choice of the road to be taken to achieve people's
democracy in Indonesia as a transitional stage preceding Socialism.
One of the fundamental differences between Marxism-Leninism and

revisionism, both classic and modern, lies precisely in the question of choosing the road to Socialism. Marxism-Leninism teaches that Socialism can be achieved by the road of proletarian revolution and in the case of colonial or semicolonial and semifeudal countries such as Indonesia, only after completing the stage of the people's democratic revolution. Revisionism by contrast dreams of achieving Socialism by the peaceful road.

How did these errors develop?

For fifteen years after 1951, the PKI conducted a legal and parliamentary struggle. The legal and parliamentary form of struggle must be used by a revolutionary proletarian party under certain definite conditions, as Lenin explained in his work *"Left-Wing" Communism: An Infantile Disorder.* . . .

The parliamentary struggle as a form of legal struggle carried out by the Party in 1951 was in the main correct and in accordance with the objective conditions existing at that time: the revolutionary tide was at low ebb, the driving forces of the revolution were not yet reawakened, and the majority of the people who had never enjoyed political independence before the August Revolution still had hopes of bourgeois democracy.

During the early years of this period, our Party achieved something politically as well as building up the Party. One important achievement of this period was the formulation of the main problems of the Indonesian revolution. The Indonesian revolution was depicted as a new type of bourgeois democratic revolution, the tasks of which were to liquidate imperialism and the vestiges of feudalism and to establish a people's democratic system as a transitional stage to Socialism. The driving forces of the revolution were the working class, the peasantry, and the petty bourgeoisie; the leading force of the revolution was the working class and the principal mass strength of the revolution was the peasantry. The national bourgeoisie was described as a wavering force which might side with the revolution within certain limits but which might also betray it. The Party also held that the working class, to fulfill its obligations as the leader of the revolution, had to forge a revolutionary united front with other revolutionary classes and groups, based on a worker-peasant alliance under the leadership of the working class.

However, there was a very important shortcoming which in later days developed into Right opportunism or revisionism, namely, that the Party had not yet come to the clearest unity of minds on the

Indonesian revolution's principal means of struggle. The Central Committee of the Party once discussed this problem in broad terms but subsequently never discussed it intensively to reach the most correct common viewpoint as a prerequisite to reaching a correct and unanimous understanding of this problem in the whole Party.

It is a great mistake for a Party such as the PKI, having a historical mission to lead a revolution, not to make the question of the principal means and the main form of struggle of the Indonesian revolution a problem for the whole Party, instead of one that concerned only a minority of the leadership and certain cadres in the Party. In this way, the thoughts of the majority in the Party were rendered passive with regard to this most important problem of the revolution.

Though the leader of the Indonesian revolution is the working class, its principal mass supporters are the peasantry. In view of the smallness of the working class in Indonesia, the method of struggle characteristic of the working class, as when a general strike leads to the awakening of other driving forces of the revolution and develops into an armed insurrection, . . . can never become the main form of struggle or the method of the Indonesian revolution.

The Chinese revolution has given us a lesson on the main form of struggle of the revolution in colonial or semicolonial and semifeudal countries, namely the people's armed struggle against the armed counterrevolution. In line with the essence of the revolution as an agrarian revolution, the essence of the people's armed struggle is the armed struggle of the peasants in an agrarian revolution under the leadership of the working class. The practice of the Chinese revolution was first and foremost the application of Marxism-Leninism to the concrete conditions of China. At the same time, it has laid down the general law for the revolutions of the peoples in colonial or semicolonial and semifeudal countries.

To achieve complete victory, the Indonesian revolution must also follow the road of the Chinese revolution. This means that the Indonesian revolution must inevitably adopt this main form of struggle. . . .

The agrarian revolution which is the essence of the Indonesian revolution's present stage is not an agrarian reform of the bourgeois type that will only pave the way for the development of capitalism in the countryside. It will liberate the farm laborers, poor peasants, and middle peasants from the feudal oppression of foreign or native landlords, by confiscating the lands of the landlords and freely distributing them to farm laborers and poor peasants individually to be their private property. Such a revolution will be victorious only when it is carried out by force of arms under the leadership of the working class. This revolution will break out on the basis of the strong consciousness and conviction of the peasants themselves arising from their own experience and their education by the working class.

It is clear that in a situation where the conditions for a revolution are still absent the task of the PKI should be to educate Party members, the working class, and the peasantry, through political work, agitation, and propaganda, as well as through organizational work with regard to the Indonesian revolution's main form of struggle. All forms of legal and parliamentary work should be subordinated to the main form of struggle and must not in any way impede the process of the ripening of armed struggle.

The experience of the last fifteen years has taught us that starting from the failure to reject the "peaceful road" and to hold firmly to the general law of revolution in colonial or semicolonial and semifeudal countries, the PKI gradually got bogged down in parliamentary and other forms of legal struggle. The Party leadership even considered this to be the main form of struggle to achieve the Indonesian revolution's strategic aim. The legality of the Party was not considered as one method of struggle at a given time and under certain conditions but was erected into a principle while other forms of struggle had to serve this principle. Even when counterrevolution not only trampled underfoot the legality of the Party but violated the basic human rights of the Communists, the Party leadership still tried to defend this legality with all their might. . . .

In order to prove that the road followed was not the opportunist "peaceful road," the Party leadership always spoke of two possibilities, the possibility of a "peaceful road" and the possibility of a non-peaceful road. They held that the better the Party prepared itself to face the possibility of a non-peaceful road, the better would be the prospects for a peaceful road. In fact, such statements show precisely the existence of dualism concerning the road followed by the Party leadership. Thus, the Party leadership planted in the minds of Party members, the working class, and the masses of working people the hope for a peaceful road which in reality did not exist. . . .

When unilateral actions began to arise among the peasants which directly attacked the domestic landlords, they were not encouraged to develop into a higher form but were diverted along different lines and transformed into various actions that were not directed against the landlords, such as the "New Culture Movement," the "One Thousand and One Campaign" to raise production, the "Rat Extermination Campaign," and so on. Naturally, it is not wrong for a revolutionary peasant movement to launch campaigns to increase production, to exterminate pests, and to raise the cultural level of the peasants. But all of this should serve the main objective of the revolutionary peasant movement, namely, the antifeudal agrarian revolution. Therefore, such campaigns should not be valued so highly that the revolutionary peasant movement is converted into a reformist movement.

In the cities, despite the increasing suffering of the workers, political actions by the workers diminished because they lacked proper leadership. It is true that there were actions by the workers that seemed big and had great political significance, such as the take-over of the enterprises belonging to the Dutch, British, and Belgian imperialists. But actually, these actions benefited only a handful of bureaucratic capitalists and could by no means improve the living conditions of the workers concerned. Besides, since the Party leadership regarded the former imperialist-owned enterprises that were controlled by the government as national property, further actions by the workers were restrained. On the other hand, many activities were organized directly by trade unions or through Enterprise Councils aimed at increasing production, raising the working efficiency of the enterprises, improving the state of the economy, and the like, which did not improve the living conditions or heighten the revolutionary spirit of the workers.

Proceeding from the erroneous view that the armed forces of the Republic are not reactionary armed forces the problem of working among the enemy's troops was interpreted as "integrating the important instruments of the state with the people," or "strengthening the links between the people and the armed forces." This plainly means integrating the instrument of violence of the oppressing classes with the oppressed classes. Such error could occur because the Party leadership had deviated from the Marxist-Leninist teachings on the state, not considering the Indonesian Republic a bourgeois state nor its armed forces the instrument of a bourgeois state. The Party leadership forgot the reality that the armed forces of the Republic, as a whole, despite the fact that they were brought into being by the August Revolution, had become an instrument in the hands of the classes which ruled the state from the time the revolution failed and state power fell entirely into the hands of the reactionary bourgeoisie. In view of their class origin as sons of workers and peasants, the rank and file of the armed forces might indeed constitute elements who would take the side of the people. But this could not in any possible way alter the position of the armed forces as a whole as an organ of the state which served the interests of the ruling classes. . . .

The evolution of the mistakes in implementing the national united front can be traced briefly as follows. In the course of rebuilding the Party in 1951, efforts were made to win the national bourgeoisie over to the side of the people. By utilising contradictions between the national bourgeoisie and the compradore bourgeoisie, the Party succeeded in gradually winning the national bourgeoisie over to the side of the people. This began during the struggle against the Sukiman Cabinet and its "August Raids." This struggle was successful and the Wilopo Cabinet was formed. At that time and in the following years the Party was still weak and the alliance of the workers and peasants was not yet established. So, the united front with the national bourgeoisie failed to grow upon a strong foundation, namely, the alliance of the working class and the peasantry under the leadership of the working class.

The Party leadership valued the establishment of a united front with the national bourgeoisie and considered that it "opened up possibilities for the development of the Party and for the realization of the immediate tasks of the Party, namely, the formation of the alliance of the working class and the peasantry against feudalism" (D. N. Aidit, "Lessons from the History of the PKI," a speech delivered at the fortieth anniversary of the founding of the PKI). This appraisal gave rise to the formulation that the fostering of the national united front was the first and most urgent task of the PKI. This formulation clearly indicated that by the national united front, the Party leadership meant first and foremost the united front with the national bourgeoisie.

How could the united front with the national bourgeoisie be maintained in the absence of a strong alliance of the working class and the peasantry? There are two reasons: first, because the national bourgeoisie in their contradictions with the compradore bourgeoisie needed the support of the working class; second, because the Party gave the needed support without arousing apprehension in the national bourgeoisie that their position was in any way threatened.

The formation of the united front with the national bourgeoisie resulted in the formation of those cabinets which, to a certain extent, pursued an anti-imperialist policy and gave a little freedom of action to the PKI and the revolutionary mass organizations. No doubt this situation was rather favorable for the work of building up the Party, especially in the countryside, the fashioning of the worker-peasant alliance. The precondition for such an alliance already existed, namely, a revolutionary agrarian program.

However, in the course of the cooperation with the national bourgeoisie, the ideological weaknesses in the Party, in particular among the Party leadership, grew and were influenced by bourgeois ideology through that cooperation. The development of the ideological weaknesses in the Party gradually deprived it of its independence in the united front with the national bourgeoisie. The Party gave too many concessions to the national bourgeoisie and lost its independent role of leadership. One manifestation of this loss of independence in the united front with the national bourgeoisie was the Party leadership's attitude toward Sukarno. They always avoided conflicts with Sukarno and overemphasized the similarities and the unity between the Party and Sukarno. As the public saw it, Sukarno had no policy that was not supported by the PKI. The Party leadership went so far as to accept without resistance the recognition of Sukarno as the "Great Leader of the Revolution" and the leader of the "people's aspect" in the state power of the Republic. In many articles and speeches, Party leaders frequently said that the struggle of the PKI was based not only on Marxism-Leninism, but also on the teaching of Sukarno, that the PKI made such rapid progress because it carried out Sukarno's idea of *Nasakom* unity, and so forth. Even the system of people's democracy in Indonesia was said to be in conformity with Sukarno's main ideas as expressed in his speech, "The Birth of Pantja Sila." So the Party leadership failed to teach the working class and the rest of the working people that the leadership of the revolution must be in the hands of the proletariat and their Party, the PKI!

The Party leadership boasted that the birth of the Political Manifesto meant that the persistent struggle of the Indonesian people led by the PKI had successfully brought the broad masses to recognize the correctness of the PKI's program, and therefore "to implement the Political Manifesto consistently is the same as implementing the program of the PKI."

The formulation of a common program for the united front is indeed a good thing, and in this sense the birth of the Political Manifesto, too, was a good thing because it could serve up to a point to unite the thinking of the various anti-imperialist classes and groups with regard to certain problems of the Indonesian revolution. However, it is not true that the birth of the Political Manifesto and its further elaboration meant that the broad masses recognized the correctness of the PKI's program, because the Party program and the Political Manifesto had only certain parts in common.

Communists should not have supposed naively that other classes which do not belong to the driving forces of the revolution would easily accept the program of the PKI. They accepted only those parts of the Party's tactical program which were not detrimental to their own interests, while rejecting those parts which were contrary to their interests, such as the leading role of the working class, revolutionary agrarian reform, and so on. There was no guarantee, either, that they would implement those parts of the Party's program which they accepted. Meanwhile, the reactionaries who assumed a dominating position in the state power accepted the Political Manifesto hypocritically, in an effort to adjust themselves to the prevailing situation. No matter how consistently the Political Manifesto was implemented, it could never be the same as the program of the PKI. Consequently, to say that consistently implementing the Political Manifesto meant implementing the program of the PKI could only mean that the program of the national bourgeoisie was accepted by the PKI and was made to replace the program of the PKI.

The abandonment of principle in the united front with the national bourgeoisie developed even further in the so-called "General Line of the Indonesian Revolution" that was formulated as follows: "With the national united front having the workers and peasants as its pillars, *Nasakom* as its core, and the Pantja Sila as its ideological basis, complete the national democratic revolution in order to advance toward Indonesian Socialism!" This so-called "General Line of the Indonesian Revolution" did not have even the faintest smell of revolution about it, because, of the three preconditions for a successful revolution, namely, a strong Marxist-Leninist party, a people's armed struggle under the leadership of the Party, and a united front, only the united front was retained. Even then, it was not led by the working class nor was it based on the alliance of the working class and the peasantry under the leadership of the working class but, on the contrary, it was based on *Nasakom.* . . .

The Party leadership said that "The slogan for national cooperation with *Nasakom* as its core will by no means obscure the class content of the national united front." This statement is incorrect, because apart from the working class party, there were political parties in *Nasakom* representing mainly the interests of the national bourgeoisie, the compradores, the bureaucratic capitalists, and the landlords. Ever since the banning of the compradore parties such as the Masjumi and the PSI, the compradores and landlords have been seeking admittance in other political parties and organizations of nationalist or religious tendency. Thus, the class content of *Nasakom* was the working class, the national bourgeoisie, and even elements of the compradores, the bureaucratic-capitalists, and the landlords. Obviously, making *Nasakom* the core meant not only obscuring the class content of the national united front but radically changing it into . . . class collaboration.

The erroneous political line which dominated the Party was inevitably followed by an equally erroneous organizational line. The longer and the more intensively the wrong political line ruled in the Party, the greater were the mistakes in organizational field, and the greater the losses caused by them. Right opportunism which constituted the wrong political line of the Party in the period after 1951 had been followed by another Right deviation in the organizational field, namely, liberalism and legalism.

The line of liberalism in the organizational field manifested itself in the tendency to make the PKI a party with as large a membership as possible, a party with a loose organization, which was called a mass Party. . . .

Now it is clear that the mass character of a party is determined not primarily by the size of its membership, but by the closeness of the party and the masses, and by the party's political line which defends the interests of the masses. And the mass line of the party can only be maintained when the prerequisites determining the party's role as vanguard are firmly upheld, when the party is made up of the best elements of the proletariat who are armed with Marxism-Leninism. Consequently, to build a Marxist-Leninist party which has a mass character is impossible without giving primary importance to Marxist-Leninist education.

During the last few years, the PKI built up the party along lines which deviated from Marxist-Leninist principles. After success in expanding the membership and organization through short-term plans, the Party successively carried out the First Three-Year Plan (Organi-

zation and Education) and the Second Three-Year Plan (Education
and Organization), and was embarking on the Four-Year Plan (Culture, Ideology, and Organization). Through the fulfilment of the
short-term plans and the First and the Second Three-Year Plans, the
PKI had spread to all parts of the country and to all islands and ethnic
groups throughout Indonesia, with a membership of more than three
million. This was a great achievement.

But at the same time liberalism was growing in the Party. Though
the Second Three-Year Plan professed to stress ideological education,
it was always the expansion of the membership and organization
which was emphasized in practice. The plan for the recruitment of
new members was carried out with complete disregard of the organization's capacity to absorb and train the new members. Since Party
organizations concentrated their efforts solely on reaching the targets
fixed in the plan, the recruitment of new members was carried out in
violation of provisions laid down in the Party constitution. The organization of the PKI had been made so loose that practically everyone who had expressed his agreement with the program of the PKI
could be accepted as a member. One could no longer clearly distinguish a Party member from a member of a mass organization led
by the Party. The conditions for membership in the vanguard of the
working class were altogether ignored.

The liberal expansion of Party membership was bound up with the
political line of the peaceful road. The large membership was intended
to increase the influence of the Party in the united front with the
national bourgeoisie. With the growing Party in continuing alliance
with the national bourgeoisie, a change in the balance of power was to
be achieved that would permit the total defeat of the diehard forces.
The interests of the peaceful road were even more graphically reflected in the organizational field in the Party's Four-Year Plan.

In this plan, the stress was no longer laid on the education and the
training of Marxist-Leninist cadres to prepare them for revolution or
for work among the peasants to establish revolutionary bases, but on
the education of intellectuals to serve the needs of the work in the
united front with the national bourgeoisie and to supply cadres for
the various positions in the state institutions that were obtained thanks
to cooperation with the national bourgeoisie. In the light of this
policy, the slogan of "Total integration with the peasants" became
empty talk. What was being done in practice was to draw cadres from

the countryside to the cities and from the regions to the center, instead of sending the best cadres to work in rural areas.

To raise the prestige of the PKI in the eyes of the bourgeoisie and to make it respected as a party of intellectuals, the Four-Year Plan stipulated that all cadres of the higher ranks must obtain academic education, cadres of the middle ranks secondary education, and cadres of the lower ranks lower middle school education. For this purpose the Party set up a great number of academies, schools, and courses. So deep-rooted was the intellectualism gripping the Party leadership that all leaders of the Party and popular movements had to write four theses in order to obtain the degree of "Marxist Scientist."

The deeper the party plunged into the mire of opportunism and revisionism, the less was its organizational vigilance and the more legalism developed in the organization. The Party leadership lost its class prejudice toward the falsehoods of bourgeois democracy. From everything the Party did, it appeared that the peaceful road was a certainty. The Party leadership did not alert the mass of Party members to the danger of attacks by reactionaries who were constantly on the watch for a chance to strike. Owing to this legalism in the organizational field, the counterrevolution has succeeded in paralyzing the PKI organizationally within a short time.

Liberalism in organization had destroyed the principle of internal democracy in the Party, destroyed collective leadership, and given rise to personal leadership and personal power, and to autonomism which provided fertile ground for the growth of the personality cult. . . . With liberalism dominating its organizational line, the Party could not do its job, namely, to combine theory and practice, to keep close bonds with the masses, and to conduct self-criticism. It was equally impossible to implement the method of leadership, the essence of which is the unity of the leadership and the masses, for which the leadership must give an example to the rank and file.

In actual fact there was no integration of the universal truth of Marxism-Leninism with the concrete practice of the Indonesian revolution, but attempts to reconcile Marxist-Leninist teachings with the views of the bourgeoisie, to systematize and develop the views and the theories of the bourgeoisie, and, under such slogans as "Indonesianization of Marxism-Leninism" and "Developing Marxism-Leninism creatively," to revise Marxism–Leninism.

PART THREE

AREAS OF CONTROVERSY

IX

National Identity

The debate on what Indonesia should take from the West and what it should do to remain true to its own history and culture is as old as nationalism itself and has always been something of a Great Debate. It was carried on vigorously in the 1930's, particularly in artistic and intellectual circles and more generally throughout the community of persons of modern education.

After 1945 it was sustained, becoming a major part of what the radical nationalists and democratic socialists argued about in the following decade. It became particularly central after 1956, when President Sukarno began to appeal for a Guided Democracy, coupling this with demands that Indonesia should return to its own identity. After the reactivation of the 1945 Constitution in 1959, "Returning to Our National Identity" became an important theme of government ideology and one of the five principles of *Manipol-USDEK*, and the government made vigorous denunciations of rock-'n'-roll, cha-cha-cha, and Dutch-sounding abbreviations of first names as well as of "Dutch thinking," "textbook thinking," and "hyper-intellectualism." Hence a good deal of the argument between the supporters of Guided Democracy and its opponents was about cultural borrowing and the proper foundations of a national personality. Then, as before, Javanese tended to favor national identity ideas, as, for instance, in Vg, which illustrates a common theme of national identity advocates, the praise of the village. Non-Javanese tended to be more suspicious, an extreme example being Kahar Muzakar (Xe).

In the first six of the following extracts "pro-Western" and "pro-national identity" views alternate with each other, with chronology largely disregarded. Hatta stands close to the democratic socialists here, Sjamsudin Kartokusumo to the radical nationalists and Javanese traditionalists. Soedjatmoko presents a further argument for the "modernizing" or "pro-Western" view, and Selosoemardjan gives a sociological explanation, and partial justification, of the tendency for Western influences to be denigrated under Guided Democracy. Another sociologist, Muhammad Slamet, writing at about the same time, provides a fully argued case against the government demand for a "Return to Our National Identity"; and this is followed by the left-wing nationalist argument of Mrs. Utami Suryadarma on the other side.

For the last two slots we have chosen extracts which do not fit easily into a view of the debate as one between two major camps. Aidit's approach is clearly closer to that of the "modernizing" or "pro-Western" groups than to the radical nationalist position of his party's current allies; it is also clearly different in emphasis from the other markedly left-wing extract here, that of Mrs. Utami Suryadarma. Mohamad Said's contribution is interesting for its individuality; the author's synthesis of Javanese moralism and Western social science is unique and endows him in many eyes with the stature of a prophet.

IXa

Mohammad Hatta Take the Core of Foreign Culture and Throw Away the Peel (1952)

This extract is taken from the opening address given by Hatta as Vice-President to an All-Indonesian Cultural Congress held at Bandung in January 1952. The address was published in Indonesia, Madjalah Kebudajaan, *III (January–March 1952), 20–30.*

If we look at the cultures of foreign nations generally known as civilized, we can detect a pattern to which the various features of each culture conform. They have a kind of unity in their cultures. With our nation this is not so. It is difficult to say that Indonesian culture has a particular character as one can in the case of those other nations. There are similarities from one region to another, but there are also differences. We would not be far from the truth if we said that the culture of our nation still has regional features.

That is why I am not surprised that many efforts are being made to find a basis for the unified development of Indonesian culture. Generally, people want to base the development of our culture on the Pantja Sila which has become the basis of our state. This can be seen, for example, in the various papers presented to this Congress, and our chairman himself, Mr. Bahder Djohan, said in an interview with Aneta News Agency that the goal of the Congress is "to arrive at criteria for cultured life which are based upon Pantja Sila, in order to create a characteristically Indonesian spirit of culture."

In this connection, one condition that is now clear is that the character of Indonesian culture varies from region to region, born as it is from the vibrations of different spirits. It is not easy to blend all this into one. From what has been said by all the experts on our way of life, we can see that great variety exists in our economic ideas, artistic ideas, views of life, and so on. Rather than compose a unified culture at this time, we would do better to create harmonious relationships between the cultural groups so that they appreciate and fertilize each other. We can cultivate such relationships within the framework of our state motto *Bhinneka Tunggal Ika,* or Unity in Diversity.

This diversity should be taken as something given in the development of our culture from which we shall proceed firmly and consciously toward a higher level. Science and technology, which are universal in nature and whose influence on Indonesian culture will grow, will increase automatically the things which unify and decrease the things which diversify. But complete unity will never be achieved. All kinds of differences will always remain as evidence of the living quality of Indonesia's vast society.

To establish a wholly unified culture, a great deal of power, dictatorial power, would have to be placed in the hands of the state. The state would have to plan, arrange, and determine from above the characteristics of the culture. Whatever deviated from its standards for unity would have to be wiped out. The result would be that whatever was living in culture would die or, at best, become technology. It is clear that such a system would be contrary to our ideals, contrary to the spirit of our society which created a democratic state on the foundation of Pantja Sila, inconsistent with the philosophical basis of the Republic of Indonesia. . . .

Often the question is posed: do we have to reject foreign cultures or filter them?

According to its nature and its sociology, Indonesian culture easily develops and enriches itself with elements of foreign cultures. Elements from Arab, Persian, Indian, Chinese, and Western cultures have made no small contribution to Indonesian culture. In the past our people have shown how to receive cultures from the whole world to enrich their own. The location of our homeland as an archipelago, a chain of islands, at the crossroads of inter-Asian and international communications has always led us to mix a lot with the foreigners calling here. Because of this and because our people are cultured and hospitable many foreigners settled here and brought various elements of their civilizations into ours. That is why it is impossible to keep foreign cultural elements from entering Indonesia. It has been proved impossible in the past, and it will be even more impossible in the future because of the progress of science and technology together with the development of economic ties with the outside world.

What is important for us is the way in which we respond to foreign culture. Historically we have accepted elements of foreign cultures without losing the core of our own. Our attitude to the foreign cultures impinging upon us at this time must, as I have often said, be one of adapting rather than adopting. Let us not receive them and swallow them whole; let us rather bend them to our needs.

We can enrich our culture by making use of foreign cultures without forgetting the basis of our own. In any case, we have been dominated and influenced by foreign nations in the past, and we feel thankful that our nation has been able to protect and cultivate the essence of its own culture. Though under pressure from foreign cultures, its roots did not die but lived. One of the main reasons is that our culture is based on a civilized and moral tradition and stands at a rather high level.

We must look after the roots of our culture because in them lies our defense. A nation which has lost its own culture cannot be strong, cannot have individuality, and quickly descends to copying. Should our culture ever become mere "civilization" (as this is conceived of in the West) it will be cut off from its roots. We will forget our own selves.

But our nation has been blessed by God Almighty. It can defend the basis of its own culture whatever foreign influence it is exposed to. Our flexible customs and traditions, the nation's heritage, are clearly not outdated; they enable us to develop without rejecting foreign cultures. If I look at the progress our culture has made since early times and at the way our people have received constructive elements from foreign cultures without abandoning their own, I have no fears that our people will forget their roots. The history of this culture of ours should be our guide in laying down cultural policy for the future.

Looking at the character of the papers we are to discuss at this Congress, it is clear that there is a strong desire to develop our culture along the lines of the Pantja Sila. This means that we have not yet looked closely enough at the possibilities of achieving various kinds of progress through building on our existing cultural foundations. The relationships between these five principles have not yet been fully clarified, but anyone who examines them thoroughly in the spirit of our culture will find a strong foundation. The Pantja Sila is not "a bundle of contradictions" as someone has called it. Pantja Sila cannot be expected to provide a single unitary basis, as it is clear from its very name that it comprises five bases. Anyone who is not committed to monism as a philosophical dogma can appreciate that it has five distinct bases and can see relationships and links among these five. Be that as it may, the Pantja Sila can be made a guide for building up culture, for developing art in its various forms, and advancing science and knowledge.

As I look at all this with faith in our capacity to arise and build a culture on the foundations we have accepted for our state, I have no fear that we will be completely submerged in foreign culture. Sometimes, of course, foreign cultural products exercise a bad influence so that we react against them. As I have said, the presence of the film censorship problem on the agenda of the Congress makes it clear that there is uneasiness about the penetration of one particular aspect of foreign culture which could undermine our morality. This reaction proves that the art and culture that comes from overseas is not all good. Something that is considered normal in other countries would possibly be scandalous and indecent in Indonesia, or a threat to public welfare. Foreign cultural influences may be good or bad, but if we look closely at the core of our culture, there is no need to fear that it will be poisoned by the bad aspects of foreign cultures. I have no fear that the Indonesian people in general can be cut off from the roots of their culture.

If there is anything to fear from bad influences, it will possibly be in the large cities which are very much influenced by the way of life of foreigners, especially Westerners. In these places, most of our people just become imitators. As usual, the easiest thing to imitate is the shallow, the superficial. Those people do not penetrate to the inside, to the kernel of the foreign culture concerned.

The reason for all this is that most of our cities did not arise from our own society but rather as appendages of a foreign economy. These cities are not centers of the creative activity of our own people but primarily distribution centers for foreign goods. They emerged before a spirit and soul capable of receiving the core of the foreign culture concerned was ready.

We can understand the shortcomings of our cities as filters of foreign cultural influences if we compare the process of their emergence with the birth of cities in the West. There the city emerged with the development of an exchange economy and grew from within, out of the womb of its own society. The city became a center of constructive work, such as small industry and handicrafts. The city dwellers were bearers of culture and governed themselves. In the West, the cities have always carried the torch of freedom.

As I have said, the Indonesian city was built from without and became a center of foreign power. It is not a place where handicrafts or national economic activities have developed but is primarily a center for the distribution of foreign-produced goods. That is why our cities are not capable of filtering the foreign cultures that come here and are receptive to all kinds of things which our people regard as bad and which are regarded in the West, too, as excesses. What is taken from the Western nations first is not their active spirit, but dancing, "free social intercourse," and so on.

Now that we are consciously building up our culture, the center of this culture-building will be in the cities, too. Let us clean them out and fill them with the national spirit. We must be cautious and selective in the face of foreign cultures. Take the core and throw away the peel! It is the core that we must hold on to and use to enrich our culture, not the skin. Western dancing, as we have seen it, is an element of Western culture; it accords with the spirit and customs of Westerners, who can practice it without endangering their morality. But in the case of our young people who lack that background dancing often stimulates desires and channels thoughts in wrong directions. That is why very many of the older generation feel anxious when they notice the behavior of some of our young people who like to imitate Western ways.

So I affirm here: if you take Western culture as a model, take not the skin but the contents. What is particularly worth taking from Westerners is their dynamism in thought and action. In order to give meaning to our independence, to achieve prosperity and spiritual well-being for our nation as soon as possible, we must become more active. Let us actively study the science which has been brought to us by Westerners and develop and spread it as widely as possible through our society.

At the present time, we are a nation which receives more than it gives. But if we continue to be active in thinking and doing, a time will come when our nation will make a valuable contribution to the science and culture of the world.

As we sift the products of their thought for our own needs, let us above all take note of their method, the way they think and analyze the problems of society and so on. Let us also look at how they depict the various features of social life in their literature. In our novels let us not just imitate the various views expressed by Westerners in their works of literature. What must be studied is their basic approach and method. Analyses of social relationships in our literature must accord with reality here. Do not merely copy Western literature; do not be a tree without roots, as in the proverb.

There is much we can learn from Western culture. If we are good at sifting it critically, there is no need for us to fear the penetration of its influences. For more than three hundred years we were dominated by the Dutch, and this did not destroy our culture.

IXb

Sjamsudin Kartokusumo Sunan Bonang and Sunan Kalidjogo (1964)

This extract is taken from an unpublished letter of September 17, 1964, to a Western friend.

This is not the first time in history that the Indonesian people have had to face a confrontation between new alien ideas and old ideas which were also once alien but have since become Indonesianized. Let us delve for a while into Indonesia's history and for our purpose let us put the fifteenth century in the spotlight, the period when new alien religious ideas, those of Islam, were brought to the shores of the Indonesian Archipelago by merchants from the Middle East and India. Coastal potentates who had embraced the new religion began to feel superior to, and to revolt against, the "pagan" king in the capital of Madjapahit. The authority of the central government waned, and finally it lost its once mighty grip on the vast kingdom, which was actually already undergoing a process of disintegration and which ultimately collapsed and split into several lesser kingdoms. But none of the Muslim coastal rulers had the ability or capability to set up in Madjapahit's stead a kingdom of the same might, vitality, and size. These rulers had not yet had time to consolidate their recently acquired political power when Western Europeans appeared on the Indonesian scene.

From that time on, relatively speaking, the Indonesian people stopped making history for about four hundred years. That episode is the history of the Europeans in Indonesia. In relation to this, Louis Fischer in his *Story of Indonesia* says: "Vital and united, the East Indies might have resisted the white intruder. Divided, they fell and gave Europe the cue which brought it onto the stage for more than four centuries."

To consolidate their political authority the Muslim rulers had to convert the Hindu-Buddhist population to Islam. For this purpose Java was apparently divided into nine operational areas in each of which a preacher was appointed to teach Islam among the people. This preacher was called a *wali* and since their number was *songo,* the Javanese word for "nine," their name was *Wali Songo,* or the nine preachers. However, I remember only two of their names—Wali Sunan Bonang and Wali Sunan Kalidjogo. Gatherings were regularly held among them to report on their individual work and successes. In one of those gatherings the Sultan of Demak, a political figure who had been converted to Islam, reported that he had sacked the capital of Madjapahit and burned down the royal palace and all the Hindu-Buddhist books that had so much "magic" for the Javanese. Sunan Bonang, commenting on the report, said: "That has been very correctly judged. As long as there are still books containing the Hindu-Buddhist world outlook, the Javanese will persist in their paganism, maybe for a thousand years, and never change their religion to following the Laws of the God's Prophet. They will not repent or invoke the names of Allah and His Prophet."

Sunan Bonang seemed to overlook the fact that the population had kept the contents of their books in the secrecy of their hearts and that history is a continuous process which can not possibly be cut off, as he wanted it to be, so as to make the past disappear. A much wiser and more mature attitude was adopted by another *wali,* Sunan Kalidjogo, who decided to reconcile Islam with Hindu-Buddhism as the best way of converting the Javanese Indonesians to Islam. This is illustrated in the following legend.

In the neighborhood of my birthplace, Purbolinggo, in the western-most part of Central Java, there is a mountain ridge which completely encircles a bowl-shaped valley. This ridge is called Gunung

Lawet. A peculiarity of this ridge is that all the hilltops are bent in-ward into the bowl-shaped valley. The story among people of that area, which has been handed down from generation to generation, tells us that Wali Sunan Kalidjogo once preached Islam there in the following way:

Brothers, do you know why all these hilltops are bent toward us? Not long ago, right here in the valley, I met Yudistira, the eldest of the Pandawa Brothers. He had been wandering through Java desperate, very much wanting to die but unable to as long as his amulet, called "Kalimo Sodo," * was still with him. He did not know of a single person fit to inherit this amulet from him, and, after all, he could not just throw it away without further ado. Then I talked to him and made him understand that I was the most fitting person to whom he could hand down his "Kalimo Sodo" amulet, because the real meaning of "Kalimo Sodo" is "Kalimat Sahadat," which runs: "Ashadu Allah ilaha illallah wa ashadu ana Mo-hammadar Rasulu'llah." † Unconsciously Yudistira had already embraced Islam. He fully understood the situation and passed his amulet to me. At last he was able to leave this earth. That, Brothers, is why all those hill-tops are bent inward toward us. They wanted to listen to my talk with Yudistira then and to my talk with you now.

That is how Wali Sunan Kalidjogo won the Javanese Indonesians over to Islam. Is this Wali not the counterpart of St. Paul who brought Christianity to the ancient Greeks, and whose theology which has been given to Christianity is no more nor less than the Greek Dionysian theology of the Savior? On seeing an altar in Athens with the inscrip-tion "For the unknown God," St. Paul immediately grasped the op-portunity to say to the Greeks that the unknown God whom they worshipped was in reality the Christian God. It is assumed that Christianity in the hands of St. Paul has become Greek while in those of St. Peter it has become Jewish. It could not have been other-wise. The assimilation of the new and the old into a growing and living synthesis is inevitable.

Our two *walis* lived in the fifteenth century. In their time they represented two different types of personalities. Let us call them, for the sake of convenience, the Bonang-type and the Kalidjogo-type. These two types of person, however, turn up in every period when the old is being confronted with the new. The Bonang-type is easily

---

* Literally, "great power of Kali," a powerful charm given to Yudistira by Kali, the Hindu goddess of destruction.

† The Muslim declaration of faith: "There is no God but Allah and Moham-med is His Prophet."

charmed, enchanted, and overpowered by the new, so that he is what he actually still is but thinks he has ceased to be. The new is unconditionally accepted as his supposed present identity. He denies his own identity and starts to adopt a new one. The continuity of the growth of his identity is broken off at a certain moment, and a start is made on the development of a quite new one which has just been adopted. Could this be possible? How could the new become a living and growing organism when there are no roots to feed it, when the individual who has taken it up has cut himself off from his ancestral culture and has become completely without culture?

Then we have the second type, the Kalidjogo-type, who is fully aware that his mind is deeply rooted in the past but remains receptive to the new, including that which has come from alien soil. He appreciates the new, but he knows that it cannot be assimilated as a growing and living element in his mind if he denies his own past and cuts himself off from the roots which have been feeding his identity up to now. Here there is no question of cutting and breaking off; the continuity of his identity remains undisturbed. The new is assimilated with the old into a harmonious synthesis which is fresh because of the new and full of vitality because of the vigorous roots that still feed it. History is a continuity.

In relation to this I would very much like to remind you of the figure of Virgil's Aeneas. The city of Troy had been sacked and burned down by the Greeks. Aeneas fled from the destroyed town in search of a better future and asked his father, a lame old man, to go with him. He carried the lame old man on his back and led his little son by the hand as he left burning Troy. This is a man who had to start his life anew but did not forget the past. When he went into the wide world in search of a better life and future, responsibility for the past was still clinging to him. Such is André Gide's interpretation of the Aeneas-figure. In this figure I clearly see the reflected image of my own people. They, too, are leaving their destroyed old world still carrying their past with them.

Let us now scrutinize the twentieth-century Bonang-type. The ancient Sunan Bonang saw the problem as it stood in principle, in the alternative: Islam or Hindu-Buddhism. He made his choice, and it fell on Islam. The modern Sunan Bonang puts himself before a similar alternative: the West or the rudiments of the remnants of the Indonesian feudal civilization. And he, too, has made his definite choice, and it has fallen on the West.

This is the prototype of the modern Sunan Bonang. Indonesians of this type seem to have lost every cord that once connected them with their past, with the Indonesian people, their own people. These men of the Bonang-type feel that they are closer to Europe and America than to the Borobudur, or the Mahabharata, or the primitive Islamic culture in Java and Sumatra. They strongly believe that in their spiritual needs they depend on the West, not only scientifically but culturally as well. Anything that Europe has accomplished in the fields of politics, economics, social affairs, literature, and art is considered as the universal standard and norm. Western values are equivalent to international values. Since European culture is supposed to be international in nature, Indonesians are seen as unable to escape from finally embracing the West in its whole totality. As science and technology could never be separated from Western traditions and world outlook and life attitude, so the West should be accepted in its totality and should be the cultural basis from which the Indonesian people set forth after they have acquired their independence. Such is the reasoning of the modern Bonang-type. I believe in the sincerity of their conviction, but I fail to see the correctness of their reasoning.

Most of them have had their education in Europe and have come back to Indonesia with their minds deeply steeped in European cultural values and traditions. When they find themselves among their fellow-Indonesians who have never been outside Indonesia they begin to discover, to their own surprise, that they get annoyed and vexed by the things that fill the lives of the Indonesian people and to which these people are so attached. Those things which to the people contain beauty and arouse their gentler emotions are considered senseless and ugly. The people's inertness and obstinacy, the people's ignorance and small shortcomings in their behavior, all these have made them impatient, desperate and mad. They are definitely not habitual schizophrenes, who are divided within themselves. No, they do not belong to a double world but positively to a single world, the Western world. They cannot be classified among people who are usually termed "marginal men" or, as Han Su-yin calls them in *A Many-Splendored Thing*, "the intellectual Eurasians."

Apparently no sweet sound and warmth of childhood binds them emotionally to their own country any more. It is only the fascinating West that has them spellbound and that has swept the last lovely memories of the past out of their minds. And then they start to complain of not being understood by their own people. But have they

ever tried to understand their people, have they ever accepted their
people as they actually are? No, in view of their feeling about the
Borobudur, the Mahabharata, the puppet-play, the "primitive Islamic
culture," * and so on. No effort has ever been made in that direction.
Finally, they wonder: Am I perhaps estranged from my people? In
fact, from the moment when they start to wonder and doubt, they
have lost every moral right to constitute themselves as leaders of
their people.

If the faith and future of this country were entrusted to men of this
Bonang-type, the political institutions of Indonesia would be mere
poor duplicates of those in Europe, quite irrelevant to the Indonesian
world of thought. They want to concentrate their activities on bringing the organization of the country's administration to perfection, but
that would be no different from the administration of the Western
colonial rulers, which was marked by its perfect efficiency. These men
would warn the Indonesian people to leave alone foreign entrepreneurs and their enterprises within the Indonesian economic framework, otherwise, the Indonesian economy would collapse; they would
warn them that Southeast Asia belongs to the sphere of influence of
the Anglo-Saxon peoples, so that the Indonesian people must not
overestimate their abilities and must check their wishes and aspirations accordingly. The Indonesians cannot subsist from "spirit" alone;
they must have a considerable dose of a sense of reality. All this is the
"Sermon on the Mount" of the modern Sunan Bonangs.

But what does this sense of reality mean to the Indonesian people
but yielding to present realities? The Indonesian people would then
continue to keep the predicate of "brown sods," sods from whom the
West thinks it should keep aloof. The Indonesians would still have
the quiet and peaceful lives of these "brown sods" and might enjoy
the agreeable rice-price of one rupiah per kilo. But Indonesia would
then be no more than an independent country of the type of Malaya,
and the Republic of Indonesia would be a mere name.

IXc

Soedjatmoko   The Courage to Try
New Ways (1954)

This piece comes from an article in the September–October 1954

* This phrase, like many others attacked and derided in this extract, comes
from S. Sjahrir, *Out of Exile* (New York: John Day, 1949).

issue of the bimonthly cultural journal Konfrontasi, *an article which was published in English by the Cornell Modern Indonesia Project under the title* Economic Development as a Cultural Problem.*

In analyzing the problem of industrialization in Indonesia we see that there is required a process of all-enveloping change, a process that is a creative adjustment of our culture. To accomplish this creative adjustment we must evoke from within our own cultural pattern appropriate stimuli which will serve as catalytic factors in our social structure, providing an impetus toward a modernization specifically Indonesian in character. Failing this, the adjustment we make will be purely passive; we will not go beyond the level of mere imitation; we will have done no more than shift from one static position to another static position, and we will always lag behind.

At the same time, in approaching the question of industrialization we cannot take the stand of being prepared to accept modern machinery and technology but unwilling to accept other expressions of modern culture. There is absolutely no justification for this narrow eclecticism advocated by certain of our cultural leaders, an eclecticism which is also vaguely found among various sections of the population. As a prerequisite condition for our mastering of machinery and of modern technology we must first understand the culture and the mental orientation which brought them into being. An understanding of occidental culture, the fountainhead of the modern world, could help us to discover within ourselves dynamic principles of our very own, such as those referred to above. . . .

The experience of India, China, and Burma shows that there does exist for us the possibility of seeking a solution for Indonesia in accordance with our own situation and our own national character. To do this, however, we must throw off the bonds of any dogma and entrust our destiny to our own creative capacities. Accepting this condition, we can see that there is, then, no need for the attempt to make an a priori definition of the future pattern of Indonesian culture before we launch ourselves on the road toward economic development. For the subsequent form and content of our culture will be evolved by a new Indonesia, by a people no longer haunted by the threat of poverty but imbued with an awareness of its national individuality and self-confidence, determined to be themselves the masters of their destiny. Naturally, the specifically Indonesian character

* Ithaca, N.Y., 1958; reprinted by permission.

of our culture will be imprinted on the solution we find to the problem of development, and thus it is pointless to insist a priori on one or other specific pattern for the evolution of our culture.

Nor is there any reason for hesitating to adopt innovations only because these may be felt somehow to be un-Indonesian. Only that cultural pattern will be meaningful to us which can secure our place in this world and which at the same time we can consider the expression of ourselves. In dealing with the problem of building our new society we must, therefore, have the courage to go about it in a practical way; we must have the courage to try new ways, and if these prove to be unsuitable or insufficient, we must have the courage to cast them aside and to try other ones. In all this the regulating principle is a desire for development, for without this desire and determination everything is meaningless.

On the other hand, an active desire for progress cannot arise unless we fully understand the purpose of development, unless we have firmly established the objectives we wish to reach, unless we have a clear conception of the changes that will take place in our ways of living, and unless we are honestly convinced that the pursuit of economic development is a legitimate and desirable purpose.

IXd

Selosoemardjan   Narrowing the Cultural Gap (1961)

This extract, * like IIIg, comes from a paper written originally in 1961 and published in the January 1963 issue of the* Review of Politics *(Vol. XXV) under the title "Some Social and Cultural Implications of Indonesia's Unplanned and Planned Development."*

Different systems of education in the prewar period promoted in Indonesian towns the development of a class of Dutch-oriented intelligentsia which felt socially superior to those having no formal education or having formal instruction only in the non-Dutch rural schools. From this basic distinction there developed other differences which extended the social and cultural distance between the two classes. Mastering the Dutch language and learning Western cultural traits were found rewarding, as to do so opened the way to higher ranks in the administration and, eventually, in well-paying foreign-owned business. This development led to an alienation of the intel-

* Reprinted by permission.

ligentsia from the indigenous Indonesian culture; it even fostered the popular notion that Western culture was superior to Indonesian. This view drew strength from the fact that Dutch and other Western languages, Western education, Western types of houses, and Western cultural patterns were associated with the dominant Dutch social elite in the colony. Great efforts were, therefore, made by members of the Indonesian intelligentsia to "go Western" and to be associated with Dutch social circles. Culturally speaking, the intelligentsia tended to drift more and more to the West and the Dutch. . . .

The present urge to rediscover the Indonesian identity may be seen as a correction of the cultural alienation characteristic of the Indonesian intelligentsia. This effect is closely related to Indonesian Socialism, for the Indonesian identity will define the Indonesian quality of the socialist society to be ultimately established in the Indonesian Republic. During the period of liberal democracy there was a persistent effort to adapt the less educated masses to the principles of Western political institutions and to adjust their life to Western standards of political and social behavior. When this effort proved to be unavailing, the President decided to narrow the cultural gap between the Western-educated class and the non-Western-oriented groups of the population by reversing the process of acculturation; the acceptance of Indonesian identity as the fifth principle in *USDEK* requires the reacculturation of the Western-educated class to the indigenous cultural patterns still maintained by the non-Western-oriented groups.

The principles are idealistic in nature, while the outlines given by the President and First Minister have not taken away very much of their vagueness. Nevertheless, in less than three years, they have proved to be useful guiding principles and broad directives which have had a unifying effect upon Indonesian society, disorganized in large measure as the result of colonial rule and of more than a decade of unplanned political and social revolution. . . .

In the light of the intelligentsia's alienation from Indonesian culture during colonial rule, the present nativistic cultural movement may be seen as negatively motivated in its flight from Western culture. But this reaction found its stimulus in the disorganizing social effects of the rapid and unbalanced process of acculturation of Western democracy which, in turn, produced a personality-centered and tradition-oriented Indonesian culture. The eight-year plan does not reject Western cultural elements but seeks to establish a firm cultural groundwork of specifically Indonesian character, so that Indonesian society in its planned development can remain integrated in its contacts with other societies that have already reached a higher stage in the development of science, technology, and industry.

IXe
Moehammad Slamet Let Us Not Crawl Back into Our Shells (1960)

This extract comes from "Some Ideas on 'Returning to our National Identity' in Indonesia," an essay which was written for the World Federation of Mental Health and published in Indonesian in February 1960 as an Occasional Paper of the Social Research Center of Padjadjaran State University, Bandung.

Since President Sukarno's Independence Day speech of August 17, 1959, in which he proposed that the Indonesian people should seek a return to their own national identity, the press has carried much discussion of his proposal, both in editorials and in readers' letters.

Although this "return to the national identity" was intended by Bung Karno as a positive and constructive movement, as a force which could reintegrate the nation in its efforts to realize its ideals, there are signs that this noble intention is beginning to be misunderstood by various persons, so that it is very possible that public opinion will be influenced and tend towards negative, conservative, and reactionary attitudes.

This paper is intended to discuss some aspects of these negative tendencies, so that we can become aware of them and thus together uphold our nation's welfare.

To introduce the subject, I will first briefly discuss the question of neurosis. There are many definitions of neurosis. The term originates from a period in the development of medical science when neurosis was considered to be closely related to the nervous system. According to the definition accepted by a school of psychiatry centering around such figures as Karen Horney, Erich Fromm, Harry Stack Sullivan, and Rollo May in North America, J. A. C. Brown in England, and Buytendijk, Rümke, and Van den Berg in Holland, neurosis is the psychic disturbance of a healthy individual or the derangement of normal human relations. Such disturbance or derangement is caused by sociological factors. In the words of Frank, "Society is sick; society is the patient," and Van den Berg suggests that the word *neurosis* be replaced by *sociosis*. That neurosis or sociosis is strongly affected by social conditions is demonstrated by the fact (among others) that the type of neurosis characteristic of the late nineteenth century in Europe was a form of hysteria, whereas now as a rule it is anxiety-neurosis that is found in Western nations. I have a hypothesis myself that before long the type of neurosis found among the Indonesian people before the Second World War—hysteria and "amok"—will give place to anxiety-neurosis, too.

Now with a person who is abnormal, neurotic, or "sociotic," the relationship with his own self and with society is one of frustration. There is a great possibility that—as a reaction—such a person will withdraw from serious social relationships and will gradually reach a state of mental isolation, which will further increase his feeling of deprivation, since his social needs cannot be fulfilled—those needs which in the literature of social psychology are known as the "four needs of W. I. Thomas": the desires for new experience, for security, for intimate response, and for recognition.

In general, one should not take the condition of the individual as an analogue for the condition of society, but in this case there are strong sociological justifications for doing so. So we may ask: Do the relationships of us Indonesians with the outside world arouse such frustration in us that we tend to hide our faces, "to crawl back into our own shell" as the Dutch put it, which is basically an irrational flight mechanism?

For example, in our policy vis-à-vis Holland, it cannot be said that we have been victorious. We are pictured in the Western press as a state in chaos. Many Indian students abroad, and even Malayans, have a bad impression of our country. There are Indonesians in Europe who pretend to be Filipinos, Malayans, or Japanese because they are ashamed to be known as Indonesians. Our cultural intercourse with the outside world, too, is not very advantageous to us. What enters as an import is "crossboyism," * "crazy" dance music, and foreign luxuries which are beyond the capacity of our economy to support, but not planning-mindedness or the mentality of science. So, too, in our relations with the international economy: we experienced a rubber boom for one or two years, and then that came to an end because of the end of hostilities in Korea. Our economic struc-

* "Crossboys" are rebellious youths of exaggerated Western tastes and sometimes delinquent tendencies found in larger Indonesian cities.

ture is gradually deteriorating, while the outside world is experiencing prosperity. Our overseas reserves are diminishing because of luxury imports—the demonstration effect is important here. Our exports are falling or are taken out by smugglers. Our inflation is accelerating, partly due to the use of credit-financed imports for unprofitable projects, and because few compensatory short-term deflationary measures are being applied.

Before the outbreak of the Second World War, and then, later, when the pure spirit of the Revolution was still generating enthusiasm in us, when the social indicators, so to speak, were still rising, we were very optimistic about our capacity to modernize our country. We were convinced that we could transform the agrarian colonial economy into a modern industrial national economy in a short space of time. Being "progressive," we regarded *adat* law and ethnology as conservative sciences, as colonial branches of study, used by the Dutch purely to preserve the outdated forms of our society, to leave us in backwardness and ignorance. What of our attitude to those studies now? We are now beginning to value them. Why? Is it out of a healthy level-headedness and a positive, adult attitude, or is it because of the injury, shame, and frustration we have suffered in our contacts with the outside world, the modern world?

If the hypothesis suggested here is correct and the interpretation of these sociological indicators valid, then it is clear that the movement to "return to national identity" in its popular negative interpretation can contain reactionary and conservative attitudes which can obstruct the entry of modern industrial culture. In the future we can no longer live with Javanese mysticism, with the ethnocentrism of Indonesia's hundreds of ethnic groups, with an already hypertrophied agrarian system, with a traditional system of mutual help which is often abused for the advantage of various groups, and so on. We must have a revolutionary attitude, not in the extremely narrow sense in which this word is usually used by the mass of the people and in the sensational press, but in the sense of facilitating and accelerating, in a well-balanced way, the revolutionary transformation of our society from a system which is economically and technologically backward into a modern industrial and democratic society.

Why has our society begun to tend toward this counterrevolutionary attitude which is contrary to man's historical progress? I believe it is because the power of our society to integrate foreign influences has greatly declined, partly owing to tensions within our own community.

In other words, it is because the interaction between our culture and foreign cultures, given the present condition of our society, only gives rise to social change of a disorganising and disintegrating kind. And what are the consequences? Among other things, we react by resenting foreign culture, and our first target is "crazy" music and dancing.

Whilst the "return to national identity" may very possibly be of a negative and conservative character, it can also be considered from the angle of the sociology of nationalism and social change.

A society undergoing rapid social change—and this has been the case throughout most of the world since the industrial revolution began two centuries ago—continually experiences social dislocation. One group loses status; another comes to the fore. "Only a few years ago A used to be my classmate at school—now he is a cabinet minister!"

"Sergeant X, who used to be one of my subordinates, is now a big businessman. He makes trips abroad, and I'm still only a Captain!"

What does this mean? It means that the feeling of frustration and insecurity holds sway, not only among those who have experienced social downgrading but also among those whose star is rising. "Can I hold on to my position? What if the day after tomorrow I am retooled [sacked]? Is my role-behavior in my new status appropriate? What do people think of me? Won't they ridicule me?"

In this situation of insecurity, status symbols and status attributes are excessively valued as forms of compensation—for instance, having the right make of car, a Bel Air or a Mercedes; joining in such forms of recreation as tennis, golf, cocktail parties, and receptions; being a member of exclusive clubs; owning luxury items such as refrigerators, tape recorders, and pickup sets; having a large home and large office; chatting in the elite language, namely, Dutch; and traveling, so that one "has been abroad." So, it is a situation which often gives rise to what Thorstein Veblen called conspicuous consumption. In such an atmosphere it is natural that jealousy, exaggerated self-promotion, gossip, *Schadenfreude*, melancholy, masochism, apathy, defeatism, and so on are rampant among the people concerned.

Another factor which arouses mass neurosis or sociosis is the gap between the "revolution of expectations" on the one hand and the continuing low level of our economic and technological capacity on the other. For the Western world the damaging consequences for mental health of this gulf between desire, which is maintained by modern advertising techniques ("the hidden persuaders"), and capacity has been demonstrated (Karen Horney, Vance Packard). The situation is the same but to a higher degree in Indonesia, the only country in Asia where levels of living are falling and a country which is subject to a very strong demonstration effect from the West.

In the first place, then, this social change generates various kinds of frustrations and insecurities, inferiority feelings and guilt feelings, which are intensified by the large- and small-scale corruption which exists at all levels of society from the top to the bottom, caused for the most part by the accelerating inflationary spiral.

Every human being has a self-image, a picture of himself, a reflection of both what he has actually done and what his conscience tells him he ought to have done. In an atmosphere so pervaded with these feelings of frustration and guilt, each person has a poor image of himself, which is generally suppressed or repressed and so exists on the subconscious level. The feelings of frustration and guilt do not disappear, but rather change into the diffuse feeling that in English is called anxiety. This feeling of anxiety is a common state for the greater part of mankind, so that Karen Horney could write a now famous book on *The Neurotic Personality of Our Time.* In my opinion this neurotic personality will become more common in countries now undergoing rapid social change, including Indonesia. The social research institutes should assemble statistical material on such symptoms of it as rates of divorce, prostitution, and suicide, on aversion to work, and on such psychosomatic diseases as stomach ulcers, high blood pressure, heart trouble, migraine, various kinds of rheumatism and diabetes.

In the second place, this process of social change and dislocation—aggravated as it is by the large-scale urbanisation which results from rural overpopulation, agrarian unrest, the activities of terrorist gangs, and so on—gives rise to what sociologists call atomization, uprooting, alienation and loneliness, and the beginnings of anomie, which can also produce such feelings as insecurity, guilt, and helplessness.

In such a neurosis-producing society, one in which there is so much feeling of frustration, people need compensations—compensations for their unfavorable self-images and compensations to help them overcome their loneliness. Such compensations are easily found in the solidarity of large collectivities and in various ideologies, including the hypernationalism or chauvinism which regards everything indigenous as perfect and everything foreign as contemptible. And so, in this century of the atom, we are returning to ethnocentrism, to an ethnocentrism which is all the more dangerous because of its capacity to mobilize the masses and its link to a modern apparatus of power. We saw this extreme nationalism with its attitudes of bitterness and vengeance, its xenophobia and its superiority complex symptoms, in Nazi Germany and Japan before 1945. And, frankly, I am uneasy lest our healthy Indonesian patriotism should gradually change into chauvinism, perhaps not visibly in constitutions and ordinances but in the realities of daily social life which already exhibit such tendencies. This chauvinism is essentially reactionary and conservative, for it hinders the growth of a modern democratic state which requires a healthy interdependence both internally among different spheres of life and among various social strata and externally in relations with other nations and peoples.

With all this in mind, I am somewhat suspicious about our being urged at just this point to return to our national identity. For in a community which is experiencing these various frustrations, it is not credible that the realization of this "identity" should take the form of a healthy and positive self-respect. On the contrary, it will inevitably take the form of a superiority complex to compensate for repressed inferiority and guilt feelings. This is a law of psychoanalysis, psychiatry, and the psychology of conflict.

Another important law is as follows: A person who truly respects himself will take a positive attitude towards others and respect their personalities. In his recent book, *The Act of Loving,* Fromm states that a person who loves another also loves his own self and that a person who hates others in essence hates himself, too. This fits with what I have written above, that if a person has an unsatisfactory self-image, he will have aggressive attitudes towards others.

Thus, what worries me about Indonesia is that an aggressive and hostile attitude to the outside world and to foreign culture will constitute a destructive factor within our own society. The beginnings of destructive symptoms are already evident. Look at the prevalence of self-will, at the attitudes of *après nous le déluge,* of *carpe diem* and "It's a mad time, but if we don't go with the crowd, we'll miss out," and at people's willingness to make accusations about each other and to look for scapegoats.

The conclusion to be drawn from this is that we should not at the present unfavorable point of our social development put too much stress on "national identity," because in such an atmosphere of discontent, dissatisfaction, and mass frustration, any such "identity" will have the character of a compensation or substitute satisfaction. Such appeals will not be able to produce a healthy identity unless there is a firm and capable leadership in our society, one which can channel popular emotions into constructive channels toward ends which embody real satisfactions.

It is better for us in this period to stress the broad lines of our national development, to seek out and do battle with what lies at the roots of social tensions rather than with their symptoms. This means endeavoring to reduce the gap between the rising expectations of the people and the real possibilities of meeting them. It means strengthening the integration of our culture by restoring our national unity without harm to other nations. And it means working conscientiously for the gradual realization of the ideals expressed in our Pantja Sila, for up till now this state ideology has not been realized in any concrete way and, indeed, has often been given mere lip service and used to blind the people to reality.

If all this can be done and a happy atmosphere pervades our country caused by the flowering of positive creative forces and healthy interpersonal attitudes throughout our society, then a "national identity" will emerge of its own accord, and in a healthy form.

As our outstanding educationalist Mohamad Said once said, our personality is revealed in our work and day-to-day behavior. Our national identity is not something to be achieved by setting up a purely ideal picture of it, as, for example, when people say, "We are an Eastern people with a lofty spirit," "We do not stress material things," "We are animated by a democratic and socialist spirit," and so on, all of which can only be construed as a form of defense mechanism, that of self-glorification. On the contrary, our identity will be shown in the real pattern of our everyday lives.

IXf

Utami Suryadarma   Fight Cultural Imperialism (1964)

This extract comes from a speech which Mrs. Utami Suryadarma made to the fourth Asian-African Film Festival, organized by the Asian-African People's Solidarity Organization, which was held in Djakarta in February 1964.

As with nations, films also may be divided into two fundamental categories: films of the new emerging forces, and films of the old established forces. Needless for us to say, this Afro-Asian Film Festival is a festival of the new emerging forces; it is not a neutral festival without a character, but one that is firmly anti-imperialist, anticolonialist, and opposed to all that is backward, obsolete, and reactionary.

As we all know, a traditional imperialist weapon for frightening people is the policy of using means ranging from education in schools to modern propaganda through the press, radio, and television to establish the belief that politics must be separated from other areas of life. But the present Afro-Asia is no longer the Afro-Asia of yesterday! We have torn down the old beliefs once and for all, including the political beliefs instilled by the imperialists.

World imperialism is well aware of the significance of films. In fact, world imperialism has been using the film as an intensive and effective propaganda weapon for decades.

They surreptitiously smuggle their ideology, the capitalist-imperialist ideology, into the plot of each film. They seek to create a confusing dream world which creates false illusions alien to the practical life and day-to-day struggle of the People. They seek to establish the attitude or belief that white people are superior to colored people, because for years they were in a position to force the peoples they dominated to accept this idea. They try to introduce this poisonous illusion little by little into the minds of our children, with alarming consequences in moral and cultural deterioration. In short, they try to use their films to build up a concept of life which is contrary to the interests of the Afro-Asian Peoples who are in the process of perfecting their national independence by formulating a concept of life based on human dignity, free from the exploitation of man by man. . . .

Whether in the hands of the imperialists or in our hands, the film is a weapon. It is up to us to use the film to the best effect as our anti-imperialist weapon. It is up to us to exploit fully the film as a tool of mass education, as a tool with which to create a concept of life which raises the dignity of mankind and which can be used to fight reaction and the ideology of reactionary imperialism.

It is a fact that, as a result and a legacy of the colonialism which we suffered under for centuries, our national film industries are not yet developed, that in many countries they have only just begun, and in one or two countries they are completely nonexistent. But this will certainly not dismay us. It is precisely because our resources are so limited that cooperation and solidarity among us Afro-Asian workers in the film industry is necessary, extremely necessary. . . .

It is the duty of our film industry to devote itself completely to this great struggle. If the artists and workers of the Afro-Asian films are inspired by the struggle of their People, and if these films reflect and speak for the struggle of the People, then the films will inspire and advance the struggle of the People.

More than anything else, our struggle is a *political* struggle.

Imperialism, forced to withdraw from Afro-Asian soil, still tries with all its strength to defend its cultural influence over music, dancing, literature, drama, sculpture, and especially films, which have a great attraction for the masses. For example, after the Dutch had been forced to leave Indonesia, they retained their influence in the cultural sphere: They left behind them a cultural penetration center known as Sticusa [Foundation for Cultural Cooperation], and they advanced money to universities. I suppose that every Afro-Asian country has had experience with cultural penetration by colonial or ex-colonial powers.

We may sneer at all this, but we cannot ignore it or underestimate it. The obvious fact is that sections of our society are being inculcated with hysteria. This imperialist "culture" poses a problem, especially among youth in the cities, particularly in the big cities. Moreover, a new development has begun: with the progress of technology, particularly transistors, imperialist "culture" can also penetrate into our villages.

What forms does our counterstruggle take? The Afro-Asian Peoples, both during and after their struggle for independence, strive to bring their old cultures back to life; they strive to recreate those cultures along new, progressive lines. Patriotic members of the film industries, from writers to workers, are beginning to organize themselves into anti-imperialistic cultural organizations; our writers and artists are devoting their talents and abilities to the struggle of their Peoples. By way of their works they also play a part in instilling patriotism and the democratic spirit into the masses.

Just look at the number of Afro-Asian countries from which the "Peace Corps" and American "foundations" have been expelled! And in the sphere of films, the governments of Ceylon, Burma, the U.A.R., Indonesia, and many other countries have forbidden this or that imperialist film. Why are these drastic actions necessary? Because films and other manifestations of imperialist "culture" are designed to force upon us a "way of life" which is not only contradictory to our own national identities but seeks to stifle them. This is the reason for the appearance of the movement to "rediscover our own identity." By developing our own identity and by rejecting the "way of life" of the imperialists, we are striving to end imperialist domination of our cultural lives.

It is our conviction that, in the last analysis, the freedom of our respective cultures cannot be separated from the political, economic, and military freedom of our respective countries. Between the struggle in the cultural sphere and the struggles in other spheres there is interdependence and complementarity. In short, the national independence of our respective countries is the basis for our cultural independence and also for the independence of our films. However, we cannot postpone our efforts at development until our countries are perfectly independent, because at the present time efforts at cultural development, including films, contribute toward our national independence in general.

And so the film represents an extremely important component in the culture of a nation. The film is not merely a medium for information, as it is often misinterpreted as being. The film is a part of culture, a vital part. Therefore, if the film is reduced in significance to the level of a mere vehicle for information, it will not only be superficial but its effectiveness as a revolutionary tool will be reduced.

We believe that in general it is the obligation of the workers and artists in our film industry not only to convey a political message to their audiences but to convey it in an artistic form of high quality. Only in this way will the appeal of our revolutionary films be great. Herein lies the importance of continually raising the artistic quality of our films, and here we have come to the crucial problem of developing film criticism in Afro-Asian countries.

Both in raising the artistic standards of films and in developing film criticism cooperation and solidarity are our prime weapons, for without cooperation and solidarity we cannot possibly exchange experiences and learn from each other.

The film is a relatively new branch of the arts and one which contains within itself various other branches of art. We raise this simple fact in order to emphasize that it is the very collaborative nature of the film industry which demands cooperation. In creating a film there is no alternative but for script writers, producers, décor men, cameramen, composers, musicians, and actors to cooperate harmoniously. And for us, too, there is no alternative to the smoothest possible cooperation between all progressive cinematic artists and workers and artists in other fields; indeed, cooperation with anti-imperialist politicians, economists, and military commanders—cooperation which must be carried out on a national scale and on an Afro-Asian scale.

IXg
D. N. *Aidit*   Which Ideology Is Native? (1962)

This piece comes from a speech Aidit made on November 12, 1962. The full speech is in Problems of the Indonesian Revolution (*Bandung: Demos, 1963*), *pp. 197–221.*

This evening we are celebrating three important historic events: first, the forty-fifth anniversary of the Great October Socialist Revolution [November 7, 1917]; second, the seventeenth anniversary of Heroes' Day [November 10, 1945]; and third, the thirty-sixth anniversary of the first national Uprising [November 12, 1926].*

I feel very happy, indeed, that we can celebrate these three events simultaneously now, since breathing the air of these three historic events at one and the same time means that we absorb as deeply as possible and renew, both our patriotic feelings and our feelings of internationalism. As revolutionary fighters we are in equal need of both, just as we need our hands and our feet. Is it not so that we can only be complete patriots if we are at the same time internationalists, and is it not so that we will only be true internationalists if we are also patriots? Patriotism without internationalism can deteriorate into stale chauvinism and is, therefore, to be condemned, whereas internationalism without patriotism can deteriorate into cosmopolitanism or national nihilism, which is no less stale and to be condemned.

Strangely enough, there are some people who think that they are born into this world as inhabitants of one particular country only and not as inhabitants of the world. And, conversely, there are some who think that they were born as world inhabitants without becoming inhabitants of one of the world's countries. We Communists and other progressive people, however, are realists; we were born with two qualities at one and the same time, as inhabitants of a particular country and as inhabitants of the world, because our country is, after all, situated on our globe. As grown-up people we have a responsibility toward the people and the world in which we live. We are patriots and internationalists at one and the same time. We are not cos-

* The Battle of Surabaja took place on November 10, 1945. The Uprising of 1926 is more usually known as the Communist revolts of 1926–1927.

mopolitans or national nihilists who have no fatherland, nor are we chauvinists whom Bung Karno calls "narrow-minded" people. . . .

Of course, there will be some people inflicted with communist-phobia who will interject: But you are a Communist; your attitude of friendship with the Soviet Union is that of an "agent"; therefore you must have a different attitude from that of non-Communists who are friends with the Soviet Union. Good gracious, where are their common sense and their feelings? Proletarians may not be friends with proletarians, Communists may not be friends with Communists? It is precisely these incomprehensible and arbitrary acts of the reactionaries that become a stimulant for Indonesian Communists to deepen further their feelings of friendship for the Soviet Union, because they are convinced that such a friendship will increase their service to the Indonesian fatherland and people. What the reactionaries dislike, is, as a rule, good for the people and for the revolution.

The communist-phobes, however, do not want to stop at this. They go on to say: Yes, but Marxist-Leninist ideology is not "native" but "imported," and that is why your patriotism is doubtful. Ah, this is the way importers and exporters talk about ideology; for them ideology is like raw material and small goods.

If we are to discuss ideology, let us do so seriously, not in the fashion of importers and exporters of raw material and small goods and not in an atmosphere of general elections, an atmosphere of feverish haste to obtain the greatest possible number of votes.

Since the beginning of this present century Indonesian politics has been marked by the development of three main ideologies and three main political trends: Nationalism, Religion, and Communism. . . .

Which of these three ideologies and political trends is "native," is really inherited from our ancestors, is the heritage of our forefathers?

In my opinion, Indonesian nationalism is much more influenced by Ernest Renan, Karl Kautsky, Karl Radek, Otto Bauer, Sun Yat Sen, Tilak, Kemal Ataturk, and others, than by the thoughts of our ancestors who began to set foot in our archipelago three or four thousand years ago and who at that time still lived in a society of primitive communism. To speak specifically of Marhaenism, that is, Nationalism according to Bung Karno's ideas, the progressiveness of which is beyond doubt, I am convinced that it is influenced also by Marxism. All this makes sense, since Nationalism is not something abstract, but concrete; it grew in the struggle against colonialism and imperialism.

At the time of our ancestors some three or four thousand years ago, such a struggle was not known.

But what is wrong in Indonesian Nationalism's taking many ideas of champions of social science and independence fighters from abroad? Why should it be looked upon as taboo to take up the universal ideas of anti-imperialist Nationalism? I think it equally correct for Indonesia to take weapons from the Soviet Union and other countries to expel Dutch colonialism or for Indonesia to import penicillin to combat various diseases. That is why it is not a question of rejecting universal progressive ideas but of integrating these ideas into the struggle of the Indonesian people, with the Indonesian revolution, as was done so well by Bung Karno when he created his progressive system of Nationalism, Marhaenism.

I think I need not say much about religion, since of all religions living and having wide influence in Indonesia, there is not one that is "native." That is the reason why one can say that religious people do not attack Marxism-Leninism from the angle of "not being native." I think that, as far as religion is concerned, it is also not a question of "native" or "not native," but to what extent these religions, or rather their followers, participate in the struggle against imperialism and colonialism, in the struggle to realise the Political Manifesto and the guides for its implementation.

Should it be really necessary to raise the problem of "being native," then the Indonesian Communists think that, scientifically speaking, it is Communism that is most "native," since our ancestors lived in a communist society, that is, the same society the Communists are at present striving for—of course, with this difference that the old society was primitive and what we are now striving for is modern communism. The situation was indeed so: three or four thousand years ago our ancestors lived in a society in which the instruments of production were common property, where exploitation of man by man was nonexistent, and where all inhabitants had a right to natural riches; they elected their heads, did not know of heads appointed from above, and did not know state power. Indeed, it is such a society in which these principles are in force that the Communists at present are striving for. One should not forget, however, that Marxism-Leninism is a weapon to put an end to capitalist society, to build socialism and communism with science and modern technique, something utterly unknown to our ancestors thousands of years ago.

Now then, how do Indonesian Communists stand in the question of "native" and "not native," in the question of "import-export" of ideology? Communists should approach this problem as they approach all social phenomena, from the angle of concrete history, from the angle of the interests of social progress, and not from abstract formulations, and, in the very first place, from the angle whether the political trend which bases itself on Nationalism and Religion promotes progress or not. Without involving ourselves in the problem of "native" or "not native" or "import-export" of ideology, the Indonesian Communists should cooperate with the Nationalist and Religious political trends within the framework of implementing *Nasakom* cooperation so as to promote the development of Indonesian society.

What counts for the Indonesian Communists is not defending the truth that the Communist society they are fighting for is in harmony with the principles valid in the society of our ancestors some three or four thousand years ago, but struggling hard to Indonesianize Marxism-Leninism, fighting for the realization of a "total integration of the general truth of Marxism-Leninism with the concrete practice of the Indonesian revolution, so as in this way to make Marxism-Leninism truly the property of the Indonesian working people, to make it the most effective fuel for the progress of Indonesian society."

IXh
Mohamad Said Honesty, That Is What We Need (1960)

This extract is taken from a paper of the same title which was presented to a Conference on the Problem of the National Personality held at Salatiga, Central Java, in August 1960. The Indonesian text is in Kepribadian Nasional *(Jogjakarta: Madjelis Luhur Taman Siswa, 1961), pp. 5–11.*

There is still a great deal of confusion about the problem of our national personality or identity because there is still no agreed-upon interpretation of the term "national personality." Because no such agreed-upon interpretation exists, there are all sorts of mutually opposed and confusingly crisscrossing views on the question.

There are, for example, those who consider that we do not possess a national identity at the present time; there are others who consider that we do; and there are others again who are of the opinion that we once had one which we have now lost or abandoned. . . .

The problem of the national identity or national personality of the Indonesian nation cannot be separated from that of the personality and character of Indonesian men and women.

According to this formulation, we have had a national identity, personality, and culture ever since we began to live together in a national community as an independent and sovereign people. To deny that the Indonesian people have a national personality is to deny that the Indonesian nation is independent and sovereign.

The very disappointing and indeed messy and chaotic condition of our society reflects disorder in our national personality, a disorder which is a product of the disorder which exists in our personalities as members of this nation.

If we want to improve our national personality and culture, let us honestly face up to this fact. Let us not run away from it by saying that this disordered national personality is not our national personality, that our national personality is good and noble but that we have left it behind or lost it as a result of colonialism and must try to find it again.

If what is reflected by the present condition of our society is not our national personality, whose national personality is it? If we once had a good and noble national personality, when was it that we had this, and just who is meant by this "we"? If it is really true that we left our national personality behind or lost it, where and when did this occur, and where and how are we to rediscover it? If it is really colonialism which is to blame for all this, why did we will to abandon our national personality and allow it to be lost?

In my opinion, personality, the condition and character of a person, is not something which the person can leave behind or lose, but rather something which cannot, by its very nature, be separated from him.

If Bung Karno, nevertheless, proposes that we return to our own personality, then this should not be interpreted to mean that we have lost our personality and must find it again. It should, rather, be taken to mean that we should not slavishly imitate everything which comes to us from foreign cultures, but rather stand firm on the foundation of our own cultural history with a critical attitude toward the values of foreign cultures.

If we desire to improve our personality, let us genuinely and honestly face the fact that our national personality is still poor and needs to be made better. Let us honestly admit that this is our own fault and that we ourselves must take the blame.

Running away from reality, dodging responsibility for a fate which we ourselves have shaped, abusing other parties and blaming the situation—all this is not only a waste of time and energy, but also shows the immaturity of our personality as individuals and as a nation.

We are, indeed, still young as a nation. But this youth should not be used as a basis for justifying the condition of our society which is disappointing in so many ways. Moreover, the maturity of a nation's personality does not depend on the nation's age in years but on the level of its capacity as a nation to face truth honestly and sincerely, and on the level of its awareness of what it means to live as a free and sovereign people.

X

National Unity and the Ethnic and Regional Groups

The problem of relating national loyalties and sentiments to those attaching to particular ethnic groups and regions was a touchy subject in the Indonesia of our period.* Ethnic group statistics were not collected by any Indonesian government in this period, and frank public discussion of what it meant politically to belong to particular ethnic groups was rare. Although this situation has close parallels in other newly independent states, in Indonesia it is closely related to a particular set of developments during the Revolution.

Between 1945 and 1949 the Dutch established fifteen federal states, large and small, in territory they had taken from the revolutionary Republic, seeking in each of these to develop a local loyalty, often ethnic in character, which would override loyalty to Indonesia as a whole and to the Republic. As a result, ethnic and regional loyalties became intensely suspect among supporters of the Republic, whose own leadership was impressively multi-ethnic (see Simatupang, Ig).

Once the Dutch decided to withdraw from Indonesia, as they did in 1949, most of those who had been associated with one of the Dutch-sponsored states made vigorous efforts to live this fact down. Few groups had an interest in upholding the federal state structure, despite the fact that the Republicans had accepted this structure by agreeing to cosponsor the Republic of the United States of Indonesia. Hence this RUSI crumbled quickly. Our first selection is typical of the arguments used against it, which concentrated on its Dutch origins rather than opposing federalism in principle. The small minority

* It also attracted considerable attention from foreign scholars, notably John D. Legge, *Central Authority and Regional Autonomy in Indonesia: A Study in Local Administration, 1950–1960* (Ithaca, N.Y.: Cornell University Press, 1961), and Gerald S. Maryanov, *Decentralization in Indonesia as a Political Problem* (Ithaca, N.Y.: Cornell Modern Indonesia Project, 1958).

who sought to uphold a federal structure in the face of the revolutionary nationalism of the Republic and the "me-tooism" of so many of the men of the Dutch-built states were either out-maneuvered, as in the case of groups in West Java and South Sulawesi, or militarily defeated, as in the case of the "Republic of the South Moluccas." Thenceforth ethnic appeals and federal arrangements were associated with the Dutch, their anti-Republican strategies, and their "time bombs."

After about 1954,* however, related issues came to the fore in a new form, with frequent demands for regional autonomy in a number of areas of Sumatra and Sulawesi, especially areas which made major contributions to Indonesia's foreign exchange earning. Regional grievances of various kinds became central problems in the country's politics after December 1956, when control of several Sumatran provinces was taken out of Djakarta's hands by leaders of regional movements, and, particularly, in February 1958 when a number of these leaders, and others from Sulawesi, formed a Revolutionary Government of the Republic of Indonesia (PRRI). The second and third of our extracts come from this period and show how demands for regional autonomy were intertwined with demands for particular policies to be pursued by the central government. See also IIh (Natsir).

During the period of constitutional democracy the ethnic balance in governmental leadership was roughly parallel to that in the population at large. The community of ethnic Javanese, constituting about 50 per cent of Indonesia's population, provided the Prime Ministers of four of the eight cabinets of this period. But with the establishment of Guided Democracy the basis of governmental power was narrowed at the expense of the Masjumi, which had been shown by the 1955 elections to be the one major party whose support came mainly from outside the ethnic Javanese provinces; so, the power of the ethnic Javanese became relatively greater. Extract Xd, by a Javanese, illustrates the official view of ethnic diversity under Guided Democracy and Xe, from an illegal document, is an extreme instance of anti-Javanese protest against the Guided Democracy settlement. A more measured view of some of the same grievances, guardedly expressed, can be seen in IIIi (Kalimantan Evangelical Church).

As our sixth extract here we have included a PKI statement which is interesting for its frankness in facing the facts of ethnic variety and

---

* This phase began somewhat earlier in Atjeh. On this unusual case, where regionalism was bound up with extreme Islamic sentiment, see VIb.

ethnic sentiment, a frankness which PKI leaders could permit themselves because their party's basic commitment to the centralist position was not questioned.

Finally, it is worth noting that we have included no essay on language problems in this section. There has indeed been much debate
about language in Indonesia, but neither arguments about the power
of Djakarta nor arguments about the role of the Javanese have involved disagreements about the language to be used in public affairs,
because the position of Indonesian (or Indonesian Malay) as the national language has been unchallenged. Working in a language of the
pluralistically minded Outer Islands rather than that of the centralistic
Javanese, Djakarta has been able to placate its potentially centrifugal-
ist critics while at the same time entrenching its own authority.

Xa

Mohamad Said   Unitarism versus Federalism
Is Not the Issue (1950)

*The State of East Sumatra, which had been recognized by the
Dutch on December 25, 1947, came under heavy attack from local
Republicans after the transfer of sovereignty to the Republic of the
United States of Indonesia two years later. The attacks culminated in
an "All East Sumatra People's Congress" in Medan, beginning April
27, 1950. This selection is part of the Congress chairman's opening
speech. The State was eventually dissolved with the proclamation of
the unitary Republic in August 1950. The author, a Medan journalist,
should not be confused with the writer of the preceding extract,
though their names are the same. The full Indonesian text appears in*
Republik Indonesia: Propinsi Sumatra Utara (*Djakarta: Ministry of
Information, 1953*), pp. 347–352.

The National Revolution which has seethed for more than four
years has resulted in conflicts of attitudes within the nation, between
those who quickly perceive the situation and acknowledge the demands
of the times and those who lag behind in word and deed. The colonialists have taken advantage of this situation, as the two "military actions" demonstrate. The Dutch were easily misled by their calculations, because they thought that they would succeed in reimposing
their colonial domination with the support of the latter group.

Meanwhile one thing is clear: that in conflicts between those in the right and those in the wrong, those in the right will be victorious in the end. Thus should it be with our revolution. Only it seems that the victory of rightness is rather long in coming, if, indeed, it has not been ambushed at a roadblock. So, to minimize sacrifices and loss of life, time, and energy, the Indonesian nation is forced to accept the facts once again.

Among these is the Round Table Conference. That Conference produced the Republic of the United States of Indonesia, which can actually be compared to a new house with concrete walls and tile floors but with a roof that leaks everywhere. In this connection I might compare the wishes of the common people who are anxious to remove the remnants of Van Mook's colonial strategy* with the wishes of the occupants of that house who scurry about trying to repair the holes in the leaky roof. Just as they must wait some time before substituting a good new roof appropriate to the style of the walls and the floors, so the Republic of the United States of Indonesia must wait for the completion of the work of the Constituent Assembly.

Even so, it is clear that to permit the roof to go unrepaired amounts to leaving the occupants in a mess. To leave the political structure of the Republic of the United States of Indonesia in the grips of the legacy of Van Mook's colonial policy is simply asking for continuation of political instability in this country.

Everywhere throughout Indonesia every politically aware element in the population has all at once rolled up its shirt-sleeves to repair the roof of the house in which it must live. This metaphor is very relevant to the political situation in our homeland since the transfer of sovereignty on December 27, 1949.

In various regions, such as West Java, Central Java, East Java, Madura, Kalimantan, and South Sumatra, the people are busily devoting their efforts to getting rid of Van Mook's colonial legacy. We thank God that the common man has quickly realized how to apply his energies in that connection. We thank God that many prominent figures who had been brought to the fore by Van Mook quickly realized that the efforts now being made to repair leaky roofs are an absolute necessity for the smooth running of our young ship of state. The dissolution of several states and their reincorporation as a part of the Republic of Indonesia has already produced political calm in the

* Dr. H. J. van Mook, as Lieutenant Governor General of the Netherlands Indies in 1945–1948, was the architect of the policy of establishing member states of a foreshadowed federation in parts of the country controlled by Dutch troops.

areas concerned. Delay in carrying out that fusion, which means delay in getting rid of elements and remnants of the Dutch colonial policy, means the continuation of political tension.

To dispel misconceptions, it must be explained that the heart of the problem of fusion is not the difference between Unitarism and Federalism. This must be made clear. Because a Federalism that was national-democratic would not constitute a leaky roof, nor would a Unitarism that was colonial-dictatorial constitute a new sail on our Indonesian ship. . . .

In other words, as long as there are in Indonesia elements which defend Van Mook's colonial legacy, it makes no difference whether they are Unitarists or Federalists; but as long as those elements are not swept out, political tensions will continue to exist like a thorn in a man's flesh.

This is confirmed by the fact that, as in other areas, so, too, in East Sumatra there is great pressure to fuse the State of East Sumatra with the Republic, in spite of the Round Table Conference agreement, because as I explained before, the Round Table Conference has produced a new house with a very leaky roof. . . .

The people have made many resolutions, motions, demonstrations, and so forth, demanding the dissolution of the State of East Sumatra, not because of the Federalist view which is espoused by the leaders who hold the reins of government, but rather because they wished to wipe out Van Mook's colonial legacy.

Xb
S. *Takdir Alisjahbana*   The Grievances
of the Regions (1957)

The following selection is taken from the text of an address which Professor Takdir gave before the All-Sumatran Adat [Customary Law] Congress which was held at Bukittinggi, March 12 to 20, 1957. This Congress was one of a number of gatherings intended to foster cooperation among regional movements in Sumatra whose leaders had tried to seize control of their areas in defiance of Djakarta three months earlier, successfully in the case of Central Sumatra [the Banteng Council or Wild Buffalo Council] and South Sumatra [the Garuda Bird Council], more or less unsuccessfully in North Sumatra. The address was published as Perdjuangan untuk Autonomi dan Kedudukan Adat didalamnja (*The Struggle for Autonomy and the*

Position of Customary Law within It) (Djakarta: Pustaka Rakjat, 1957).

The creation of a unitary state in 1950 signified the achievement of the best possible compromise between national ideals and aspirations and the practical difficulties inherent in any attempt to create a united state and nation in an area as large as Europe. It not only retained the ideal of unity which had fired the minds of Indonesians for twenty-five years, thereby satisfying those who had sacrificed so much in the name of that ideal, but, in granting the widest possible autonomy to the regions, it opened the way for them to progress and derive satisfaction from their own development no less than had the Federal State, which had carried the stigma of being a colonial device aimed at keeping the nation divided.

Although we have experienced almost seven years as a free and unitary state, in the light of this history and of the present situation of deep crisis we cannot but admit that we have failed to make our Constitution work. Not only have we failed to fulfill the promise of regional autonomy clearly expressed in Article 131 of our Constitution, but we have also misused our slogans of unity to satisfy a whole lot of egotistical desires—desires for power, wealth and position, and even regional advantage. Instead of providing freedom and equality of opportunity to all Indonesians, the central government, under the slogan of unity, now operates in the same centralized fashion as did the Dutch colonial government.

During the struggle against the Dutch, most of the leaders were dispersed throughout the regions, especially in Jogjakarta. After the transfer of sovereignty they hurried to Djakarta to take over the government of the whole Indonesian state. Then, after all their sufferings in the long and arduous struggle for independence, they were suddenly confronted with opportunities to gain positions, power, and wealth. The outcome was that most of them lost their sense of direction and instead of a concentration of energy and thought upon carrying out the tasks involved in uplifting and advancing the people of all Indonesia who had suffered so much, there has been a scramble for power, position, and wealth unparalleled in Indonesia. Leaders flocked to Djakarta to fill top positions in the governmental hierarchy of the unitary state which they had inherited from the Dutch. Alongside this they created various new positions from which to control the whole country.

Not only has most of the revenue of the new State accumulated in Djakarta, but most of it has also been spent there. Djakarta has become the center where the money collected from the rest of the country is divided up. It is not surprising that anyone who wants to do business of any kind must make his way to Djakarta because only there . . . is there access to finance; only there are decisions made. Consequently, the city has expanded at an astonishing rate, far more rapidly than at any time during the colonial period. The prewar population of half a million has already increased to three and a half million, and along with this population growth has gone a corresponding increase in multistoried buildings, beautiful villas, . . . and fine cars. It can be said that, due largely to this increased affluence, Djakarta has grown so as to encompass not only the glittering new satellite town of Kebajoran, but also the large area between Bogor and Tjiandjur, where the Djakarta rich spend their leisure time.

Undeniably Djakarta, as the center of government and business, has exhibited extremely rapid progress during the last seven years. If Djakarta conditions were a gauge to the condition of the country as a whole, we could well be proud of Indonesia's progress and development. But what are we to say of the real situation, in which Djakarta, with its population of top officials and business leaders who are all tied to each other by a whole range of political and financial connections, is like a fat leech sucking on the head of a fish, the fish being Indonesia? The leech sucks blood from the body of the fish and so grows fatter and fatter while the fish, losing blood, gets thinner.

This is no exorbitant analogy. Djakarta can really only be compared with such Chinese cities as Shanghai just before the fall of Chiang Kai-shek. Everybody, even Djakarta people themselves, is aware of the situation, but so many groups and individuals have become involved in this exploitation of the regions during the past seven years and such a complicated fabric of vested interests has been woven, that it is no longer possible to find a way out. This is principally because the political struggle which called for such great sacrifices during the revolution has been replaced by a scramble to pick the fruits of victory. It is precisely because politicians have become involved in exploitation of the regions on such a scale that the crisis now confronting our nation is so grave.

We all know that because Djakarta is the sole center of power, political parties playing the game of power have all established their headquarters in Djakarta. The presence of so many political party leaders in Djakarta has increased the total amount of wealth and power there so that it is no longer possible to change the situation by legally proper means. Each new leader who appears in the provinces regards the achievement of a position in the national capital as his goal and is, in fact, welcomed to Djakarta with open arms. But his removal to the center only serves to strengthen the ranks of the rulers at the center who join in the feast of sharing up Indonesia's power and wealth. . . .

Thus we see that the struggle between parties is not merely for ministerial positions—especially Finance Minister and Minister of Economic Affairs—but is equally directed toward gaining strategic administrative positions such as secretary-generalships, bank directorships, governorships, and so on. The holders of such strategic posts are able to channel the wealth of the State into public foundations, corporations, and other business organizations where their party colleagues are able to use them as if they were their own. The "horse-trading" which is so much discussed in the case of the division of cabinet posts in fact occurs over other offices and positions in our public life as well.

Thus financial corruption goes hand in hand with large-scale political corruption, and the interests of the people and the State are lost from sight. The high point of political and financial corruption was reached some time before the general elections, when the parties were in great need of money for the elections, success in which was to mean four years of power and spoils.

The result was that instead of the elections representing the crowning achievement of our struggle for democracy and popular sovereignty and producing, as was anticipated, the respite from political conflict necessary for any large-scale development of the country as a whole, they hastened the onset of our present serious crisis. This was because our faith in the elections was misplaced. The selfishness of groups and individuals predominated rather than any sense of responsibility. . . .

The result of the interaction of all the factors briefly outlined here is that the regions, which produce all the wealth absorbed by the center, are increasingly neglected as a result of the center's selfishness, as much as, indeed more than, during the Dutch colonial period. Not only is the share of the budget allocated to the regions pitifully small, but methods and conditions applied in the remission of this small share are such that most of it can never be used effectively when it is received. All this is accompanied by such unbridled negligence and bureaucracy, and such offensive favoritism, that no one can be surprised that the sense of frustration in the regions has reached a point of climax. Under the circumstances, nothing could be gained by more polite warnings, protests, and resolutions. In the prevailing atmosphere in the capital of struggle for power, rank, and riches there is no possibility of the problems of the regions receiving a sympathetic hearing.

With all this in mind, we should regard the tumultuous events of the last three months—the actions in Central Sumatra of the Banteng Council and in Medan of Colonel Simbolon,* the formation of the Garuda Council in South Sumatra and the announcement of military rule in the seventh military region [East Indonesia]—as evidence that our people in the regions still retain their balance and good sense. They do not want and will not tolerate the political game and the financial debauchery in the capital which causes what is potentially one of the world's richest countries to retrogress and decline. . . .

We in South Sumatra are keenly aware of the disparities existing between Djakarta, where construction is on a wasteful scale, and our region, which is one of the chief foreign-exchange producing areas in the country. To say nothing of electrification and factory construction, there is not one stretch of good road in all South Sumatra, an area as large as Java, so that villages become isolated, crops rot in the fields because transport costs are higher than the value of the yield, and economic activity ceases. On all sides the more energetic and spirited young people leave their villages to seek a livelihood elsewhere.

Despite the anger aroused by the sight of such unlimited confusion, incompetence, injustice, corruption, and political conflict, and despite our vexation at seeing how much work there is to be done, while all our efforts are stultified by the failures, chaos, and corruption in the capital, we must, at all costs, approach the problems besetting our nation calmly. We must believe that the present situation is merely a passing mistake, like a sickness in childhood. We must believe that our nation still has the resources to surmount this grave crisis.

I believe that it is this conviction that has endowed all the participants in the antigovernment actions in the regions over the last three months with a sense of responsibility and solidarity in stating

---

* The leader of the unsuccessful attempt to establish rule by an anti-Djakarta regional council in North Sumatra.

their grievances against Djakarta. In each case it has been clearly stated that the purpose of such action was to prevent further deterioration in the condition of our nation in order to preserve its unity. In every instance the opportunity for negotiation with the central government has been clearly, indeed eagerly, provided.

In this period of conflict and great danger it is desirable that we renew our faith in one country, one nation, one language.* Both from our own point of view . . . and from the point of view of the world as a whole . . . the political fragmentation of the Indonesian archipelago would appear as a loss and indeed a danger, especially if the several fragments came under foreign influence or control. May our fate not be that of Korea, which has become the cockpit for the great powers, for the suffering and misery that this would bring upon us is greater than we can imagine.

Xc

Sukarno   There Is Something Else behind
This Problem of the Regions (1958)

This extract comes from a public lecture which the President gave on April 3, 1958, under the auspices of the Students' Mass Action Committee against the PRRI. By this time military action against the PRRI's countergovernment had begun. The full text appeared as Mahasiswa Indonesia mendjawab Tantangan Zamannja *(Indonesian Students Meet the Challenge of the Times)* *(Djakarta: Ministry of Information, 1958).*

Look at the development of this regional problem, of this thing called the regional problem. I say "this thing called the regional problem" because I was never willing from the beginning to regard this as just a problem of autonomy. No! No! I said from the beginning that there was something else behind this. Look, when this so-called regional problem first came up, they talked about autonomy and development. That was the first stage. Not long afterwards, they came out with an anticommunist statement. They gathered *ulama* together from all over Sumatra. Do you remember that *Ulama's* Congress? An anticommunist resolution was passed at that *Ulama's* Congress. That was where it went into the second stage, because that congress was held at the urging of people I call adventurers.

* The language here is that of the youth pledge of 1928, a landmark in the development of Indonesian national consciousness.

And then it went into stage number three. What was stage three? At that point the picture changed from simple anticommunism, and they gave democracy away. They started arresting people. They started, they or the people in their group or some of the people in their group, to practice terrorism. I myself am one of the people who have experienced this. They attacked me with a hand grenade. When the Tjikini Affair* comes before a public trial perhaps you will hear from the defendants that the person who put them up to that act is one of that group. I am not going to give you his name, because I do not want to anticipate the trial, nor am I allowed to.

So they started to go in for terrorism. Very briefly, they abandoned democracy. And they went on to proclaim the Revolutionary Government of the Republic of Indonesia, which as I said was revolutionary all right, but counterrevolutionary. They abandoned democracy; they clearly left democracy behind. If they were still true to democracy and they did not like the Working Government, the Working Cabinet,† why did they not bring the cabinet down by democratic means, by parliamentary means? Why did they use means like this? That was stage three: abandoning democracy, practising terrorism, acting against the constitution, making their own proclamation.

By the fourth stage, they were clearly being used, working with people from a group which does not like neutralism but wants to pull us or part of us into one of the blocs. There is one piece of evidence here that I have already talked about elsewhere, in Tokyo among other places. I was talking before about Sumual.‡ That Sumual was not only talking against the Republic, blackening the name of the Republic, making threats against the Republic, and so on. Do you know what else he was doing in Tokyo? He was trying to get arms, buying arms from Japanese adventurers, arms to strike at the Republic of the Proclamation, arms to strike at Djakarta. Walandouw§ was saying, "We can walk into Djakarta easily, we can swing into Djakarta." They were trying to buy arms, their talks with a particular Japanese adventurer were under way. . . .

The deal was all arranged. It was just a matter of delivering the copra and receiving the arms. Suddenly, someone else, someone from another quarter said to Sumual, "Sumual, you don't need to buy arms

---

* The attempted assassination of President Sukarno on November 30, 1957.

† These were names given to the Djuanda Cabinet, in office since April 1957.

‡ A colonel, one of the principal leaders of the regional movement in East Indonesia.

§ One of Sumual's associates.

in Japan; that's unnecessary; you can get arms from us, from closer to Indonesia." So what happened? Getting an offer like that, being able to get arms from nearer to Indonesia, Sumual canceled the deal with the Japanese. And what happened then, what was the result of all this? The Japanese man was angry; he was furious. So he passed on all the documents, all the correspondence, in black and white, to another Japanese, with the request that it be sent on to President Sukarno. So I received the lot.

Well, Brothers and Sisters, I knew it from the beginning. I knew that this business was not straight, that these people wanted to hit at the Republic. It was never just a matter of autonomy and development. No! No! And now it has reached its fourth stage. First it was a matter of autonomy and development. Then came the anticommunist slogan. Then, the terrorism and the abandonment of democracy. And then the blatant cooperation with a party that wants to drag our state or a section of it into one of the blocs.

We in Djakarta were working patiently to settle this problem, working by peaceful means, by *musjawarah,* through the National Consultations, through the National Development Consultations.* But they for their part went straight ahead from stage one, to stage two, to stage three, to stage four.

As I said in my speech of February 21, there is now no other way open to our government than to act firmly. And I ask you now, you, students, can you take any other position? For this is a challenge, a challenge to your state, to the state you proclaimed on August 17, 1945.

Xd
Prijono Nation Building and Education (1959)

This piece comes from a statement which Professor Prijono issued in late 1959 in his capacity as Minister of Basic Education and Culture. The statement was sometimes regarded as a kind of educational supplement to the Political Manifesto of August 1959 (see IIIa and IIIb). It was published in English in Reform Measures Aimed at the Development of a National Educational System in Indonesia (*Djakarta* [?]: *n.p., 1962*).

* These two conferences were held in September 1957 and December 1957 in an attempt to reach a settlement between the central government and the regional councils.

In order to improve the education system, which is still far too intellectually oriented and exhibits the characteristics of a system inherited from the colonial period, we have tried to find a new course by which to make the system accord better not only with our national ideals but also with the current stage of our revolution. As well as having enduring national aspirations, we must concern ourselves at this stage of our revolution with the all important task of national construction, or "nation building." By nation building is meant not just material construction, but also and more particularly construction of the spirit.

According to political science a nation is a group of people possessing its own independent state and its own fully sovereign government. But seen from another vantage point a nation is a spirit, the spirit which causes a group of people to want to live together in a sovereign, self-governing state.

People may ask, "If the Revolution has proven that the Indonesian people are already a nation in the spiritual sense and if we now have a sovereign state and are self-governing, if we form a nation in every sense, is there still a need for 'nation building,' especially in its spiritual aspect?"

We reply, "Yes, because the Revolution was waged by only one part of the present Indonesian nation, even though that part was not small. It is the duty of the Leadership of the Revolution and the Government, and of the Department of Education and Culture in particular, to strive to infuse into the breast of each and every Indonesian citizen the patriotism and nationalism that burned in the breasts of the Leadership of the Revolution and of all those who pledged themselves body and soul to win back our freedom."

Patriotism, love of homeland, nationalism—for us this means primarily that all the *sukus* in our homeland desire to become one large indivisible unit, the Indonesian national unit, inseparable from the country called the Republic of Indonesia, whose freedom they will all guard, defend, and perfect together.

As long as our consciousness of *suku* is strong and constitutes a solid moral foundation, our national consciousness will remain relatively weak. Therefore, we must, if possible, abolish *suku*-consciousness and raise men's consciousness to the level of the nation. Where this remains impossible, we must at least combat the demon of *suku*-ism exposed by the President in the speech now well known as the Political Manifesto. National consciousness must become stronger than consciousness of any other kind, stronger than consciousness of *suku*.

Bhinneka Tunggal Ika [Unity in Diversity] does not mean that we may adopt differing forms of national consciousness, but rather that we possess a single national consciousness, one Indonesian nationality, despite minor variations in our names and appearances due to *suku* and culture. In our opinion, there can be no more haggling about this matter. We must continue to work at "nation building"—in the spiritual as well as the material sense—diligently and with all our energy.

One thing which must be understood is that Indonesian nationalism, denoted by the principle of "Nationalism" in the Pantja Sila goes together with another principle of the Pantja Sila, Humanity; and according to President Sukarno's explanation Humanity includes the notion of internationalism. So our nationalism does not conflict with internationalism.

As well as "nation building" in the spiritual sense, that is, the raising of consciousness from the *suku* level to the level of the nation, we must also strive to fashion a national morality, a conception of the general good which will be accepted by all Indonesians. We need to have such a conception of the general good in order to overcome conceptions of the good of particular *sukus*, parties, or other groups which sometimes conflict with the national morality and detract from our life as an indivisible nation. If we are faithful to the spirit of Pantja Sila our national morality will not conflict with good international morality but only with bad international morality, with colonialist, capitalist, and imperialist morality. . . .

One other thing which conflicts with our morality is feudal morality; this clearly cannot be permitted to exist, in view of the Pantja Sila's principle of the Sovereignty of the People. The oppressors in all areas of oppression keep feudalism alive in order to obtain strong support from a small section of the oppressed nation and so be able to continue their oppression.

One consequence of the spirit of feudalism perpetuated by oppressors is that the intellectuals, whom the oppressor was forced to educate in order to have cheap personnel for his administration, were kept away from manual work, the justification being that manual labor—with the exception of the labor performed by typists or clerks—was incompatible with the aristocratic spirit. In order to undo this legacy we must make manual work an important subject in schools.

It is not enough for love of nation and country to be fostered by the study of civics; this must be reinforced by emotional and artistic development, by teaching concerning the freedom of our ancestors, the beauty of our motherland, and our culture and art. This should not merely be learned by rote, but should become a beloved idea, a practised skill.

Of great importance for strengthening our desire to live together as an indivisible nation are what are termed in English "common cultural goods," that is, cultural features which we all, as a nation, possess, or elements which, taken together, constitute our common national culture. The need for such "goods" is urgent because our historical legacy and the consequence of our democracy and tolerance is that our nation embraces a variety of religious and political ideologies. Because of this firm ties must be established within which all Indonesians, regardless of religion, ideology, or *suku*, may feel content and free.

It is our conviction that an Indonesian national culture, accepted, loved, and given life by the whole nation irrespective of religion, ideology, or *suku*, can provide these ties, and that the creation of such a culture is therefore the important duty of our government and the people in general, and of the Department of Education and Culture in particular. Because of this the Department of Education and Culture must direct its efforts, both within the schools and outside them, toward this goal. However, it should not neglect or oppose regional cultures and art, as long as these do not threaten national unity.

Xe
Kahar Muzakar Down with the New Madjapahitism! (1960)

This extract is translated from the illegally circulated booklet, Konsepsi Negara Demokrasi Indonesia [A Plan for a Democratic State of Indonesia] (*n.p., 1960*), *which was presumably written in a guerrilla camp in the mountains of South Sulawesi.*

History bears witness that the Dutch and other foreign nations wanting to hold power over rich Indonesia were able to exercise colonial domination for centuries by the tactic of fostering dissension among the ethnic groups of Indonesia. History witnesses, too, to the violence which was Japan's domination of Indonesia, for all its tyranny being hidden by the song of "Japanese-Indonesian equality" sung by a chorus of loud voices proclaiming Indonesia as the blood brother of Dai Nippon.

And history will bear witness shortly to the final act of Sukarno and his fanatically pro–Republic of Indonesia followers, of this Sukarno who is foisting civil war on Indonesia with a particular goal in view, namely, realization of the aspirations of the Madjapahit Kingdom to colonize the people of Indonesia.

Whether or not the imperialism of Sukarno's Republic will be successful, whether the idea of Madjapahit's controlling all of Indonesia will be brought about or not, is a question which history will soon answer. Let us leave it to history to judge.

According to history as written by the Javanese themselves (who have no historical evidence as proof), Indonesians are a nation of common origin, originating in Indo-China or Vietnam countless centuries ago, who later came to occupy Indonesia, that is, the archipelago stretching from Sabang to Merauke. The Indonesian people, a single people living scattered through the entire Indonesian archipelago, were united by Javanese kingdoms of early times, namely, at the time of Darmawangsa, at the time of Madjapahit's struggle for empire with Sriwidjaja, and at the time of Raden Widjaja, Hajam Wuruk, and Gadjah Mada. Such is the formulation of Indonesian history as written by Javanese who are fanatics for Madjapahit imperialism.

Anyone who studies the history of the Madjapahit Kingdom carefully and thoroughly will certainly know that Madjapahit's struggle was not a struggle for independence but a struggle for power, a struggle for empire, to control and dominate the whole of Indonesia.

Anyone with sharp wits who has frequently watched, heard, and paid attention to Sukarno's words, who has heard his speeches boasting of Sandjaja, Darmawangsa, Raden Widjaja, and Hajam Wuruk, and of Gadjah Mada and his Madjapahit Kingdom, will know that Sukarno is, in fact, a Nihilist, a visionary who continues to dream of the realization of Madjapahit's imperial ambitions.

Sukarno and his Madjapahitist group found a good argument for putting the idea of Madjapahit domination into effect by using the tragedy of foreign imperialism in Indonesia as their disguise and talking about national unity, national independence, and the prosperity and well-being of the entire Indonesian nation which were entailed in the proclamation made on August 17, 1945.

It is certainly true, and no one has reason to deny this, that the August 17 proclamation was the basis of the independence of the Indonesian people and the cause of groups of people throughout

Indonesia freeing themselves from Dutch domination. Therefore the August 17 proclamation was accepted by all of the ethnic groups of Indonesia as the proclamation of independence of the Indonesian nation. This is acknowledged; it is recognized by all of us, by the entire Indonesian nation.

But on the other hand, there are no grounds for Sukarno and his group's denying that all of the ethnic groups of Indonesia rose together in response to the proclamation of August 17, 1945. This was not because of an awareness of being a people descended from Madjapahit and certainly not to realize the imperialistic aspirations of Madjapahit.

Sukarno and his group certainly know the truth, that from early times on, from before Indonesia was colonized by the Portuguese, the Spanish, the Dutch, the English, the Japanese, or any other foreign nation, all of the Indonesian ethnic groups had their own independent states with their own territorial borders and sovereignty.

With the evidence of history, I shall make it clear in this booklet that the struggle for independence of the people of Indonesia which began on August 17, 1945, and which Sukarno and his group called a National Struggle and a National Revolution was not this. I shall show that the struggle for independence of the Indonesian people of August 17, 1945, was not an Indonesian National Struggle, not a National Revolution, but an outburst of the spirit of freedom of all the Indonesian ethnic groups, that it was an individual revolution, that is, a revolution brought about by the spirit of independence of all the Indonesian ethnic groups together, spontaneously freeing themselves from the oppression of Indonesian feudalism and from the colonial domination of Holland and Japan.

This view of mine may well be denied by Sukarno and his group. But before Sukarno and his group try to advance grounds for a denial, let me first ask why it was that the regions rose in opposition after the August 17, 1945, proclamation and after the surrender of sovereignty by the Dutch in 1949? Why did the Islamic community of Indonesia organize a struggle of their own, their own Islamic revolution? Why did the Indonesian communists, who had also responded to the proclamation of August 17, 1945, organize their own struggle? Why did the leaders of the South Moluccas declare the independence of the Region of the South Moluccas? Why was civil war foisted on Indonesia?

I can give detailed evidence of the way in which Sukarno and his group have violated the right to independence of the other Indonesian ethnic groups in the cultural, political, and economic spheres.

In the cultural field, Sukarno and his group affect to denounce Western culture up hill and down dale, to reject the culture coming from the outside. And they condemn the cultures of many Indonesian ethnic groups, branding these as foreign-infiltrated and as a basis for foreigners to use in their efforts to regain colonial domination in Indonesia. These are some of the arguments Sukarno and his group have used to force all the Indonesian ethnic groups to return to the Indonesian identity, to the original Indonesian culture, of which, according to Sukarno and his group, there was only one.

But it is surprising, in fact astonishing, that what has been done in the primary, secondary, and tertiary schools to encourage all Indonesian ethnic groups to return to this original Indonesian culture, involves deepening understanding of the history and culture of one ethnic group, the Javanese, and promoting comprehension on the part of people outside it of Brahmanic culture with all its *Hijang Palawa* terms which people of other ethnic groups of Indonesia find hard to pronounce. [*Hijang Palawa* apparently means here the Hindu gods.]

It is really surprising that, in making their appeals for a return to the genuine Indonesian culture, Sukarno and his group are shameless about saying that the Borobodur, the shrines at Prambanan and Mendut and all those in Bali, are cultural symbols of the ancestors of our entire Indonesian people.

It is the same story when one looks at the way in which Sukarno injected the needle of cultural imperialism into the body of all Indonesian ethnic groups, before the risings in the Outer Islands began, by celebrating Javanese heroes in the naming of army units, warships of the navy, universities, and so on—for instance, the Brawidjaja Division, the Diponegoro Division, the Siliwangi Division, the navy ships "Hang Tuah" and "Gadjah Mada," Gadjah Mada University, and so on. In all this the names of Javanese heroes were pushed forward. The names of heroes from outside Java were deliberately ignored, because it was considered that the level of their heroism was lower and not to be compared with that of Javanese heroes descended from the *Hijang Palawa*. [Neither Siliwangi nor Hang Tuah was Javanese.]

These events remind us all of the policy of cultural imperialism of the Dutch in Indonesia, who invariably used various very Dutch names with a view to eliminating the spirit of culture of the Indonesian people. . . . Politically Sukarno and his group have been conspicuous about using their power to put in high officials in all branches of government who are well known in the Outer Islands as "o men," that is, men called Hartono, Subroto, and Djojo, and others like Sukarno, Sugito, and Kartolo, and others, again, like Sandjojo, Darmowongso, Muljono, Susilo, Sujono, and so on.* Of course, the system of "o" power is justified, as it was by the Dutch, on the grounds that the Indonesians are as yet incapable of governing their own country.

Moreover, it has become customary since the rise of unrest in the Outer Islands to use such tough arguments as that the people in the Outer Islands are very provincially minded, that they are trouble makers who cannot possibly be trusted to hold positions of authority. And various other arguments are used to hide their real intentions. In the economic field, Sukarno and his group are using their power to control all sources of mineral wealth, to hold tightly onto all mining throughout the Indonesian archipelago, and onto all the large enterprises which produce the basic necessities for the Indonesian people.

Sukarno has given false comfort to Indonesian ethnic groups in the promise of "broad rights of autonomy," and at the same time has made all sorts of regulations to tie up the sources of wealth in the regions outside Java. The system of state enterprises and various other systems were devised to siphon off as much as possible of the profits of Indonesia for the benefit of the central government. This is the proof of all proofs that Sukarno's Republic of Indonesia is perpetrating colonial domination on the people of Indonesia and using the August 17, 1945, proclamation as a basis for realizing the imperialist ambitions of Madjapahit.

The fact that I am raising this matter of the goals of Sukarno's Republic of Indonesia in this booklet certainly does not mean that I hate the Javanese or that I am anti-Javanese. This is not so, I repeat it is not so. . . .

Sukarno is using the problem of overpopulation in Java and the need to move people to other areas as a disguise to achieve Javanese–Madjapahit domination over the rest of the Indonesian people, and he is playing a democratic numbers game in which the Javanese comprise more than half of the number of votes and so outnumber other ethnic groups.

The Indonesian Communists are following the strategy of riding on the back of the Sukarno Republic of Indonesia in all affairs of government policy. They are getting their people into the ranks of those

* All these, and most other Indonesian names ending in "o," are Javanese.

being moved as part of the policy of shifting Javanese population to areas outside Java, with the purpose of agitating against the authorities and eventually communizing Indonesia.

This policy of shifting Javanese to regions outside Java, which is being pursued to the accompaniment of the sweet music of *USDEK* to realize the imperialist aspirations of Madjapahit and amid the hateful and envious agitations of the Communists, will lead to bloody tragedy, to an unending civil war.

Xf

M. H. Lukman   Recognizing the Ethnic Factor (1960)

This piece comes from Tentang Front Persatuan Nasional* (*On the National United Front*), *a pamphlet which was first published in June 1960 by the Unity Front Department of the PKI's Central Committee.*

In the past the ethnic factor has not had enough attention in relation to the national unity front, and it has often been misunderstood. At the present time the slogan that we are one people, in the sense of one nation, is popular and continues to be popularized, and so someone who raises the ethnic problem is regarded as wanting to stir up ethnic feelings which are seen to have disappeared long ago. There certainly are groups who deliberately push the ethnic problem forward just to play one ethnic group off against another and so split the national unity of the Indonesian people. The Netherlands Indies government also played ethnic groups off against each other, as part of its policy of divide and rule. The Dutch colonialists fostered differences between the ethnic groups just to create antagonisms between them. But because the effects of oppression and exploitation by the Dutch colonialists were directly felt as greater by the whole Indonesian people as one nation, the inter-ethnic conflicts created by the Dutch were subordinated to the conflict between the Indonesian people as a whole and the Dutch colonialists.

After Indonesia gained political independence the situation became rather different, with the Dutch no longer holding power directly. Using the compradore bourgeoisie, the imperialists succeeded up to a certain point in fanning the spirit of separatism and exploiting the dissatisfaction of the people in the regions. They misled the people by

* Djakarta: Jajasan Pembaruan.

concealing the fact that differences between one region and another, especially differences in the advancement or backwardness of particular regions or ethnic groups, are a result of Dutch colonial policy in Indonesia over hundreds of years.

It is natural that the people hoped for a more rapid improvement in their standard of living after Indonesia achieved political independence. For political independence is certainly a weapon, and must be used as a weapon, to raise the people's standard of living. But it is clear that what is called regional unrest, or antagonism between the region and the center, is primarily the result of imperialist policy and of the greed of high-level figures from the regions or ethnic groups who want to use our present political independence to gain power and wealth for themselves.

The prerequisite for bringing about a radical improvement in the living standards of the people and the beginning of real development in the interests of the people of all the regions, is a radical liquidation of imperialist economic power and the remnants of feudalism. But the fact is that the separatist leaders and the PRRI-Permesta rebels, who are always shouting the slogan of regional development, are doing nothing to bring the people to struggle against imperialism and landlords, but, indeed, join these and carry out their policies.

By contrast with the separatists, if we Communists bring up the ethnic problem, it is simply because we know there are differences between ethnic groups—differences of size, language, culture, and customs. These differences do not need to become the grounds of dissension, providing that one observes the principle of equal rights and mutual respect among all the ethnic groups, regardless of size and advancement or backwardness. If this fact of ethnic differences is ignored and there is no attempt to find an appropriate solution of it, the differences will grow to become the seeds of conflict and division and will be capable of cracking, indeed of destroying, the national unity of the Indonesian People.

How should the policy of equal rights and mutual respect among all ethnic groups be implemented? In a Politburo report to a Plenary Session of the Central Committee, Comrade Aidit declared:

A policy of equal rights for all ethnic groups is a policy of autonomy for ethnic groups under a unitary government. The right to autonomy means the right of the ethnic groups to run their own affairs, for example, the right to manage political and economic affairs in the environment of each ethnic group, the right to use their own language alongside Indonesian, and the right to develop their respective cultures. The policy of ethnic autonomy is the only policy which can solve the problem of the ethnic groups.

Concerning what it is that is called autonomy in Indonesia, Comrade Aidit explained:

The question of autonomy which is now much discussed is not autonomy based on ethnic groups but autonomy based on administrative areas and is called "regional autonomy." The present government's division into administrative areas is basically a continuation of the administrative divisions of colonial times. In the framework of its present program of demands, the PKI is able to agree to "regional autonomy," that is, to something less than ethnic group autonomy, as long as elections for the regional legislatures are held on a democratic basis, and as long as regional executive bodies are formed on a basis of proportional representation. But this is an interim solution to be used until autonomous units based on ethnic entities can be formed.

So we should not stop at "regional autonomy." At the same time as we accept regional autonomy we must be examining and arriving at conclusions of the problems of the ethnic groups, for example, questions to do with the boundaries of an ethnic group's territory, the question of the linguistic and cultural unity of each ethnic group, and so on. On the basis of the results of this study we shall gradually establish autonomous units based on ethnic groups, in accordance with the interests of the entire nation. . . .

In dealing with the ethnic problem we must prevent the growth of a feeling of superiority on the part of the large ethnic group; we must prevent the growth of large ethnic group arrogance. Further, we must guard against the large and more advanced group's looking down on other ethnic groups and imposing its own wishes on them even though its intentions may be to advance the other ethnic groups. In brief, every ethnic group must advance another ethnic group. The ethnic group which is already advanced must have a sense of obligation to help the other ethnic groups, but the discharging of the obligation cannot be force. The major ethnic group must respect the small groups. If there are shortcomings in the work of administering the country, the first to practise self-criticism must be the large and advanced ethnic group.

Among the small ethnic groups we must guard against the growth of narrow ethnicism of the kind which leads a group to refuse to accept anything from another group. Narrow ethnicism slows down the advance of the group itself. Besides that it can easily be exploited by the imperialists to play ethnic groups off against each other and destroy the unity of the Indonesian people. This would mean splitting and greatly weakening the position of the unitary Republic of Indonesia. Feelings of inferiority must also be guarded against in these small ethnic groups, because these are also obstacles to the advancement of the groups concerned.

Experience shows that religious and ethnic factors are often tied together in unity front work. If one takes an incorrect attitude to a religion which happens to be professed by the majority of the masses of a particular ethnic group, this can be interpreted as a direct insult to the entire ethnic group. Conversely, when their ethnic group feelings have been offended, people may feel that they have been affronted in their religious beliefs. That is why there are prominent religious and ethnic group figures who are not opposed by the mass of the people of their religion or ethnic group, despite the fact that they are known to be reactionary in their politics.

Arousing political awareness among the backward masses which are under the influence of religious or ethnic group leaders is very difficult without the support of these men and particularly in the face of opposition from them. Hence, to be able to operate the national unity front policy, it is extremely important for us to attract and co-operate with religious and ethnic group leaders, from the center to the outer regions.

Stressing the importance of efforts to attract and cooperate with religious and ethnic group leaders does not mean that the work of arousing the backward masses who adhere to a certain religion or belong to a particular ethnic group must always be with the mediation of religious and ethnic group figures. The important and decisive matter here is that we should have the correct position and attitude towards religion and ethnic groups. . . .

All of this discussion of the question of ethnic groups is intended to show convincingly that the ethnic group problem and the problem of minority groups of foreign descent are very serious problems which must be correctly solved. It is mistaken and dangerous to talk as if there were no ethnic and minority problems, as if these problems existed because our own policies have brought them into being.

The fact that the reactionaries of the Masjumi and PSI have been able to use ethnic sentiment to establish separatist movements and the PRRI-Permesta rebellion and to use anti-Chinese racial sentiment to destroy the unity of citizens of the Republic of Indonesia—this fact should suffice to dispel the mistaken notions which suggest that the ethnic group problem and the problem of minorities of foreign descent are unimportant.

The only policy by which the ethnic problem can be solved is one of autonomy for ethnic groups, which would serve to implement the principle of equal rights and mutual respect among all ethnic groups irrespective of size and advancement or backwardness. . . .

The aspirations or goals of each ethnic group, for example, its desire to see the advancement of its culture and to see members of the group as leaders of the people or of the government, at least of the regional government—these can only be fulfilled if ethnic group autonomy is granted. If ethnic group autonomy is put into practice under the unitary government of the Republic of Indonesia, the effect cannot be other than equality of status, mutual trust, and cooperation and closer and firmer unity of all the ethnic groups in the Indonesian nation.

XI
National Unity and the Chinese Minority

What we have reproduced in the foregoing section on Indonesia's ethnic and regional variety refers scarcely at all to the Chinese minority. The omission is characteristic, for Indonesian political thinking in our period distinguished sharply between diversity within the *bangsa Indonesia* (Indonesian people or nation) on the one hand and relations between the *bangsa Indonesia* and "minorities of foreign descent" on the other.

The provisional constitution of 1950 gave formal recognition to three minority groups. It provided for Indonesian citizens of Chinese, European (and Eurasian), and Arab descent to be assured nine, six, and three seats respectively in the parliament to be elected. But the number of Indonesian citizens of European and Arab descent was always small, never as high as fifty thousand persons; and the counterpart communities of Europeans and Arabs of foreign citizenship were either small from the beginning, as in the case of the Arabs, or rapidly dwindling, as in the case of the Europeans after 1949.

The Chinese, on the other hand, were a large group; 2,450,000 by G. William Skinner's estimate of 1963.* The number of these who could claim Indonesian citizenship changed over our period and was never precisely known. But Skinner's estimate is that between 600,000 and 800,000 became, or were confirmed, as Indonesian citizens between 1960 and 1962, under an option procedure based mainly on the

* "The Chinese Minority," in Ruth T. McVey, ed., *Indonesia* (New Haven: Yale University, and Human Relations Area Files, 1963), p. 111. On the position of the Chinese, see Donald E. Willmott, *The National Status of the Chinese in Indonesia, 1900–1958* (Ithaca, N.Y.: Cornell Modern Indonesia Project, 1961), and Mary F. Somers, *Peranakan Chinese Politics in Indonesia* (Ithaca, N.Y.: Cornell Modern Indonesia Project, 1964).

Sino-Indonesian Dual Nationality Agreement of 1955. Of the rest almost all were citizens of the Chinese People's Republic.

By no means all of the Indonesian Chinese are in business. Many are wageworkers, and a minority are in professional or clerical work or work as farmers. But a large part of the community are business people, and their role in urban business, particularly large- and small-scale trade and manufacturing, is major. The strong economic position of this part of the Chinese community, combined with the social separateness of the community as a whole, has made it a target for envy and hostility. Among indigenous Indonesian trading groups particularly, and among many strong Muslims, anti-Chinese sentiment has long been strong.

Chinese persons have never played any very important roles in Indonesian politics and the position of the Chinese community was not a controversial issue in the politics of our period taken as a whole. But this question did assume importance at particular times, when anti-Chinese measures were advocated or actually effected. The anti-Chinese violence of the early days of the Revolution provided the occasion for our first extract here. In the next decade there was administrative discrimination against the Chinese but virtually no anti-Chinese politics. However, anti-Sinicism became a political issue in 1956 as a result of the "Assaat movement"—see XIb—and particularly in 1959–1960, when Chinese citizens were banned from retail trading in rural areas and over 120,000 persons left Indonesia for China. This latter measure is discussed in VIIIc (Aidit).

The 1959–1960 crisis led members of the Chinese community, and especially the Indonesian citizens among them, to an anguished reconsideration of their position in Indonesia. One group of them, whose view is expressed in our third extract here, that of Onghokham, insisted that it was up to the Chinese to assimilate if they wanted to stay in Indonesia; this group, organized in the LPKB (Institute for Building National Unity), was supported by a number of the anti-Communist leaders of the army. The larger group, whose view is represented by our fourth extract here, opposed assimilation, arguing that the Chinese community had as much right to cultural distinctiveness as the community of the Bataks or that of the Sundanese; this group, organized in the Baperki, had support from the PKI and to a large extent from President Sukarno. The PKI's interpretation of anti-Sinicism as "destroying one's own house to let the burglar in" appears in VIIIc.

In the last two years of Guided Democracy the pressure on the Chinese community eased somewhat, with the result that the influence of the assimilationists within the community diminished. But there were periodic reminders that anti-Sinicism was a weapon of great potential value against the increasingly Peking-aligned government. Our fifth extract here expresses PKI apprehensiveness about these possibilities. Predictably, the rightward trend in Indonesian politics after 1965 brought a new wave of anti-Chinese violence.

XIa

Sjahrir   On Hatred of Foreigners and Internal Minorities (1945)

This item is translated from Our Struggle,* *written in October 1945 at a point in the early days of the Revolution when violent acts against Dutch people, Eurasians, Chinese, and Indonesians from Christian and traditionally pro-Dutch areas such as Ambon and Menado (North Sulawesi) were frequent.*

One very important matter in our struggle is our attitude and policy toward the more or less alien groups in our population, that is, foreigners and people of foreign descent, whether European or Asian, Christians from Ambon and Menado, and so on. So far we do not have any satisfactory position or policy in relation to all these groups. On the contrary, there have been happenings in the recent past which are clearly wrong and damaging to our people's struggle. Hatred for foreign groups and peoples is indeed something one finds voiced in every nationalist movement, especially hatred directed against groups or peoples which seem to hold positions of privilege. But every national movement which intoxicates itself with a passionate hatred of foreigners in order to gain strength must ultimately come face to face with the whole world and the humanity of man. The same nationalist passion which may, at first, be a source of strength must later lead into a dead end and, finally, to self-destruction. The strength we have been looking for is strength at the expense of justice and humanity. But it is only a spirit of nationalism tempered by justice and humanity which can carry us forward in world history.

For, eventually, all nations must realize their destiny in one humanity embracing all the world, must join together to become a single

* *Perdjoeangan Kita* (Palembang: Residency Information Office, 1946?).

nation, a nation of all mankind living together on the basis of justice and truth, where there are no longer any narrow-minded notions dividing man from man on the basis of skin color or descent. It is only when such narrow-minded attitudes have ceased to prompt our actions and behavior, that we will be free from blind ties to our primitive history. Only then will we be able to see clearly the difference between patriotism on the one hand and on the other feelings of dislike toward foreigners and internal minorities which are isolated as a result of history or isolate themselves because of their blood, because of a stupid and barbarous notion of blood.

Our attitude to all this must be based on a study of society, on an honest investigation and consideration of what will serve the ideals of humanity and social justice.

XIb

Assaat The Chinese Grip on Our Economy (1956)

This comes from a speech made to the All-Indonesian National Importers Congress of March 1956, a speech which expressed frankly ideas previously discussed only in private. The full text can be found in Badan Pekerdja KENSI Pusat (Central Working Committee of the All-Indonesian National Economic Congress), KENSI Berdjuang (The Struggle of the All-Indonesian National Economic Congress) (Djakarta: Djambatan, 1957), pp. 51–62. This congress gave birth to what was known as the Assaat Movement, a movement for preferential treatment in economic affairs to be given to ethnic Indonesians rather than to the larger category of persons of Indonesian citizenship.

The Chinese as an exclusive group resist the entry of others, whether in the cultural, social, or, especially, the economic sphere. In the economic sphere they are so exclusive that in practice they are monopolistic. Every Indonesian businessman experiences the Chinese monopoly in practice. Let me mention several examples. An Indonesian shopkeeper who wants to sell rice in his shop is forced to buy from a Chinese rice dealer. There he is treated differently from a Chinese shopkeeper. The rice dealer gives better facilities to the Chinese shopkeeper as regards credit, price, and quality. . . .

An Indonesian shoemaker who needs materials such as leather, nails, thread, needles, and so on has to get his supplies from a Chinese dealer who controls these goods. He will experience the same sort of discriminatory treatment as the shopkeeper. . . .

An Indonesian importer who wants to operate properly has to sell the goods he imports to wholesalers. Wholesaling is almost 100 per cent in Chinese hands, so when imported goods are plentiful, the Indonesian importer really feels the competition with the foreign importer who has good relations with the wholesaler. The Indonesian importer is easily pushed around by the Chinese wholesaler.

What happens to the Indonesian importer happens to the Indonesian manufacturer. . . .

If we look at Chinese businesses, we see at a glance that the office staff are always Chinese. Only menial and unimportant work is given to Indonesians. . . .

What about the group called new citizens, or citizens of foreign descent—in this case, of Chinese descent? To answer this, we must investigate just who these new citizens are under the present regulations in our country. Chinese who were Netherlands subjects and did not refuse Indonesian citizenship automatically according to the law become Indonesian citizens.

Who was included among these Netherlands–subject Chinese? Anyone born in Indonesia whose parents were Chinese foreign orientals living in Indonesia was a Netherlands–subject Chinese. So a child born in Indonesia of a Chinese *totok** father and a Chinese *totok* mother living here, became an Indonesian citizen unless he objected.

Totok father, *totok* mother, capital from his father. Such a man is a foreigner. Socially and economically he is still part of the Chinese *totok* community; yet he could become an Indonesian citizen.

Do these people feel themselves Indonesians? Do they feel one with the Indonesian people? Would they be prepared to defend the interests of Indonesia if there was a dispute with another country, even if it was the Chinese People's Republic or Taiwan? Our brief history since the outbreak of World War II shows that their attitude is appropriate to their objective in coming here to seek a living, namely, to be always on the side which appears to be strongest. During Dutch colonial times they were pro-Dutch; during the Japanese regime they were pro-Japanese; with the return of NICA they were pro-Dutch again. When the Kuomintang was in power they sided with Chiang Kai-shek; now, with the Chinese People's Republic in power, they side with Mao Tse-tung.

* Chinese born in China or strongly China-oriented.

This sort of citizen cannot be separated from the Chinese group, especially in the economic field. In trading in the Pasar Pagi and Pintu Ketjil business districts, no one asks whether Mr. Liem is a citizen or not. These people are not hit by the effects of the exclusive and monopolistic nature of the Chinese group in the way that native Indonesians are. . . .

To extend special protection to this sort of citizen means enabling the Chinese to maintain and entrench further their position in politically independent Indonesia; all the various regulations aimed at advancing the interests of the Indonesian people will be evaded and circumvented by the Chinese via these new citizens. . . .

Once again I stress that if I believe that there is a need for special protection in the economic field for indigenous Indonesian citizens, this feeling does not arise from jealousy or race-hatred of the Chinese as a people but from calculation based on the facts I have put forward. Advancing the interests of the weak group over those of the strong group with the aim of all equally sharing happiness and prosperity in our country is in my opinion just and wise. On the other hand, treating the weak and the strong group the same means strengthening the position of the strong group—something which is contrary to justice. Our government, based on Pantja Sila, which includes social justice, not only may but must favor the weak group over the strong group. Not to do so would be contrary to the constitution of the Republic of Indonesia. . . .

Since it happens that the weak group and the strong group in the economic field are identical with the native Indonesian citizen group and the Chinese group, it would be easy for the Chinese to hurl accusations at the government that it is following a policy of racial discrimination. . . .

A government confident of its strength and the rightness of its policies would not heed these ill-founded accusations. The attitude of giving in to the threats and accusations of the new citizens who are supported by the Chinese group as a whole, does great harm to the struggle of the Indonesian people in the economic field, seriously obstructs Indonesian enterprise as I have explained, and, moreover, strengthens the position of the Chinese group in our country. If we give in now, then the revolution which has claimed the lives of hundreds of thousands of Indonesians will have been in vain. Economically we will still be oppressed by the Chinese.

The privileged position of the Dutch businessman is acknowledged and regulated in the Round Table Conference agreement. It is therefore easy to liquidate his special privileges by canceling this agreement. The power of the exclusivist and monopolistic Chinese in the economic field is far more dangerous for the progress of the Indonesian people, but that power is not regulated in any agreement; rather it has been rooted and entrenched in society for centuries. Therefore, liquidation of this legacy of Dutch colonialism is very difficult. We must face this danger together. The entire people and the government must face it consciously and systematically, as we have struggled to liquidate all other aspects of Dutch colonialism.

Although this Congress is called the All-Indonesian National Importers Congress, not only importers but also people from industrial, banking, and cooperative groups were invited and are attending. So the problem which I have outlined, which I consider to be an important national problem in the economic field, I place before this assembly, in the hope that this Congress will be ready to take the initiative in striving to liquidate this legacy of Dutch colonialism which still oppresses us in the economic field. Therefore, I urge the Congress to consider and eventually to accept three propositions as a basis for this struggle. They are:

1. The power of the exclusive Chinese group in the economic field, especially in the trading sector, hinders the progress of Indonesian business in all sectors of economic life.
2. In economic life it is not possible to differentiate between foreign Chinese and Chinese who are citizens of Indonesia according to the present citizenship regulations.
3. Native Indonesian citizens must receive special protection in all their endeavors in the economic field, from the competition of foreigners in general and the Chinese especially.

XIc

Onghokham   The Case for Assimilation (1960)

This extract was published under the title "Assimilation and the Political Manifesto" in the Djakarta Star Weekly *of April 2, 1960.* Star Weekly, *published in the Indonesian language, was edited by Indonesia-minded Chinese, and it was to Indonesia-minded Chinese that this article was principally addressed. The way in which the author*

relates the current position of the Chinese to Dutch colonial policy
bears comparison with Roeslan Abdulgani's view in IVd.

It is now quite feasible for the government to plan for the assimilation of Indonesians of Chinese descent into the majority community.
The government could create an atmosphere favorable to the improvement of minority-majority relations. For example, without regarding
the minority as a distinct group, it could institute mixed schools in
which both majority and minority were represented among the students, and establish mixed associations which could play an active
role in the guided economy, in cooperatives, and in other social
activities.

The distinction between guidance and compulsion is one of degree,
and the boundary between the two is laid down in and guaranteed by
the Pantja Sila, which includes the principle of humanity. Perhaps the
distinction between the two concepts will become more obvious in
the following examples. If the government selected partners for people who wished to marry, then this would be compulsion. If the government passed laws making illegal marriages other than those
between people from different groups, this also would be compulsion.
But if the government improved intergroup relations so as to create an
atmosphere in which members of the minority could meet with members of the majority, then this would be not compulsion but guidance.

When the government as at present forbids Indonesians to study in
foreign schools, it is, in a guided manner, focussing the full attention
of Indonesian children upon the homeland rather than upon foreign
countries. It is often said that this regulation conflicts with the principle that parents should be able to send their children to schools of their
own choosing. People who voice such opinions forget that before they
can become Indonesian citizens they must know about the ideals of
the Indonesian nation, that is, nationalism which, among other things,
demands that the children of Indonesian citizens be educated in a way
which orients them toward Indonesia and which teaches them to love
their homeland.

It is frequently forgotten by the minority group that the policies
and aims of the state are concerned not only with the majority but
also with the minority. Such an attitude on the part of the minority is
influenced by the idea that the minority group can live as a separate
group that needs take no interest in affairs of state just so long as this

group can live in a "prosperous" and "just" manner according to its own standards. It is as if, taking the motto *Bhinneka Tunggal Ika* [Unity in Diversity], they want to remember only the *Bhinneka* [Diversity], as if they still lived in the period of the Dutch political slogan *Rust en orde* [peace and order].

It is important that the minority should think about the *Tunggal Ika*, too. This expresses the aspiration for national unity, which includes unity between minority and majority. National unity means that the concepts of minority and majority disappear, as will the "devil of *suku*-ism and the devil of group-ism" (in the words of President Sukarno's August 17, 1959 speech called the "Political Manifesto"). The minority group cannot merely aim at a just and prosperous society, but must also fulfill and implement the principles of the Indonesian state, that is, they must work toward unity.

Progress toward this unity can only be achieved by means of assimilation, so that the exclusiveness of the minority is destroyed and the relations between minority and majority are improved and mixed marriages increase. In this way assimilation can be achieved: biological, economic, social, political, and so on. In the opinion of the writer, it is this sort of assimilation which accords with the ideals of the Indonesian nation which rejects groupism and *suku*-ism. We should not forget that Van Mook's policy consisted of two elements, that is, emphasizing regional and ethnic differences among Indonesians and accentuating the differences between groups of foreign descent and the rest of society. Proceeding toward assimilation means participating in the destruction of the policy of Van Mook.

Apart from the fact that assimilation accords with both the slogan *Bhinneka Tunggal Ika* and the aim of the state as it is clarified in the Political Manifesto, assimilation also represents the solution to the minority problem. Assimilation means the abolition of distinctions between one group and another, so that discrimination naturally disappears because the differences are no longer visible. The minority group that always emphasizes the problem of discrimination conveys the impression that the fault lies with the majority which practices the discrimination. However, the matter may be seen from a different angle, that is, that the minority remains aloof from the society and does not wish to join in the activities of the state. The minority still wishes to continue to defend itself as a group by exclusiveness. For the minority to differentiate and separate itself is to invite discrimination.

Some people say that assimilation is a long process and cannot possibly happen; and they then produce examples of minorities which have not been assimilated. Indeed, their first point is correct; however, the formation of a united nation always requires a long time, and it is possible that it would not take as long in Indonesia as many people think. Indonesia is free of racial prejudice, and it is free of religious prejudice. Even the problem raised by the physical characteristics of the minority group cannot become a great obstacle, as narrow eyes, yellow skin, and other Mongoloid features are also characteristic of "native" Indonesians. What, in fact, causes the existence of the minority group is not racial prejudice, as in America, nor religious prejudice, as in Europe with the Jews, but politics and history which have made the Indonesian–Chinese a distinct group within the society. By doing away with relics from the past, by doing away with obvious differentiating characteristics, such as names, assimilation can be encouraged.

Antiassimilationists often use examples of Negro and Jewish minorities to argue that the minority problem cannot be solved by assimilation. To do this is to forget the fact that every nation is composed of minorities which have been integrated so as to produce one nation or of minorities which have been merged into another group. We do not need to travel far to find examples: ethnic groups in Indonesia itself contain Indian, Chinese, Arab, and other elements. In Europe, where the Jews form a minority, the French, German, and other nations consist of a variety of ethnic stocks. America, where the Negroes have not been integrated, presents another prominent and living example. To say that minorities cannot be absorbed is to refuse to acknowledge or else to forget completely that throughout history there have been national migrations. The groups which have not been integrated are only exceptions, and each such exception is explicable in terms of special causes.

In America there is racial prejudice toward people with colored skin. All the immigrants from Italy, France, Germany, Poland, England, Scotland, and so on were absorbed, some easily, others less so; the Negroes, Chinese, and Japanese were not absorbed because of the existence of this racial prejudice. Thus, it is not that a minority cannot be absorbed by a majority, but that the characteristics of American society were unfavorable.

But, thank God, Indonesia is not America. In Europe a similar situation exists, that is, there is religious prejudice against the Jews. Apart from this, the Jews themselves do not want to be assimilated and always defend themselves as a group with all their might. The Jews feel

that they are a nation "chosen by God," "God's favored nation." This
feeling is strengthened by religious teachings in Europe and by other
factors, so that their hope that they will be freed by God's Messiah is
increased, which, in turn, causes them to intensify their group consciousness.

The failure of a minority to be absorbed is also often the fault of
that minority itself, which maintains its group identity. Of course,
there are also barriers between Christianity and Judaism in Europe,
and so on. However, in Indonesia the obstructions created by the
majority are few, and, in the opinion of the writer, the greater difficulty is caused by the minority. In Indonesia obstacles, such as religion,
are small. Other obstacles, such as customs and beliefs, restrictions on
certain kinds of foods, and the like, are of decreasing significance in
the cities and, anyhow, do not represent great obstacles.

The problem now is that the minority has to realize that they cannot remain here as Indonesian citizens and continue to behave like
foreigners. They must realize that absorption into the society is the
only road for them.

The greatest obstacle to the absorption of the minority is the weakness of its own orientation toward Indonesia. This is a legacy of the
colonial period, when the colonial government indeed gave the impression that improvement of the group's position could only come
from China. This sort of thinking must now be abandoned because it
no longer accords with the times.

XId
Baperki For Nation Building through
Integration (1963)

*This is the General Resolution issued by Baperki after its Eighth
National Congress at Semarang in December 1963, over the signature
of its chairman, Siauw Giok Tjhan. It was published in* Madju Terus,
Pantang Mundur (*Ever Onward, No Retreat*) (*Djakarta: Baperki,
1963*).

BAPERKI! FORWARD, NO RETREAT, FOR NATION BUILDING THROUGH IN-
TEGRATION WITH THE REVOLUTIONARY RANKS OF THE PEOPLE!

At its plenary session held in Semarang from December 26–28,
1963, Baperki thoroughly discussed problems connected with nation
building, in keeping with its struggle for the development of a solidly

united nation based upon Pantja Sila nationalism or *Gotong Rojong* nationalism. As is stated in the Preamble to the Baperki Constitution, this can only be successfully implemented by completing the transformation of Indonesian society, that is to say, by establishing and strengthening Indonesian socialism, where there is no exploitation of man by man.

In his address at the opening reception of Baperki's Eighth National Congress, His Excellency the President–Great Leader of the Revolution said in essence that within the mold of Indonesian culture, the form and content of which is *Bhinneka Tunggal Ika*, each of the various ethnic groups making up the single Indonesian nation display specific features of their own, as is evident, for example, from the names characteristic of each group.

Some people hold the opinion that the unity of the Indonesian nation must be attained by means of what they term "total assimilation," the complete merging of all the ethnic groups that make up the Indonesian nation by means of open or concealed pressure aimed at completely obliterating the specific features of each of the ethnic groups. This opinion clearly conflicts with the basic principle of the State, Pantja Sila, and the broad lines of State policy, *Manipol* and *USDEK*.

The political groups that advocate "total assimilation" have in their activities resorted to compulsion openly or covertly; for instance, by forcing school pupils in some towns of West Java, Central Java, and elsewhere to change their names so as to be able to take the elementary and secondary schools examinations, by discreetly or bluntly forcing sportsmen to change their names as the condition for participation in the Fourth Asian Games held some time ago, and by compelling businessmen to implement the principle of "voluntary participation" which is, in fact, compulsory. Such acts of compulsion retard the natural process of intermingling that has been taking place spontaneously since ancient times.

Besides resorting to force, it is clear that the "total assimilation" movement wants to divert the revolution from its course; this is apparent from their declaration issued following the May tenth incidents* of racial terrorism. In that statement, they did not condemn this terrorist movement which has been described by President Sukarno as a counterrevolutionary movement aimed at destroying the State; on the contrary, they called upon the innocent victims of this terror to

* On May 10, 1963, there was large-scale anti-Chinese rioting in Bandung, apparently instigated by anti-Sukarno groups.

carry out "total assimilation," creating the impression that "assimilation" can eradicate the contradictions in society. Objective investigations undertaken by scientists reveal that racialism is a weapon used by the most reactionary and counterrevolutionary groups to attain political aims that have been strongly denounced by civilized mankind. These reactionaries and counterrevolutionaries are in essence not national revolutionaries but social-reactionary chauvinists.

Modern history provides us with dismal proof that the policy pursued by the racialists, reactionaries, and counterrevolutionaries in fact aims at the annihilation of an entire group in society; this is known as genocide. Notwithstanding the fact that in all the history of the Jewish nation, the German Jews were the ones who most thoroughly "assimilated" themselves physically and spiritually with the German nation, six million of them were annihilated by the excesses of Fascism. Another grim example revealing that so-called "total assimilation" cannot under any circumstances eliminate the more basic social and economic contradictions within society is the life story of Edith Stein (a 100 per cent German name). She was a Jewish girl who abandoned the religion of her parents and was converted to Hitler's religion, Catholicism. Though Edith Stein had gone so far in this process of "assimilating" herself and had even entered a Catholic order and become a nun, she met her death in a gas chamber. The Catholic Church in Germany is now collecting material about her life to back up a proposal that she be canonized as a saint.

The social and economic contradictions still plaguing Indonesian society as a legacy from colonial times can only be solved by consistent implementation of the *Manipol-USDEK* which has provided our Revolution with a line leading toward the creation of a just and prosperous society: Indonesian socialism, a society that differs basically in structure from present-day society.

On the basis of the above facts, serious note should be taken of the fact that the "total assimilation" movement is none other than a racial movement classified by President Sukarno as a counterrevolutionary movement because it does not tend to unite the nation on the basis of a unified progressive national ideology. This was pointed out by Deputy Prime Minister–Foreign Minister Dr. Subandrio in his explanatory remarks about the recent Government Statement to Parliament.

The progressive national ideology referred to here is none other than *Manipol-USDEK.*

In view of this standpoint of ours, we enthusiastically welcome the statement made by the President in his *Gesuri* address* where he said among other things that the task of the Institute for Building National Unity (LPKB) is first and foremost to disseminate a correct understanding of the errors of such phobias as Communist-phobia, worker-phobia, peasant-phobia, and *Nasakom*-phobia.

Hence, the LPKB which has been set up by the President under the leadership of Minister-Coordinator-Minister of Information Roeslan Abdulgani must be cleaned of all elements harboring such phobias and its personnel must be overhauled in order to guarantee implementation of the *Gesuri* address in a way favorable to the development of the nation toward implementation of the principle of *Gotong Rojong* with *Nasakom* as its core for the implementation of the Message of Suffering of the People.

This is why Baperki, as a tool of the revolution, calls upon its masses to speed up the process of integration with the revolutionary political parties and mass organizations as the best possible way of achieving the unity of the nation based upon one progressive national ideology, Pantja Sila and *Manipol-USDEK*. This will make the Baperki masses active participants in the struggle for the completion of the Indonesian revolution.

Finally, Baperki believes that in implementing the tasks of the revolution which are continuously mounting at the present time, we need to reinforce our national vigilance because the counterrevolutionaries are, to use the term coined by President Sukarno, quite "unruly" and are constantly striving to carry out counterrevolutionary activities in a variety of forms such as racial terror, arson, seizing school buildings owned by revolutionary progressive organizations, murders, and the like!

XIe
Harian Rakjat   In Defense of Foreign Traders (1965)

An editorial from the May 14, 1965, edition of the PKI's Djakarta daily, Harian Rakjat.

One newspaper in the capital has proposed, very surprisingly, that all trade and distribution still in foreign hands be taken over by the

---

* *Gesuri,* an abbreviation of "The Resounding Echo of the Indonesian Revolution," was the title of the President's Independence Day address of 1963.

government. Since the "Big Five" have already long been taken over, it cannot be doubted that what this newspaper refers to is the trade and distribution carried on by citizens of India, China, Pakistan, the Arab countries, and so on.

This proposal, contrary to the Political Manifesto and the Economic Declaration, does not make any distinction between foreign capital and domestic capital. This latter category refers to capital which is indeed owned by citizens of other countries but the income from which is not transferred abroad but continues to circulate within our national economy. In the Political Manifesto and the Economic Declaration it is laid down clearly that such capital is among the progressive "funds and forces" which are guaranteed a part in development. So also in his *Tavip* speech, and even in his *Berdikari* speech before the Provisional People's Consultative Assembly, the President very clearly held up the possessors of this foreign capital as an example to be imitated by our parvenus, who with little expenditure of time and effort expect bungalows, automobiles, refrigerators, and all kinds of consumer goods. "Only with shorts and singlet"—by hard work—said the President.

Apart from this, when foreign capital was forbidden to engage in trade and distribution in the rural areas, we saw for ourselves, indeed, we felt directly, how trade was disrupted and how quickly the economic situation deteriorated. The same thing is happening in Burma at the present time, where the government has too hastily taken over all enterprises right down to shops and street-stalls, so that trade has largely ground to a halt, as these shops and stalls rapidly fell into the hands of certain bureaucratic capitalists. The main stumbling block of our economy at present is the economic dynasty of the bureaucratic capitalists, so let not our problems be presented in another way, a way which can succinctly be called neo-Assaatism* or neo-Sumitroism.†

* See Assaat (Biographical Notes) and XIb.
† See Sumitro (Biographical Notes).

XII
National Unity and
the Communists

Communism had shown by the early 1920's that its appeal in Indonesia was wide. Ruth McVey writes that the PKI was the most influential of all Indonesian parties in 1924 though its membership was then barely over a thousand.* Equally important, however, the bitter conflicts within the Sarikat Islam had shown that communism tended to arouse strong hostility in other Indonesian groups. It was in the knowledge of both of these facts that the young Sukarno formed his views on how unity was to be achieved in the nationalist movement; see XIIa.

Sukarno's views were not tested for a long time, for the Communist Party was effectively suppressed after its abortive rebellion of 1926–1927, but they were subjected to a severe test with the rapid revival of Communist strength after 1945. Conflict between Communists and Anticommunists proved to be a major barrier to the unity of the revolutionary Republic from late 1947 onward, and the following year saw the quick development of a polarization of forces: the Hatta Cabinet and its supporters on the one hand, the PKI-led People's Democratic Front (FDR) on the other. In September 1948 a group of second-echelon leaders of the PKI at Madiun in East Java raised the flag of revolt against the Sukarno-Hatta government, and bloody battles were fought in the following two months before the PKI forces were crushed. President Sukarno condemned the Madiun uprising in no uncertain terms, as XIIb shows, but he did so in a way which left the Communist Party with a legitimate role to play, and in a way which was compatible with his progressivist view of history as a leftwardly unfolding series of stages of advancement. Indeed XIIb is a good presentation of this view, expressing both Sukarno's debt to Marxism

* *The Rise of Indonesian Communism* (Ithaca, N.Y.: Cornell University Press, 1965) p. xiii. For literature on Indonesian communism, see p. 245.

and the way in which he has fused elements of Marx's historical materialism with aspects of the Javanese view that history consists of a series of successive epochs, to which the men of that epoch should be attuned.

Our third extract, too, was written against the background of the Madiun affair and the legacy of bitterness it had left. But it also shows how the Communists became part of the national community again, because of the Republic's need to wage its bitterest struggle against the Dutch within a few months of Madiun.

During most of the "liberal period" the Communists were legitimate participants in the framework of politics without threatening it. But their rapidly expanding numbers and impressive organisation made their enemies more and more restive. Their right to full equality with other parties was vigorously asserted by President Sukarno in his Concept of February 1957, when he argued that they should have representation in the cabinet (IIg); but this was equally vigorously denied in Hatta's response to the Concept (XIId). However, Hatta and his supporters lost out in the maneuvers of the following year, and so the transformation of the political system which followed the disintegration and overthrow of parliamentary democracy was accomplished at the expense of the Masjumi and PSI rather than the PKI.

Under Guided Democracy the PKI's prestige was high, and it seemed to be successfully erasing the earlier stigmas of atheism and a-nationalism; see IXg (Aidit). But from 1963 onward its position as part of the legitimate framework of politics became highly controversial once more. There is irony here, for this was a period in which President Sukarno's ideas of *Nasakom* unity (Unity of Nationalists, Religious People, and Communists) were strongly ascendant—see XIIe—a period when Anticommunist ideas could only be expressed in the most covert and indirect ways—as in XIIf. In fact, however, the *Nasakom* assertions were made so frequently and with such great emphasis precisely because belief in them was flagging. By this time the Communists' strength was very great indeed, perhaps greater than ever before, thanks partly to the favor with which President Sukarno looked on them; and so there were many noncommunist leaders who felt that the PKI had to be dealt a major setback if it was not to be permitted to inherit the Republic. The Communists were receiving just such a setback in mid-October 1965, when XIIg was written.

XIIa

Sukarno Nationalism, Islam, and Marxism (1926)

This extract comes from an essay of the same title which Sukarno published in the Bandung paper Indonesia Muda (*Young Indonesia*) *in 1926 as one of his first major pieces of writing. The most accessible Indonesian version of the full text is in* Dibawah Bendera Revolusi (*Under the Banner of the Revolution*) (*n.p.: Panitya Penerbit Dibawah Bendera Revolusi, 1959*), *I, 1–23.*

The Boedi Oetomo, the "late" National Indische Partij which is still "alive," the Sarikat Islam, the Minahasan Federation, the Indonesian Communist Party, and many other parties—each of these has either the spirit of Nationalism or the spirit of Islam or the spirit of Marxism. Can these three spirits work together in their policies facing the colonial authorities and combine to form one great spirit, the spirit of unity, a spirit of unity which will bring us to greatness?

Can it happen in a colony that a nationalist movement joins with an Islamic movement which, properly speaking, is not tied to any one nation, and with a Marxist movement, which is engaged in an international struggle? Can Islam, a religion, work together in facing the colonial authorities with Nationalism, which attaches prime importance to the nation, and with Marxism, which is based on teachings of materialism? . . .

We say with firm conviction: "Yes, it can be done!" It is true that Nationalism does not concern itself with groups which do not follow it in "the desire to live as one" with the people. It is true that Nationalism belittles all groups which do not feel as "one group, one nation" with the people. And it is true that Nationalism fundamentally rejects all modes of action which do not spring from "the common experiences of the people." But we must not forget that the men who built the Islamic and Marxist movements in this country of ours shared a "desire to live together as one" with the men who built the Nationalist movement, that they felt they were "one group and one nation" with the Nationalists, that all groups of this movement of ours, Nationalists, Muslims, and Marxists alike, have a history of shared circumstance behind them, that they have shared for hundreds of years a common fate of being deprived of freedom. . . .

The Nationalists who are reluctant to get close to Marxists and work together with them display great ignorance of history and of the way in which the world's political wheel has been turning. They forget that the Marxist movement in Indonesia and Asia generally has its origins in common with their own movement. They forget that the direction of their own movement is often in conformity with that of the movement of their country's Marxists. They forget that to oppose those of their nation who are Marxists is to reject comrades of the same path and to add to the number of their enemies. They forget or do not understand the significance of the standpoint of their fellow fighters in other Asian countries, for example, the late Dr. Sun Yat-sen, that great Nationalist leader who happily and wholeheartedly worked together with the Marxists, even though he was convinced that a Marxist organization of society was still impracticable in China because the necessary conditions did not exist. . . .

Also we are convinced that we can bring the Muslims and the Marxists together, even though the differences of principle between these two are really very great. Our hearts ache when we recall the darkness in the Indonesian sky several years ago when we witnessed a civil-war-like clash, an outbreak of enmity between Marxists and Muslims, when we saw the army of our movement split into two parts warring with each other.

This conflict represents the blackest pages in our history. Whereas our movement should have been growing in force, this conflict meant that we were throwing away all of its strength for nothing. It set our movement back by decades.

Alas! How strong our movement would now be if this conflict had not occurred. Our organization would certainly not be as inadequate as it is now; our movement would undoubtedly have advanced further than it has, no matter how great the obstacles in its path.

We are convinced that there are no important obstacles to Muslim-Marxist friendship. As we have explained, true Islam has some characteristics of socialism. It is true that socialism is not necessarily Marxism, and we know that this Islamic socialism is different from Marxism —because Islamic socialism is based on spiritualism, whereas Marxist socialism is based on materialism. But it is sufficient for our purposes to show that true Islam is socialistic in character.

Muslims should not forget that Marxism's materialist interpretation of history can often serve them as a guide when they are faced with difficult problems of economics and world politics. Moreover, they should not forget that historical materialism as a method explains events that have taken place in the world, that it is a means of predicting future events, and that it can be extremely useful to them!

Muslims should not forget that capitalism, the enemy of Marxism, is also the enemy of Islam! This is so because what is called surplus value in Marxism is fundamentally the same as usury in the teachings of Islam. Surplus value is that portion of profit which rightly belongs to the workers who produced it. This theory of surplus was worked out by Karl Marx and Friedrich Engels to explain the origins of capitalism. It is this surplus value which constitutes the essence of capitalist systems; in attacking surplus value, the Marxists are attacking capitalism at its very roots!

For the true Muslim it should quickly be obvious that it is wrong to regard this Marxism which opposes surplus value as an enemy. Such a person cannot forget that true Islam also fights against such things; he does not forget that true Islam strongly forbids usury and the taking of interest. . . .

Marxism, which was previously so violently antinationalist and antireligious, has now altered its tactics, especially in Asia, so that its previous bitter opposition has turned into comradeship and support. We now witness friendship between the Marxists and the Nationalists in China, and we see friendship between Marxists and Muslims in Afghanistan.

Marxist theory has changed, too. Indeed, it had to change! Marx and Engels were not prophets who could produce eternally valid laws. Their theories must be changed as the times change; they must be adapted to fit a changing world if they are not to become bankrupt. Marx and Engels themselves perceived this; in their writings they often showed that they had changed their minds or changed their interpretation of particular events of their time. If you look at the views they held before 1847 or compare their use of the term "increasing misery" in the *Communist Manifesto* with the way in which they used this term in *Das Kapital*, you can immediately see a change of attitude or difference of emphasis. Indeed, the Social Democrat Emile Vandervelde was right when he said that "Revisionism did not start with Bernstein, but with Marx and Engels."

This capacity to make tactical and theoretical changes explains why the "younger" Marxists, whether they are "patient" or "tough," especially the "younger" Marxists in Asia, are all supporters of nationalist movements where these are real. They know that in Asian countries, where there is no proletariat in the European or American sense, their movement must change its character to fit in with prevailing conditions of life. They know that the Marxist movement in Asia must employ different tactics than do Marxist movements in Europe, and that they must "work together with petty-bourgeois parties," because what is primarily required here is not getting into power but fighting against feudalism.

For the workers in Asia to be free to organize a socialist movement, it is necessary that these countries should be free, that the workers should have national autonomy. As Otto Bauer said, "National autonomy is a goal which must be pursued by the proletariat in its struggle, because it is very necessary for its policies." That is why national autonomy is something which must be sought before all else by the workers' movements of Asia. That is why it is the duty of the working class in Asia to work with and support all movements aimed at achieving national autonomy, irrespective of the philosophies of these movements. That is why the Marxist movement in Indonesia must support our Nationalist and Islamic movements which also have national autonomy as their goal.

Marxists must remember that their movement necessarily gives rise to feelings of Nationalism in the hearts of the Indonesian workers, because most capital in Indonesia is foreign capital and because the struggle itself produces dissatisfaction in the hearts of the workers who are "at the bottom" against those who are "on top" and so produces a desire among the people themselves to be able to wield national power. They must remember that the feeling of internationalism is not nearly as strong in Indonesia as it is in Europe, that the Indonesian working class accepts internationalism primarily as a tactic. Because of their attachment to their country and because of their lack of the necessary wherewithal, few Indonesians leave their country to look for work in a spirit of *ubi beni ibi patria*, or my fatherland is where working conditions are good—unlike the workers in Europe who then come to have neither a fixed place of abode nor a single fatherland. . . .

The Marxists have taken their hatred of religious people, which arose as a result of the reactionary attitude of the Church in Europe, and applied it to the Muslims, whose position and attitude is completely different. The Islamic religion here is the religion of the unfree, the religion of the underdog, whereas those who profess Christianity are the free. Christianity is the religion of the people on top.

If what one is dealing with is an anticapitalist religion, a religion of the unfree, a religion of the underdog, a religion which demands the achievement of freedom, a religion which forbids that men should endure oppression—such a religion cannot possibly issue in a reactionary standpoint but must necessarily produce a movement whose struggle is in some respects parallel with Marxism.

If the Marxists bear in mind this difference between church people in Europe and Muslims in Indonesia, they will stretch out their hands and say, "Brother, let us unite." If they take notice of the examples of their fellow Marxists in other countries who are cooperating with Muslims, they will follow these examples. And if in doing this they also cooperate with Nationalists, they will have the right to say with their minds at rest, "We have done our duty."

If they do all of these things which are required of the "younger" Marxists, if they concern themselves with the changes in their basic theory and follow out all the changes in their movement's tactics, they will have the right to call themselves the true defenders of the people. Indeed, they will have the right to call themselves the people's salt.

But Marxists who do not concern themselves with unity, who stick to the old theory and the outdated tactics and treat our Nationalist and Muslims movements as enemies—Marxists like this should not feel offended if they are called the people's poison!

XIIb
Sukarno The Madiun Affair (1948)

This extract, translated from "Sarinah," a long article on the emancipation of women, was written shortly after the Communist revolt attempted at Madiun in September 1948 against the leadership of the then embattled revolutionary Republic. The full Indonesian text can be found in Kepada Bangsaku (*To My People*) (n.p.: Panitya Pembina Djiwa Revolusi, 1962), pp. 367–423.

What are the stages of our Revolution? We have been going through its national stage, and we will go through its social stage; the national stage is the one in which we are establishing a National State, and the social stage the one in which we will establish socialism. In the national stage the destructive and constructive forces have been working simultaneously; in the social stage the destructive and constructive forces will also work simultaneously. The epic of interplay between the *amok* of the destructive forces and the forces of construction is

now going on in all its awesomeness. So tumultuous is it that it shakes
the whole world. In the present national stage, political chains, economic shackles, oppressive colonial laws are being battered and
crushed to little pieces. But simultaneously a New State, a New
Government, new laws and concepts are being forged into shape.

And they are not being forged for the present stage alone! In the
course of the present stage, conditions are being prepared gradually
for the implementation of the social stage to come, for instance, the
technical and spiritual tools I mentioned above. In the same manner,
not only will all capitalist elements be crushed and destroyed in the
social stage, whereas elements of social welfare will be built up and
nurtured, but several elements which have been shaped in the preceding stage, that is the national stage, will also be maintained. Thus,
the stages are not sharply marked off from each other, as the sea is
separated from the land, but fit together closely, as adolescence merges
into maturity in the life of a human being or an animal.

Mind you: as the stage of adolescence and the stage of maturity in
the life of a human being or an animal! This means that the two
stages themselves must exist—that one stage must precede the other,
and one stage follow the other. The two stages cannot occur together
at the same time. . . .

How horrible and inhuman was this "social revolution" provoked
in Madiun and other districts by those irresponsible people! It was
completely devoid of noble sentiment. The reason for this is that the
"social revolution of Madiun" was a *provoked* social revolution, a
social revolution that was forced years, perhaps decades, before its
time. The "Madiun social revolution" was cruel and barbarous because
our society generally was not ready for a social revolution and in general did not yet *want* a social revolution—so that those troublemakers
(who, because of their inadequate understanding, felt themselves
"obliged to lead a social revolution now") felt "obligated" to push
out those who did not want this, by torturing them, murdering them,
and hacking them up, as butchers slaughter animals.

This lack of understanding made men into creatures of Ksetra Gan-
damajit.* And yet, despite the fact that they shot and slaughtered
hundreds, indeed thousands, their revolution still failed. They
brought about nothing but destruction and condemnation. Their cruel

---

* Literally, the plain of the smell of death, the jungle of Kali, the Hindu goddess
of death.

history is the only thing that remains written of them in the book of yesterday. There were no masses or millions of people who responded to their call; no mothers who gaily shouted their support for them. Ninety-nine per cent of our people did not approve of their revolution; indeed, a very large proportion of them actively opposed it. This was a sign and clear evidence that their revolution had to fail; a sign and clear evidence that a revolution cannot just be made at will; a sign and clear evidence that revolutions wait until their own time has come; a sign and clear evidence that the "Madiun Revolution" was not based on objective conditions but rather something that was forced as a result of the subjective desires of its leaders.

In fact, the "Madiun Revolution" was not a revolution at all. The word "revolution" is too glorious; it accords too much respect, to be applied to what people did there. The "Madiun Revolution" was an upside-down revolutionary act. In terms of its execution it was a rebellion; in terms of its significance it was a *putsch*. For those who really understand revolutionary literature and terminology, that is, people well versed in socialist theory, the term *putsch* implies criticism and condemnation.

It is true that they cruelly spilled a lot of blood. But whether what they wrought was revolution or not does not depend on the quantity of blood they spilled. *Putsches* are often extremely bloody. The fact that the rebels spilled the blood of innocent people does not establish that their actions constituted a revolution. As I have said, "It is not bloodshed or its absence that determines whether an event is revolutionary or not," and "It is often precisely the reactionary elements who spill a lot of blood!"

What I mean by the term "Social Revolution" is a Social Revolution that proceeds from "a solid steppingstone," one which proceeds after the National phase has been completed. This Social Revolution will not be one which entails slaughter, because, as I have said, it will take place after we have given content to our National Independence (of all Indonesia) in a way which establishes the spiritual and material conditions for National Independence, and thus establishes a solid steppingstone from which to proceed to Social Independence in the future. At the point at which our National Revolution has been completed, in the sense that I intend, we will have established the material preconditions for social welfare, and the spiritual preconditions as well! The minimum technical requirements will have been met, and many Indonesians will have been imbued with the spirit of New Man. By that time society will be "pregnant" with Social Welfare, and then the Social Revolution will be born "smoothly."

XIIc
Sudirman All Groups Must Unite
to Face the Common Enemy (1949)

This message by the Supreme Commander of Indonesia's Armed Forces during the Revolution speaks for itself. The date is significant, May 1949. In December 1948 the Dutch had launched their second "police action" intended to bring the Indonesian Republic to its knees, and this had inaugurated a period of intensive guerrilla retaliation. It had also led to the release of a large number of Communists who had been arrested following the Madiun revolt, many of whom now fought with the Republic against the Dutch. During the Madiun affair there had been a good deal of fighting in the Ponorogo-Sumoroto area, especially between the Communists and the local Masjumi. The Indonesian version is in Solichin Salam, Djenderal Soedirman: Pahlawan Kemerdekaan (General Soedirman: Hero of Independence) (Djakarta: Djajamurni, 1963), pp. 67–69.

SECRET
TO: The leaders of the PKI/FDR
                         The leaders of Masjumi
                         Major Soeprapto Soekowati
                         In the Ponorogo-Sumoroto region.
DATE: May 9, 1949.
Merdeka!
                   Comrades and fellow fighters!

I, being responsible for the over-all execution of battle in our struggle, feel obliged to issue this command to you all with the intention that our defenses be truly strong in the face of our enemy.

Our State is a state based on democracy and provides complete freedom for people to choose and adhere to their own religion or beliefs. This freedom is provided for in the Constitution of the Republic of Indonesia.

However, all faiths or ideologies embraced must serve the welfare of the country and the nation so that the people of Indonesia who have suffered and sacrificed for hundreds of years can be independent and free from imperialist-capitalist influence. The main thing is that, despite our professing a variety of ideologies, there is one obligation which must be fulfilled by all of us together, that is: "Free the soil of Indonesia from the threat of colonial imperialism."

At present we all face a common enemy, the Dutch. Therefore, all groups must unite: the events of the past must be completely forgotten so that we can be truly solid and united and the people of Indonesia form one impregnable fortress capable of resisting attack from any quarter. Total war, that is, war waged by all sections of society under one command, as has often been advocated by the leaders of both the right and the left, must be resolutely waged, especially at the present moment. If we are colonized again, then not only one or two groups will suffer, but all groups, regardless of ideology.

If we want to win in this sacred struggle, we must be strong; to be strong, all petty differences must be discarded and all groups of all ideologies must be united in mind and deed. My only hope is that we can quickly achieve the unity of the people of Indonesia so that we can carry on total war.

We must realize and believe with all our hearts that no earthly power can destroy the freedom of a nation if that freedom has been bought with the blood and treasure of thousands of its people.

To conclude: I trust that you will all strive with singleness of purpose to carry out this order of mine which is issued with no other end than to assure the safety of our beloved country.

Fight on! Freedom for ever!
May 9, 1949
Supreme Commander of the Armed Forces
of the Republic of Indonesia
Lt. Gen. Sudirman

XIId
Mohammad Hatta Oil and Water Do Not Mix (1957)

This excerpt comes from "Assessing Bung Karno's Conception," an article commenting on the President's Conception speech of February 21, 1957 (IIg), which was published as a supplement to the Djakarta daily, Indonesia Raja, of March 5, 1957.

When we come to examine Bung Karno's conception of a *Gotong*

Rojong Cabinet, we are faced with an idea which is intrinsically good and idealistic but in practice cannot be put into effect. It could only be put into effect if all parties represented in parliament shared a common goal and if their political differences concerned only how this goal was to be attained.

But it is this common goal which is lacking. Especially as between the PKI on the one hand and the religious parties and some nationalist groups on the other, there is a difference of ideology and goals which is very fundamental, so that it is difficult to bring these two together in a *Gotong Rojong* Cabinet. We can leave for the moment the question of how portfolios would be divided between these mutually suspicious groups.

Some will concede that there are indeed differences of principle between the PKI and the religious and nationalist parties as regards their ideology and view of life but go on to ask whether there are also such differences as regards goals. Yes, as regards goals, too, there are differences of principle! The aim of the religious and nationalist parties is the building-up of one national state, an Indonesian nation which will be just and prosperous. The PKI is basically part of an international movement which aims at world revolution. Its means of realizing this is by setting up proletarian dictatorships everywhere.

From time to time the Communists are allowed to adapt their tactics to accord with a particular situation, but fundamentally their struggle may not deviate from the principles laid down by Lenin which are known as democratic centralism. This means absolute obedience to the leader, and no right to disagree, in the interests of the whole. And this leader is, for Communists all over the world, Moscow. For a Communist, the Soviet Union is the capital with which all his ideals can be realized, for the Communist struggle stands or falls by the success of the Soviet Union.

Because Soviet Russia is the pioneer of the realization of his ideals, the Communist puts the interests of its international political struggle first. In order to strengthen the position of the Soviet Union, he will, if necessary, sacrifice all other interests, including those of his own country's freedom. This has been shown by the history of the last thirty years. As they see it, once Russia has achieved victory in its struggle against imperialism, the freedom of other countries will come of its own accord.

Absolute obedience to the leadership of Moscow is a fundamental law of life for a Communist. It is the foundation of the Communist movement's strength. A person cannot be a real Communist unless he understands and can adapt himself to this iron discipline. So an Indonesian government in which Communists are participants cannot carry out an independent foreign policy. Whatever his personal feelings may be, a Communist will be betraying his ideals if he does not put the interests of the Soviet Union first, even where these conflict with the interest of his own country.

Because of this, Bung Karno's efforts to bring the PKI and the religious and nationalist parties together in a cabinet must fail. It is like trying to mix oil and water. There are, indeed, some among us, opportunists, who hope that the PKI can be made into a Titoist communist movement and argue that this could be done by bringing it into the cabinet to participate in carrying out national policies, including our independent and active foreign policy.

That possibility is not reasonable! The PKI will continue to take Moscow as its guide, will continue to hold fast to the fundamentals of Leninism and Stalinism. Quite apart from considerations of ideology, there is no advantage for the PKI in becoming a Titoist communist organization, a body standing by itself and competing with other parties, without any ties to international communism. This would only weaken it. The possibility does not exist, especially in view of Moscow's present position of returning to the centralist principles of Stalin.

Bung Karno is afraid that a movement such as the PKI, which obtained six million votes in the recent elections, cannot just be left to be in the opposition. Quite apart from the question of what value one places on those six million votes, what are we to do if the groups which obtained more than three times as many votes as the PKI are unwilling to accept the PKI? To force them to accept it would sharpen the conflict and take us further away from our ideals of national peace and national unity.

But what is wrong with the PKI's sitting in parliament as an opposition party? A good democratic government consists of government and opposition. The government acts and the opposition acts as a check on it. If the PKI acts as a good and firm opposition in parliament and does not merely obstruct and make trouble, it can influence the course of government and turn it in a favorable direction. It can prevent corruption in the government parties and so help to raise the present low level of political morality. In this way the government parties will be forced to give proper attention to the improvement of the lot of the common people.

Only a good and responsible opposition, one with a sense of responsibility for the welfare of the government and the people can contribute to the healthy development of democracy, which is apparently struggling to survive.

XIIe
Sukarno   The Unity of All Revolutionary Forces (1964)

This excerpt is taken from the President's address of August 17, 1964. The address was given at a time of increasingly acute conflict between procommunists and anticommunists, at a time when Sukarno was frequently criticized for showing too much favor to the former. The full English text is in Sukarno, Indonesia's Political Manifesto, 1959–64 *(Djakarta: Prapantja, 1964?), pp. 281–326.*

Do not think that Sukarno is in the possession of some magic power. No! Whenever I predict this or that, my prediction is based on my knowledge of the objective laws of the history of society. If there is any "magic" in my possession, it is because I know the Mandate of the Sufferings of the People, because I know conditions, and because I know a science which is efficacious, namely Marxism. Therefore, when I ordered the ban on those reactionary parties and newspapers, I imagined that the leftist-progressive people would be even more convinced of the correctness of the Political Manifesto, the "middle-of-the-roaders" would be able to see the truth of my policy, while the right-wing people would not dare any more to be openly hostile to it.

Yes, they would not dare to be openly hostile to the Political Manifesto, because they were afraid of prison, or afraid of the People. This was the beginning of the appearance of the double-faced Manipolist: the hypocrite Manipolist, the pseudo-Manipolist—the false Manipolist! In my address "The March of our Revolution" I warned: "One of the characteristics of a person who is truly revolutionary is oneness of word and deed, the oneness of what his lips say and what he does." I also explained there about the "three big groups of revolutionary powers" whose "reality cannot be denied even by the Gods in heaven," and that, therefore, "the bundling together of the three large groups of revolutionary powers is a must in the struggle against imperialism and capitalism." I said at that time: "We should not be afflicted by the diseases of Islam-phobia, nationalist-phobia, or communist-phobia," and "I work my fingers to the bone to unify all forces which are revolutionary—work my fingers to the bone to unify all *Nasakom* forces, all nationalist, religious, and communist forces!"

Was my prediction wrong? Did it not later turn out to be true that there were indeed people whose lips muttered Manipol but whose practices sabotaged the Political Manifesto? People whose lips muttered *Nasakom* but whose practices sabotaged *Nasakom?* If I criticized them, it was not because I was making things up, it was not because I wanted to "disrupt our unity," of which I have been accused by some people. No! It was they who disrupted unity, and it was my action in criticizing them which saved it! Because our unity is not just unity for the sake of unity, our unity is the unity of all revolutionary forces. It is indeed, therefore, very amusing that there are people who call themselves "propagators of the teachings of Sukarno" who do not speak of "the bundling together of all revolutionary forces" but talk of "the bundling together of all forces"! They have "only" corrupted the word revolutionary, which means that what they have corrupted is the very spirit, the very soul of the teachings of the Revolution! . . .

In Indonesia whose people are of wrought iron and tempered steel only progressive efforts can be successful, whereas efforts, steps, and actions which are contrary to the laws of history not only can fail but are certain to fail. They are certain to fail! Is this not true? They are certain to fail! If you want to swim in the sea, you must know the laws of the sea! One can commit suicide by going against the laws of the sea, but one cannot kill the laws of the sea! One cannot kill the laws of History; one cannot kill the laws of the Revolution! . . .

Still there are people who accuse Sukarno of "taking sides," who accuse Sukarno of "favoritism." Sukarno taking sides? Taking sides with whom? If it is against imperialism, feudalism, and the enemies of the Revolution in general, yes! Sukarno is certainly taking sides, Sukarno certainly has favorites, that is, he sides with the People and with the Revolution itself. Have I not said before that a Revolution cannot possibly be uncommitted, which means that a Revolution must always be committed, that it must take sides? Yes, indeed! As far as being against imperialism, against feudalism, against the enemies of

the Revolution in general is concerned, I certainly have favorites, I
certainly take sides, because I cannot possibly favor imperialism and
feudalism, I cannot possibly follow the lackeys of imperialism and
feudalism, and, therefore, I have favorites, and my favor is for the
People, for Marhaen, for Sarinah, for Djelata, for Proletar, for the
"humiliated and the hungry."

I have been accused of bringing advantage to one group only among
our big national family? My answer here also is, yes. Yes, I am giving
advantage to one group only, namely, the revolutionary group! I am
a friend of the nationalists, the revolutionary nationalists! I am a
friend of the religious group, the revolutionary religious group! I
am a friend of the Communist, because the Communists are revolutionary people. What is more, as I said some time ago in the Sports
Palace at Senajan, I am a friend of the very revolutionary people! . . .

The political atmosphere in our country has lately been clouded by
various discussions, polemics, and debates. Is this a good symptom or
a bad one? It is bad if it weakens national unity. But it is good if it
strengthens national unity. It is true that I am a man full of dynamism!
I do not like tranquility which is frozen and dead; I do not like sluggishness. What I like is dynamism, vitality, militancy, activity, a revolutionary spirit! . . .

In the People's Republic of China, Chairman Mao Tse-tung has a
motto: "Let a hundred flowers bloom together." Here I have a motto:
Let the *melati, mawar, kenanga,* and *tjempaka* and all flowers bloom
together in the flower garden of Indonesia! I said, all flowers—not
elephant grass, not weeds, not parasitic plants, not waterweeds.

There has been a polemic about culture. On culture, my standpoint
is clear: Wipe out the foreign culture that is crazy! Return to our own
culture. Return to our own identity. Get rid of the "Cultural Manifesto";* it weakens the Revolution!

And there has been a polemic on political parties. It is true that
I spoke in the Political Manifesto of "the evil of the multi-party
system," but I have never been hostile to political parties as such.
I have seen the merits in political parties since before the war; I
even set up a political party myself and was chairman of a political
party. Those political parties took part in preparing and later serving
the Revolution. What I do not like are the political parties which
people use to enrich themselves or to give full rein to their voracious

* This was a document issued by a group of humanist and Anticommunist
writers in 1963, pleading for greater freedom of cultural activity.

personal ambitions. With the banning of the two reactionary parties*
and with the failure of other parties to meet the conditions of Presidential Decision No. 7 and Presidential Regulation No. 13 of 1959,†
there are ten parties left. They are not only legal; their right to exist
and right to representation are guaranteed. Of course, if there are
later some among these ten political parties which deviate, which
become anti-Manipol or become Manipol-hypocrites or which suffer
seriously from the disease of phobias, the President–Supreme Commander will not hesitate to ban them, too! . . .

At present I am satisfied with the retooling for simplification that
I have effected among the political parties. What I am now asking, as
I proposed before the Nationalist Party Congress in Purwokerto, is
that the political parties hold a Manipolist competition. The party
which gives more and better service to Country and Revolution, which
gives more and better service to national revolutionary unity, which
is more consistent in mobilising the mass of the People to wipe out
imperialism, colonialism, neocolonialism and feudalism, whichever
party excels in this Manipolist competition is the best party.

And there has been a polemic concerning the implementation of the
Basic Agrarian Law and the Basic Law on Crop Sharing, especially
concerning "unilateral actions" by the peasants. . . .

I know that efforts have been made to implement land reform, but,
frankly, I am not satisfied! I have received many reports about slug-
gish implementation, about obstructions, and even about sabotage of
land reform. The Minister of Agriculture promised implementation
within a period of three years for Java-Madura-Bali, and within five
years for the other regions. Now we are in the fourth year. In short, I
support every effort to smash the obstructions, including the initiative
of the Minister of Justice to establish Land Reform Courts. . . .

At my side, at this present moment, witnessing with us the anniversary of the August Revolution (which also means witnessing the
revolutionary determination and spirit of the Indonesian People) are
my friends, the Head of State of the Kingdom of Cambodia, Prince
Norodom Sihanouk, and a Representative of the Prime Minister of
the People's Democratic Republic of Korea, Kim Il Sung. Prime
Minister Kim Il Sung himself was suddenly unable to come, because
of the critical situation in the regions to our north. But observe our
guests: one is a Prince and the other a Marxist-Leninist. Let the im-

* The Masjumi and Socialist party (PSI), which were banned in 1960.
† These were measures to eliminate the very small parties.

perialists look at the three of us: one who is a Prince, one who is a Marxist-Leninist, and the third one *Nasakom* compressed; but all three are patriots; all three fight imperialism!

Is there anything strange about this? No! If there were no imperialism, we three might perhaps never have appeared together on this platform. Yes, it was in fact imperialism which gave us birth, which made us, which molded us. It is true, my standpoint has always been that whosoever, *whosoever*, opposes imperialism is objectively a revolutionary. In our struggle for independence there have been aristocratic elements side by side with the peasants, but so long as they oppose imperialism so long are they revolutionary. While the picture in Asia is similar to this, it is much the same in Africa and Latin America, too. In this way, Haile Selassie stands shoulder to shoulder with Modibo Keita and Ben Bella, with Sekou Toure, with Nkrumah, with Jomo Kenyatta, with Gamal Abdel Nasser. In this way, Arbenz Guzman stands hand in hand with Cheddy Jagan, with Fidel Castro, the Bolivar of the twentieth century! Yes, in this way Sukarno became the comrade in arms of Ayub Khan and Sirimavo Bandaranaike, the comrade in arms of Ne Win and Macapagal, the comrade in arms of Ho Chi Minh and Mao Tse-tung, the comrade in arms of Norodom Sihanouk and Kim Il Sung!

XIIf
Sajuti Melik   Nasakom or Nasasos? (1963)

This fragment is from the booklet Pembinaan Djiwa Marhaenisme *(Fostering the Spirit of Marhaenism)* (Djakarta: Pantjaka, 1963). *It illustrates the idiom in which many Anticommunists wrote in the late years of Guided Democracy when the Communists were playing a leading public role and outright condemnations of them were impermissible. Some time after writing this booklet Sajuti became a leader of the (covertly Anticommunist) Body for the Promotion of Sukarnoism.*

In 1926 Bung Karno urged that there be as much cooperation as possible between the ideologies or doctrines of nationalism, Islam [religion], and Marxism [socialism], and his ideal was to become the Son of Mother Indonesia who could unify these three ideologies or doctrines. At that time, each was personified in an individual: Tjipto

Mangunkusumo [nationalism], Tjokroaminoto [Islam], and Semaun [Marxism]!

In 1927, Bung Karno founded the PNI [the Indonesian Nationalist Party] based on Marhaenism, Bung Karno's Marhaenism, which contains the essences of these three doctrines, the national, religious, and socialist essences. These three can be compressed into the spirit of *Nasasos* [*Nasionalis, Agama, Sosialis*], or, as has become popular now, the abbreviation *Nasakom* [*Nasionalis, Agama, Komunis*], although their conceptions differ a little—a little but profoundly!

So, not only did Bung Karno urge the union or the co-operation of *Nasasos* or *Nasakom*, but also he himself straight away upheld that cooperation by establishing a party and formulating a doctrine which contained *Nasasos*—that is, Marhaenism.

So Marhaenism is the embodiment of *Nasasos!* Bung Karno is a *Nasasos* person. Every Marhaenist disciple or supporter of Bung Karno should also be a *Nasasos* person! . . .

Bung Karno teaches *Nasasos*. It is a positive fact that Bung Karno himself is a *Nasasos* person. That is why all his pupils who are loyal should become *Nasasos*, too.

Certainly there are differences in conception between *Nasasos*, which has manifested itself as Marhaenism, and *Nasakom*, which is so well known today. If we use chemical terms, *Nasasos*, which became Marhaenism, is a chemical compound, whereas *Nasakom*, which is popular today, is a solution. A chemical compound cannot be broken up any further and has taken on a new form. It can only be separated by a chemical process. A solution, on the other hand, can still be separated without having to go through a chemical process.

A Marhaenist or *Nasasos* person can be pictured like this: his body is nationalist; his soul is religious; his thoughts are socialist! But what is meant by the mutual help of *Nasakom* today is pictured as three people: a nationalist, a religious person, and a Communist; three people who work together helping each other in order to complete the multi-complex national revolution of Indonesia.

XIIg

Soerasto Sastrosoewignjo You Have Stabbed Us in the Back Again (1965)

This is part of an article in Mertjusuar, *a Djakarta daily of the Muslim reform organization Muhammadijah, of October 15, 1965, and reflects the dramatic change of political climate which followed the unsuccessful coup of October 1. The author used the pseudonym S. S. Kelana.*

Puppet-master, how many times have you practiced your craft to stab our revolution from behind? In 1948 in the midst of the armed revolution, a shameful and accursed treachery was perpetrated, aimed at changing the goal of the revolution by brutal force. . . . How many thousands, tens of thousands, and hundreds of thousands of patriotic folk, of religious leaders, and true nationalists fell victims in that famous Madiun Affair of yours? Mass burials in disused wells are no innovation for you! You pumped the gentle spirits of a humane and patriotic people full of "progressive revolutionary" notions, which, however, tended basically toward a cruel and uncivilised anarchism. The memory of this dearly bought experience still festers in the breasts of all true patriots and nationalists.

In our mental revolution until now you have despicably slandered whatever groups or individuals have not submitted to your commands. Your puppets have shrieked that their opponents are splitters, economic dynasts, bureaucratic capitalists, exploiters of the people, anti-people, compromisers, hypocritical Pantja-Sila-ists, false *Nasakom*-ists and whatever other filthy epithets you and your accomplices could dredge up. In reality there is no one whom these labels fit better than you and your friends.

You seek out a term of abuse for every group, to be used as an excuse to destroy it. Is all this done merely for the glory of the dialectical philosophy you espouse? As a result of this indoctrination the breasts of all your followers burn with a thirst for battle—battle to maim and destroy the integrity of this nation. You darken the future of the young and innocent with practices of seizing other people's property. What actually is their work? Where actually is the theory of labor to which you profess to adhere? You always see others as exploiters of surplus value. What surplus value? Your puppets launch agitations to reduce the amount of work done, with "slow downs", at the same time as your trade unions are interrupting the process of production and demanding unlimited increases in wages. Good! Let us, indeed, raise wages, provided the work done does not fall. How can national investment and economic betterment come from this kind of work? Indonesian socialism must be built on a foundation of mutual agreement.

At the same time the mass media you control, which should be act-ing as enlighteners of the people, serving the revolution with honest reporting, have been turned into sources of lies to exacerbate cun-ningly the conflicts existing among the people. . . . When one of your group of papers cries "a mouse!" all of the evil group take up the same cry in unison again and again and do not stop till whoever has been branded a mouse is mobbed and left for dead. Many are the groups which have thus wantonly, humiliatingly, and offensively been made victims. Their treatment has been inhuman, worse than one would expect in a slaughterhouse. . . .

Still fresh in our minds are the remarks about Pantja Sila which one of your puppets made at the first *Nasakom* cadre course, when he said, among other things, "We only need the Pantja Sila as a unify-ing instrument. When we are thoroughly united, we can leave the Pantja Sila behind." * These words evoked a strong reaction. Then later in a base and shameless fashion this puppet of yours backed down and washed his hands of what he had said. But remember that the witnesses were from all levels of society—dozens of generals, hun-dreds of officers of all services, and party leaders, and thousands of progressive-revolutionary people, patriots all, with the exception of the cockroaches who crawled in on your own sponsorship.

We want to know: Who in fact deviated from the spirit and mean-ing of *Nasakom* unity? . . . You know the answer well. The group responsible are those who were always shouting that other people were hypocritical *Nasakom*-ists. Yet this cap fits no one better than you and your friends. . . .

The peak of this hypocrisy is visible in the terrorism of the tragic September 30 Movement. . . . On a previous occasion you made ac-cusations in your White Book and made your opponents responsible for the bloodshed of the Madiun Affair of 1948. But now fresh evidence has been piled up against you in the tragic happenings at Lobang Buaja on October 1, 1965. In truth your hands are so stained with the blood of patriots that you would not be able to cleanse them in the next world, even if you did believe in its existence. . . .

And now to the harvest of these acts you are now reaping. You, the puppet-master, flee like a cat before the broom. You disappear from view while your puppets are scattered in confusion. We are surprised. It was always you and your friends who shouted loudest about de-

* Aidit was reported to have said something like this in October 1964.

fending the people and standing in the midst of them. Now it turns out that you fear the people and hide from them. You posed as the patriot and revolutionary. Since October 1 it turns out that the puppet-master has just been talking big and is really a counterrevolutionary. And you know what the punishment for counterrevolutionaries is?

XIII
The Economic Order

In selecting writing on economic goals and problems we have had to be more restrictively selective than in relation to any other area of controversy. In fact, we have had to leave large areas of controversy out altogether: for instance, controversy about the policies of fostering a "national" (private) business group,* about the seizure of the large Dutch business establishment in December 1957, about private Indonesian enterprises and government firms, about the ban on Chinese retailers in rural areas, about industrialization and the siting of industries, about the Eight-Year Overall Development Plan, about cooperatives, about land reform, about the army's role in economic management,† and so on. On the whole we have chosen items concerned with economic goals broadly conceived, but there are also two or three pieces here dealing with current policy.

The climate in which economic matters were discussed in the political world was dominated by the consideration of ends, of broad social and political norms such as *sama rasa sama rata, gotong rojong,* antiliberalism, the principle of the family relationship, national In-

---

* Indonesian views on this and some other aspects are quoted at length for the first half of our period in John O. Sutter, *Indonesianisasi: Politics in a Changing Economy, 1940–1955* (Ithaca, N.Y.: Cornell Southeast Asia Project, 1959). For the quite extensive literature on the Indonesian economy since independence, see George L. Hicks and Geoffrey McNicoll, *The Indonesian Economy, 1950–1965: A Bibliography* (New Haven: Yale University, Southeast Asia Studies, 1967), and the supplementary volume (1968). Two excellent surveys are by Douglas S. Paauw, in Ruth T. McVey, ed., *Indonesia* (New Haven: Yale University and Human Relations Area Files, 1963), pp. 155–247; and J. A. C. Mackie, "The Indonesian Economy, 1950–1963," in D. Rothermund, ed., *Studien zur Entwicklung in Süd- und Ostasien: Indonesien* (Frankfurt-on-the-Main: Metzner, 1964), pp. 115–155.

† But see XIVf for one army view on this problem.

donesian control, an economy in revolution, and so on. The underlying assumption of those who set the tone seemed to be that Indonesia was a rich country and that the task of political leaders was therefore not to make the economic wheel go around (which it would do anyway), but rather to see that it was headed in the right direction. See our first and fifth extracts here and also IVb and IIIc.

As our second extract of this section suggests, the professional economists, who believed that economic management was a difficult business and that Indonesia's economic problems could only be solved by a heavy concentration of effort upon them (one in which the laws of economics were taken seriously), were also obliged to talk in terms of goals and norms, or at least to use these as a point of departure for discussions of appropriate means.

In fact, the central dialogue about economic matters in our period was about the importance of economic advancement as such. It was a dialogue about whether one should put prosperity first or justice first, whether one should work for higher production or for a greater degree of "national" Indonesian control of this production, for a larger cake to be consumed or a fairer division of the cake. This debate was sometimes one between politicians and professional economists—as in XIIIa and XIIIb—and sometimes one between the radical nationalists and their allies and the democratic socialists and theirs—as in XIIId and IVb. And it was often intertwined with arguments between supporters of foreign capital and its opponents, as in XIIIc, or with arguments between advocates of regional autonomy and its opponents, as in Xb. But it was rare for the discussion to be in the form of an argument about means, of an argument about alternative paths to economic progress. In fact, several of the political groups which played a major role in the making of economic policy, notably the PNI, persistently refused to defend their policies with distinctively economic arguments, preferring a justification in terms of broader social and political ideals.

The last four extracts here were born of the situation between 1963 and 1965, when the economy was by general agreement in a serious condition, with production falling in most parts of the modern sector, inflation proceeding at more than 100 per cent per year, roads and shipping in a far-gone state of disrepair, foreign debts mounting at an alarming rate, and urban wages and salaries at lower real income levels than at any time since the last year of the Japanese occupation.

In this situation there was a good deal of discussion of alternative paths to economic regeneration, thanks largely to the fact that the Communists now became vigorous participants in an argument which had previously been almost exclusively between radical nationalists and democratic socialists. The Sadli and Aidit pieces below may be taken as representing the two principal alternatives as they were presented in this period, with the Sukarno extract representing the political idiom of the day to which both Sadli and Aidit were obliged to defer. Mrs. Slamet's piece, complementing perhaps that of Aidit, looks beyond the troubles of the modern sector of the economy to the most basic of Indonesia's economic problems, the deepening crisis of poverty and overpopulation in the countryside.

XIIIa
Wilopo The Principle of the Family Relationship (1955)

What follows is part of a contribution* to a symposium held at the University of Indonesia, Djakarta, on September 23, 1955. On that occasion former Prime Minister Wilopo discussed with the economist Widjojo Nitisastro the interpretation of Paragraph I of Article 38 of the Provisional Constitution then in operation, the constitution of 1950. This paragraph, which is to be found also in the constitution of 1945, reads as follows: "The economy shall be organized as a joint endeavor based on the principle of the family relationship."

The implementation of liberalism in Asia by the Western nations gave rise to the same features and the same problems that the practice of this doctrine had evoked in the European countries—exploitation of man by man, diminution of liberty for the economically weak mass of the people, and large disparities in the ownership of wealth in the society. These consequences of the growth of a liberal economy were explained by Asian leaders in the same terms as employed in Europe, these explanations being in accordance with philosophical and economic teachings of universal relevance.

However, the negative consequences of liberalism in the colonial countries were far more pronounced and far more depressing than

* Reprinted, by permission, from Wilopo and Widjojo Nitisastro, *The Socio-economic Basis of the Indonesian State* (Ithaca, N.Y.: Cornell Modern Indonesia Project, 1959).

was the case in Europe, so that the reaction was inevitably more intense. It was for this reason that, with the achievement of independence, we wished to change completely the basis of the country's economy.

The pattern of economic development in the past, particularly since 1870, had produced misery and injustice among the great mass of the Indonesian people. This pattern was based on economic liberalism. Article 38 of the Provisional Constitution formulates a new principle, and this principle is opposed to liberalism. The antagonism between the principle laid down in Article 38 and the concept of liberalism is not only evident from the Government statement at the time of the Provisional Constitution but is also in conformity with the background of the Indonesian revolution.

Having established that the principle laid down in Article 38 is in opposition to liberalism, we can go on to formulate the interpretation of this article in terms of antiliberalism and in relation to those other provisions in the Constitution which are related to the question of economic systems. The term "joint endeavor" conveys the idea of a form of enterprise that is quite distinct in character from that of private enterprise; in the latter all decisions are in the hands of the entrepreneur and all the worker's life and work depends on the employer. It is because liberalism produced a situation in which the workers in general are subjected to pressures of social compulsion that we object to such a system.

Our ideal is of a type of enterprise in which all participants can be freely accorded "to all in accordance with their nature, aptitude, and ability to take part in the development of the sources of prosperity of the country." These words are the formulation of the guarantees accorded to the individual human being in Paragraph II, Article 37. The term "based on the principle of the family relationship" signifies a basis of collective responsibility directed toward achieving a common effort which will ensure progress for each participant. It is in this collectivist feature that one sees the difference between the envisaged economic system and the principle of individualism. Economic activity has no longer the motive of personal gain but rather the motive of serving the community for the common good.

Encouragement must be given to the development of the forms of enterprise fulfilling these requirements, particularly where traditional practices exist which can be adapted to the new concept.

In this respect co-operative forms of enterprise are of special importance since the population is sufficiently familiar with undertakings of this nature, and because it already plays a role in different fields of activity, such as agriculture, fishing, and so on.

Now that it has been demonstrated that the principle formulated in Article 38 is a rejection of economic liberalism, further interpretation of this article is facilitated. The term "joint endeavor" indicates the difference with private enterprise, while the term "principle of the family relationship" expresses the idea of joint responsibility for ensuring the advancement of all. The purpose of developing joint endeavor is not private profit but the advancement of the entire community. The sense of community responsibility ensures that justice prevails.

It is, of course, obvious that efforts to develop an economic system of joint endeavor as prescribed in Article 38 are not to be left to develop of their own accord. By the terms of this article certain obligations are placed on the state. . . .

In actual fact this article is an assertion of the conviction that the economic system it prescribes is the most suitable for achieving the desired development of the country's economy. Whereas a liberal economy entrusts the achievement of prosperity to the functioning of private enterprise, in principle without state interference, Article 38 of the Provisional Constitution provides for a "joint endeavor based on the principle of the family relationship," this pattern to be developed with the assistance and protection of the state.

The envisaged economic pattern of joint endeavor must be accepted as the guide for all legislation dealing with economic questions and recognized as the basis for all policy decisions of the central government and the regional authorities. All enterprises established by the population in accordance with this pattern must be given every encouragement and assistance.

At the same time, other forms of enterprise, although still permitted, must not be allowed to obstruct or prejudice the undertakings based on the principle of joint endeavor. Failure to provide this protection would be a neglect of the general interest.

Whatever measures are taken by the state must, however, be free of any element of inequitable compulsion, for, after all, it is the liberty of choice of employment and the opportunity for the individual to perform work in accordance with his abilities which ensure the most effective development of human energy.

XIIIb

Widjojo Nitisastro   Raising Per Capita Income (1955)

This passage* is taken from Widjojo's reply to Wilopo in the university symposium of September 23, 1955. See the preceding extract.

In further criticism of the main speaker's approach it may be noted that his interpretation was concerned unduly with the question of redistribution of income, while little or no attention was given to a consideration of the article under discussion from the viewpoint of raising per capita income, which is, in fact, a reflection of the rate of increase in the national income taken in relation to the rate of increase of the population. When it is a matter of analyzing an economic system which is intended to provide a guarantee of successful economic development, the question of redistribution of income and the question of raising the per capita income are inseparable. In the course of economic development both of these ends, redistribution of income and increasing of per capita income, should be realized concurrently since they are complementary and integrally related. Consequently, an analysis of both of these two factors is essential to the study of economic systems. Redistribution of income, unless accompanied by efforts directed toward raising the level of per capita income, would almost certainly act as a restraint on initiative and thus result in a general decline in the rate of expansion of production. Moreover, there would ultimately be a diminution in each individual's share as a consequence of population increase if redistribution of income were to be effected without being related to provisions for raising the average income level. Conversely, the raising of per capita income without an accompanying redistribution of income would ultimately inhibit a rise in per capita income as a consequence of falling enthusiasm for work and also very possibly because of rising social tension.

For these reasons an interpretation of Paragraph I, Article 38, of the Provisional Constitution cannot be arrived at from an approach which takes into consideration only the question of redistribution of income. . . . Given that the principle formulated in Paragraph I, Article 38 is contrary to the principle of economic liberalism, it be-

* Reprinted, by permission, from Wilopo and Widjojo Nitisastro, *The Socioeconomic Basis of the Indonesian State* (Ithaca, N.Y.: Cornell Modern Indonesia Project, 1959).

comes necessary to analyze the operation of the economic process, first, in a liberal economic system, and, then, in an antiliberal system.

Private enterprise is the legal basis of economic liberalism. A liberal economic system operates on the basis of the freedoms inherent in such a system, that is, freedom of production, freedom of consumption, freedom of exchange, and freedom of competition. In consequence, the establishment of prices, including wages, is left to the free play of economic forces. Ultimately, this results in the fixing of prices by the monopoly and oligopoly forces which come into being by the very reason of the liberties prevailing in such a liberal economic system.

An antiliberal economic system can be such that the economic process operates without price mechanisms, since all enterprise is conducted by the State. In other words, in an economic structure of this nature there is no place for private enterprise.

However, an antiliberal economic system can also be such that price mechanisms continue to operate, also in the determination of wages, but under the control of the state, so that there is a guarantee of equitable distribution of income through the entire community.

Various forms of control can be exercised: controls in the field of fiscal policy, budgetary policy, balance of payments policy, price and wage policy, and so on. Moreover, it is possible to use direct methods to crush the forces of monopoly and oligopoly. Under these circumstances the existence of private enterprise does not constitute an anomaly. At the same time the existence of collective and cooperative enterprises constitutes one of the factors of utmost importance, especially in strengthening the bargaining position of the small producers in relation to the middlemen, so that the former are assured of securing a just return. Moreover, these collective and co-operative enterprises are institutions for mobilizing savings for investment purposes. Most important, however, is the fact that in an economic system of this character, the state is obligated and empowered to play an active role in pursuing an equitable distribution of income for all members of the community.

In this connection it may be recalled that for us any reference to private enterprise usually evokes the names of large concerns such as BPM [Royal Dutch Shell], KPM [Royal Dutch Steamship Company], or Stanvac [Standard Vacuum Oil]. But we forget all too easily that the small peasant with a holding of no more than 0.1 hectare is also engaged in free enterprise. Similarly, we often fail to recognize that cooperatives are also privately owned undertakings (in the sense of not being state-owned).

Besides causing an inequitable distribution of income, liberalism also brought about a low level of income in our economy. The level of income is a matter of output, which is a function of investment. An economic system based on liberalism allows complete freedom as regards the volume and directional flow of investment. This absence of control of investment has created structural debilities in our economy, which are reinforced by sharp short-run fluctuations.

An economic system based on antiliberalism is one which ensures structural changes in our economy and which directs the appropriate volume and flow of investment to those sectors which ensure an increase in output and, consequently, an increase in the level of income. In an antiliberal economic system which also abolishes private enterprise, the only source of investment is public saving. On the other hand in an economic system which is based on anti-liberalism but which does not eliminate private enterprise, although investment comes in large part from the state, a not inconsiderable proportion of it is contributed by private enterprise. The essential point is that the volume and directional flow of investment is not left for private enterprise to determine, but that this is the responsibility of the state, for which purpose a variety of policy instruments can be used.

These are the fundamental aspects of an economic system based on antiliberalism which does not do away with private enterprise.

Proceeding from this analysis, we can see that Paragraph I, Article 38, when interpreted in relation to the other provisions of Article 38 and in relation to the full text of the Provisional Constitution, is to be understood as expressing the concept of an economic system based on the joint efforts of the entire community, with the objective of achieving a higher level of per capita income and an equitable distribution of income, with the state playing an active role in guiding and implementing economic development. An equitable distribution of income is one with the highest possible degree of equality compatible with not hampering the production process but, on the contrary, allowing the highest possible rate of expansion of production.

The terms of this interpretation do not make the existence of private enterprise an incompatible element in the economic system under discussion. On the contrary, private enterprise is allocated a specific role. Cooperatives and similar forms of enterprises are allotted the role of ensuring an equitable return for the small producers and of acting as an institution for mobilizing savings for investment. It is thus evidence that the principle of the family relationship cannot be taken as identical with the principle of cooperative enterprise and it is also clear that in interpreting Paragraph I, Article 38, the primary consideration is not the form of enterprise or the type of undertaking which will operate, but rather the functioning of the economic process within the envisaged economic system.

XIIIc

Sjafruddin Prawiranegara The Causes of Our Falling Production (1953)

This piece is part of the "Report of the President for the Financial Year, 1952–1953," issued by the Java Bank, Indonesia's central bank (subsequently renamed Bank Indonesia). Sjafruddin, as the Bank's first Indonesian head, was continuing the tradition of using the annual report as an opportunity to express general views about the problems of the economy.

I come now to an elaboration of the reasons which have led to a slowing down in production.

As a first cause I would mention the unbalanced financial and economic policy which concentrates on the development of new, secondary branches of production (trade and transport concerns run by newcomers) instead of on rehabilitation of the equipment for primary production (particularly indigenous agriculture and home industry).

It must be acknowledged that this unbalanced economic policy is based on highly idealistic views, but these views are definitely not practicable. The interest of many people is attracted by the idea of an "economy established according to plan," by an impressive and comprehensive scheme which covers important and spectacular objects. Though such a plan is undoubtedly very important and valuable, I, nevertheless, consider it far more desirable that the Indonesian people should receive assistance and support as quickly as possible in the production of goods out of the resources and materials existing in their own country, goods for the most essential necessities of life, without having to wait upon the execution of vast schemes which are dependent on assistance and raw materials from abroad.

In addition, it is necessary to point out that too little attention has been given—by the people as well as by the Government—to the middle-class industries. We are far too preoccupied with the large enterprises and industrial concerns. Because these are in a position to make big profits and because they are for the most part in the hands of foreign organizations, there is a natural desire to replace them as soon as possible by similar Indonesian industries. In this plan for position-changing, however, too little consideration is given to the fact that these big organizations are closely connected with small and medium-sized businesses, which to a great extent are also in the hands of foreigners. So long as an adequate settled basis is lacking, in other words, until such time as an Indonesian "middle class" has been built up out of trading organizations and industries of medium size and significance, established either directly or by way of small industries in our community, it cannot be expected that prosperous Indonesian major industries can be established or maintained. Healthy and lasting development grows upward from below, not the other way round. The formation of an Indonesian middle class will undoubtedly take time. If, however, we do not give attention to this matter forthwith, the development of Indonesian major industry will be delayed accordingly.

It also appears, in view of the desire to grant assistance to businesses of newcomers, that insufficient weight has been given to the consideration that capital alone is not enough for the successful development of any firm. Good organization is probably of more importance than capital, and such organization is, after all, entirely dependent on the professional knowledge and experience of the individuals in control of such a business. Experience acquired in small and medium-sized businesses can be of paramount value for the management of larger organizations, and, indeed, Western concerns can act as training institutions for Indonesian entrepreneurs.

It also needs to be realized that apart from experience and professional knowledge, there are certain other factors, that is, qualities of character such as reliability, zeal, sense of responsibility, stability, and so on, which have a decisive influence on whether a business will succeed or not.

Industries which are entirely dependent on Government subsidies are generally not the best places to learn to take business risks. It has often become clear that money advanced by the Government has been wasted, because the newcomers who borrowed it did not possess the above-mentioned qualities.

The second factor acting as a brake on economic development is the unwieldy centralization of authority in Djakarta.

After the federal State structure embodied in the Republic of the United States of Indonesia was abolished and the unitary State took its place, the Government should, in fact, have acted as quickly as possible to grant a clearly outlined measure of autonomy to the regions for whom this was intended. Although regional autonomy forms part of the program of every new cabinet, virtually all official authority concerning almost every kind of control is still concentrated in the central Government, in consequence of which the provincial governors have to consult Djakarta on even the most urgent matters, not infrequently coming in person. The result is that in those regions where peace and order has been restored and, consequently, excellent possibilities exist for further development in a variety of spheres, for instance, in Sumatra, such possibilities have been exploited only to a very small extent. It is only because of the capacity of the governors and those working with them to find ways of getting around this situation, which has at times been intolerable because of the bureaucratic attitude of certain Government circles, that any progress was able to be achieved in the work of reconstruction.

As the third factor impeding production—especially in foreign concerns—and resulting in total exports lagging far behind what is potentially attainable, I would mention the feelings of hatred and aversion evinced by the Indonesian community in regard to foreign enterprises in general. Although the asperity of these sentiments has gradually become somewhat less intense, they are still to be found everywhere, even among responsible Indonesian leaders. As regards foreign industries the economic problem in Indonesia must therefore be regarded as primarily psychological. These feelings of hatred date back to colonial days and the subsequent revolution and are based on a false notion of the position and function of foreign capital in the present-day Indonesian economy.

Foreign industries are identified with the Netherlands colonial power. That power has, of course, been transferred entirely to the Indonesian people, but so long as foreign capital is still present and operative in Indonesia, most Indonesians cannot help feeling that complete independence has yet to be achieved. "It is true that the

Dutch lion is dead, but his claws are still embedded in the body of Indonesia" is frequently the sentiment, even in the highest and most authoritative circles. "The sooner foreign capital and foreigners clear out of Indonesian territory, the better for Indonesia. Not until Indonesia is completely rid of them will the Indonesian people be able to prosper."

Among certain sections of those who played an active part in the fight for freedom, these feelings of hatred did not only not diminish after the transfer of sovereignty but became more pronounced as it became apparent that the expectations aroused by the freedom could not all be realized at once. All misunderstandings and wrongs which have appeared since freedom was won are attributed to foreign capital and foreigners and to the Government which "protects" foreign capital. The resistance of groups which have openly or surreptitiously opposed the Government is based in large part on these feelings of aversion and hate, even though, of course, there are factions which are simply gangs of common criminals.

When such sentiments prevail, it is easy to induce workers to come out on strike. It is likewise easy to incite the people to rob and destroy the property of foreign industrial concerns, as these acts provide an outlet for the feelings of hatred toward such concerns. It is, therefore, not always right to regard low wages and poverty as the only real cause of the deplorable vandalism and of the strikes that at one period almost crippled the economic life of Indonesia and even now present a very real danger. The cause is often resentment of the foreign industries against which strikes and vandalism are aimed.

Why is it that there was more peace and order and fewer strikes during the revolution, in the Republican region, notwithstanding the fact that workers and the people in general were living under worse conditions? It is because the loyalty which people cherished toward the struggle for independence was a far stronger motive than the poverty and privations they were experiencing. Men and women were willing to suffer, to work, and to make sacrifices for the salvation and welfare of the nation and of generations to come.

In order to counteract this resentment toward foreign capital and foreign activities, thus enabling production to proceed more smoothly, it is essential to educate the public thoroughly to the fact that foreign capital and foreign workmanship are nothing more than a means to an end in our effort to achieve prosperity for our people and our descendants. As an economic instrument they have to be treated as well as possible in order to obtain the highest possible output from them.

XIIId
Soedjatmoko On Equivocating about Economic Advancement (1954)

This piece is taken from Economic Development as a Cultural Problem, *which was originally an article in the September–October 1954 issue of the cultural journal* Konfrontasi *and was published in 1960 in the Translation Series of the Cornell Modern Indonesia Project.* *

Although we have, in the course of the last few years, registered some measure of economic progress, there is, nevertheless, the impression that this progress has failed to catch the imagination of the Indonesian people. Moreover, it must be conceded that the progress achieved up till now is far from sufficient to meet the demands of our time. The results up to the present are also too limited to strengthen our self-confidence and enthusiasm and to inspire us to further efforts. It seems that the economic development plans emanating from the Government have failed to come to life in our society as a whole, although the areas directly involved are aware of the importance of these plans. There is a general feeling that the projected developments will remain mere Government schemes, in which each Ministry will go its own separate way, not as a constituent part of an integrated over-all development plan. At the same time the political parties likewise suffer from a similar failing. Although their leaders pay lip service to the idea of economic development, there is no evidence of any real concern for this issue. In the present situation in Indonesia party maneuvering for political advantage takes priority, whereas the question of economic development is apparently treated as a matter of little urgency. It is hardly surprising, then, that there does not exist among the public any clear idea of the meaning of economic development or of the public's role in this process. . . .

The forces resisting change are manifested in a diversity of forms. There is, for example, the attitude—encountered not infrequently among high officials, political leaders, and even professors—conveyed in voicing doubts as to the need for economic development, in asking whether it is desirable that the Indonesian people should be recast in

* Ithaca, N.Y.; reprinted by permission.

a Western mold, whether we must lead the people toward an existence dominated by unrestrained competition where each is the prey of the other, and the individual no longer has any personal relationship to his work or his fellow workers, and whether such a spirit should be introduced into our culture and social structure.

This attitude, in fact, embraces two elements. First, there is the rejection of Western capitalism—no new stand this, for in Asia rejection of Western capitalism is general. But more important in relation to our basic problem is the second element, the rejection of the pattern of existence that will evolve with industrialism. It is in this rejection of industrialism in all its consequences that the source lies of the varying degrees of opposition in official circles to the carrying out of economic development in Indonesia. The point merits further examination. In one sense it is true to say that the ultimate of happiness is ideally achieved when an equilibrium exists between needs and the possibility of satisfying them. To achieve this happiness man can, on the one hand, endeavor as intensely as possible to fulfill those needs, however high their level. Equilibrium is then achieved on a high material level. Conversely, he can also endeavor to attain happiness by lowering the level of his needs so that no special effort is required in order to fulfill them. Equilibrium is then achieved on a much lower material level.

In general this second alternative is found where the general attitude to life is essentially one of *Weltverneinung,* i.e., the rejection of enjoying worldly life in its fullness. In various parts of Asia, particularly where the cultural pattern bears the stamp of Hindu philosophy and in general where there is a tradition of mysticism, this attitude is frequently encountered, and in these regions lowering one's material aspirations often constitutes a powerful ideal. . . .

Among the advocates of this outlook was Gandhi, who perceived the pattern of modern existence as based on an excessive preoccupation with purely material demands. In the Gandhian view, the insistence on what was considered an unnecessarily high standard of material satisfaction reduced man to a mere slave of the machines that were the prerequisites for the fulfillment of modern requirements. It was, therefore, in his view extremely dangerous for India and for the Asian peoples in general if they wanted to compete with the Western nations on the basis of western industrial life. He therefore urged the rejection of this dangerous road toward happiness, and he advocated that India's struggle for independence should be waged not by the adoption of Western industrialization but by a return to the spinning wheel. The Gandhian rejection of industrialization was based mainly on moral considerations, on the contention that a spiritual decline must result from the increasing acceptance of industrial life.

Obviously, such a standpoint could only have grown out of the relative isolation of Gandhi and of India from the outside world; it could hardly be objectively defended in the face of the dire poverty of the Indian people, nor could it prevail against the external forces acting on the situation in India. It is, consequently, not surprising that despite the still widespread influence of Gandhi's ideas, in the field of economic life India has not followed the footsteps of Gandhi but has chosen to follow the road of industrial development advocated by Nehru.

Certain groups in Indonesia also express in varying degrees a hostility to modernization, and this is one of the causes of the inadequate recognition in official circles of the pressing need for economic development. Except where some specific project is directly related to the particular interests of one or other party, the question of economic development as a whole is not given any real consideration by most of the political parties in Indonesia. If there is to be positive action taken to bring about economic development—and every political party pays lip service at least to this aim—it is essential that the urgency of the issue be felt sufficiently so that the will to act is awakened. Similarly, it is necessary that there should exist a realization of the speed with which measures for economic development must be put into effect. There must no longer be any moral equivocation as to the virtues or disadvantages of economic advancement. It must also be recognized that economic development is in the final analysis related to a rise in the level of consumption and, therefore, to the growth of the desire of the population to possess and to use the products of industrial life.

In other words, acceptance of the principle of economic development means the prior rejection of the idea of *Weltverneinung* and an acknowledgment of man's title to enjoy from life the fullest possible material and spiritual satisfaction as a legitimate purpose in life. It must be recognized that the concepts of our traditional philosophies and of the *Wedhotomo** ethics, whatever the nobility of values these embody, were rooted in a feudal-agrarian pattern which can no longer

* A Javanese book of ethics.

endure now that the old social structure is collapsing. The task of the
Indonesian nation at the present stage of its history lies in this world
and not in the world hereafter.

Again we see that the problem of economic development in Indonesia is essentially related to the outlook of the Indonesian people. As
long as our attitude on this subject is not clear, the implementation
of any program of economic development will be unsatisfactory because there will still be resistance in the form of the hostility en-
gendered by the old concepts of life.

XIIIe
Sukarno   The Economics of a Nation
in Revolution (1963)

*This item comes from the President's Independence Day address of
August 17, 1963. In the first half of that year a great deal of attention
had been given to economic questions. The President had proclaimed
an Economic Declaration (Dekon) in March, and on May 26, First
Minister Djuanda had issued a series of fourteen regulations intended to serve as the basis of a program of economic stabilization.
The full English text is in Sukarno,* Indonesia's Political Manifesto,
1959–64 *(Djakarta: Propantja, 1964?), 231–271.*

The economic question demands our full attention. Is not food and
clothing one of the points of the Government's Three Point Program?
And is not the economy one of the "points" of our Revolution?

As the Great Leader of the Revolution, I devote very great attention to this economic "point." But let me be frank: I am not an
economist. I am not an expert in economic techniques. I am not an
expert in the techniques of trade. I am a revolutionary, and I am just
a revolutionary in economic matters.

My feelings and ideas about the economic question are simple,
very simple indeed. They can be formulated as follows: If nations
who live in a dry and barren desert can solve the problems of their
economy, why can't we?

Why can't we? Just think about this:

One: our natural riches, both those that have already been exploited and those that have not, are abundant.

Two: We have an abundance of labor power, with a population of
100,000,000!

Three: The Indonesian people are very hard-working and possess very great skill; this is recognized by everyone abroad.

Four: the Indonesian people possess the spirit of *gotong rojong,* and this can be used as the basis for gathering together all funds and forces.

Five: The ideals and the creativity of the Indonesian Nation are of a very high order—in political affairs, in social affairs, in cultural affairs, and certainly, too, in the field of economics and trade.

Six: The traditions of the Indonesian Nation are not insignificant traditions! In ancient times we controlled trade throughout the whole of Southeast Asia and plowed the seas to trade as far afield as Arabia, Africa, and China.

What else do you want? This, then, is how simple my thinking is on this matter. If we effectively exploit all these favorable characteristics and assets, the problem of providing the people with enough food and clothing, simple food and clothing, will undoubtedly be solved early, within a short period. Desert people can live, so why can't we? The people of Mongolia—that is a desert—can live. So, why can't we build a just and prosperous society—*gemah-ripah loh djinawi, tata tentrem kerta rahardja,* hospitable, fertile, orderly, peaceful, hard working, and prosperous—where Dullah has enough clothing and enough food and Sarinem has enough clothing and enough food? If we are unable to provide food and clothing in this rich country of ours, then in fact it is we ourselves who are stupid, we ourselves who are completely stupid!

In fact in this simplicity of my thinking, I rejoice that our Nation is not a Nation that is already too far gone with the wrong form, that we are not a Nation too far gone with the wrong structure, that we are not a Nation whose social structure is difficult to change.

To solve the economic problems of nations that are already fully formed, especially for what are called *nations arrivées,* persons of outstanding skills in the routines of economics are perhaps required, very precise knowledge of economic science, very highly technical, very "expert" knowledge of economics.

But, Praise be to God, I know that our economic problems do not have to be solved in routine fashion. Our economic problems are the problems of the economy of a Revolution. We are indeed a Nation in Revolution and a Revolution is not routine, none of its problems are routine, its economy too is not routine.

We are a Nation in a multi-complex Revolution, which includes among other things an economic revolution. Therefore: we must tackle the economic problem as a part of the Revolution! Therefore: we must tackle the economic problem as an instrument of the Revolution. Therefore: we cannot and must not tackle the economic problem in a routine fashion. I think this is clear, this is plain.

It was with the background of this simple thinking that I stated last year that we could surmount the problem of food and clothing— of the basic necessities—in not too long a time. And now one year has passed. What do I say now? I still say: God willing, we shall solve the problem of *sandang-pangan* [essential food and clothing] before too long. Meanwhile, just as last year, I say with regard to what is not yet in order in the food and clothing situation: "Go ahead, please go ahead, be angry with me, go ahead, point your finger at me, go ahead, pour your wrath upon me—and I will accept it all with a calm heart."

What more can I say other than to ask you to be patient for a while longer? I have already issued the Economic Declaration known as *Dekon,* and fourteen Government Regulations are also out. Now I say only: be patient a while longer, be patient, wait and see!

What is *Dekon?* Whereas the Political Manifesto said "stop" to deviations in the political field, *Dekon* says "stop" to deviations in the economic field. In short, I can say that *Dekon* is the Political Manifesto of the Economy.

Understanding *Dekon,* people can no longer confuse the two stages of the Revolution.

On the one hand, the opinion is not to be tolerated which denies that our future is socialism. Thus: concepts, intentions, and actions proceeding in all sorts of ways towards capitalism will not be countenanced.

On the other hand, the opinion is not to be tolerated that socialism can be put into effect at a single blow—that is, from the present situation, one-two-three-jump into socialism, like someone one-two-three-jumping across a water channel—except after completing the national-democratic struggle, that is, until we have eliminated the remnants of imperialism and feudalism.

Dekon states this clearly and firmly. Therefore, too, I often emphasize that we are not as yet in the socialist stage.

And in connection with the need to give priority to increasing production I affirm here, also for the umpteenth time, that the most important source of production is the workers and peasants. The workers and peasants are the mainstays of the Revolution! For that reason it is not enough to say negatively that efforts to increase production must not be hostile to the workers and peasants. These efforts must develop the productive powers of the workers and peasants in a positive way. Without the manpower of the workers and peasants increasing production is impossible!

Besides that, we are now also using the energies of the Armed Services to step up production. The Armed Services are now being instructed also to carry out what are called "civic missions." With regard to these I have a good report in my hands from Deputy First Minister–Chief-of-Staff of the Armed Services, General Nasution, but due to lack of time, I cannot read this report here. . . .

I am now paying full attention to the voice of the People with regard to the way in which *Dekon* is being implemented. I have often said—I said this in Manila, too—that I am merely the mouthpiece of the People. After a while when I am fully convinced as to the true voice of the common people, then, God willing, my own tongue shall utter that cry from their hearts.

I am extremely happy that the desire to build our national economy by standing on our own feet has recently become more intense. This is what I call economic patriotism, and I am indeed very happy about it. A Nation can become strong only if its patriotism encompasses economic patriotism. This is indeed the correct path to national strength, the path that is right, the path that is exactly suitable.

In the Colombo Plan Conference in Jogjakarta several years ago, I said: "Our economy will be Indonesian; our political system will be Indonesian; our society will be Indonesian, and all will be securely founded on our own cultural and spiritual heritage. That heritage may be fertilized by assistance from beyond the seas, but its fruits and flowers will be our own. Thus, please do not expect that any form of assistance will produce a mirror image of yourselves."

Of such a kind is the economic patriotism which I depicted in my address to the Colombo Plan Conference in Jogja. Yes, the world today is indeed a world which cannot live without mutual help. But we do not want help from anyone at all, and we are not going to beg for it. We are a Great Nation; we are not an insignificant nation. We are not going to beg, not going to ask for this and ask for that, especially if aid has this condition and that tie tacked onto it! Better to eat poverty rations of cassava and be independent than eat beefsteak and be enslaved!

XIIIf

Mohammad Sadli   Inflation, the Drifting Kite (1963)

This is part of Dr. Sadli's inaugural lecture as Professor of Eco-
nomics at the University of Indonesia, delivered on August 31, 1963
when the effort at economic stabilization launched in May was al-
ready foundering. To our knowledge, the lecture has not been pub-
lished.

What is meant by a policy of economic and monetary stabilization? Is it necessary to carry it out at this time?

By a policy of economic and monetary stabilization I mean in
general a government policy in a period of inflation which has for
its object the prevention of further price increases. Basically, a
stabilization policy as presently desired is an anti-inflation policy.

This stabilization policy which curbs inflation still requires further qualification. Is the aim to prevent absolutely further movements of the general price level? Although ultimately 100 per cent
stability of the general level of prices is what is ideal, such a condition may not in present circumstances serve the interests of economic rehabilitation. We must not forget that the end object is
not to solve monetary problems as such but to enable economic development to go more smoothly so that the national income will
gradually rise. In the last analysis, the most essential thing is what
will happen in real terms, namely, measures of production and investment, and not monetary measures. Monetary problems must be
solved in order that the monetary climate will be favorable.

Since monetary stabilization is not the absolute objective, the
question now is: what monetary climate is the most advantageous
for economic development within the next one or two years? In general we can rule out deflation as the most suitable climate. First, because of practical reasons: we do not think it possible politically and
administratively to change a state of inflation as strong as we have
gone through in these past years into a deflationary state, that is,
where the general level of prices show a tendency to go down for
a sufficiently long period of time. Second, it is accepted often enough
theoretically that in an economy which has the character of a market
economy, a light inflation is more advantageous to production and
investment than a state of deflation. . . .

We do not want a strong inflation because such an inflation often has characteristics tending to defeat economic development. . . . Strong inflation always forces the government to employ strict and extensive control of prices and wages. This in itself could be disastrous for production incentive. Exports which run up against an official rate of exchange which is not adjusted to the domestic price increases will ultimately also become slack and decline. Public utilities whose rates are frozen for long periods of time will in the end require large subsidies and in such circumstances maintenance of their equipment is often disturbed, also. The domestic industry and service enterprises such as cinemas, hotels, and other enterprises requiring many capital goods cannot guarantee replacement of these goods because often the price control formula does not allow it. Thus, strong inflation, which always requires widespread price control, will in the end kill production incentives and annihilate the positive production effects that may still be brought about by an inflation.

This last argument is for our country not just a theoretical one: we have experienced the reality of it for several years. Because of sustained and ever-increasing inflation our economy is hit at its most vulnerable point, at its Achilles' heel namely, exports. During the last decade our exports have declined by about 27 per cent. In 1952 exports including petroleum, reached U.S. $935 million; last year [1962] our exports reached only U.S. $682 million, which means a decline of $253 million, partly owing, admittedly, to falls in world market prices. Just imagine how many factories we could have erected with such an amount of money in one year! The investment cost of a cement factory is about twenty million dollars, a fertilizer factory about thirty million dollars. Because of the decline in exports the foreign exchange available for our import requirements has become very limited. After we have used up the largest portion of these funds to meet our requirements for food and clothing and for the government's requirements, not much remains for new development projects and raw materials and spare parts for industry and transport. Work is continuing on a number of development projects because of foreign credits. But the problem of settling these debts will become very difficult unless our exports recover. . . .

Before continuing I must lightly touch on the problem of price control in a time of inflation. Generally, price control in a time of inflation has two objects. The first object is to prevent inflation from becoming stronger because of spiral effects, that is, the spiral of price and cost and the spiral of price and price. This spiral process is feared since it can strengthen inflation due to its cumulative and accelerating influence. The second object has more of a social character, since inflation always hits one class of workers and consumers more than other classes. For instance, those classes of workers who receive fixed incomes, namely, salaries and wages, are hit harder than the classes whose income can follow the rises in price, such as the traders, farmers, and the like. To prevent inflation from changing too greatly the distribution of income in the society, the government often applies price control. And since price control alone is not enough to ensure this, the government is often forced to concern itself also with the physical distribution of goods.

If the government in a time of inflation is no longer willing to use the mechanism of market and price for the requirements of allocation and distribution, and wants to replace it with an administrative mechanism with frozen prices, the first requisite for the success of this method is that the government be able to control a large portion of the supply of goods it wants to distribute. This prerequisite can often not be fulfilled in our country, so that although there is a rationing system, it covers only a small portion of the volume of the goods, the distribution of which is to be controlled socially. A classical example is rice: the government has control of at most only about one-sixth of the total amount of rice consumed by the people within one year, or at most only half of the rice which is estimated to enter the market annually.

It is characteristic of the distribution system in our country at present that those who are protected by it comprise only a small part of the total of consumers: i.e., in general government employees, members of the armed forces, laborers and employees of state enterprises, and the inhabitants of several large towns. Formally other classes of citizens, such as those in villages and small towns, are also included in the rationing system, for example, to obtain kerosene, but the actual implementation of this is patchy so that only occasionally do they get their rations at low prices.

From a political viewpoint, this distribution system is looked upon by some people as being fairly capable of attaining its objective. The classes which are politically strong and vocal can to a certain extent enjoy its benefits, but millions of other citizens do not or only rarely participate in the enjoyment of these benefits. Such a condition can in the long run arouse the annoyance and sometimes wrath of the villagers, which can bring about politically sensitive situations. On the one hand, price control and distribution of insufficient effectiveness hit the producer; on the other hand, they allow a large number of people to obtain abnormal profits from black-marketing, fighting for a larger allocation, and the like. The distribution system intended to ensure social justice, therefore, in the end will be looked upon by many as a means of pampering the politically stronger groups in the population. . . .

If we are compelled in the coming years to live in a situation that is somewhat inflationary, we must dare to consider another formula, namely, to strive to ensure that the inflation will only be light, for instance, that its rate does not exceed 10 per cent per annum, and not to indulge in stringent price controls. I do not dare to offer guarantees that this formula will be better than the old one, since a theoretically correct formula will still be subjected to other influences when put to practice; but it seems we have sufficient proof that the formula we have used so far has become outdated and blunted in its effect. It is possible that the formula is a priori not too correct, and even if it were valid in an a priori sense, it has already undergone the same fate as some varieties of DDT, sulfa drugs, or antibiotics; namely, if they are used too long, their effectiveness decreases and in the end disappears as the germs they were to eradicate have become immune.

What we must try is, first, to decrease the severity of the inflation—for this we must carry out a stabilization program; and second, to establish a policy which gives the producers more freedom in determining their prices. Both social functions of price in a market economy, namely, the function of giving incentives to the producer and the function of limiting consumption, must be allowed to operate again. There are, of course, a number of government officials who are afraid of the consequences. They have lived too long in a system in which the economy is administratively managed and price-forming strictly controlled; besides, during that time vested interest groups have grown up whose members are afraid that the new policy will cost them many of their privileges. The government must therefore be thoroughly convinced that the old policy is no longer workable and that the new policy must be carried out uncompromisingly; if certain officials cannot adjust themselves to this line of thought, their policies must be corrected.

Exports and imports have suffered too long from inflation due to the curbing of prices and now is the time for them to be freed from dis-incentive influences. Exports and production must be made "inflation-proof."

I do not suggest that the government turn liberal, that is, take a hands-off attitude toward the economy. Far from it. The principle of Guided Economy remains essential to promote the development of our national economy. What I am concerned with is how this is to be managed. Managing the national economy with little discipline and self-discipline in handling governmental budgets, so as to give rise to those large deficits which are the main cause of strong inflation is not an example of the most effective implementation of the Guided Economy. The large deficits in the budget can be likened to a kite with a broken thread. Given such deficits, all the government's efforts to rescue the economy are like chasing a drifting kite. To make Guided Economy effective a start must be made with settling the affairs of the nation in a more orderly way, based on careful planning and fiscal and monetary discipline.

XIIIg
D. N. Aidit   Mismanagement, Corruption, and the Bureaucratic Capitalists (1964)

This extract comes from an address to a bank employees' conference and appeared in the PKI daily Harian Rakjat 9–10 *June 1965.*

For quite a long time now we have all felt that whenever we begin to analyze economic problems we have always to deal with the same things, the same unchanging problems—there are mismanagement, corruption, confusion, stifling bureaucracy, and over and above all this mess are the bureaucratic capitalists, who always seem able to profit abundantly from it. However, even though in general these problems do not change but merely increase in complexity, we must not take the attitude that they cannot possibly be solved, and that, therefore, we had best not get too concerned about them. This is precisely what the bureaucratic capitalists want! The economic problems now faced by the Indonesian people are indeed complex and have many aspects which require attention. But this in no way implies that those problems cannot be overcome. Our Nation is naturally rich and her People are both industrious and increasingly fired with anti-imperialism and antifeudalism. This is the guarantee that, no matter how energetically incompetent officials and bureaucratic capitalists damage our economy, the People of Indonesia will finally be capable of solving all the problems these groups have created.

What is extremely important for us now is to understand what are the origins of the current problems, and, after having analyzed these origins, to point out what must be done to improve the situation.

Basically, the factor obstructing economic progress in our country is that we have still not eradicated the last vestiges of imperialism and feudalism. These remnants represent strategic obstructions and must be completely destroyed precisely because they block economic progress and prevent the growth of productive forces in our country. To give just a simple example, we must do away with feudalistic remnants so as both to release the productive energies of the peasants in the villages and to create a reasonable possibility for industrial development in our country. As long as the peasants carry the heavy burden of the vestiges of feudalism, they cannot wholeheartedly work to increase food production. And as long as the peasants generally live in poverty, the industrial sector in our state will never develop.

However, alongside these objective factors we must also consider subjective factors, such as the ability of officials to carry out their designated tasks in the economic sphere. This includes the management both of the economy as a whole and of particular sectors and enterprises. If we analyze the management of the economy as a whole, we learn that there are basically three sources of inflation, namely, deficits in the state budget, the unplanned and indiscriminate expansion of bank credit both state and private, and the external balance of payments. In analyzing these three problems we would undoubtedly come across many factors requiring concrete and exhaustive study in order to find what course of action was required. For now I can only touch upon a few key problems.

Take, for example, budgetary problems. There are people who would like to make us believe that the main cause of budgetary deficits is the expenses of the revolution. I do not deny that our revolutionary activities do indeed require money, which we, of course, must pay. However, why is it that these people always talk about "the economic losses" occasioned by the revolution? Why do they always close their eyes to the fact that the revolution also

carries economic advantages of no mean proportions, indeed advantages which more than compensate for any possible "losses" we
experience. We must not forget that it was precisely because of our
revolutionary activities that our country gained a very broad state
sector, which includes such areas of production as agriculture and
industry, trade, banking, shipping, and many others. But for our
revolutionary actions I doubt that we could have gained such wealth
as this within the space of a few years. And we can be sure that in
the not too-distant future our country will "harvest" again by carrying out even tougher actions against the U.S. businesses.

I think that if these many enterprises had been handled properly,
without mismanagement, our country would have felt the economic
benefits long ago, instead of experiencing the shift to the right that
has taken place in our economic system. If these enterprises had
been properly managed, I think we could have achieved the goal
laid down in the Economic Declaration—that is, to make the State
Enterprises the prime source of state income—long ago. These are
the positive benefits of our revolutionary activities which we have
not yet been able to enjoy because of the operation of subjective
factors in this State sector of the economy.

Confronted with the growing budget deficit, there are those who
advocate the immediate abolition of the subsidies paid to cover
public utility costs, which would necessarily mean that tariffs and
prices on certain goods and services would have to be raised. This
view was reflected in the actions taken by the Government several
months ago in increasing the rates charged by Pelni Shipping and
Garuda Airways by 250 per cent and 200 per cent respectively.
The PKI made it clear that it did not agree with those actions, and
it urged the Government to reconsider the actions already taken to
raise certain service charges and to refrain from raising any others.
This attitude was based on past experience and on the belief that
although it can happen that service charge increases make temporary reductions of subsidies possible, in a very short time such actions push prices up to the point where the Government must
assume as heavy a financial burden as it had shed by reducing the
subsidies.

And if there are those who believe that increased service charges
will do away with the disparity between official and black market
prices, I maintain that such people have very short memories and
must have forgotten the experiences after the May 26 regulations of

1963.* The liberal price policies pursued since those regulations have been completely incapable of eliminating black market prices. As long as the state sector cannot ensure the availability of vital goods and guarantee their uninterrupted distribution to the consumer, as long as our economic apparatus is riddled with the disease of mismanagement and chronic bureaucratic capitalism, the disparity between official prices and black market prices cannot be abolished.

There are those who say to us: "Why do you always make such a fuss? The increased transport costs only account for 1 per cent of the cost of production of this commodity or that commodity." In fact their 1 per cent is calculated from the official exchange rate, whereas it is a very different matter if the calculation is based on the black market prices. Moreover, in an economic situation characterized by constantly and generally rising prices, it is understandable that a rise in the price of just one commodity will exert a pressure on other prices that is far in excess of that arrived at by such "logical calculation."

If we do not agree with service charge increases such as those carried out by the Government, there are sure to be those who ask: "All right then, what should be done? Do you people believe that we should just allow subsidies to increase every month until finally the greater part of Government income is being used to finance subsidies?"

Of course we do not believe this. Basically, I believe that State Enterprises in almost all fields need to and must run on their own power and not be dependant upon subsidies and credits which grow from one month to the next. However, subsidies need not necessarily be reduced or abolished by means of increases in prices and charges. What is required is that all outlays of the Enterprises be subjected to close scrutiny to stop the various widespread forms of extravagance, inefficiency, and corruption which now occur.

One characteristic of the inflation in our country is that the costs of distribution are very great, often causing the end price to be many times the initial cost. To give some examples: When fertilizer is produced by a State Enterprise—the Sriwidjaja fertilizer factory in Palembang—and sold to the distributor—the State Enterprise Pertani—at Rp. 69 per kilo, why is it that it must be bought by the

---

* These provided for liberalization as part of a plan for price stability. They were originally to be underwritten by credits from a consortium of Western countries.

peasant at Rp. 300 or 400? That is a cost of distribution four times greater than the factory price. Why is it that copra sold to a primary cooperative by the copra-farmers of South Sulawesi for Rp. 18,000 a quintal and then sold to a regional cooperative for Rp. 22,500, brings a price of Rp. 50,000 when sold to coconut oil factories in Djakarta and Surabaja, despite the fact that the cost of sea transportation from Menado to Java is no more than Rp. 2,000? Why is it that spare parts imported by State Enterprises to be used in Pelni boats are sold to Pelni by certain agents at a price far higher than their import cost? These are things which we meet everywhere, causing each State Enterprise to be burdened with a variety of concealed costs. Such practices must necessarily be attacked directly and not by way of granting subsidies or by raising prices.

I have looked into this problem of collection and distribution costs at some length because I regard this factor as one that is extremely obstructive to both the production sector and the State budget. Such very unhealthy symptoms as these represent manifestations of the despicable activities of the bureaucratic capitalists, and must be attacked immediately. I am convinced that if this is done the problems of subsidies will be greatly reduced and the level of Government expenses will be pushed down. . . .

Time does not permit me to deal with budgetary and balance-of-payments problems at greater length, but I feel that the examples I have given have been sufficient to prove that what is needed at the present time is not official price rises by the Government—no matter what the pretext used may be—but actions aimed directly at stopping widespread mismanagement, corruption, and uncontrolled spending, and executed in such a way as to produce a direct downward pressure on prices and Government expenditures. And to deal with this problem, those who must be attacked are the parasites, the large-scale corruptors, the bureaucratic capitalists.

XIIIh

Ina E. Slamet Youth and Village Development (1963)

This is taken from Mrs. Slamet's book Pokok-pokok Pembangunan Masjarakat Desa: Sebuah Pandangan Antropologi Budaja (*Principles of Village Community Development: A Cultural-Anthropological View*) (*Djakarta: Bhratara, 1963), pp. 104–108.*

For hundreds of years the village people of Java, working a soil which is among the richest in the world, have experienced oppression, deception, and exploitation. Their dreams of a *Ratu Adil,* a just king who would bring for them an era of prosperity and happiness, were never realized, and indeed the colonial period saw increasingly intense exploitation of the fertile land and the men who worked it.

Now the power of the kings and the power of Dutch colonialism has been broken, and with that the vision of a *Ratu Adil* has vanished from the Javanese cultural sky. What has not vanished is the longing for an era of justice, prosperity, peace and love, a longing which has not as yet been fulfilled in this period of independence.

Certainly, all villagers agree that this period of independence has brought an important improvement in their conditions as compared with the colonial period—at least in the Klaten area in which we have carried out investigations ourselves. In the old days a villager might work as hard as he could with the help of his wife and children and still not be able to plant rice twice a year and grow garden crops around his house. Moreover, he was always mentally oppressed by fear of falling victim to the arbitrariness of his overlord, and he had no perspective of hope for the future.

His bitter experience in feudal and colonial times has left its legacy in his attitude of suspicion toward all city people he does not know. In the eyes of the peasant who possesses only a few tools or other belongings, there appears behind everyone who comes from "above" the specter of increased taxes. Even today many peasants are unable to think of any reason why a city person should come down to the village other than to rob the village of its wealth on one or other pretext.

And what is the real situation today of the poor peasants—that is the majority of peasants—in the most densely populated regions of Java? With land and work opportunities in short supply, food is short, that is, there is too little of it to enable men to work hard, and there is far too little protein. Moreover, one's food supply is never certain. A landless peasant once explained to us that his life and that of his fellows is like that of the *djelatik* bird, which perches first in one place and then in another looking for food. Sometimes he finds some; sometimes he does not. If he does not, he may borrow from a neighbor or friend or not eat for a day.

The situation of those who still possess a buffalo, or a piece of land, large or small, is a little better, although their lives are generally also very frugal. They still try to put something away in the form of gold as a guarantee against times of misfortune. Or, as is the case in the Klaten area, they may save in the form of building material, perhaps to replace their own old house but more often to help their son or son-in-law who is poor; and for this they are not against saving for years, up to seven years, to build a house worth no more than Rp. 10,000.

This situation of poverty would certainly have resulted in disaster if the essentials of life for the poorest villagers were not still taken care of by mutual help among their *sanak keluarga,* i.e., their neighbors and relatives. The position of the poor peasants would have become unbearable long ago if there was not among fellow villagers of similar fate the moral conviction that a person's poverty should not sink to the point where it is embarrassing for him according to the norms of village society, for instance, to the point where he cannot afford to hold a *selamatan** for a son's circumcision or to the point where it causes him to go hungry.

But the possibilities of mutual help are limited, and, with the population growing rapidly, with the prices of necessities rising higher and higher, and with no expansion of work opportunities outside agriculture, the situation becomes more critical every day. So the promotion of village community development in this region has become a matter of extreme urgency.

We have described the ways to realize this development. . . . It can be promoted by raising agricultural production in general and, particularly, the production of gardens around houses. It can be promoted by forming simple producers' and marketing cooperatives on a *gotong rojong* and fully democratic basis, using surpluses to change to more rational methods of production, and increasing the capacity of small farmers to organize themselves so that they can bypass the middlemen as regards both buying and selling. Increased production and cooperative effort should yield capital and provide a wider market within village society itself for the expansion of handiwork and village small industry. Moreover, village development can be promoted by using land in the best possible way and on the basis of justice, as a result of a radical change in land tenure relationships. It can be promoted by a democratization of village government, and by establishing third-level autonomous regions as quickly as possible

* A ritual meal of great importance among *abangan* Javanese, at which foods are presented to the spirits.

and charging them with village community development as their principal task, village community development which is to be effected in a truly democratic way. Finally, it can be promoted by transmigration and large-scale industrialization.

All these things should be done simultaneously as far as possible. But a movement to increase production and gain a more just division of the yield between those who own land and those who work it and so on need not be delayed until all of the other efforts suggested here are being attempted.

What do all these desired changes mean for the villager, as a man who holds to certain customs and whose character cannot be separated from the influence of the society and environment around him, as a man concerned with his current lot, who also has certain aspirations for his own future and that of his children? What is asked of such a man is a thorough-going mental transformation.

Our revolution has in its fifteen years made an impression on the peasants' view of life and begun to change it significantly, but it has not really filtered through to the roots of our village society. Bringing the revolution to completion means neither more nor less than a basic transformation of our whole economic system as it has existed since the formation of the first feudal kingdoms in Java. If this is not fundamentally changed, the dreams of justice and prosperity for the people will never be fulfilled.

But this means that the peasants of Java must rid themselves of all remnants of the patriarchal, slave, and feudal traditions which have filtered down into the village over the last twenty centuries, and of all traces of the wounds of contempt and deception which have undermined their self-confidence. It means that they must break the chains of superstition and ignorance fostered by the feudal and colonial authorities in order to bind them to their lowly positions. It means that their dreams of a *Ratu Adil* must be converted into a firm belief that they, the millions of small farmers, themselves are the *Ratu Adil* who can create an era of justice, prosperity, and tranquility, an era unparalleled in history but in keeping with the stage of technical development reached in the modern world.

Such profound changes can only be effected gradually as a result of a peasant's day-to-day experience in working to improve his lot, helped by the traditions of *gotong rojong, kerukunan* [neighborhood solidarity], and indigenous village democracy, as well as by the peasants' more recently born revolutionary traditions; for the material and spiritual aspects of such development need to be tied to one another as closely as possible.

In this connection, the role of youth in the process of changing village society and rejuvenating the spirit of its members requires special consideration. According to my own observations in a study carried out in the village of Dj'omboran, the youth is the most dynamic group in the village and one which plays a large role in the life of the community. I do not know whether this applies generally to the Javanese village areas under discussion here. But I consider the matter important enough to warrant putting it forward here, in the hope that our observations and analysis will be tested in relation to the situation in other places.

These young people do not much hold to the old customs and beliefs of the generations of their parents and grandparents, but it is they who are the strongest upholders of the traditions of *sambat sinambat** and *kerukunan,* both among themselves and among the village inhabitants in general. It is they above all others who uphold moral norms in the village and discuss them. It is they who actively protect the village, as regards both its physical safety and its reputation. It is they who enthusiastically throw their efforts into art groups and also into the *sinomans,* traditional youth groups which have been re-established as a result of the initiative of young people and given the function of supplying labor for *gotong rojong* activities, which is wider than their old function of helping with the work connected with *selamatans* and so on.

These characteristics of young people surprised us at first, but if one thinks the matter out more thoroughly, they are understandable. They are the product of some factors of long standing and of several new ones. The older factors are connected with the structure of the Javanese family and the conditions of economic life in the village. Javanese villagers live in nuclear families, and authority within the family is divided almost equally between husband and wife. Moreover relations between children and parents are not authoritarian in character, although respect for all older persons is greatly stressed (with nuances resulting from the operation of a "classificatory kinship system").

The result is that relations between a young person and his parents and parents-in-law are generally good and do not act as a form of

* Mutual assistance at the request of one party.

pressure on the personality of the young. Besides, children are given simple jobs to help their parents in their day-to-day work of making a living from the time they are eight, so that they develop a serious and responsible quality early.

One of the new factors is that young people can mostly read and write and have a fair command of Indonesian, because they have had primary education. So it is not unusual for them to be asked for help by their own parents who are for the most part still illiterate.

In addition we must remember that this generation of youth has not had any conscious experience of the pressure of colonialism and that their thinking has been influenced by their own parents' stories of their experiences of the Japanese occupation and the revolution. These stories, however sad, contain the lesson that two giant despotisms were destroyed and that their destruction within a few years was made possible in part by the struggle of the peasants of their own nation. These two types of factors have undoubtedly strengthened the self-respect and self-confidence of the young people—and in a way which is all the more conspicuous in view of the fact that their standard of living is so terribly low. And it is these living standards which exercise a decisive influence on their relationships with their friends whose lot is similar.

The number of peasants who no longer have any land is relatively high in this young group, among its married as well as its unmarried members, because of population increase and because their parents' land is still often being used to provide for the needs of the parents themselves and of younger brothers and sisters. Thus, the number of landless laborers and of people who own only a small piece of house-garden is very great among the young, with the result that their livelihood is extremely insecure.

In such circumstances it is understandable that they hold fast to *gotong rojong*, especially in the form of *sambat sinambat* and to *kerukunan;* these are their principal weapons against unemployment, pauperization, and hunger. And this tendency is strengthened by the influence of labor unions and peasant organizations, which have particularly large numbers of members among the youth.

In connection with their dynamic character and their important role in village society, there arises the question of how the young can be involved in village community development. The difficulty is that a large proportion of them have no direct interest in efforts to increase agricultural production because they own little or no land, with the result that *gotong rojong* and co-operative activities directed at rationalizing and expanding agricultural production have little direct benefit for them. Their primary need is for an expansion of work opportunities outside the field of agriculture, and such an expansion is hard to achieve at the first stage of village community development, at least within village society.

This again points to the great importance of having a unit of development at the third level of autonomy, for within an autonomous area of the third level, whose funds are far greater than those of the village, the youth could far more easily be involved in development as workers in various fields. Moreover, in view of the characteristics of the youth and their position in society in their period, they could become a very important source of pressure for development.

Naturally, there is no objection to including some of them in resettlement schemes if possibilities have been opened up for them and they are prepared—this would also contribute to development in other areas of Indonesia. But, at least in the village I studied, they form a pioneering force which is very valuable in opening up, advancing, and modernizing the village, while at the same time safeguarding its integration and, most important, safeguarding the essential unity of its culture in the process of mental and spiritual rejuvenation which will inevitably accompany development in the economic field.

The task of village community development is certainly gigantic. But by allowing patriarchal and semifeudal ties to remain in existence in the villages, by allowing land concentration to continue, and with it the pauperization of the small peasants, one is only delaying the transformation of village society and making it slower and more difficult. And this transformation cannot be evaded if we desire that the highest human values in Javanese culture and the values of humanity in general should be preserved and brought to fruition in the modern, industrial society which we want to create.

XIV
The Place of the Army

The origins of the Indonesian army of our period lie less in the Netherlands Indies army, whose Indonesian members were recruited largely from a few outlying and predominantly Christian ethnic groups, than in the Fatherland Defense Corps (Peta), a kind of auxiliary army which the Japanese established under Indonesian nationalist pressure after 1943. Peta, however, had no general staff; its highest officers were battalion commanders. So when the Indonesian National Army was established on the basis of a Peta core in 1945, its center of gravity lay in the battalions. Its general staff remained relatively weak for many years, both during and after the Revolution, finding it difficult to impose its authority on its subordinate commanders.*

Vis à vis the civilian political leaders, however, the leaders of the army were in a fairly strong position, particularly as the political leaders were not organized in a single revolutionary party. Outsiders may continue to argue whether Indonesia's victory over the Dutch was predominantly a military achievement or predominantly a political and diplomatic one; but among Indonesians there is widespread agreement that the military aspect was the overwhelmingly important one. And so the army leaders' prestige was very high at the end of the Revolution. Their moral position relative to the civilian leaders was particularly strong because most of the latter had allowed themselves to be taken prisoner at the time of the Dutch capture of the Republican capital of Jogjakarta in December 1948. Moreover, army officers

---

* Scholarly literature in English on the army is extremely limited. Two brief discussions are Guy Pauker, "The Role of the Military in Indonesia," in John J. Johnson, ed., *The Role of the Military in Underdeveloped Countries* (Princeton, N.J.: Princeton University Press, 1962), and Daniel S. Lev, "The Political Role of the Army in Indonesia," *Pacific Affairs*, XXXVI (Winter 1963–1964).

had borne considerable responsibility for regional administration in the course of the Revolution.

The army leaders were never well disposed toward the political parties. As our first two extracts show, there was a good deal of tension between them in the course of the Revolution about the role of the various irregular fighting organizations based on particular parties and ideologies, organizations which were little disposed to accept the need for negotiations with the Dutch, and over whom the army leaders had less control than they sought.

During the "liberal" period this tension remained. The army leaders accepted the system of parliamentary government and the much diminished political and administrative role which this assigned to them and concentrated on building-up their organization more or less in isolation from civilian affairs. But they did this without any enthusiasm for parliamentary government—see XIVb—and with the repeatedly asserted qualification (and threat) that the army was the ultimate guardian of the independence for which its members had given their lives.

Thanks partly to the army's divisions and partly, too, to a situation of balance in which the army and President Sukarno stood at opposite sides of the political arena, each willing to remain outside it as long as the other did the same, the army's direct political role was fairly small in the "liberal" period. But as the conflicts within the parliamentary arena grew sharper, the pressure for army intervention became overwhelming. Extract XIVc shows how one of the most successful of such acts of intervention was defended. It is also an excellent statement of the highest common factor of army views on the role the army should play.

In the years 1956–1958, when parliamentary government was breaking down, groups of the army became involved in a number of contending political causes, with civil war a constant threat and one which eventually materialized, albeit in a relatively minor form. Our next piece, by the reflective Major General Simatupang, discusses some of the alternative sets of military-political arrangements which seemed to be available at that time.

Finally, we are reproducing three views of the role which the army and the armed forces generally came to fill under Guided Democracy. This role involved the blurring of civilian-military divisions, with military officers occupying a great variety of nonmilitary posts, as cabinet members, parliamentarians, ambassadors, provincial governors, senior civil servants, university rectors, and executives in government firms, and with large numbers of civilians being trained in military affairs. It did not, however, put an end to tension between military men and civilians. Between the top army leaders and President Sukarno, in particular, conflict persisted. It was growing sharper and sharper in the two years before the coup of October 1, 1965.

XIVa
Tan Malaka   The Army and the Guerrilla Forces (1948)

This passage is taken from Gerpolek (*Guerrilla Politics and Economics*), *a book written by Tan Malaka while in a Republican jail in 1948. He had been active in 1945 and 1946 as a leader of groups which opposed the Sjahrir cabinet's policies of negotiation with the Dutch (see XVd), and his arrest was connected with the attempted coup d'état of July 3, 1946. Much of Tan Malaka's political support came from irregular fighting groups outside the army, and he is speaking for them here.* Gerpolek *was reprinted by Jajasan Massa of Djakarta in 1964.*

The kind of army we want is a people's army, an army made up of the people, fighting for the interests and aspirations of the people.

In a time of revolution the responsibility of a people's army is fighting the revolution. A people's army is, then, a revolutionary army, that is, an army with revolutionary policies, one whose training, arming, organization, administration, and strategy are effected by a government of the people, that is, by a government whose will and policies accord with the will and policies of the revolutionary people.

A guerrilla irregular force is a people's force, one which specializes in the tactics of guerrilla warfare and consists of small units or combinations of small units. A guerrilla force can be disguised as peasants or workers. It is ready to launch lightning attacks and then disappear into the working masses. Guerrilla irregular forces assist the people's army at either flank of the front line or behind the enemy's lines, harassing the enemy's posts, convoys, supplies, and preparations.

Guerrilla forces are established on the initiative of the working masses and financed by them. Where there is no people's army, guerrilla forces can provide leadership to deal with everything. In such situations guerrilla units can be formed, led, and deployed on a large scale on the basis of guerrilla tactics and with trained guerrillas in the vanguard.

Guerrilla irregular forces must be able to gain acceptance into the people's army. On this basis the people's army will be able to lay a great deal of emphasis on guerrilla tactics.

People's army, people's forces, and guerrilla forces—all these have nothing to do with any proposed federal army or any sort of army formed by co-operation with the Dutch. Throughout the revolution officers trained in the Royal Netherlands Indies Army and its military academy have never shown more initiative, ability, or achievements than officers given three to six months' training by the Japanese. Almost all of what has been achieved by the army, the irregular units, and the people's forces is the result of the initiative and sacrifices of the masses, and particularly the young.

Officer training of the type given in the Royal Netherlands Indies Army and its military academy is too expensive and cannot be afforded by the people who are poor enough already. The sort of training to be given to the officer trainees of the Republic after 100 per cent independence has been achieved should be determined by the character and political philosophy of the Republic of Indonesia, and also by the progress of Indonesian industry. This is a matter for the Indonesian people alone to decide. It is not a matter for the Dutch to decide or meddle in! The Dutch did not demonstrate any great military prowess in the World War just over. We cannot permit the Dutch to participate in establishing an army in Indonesia. Any army formed by the Dutch, whether it is called a federal army or whatever it is called, will be colonial in nature. A federal army means an army separated from the people, an army paid for by the people to oppress the people. Entrusting our seventy million people to an army formed by the Dutch shopkeepers means asking for another disaster such as that of March 8, 1942! *

People can become members of a guerrilla force regardless of the class or group they belong to. Children of aristocrats, traders, workers, and peasants can equally become members or leaders of guerrilla forces, as long as they believe in 100 per cent independence. The final criteria by which they will be judged are honest commitment to independence and ability as fighters and leaders. But, generally, the maxim of "Oil to oil and water to water" applies. A factory worker

* The day on which the Governor-General of the Netherlands Indies surrendered to the Japanese.

prefers to mix with other factory workers and a miner with other miners. Plantation workers and peasant villagers mix more easily with other plantation workers and peasant villagers. A town slum dweller mixes most easily with other town slum dwellers. Having similar work, similar interests, and similar problems means finding it easier to understand each other and feel for each other, and so they quickly become close friends. Men's capacity to understand and feel for each other is the central requirement for any co-operative effort, and co-operative effort is essential for every kind of organization, particularly a fighting organization.

It is also best if commanding officers belong to the groups they command, if a worker unit is led by a worker officer, a peasant unit by a peasant officer, a unit of the urban poor by an intellectual of urban poor background and so on. Naturally, a person of any group can be an officer as long as he is honest and loyal to his men.

In view of the way in which the situation around us has developed, it is permissible that units be formed on the basis of a particular view of life and political orientation. What we have at present is a variety of irregular units and formations based on religion or on a nationalist or proletarianist ideology. The strength of the Hizbullah forces is rooted in religion. The strength of the Barisan Banteng and the power of the Barisan Pemberontak, the Lasjkar Rakjat, and others of that group are based on the ideologies of nationalism and Murba-ism respectively. All this is no obstacle to the formation of a guerrilla force or to establishing coordination between the various guerrilla forces. What is important for a guerrilla force is its characteristic tactics and the way it allies itself with the community around it. In short, a guerrilla force can be organized either along work or group lines or along the lines of *Weltanschauung* or political ideology, religious, nationalist, or proletarian.

In battles fought in Republican territory the guerrilla force must do its best to co-operate with the leaders of the army of the Republic, must assist the regular army in all positions indicated by the regular revolutionary forces. In such cases the guerrillas can do their work on the enemy's right or left flank or behind his lines.

But the guerrilla forces must hold firm to their position, that is, to the demand for 100 per cent independence. They must fight on, openly or otherwise, until 100 per cent independence is achieved. In a cease-fire situation they should continue to be guided by the goal of 100 per cent independence. They will be willing to stop when 100 per cent independence is guaranteed. They will continue their struggle, an open struggle or a hidden one depending on their strength, if a "cease fire" means anything less than 100 per cent independence, that is, independence as regards politics, economics, external affairs, military affairs, and financial affairs for the whole of Indonesia.

XIVb
A. H. Nasution   Unity of Command (1955)

These two extracts come from Tjatatan-Tjatatan Sekitar Politik Militer Indonesia (*Notes on Indonesian Military Policy*), *a volume which Colonel Nasution, as he then was, published in May 1955.** It was written while he was a nonactive officer, that is, between his two periods as Chief of Staff of the Army, 1950–1952 and 1955–1962.*

Historically, it is obvious that there have often been tensions and conflicts between political and military leaders, because of personal backgrounds as well as policies.

In the recent World War it was apparent that Hitler as Head of State and Supreme Commander was unable to restrain himself and interfered too much in operational matters, tying the hands of his commanders to the point where they were unable to apply their full energies to the fighting. After the Allied landing in Western Europe, for instance, he ordered that every speck of land be defended to the end, so that his commanders were no longer able to act according to the essential principles of war.

We ourselves have seen such things during the revolution. Political agitators made demands such as "Continue the attack," "All arms to the front," and "Don't retreat a single step" which resulted in the loss of no small number of our young men's lives and meant that we were wasting men and arms in battles which were of no significance for our strategy. We are familiar with the giving of orders via public radios, too.

At the other extreme is the situation in the period of the German Empire where the military, the famous General Staff, always ignored political considerations, with the result that their country eventually suffered defeats.

We have been experiencing this sort of thing in the present period, where military people have treated antiguerrilla warfare "too mili-

* Djakarta: Pembimbing.

tarily," to the point of ignoring political factors. This has often led eventually to failure. The problem of relations between political and military leadership is on the one hand a political and constitutional problem, but on the other hand it is also a military problem, a question of the science of war.

Under the system of Western democracy, which we have taken as a model in our present constitution, it is difficult to deal with this problem properly. Comparing our various constitutions—the Constitution of the Proclamation, the Constitution as altered by the Central National Committee,* the Constitution of the Federal Republic of Indonesia, and the 1950 Constitution of the Republic of Indonesia— it is the Constitution of the Proclamation which is the simplest and the one which best facilitates the efficiency of military leadership, especially in providing for smooth relations between the politicians and the military. For under this Constitution leadership of the overall people's war is in the hands of the President and Supreme Commander, who is responsible and assisted by ministers, and the operational leadership is held under his orders by the Commander in Chief.

The factor which has been of decisive importance in the matter of relations between military and political leaders during the short lifetime of this Republic is internal politics, that is, the efforts of the politicians to establish complete control over the army. Indeed, our army was born before the political parties. Indeed, the battalions, regiments, and divisions of our army and its general staff existed before there was a Minister of Defense. Indeed, our army headquarters was operating before there was a Ministry of Defense. Indeed, it was armed units which pioneered the seizure of power, civil as well as military power, in the first stages of our revolution.

The political parties were born later but they soon formed their own irregular military units, which often competed with and fought against the state forces. We experienced occurrences like this in Atjeh, in East Sumatra, in West Sumatra, in West Java, in Central Java, and in East Java. The leaders of the irregulars were generally politicians who held power in the provisional parliament and the defense councils.

We were able to avoid difficulties and mistakes in the matter of leadership during the second guerrilla war or second Dutch military action, of 1948–1949. With the cabinet and provisional parliament

---

* This is a reference to the de facto constitutional change of October–November 1945 from presidential to parliamentary government.

nonactive, their members captured or living in occupied towns, and with full power vested in the President because of the still unfinished Madiun revolt, the top military leadership put aside old organizations and regulations and created a unified war leadership in the hands of the Commander in Chief under the supervision of the guerrilla Prime Minister, Sjafruddin Prawiranegara. In Java the old defense councils and people's defense organizations were abolished and leadership of the "over-all people's war" or "territorial war" was held by the island commanders, and under them by the regional commanders who doubled as military governors.

In fact the war was a single unified effort. The people's war or over-all war was not just an operation in the military field, but an all-embracing one involving the political and economic fields as well. Therefore, it was not possible for the leadership to be diffused piece by piece into the hands of various officials operating alongside each other. There had to be a single man at the national summit bearing full responsibility. This was the position of the President and Supreme Commander in the [Proclamation] Constitution of the Republic of Indonesia, but the position became blurred after the relevant sections of that constitution were "frozen" by the Central National Committee. . . .

[Under the present constitution] there is no unified leadership in the matter of preparing for war because the chiefs of staff of the three forces act independently and are coordinated only by a minister, a civilian politician who usually cannot possibly have a deep understanding of defense problems, as has been shown in the short lifetime of our state.

This policy of dividing responsibility resulted from particular political views. It has its roots in the competition between the parties and the army, which has existed ever since the government urged the establishment of parties as widely as possible, and each party formed its own defense department and army. . . .

Excesses are certainly possible on both sides. On the one hand, as we have often found, the politicians want to meddle in military affairs, politicizing military problems. But there is also the tendency on the other side of military men wanting to meddle in political affairs and, to put it simply, to militarize political problems. But in the end each side must realize that it cannot just ignore the considerations of the other. For the politicians cannot possibly determine state policy without considering the military aspects, and on the other hand the military cannot possibly ignore the basic lines of state policy which must be the foundation of their plans. There must be coordination.

Excesses of politicization of military affairs occur in France, where a party temporarily in power will immediately change the previously existing military leadership. The result is an unstable military leadership. Our constitutional system being based on the French model, we have experienced a tendency to these same excesses. . . .

Such tendencies will certainly continue to exist while the system of state leadership is one which forces a separation of military and political leadership as in the constitutions of Western states.

In the absolute monarchies of former times these difficulties did not exist, because the king was a statesman and a military man at the same time, both head of government and supreme military commander with direct control. This was the position of Emperor Napoleon, Emperor Alexander, and others in Europe, of Washington, who acted as both political and military leader in the American War of Independence, and, in old Indonesia, of Sultan Iskandar Muda in Atjeh, Imam Bondjol in Minangkabau, Singamangaradja in Tapanuli, Diponegoro in Java, Sultan Hasanudin in Sulawesi, and so on.

Kings who did not have military expertise usually had a deputy or chief of staff who did have such expertise, in order to have effective leadership in war. Thus the German Kaiser appointed Hindenburg as his commander in chief and Ludendorff as his Chief of Staff. Stalin as Supreme Commander in Russia appointed Zhukov as his Chief of Staff. President Mao Tse-tung has Supreme Commander Chu Teh as deputy chairman of the War Council.

In the history of Islamic wars, too, one finds examples of heads of state who are leaders in both state and military affairs. Indeed, this is the case with Kartosuwirjo, who is both *Imam* [religious and political head] and Supreme Commander [of the rebel Islamic State of Indonesia]. King Ibn Saud is a well-known example of one who is both head of state and military commander.

But in our constitutions, with the exception of the Proclamation Constitution of 1945, political leadership and military leadership have been firmly separated from each other.

In a system of government such as under this second constitution of the Republic of Indonesia the situation of the head of government is not clear. The President has no power, only a title, and the Prime Minister is not the head of government either, but merely the chairman of meetings of ministers. It is the cabinet in its entirety which holds power. Under this system it is impossible to establish a unified war leadership such as existed in the American, British, German, and Chinese examples quoted above, where the head of state or Prime Minister has full power in his own hands, which is an essential requirement of war leadership.

The Proclamation Constitution on the other hand, does meet this requirement, for under it the President is the responsible head of government. He is no mere symbol like the Queen of England, the Queen of Holland, or the President of France or Italy. From the point of view of the requirements of war and leadership in war, this is the best system. On the basis of this Constitution, a war leadership was able to be established which made it possible to wage a people's war on an integral basis. But as history shows, we abandoned this system just as we were on the threshold of the colonial war. We returned to it at periods of internal crisis, at the time of the July 3, 1946, coup of Muhammad Yamin, Iwa Kusumasumantri, and their associates,* and at the time of the PKI rebellion of September 18, 1948, the rebellion of Muso, Amir Sjarifuddin, and the others.

One other difficulty which resulted from the change is that Sukarno and Hatta, the men who had real authority, were made into symbols, and their power taken by party men with far less authority. This has remained a problem right up to the present time.

XIVc
Zulkifli Lubis Militarism and Civilianism (1955)

This Order of the Day, of July 17, 1955, was published in the Djakarta daily Indonesia Raya *on the following day. It was issued in the wake of the "Affair of June 27," when the Army leadership, under Deputy Chief of Staff Colonel Lubis, had organized an almost complete boycott of a ceremony in which a nominee of the first Ali Sastroamidjojo Cabinet was being installed as Army Chief of Staff. By July 17 the army leadership under Lubis had forced the resignation of the Minister of Defense, and it was widely believed that the cabinet could not survive. It fell on July 24. With the parliamentary elections due in September, mid-1955 was a period of intense party conflict. The Army leaders reportedly discussed the possibility of a military take-over at this time but decided against immediate action of this kind.*

* This refers to an abortive attempt to seize power which was made under the leadership of the "Tan Malaka group" of national-communist leaders opposed to the Sjahrir cabinet's policies of negotiations with the Dutch.

(1) Provocative accusations have been and continue to be hurled at us in connection with the affair of June 27, 1955, insinuating that the Army intends to destroy the basis and structure of democracy and to establish a military dictatorship upon the rubble left by this destruction.

(2) Bearing in mind the principle of military science which teaches "never lose sight of your goal," we must not allow such accusations and provocations to cause us to deviate from the goal the Army is pursuing. That goal was put forward in the explanatory note accompanying the Decision of the Meeting of the Leadership of the Army of July 2, 1955. It needs to be achieved . . . in order to make it possible for the Army to lay the foundations for carrying out its role within the framework of the ideology and struggle of the nation. The first step in pursuing this goal is to settle the affair of June 27, 1955, whose causes lie in the matters of principle discussed in the Decision of the Meeting of July 2, 1955.

(3) It would not be surprising if the taking of this first step led to the development of a situation whose effect on the continued life of the cabinet accords with history's dynamism and capacity for movement. Seen in relation to the living and growing processes of nature, a parallel development of this kind would not be peculiar or anomalous. Yet it could not be said that such a parallel development was deliberately brought about simply by the attitude and actions of the Army. Such a conclusion would not only be unhelpful; it would also be wrong. A parallel such as this is an "imponderable," that is, an element whose influence cannot be weighed in any easy or certain way.

The attitude and actions of the Army which contribute to the parallel are difficult for people who are not members of the Army to understand. The Army's task and function in relation to the national ideology and constitutional structure, the course of its living history to date, and the fact that it is a military body with particular characteristics—these combine to give the Army a mode of thinking which is difficult for outsiders to comprehend.

(4) The attitude and actions of the Army cannot be interpreted as meaning that the Army wishes to destroy the foundations and structure of the parliamentary democracy of the Republic of the Proclamation. The problem must be seen in the light of the Army's broad responsibility to the Homeland and the Nation for national welfare in general, and the defense of the state in particular. The Army is like a

nationally owned firm in which the eighty million people of Indonesia are the shareholders. Therefore, the Army is responsible to those eighty million shareholders. Only, as the state is based upon the principle of democracy, this responsibility is channelled through a board of directors and a board of shareholders, i.e., the highest executive body and the people's consultative assembly. If there is a disturbance in the harmonious relationship between the Army and the executive, then the Army must concentrate on the shareholders in defense and the armed forces. An imbalance of this kind reached its peak in the affair of June 27, 1955. Bearing in mind the mode of thinking outlined above, it is clear that the Army did not threaten or destroy the foundation or structure of democracy. The situation was rather that the Army confronted individuals occupying positions within that structure who, in the opinion of the Army and the common people, have been using that foundation and structure in a way which does not accord with the principles, rules, norms, and criteria shared by us all. These people have not abided by the "rules of the game" which we all accept. And they have misused the democratic structure in order to pursue interests other than those of the nation. In short, they have not used this structure to realize the purposes of the state.

The attitude and actions of the Army are not only intended to defend the procedures of democracy, such as that the people participate in the making of decisions and in the formation of the broad policies of the state, but also intended to guarantee that the decisions which are taken are concerned with the aim of democracy, that is, the interests of the nation.

(5) In terms of relationships between politics and the military, there are two extreme forms of government. The first emphasizes the importance of the military element and is expressed in the idea of militarism, the stream of thought which places military matters above political ones, and is given concrete form in military dictatorship. The second emphasizes the importance of politics, does away with the military element, and is expressed in politicism or civilianism, which is given concrete form in the government of unarmed democracy. What the Army wants is balance and harmony between the political and the military, between statecraft and strategy.

(6) The history of the Army is evidence that the Army has itself taken the initiative to do away with or lessen the possible danger of militarism in our country. The first instance of this was in 1951 when

Army headquarters drew up a plan for preliminary military development. This was designed to make possible the introduction of compulsory military service, a militia system, by the middle of 1956. With that plan the top leadership of the Army aimed at abolishing the professional army system and replacing it with a militia cadre system, which would lighten the burden borne by the nation and open the ranks of the army to the whole nation, thus making it difficult for militarism to appear. But the 1951 preliminary development plan foundered on the reefs of the events prior to, during, and after October 17, 1952,* and so has remained uncompleted right up until the present.

A second instance came in the first quarter of 1955 when the officers of the Army General Staff argued before the Ad Hoc Committee set up by the Ministry of Defense for the Army's view of compulsory military service, compulsory training, and basic defense education for the people.

(7) The Army does not believe in militarism, but it also rejects the politicism, or civilianism, which is clearly raging unchecked in our country. The Army opposes the way of thinking which regards politics as the only important factor in all assessments and considerations and pushes aside military and other factors—especially if such politicism shows signs of being influenced by individual and group interests.

The sequence of events within the Army has made it sufficiently clear that efforts are being made by followers of politicism to put the "political" considerations and calculations of individuals and groups, in one form or another, before military considerations, whether these be strategic, tactical, administrative, logistical, or technical. Consequently, the allocation of materials and funds to the Army is effected according to politicism, not on the basis of efficiency, of honesty, or of justice for the ever-suffering soldier. The result is that after ten years of independence and sovereignty the Republic has still no defense policy or basis for national defense.

(8) Our top military leaders should be appointed by the President in accordance with decisions taken by Cabinet, which must aim at maintaining a balanced and harmonious relationship between the

---

* On that day a group of army leaders sought to force President Sukarno to dissolve parliament in what was seen by some as the intended first stage of a coup d'etat. The President, however, refused to accept the demand. One consequence was exacerbated division within the Army.

political and the military, not at politicism. Such an arrangement would ensure that there are no disturbances of the constitution caused by the military. The leaders of our state should be chosen in general elections and in the Parliament, not in military staff meetings or military councils. Therefore—and because political power is enthroned upon military power—the maintenance and guaranteeing of balance and harmony between matters political and matters military, between statecraft and strategy, and between the leaders of the state and the leaders of the Armed Forces, is the responsibility first and foremost of our leading politicians, who exercise the power of the state. It is they who form Cabinets, and they who can dissolve them, certainly not military leaders.

(9) Relations between the political and the military, between state-craft and strategy, and between the leaders of state and the leaders of the defense forces can easily be formally set down, in any of a variety of laws and regulations. But, the philosophy of the military makes it clear that the human element is basic.

Therefore, because the machinery of the state in general, and of defense in particular, is operated and guided by men, and as men remain guided by their emotions, balance and harmony between the political and the military can in practice only be guaranteed by a spirit of mutual respect, mutual trust, and an honest interpretation of the reality and responsibility involved in their respective duties and functions. This spirit and this responsibility must be fostered in the body and soul of Indonesian Man from the time he enters kindergarten. Thus, the problem is one of national education, which must lay the foundations for a system in which the people of Indonesia are organized as a national team.

(10) Finally, I want to deliver a principle of military philosophy to all soldiers in the National Army, one which should be a guiding principle for you all: "When political leaders say 'yes' and military leaders say 'no,' the reply must always be 'yes.'" Nevertheless, this does not imply that such a "yes" is automatically the correct answer, nor does it mean that political leaders are better citizens than military leaders.

In short, the essence of this Order of the Day is that accusations to the effect that the Army is violating the procedures of democracy— that is, the participation of the people in determining the destiny of the nation—are not true. The Army is struggling precisely in order to give the Armed Forces the position which they, as national forces, must have in the interests of the nation, and in so doing is helping to give content to democracy.

My message to all Army members, no matter where they are or what they are doing is to remain calm in body and mind in the face of these provocative accusations. Prove, in your everyday attitudes, in your words, behavior, and actions that you are citizens like all other citizens in the society, so that the people will realize that the Army is a national asset.

XIVd

T. B. Simatupang   The Army amid Upheaval and Conflict (1957)

This extract consists of portions of two essays from Major General Simatupang's book Pemerintah, Masjarakat, Angkatan Perang *(Government, Society, Armed Forces) (Djakarta: Indira, 1960). The essays were written during 1957 against a background of abortive coups in Djakarta and successful ones in the provinces, of increasingly frequent violations of constitutional norms, of calls for a radically different political order—including President Sukarno's for a "Guided Democracy"—and of fears of civil war. Simatupang had lost his position as Armed Forces Chief of Staff three years earlier.*

In Indonesia since 1945 we have taken the view that there should be freedom to form parties and that parties should be free to compete with each other in and outside a freely and secretly elected parliament. Therefore, the operative formula in our country is: "Hands off the army" for the parties and "Hands off party politics" for the army.

There are several factors which have continued to make it difficult to apply this formula fully; but no matter how great these difficulties have been, we have never abandoned the formula and have always judged deviations by taking this formula as our criterion. It is only recently that voices have been raised to demand the abandonment of the system of freedom to form parties and of freedom for parties to compete. If this system should at some point be abandoned, this in itself would mean that a new formula would have to be adopted on the position of the army in the state; for a decision to abandon a particular constitutional system means that the formulas rooted in that system are rendered indefensible.

Other difficulties have arisen as a result of the fact that the at-

mosphere has been dominated by suspicion and fear in the past few
years. Each party is afraid of the others, suspecting that they will
come to dominate the army and thereby gain a monopoly of power
in the state and society. The parties are fearful and suspicious that
the army will at some point establish a kind of militarism in Indonesia;
and the army for its part is afraid of the parties because it suspects
them of wanting to weaken and politicize it. Much of the activity
within and around the army in the last few years owes its origin to
these feelings of fear and suspicion.

These fears and suspicions, whether harbored by the parties or the
army, are consequences in their turn of each group's realization of its
own weakness, for it is true that there are weaknesses within each of
these organizations. And we know that suspicion and fear are generally the twin-children of weakness.

Apart from this, there are problems involved in applying the above-
mentioned formula which result from the particular characteristics
of our army at the present time. Our revolution and war of independence brought forth a great surge of strength in our nation, strength
which had remained buried during the colonial period. Our army
is a part of that strength; it is the part which was channeled into the
military organization of our nation.

So the spirit of the army has two poles. The first pole is the realization that it is part of the new strength which emerged as a result of the
revolution and the war of independence. The other consists of the
realization that, as the military organ of the state, it is tied to formal
arrangements.

So long as everything goes well there will not be felt to be any
conflict between these two poles. But once the belief arises that extraordinary measures are needed to move the dynamic of the revolution back into its proper direction—and this belief has apparently
arisen in a section of the army in recent months—then tensions appear.
Yes, seen from the outside it even looks as if there are conflicts. On the
one side there are those who adhere firmly to the formal pole and feel
themselves to be in the right because of this, and on the other there
are those who adhere to the second pole, that is, regard themselves
as a part of the strength released by the revolution and the war of
independence—and are convinced on this ground that it is they who
are right.

There could be no more tragic course of developments for our
army and state than that all this should lead to the forces aroused

by our revolution and our war of independence annihilating each other.

Sometimes people suggest that India—like Indonesia, a democratic state based on law in which there are many parties and differences among the peoples of the various regions—should be taken as a guide. But as well as these similarities between the two countries, there is one major difference: In India the politicians achieved independence and the British government handed the Indian army over as assets to the leaders of the Congress Party, whereas in Indonesia the army was the product of revolution and waged a war of independence against the Dutch.

Sometimes, too, there are people who want to copy the situation in China. However, the characteristics, culture, and history of the Chinese are completely different from those of the Indonesians. The present Chinese army was formed by the Chinese Communist Party more than thirty years ago, and it fought for more than thirty years under the leadership of that party. In Indonesia the army was not formed or led by a party; the Indonesian army arose and grew in a country where there were many parties, and at those times during the war of independence when the parties could function no longer, the army carried on the war.

At first sight there appear to be many similarities between the problems faced by our army now and those faced by the German army in the post–First World War Weimar Republic. The German army at that time also had to find a place within a highly unstable state and a society riven by sharp interparty conflicts. It safeguarded itself by adopting a policy of isolation. In the midst of that social and political turmoil and taking the traditions of the German army under the Kaiser as its guide (even though Germany had become a Republic), the army focussed its attention on military matters alone and prepared itself to become the core of an expanded German army of the future. The army regarded itself as the bearer of the idea of the Empire (*Träger des Reichsgedankens*) and not as supporting any particular one of the continually changing governments which it labeled "governments of accident" (*Zufallsregierungen*), and its leaders refused to allow it to be used for policing purposes because such a role would, they said, alienate the army from the people. The army came to be a kind of "state within a state." In this way the German army was indeed able to make its way safely through that stormy era, but the German state and society meanwhile fell into the hands of the Nazis, and finally the army became a tool of the Nazi government, too.

Although there are surface similarities between the problems faced by the German army then and those faced by our army at the present time, there are clearly important differences at a more fundamental level. It is true that both armies had to find themselves a position within states and societies rent with turbulence and extremely sharp conflicts. That is the similarity between their situations. However, there is this important difference: The German army, which approached the situation by taking old traditions as its guide and with the support of an officer corps with a common set of basic ideas—and especially of the famous *Generalstab* corps—was able to isolate itself. The Indonesian army, on the other hand, cannot isolate itself —how, for instance, could it refuse to let itself be used for policing purposes, that is, for duties to do with internal security?—and, as a young revolutionary army, cannot take old traditions as its guide but must look to the future, that is, to the fulfilment of the ideals of the revolution.

Our army cannot pursue a policy of isolation. It stands in the midst of the upheaval taking place in our society and state. It cannot be guided by the traditions of a past age. It looks to the future and seeks to contribute actively and positively to realizing the ideals of the revolution, while at the same time doing its best to ensure that it is not swallowed-up or split by the ferment and conflicts around it. It is a problem that is more difficult than the one which the German army faced in the Weimar Republic.

XIVe

A. H. *Nasution* The Army as a Functional Group (1962)

This excerpt is part of the speech delivered by General Nasution when receiving an honorary doctorate at Andalas University, Padang (Sumatra), on July 16, 1962. It sets out most of the principal themes of the army leadership's political doctrine in the guided democracy period. The full speech may be found in Towards a People's Army *(Djakarta: Delegasi, 1964), pp. 93–114.*

In its essential nature, the TNI is a People's army, a freedom army, a national army and an army of partisans, charged with achieving the goals of the Revolution. . . .

Because it is a people's army, an integral part of the people, and because of its responsibility to fulfil the Message of the Suffering of the People, the TNI is progressive and dynamic and has been accorded a proper role by society in guarding the Revolution and thwarting deviations from it; it is not only a stabilizing force but a dynamic force for the completion of the Revolution. . . .

The unity of the people and the army, which is a vital part of the essential nature of our state and armed forces, is a source of strength to the TNI and makes it invincible. . . .

Since the outbreak of the Revolution on August 17, 1945, our state and nation have repeatedly experienced dangerous crises. In all these crises, the TNI has revealed its character as a part of the nation's assets, as an instrument of struggle ever ready to defend the Revolution of August 17 from any assailant whatsoever. This may be seen in the cases of the "July 3 Affair" of 1946 and the Madiun revolt of 1948, when the state called upon the army to save the Revolution. This task of saving the state and the Revolution was entrusted to the TNI again during the second military phase of the war of independence, when the supreme political authority could not discharge its obligations because it had fallen into enemy hands.

At that time the TNI not only carried on guerrilla warfare but also operated in other fields, including the administrative, the social-economic, and the cultural, in its efforts to uphold the government's prestige, to improve the village economy, to keep basic education from breaking down, and so on. Most recently we have contributed to the surmounting of a crisis of state by putting an end to the PRRI-Permesta rebellion.

From these facts it is clear that the TNI is a legatee of the Revolution which remained true to its first task to save the course of the Revolution. The Armed Forces of the Republic of Indonesia have never been absent from any effort to save our nation's struggle from dangers without or within. One by one these dangers have been overcome, but not without great sacrifices.

History has shown that our duties in saving the state and the Revolution have not been purely military but have extended to all spheres of public life including the social-economic. We recall the proclamation of a state of emergency at the time of the seizure of Dutch property, in which the TNI played a leading part. So it does, too, in the Prosperity Operation Movement, the National Cleanliness

Movement, in this committee and that council, and many other state institutions. . . .

The role of the TNI as a tool of the state for defense is distinct from its role as a functional group. . . . Guided Democracy divides society up on the basis of function and distinguishes functional groupings. The TNI is officially recognized as one such functional grouping. Therefore, besides its defense task, the TNI must be actively involved in carrying the Revolution of August 17, 1945, to its successful conclusion. . . .

The placement of members of the Armed Forces as functional group representatives in the government organs of the Republic of Indonesia is a feature of our state organization which is unique in the world. But though we describe it as unique, it is historically logical, a natural outcome of the development of our struggle for independence.

The basis of Indonesian society is a family basis, not one of class difference. From this family basis arises the spirit of mutual discussion and mutual assistance which we have inherited from our ancestors and which we have now begun to practice again.

So the Armed Forces both as a functional group and as an instrument for the salvation of the Revolution takes part in discussing problems within the great family of the Indonesian nation. . . .

The TNI as a functional group is not the same as the TNI as an instrument of the state for defense. As an instrument of the state, it is only active in one sphere of the state's activities. As a functional group it takes part in all aspects of the national struggle, along with other functional groups. This particular functional group, it is true, only represents one particular social function, but it must pay attention to the whole and take part in drawing up state policy in concert with other functional groups. This is the function and status of the TNI in the state and its struggle at the present time.

For this reason we must transform our modes of thinking and working. Whereas in the liberal period the military and civilian officials were mere lifeless depoliticized instruments of the government of the day (instruments over which the parties nevertheless quarreled), now military and civilian officials must be politicized in the sense that they must positively uphold the policy, ideology, and program of the state, though they must also be freed from party influence. . . .

Many members of the TNI as a functional group at present have tasks in other fields—as members of legislative bodies, as Ministers, as high officials in Departments and in State Enterprises, and so on. . . .

There are still people who make an issue of whether such people with assignments in other fields ought to be allowed to wear uniform. This is a result of "separation of powers" thinking according to which the civil and the military should be kept distinct. Now if a Governor happens to be a military man and the wearing of uniform helps him to command respect and discharge his duties better, then there is nothing wrong with his wearing uniform. What is necessary is to consider what is useful and to beware of abuses.

And, indeed, in this whole question of the assignment of military men to other fields, it is the usefulness or otherwise that must be considered. There may be an officer who is not so good at leading troops but who makes a good district administrator. And there may be a good commander who would not pass muster as an administrator.

In connection with the first stage of over-all planned development, the TNI, in addition to its own internal development, must also participate in development outside its own field, for instance in the process of production, starting off new projects, and so on. . . .

The essential character of the TNI has conferred upon it the task of leading the Indonesian people toward the attainment of their national aspirations, and, consequently, it is fully conscious that it is a binding obligation on the Armed Forces to participate in the implementation of over-all development, which is one aspect of the fulfillment of the Message of the Suffering of the People.

XIVf

Suharjo The Army in Regional Development (1962)

This passage is from the Introduction to a book of speeches written when Suharjo (then Colonel) was military commander in East Kalimantan (Borneo) in 1962. The book was called Tanah, Rakjat dan Tentara (*Land, People, and Army*) (*Djakarta: Pentja, 1963*).

As military head of the region, I must naturally be as familiar as possible with the region and its people. So I have to make thorough inspections, hearing the voices and tales of the people deep in the interior, to fill out the information I have obtained scientifically.

These voices of the people are often an inspiration and stimulus for me and not infrequently contain important facts for those who are able to hear them. Do not such notes as these enhance the beauty of music? For instance, I once asked a farmer who it was who had taught him to plant cloves so that they yielded so well. The answer was brief: "The clove tree itself." It turned out that he had experimented continually for five years till he discovered the right way. Such were his energy and perseverance. But it also follows that we as leaders were not active enough, for that long period of time need not have been wasted.

I do not want to discuss military problems . . . because one can read about those in all the many military textbooks and because my friends did not ask this of me. What is important for me is knowledge about conditions as they really exist, which permit or prevent the implementation of the theories.

The vast land of East Kalimantan, property of the state, not developed and exploited, and so as yet without any role in production—in the production of food, clothing, and the goods useful in a modern and progressive society; and its people as yet few and scattered—these factors have to be brought together. And the army, too, an army of men who must be willing to sacrifice, work, lead the way, and provide the example—this factor, too, must be placed in a proper relationship with the other real factors just mentioned.

The ways we take must be consistent with the existing conditions— and these conditions are revolutionary conditions. We may not dream of a strong national defense in isolation from the socio–political structure and economic system we want to achieve. The matter of such doctrines as territorial defense, people's defense, and over-all warfare, cannot be separated from the basic elements of our state. We may not dream at all, because dreams fade as soon as we become conscious. We must remain conscious; there is no room for false dreams.

The vast region of East Kalimantan with its small and scattered population in tiny village communities, mostly situated on the banks of rivers large and small which serve as lines of communications; rulers who for decades have operated a feudal system very injurious to the people; a people whom the Dutch colonialists through the feudalists and other agents exploited and allowed to live in ignorance—such a society as this has to be mobilized and built-up into a community which is strong politically, economically, and mentally, and strongly defended.

We are dreaming if we want to achieve this by liberal means, if our means are the means of compromise. We must be thankful that the Great Leader of the Revolution has laid down the way for us in

Manipol-USDEK! On this foundation we can carry out an overhaul of the governmental apparatus of East Kalimantan and abolish the system of economic exploitation of the people. . . .

When I first came to East Kalimantan, I wept to see in the interior officials who ought to have been leading but were, on the contrary, exploiting and oppressing the people for their personal gain. Do not imagine that an area like this can be made into a stronghold of people's defense without transforming radically the system which brings suffering to the people.

On such a basis we have mobilized the progressive-revolutionary energies of the people to demolish the system of usurious loans and phony cooperatives, to organize the farmers . . . and spread understanding of Indonesian socialism. We have to be quick, for delay means retrogression. With the establishment of the National Front we can bring together the progressive-revolutionary people to do all this!

Many problems are bound up together in an effort to improve the people's economy. For instance, the State Trading Enterprises have to be capable of handling the people's products—rattan, gums, salted fish, rubber, copra, and so on. They can do this if they are properly run in accordance with the government regulations and if the people really feel they share in their ownership—so that, for instance, they do not degenerate into commercial commission agents. The State Trading Enterprises have to consider, too, the distribution of essential commodities for the people. To put all this in order we have carried out "retooling," replacing corrupt and obstructionist personnel with people who are willing to work properly. Simultaneously we have set up rubber co-operatives, fishing co-operatives, and the like. All this we have done with the participation of the masses and the National Front.

What is the role of the army in this matter? In the first place, it must firmly retool those of its own members in the State Trading Enterprises or other organs whose hands are not clean! Second, the army organization from the Regional Command level downward must be a pacesetter and actively participate in supervising the implementation of programs. The job of the military emergency government is to break through any obstructions that appear—not to take over all work but, on the contrary, to make it possible for the existing civil apparatus to work—and sometimes to coordinate different branches to overcome difficulties. The military emergency government limits its staff to as few people as possible. In remote districts it is the army's task to make good the manpower shortage in village schools, anti-illiteracy campaigns, and so on. This is the easier because members of the army are often also members of local branches and sub-branches of the National Front.

Because of all this activity, the army is integrated with society, understands society's needs, and, because it understands, can uphold the interests of the community, of the common people! In the long run, when a soldier leaves the army, he will not be isolated and he will feel one with the common people who are struggling and will go on struggling.

The army is not a separate class! In a free state such as Indonesia, every adult is liable to military service. In the years to come there will be nothing unusual about military life for the Indonesian people. In the Indonesian Socialist society, there will be no great differences in the standard of living of an Indonesian whether he is in military service or outside it. We must take that as our aim; we have to move toward it now; our mental attitude must be brought in line with that goal. Every military problem, from the highest doctrines down to, for example, the channeling of discharged men back into the community has to be adapted to the over-all orientation of our state. When such men are returned to the community, we must place them in a suitable position within the framework (for instance) of guided economy; let us not give them facilities which may lead to their becoming a negative element in the economic field, becoming opponents of guided economy and obstructions to its establishment.

XIVg
Sukarno The Armed Forces as an Instrument of Revolution (1961)

This selection comes from the President's Independence Day address of 1961, a year in which there had been a great deal of tension between him and the principal army leaders. The full English text is in Sukarno, Indonesia's Political Manifesto, 1959–64 *(Djakarta: Prapantja, 1964?), pp. 129–177.*

It is on the basis of political activity, in the sense of everyone's together actively carrying out the Mandate of the People's Suffering on the basis of the principles of Revolution, Indonesian Socialism, and Leadership, or the New Order, that we are giving the Armed Forces a place in political life. It is on this basis that we have abandoned the principle of the Separation of Powers, that sacred cow of Western-baked constitutional experts. Under Guided Democracy, we need not be afraid that the bayonet will seize power, because in Guided Democracy politics is not a matter of getting into power. Under Guided Democracy, we take every advantage of and gather together all the political abilities of the Armed Forces, which were, indeed, born in a People's Revolution, which fought against Dutch bestiality during the guerrilla war, which have carried out military operations to smash the rebels and bandits, and which must always live and struggle side by side with the People. They certainly understand the cry of the People. They certainly understand the sufferings of the People. They certainly understand the Mandate of the People's Suffering!

They are an instrument of the Revolution, they are the Armed Forces of the Revolution. They must be faithful to their origins, to the Revolution, to the People. They must serve the People, they must put the interests of the People above all other interests. They must not hurt the feelings of the People; they must be Armed Forces which are admired and loved by the People. As I have said, the People have already accepted the Political Manifesto as their compass in politics; thus, the Armed Forces must also accept the Political Manifesto and accept it wholeheartedly. The People are already guided by the Political Manifesto, so the Armed Forces must also be guided by it. I repeat again: It is not the Armed Forces or the rifle which guides the Political Manifesto. It is the Political Manifesto which guides the Armed Forces and the rifle!

Do not twist this around; do not turn it upside down! To twist it around is to deviate toward fascism. The rifle in the hands of the Armed Forces must be like a rifle in the hands of the People, to protect the rights of the People and defend the People's State and Revolution. There must not be antagonisms or contradictions between the Armed Forces and the People in our Revolution, today or in the future.

XV

Indonesia in the World

Overseas observers whose principal interest lies in Indonesia's foreign policy have sometimes asserted that Indonesians are broadly at one in their view of the role which their country has played in the world in the past and the role they believe it should play in the present and the future. We for our part, looking first and foremost at the domestic scene, are impressed by the contrasts far more than by the consensus. The earlier sections of this volume contain several references to the great fourteenth-century empire of Madjapahit to which advocates of a "Greater Indonesia" have often harked back; but they also contain numerous references to old Indonesia as a center of international trade, hospitable to cultural currents from all over the world.

As for what Indonesia's relations with other countries should be in the present and future the prevailing view on this was markedly different at different points in our twenty-year period. And there were persistent contrasts between men of different ideological tendencies, particularly radical nationalists and democratic socialists. As in so many other areas of controversy, the Muslims and Javanese traditionalists were without distinctive views on what Indonesia's external role should be, and the Communists' views were clear-cut but several notches removed from the central focus of the argument.

Something of the dominant contrast between the moderate "internal consolidation" view and the more assertive "realize our national destiny" one is manifest in our first two extracts here, both taken from the series of debates which preceded the proclamation of independence.

The next two pieces also form a pair. Behind the armed forces of Britain and Holland which the miserably equipped new Republic was facing loomed the power of the United States. Using the same arsenal of Marxist concepts, Sjahrir and Tan Malaka for reasons perhaps more temperamental than intellectual arrive at contrasting diagnoses. To Sjahrir's mind the logic of Indonesia's position within the orbit of Anglo-American power forced her to seek American support by diplomatic means, but this policy ran afoul of the dominant nationalist sentiment which Tan Malaka expressed.

Once the Cold War had begun, a new way of dealing with this problem opened up. From 1948 or so onward, men like Sjahrir and Hatta, like India's Nehru, were able to justify policies of limited cooperation with the U.S. and other Western countries by arguing that "We have good relations with countries of both blocs and so are contributing to lessening world tensions." Indonesia's central posture in foreign relations throughout the 1950's, the "independent and active" foreign policy, developed out of this situation. Our fifth extract here, Hatta's, and our sixth, by Sukarno, express this posture in the prosaic and heroic styles characteristic of these two leaders, and in the three forms which were competitively intertwined with each other: staying out of the big powers' quarrels to concentrate on one's own affairs, staying out of these quarrels to preserve world peace, and staying out of them to fight the more important battle against colonialism.

With the establishment of Guided Democracy foreign policy activities came to be of much greater importance in national life than ever before. From 1958 onward President Sukarno traveled widely overseas, with large delegations, and received numerous foreign dignitaries in Djakarta; and Indonesia frequently played host to international conferences, particularly of Asian-African organizations. At the same time it waged a vigorous campaign of diplomacy in favor of its claim to West Irian.

All this was done initially within the framework of nonalignment, of the "independent and active" foreign policy. But after 1961 or so, the "independent and active" policy was gradually abandoned, to be replaced by the doctrine of the New Emerging Forces. In President Sukarno's words in September 1962, the world should not be seen as divided into three camps but rather as divided into two, the Old Established Forces of imperialism, exploitation, and oppression, and the New Emerging Forces of justice and freedom (in which he included the newly independent nations of Asia and

Africa, the socialist countries, and the progressive forces in capitalist countries). Our last three extracts here are taken from the period when this newer doctrine held sway, which was also the period of "confrontation" of Malaysia, a period of increasingly strained relations with the United States, and of increasingly cordial relations with China.*

XVa
Muhammad Yamin Unity of Our Country and Our People (1945)

This is part of an address given on May 31, 1945, to a plenary session of the Investigating Committee for the Preparation of Indonesian Independence, a committee which had been proclaimed by the Japanese Military Government in March. The Indonesian text may be found in Muhammad Yamin, ed., Naskah Persiapan Undang-undang Dasar 1945 (*Drafting the 1945 Constitution*) (*n.p.: Jajasan Prapantja, 1959*), *I, 126–135.*

Mr. Chairman, what should be the basis of our stand in determining the territory of Indonesia? My considered opinion is that we have two guiding principles for the determination of a firm and honest attitude, because we must be free from wild ambitions.

The first guiding principle is that the areas which should be included in Indonesian territory are those which have given birth to the Indonesian people: the motherland of a people should become the territory of its State. We shall reach this stage of development when we attain our independence. In following this guiding principle we are not only unifying the people in our own country; we are also seeing to it that all the areas of our motherland are under the Indonesian State, and that there are no enclaves.

History has shown how Poland and Turkey have had their territories divided, and how Czechoslovakia has been united. A second example is not hard to find; we need only look at our own situation. For 350 years our country has been the victim of territorial division, at the hands of the Portuguese, the Spanish, the French, the British, the Australians, the Germans, and the Dutch. I do not need to go

---

* For additional material from this period, see George A. Modelski, ed., *The New Emerging Forces: Documents on the Ideology of Indonesian Foreign Policy* (Canberra: Department of International Relations, Research School of Pacific Studies, Australian National University, 1963).

through this history any more because we do not want to follow the same methods.

In the present period our country has been united under the rule of the Japanese army. With the elimination of the policy of divide and rule, we, the Indonesian people, should pursue a policy of complete unification because we are now united physically and psychologically for the establishment of a unitary State of Indonesia. We do not want to suffer the same fate as has befallen Poland. In this policy of achieving the unity of our country and our people, it should be our aim to preserve our territorial integrity, that is, we must be prepared to safeguard every inch of our territory, taking all the consequences which that position involves. At the same time we do not want any of the territory of others. Although we want to promote the sovereignty of our country, we do not want to encroach upon others. . . .

As history shows, Papua and the islands adjacent to it have been inhabited by the Indonesian people since time immemorial. Part of Papua was once within the sphere of Tidore-Halmahera. Papua is within the sphere of Austronesia* which is centered on Indonesia. In the last thousand years Papua has been united to the Moluccas, at one with Indonesia. The names Merauke, Fakfak, and Digul have a familiar ring in our ears. Before the war, the island of Papua was divided into two parts, one part being ruled by the Dutch and the other being part of Australian territory. What I mean by Papua in this context is that part which used to be ruled by the Dutch. . . .

Portuguese Timor and North Borneo, being outside the territory of former Dutch rule, constitute enclaves, and enclaves should not be allowed to exist in the territory of the State of Indonesia; so, these areas should come within the control and complete the unity of the State of Indonesia. They are not only physically part of us but have been inhabited by Indonesian people since history began, forming part of our motherland.

Mr. Chairman, let me now give special attention to Area 4, namely the Malay Peninsula, including the four states of the peninsula.† The whole peninsula was part of Indonesia proper, and its original inhabitants were from the same stock as ours.

* The area of the Austronesian family of languages.

† The reference here is to Perlis, Kedah, Kelantan, and Trengganu, the four northern (unfederated) states of Malaya, which Japan ceded to Thailand soon after the Japanese conquest of Malaya.

The Chinese occupy a strong position in Malaya and a large part of the economy is in their hands. The lower positions in the country's social structure are held by Indonesians, and the country is divided into a number of states with their own governments. Before the war Perak, Negri Sembilan, Pahang, and Selangor were associated in what was called the Federated Malay States, while the others were separated from one another, with the British exercising control over all of them. The boundaries of Malaya were fixed by international agreement.

From a geo-political point of view, Malaya serves as a bridge for any power in Indo-China to proceed toward Indonesia. Conversely, the peninsula has in the past provided a bridge for Indonesian powers to cross over to the Asian mainland. It is like a natural dike separating the China Sea and the Java Sea from the Indian Ocean. The Straits of Malacca provides a passage to our islands, while the Malay Peninsula forms the neck of our Archipelago. Separating Malaya from the rest of Indonesia amounts to deliberately weakening the position of the People's State of Indonesia from the outset, as far as its international relations are concerned. On the other hand, uniting Malaya to Indonesia would mean strengthening our position and perfecting our unity in a way which accords with our national aspirations and is consistent with our geo-political interests as regards air, land, and sea. It has been the express and sincere wish of the people there to join with us. I feel that this is a most opportune moment for the people of Malaya to be reunited with the people of the State of Indonesia. . . .

The conflicts between Indonesia and Siam over Malaya will be removed, giving rise to a sense of justice, once the four states of Perlis, Kedah, Kelantan, and Trengganu are returned to their original status,* as a first step toward their reunion with the Indonesian motherland.

Mr. Chairman, let me not be accused of a policy of imperialism. If I have advocated a policy of unification extending to the northern part of Malaya and elsewhere, my efforts have not been motivated by imperialistic designs. On the contrary we are persisting in our struggle to overthrow imperialism. Every Indonesian who is dedicated to the overthrow of imperialism should fulfill his duty now. I say to the Indonesian nationalists that they should not accept a policy of allowing any part of Indonesia to be under the sovereignty of Thailand, because that represents eastern imperialism under which

* That is, taken from Siam to become part of Malaya once more.

people suffer. To the Muslims I say, let me urge upon your scholars that Malaya is part of Islamic Indonesia. Let no Muslims be ruled by Buddhist Thailand.

I know for certain that the whole population of Malaya wants to join with us. . . . I ask the learned Muslims, have you forgotten about the unity of the territory of Islam? Have you forgotten how the youth of Malaya have joined with the youth of Indonesia in Mecca and Egypt? What about the group of Indonesians who recently went to Japan? Your names are held in high esteem by the people of Malaya because you stand for unity. And our leaders, Drs. Mohammad Hatta and Ir. Sukarno, your names have spread a fragrance as far as North Borneo and Timor and throughout Malaya, springing from faith in the national policy which you have pursued, which is based on unity of territory and people, a policy broad and sincere. Let the people of Malaya not be disappointed, and let the hopes of the Indonesian youth be fulfilled!

XVb
Mohammad Hatta Let Us Not Encourage the Spirit of Expansion (1945)

This extract comes from an address of July 11, 1945, to a further plenary session of the Investigating Committee for the Preparation of Indonesian Independence. The full Indonesian text may be found in Muhammad Yamin, ed., Naskah Persiapan Undang-undang Dasar 1945 (*Drafting the 1945 Constitution*) (*n.p.: Jajasan Prapantja, 1959*), *I, 201–224.*

At the first meeting of the Investigating Committee I put forward a moderate demand on the territorial limits of Indonesia. I said then that I was asking for no more than the territory that was previously under Dutch rule.

If all that we ask for is given to us by the Japanese Government, I shall be quite happy. I have presented my views on Malaya before; as for me I would prefer to see Malaya become an independent state within the sphere of Greater East Asia. However, if the people of Malaya themselves desire to join with us, I shall have no objection to that.

Yesterday, I heard statements made about Papua which worry me somewhat, because they may very well create the impression outside that we are starting to make demands which may be regarded as imperialistic. I also heard the theory put forward yesterday that Malaya and Papua should be asked to be included in Indonesia on grounds of strategy. I am not a strategist, but my study of international politics tells me that strategy cannot stand by itself but depends on political groupings within the international sphere. For instance, Chamberlain might say that the boundary of England does not extend to the English channel only but as far as the Rhine. If this sort of argument is proceeded with, it is possible that we shall not be satisfied with just Papua, that we may want to include the Solomons and so on as far as the middle of the Pacific Ocean. Can we possibly defend such a large territory? Have we the capacity to administer the whole territory of our motherland including these new areas?

For these reasons I maintain that territorial limits are not a question that can be determined with any exactness but are merely a question of opportunity and efficiency, that is, of precise objective. Our precise objective is that area of Indonesia which was previously ruled by the Dutch. This is not only right but also corresponds to the facts of international politics; and these facts must first be recognized. So, the only question that needs to be discussed now is the transfer of power from Dutch hands to ours, which transfer will be arranged by the Japanese Government.

Besides, we should be careful about applying the theories expounded by Mr. Muhammed Yamin yesterday as regards land of birth, which in German are called theories of *Kultur und Boden.* There are great dangers here because we have seen the result of the imperialistic policies pursued by the Germans, which sprang from unrestrained passion culminating in the annexation of Austria and Czechoslovakia. In the end the Germans are suffering for their greed. So we must persuade our youth—and I myself value our youth—to think realistically, to do away with uncontrolled passion for expansion of the country and to convert that passion into constructive efforts toward the development of the nation and the defense of the country. As far as our youth are concerned, I feel that their enthusiasm should be directed to national defense. For that reason I said that the question is merely one of efficiency, of precise objective. . . .

Let us live within our own country. We have opposed imperialism all our lives. Let us not encourage our youth toward imperialism or give them the spirit of imperialism, the spirit of expansion. Let us educate our youth so that their expansive enthusiasm is converted into constructive work for the good of the country, for which so much has yet to be done.

XVc
Sjahrir   The American Orbit (1945)

This excerpt is taken from the pamphlet Our Struggle,* *written in October 1945, which presented a number of the political aspirations and diplomatic analyses on which Sjahrir was to act on assuming the Prime Ministership in the following month.*

Indonesia is situated within a circle of Anglo-American capitalist-imperialist influence. Indonesia's fate depends on the fate of Anglo-American capitalism-imperialism.

For more than a century the Dutch have controlled our country and people as a result of the calculations and determinations of British foreign policy. We know that the British took Indonesia from the Dutch in the early nineteenth century and then returned it to them; in fact, the Dutch were no longer in our country by dint of their own strength but rather by the grace of Britain and absolutely dependent on British policies. Britain pursued the same line of policy toward East Asia for more than a century, despite the rise of new powers such as Russia, Japan, and the United States and despite such new developments as the Chinese revolution. But the position did continually change, especially with respect to China.

The great change affecting our region occurred with the eviction of the Dutch from our country by the Japanese military. Japan, having been defeated, will temporarily disappear from the Southeast Asian political scene. But on the other hand, it can be said that all of Japan's position will fall into the hands of the United States, which has now become by far the largest Pacific power.

In contrast with Britain with its more than a century-old policy, America is making itself felt throughout Asia, including our country, as an innovator and champion of change. If Britain fails to adapt itself to American policies, which are themselves controlled by the laws of capitalism in America, it will certainly succumb before American power in the long run. It is clear that the power the Dutch have wielded to date has been given to them as part of the

* *Perdjoeangan Kita* (Palembang: Residency Information Office, 1946?).

British political game. It is also clear that Dutch control over our country does not have the same significance for the United States as it has for Britain. In these facts lies the possibility that we will get a new position which fits in with the political goals of the giant of the Pacific, the United States.

But these same facts limit the possibilities open to us as long as the world power structure remains imperialistic and capitalistic. So long as this remains the case, we will certainly be in and enveloped by the Anglo-American environment of imperialism-capitalism, and, however much we try, we will not be strong enough of ourselves to smash that environment to obtain complete independence for ourselves. So, the fate of Indonesia, more than that of other nations in the world, depends on the international situation and international history, and, more than other nations in the world, we need change in the basis of human society such as will do away with imperialism and capitalism.

Until this has occurred, our people's struggle will not be able to be brought to full fruition, and so, even if we obtain full independence from the Dutch, this will only be independence such as one finds in other small countries which are under the influence of the great capitalist countries, that is, independence in name only.

XVd

Tan Malaka Fighting Diplomacy (1945)

After the Japanese surrender, parts of Indonesia were occupied by British troops for limited purposes, chiefly for disarming and evacuating the Japanese. However, in the absence of de jure British recognition of the Indonesian Republic, Dutch authorities (NICA or Netherlands Indies Civil Administration) were able to return under cover of the British forces. Violent incidents occurred at many places, particularly Surabaja, where the British General Mallaby was killed on October 30, 1945. On November 10, the British launched a full-scale attack on the city. The stubborn bravery of the defenders, unavailing though it was, impressed both friend and foe. While this battle was still raging, Tan Malaka wrote his Muslihat (Strategy) *(Bukittinggi: Nusantara, 1945), of which this extract is a part.*

Britain insists, brothers, that the Indonesian people and the army of the Republic lay down their arms. The people and the army of the

Indonesian Republic have to get down on their knees and hand over all their weapons. Only the people of a state willing to give up the right to freedom and willing to be humiliated and treated like slaves would be prepared to comply with such a demand. The British were not asked by the Allied Forces to disarm the Indonesian people but to disarm the Japanese army. Even if they had been asked to disarm us, there would be no necessity whatsoever for Indonesia to humiliate itself by acquiescing to a British demand of this kind which conflicts with the sovereignty of an independent people. Since August 17, Indonesia has been an independent country. The seventy million people of Indonesia affirm and support this independence with all that is in them.

Is it fitting for the people of an independent state to allow themselves to be disarmed? One of the first prerequisites for an independent country is the freedom to want to and to be able to defend its independence. This freedom will cease to exist altogether if the people no longer have their arms.

The British came here not to disarm the Japanese army but to disarm the Indonesian people. It would be very easy for them to intimidate an unarmed people, and it would be easy for the Dutch administration which British Imperialism is now readying to colonize Indonesia, to trample on such a people and cut them to pieces. Once the NICA Government has been firmly reestablished and is again colonizing Indonesia, then the British hope to get back their estates, mines, factories, and shops. These are the real motives of the British.

However much the British may deny the charges made by us and many others in the world that they are trying to restore colonialism to Indonesia, all the evidence reveals that this is in fact what the British want to do. And furthermore, all the British possessions in Africa and Asia bear witness to the lies, cunning, and brutality of the British in matters of colonialism.

The words of British imperialism are like the words of a prostitute: they should never be believed. Indonesian independence will be crushed if we listen to their pretexts and their advice. As long as British troops remain on Indonesian soil, we must regard their promises as nothing but tricks.

But the people of Surabaja refuse to listen to these demands and pretexts of the representatives of British imperialism. Although they are not jurists, the people of Surabaja are fully aware of the rights of an independent people. The people of Surabaja are holding weapons in their hands; and with weapons in their hands, they will defend their independence. This is a manly stand to take. It is a wise attitude, based on consciousness of one's own rights, of one's own responsibilities, and of one's own self-respect. Anyone who fails to adopt such a stand does not want to be free and has no self-respect whatsoever. Such a person is a slave or a secret agent of NICA. Basically he is a traitor.

Some people complain that we cannot resist the mighty tanks, the warships, and the airplanes of the British. My answer to that is: Have we not withstood a continual shower of bullets for three weeks already? How many losses has the enemy sustained during those three weeks? What victory has the enemy won during those three weeks? Can the British and the Dutch run their factories, shops, or estates in the regions they occupy? For as long as they are unable to make profits from exploiting the blood and sweat of the Indonesian people, the seizure of a few hectares of land will only add to their difficulties. Every single piece of land that they wrest from us must be defended night and day against the onslaught of the Indonesian people and army. The costs of defending all this grow larger and larger every day. Day after day, the British and NICA will feel the sharpness of Indonesian people's weapons which are no less sharp than any other weapons. Economic weapons employed together with uninterrupted guerrilla attacks are not weapons to be ignored, despite the fact that the British are thoroughly well armed.

Even should the British and NICA be able to capture all the towns along this coast, this would still not mean that they have been victorious! They would still have very far to go. As long as the Indonesian people are united, disciplined, and well aware of the tactics they must employ and also absolutely convinced of the righteousness of their cause and the wrongness of the enemy's cause, the British and NICA will never get farther than the beginning stage. In Magelang where naval forces can play no part, the British have been defeated. Defeated, Brothers! What does it mean if the most modern army in the world, an army that has had much experience in modern warfare, is being defeated, driven out, or destroyed by the Indonesian people and an army who have no officers, no weapons, and hardly any training?

There is no need for me to speak to our Indonesian soldiers about the events in Magelang, events that are of profound importance to Indonesian history, but I should like once again to ask all those grumblers, moaners, and cowards who are full of doubts about anything vaguely connected with Indonesia: what is the significance of the Magelang victory? And, I should like to add, it is not only in Magelang that the Indonesian people and army have scored victory in battle against the British-NICA army. Wherever troops fight against troops, Indonesia wins. There are no exceptions. The British and NICA have never scored a single victory against the Indonesians. The only victories that have been scored were won by extra special weapons such as cannons on warships firing from right out in the middle of the sea or planes flying very high.

Things will be even worse for them in our last bulwark, in the mountains that span the entire Indonesian Archipelago, for there the British and NICA will be face to face with the real thing. In those places, their cannons and fleets of warships will be quite meaningless. In the mountains, the bombs dropped by planes will be quite insignificant. In the mountains, the Indonesian army will lie in waiting like tigers waiting for their prey in places advantageous to them and highly disastrous to the enemy. Should the British-NICA succeed in occupying all the towns, the Indonesian guerrillas will launch continual attacks against these towns from the mountains. That is to say, if the British and NICA can occupy towns destroyed by fire and deprived of food and water. In these burnt-out towns, the British-NICA will have to suffer guerrilla attacks at night and hunger in the daytime.

Who can believe that the British-NICA would be able to occupy such hellish towns for even a year? To live by day and by night in danger, lacking food, sleep, and pleasure? And to have the complaints and condemnation of the world drumming on your ears? . . .

Do not forget that besides being important for international communications, Indonesia is also an important factor in the reconstruction of the badly-damaged world economy. Raw materials from Indonesia are needed in all the civilized countries of the world. The civilized world's longing for peace, the Indonesian proletariat's hatred, the colonized peoples' hatred for imperialism, and their desire for independence are all favorable to the struggling Indonesian people.

This is our diplomacy! Fighting diplomacy! In this way we arouse a sense of righteousness and justice abroad as well as at home. In this way, we shall separate the imperialists from the peace party. Not the diplomacy of compromise, the diplomacy of the bended knee, which would bewilder the world proletariat and the colonized peoples. The diplomacy of the bended knee is anathema to the civilized people of the world who are conscious of the right of every nation to independence and are full of respect for other nations that defend their own dignity.

The weaklings, the doubters, the pessimists, just like the traitors, have all sorts of excuses. "Oh," they say, "have pity on the people who must make all the sacrifices!" But are not the British and NICA to blame for all these sacrifices? Is it not imperialism that is always ready to sacrifice tens of millions of human beings in the pursuit of its policies? In what era, in which country has "independence" been won and defended by the diplomacy of the conference hall and not with the sacrifice of dozens, nay, often millions of human beings?

And furthermore, what does it matter if Indonesian "weapons" bring about the sacrifice of two or three million people for the cause of independence of the remaining sixty-eight million? Is it not a fact that during the security (!) and calm of the Japanese occupation, three or four million people fell victims?

If Indonesia were afraid to sacrifice one or two million people today, assuming that such great sacrifices would indeed be necessary in our struggle which, of course, is not what the Indonesian people themselves want, then in the future, the seventy million people of Indonesia would be sacrificed forever to enslavement in the estates, factories, and mines of foreigners.

And Indonesia is not the only one to make sacrifices in the struggle to defend its inalienable right to independence, the natural right of all people. Those who violate our independence must also make sacrifices. They, too, must sacrifice material wealth, lives, and time. And finally, you should not forget that the British and the Dutch are sacrificing their reputation as civilized nations. The moment the civilized world denounces them for their actions against a nation whose only fault is to defend its right, then victory is in the hands of Indonesia.

Indonesia will struggle on till that moment comes, till the desperados and the colonizers give up!

The tactics of the Indonesian people are to wage a protracted struggle, to reject doing anything reckless, hasty, fanatical, or impetuous. With hearts as steady as iron, with cool heads and finally, with strong wills and powerful conviction, the Indonesian people wait for the dawn of victory to break!

XVe
Mohammad Hatta An Independent Active
Foreign Policy (1953)

*As Prime Minister of Indonesia in 1948, Mohammad Hatta had pre-
sented what was perhaps the earliest full formulation of the "independ-
end foreign policy," the policy of nonalignment in the world's power
blocs which was taken as central to foreign policy action until, roughly,
1962. In this extract from the American quarterly* Foreign Affairs *of
April 1953,* he presents a fairly full range of arguments for the policy
from a rather anticommunist point of view.*

The Republic of Indonesia realizes that cooperation with other countries is essential if [the twin ideals of social justice and prosperity] are
to become a reality. It has made the United Nations the focal point
of its over-all policy of seeking good relations with all other nations.

More specifically, its objectives in foreign policy are: (1) to defend
the freedom of the people and guard the safety of the state; (2) to
obtain from overseas those articles of daily necessity required for increasing the standard of living of the population—food, especially rice,
consumer goods of various kinds, medicines, and so on; (3) to obtain
capital equipment to rebuild what has been destroyed or damaged,
and capital for industrialization, new construction, and the partial
mechanization of agriculture; (4) to strengthen principles of international law and to aid in achieving social justice on an international
scale, in line with the United Nations' Charter, with special reference
to Articles 1, 2, and 55, in particular by endeavoring within the U.N.
framework to help people still living within the colonial system to
achieve freedom; (5) to place special emphasis on initiating good
relations with neighboring countries, the majority of which have in
the past occupied a position similar to Indonesia's; and (6) to seek
fraternity among nations through realization of the ideals enshrined
in the Pantja Sila which constitute the basic Indonesian philosophy.
In short, Indonesia will pursue a policy of peace and of friendship
with all nations on a basis of mutual respect and noninterference with
each other's structure of government.

As a people just become free from colonialism, Indonesians are

* Excerpted by special permission from *Foreign Affairs*, XXXI (April 1953);
copyright by the Council on Foreign Relations, Inc., New York.

jealous of their country's independence. Slogans such as "liberty," "humanity," "social justice," "the brotherhood of nations," and "lasting peace," which were a sustaining force in the Indonesian national movement, are looked upon as ideals to be translated into practice. The Indonesian people, therefore, place a high value on international intercourse and are confident that what they long for in this respect will eventually become a reality. All these feelings help determine the country's foreign policy and the means employed to carry it out.

It is possible that, viewed from the angle of *Realpolitik*, some of these aims seem to lie outside the realm of "real and practical policy." The student of history, however, is conscious that much which was previously considered Utopian or impossible has come to pass. Who would have believed fifteen years ago that India, Burma, Ceylon, Pakistan, and Indonesia would become independent and sovereign? Who would then have thought it possible that Indonesia, assisted by the Netherlands itself, would be accepted as a member of an international organization such as the United Nations? . . .

Talk of the brotherhood of man in a world in which racial discrimination makes possible the existence of such a policy as apartheid, or talk of everlasting peace in the atmosphere of the Cold War indeed seems incongruous. Be that as it may, the Republic of Indonesia feels it its duty to strengthen the ideals of peace, however weak its voice or feeble its power. It believes that these ideals will become reality in the long run. It believes in the common sense of mankind. The people's desire for peace, as opposed to their lust for war, becomes stronger from century to century. Evil often prevails over the forces for good and destroys what civilization has built up over the ages. But man, rational by nature, will eventually make a positive and definite choice of good over evil, peace over war. The discovery of weapons of war which become progressively more terrifying and destructive will strengthen men's love of peace and arouse hatred of war. It is this conviction that leads the Republic of Indonesia to believe that the struggle for world peace is today a policy based on reality.

This explains why the Republic of Indonesia has not aligned itself with either the American bloc or the Russian bloc in the existing conflict, and why it is not prepared to participate in any third bloc designed to act as a counterpoise to the two giant blocs. To do that would merely create new suspicions and new enmities. And though Indonesia's policy has often been termed one of neutrality, it is not that, either. "Neutrality" has a precise meaning in international law, defining a condition of impartiality toward belligerent states. Writing in the *Encyclopaedia of Social Sciences,* Philip C. Jessup states that "the modern legal status of neutrality implies the impartiality of one state toward two or more belligerent states." And he says, truly, that "It may well be argued that in the present or future conditions of world solidarity, neutrality is an antisocial status." As a member of the United Nations, the Republic of Indonesia cannot adopt an attitude of neutrality. It is committed to international solidarity. Articles 41 and 43 of the U.N. Charter do not give any option to the course of action open to a member when the Security Council has declared the behavior of another state to be unlawful.

But in practice, of course, international solidarity has not been achieved; world solidarity has cracked into two pieces. Under present conditions it would not be possible for Indonesia to be other than neutral if a war broke out. The existence of war is a special case in the life of nations.

Unfortunately, Indonesia has to face a situation entirely different from the one forecast during the years of World War II. The world envisaged then is reflected in the ideology of the Charter, but the postwar world is characterized by the conflict between the American and the Soviet blocs. The opposition between the two, due to different economic systems, has been heightened by a conflict of ideologies in every particular. The Cold War is an ideological war—the "free world" versus "the people's democracies." The Western countries with similar culture and political concepts seek safety alongside the United States, which possesses great economic and industrial power. The Communist states behind the Iron Curtain form a compact bloc stretching from Central Europe to the Pacific Ocean and covering a large portion of Asia, with a total population of not less than eight hundred million souls—an almost limitless reserve of manpower for their armed forces. In such a situation, international life is dominated by power politics.

Western nations tend to hold that there is no middle position for the weaker countries, and that they must choose between the one bloc or the other. It seems logical to them that nations which desire to enjoy independence should choose the free world, and they remind neutral countries of the fate of Belgium and the Netherlands in the Second World War. As already stated, however, the policy of the Republic of Indonesia is not one of neutrality because it is not constructed in reference to belligerent states but for the purpose of strengthening and upholding peace. Indonesia plays no favorites between the two opposed blocs and follows its own path through the various international problems. It terms this policy "independent," and further characterizes it by describing it as independent and "active." By active is meant the effort to work energetically for the preservation of peace and the relaxation of tension generated by the two blocs, through endeavors supported if possible by the majority of the members of the United Nations. As an illustration of this policy may be cited the efforts made by Indonesia, in concert with the Arab and Asian countries, to put an end to the war in Korea.

This island archipelago is in a very different kind of position from that in which the Netherlands and Belgium found themselves at the beginning of World War II. It does not share a common boundary with any of the possible belligerents. Indonesia, it may be said, is bounded by the British Navy and the American Navy, which control the Indian and Pacific Oceans. But no one can say that Britain and the United States have evil designs on Indonesia. On the contrary, they are desirous of seeing Indonesia remain independent and become prosperous. Are they not the very people who hold that the infiltration of Communism can be prevented only by raising the economic level of the masses?

Further, Indonesia does not have common frontiers with Soviet Russia or China. A direct threat from that direction to Indonesian independence neither exists nor is possible. Only the domestic Communist movement is a political factor in Indonesia, but in this regard Indonesia's position is no different from that of the other democratic countries. Consequently, there is no pressing need for her to make a choice between the two big blocs. Her independent policy keeps her from enmity with either party, preserves her from the damage to her own interests that would follow from taking sides, and permits her to be friends with all nations on a basis of mutual respect. The desire to put political relations with other nations on a footing of mutual respect, despite differences of governmental structure and ideology, is a primary factor in this approach to international relations. Nations recently become independent are strongly influenced by national sentiment and feel the need to maintain their self-respect. The memory of the colonial status that bound them for centuries makes them resist anything they consider an attempt to colonize them again, whether by economic or ideological domination. This psychological factor profoundly influences Indonesia in her insistence upon an independent policy. . . .

As a young state not possessed of sufficient military strength to defend the multitude of islands, large and small, which compose its territory, the Republic seeks to safeguard its independence. Its armed forces are wholly defensive; its foreign policy aims to prevent the country from being attacked. Indonesians believe that the possibility of attack will be minimized so long as the country adheres to its independent policy and actively tries to prevent the outbreak of World War III. . . .

Internal consolidation is the primary task. The Government must concentrate on the task of building-up the nation, and it must show evidence of economic and social betterment if it is to offset the influence of agitation by radical circles. A foreign policy that aligned the country with either bloc of the Great Powers would render this internal task infinitely more difficult.

Influencing this decision to pursue an independent policy is, again, the historic ideal of peace and friendship with all races which is so deeply imbedded in the Indonesian people. And it is reinforced by the objective facts of Indonesia's geographical situation. Nature has ordained that Indonesia, lying between two continents—the Asian mainland and Australia—and washed by the waters of two vast oceans—the Indian and the Pacific—must maintain intercourse with lands stretching in a great circle around it. From time immemorial, it has had relationships with all of them, varied as they are. Its position at the very heart of a network of communications has for centuries made the archipelago a halting place for all races and a staging base in international travel. When one considers that the territory of Indonesia extends for more than three thousand miles and is composed of thousands of islands, large and small, the magnitude of the problem of maintaining the security of the country is apparent. So extensive an area cannot be defended purely by military strength.

For economic reasons, also, Indonesia must have relationships with diverse countries. The land is rich in natural resources and raw materials, but the country has not reached the stage where it can convert its raw materials into finished industrial goods. A large portion of its economy is still dependent on exports. Indonesia cannot possibly reconcile herself to being tied to the economies of a few nations, all the more so because certain articles of export such as rubber are subject to much fluctuation in price. Only by adhering to a peaceful yet independent policy can Indonesia adequately safeguard its economic interests.

XVf

Sukarno   Let a New Asia and Africa Be Born (1955)

President Sukarno spoke these words in his opening address to the Asian-African Conference held at Bandung in April 1955. The full text is available in Selected Documents: Some Aspects Concerning Progress and Principles of the Indonesian Revolution (*Djakarta-Department of Information,* 1961[?]).

As I survey this hall and the distinguished guests gathered here, my heart is filled with emotion. This is the first intercontinental conference of colored peoples in the history of mankind! I am proud that my country is your host. I am happy that you were able to accept the invitations extended by the five Sponsoring Countries. But, also, I cannot restrain feelings of sadness when I recall the tribulations through which many of our peoples have so recently passed, tribulations which have exacted a heavy toll in life, in material things, and in the things of the spirit.

I recognize that we are gathered here today as a result of sacrifices. Sacrifices made by our forefathers and by the people of our own and younger generations. For me, this hall is filled not only by the leaders of the nations of Asia and Africa; it also contains within its walls the undying, the indomitable, the invincible spirit of those who went before us. Their struggle and sacrifice paved the way for this meeting of the highest representatives of independent and sovereign nations from two of the biggest continents of the globe.

It is a new departure in the history of the world that leaders of Asian and African peoples can meet together in their own countries to discuss and deliberate upon matters of common concern. Only a few decades ago it was frequently necessary to travel to other countries and even other continents before the spokesmen of our peoples could confer. . . .

Indeed, I am proud that my country is your host.

But my thoughts are not wholly of the honor which is Indonesia's today. No. My mind is for a part darkened by other considerations.

You have not gathered together in a world of peace and unity and cooperation. Great chasms yawn between nations and groups of nations. Our unhappy world is torn and tortured, and the peoples of all countries walk in fear lest, through no fault of theirs, the dogs of war are unchained once again.

And if, in spite of all that the peoples may do, this should happen, what then? What of our newly recovered independence then? What of our culture, what of our spiritual heritage, what of our ancient civilization? What of our children and our parents?

The burden of the delegates to this Conference is not a light one, for I know that these questions—which are questions of the life or death of humanity itself—must be on your minds, as they are on mine. And the nations of Asia and Africa cannot, even if they wish to, avoid their part in finding solutions to these problems.

For that is part of the duties of independence itself. That is part of the price we gladly pay for our independence. For many generations our peoples have been the voiceless ones in the world. We have been the unregarded, the peoples for whom decisions were made by others whose interests were paramount, the peoples who lived in poverty and humiliation. Then our nations demanded, nay fought for independence, and achieved independence, and with that independence came responsibilities to ourselves, and to the world, and to the yet unborn generations. But we do not regret them.

In 1945, the first year of our national revolution, we of Indonesia were confronted with the question of what we were going to do with our independence when it was finally attained and secured—we never questioned that it would be attained and secured. We knew how to oppose and destroy. Then we were suddenly confronted with the necessity of giving content and meaning to our independence. Not material content and meaning only but also ethical and moral content, for independence without ethics and without morality would be, indeed, a poor imitation of what we sought. The responsibilities and burdens, the rights and duties and privileges of independence must be seen as part of the ethical and moral content of independence.

Indeed, we welcome the change which places new burdens upon us, and we are all resolved to exert all our strength and courage in carrying these burdens.

Sisters and Brothers, how terrifically dynamic is our time! I recall that, several years ago, I had occasion to make a public analysis of colonialism, and that I then drew attention to what I called the "life line of imperialism." This line runs from the Straits of Gibraltar, through the Mediterranean, the Suez Canal, the Red Sea, the Indian Ocean, the South China Sea, and the Sea of Japan. For most of that enormous distance, the territories on both sides of this life line were colonies; the peoples were unfree, their futures mortgaged to an alien system. Along that life line, that main artery of imperialism, there was pumped the life blood of colonialism.

And, today, in this hall, are gathered together the leaders of those same peoples. They are no longer the victims of colonialism. They are no longer the tools of others and the playthings of forces they cannot influence. Today, you are representatives of free peoples, peoples of a different stature and standing in the world.

Yes, there has indeed been a "Sturm über Asien"—and over Africa, too. The last few years have seen enormous changes. Nations, states, have awoken from a sleep of centuries. The passive peoples have gone, the outward tranquility has given way to struggle and activity. Irresistible forces have swept the two continents. The mental, spiritual, and political face of the whole world has been changed, and the process is still not complete. There are new conditions, new concepts, new problems, new ideals abroad in the world. Hurricanes of national awakening and reawakening have swept over the land, shaking it, changing it, changing it for the better.

This twentieth century has been a period of terrific dynamism. Perhaps the last fifty years have seen more developments and more material progress than the previous five hundred years. Man has learned to control many of the scourges which once threatened him. He has learned to consume distance. He has learned to project his voice and his picture across oceans and continents. He has probed deep into the secrets of nature and learned how to make the desert bloom and the plants of the earth increase their bounty. He has learned how to release the immense forces locked in the smallest particles of matter.

But has man's political skill marched hand in hand with his technical and scientific skill? Man can chain lightning to his command— can he control the society in which he lives? The answer is No! The political skill of man has been far outstripped by his technical skill, and what he has made he cannot be sure of controlling.

The result of this is fear. And man gasps for safety and morality.

Perhaps now more than at any other moment in the history of the world, society, government, and statesmanship need to be based upon the highest code of morality and ethics. And in political terms, what is the highest code of morality? It is the subordination of everything to the well-being of mankind. But, today, we are faced with a situation where the well-being of mankind is not always the primary consideration. Many who are in places of high power think, rather, of controlling the world.

Yes, we are living in a world of fear. The life of man today is corroded and made bitter by fear: fear of the future, fear of the hydrogen bomb, fear of ideologies. Perhaps this fear is a greater danger than the danger itself, because it is fear which drives men to act thoughtlessly, to act dangerously.

In your deliberations, Sisters and Brothers, I beg of you, do not be guided by these fears, because fear is an acid which etches man's actions into curious patterns. Be guided by hopes and determination, be guided by ideals, and, yes, be guided by dreams!

We are of many different nations, we are of many different social backgrounds and cultural patterns. Our ways of life are different. Our national characters, or colors or motifs—call it what you will—are different. Our racial stock is different, and even the color of our skin is different. But what does that matter? Mankind is united or divided by considerations other than these. Conflict comes not from variety of skins, nor from variety of religion, but from variety of desires.

All of us, I am certain, are united by more important things than those which superficially divide us. We are united, for instance, by a common detestation of colonialism in whatever form it appears. We are united by a common detestation of racialism. And we are united by a common determination to preserve and stabilize peace in the world. Are not these aims mentioned in the letter of invitation to which you responded?

I freely confess it—in these aims I am not disinterested or driven by purely impersonal motives.

How is it possible to be disinterested about colonialism? For us, colonialism is not something far and distant. We have known it in all its ruthlessness. We have seen the immense human wastage it causes, the poverty it causes, and the heritage it leaves behind when, eventually and reluctantly, it is driven out by the inevitable march of history. My people and the peoples of many nations of Asia and Africa know these things, for we have experienced them.

Indeed, we cannot yet say that all parts of our countries are free already. Some parts still labor under the lash. And some parts of Asia and Africa which are not represented here still suffer from the same condition.

Yes, some parts of our nations are not yet free. That is why all of us cannot yet feel that journey's end has been reached. No people can feel themselves free, so long as part of their motherland is unfree. Like peace, freedom is indivisible. There is no such thing as being half free, as there is no such thing as being half alive.

We are often told "Colonialism is dead." Let us not be deceived or even soothed by that. I say to you, colonialism is not yet dead. How can we say it is dead, so long as vast areas of Asia and Africa are unfree.

And, I beg of you, do not think of colonialism only in the classic form which we of Indonesia and our brothers in different parts of Asia and Africa knew. Colonialism has also its modern dress, in the form of economic control, intellectual control, actual physical control by a small but alien community within a nation. It is a skilful and determined enemy, and it appears in many guises. It does not give up its loot easily. Wherever, whenever, and however it appears, colonialism is an evil thing and one which must be eradicated from the earth.

The battle against colonialism has been a long one, and do you know that today is a famous anniversary in that battle? On the eighteenth day of April, 1775, just one hundred eighty years ago, Paul Revere rode at midnight through the New England countryside, warning of the approach of British troops and of the opening of the American War of Independence, the first successful anticolonial war in history. About this midnight ride the poet Longfellow wrote:

> A cry of defiance and not of fear,
> A voice in the darkness, a knock at the door,
> And a word that shall echo for evermore.

Yes, it shall echo for evermore, just as the other anticolonial words which gave us comfort and reassurance during the darkest days of our struggle shall echo for evermore. But remember, that battle which began 180 years ago is not yet completely won, and it will not have been completely won until we can survey this our own world, and can say that colonialism is dead.

So, I am not disinterested when I speak of the fight against colonialism.

Nor am I disinterested when I speak of the battle for peace. How can any of us be disinterested about peace?

Not so very long ago we argued that peace was necessary for us because an outbreak of fighting in our part of the world would imperil our precious independence, so recently won at such great cost.

Today, the picture is more black. War would not only mean a threat to our independence; it could mean the end of civilization and even of human life. There is a force loose in the world whose potentiality for evil no man truly knows. Even in practice and rehearsal for war the effects may well be building-up into something of unknown horror.

Not so long ago it was possible to take some little comfort from the idea that the clash, if it came, could perhaps be settled by what were called "conventional weapons"—bombs, tanks, cannon, and men. Today, that little grain of comfort is denied us, for it has been made clear that the weapons of ultimate horror will certainly be used, and the military planning of nations is on that basis. The unconventional has become the conventional, and who knows what other examples of misguided and diabolical scientific skill have been discovered as a plague on humanity.

And do not think that the oceans and the seas will protect us. The food that we eat, the water that we drink, yes, even the very air that we breathe can be contaminated by poisons originating from thousands of miles away. And it could be that, even if we ourselves escaped lightly, the unborn generations of our children would bear on their distorted bodies the marks of our failure to control the forces which have been released on the world.

No task is more urgent than that of preserving peace. Without peace our independence means little. The rehabilitation and upbuilding of our countries will have little meaning. Our revolutions will not be allowed to run their course.

What can we do? The peoples of Asia and Africa wield little physical power. Even their economic strength is dispersed and slight. We cannot indulge in power politics. Diplomacy for us is not a matter of the big stick. Our statesmen, by and large, are not backed up with serried ranks of jet bombers.

What can we do? We can do much! We can inject the voice of reason into world affairs. We can mobilize all the spiritual, all the moral, all the political strength of Asia and Africa on the side of peace. Yes, we! We, the peoples of Asia and Africa, one billion, four hundred million strong, far more than half the human population of the world, we can mobilize what I have called the Moral Violence of Nations in favor of peace. We can demonstrate to the minority of the world which lives on the other continents that we, the majority, are for peace, not for war, and that whatever strength we have will always be thrown on to the side of peace.

In this struggle, some success has already been scored. I think it is generally recognized that the activity of the Prime Ministers of the Sponsoring Countries* which invited you here had a not unimportant role to play in ending the fighting in Indo-China.

Look! The peoples of Asia raised their voices, and the world listened. It was no small victory and no negligible precedent! The five Prime Ministers did not make threats; they issued no ultimatum; they mobilized no troops. Instead, they consulted together, discussed the issues, pooled their ideas, added together their individual political skills and came forward with sound and reasoned suggestions which formed the basis for a settlement of the long struggle in Indo-China.

I have often since then asked myself why these five were successful when others, with long records of diplomacy, were unsuccessful and, in fact, had allowed a bad situation to get worse, so that there was a danger of the conflict spreading. Was it because they were Asian? Maybe that is part of the answer, for the conflagration was on their doorstep, and any extension of it would have presented an immediate threat to their own houses. But I think that the answer really lies in the fact that those five Prime Ministers brought a fresh approach to bear on the problem. They were not seeking advantage for their own countries. They had no axe of power-politics to grind. They had but one interest—how to end the fighting in such a way that the chances of continuing peace and stability were enhanced.

That, my Sisters and Brothers, was an historic occasion. Some countries of free Asia spoke, and the world listened. They spoke on a subject of immediate concern to Asia and in doing so made it quite clear that the affairs of Asia are the concern of the Asian peoples themselves. The days are now long past when the future of Asia could be settled by other and distant peoples.

However, we cannot, we dare not, confine our interests to the affairs of our own continents. The states of the world today depend one upon the other and no nation can be an island unto itself. Splendid isolation may once have been possible; it is so no longer. The affairs of all the world are our affairs, and our future depends upon the solutions found to all international problems, however far or distant they may seem.

---

* The "Colombo Powers": Burma, Ceylon, India, Indonesia, and Pakistan.

XVg
Subandrio Revolutionary Diplomacy (1962)

This is part of an address which Dr. Subandrio, as Minister of Foreign Affairs, gave to trainees of his Department on February 8, 1962, at a time when the politico-diplomatic struggle for West Irian was being waged with great intensity. The full English text is in Subandrio, Indonesia on the March *(Djakarta: Department of Foreign Affairs, 1963), II, 266–292.*

The idea of diplomacy as an instrument of revolution is something new, arising in the twentieth century. We will not come across this aspect of diplomacy in either the textbooks or diplomatic manuals of the West. So, in this matter we are certainly able to contribute new thinking to the ideas and practices of diplomacy as these have been developed up to now by Western states. We should recognize that there are no written rules for us as yet for the practice of this aspect of diplomacy. We still have to formulate them ourselves on the basis of the experiences we gather as we go along.

But it is obvious that, first of all, our diplomatic officers must truly understand and comprehend that we are conducting two aspects of diplomacy: conventional diplomacy and diplomacy as an instrument of revolution, the one complementing the other, each giving content to the other. Without this to hold by, our diplomats will float rudderless between the magnetism of the two great ideologies now clashing one against the other or will be influenced by one or other of those two ideologies. Without an understanding of the character and the basic objectives of the National Revolution of their own state, without an understanding of the character and the basic objectives of the Revolution of three-quarters of mankind, without an understanding of the direct connections between national interests and the principles of the National Revolution, which must be reflected in the field of international relations in the diplomacy of a given state, our diplomats will be drowned in the mere formalities of conventional diplomacy.

Therefore, should it, for instance, be necessary to choose between a candidate diplomat who is skilled only in the technical knowledge of diplomacy and a candidate who understands only this second aspect of diplomacy, my choice would fall upon the second candidate, since technical knowledge can be learnt in six months, but for a true understanding of this second aspect conviction and comprehension are needed, and these cannot be taught.

Thus, we should not concern ourselves with whether a person is a career diplomat or not, for it is not important, and for us it is beside the point. What is important is a thorough awareness of these two aspects in our diplomacy.

In the conduct of diplomacy in these two aspects, it is not enough if we only make careful investigations of developments in the economic and financial sector of some state and of current trends in its policies or its public opinion, and then, upon the basis of those factors, struggle for our interests in the best way possible. This is certainly the basis of conventional diplomacy, namely a prudent reckoning up of known and unknown factors, on the assumption that the more known factors that can be obtained, the more telling will our diplomacy be and the better will our national interests be served. But over and above this we need to study fully the great currents alive in the world, to fathom the administrative and economic systems of other states with an independent eye and an approach directed to their sources. . . .

This study must not be motivated by and based upon some negative attitude, of looking for mistakes or shortcomings, of developing an attitude of anti-this or anti-that. This investigation must be based solely upon the search for new thoughts, new ideas which can be useful for us ourselves, which can enrich our own system. In the reverse direction, our diplomats should also make contributions from the ideas and formulations which we have found for ourselves and the validity of which has been tested in our national way of life, so that in this way a two-way traffic of ideas will be obtained. This is a positive attitude and an example of the practice of diplomacy as an instrument of revolution.

In studying the great currents that are alive in the world, all of which seek true happiness and equilibrium based upon justice— whether justice based upon religion or justice based solely upon logic —it is certain that the newest current which has great influence in the world needs to obtain our special attention. I refer to the current of Marxism. In this matter I wish to remind you not to belittle Marxism too readily, not to turn too stony a gaze upon the "specter" of communism. To adopt a negative attitude is indeed easy. Establishing a positive attitude, no matter what it is, is far more difficult. This is why in our own politics we do not go in for anticommunist crusades but give the people a progressive national ideology of our own. Certainly, it is easy to be anticolonialist but to give content to a national independence that has been taken by storm through an anticolonial struggle is far more difficult. A study of the current of Marxism is strongly to be recommended, not for negative aims, but precisely in order to obtain new ideas that can be useful for the development of our own national way of life.

Once we have understood the way of thinking that lies at the back of our national way of life and which we then project abroad in our international relations, we should study what it is that is the basis of our national way of thinking. We will see that what we desire is basically a society that is socially just and prosperous, materially and spiritually, based upon both religious and logical understanding. This is implied in our Pantja Sila and in our Political Manifesto. And there is not a person in the world who can raise objections to this aspiration.

What happens when this line of thought is projected into the field of international relations? It means that we wish for international relations that are likewise based upon justice; in other words, relations among nations that are not based upon power, power politics, or the "law of the jungle." In our diplomacy it is certain that we will oppose, for instance, the opinion that contracts from former times that were customarily applied on the basis of compulsion by states of larger size continue to possess legality. According to the old view, even colonialism itself was "legal," similarly also with "protectorates" and the rest. In this connection, also, all the old concepts in international law need to obtain our very careful reconsideration.

Continuing our thinking in this direction, we reach the conclusion that Indonesia's ideals for a just and prosperous society are dependent on the growth of other states in the direction of a new world based upon that justice. We cannot bring about the growth of a just and prosperous Indonesia if the world does not also grow in that direction. *Men kan geen rijkdom kweken in een zee van armoede.** In other words, in our diplomacy we struggle for the practice of international relations based not upon power but upon justice, for the sake of our own growth.

That is why, apart from the question of which ideology is followed, we refer to ourselves at the present time as being grouped in "the new emerging forces," opposing "the old established forces"; the one positive, struggling toward a new world based upon justice; the other negative, trying to maintain itself as far as possible but, nevertheless,

* You cannot grow riches in a field of poverty.

being gradually forced to adapt itself to the rapid developments in the world.

This concept does *not* mean that we attack some specific state or nation or a particular group of states. Within the very body of a given nation, no matter how conservative it may be, it is certain that there are new emerging forces, and with them we have a common basis of struggle.

These aspects ought to be thoroughly understood by our diplomats in order that their outlook does not become foggy. To give an example, it can probably be said that in conventional diplomatic relations we are closer to West Germany or the United States of America, but that with, say, the Soviet Union, we have relations based on the other aspect, namely, that we are together grouped with it in "the new emerging forces."

XVh

Achmad Yani The Doctrine of Revolutionary War (1965)

This piece is taken from an address of March 3, 1965, given to the Command and Staff College, Quetta, Pakistan, and expresses the new military doctrine being developed at this time as a counterpart to the doctrine of the New Emerging Forces. Lieutenant General Yani spoke as Minister and Commander in Chief of the Army. The speech was published as The Indonesian Army's Doctrine of War (*Djakarta: Indonesian Army Information Service, 1965*). *We have made minor verbal changes in the text.*

After we acquired international recognition of our Republic (1949), we had to face what we call "time bombs" left by retreating colonialism. On top of that came a serious uprising in 1958, supported (as was admitted later on) by those Western powers dominating Southeast Asia. This finally and thoroughly convinced us that we still have a long, long struggle ahead of us, which for us can only end with the final retreat of those powers trying to regain their domination. We are fully involved in this struggle right now, as we have been constantly for the past twenty-five years. (Since 1940, Indonesia has never known real peace.)

With all that ahead of us, we were compelled to formulate a defense concept or rather a doctrine to serve our Revolution and its objectives. It must be aimed not only at the pure defense of our Republic but at our national security in general, which includes the elimination of any direct threat to that security.

What then constitutes that threat?

As I have stated before, no class or power has ever surrendered its privileges voluntarily; so, neither do we expect the dominating powers to do. They will try to maintain their political and economic domination, if necessary by the threat or use of military force. The presence of foreign bases with their striking forces around us we consider to be this very threat, as we have experienced several years ago.

Now, one may maintain that those foreign bases are designed to protect us against communism. You as well as I know that never have steel walls succeeded in preventing an idea or ideas from penetrating and developing. It is in men's minds that battles of ideas are won or lost and not along frontiers of steel and concrete. Look only at what has happened in China and Algeria and at what is still happening in Vietnam to see if this holds true. So, although not capable of preventing what they are intended to, those foreign bases do constitute a real threat to us. They will not seriously and immediately endanger our very existence, but being used to assist in maintaining the old order, they do impose serious limitations on our free development.

Therefore, our defense doctrine consists of two main aspects: the defense of the country itself, if ever attacked; and the elimination of any direct threat to our security. We are fully aware that the second aspect does present a certain danger, but we just cannot escape it, for the sake of our own security. We do not seek war, since this is incompatible with the philosophy of Pantja Sila and with the very character of our Revolution; we will constantly seek for peaceful ways, but if war is forced upon us, we will accept it without hesitation.

It this doctrine aggressive?

Let us define what is called aggression. A century ago, when the speed and range of weapons of war were very limited, an act of aggression always coincided with crossings of a border. With the modern tools of today, however, with their enormous speed, range, and destructive power, we do not any more enjoy the comfort and safety of former space and distance factors. In this sense the mere presence of a striking force within striking distance already constitutes a serious threat and is, thus, in other words, an act of aggression. In this context any effort to eliminate this threat is nothing else but a defensive effort. That it must take a positive form to attain results is clear. It does not follow, however, that this should always be done by military violence.

On the other hand, diplomacy only, without any force, never led to a real solution. And so it is that other ways are used, which might be termed revolutionary ways, in which force is applied in subtle forms, as long as possible without provoking war. At the same time a deterrent for war must be provided in the form of regular forces capable of inflicting damage to any enemy to an extent he is unwilling to sustain.

The purely defensive aspect is covered by a specific doctrine of ours, the so-called Concept of Territorial War, based on the principle of "No surrender whatsoever." It calls for the total mobilization of all available military and nonmilitary potential in a given area or territory to absorb the shock of any enemy attack, to tie and wear down his forces in a protracted war, while creating the conditions to defeat them in a final counteroffensive.

This doctrine of our defense we call the Doctrine of Revolutionary War, because it is meant to be closely associated with our Revolution, thereby assuming its philosophy and character. In Western terminology, Revolutionary War is normally identified with Communism and aggression. I will not comment on this, but let it be clear that our Revolutionary War is against aggression, is not inevitable but only accepted if no alternative is available. Its objective is the elimination of foreign threat of domination and not the domination of other nations. It is based on Pantja Sila and aimed at the fulfilment of our Revolution. It is, therefore, not aggressive, not hostile to the Asian and African nations or other New Emerging Forces, but seeks to be integrated into the revolutionary struggles of those nations in order to achieve the ideals of the Revolution of Mankind.

XVi

Sukarno Storming the Last Bulwarks of Imperialism (1965)

This comes from President Sukarno's opening speech on April 18, 1965, at the large international gathering in Bandung which was held for the tenth anniversary of the Bandung Conference. At this gathering, as at a number of similar ones held in Indonesia between 1963 and October 1965, representation was particularly heavy, and at a relatively high level, from the Communist states of Asia. The address was published as After Ten Years, Still Onward, Never Retreat (*Djakarta: Department of Information, 1965*).

Our century is the century of intervention, subversion, aggression. Imperialists now living in the pangs of death cannot live without intervention, cannot live without subversion, cannot live without aggression. But on the other hand, this century of ours is a century of anti-intervention, anti-subversion, antiaggression; yes, how can we possibly live if we do not fight against intervention, if we do not fight against subversion, if we do not fight against aggression?

Imperialism, despite the inner conflicts dividing the imperialists, is a system that makes up a single whole. They claw at each other like wolves when they are fighting over riches and loot, but they help each other when they have to deal with us. Just see how the United States, West Germany, Israel unite to humiliate our brothers the Arab nations! Just see how the British and the Americans unite to preserve "Malaysia," that puppet state, as a force hostile to the Republic of Indonesia! Yes, just see how virtually all the imperialists unite to defend the racialist Verwoerd government and defend apartheid in general! Thus, the wisest thing for us to do is unite, link arms, express solidarity for each other, help each other in our mighty struggle to storm imperialism, colonialism, and neo-colonialism. Let us settle the problems that arise among us as problems within the family, and let us close our ranks, let us be like *one*, joined in indestructible unity! Let us regard our struggle as one single whole, let us wage it as one single entity, for in this way our powers of perseverance and resistance will soar to great heights!

There still are some people who try to make us believe that "Imperialism is dead." And some Americans even asked me recently "Why are you obsessed with the colonial problem now when the battle is won?" I always reply to such remarks: No, no! Imperialism is not yet dead, the struggle against colonialism and neo-colonialism is not yet over!

Just think! How many people living in this world of ours are still starving? How many people in this world of ours never wear any shoes on their feet? How many people in this world of ours are still illiterate? And it is against these "backward" nations that the imperialists set up their military bases all over the world, station their troops all over the world, their fleets all over the world! How could anyone in his right mind say, that "Imperialism is dead," and that "The struggle against imperialism is over?" Let me call people who think in this way what they really are; they are mad—madmen!

We should never try to understand foreign domination in a narrow sense. And in the same way, too, all our efforts, all our struggle to throw off foreign domination must be interpreted in a broad sense. And anyhow, who is there among us who will not oppose foreign domination? Do not the Philippines and Japan, India and Turkey, Tunisia and Morocco, or all of us for that matter, strive to free ourselves from all forms of foreign domination—political domination, economic domination, military domination, cultural domination?

Self-satisfaction is our foe and imperialism's friend. The most "useful" people of all for imperialism are people overloaded with self-satisfaction. Just listen for a moment to the drivel spoken by Tshombe or by Tengku Abdulrachman; just listen to the drivel spoken by the leaders of Israel! According to them, "All is running well" in their countries. They boast of their grand highways; they boast of their schools; they boast of their hospitals; they boast of their mosques; and they boast of their churches. Yet, these roads of theirs are colonial roads; these schools of theirs are colonial schools; these hospitals of theirs are colonial hospitals; these mosques and churches of theirs are colonial mosques and churches! So impoverished are the souls of these puppets that they have nothing to be proud of except the very things that are the pride and joy of their masters. We have heard such drivel for hundreds of years, and now we are told to listen to an imitation. Oh, his master's voice! These imperialist puppets boast that their per capita income is higher than ours! This, too, is an old tale! Formerly, when we calculated Indonesia's national income, I did not include the earnings of the oil companies, because these oil companies were foreign; they were controlled by Dutch, British, and American monopoly capital. But now, foreign monopoly capital in Indonesia, including the capital invested in oil, is controlled by the Republic of Indonesia. Naturally, I count that which still belongs to foreigners as being foreign property. How much of the national incomes of Israel, the Congo, and "Malaysia" flows to foreign countries? And we might as well add: how much of it is pocketed by the gentlemen who serve the imperialists so faithfully?

The imperialists accuse our countries of being "unstable" and of having "hopeless economies." But I think I should make it clear that national instability is a thousand times better than colonial stability! Yes indeed, our times are dynamic and only the arrived think in terms of "stability," "harmony," or "comfort." And as regards our economies being "hopeless," if there is any truth in this—then who is to blame? When we compelled the colonialists to quit our countries, they bequeathed us an impossible situation the like of which it would be difficult to imagine. But, nevertheless, we accepted this "legacy" in all consciousness and responsibility. Yet, why is it that after that these gentlemen carry out machinations, sabotage? Of course, you are quite entitled to do such things, but we are quite entitled to oppose your brutal ways!

All manner of artificial barriers have been created to make things difficult for our economic growth: blockades, embargoes, pushing down the prices of our raw materials, and so on. But bad things never last long. Who can prevent Cuba from selling its sugar and tobacco to other countries? Who can prevent two Asian countries, Japan and China, both with high levels of civilization, from trading with each other?

For us, economic independence is the prerequisite for real independence in political and cultural affairs. It is indeed so that we seized our political independence as a weapon with which to establish economic independence. Without economic independence, in fact, we are not politically independent; we do not have cultural independence; we do not have independence in diplomacy; we do not have independence in military affairs; yes, without economic independence in fact we do not have any independence at all. This is the stage we have reached. Herein lies the absolute correctness of the decision adopted by the Meeting of Ministers in Preparation for the Asian-African Conference, namely that we must stand on our own feet in economic affairs as the precondition for political sovereignty and cultural self-assertion.

Let us build anti-imperialist economies, genuinely national economies that stand on their own feet, mutually assisting each other, and not relying upon the so-called aid of the imperialists! . . .

No one today doubts that if the peoples of Asia and Africa unite, they do this not for any reasons of racialism—as the imperialists always charge—but because the historical destiny of our peoples is the same. The people of Europe, the Australian people, the American people, other peoples, still suffer as a result of economic crisis, of moral crisis, and the like, but the peoples of Asia, Africa, and Latin America suffer far more. The only time the atom bomb has been used, it was used against an Asian nation. We ask ourselves today: would the vicious bombing raids now being perpetrated against the Vietnamese people twenty years after the end of the Second World War, ever be launched if the nation being attacked were not of Asia, or Africa or Latin America?

A mighty storm against imperialism is now raging in Asia, Africa, Latin America. These continents of ours, so long subjected to humiliation, enslavement, plunder, are no longer prepared to bear the crazy burden of imperialism upon their shoulders. We have cast this burden aside! We today stand firmly upright in the mighty ranks of the new emerging forces, and we are now storming the last bulwarks of imperialism! There is no power in the world that can prevent the peoples of Asia, Africa, Latin America from emancipating themselves! It is no longer possible for the imperialists, colonialists, and neo-colonialists to rule over us, as they did in days of yore, and we are no longer prepared to be ruled over as we were in days of yore. This means that a revolutionary crisis on a world scale has occurred. We must grasp, grasp this opportunity, for if not, if we lose this opportunity, we will never get it back again!

A new Asia and a new Africa has arisen!

Let us build the world anew!

Let us create a new world, free from the exploitation of nation by nation, free from the exploitation of man by man!

Let us build a new world free from imperialism, free from colonialism, free from neo-colonialism!

Onward, no retreat! Ever onward, never retreat!

APPENDIXES

Appendix I
Biographical Notes
on Authors

Aidit, Dipa Nusantara (1923–1965)

Born at Medan, the son of a minor official of the forestry service who was later a member of parliament, Aidit was educated to commercial secondary school level. His political activity began in nationalist organizations in 1939. In Djakarta during the Japanese occupation he belonged to a youth group (Angkatan Baru Indonesia or Indonesian New Generation) which combined legal political education with clandestine anti-Japanese activities. In 1945 he was one of the young men associated with the proclamation of independence and seizure of power from the Japanese in Djakarta and suffered imprisonment at Japanese, British, and Dutch hands, being released in mid-1946. He then worked at the Solo headquarters of the PKI (Indonesian Communist party), which he claimed to have joined in 1943. In 1947 he became secretary of the People's Democratic Front, a member of the PKI Central Committee, and chairman of the PKI fraction in the Republic's parliament. On the eve of the Madiun revolt in 1948 he was elected to the Politburo and following its suppression fled abroad, spending time in China and Vietnam.

After his return in 1950 he and a group of young leaders including Njoto and M. H. Lukman took over control of the PKI from the older leaders Alimin and Tan Ling Djie. He became joint Secretary General of the party in June 1950, was made Secretary General in October 1953, and became the party's first Chairman in 1959. In 1962 he achieved ministerial status as a Deputy Chairman of the Provisional People's Consultative Congress. The circumstances of his death in the aftermath of the October 1965 coup are obscure.

Many of his speeches and pamphlets have been translated into English, especially in the collection *Problems of the Indonesian Revolution* (Bandung: Demos, 1963).

Assaat (1904———)

Born in West Sumatra, Assaat graduated from Leiden University in 1939 as a lawyer. During the Revolution, he was chairman of the Central National Committee (KNIP) and its Working Body, the Republic's principal legislative organ. As a nonparty man, he was made Acting President of the (member state) Republic of Indonesia in the period of the Republic of the United States of Indonesia (1949–1950), and with the formation of the unitary Republic of Indonesia he became Minister of the Interior (1950–1951). In 1956 he was prime mover in a campaign for discrimination (known as the "Assaat Movement") against the Chinese business community. In 1958 he served as Minister for the Interior in the PRRI rebel government and was imprisoned or under city arrest from 1961 (the end of the rebellion) until 1966. He is the author of a book on constitutional law.

Atmodarminto (1894———)

After having been a member over the decades of such varied organizations as Sarikat Islam, Budi Utomo, and the People's Democratic Front (FDR), Atmodarminto, who was born at Jogjakarta, was elected to both Parliament and the Constituent Assembly in 1955 as the representative of Gerinda, a traditionalist party of the Jogjakarta region headed by Prince Surjodiningrat, an uncle of the Sultan of Jogjakarta. Atmodarminto was on the editorial staff of a number of newspapers and periodicals and for a time an official of the Jogjakarta regional Information Service.

Hatta, Mohammad (1902———)

Born in West Sumatra, Hatta, as a student at the Economic University of Rotterdam, was active in the nationalist "Indonesian Association," served for a time as its chairman, and also was associated with Nehru in the League against Imperialism. On his return to Indonesia in 1932 he became Chairman of the "New PNI," or Nationalist Education Association. For this activity he was sent, with Soetan Sjahrir, to an internment camp in West New Guinea in 1934; they were later transferred to the island of Banda.

Released on the eve of the Japanese occupation, Hatta subsequently became Sukarno's principal lieutenant in the leadership of nationalists cooperating with the Japanese. In 1945 he signed the Proclamation of Independence with Sukarno and became Vice-President of the Republic. During 1948–1950 he held the Prime Ministership as well as the Vice-Presidency and was the principal Indonesian negotiator of the Round Table Conference settlement of 1949 which led to the final Dutch withdrawal from Indonesia.

After 1950 he became increasingly associated with the Masjumi and Socialist parties in opposition to President Sukarno and the parties supporting him, and in 1956 resigned as Vice-President. As his partnership with Sukarno had often been seen as symbolizing the unity between Java and the other islands of Indonesia, the resignation intensified non-Javanese dissatisfaction with political affairs in Djakarta, and in 1957 and 1958 there were repeated calls from the Masjumi and various groups in Sumatra and Sulawesi for Hatta to be brought back to high office. It was the failure of a series of Sukarno-Hatta talks in March 1958 which led to the first fighting between the Djakarta government and the rebel PRRI government in Sumatra. His public role was very small after 1958, except momentarily in 1960 when he published "Our Democracy" (see IIIj), but he re-emerged as a public figure after October 1965. Of his many political and economic writings two are available in English, *The Co-operative Movement in Indonesia* (Ithaca, N.Y.: Cornell University Press, 1957) and *Past and Future* (Cornell Modern Indonesia Project, 1960).

Kahar Muzakar (c. 1919–1965)

Born in the Luwu region of Sulawesi and educated at an Islamic secondary school in Solo, Kahar Muzakar became in 1945 a leading figure among the youths of Sulawesi origin in Java supporting the newly proclaimed Indonesian Republic. He organized the despatch of small groups of guerrillas to Dutch-occupied South Sulawesi but did not go there himself until 1950. Then he assumed leadership of the guerrillas and when his demands that they be received into the army as a separate regiment were rejected, he led them into open revolt. In 1953, Kahar Muzakar, till then a radical nationalist in ideological orientation proclaimed his movement part of the Islamic State of Indonesia headed by Kartosuwirjo in West Java. For fourteen years he terrorized large parts of South Sulawesi. Negotiations to "return to the fold" were held in 1951, 1957, and 1961 but broke down in each case. When he was killed by government forces in February 1965 only a small following remained to him. It is difficult to assess the relative weight of regional sentiment, religious fanaticism, and simple banditry in the motivation of his guerrilla campaign.

Lubis, Colonel Zulkifli (1923———)

Born in North Sumatra and educated at a Jogjakarta secondary school before the war, Zulkifli Lubis was trained as an intelligence officer by the Japanese and became first Chief of Intelligence of the Indonesian Army in 1945. In the later part of the revolutionary war he was with the guerrillas in Sumatra. As Chief of Intelligence in 1952, he was one of the leading members of the anti–October 17 faction in the army (the pro–October 17 group included Simatupang and Nasution). As Deputy Chief of Staff and then Acting Chief of Staff in the following years, he played an important political role. In 1956, he resigned his post and then made an unsuccessful attempt to effect a coup. After its failure he went into hiding, emerging as a leader of the PRRI-Permesta rebellion in 1958. He gave himself up with other rebel leaders in 1961 and was imprisoned until 1966.

Lukman, M. H. (1920–1966)

The son of a Javanese Muslim religious teacher who was exiled to West New Guinea for procommunist activities, Lukman was brought up in and around the jungle prison camps on the Digul River. He returned to Java in 1938 and during the Japanese occupation was, like Aidit, a member of a youth group called Angkatan Baru Indonesia (Indonesian New Generation) with which he took part in the incidents surrounding the Proclamation of Independence in 1945. He was briefly imprisoned by the Japanese and in 1946 by the Republican government for participating in the "Three Districts Affair," a radical movement in part of Central Java. From mid-1946 he was active with Aidit in the agitation-propaganda department of the PKI and was elected to the Politburo on the eve of the Madiun uprising in 1948. He went abroad after the uprising and on his return was (with Njoto) one of Aidit's two leading associates in winning control of the PKI. In 1950 he became First Deputy Secretary General of the PKI and was a member of parliament from 1954, reaching ministerial status as Third Deputy Chairman of Parliament in 1963. He attended some official functions after the October 1965 affair and then went into hiding; according to one report he was shot while being arrested in May 1966.

Nasution, General Abdul Haris (1918——)

Born in North Sumatra, Nasution was a cadet at the Dutch military academy at Bandung in 1940–1942 and was a youth organizer in that city during the Japanese occupation. In the early stages of the war against the Dutch he commanded the Siliwangi Division in West Java and in 1948–1949 was Commander for all Java. In 1950, when only thirty-two years of age, he became Army Chief of Staff, a post he retained until 1962, except for a period from 1952 to 1955 when he was forced to withdraw because of his association with the anti-parliamentary demonstration known as the "Seventeenth October Affair." From 1962 to 1966 he was Chief of Staff of the Armed Forces and Minister of Defence, but it was widely believed that his influence was diminished.

He was a principal target of the conspirators of October 1965 but escaped with a foot injury; however, his little daughter was shot dead. He played very important roles in government after this coup attempt, especially in the suppression of the Communist party. Though dismissed by Sukarno as Minister of Defence in February 1966, he was elected Chairman of the Provisional People's Consultative Congress (Indonesia's highest legislative body) in June of that year. His *Principles of Guerrilla Warfare* is available in English as are several collections of speeches. Still untranslated are his *Notes on Indonesian Military Policy* and a history of the first years of the Indonesian Army.

Natsir, Mohammad (1908———)

Born in West Sumatra, after a secondary school and teachers' college education, Natsir worked in Islamic organizations and schools in Bandung from 1932 to 1945, under the influence of the prominent Islamic scholar, A. Hassan. After the Revolution he quickly came to the fore as leader of the modernist wing of the Masjumi and, subsequently was party chairman for a number of years. In 1946–1947 and 1948–1949 he was Minister of Information, and in 1950–1951 Prime Minister. In February 1958 he joined the PRRI rebel government in Sumatra and was subsequently made its Deputy Prime Minister. After the rebels returned to the fold in 1961 he was in prison or under city arrest until 1966. Since his release he has devoted much of his time to the educational organization Dakwah Islamijah. Though he plays no public political role, his great personal authority as a principal leader of the Muslim community is often brought to bear in political contexts. He has written many articles and books on political and religious subjects, but little has been translated into English except *Some Observations Concerning the Role of Islam in National and International Affairs* (Ithaca, N. Y.: Cornell Southeast Asia Program, 1954).

Nugroho Notosusanto (1931———)

Nugroho Notosusanto left a Jogjakarta secondary school to fight with the Student Army in the Revolution. In the early and middle 1950's he was well known as a student leader and short story writer. After postgraduate study at London University in the late 1950's he became a lecturer in history at the University of Indonesia. As Deputy Rector for Student affairs in the University of Indonesia, he was a target of Communist criticism in the months before October 1965.

Onghokham (1933———)

A member of an established Indonesian-Chinese family in East Java, Onghokham was a history student in the University of Indonesia when he wrote the article excerpted here. He was active in the assimilationist organization LPKB (Institute for Building National Unity).

Prijono (1907–1969)

The holder of a doctorate from Leiden University and long Dean of the Arts Faculty of the University of Indonesia. Though generally classed with the Murba party, Professor Prijono received the Stalin Peace Prize in 1955 and was Chairman of the Indonesia-China Friendship Association 1955–1957. He became Minister of Education in 1957 and retained major though not sole responsibility for that field throughout the Guided Democracy period. He came under attack after October 1965 and was dismissed in March 1966. In 1954 he published a book called *M.M.M. and Other Modern Animal Stories* (in Indonesian), which satirized political, social, and academic life in Djarkarta.

Roeslan Abdulgani (1914——)

Trained as a notary and leader of a small underground group in Surabaja during the Japanese occupation, Roeslan Abdulgani was active in establishing the Republic of Indonesia's control in that region in 1945. After many years as Secretary-General of the Ministry of Information he became Secretary-General of the Foreign Ministry in 1954 and Minister of Foreign Affairs in 1956. As Deputy Chairman of the National Council (1957–1959) and the Supreme Advisory Council (1959–1962) he was President Sukarno's leading aide in the development and propagation of the ideology of Guided Democracy. After 1963 he was less influential though still in the Cabinet. Though much criticized after the eclipse of President Sukarno, he has served the Suharto government as Ambassador to the United Nations.

In the early stages of his career a follower of Sjahrir, he subsequently joined the PNI, and his later writings reflect a strongly radical nationalist orientation. A number are included in *Select Documents: Some Aspects Concerning Progress and Principles of the Indonesian Revolution,* I (Djakarta: Department of Information, 1961[?]), and others are to be found in Roselan Abdulgani, *Pantja Sila, The Prime Mover of the Indonesian Revolution* (Djakarta: Prapantja, 1964).

Rosihan Anwar (1922——)

Born in Padang, Sumatra, Rosihan Anwar was a writer of the "1945 generation" and a leading journalist during the 1950's. Under his editorship the Djakarta daily *Pedoman,* independent but closely affiliated to the Socialist party, was a paper of great prestige, his own editorials maintaining a high standard. After *Pedoman* was banned in 1961, he devoted himself to the study of Islam. He has been a prominent columnist since 1966.

Sadli, Mohammad (1922——)

Born in Sumedang, Java, Sadli had his education as a civil engineer interrupted by the Japanese occupation and revolution, and though he graduated from Gadjah Mada University in that field in 1952, he has since devoted his attention to economics, which he studied at the Massachusetts Institute of Technology and the University of California, Berkeley. Since his return in 1957 he has taught economics at the University of Indonesia. He has been a principal architect of the Suharto government's economic policy.

Said, Mohamad (1917———) (author of IXh; no kin of the following)

A member of a high family in Central Java, Mohamad Said broke off his studies after three years in the Medical School in Djakarta, and became a teacher in Taman Siswa schools, which he has remained. He was arrested by both the British and the Dutch after 1945 but nevertheless succeeded in keeping the Taman Siswa schools open in Dutch-occupied Djakarta. Since 1949 he has been influential as a Taman Siswa leader, an educational philosopher, and a social critic. In 1966 he was briefly Deputy Minister of Basic Education.

Said, Mohamad (1907———) (author of Xa)

Born at Labuhan Bilik, North Sumatra, and educated at a teacher-training school, Mohamad Said worked for various newspapers before the war. Since 1947 he has been continuously associated with the Medan PNI daily *Waspada*. In 1950 he was chairman of the central committee of the All East Sumatra People's Congress, a movement aimed at abolishing the Dutch-sponsored East Sumatra state. In 1951 he became chairman of the regional board of the PNI. He has written on the history of Sumatra.

Sajuti Melik (1908———)

Probably none of the writers in this book has been imprisoned more often and by more regimes than Sajuti Melik. Originally a communist, he was later converted to the national-communism of Tan Malaka and the radical nationalism of Sukarno. Expelled from a teachers' college in Solo for his political writings in newspapers, he was exiled to the internment camp at Boven Digul in West Irian after the communist revolt in 1926. Released in 1933, he fled to Malaya the following year and was there jailed by the British in 1936. Returning to Java in 1938 he established the periodical *Pesat*, but was imprisoned again during 1939–1941 and by the Japanese throughout most of the occupation. During 1946–1948 he was jailed again by the Republic and finally by the Dutch again in 1949. From the early 1950's he was a member of the PNI. During 1964 he wrote a series of articles on "Sukarnoism" in the Djakarta daily *Berita Indonesia* which expressed the views of the anticommunist group who inspired the BPS (Body for the Promotion of Sukarnoism) movement at that time.

Sakirman (1911——)

After graduating as an engineer from Bandung Technical University in 1939, Sakirman was headmaster of a technical secondary school till 1942 and an official of the Economic Affairs Department during the Japanese occupation. During the Revolution, he organized a procommunist auxiliary military force and became a Major General of the army. A member of the Central Committee of the Communist Party from 1951 and of the Politburo from 1954, he was chairman of the communist group in the provisional parliament (1950–1956) and a PKI spokesman on economic and defense questions. After the October 1965 coup (in which his brother, the anticommunist army intelligence chief General Parman was killed), he went into hiding. He was reported killed in 1967.

Sawarno Djaksonagoro (1903——)

After obtaining a law degree from Leiden, Sawarno Djaksonagoro held a series of positions as a judge of the Netherlands Indies, as Chief Justice of the princely State of Surakarta (Solo), and as a senior official in the *pamong pradja* corps of the Republic of Indonesia. He is known as an authority on Javanese music, theater, philosophy, and mysticism.

Selosoemardjan (1915——)

Born in Jogjakarta, Selosoemardjan worked in the administrative service of the Jogjakarta region under the Dutch and the Japanese and in the early years of the Revolution and, later, as a high official of the central government. He studied sociology at Cornell University, where he obtained a doctorate in 1959, and was subsequently appointed Professor of Sociology at the University of Indonesia. Private secretary to the Sultan of Jogjakarta at various times since 1947, he became his official secretary at the time of the Sultan's appointment as Deputy Prime Minister in 1966. His writings in English include *Social Changes in Jogjakarta* (Ithaca, N.Y.: Cornell University Press, 1962), *The Dynamics of Community Development in Rural Central and West Java: A Comparative Report* (Cornell Modern Indonesia Project, 1963), and a number of journal articles.

Simatupang, Major General T. B. (1920——)

Born in North Sumatra and having graduated from the Military Academy at Bandung shortly before the Japanese invasion, Simatupang played an important role in the establishment of the Indonesian army after 1945, becoming successively Deputy Chief of Staff of the Armed Forces, Acting Chief of Staff, and, finally, Chief of Staff (1951–1954). He was criticized by radical nationalists and others for his rationalizing policies and, especially, his alleged association with the Socialist party and the "October 17 Affair" of 1952, an abortive military move against parliament. After 1954, Simatupang wrote several books on military subjects, of which his memoir of the revolutionary war, *Report from Banaran* (Ithaca, N.Y.: Cornell Modern Indonesia Project), is forthcoming. In the 1960's much of his time has been devoted to the affairs of the Council of Churches in Indonesia of which he is a Chairman.

Sjafruddin Prawiranegara (1911———)

Graduating from the Djakarta Law School in 1940, Sjafruddin Prawiranegara served as a financial official until the Revolution. He then emerged as the leading economic expert of the Masjumi party, holding Finance or Economics portfolios almost continuously from 1946 to 1951. During the second Dutch "police action" against the Republic in 1948–1949 he headed an emergency government in Sumatra. He was head of the central bank (Java Bank, later Bank Indonesia) between 1951 and 1958, exercising a powerful influence on Indonesian economic policy. In early 1958 he left Djakarta to become Prime Minister in the rebel PRRI government in Sumatra. In 1961 he ordered remaining PRRI guerrilla elements to give themselves up. He was kept under close or loose confinement in Java from then until 1966.

Sjahrir, Soetan (1909–1966)

The son of a government official in West Sumatra, Sjahrir attended secondary school in Bandung and studied law at Amsterdam from 1929 to 1931. On his return he joined Hatta in founding the "New PNI" but was arrested in 1934 and exiled to New Guinea and later Banda Island. Freed shortly before the Japanese invasion, he organized a small underground group. As one of the few prominent nationalist leaders who did not cooperate with the Japanese, he sprang into prominence after the Proclamation of Independence, heading three cabinets between November 1945 and June 1947. During the first Dutch "police action" he flew dramatically to Lake Success to present Indonesia's case to the Security Council, and in the second he was captured at Jogjakarta. At that time he was special advisor to the President, but he was never again to hold public office. He led the Indonesian Socialist Party (PSI) throughout the fifties. In January 1962 he was arrested and after suffering increasing ill health in prison was permitted to fly for treatment to Zurich, where he died in April 1966. His writings available in English are *Out of Exile* (New York: John Day, 1949) and *Our Struggle* (Ithaca, N.Y.: Cornell Modern Indonesia Project, 1968).

Sjamsudin Kartokusumo (1918——)

Born in Purbolinggo, Central Java, Sjamsudin Kartokusumo studied English literature at the University of Indonesia. A former Taman Siswa teacher, he now works with a firm of importers.

Slamet, Mrs. Ina E. (1928——)

Born in the Netherlands, Ina Velsink married an Indonesian journalist, Sukotjo Slamet, in 1952 and acquired Indonesian citizenship. Originally a student of French language and literature, she studied cultural anthropology at Leiden University, graduating in 1955, and taught it at the University of Indonesia, Djakarta, from 1956 to 1965. In that year she was suspended because of her membership in HSI (Indonesian Association of Scientists), a Communist-dominated organization, and later imprisoned.

Slamet, Moehammad (1922——)

Born in Garut, West Java, Moehammad Slamet studied sociology at the University of Leiden in the early and middle 1950's and then returned to lecture at Padjadjaran University, Bandung, where he subsequently became head of the Social Research Institute. From 1963 to 1966 he was working in the field of social research and economic development in India under the auspices of UNESCO, and has more recently been lecturing at Melbourne University.

Soedjatmoko (1922——)

The son of a surgeon and mystic, Soedjatmoko became involved in underground politics while a student of the Djakarta Medical School in the Japanese period. As one of the young men around Sjahrir (who was later to become his brother-in-law), he became an official of the Information Ministry in the beginning of the Revolution and subsequently of the Foreign Ministry, representing Indonesia in the U.N. and also in London and Washington during 1947–1951. Thereafter he was known as a publisher, as an editor of the daily *Pedoman* and the weekly *Siasat,* and a leading intellectual of the Socialist Party. He was a Visiting Lecturer at Cornell University in 1961–1962 and Director of the Seminar on "Cultural Motivations to Progress in South and Southeast Asia" which was sponsored by the Congress for Cultural Freedom and the University of the Philippines in 1963. In 1968 he was appointed Ambassador to the United States.

His writings in English include "The Rise of Political Parties in Indonesia," in Philip W. Thayer, ed., *Nationalism and Progress in Free Asia* (Baltimore: Johns Hopkins Press, 1956); *Economic Development as a Cultural Problem* (Ithaca, N.Y.: Cornell Modern Indonesia Project, 1958); *An Approach to Indonesian History: Towards an Open Future* (Cornell

Modern Indonesia Project, 1960); "The Modern Indonesian Historian and His Time," in Soedjatmoko *et al.*, eds., *An Introduction to Indonesian Historiography* (Cornell University Press, 1965); "Cultural Motivations to Progress: The 'Exterior' and the 'Interior' View," in Robert N. Bellah, ed., *Religion and Progress in Modern Asia* (New York: Free Press, 1965); and "Indonesia: Problems and Opportunities" and "Indonesia and the World," in *Australian Outlook*, XXI (December 1967), 263–306.

Soerasto Sastrosoewignjo (1937——)

A native of Solo and a graduate in economics from Gadjah Mada University, Jogjakarta, Soerasto Sastrosoewignjo had not long begun his career as an employee of a state bank in Djakarta when he wrote the passage excerpted here. His organizational affiliations have been those of the reformist Islamic stream. In August 1965 he became a member of the editorial staff of the daily *Mertjusuar*.

Soeriokoesoemo, Raden Mas Soetatmo (1888–1924)

A member of the princely house of the Paku Alam at Jogjakarta, where he was born and worked for some years as an irrigation superintendent, Soeriokoesoemo wrestled early with the cultural and political problems created by the impact of the West on Javanese society. He was a member of Budi Utomo when that organization shifted its attention from culture to politics during the First World War, and from 1921 until 1924 sat, by nomination of the Governor General, in the Volksraad. He was coeditor of the magazine *Wederopbouw* (Reconstruction), a member of the intellectual circle from which the Taman Siswa educational movement was born in 1922, and first chairman of Taman Siswa. Through his Taman Siswa associate Ki Hadjar Dewantoro, his ideas on democracy and leadership were to influence political thinking in independent Indonesia.

Subandrio (1914——)

A graduate of the Djakarta Medical School and a high official of the Ministry of Information in the first years of the Revolution, Subandrio was the Republic's representative in London from 1947 to 1954. He then served as Ambassador in Moscow (1954–1956) and Secretary General of the Ministry of Foreign Affairs (1956–1957). From 1957 till 1966 he was Minister of Foreign Affairs. He was particularly powerful in the last two years of Guided Democracy (1963–1965) when, as First Deputy Prime Minister, he was President Sukarno's senior minister and often regarded as his likely successor. An associate of Sjahrir in the early years of independence, Dr. Subandrio adopted a radical nationalist position in the 1950's and joined the PNI. After the unsuccessful coup of October 1965 he came under heavy attack from army, student, and Muslim groups as procommunist and pro-Chinese. His political use of the central intelligence bureau (BPI) which was under his direction was criticized and he was widely accused of implication in the coup. In March 1966 he was arrested on the orders of General Suharto and after trial in an extraordinary military court in October, was sentenced to death. Two volumes of his speeches have been published under the title *Indonesia on the March*.

Sudirman (1912–1950)

Sudirman, a teacher in a Muslim primary school in Central Java before the war, first displayed his talent for leadership in the Peta, the auxiliary military force which the Japanese created in Indonesia in anticipation of an Allied invasion. When in November 1945 representatives of the newly created Indonesian army met to elect a Commander in Chief, the choice fell on him, despite his youth and the paucity of his formal military education. During the final stages of the guerrilla conflict with Holland in 1948–1949 he continued his leadership of the army though so ill with tuberculosis that he had to be carried from village to village on a stretcher. He died a few weeks after the Dutch recognition of Indonesian sovereignty.

Suharjo (ca. 1927——)

A Javanese who as a young man fought in the revolution, Suharjo rose in the army to be military commander in East Kalimantan (Borneo) during the Indonesian "confrontation" of Malaysia. He was then regarded as being in better standing with President Sukarno than with his military superiors. In early 1965, with the rank of Brigadier General, he was sent to the U.S.S.R. to study at the Frunze Military Academy. He subsequently became an opponent of the government of General Suharto, and there are conflicting reports of his activities abroad or possibly within Indonesia.

Suharto (1921——)

Born near Jogjakarta, the son of a village trader, Suharto, after working briefly as a bank clerk, entered military school in 1940. He became a Captain in the Peta and rose through the ranks in the national army after 1945 to become Commander of the Central Java Military Region in 1956 and Director of Intelligence in the office of the Army Chief of Staff in 1960. In 1961 he was assigned abroad to maintain contact between Indonesian Military Attachés in Belgrade, Paris, and Bonn, but was recalled the following year to command the force for the recovery of West Irian. In 1963 he became Commander of the Strategic Command in Djakarta. He took the initiative in putting down the attempted coup of Lieutenant Colonel Untung in October 1965 and was assigned by President Sukarno the task of restoring order. He succeeded the murdered Yani as Army

Minister and Chief of Staff, and by a gradual process superseded Sukarno as national leader. In March 1966 he extracted extraordinary powers from Sukarno; in July he became Chairman of the Cabinet Presidium; in March 1967 Acting President; and in March 1968 President. Ruthless in his suppression of the Communists, Suharto has been conciliatory in his relations with other political groups and with factions in the armed forces. Terminating the confrontation of Malaysia, he has reoriented Indonesia's foreign policy toward friendship and economic relations with Western countries and made economic stabilization the major plank in his platform.

Sukarno (1901———)

Born of a Javanese father and a Balinese mother Sukarno was brought up in the small East Java towns of Blitar and Sidoardjo, where his father was a school teacher. His family being poor though genteel, he owed his education to benefactors, including the pioneer nationalist and Islamic leader H. O. S. Tjokroaminoto, in whose Surabaja household he lived while at secondary school. Influenced by the atmosphere of politics there, he joined the Jong Java youth movement in 1915. In 1920 he was among the first twelve students enrolled in the architecture course at the Bandung Technical University, one of the first institutions of higher education in Indonesia. As a student he founded the Bandung Study Club; in 1927 this was transformed into the nationalist party, PNI, of which Sukarno, then already known as a magnetic public speaker, became chairman. In December 1929 he was arrested and imprisoned for two years. On his release he became leader of the PNI's successor organization, Partindo, but in August 1933 was arrested again and exiled without trial, first to the East Indonesian island of Flores and then to Sumatra.

Released by the Japanese, Sukarno agreed (under an understanding with other nationalist leaders) to co-operate with them in the hope of advancing the cause of independence. In 1943 he was made chairman of Putera (Center of People's Power), an organization for mobilizing nationalist sentiment behind the Japanese war effort, and in 1944 of Djawa Hookookai (People's Loyalty Organization), which was similar but more firmly under Japanese control. As the Japanese saw the fortunes of war turning against them, they allowed Sukarno and the other Indonesian nationalists greater power. An Independence Preparatory Committee chaired by Sukarno began work on August 7, 1945. Ten days later, however, under pressure from anti-Japanese youth leaders, he and Hatta proclaimed Indonesia's independence in defiance of the Japanese, whose capitulation to the allies had just been announced. Throughout the revolutionary struggle against the Dutch from 1945 to 1949, Sukarno used his powers of oratory to great effect and served as a potent symbol of national unity, although he was not in direct control of policy after October 1945. He was a Dutch prisoner again for some months after their capture of Jogjakarta in December 1948.

During the next seven years he was a figurehead president but used his considerable influence behind the scenes, in good part to combat the power and frustrate the policies of the Masjumi and Socialist parties. From late 1956, when parliamentary democracy was under threat from regional and military dissidents, Sukarno used his prestige to urge a new system of Guided Democracy which would restore the supposed unity and zeal of revolutionary days. A series of changes introducing the new system culminated in the presidential decree of July 5, 1959; this decree restored the presidential government envisaged in the first republican constitution but in abeyance since late 1945. Thereafter, the personal power of Sukarno rose steadily and he was deluged with adulatory titles: Great Leader of the Revolution, President for Life, Supreme Elder, Spokesman of the People, and so forth. As a result of the coup of October 1965 and the manner of its defeat, his power and prestige fell greatly, and in March 1966 the effective direction of national policy was taken out of his hands. He has been a virtual prisoner since early 1967, and in March 1968, the Provisional People's Consultative Assembly formally divested him of all his powers.

Sukarno has been married six times (although in accordance with Islamic law, he has never had more than four wives at one time). He has made numerous and protracted trips abroad. Born a Raden (a minor aristocratic title which he discarded), he became Ingenieur by graduation, Hadji in virtue of his pilgrimage to Mecca, and Doctor through receiving honorary doctorates from dozens of universities at home and abroad. Of his writings, which date mainly from the prewar period, few are available in English at the present time, though this gap will probably be filled soon. Of his speeches, many are available in English, especially the series of August 17 speeches, which were the central feature of Indonesia's celebration of her independence anniversary throughout the 1945–1965 period. His political ideas show a remarkable consistency from his formative years in the 1920's until the peak of his career in the 1960's. An autobiography of Sukarno "as told to Cindy Adams" appeared in 1965, and a study of his political ideas by Bernhard Dahm, originally published in German, has been published in an English translation, *Sukarno and the Struggle for Indonesian Independence* (Ithaca, N.Y.: Cornell University Press, 1969).

Sumitro Djojohadikusumo (1917——)

The son of a high official of the Netherlands Indies Economic Affairs Department, Sumitro obtained a doctorate from the Economic University of Rotterdam during the German occupation and, after a brief period as adviser to the Dutch government, returned to Indonesia in 1946. Quickly gaining a reputation as a brilliant economist, he was a member of the Indonesian delegations to the United Nations and the Round Table Conference in 1949, and in 1950 Chargé d'affaires in Washington. In 1951 he became the first Dean of the Faculty of Economics of the University of Indonesia. Between 1950 and 1956 he represented the Socialist party in every other Cabinet, being once Minister of Trade and Industry and twice Minister of Finance. In 1957 he fled Djakarta and joined the dissident elements who proclaimed a revolutionary government (PRRI) in Sumatra the following year, one of the very few Javanese to do so. He was roving ambassador for the PRRI and continued his anti-Sukarno activities (mainly in Malaya) after the rebellion was terminated in 1961. In 1967 he returned to Indonesia, and in June 1968 re-entered the Cabinet as Minister of Trade. He has written widely, particularly on economic subjects.

Supomo (1903–1958)

Holder of a doctorate from Leiden University, Supomo became one of Indonesia's leading authorities on *adat* or indigenous customary law. He was on the Investigating Committee for the Preparation of Independence in 1945 and, subsequently, served as Minister of Justice (twice), President of the University of Indonesia, and Ambassador in London. Before the war he belonged to moderate nationalist organizations (Budi Utomo and Parindra) and later he joined the conservative Persatuan Indonesia Raya (Greater Indonesian Union). He is the author of several legal studies in Dutch and Indonesian.

Takdir Alisjahbana, S. (1908——)

Born on the west coast of Sumatra, during the 1930's Takdir Alisjahbana wrote a number of novels and worked as an editor of the state publishing agency, Balai Pustaka. Prominent also as an editor of the literary magazine *Pudjangga Baru* (New Writers), he was a principal spokesman for the Westernizing group of Indonesian intellectuals. He graduated from the Djakarta Law School in 1941. In the late 1940's he lectured in Indonesian language and literature at the University of Indonesia and from that time onward was the head of a private publishing firm. During 1956–1957 he represented the Indonesian Socialist Party in the Constituent Assembly. After 1957 he was abroad at various universities, including Stanford, Hawaii, and the University of Malaya at Kuala Lumpur where he was Professor of Malay Studies. Under Guided Democracy his writings were severely criticized and banned from school curricula. He recently returned to Indonesia. Among his works available in English are *Indonesian Lan-*

guage and Literature: Two Essays (New Haven: Yale University Graduate School, Southeast Asia Studies, 1963) and *Indonesia: Social and Cultural Revolution* (Kuala Lumpur: Oxford University Press, 1966).

Tan Malaka (c. 1894–1949)

Born in West Sumatra, Tan Malaka was converted to Marxism while studying in Holland. In 1921 he became Chairman of the Indonesian Communist Party for two months before the first of his many imprisonments. In 1923, in Moscow, he was named director of Comintern activities for Southeast Asia and Australasia, but he fell out with the main body of the Indonesian Communists over their unsuccessful risings in 1926–1927. Thereafter the Indonesian Communist Party branded him a Trotskyist.

Returning to Indonesia during the Japanese occupation, Tan Malaka quickly rose to prominence after independence was proclaimed in 1945 and led an opposition coalition against the leadership of Sukarno as President and Sjahrir as Prime Minister, criticizing their policy of negotiation with the Dutch.

Tan Malaka's life of itinerant revolutionary activity is surrounded by an aura of mystery. The circumstances of his death during the Republic's final guerrilla struggle with the Dutch are obscure. His followers, mostly grouped around the Murba party, remained a distinctive group in Indonesian politics; among them was Adam Malik, who became Foreign Minister in 1966. Tan Malaka's fairly extensive political writings have not been translated into English.

Utami Suryadarma, Mrs. (ca. 1921——)

Born into a high Javanese family, Mrs. Utami Suryadarma married a graduate of Breda Military Academy (in the Netherlands), who was to become Chief of Staff of the Indonesian Air Force. Active in many women's and left-wing causes, she was a leading figure in the government's film censorship organizations and an active promoter of the boycott of American films in 1964–1965. She was also Rector of Res Publica University, which was operated by the Indonesian-Chinese organization Baperki until October 1965.

Widjojo Nitisastro (1927——)

Born at Malang and a member of the student army (TRIP) in East Java during the Revolution. Widjojo graduated in economics from the University of Indonesia in 1955, and from the University of California, Berkeley, in 1961. He taught at the University of Indonesia economics faculty, of which he was Dean from 1965 to 1967, and has been a principal architect of the Suharto government's economic policy. In 1968 he became chairman of the National Planning Council. His research, above all in the field of demography, has resulted in a book, *The Population of Indonesia: Past and Future* (Ithaca, N.Y.: Cornell University Press, 1970).

Wilopo (1909——)

A native of Central Java, Wilopo graduated from the Law School in Batavia in 1942. Before the war he was a founder of the nationalist party Gerindo and after independence was one of a group of younger leaders of the PNI who were close to the democratic socialists in many of their ideas. After holding several cabinet posts in the fields of labor and economic affairs, he became Prime Minister in 1952. After his government fell in 1953, he lost influence in the PNI, but served as chairman of the Constituent Assembly (1956–1959) and board member of some state enterprises. In 1968 he became chairman of the Supreme Advisory Council.

Wiranata Koesoema, R. A. A. (1888–1965)

A high aristocrat of West Java, Wiranata Koesoema studied in Europe, was for many years a regent (*bupati*) under the Dutch, and was a member of the Volksraad between 1922 and 1935. Late in the Japanese occupation, as advisor on internal affairs he held one of the highest positions accorded an Indonesian. He served as Minister of the Interior in the first cabinet of the Republic and was subsequently chairman of its Supreme Advisory Council but in 1948 became Wali Negara (head of state) of the Dutch-established state of Pasoendan in West Java. With the dissolution of this state in early 1950 he withdrew from public life.

Yamin, Muhammad (1903–1962)

Born in West Sumatra and educated at the Djakarta Law School, Muhammad Yamin became a prominent figure in prewar nationalist politics, serving in the Volksraad from 1939 to 1942. During the Revolution he was a partisan of the national-communist Tan Malaka and was imprisoned for a time. He was an advisor of the Republican delegation to the Round Table Conference at The Hague in 1949, a leading parliamentarian in the next six years, minister of Justice, Education, and Information in three of the more radical-nationalist Indonesian cabinets, and Chairman of the National Planning Council, 1959–1962. He was a poet, historian, and supporter of *adat*. The principal theme of his political career was a highly romantic nationalism.

Yani, Lieutenant General Achmad (1922–1965)

Having been trained in the Peta during the Japanese occupation, Lieutenant General Yani fought as a batallion and then brigade commander in his native Kedu region of Central Java during the war of independence.

He attended the Fort Leavenworth Staff College in the United States in 1955 and in 1958 commanded the successful campaign against the PRRI rebels in Central Sumatra. In 1962 he was appointed Minister and Chief of Staff of the Army, a post he retained till he was murdered on October 1, 1965.

Appendix II
Glossary of
Unfamiliar Terms

abangan. Element in Javanese society which is nominally Muslim but adheres to a syncretism including Hindu, Buddhist, and animist beliefs and practices as well as Muslim ones.

adat or *adat-istiadat*. Custom, tradition, customary law.

amok. Berserk.

"August Raids." In August 1951, the Sukiman cabinet arrested hundreds of political figures, mainly Communists. Most were released during the following months.

Banten or Bantam. Muslim kingdom of West Java, during the sixteenth and seventeenth centuries.

banteng. Wild buffalo.

bapak. Father.

Baperki. Badan Permusjawaratan Kewarganegaraan Indonesia, or Body for Consultation on Indonesian Citizenship; a predominantly Chinese organization and the major representative of Chinese of Indonesian citizenship until its banning in October 1965. See XId.

Berdikari. Berdiri diatas Kaki Sendiri, or "Standing on Our Own Feet"; the title of a speech given by President Sukarno to the MPRS on April 11, 1965, which then became a central economic slogan, gradually falling into disuse after October 1965.

Bhinneka Tunggal Ika. Unity in Diversity, the national motto of the Republic of Indonesia.

"Big Five." The five largest Dutch firms (mainly in exporting, importing, and estate agriculture) before their take-over in December 1957.

Bintara. Same as Demak.

Boedi Oetomo. See Budi Utomo.

Borobudur. Massive Central Javanese monument in stupa form. Its huge terraced galleries are adorned with bas-relief sculptures illustrating Mahayana Buddhist texts. Built during the latter half of the eighth century, it stands near present-day Jogjakarta.

BPS. Badan Pendukung Sukarnoisme or Badan Penjebar Sukarnoisme, Body for the Promotion of Sukarnoism; an organization established in September 1964 to fight the Communists and wean President Sukarno away from them. It was banned in early 1965.

BU. See Budi Utomo.

Budi Utomo. Noble Endeavor; formed in 1908, originally chiefly to promote Javanese cultural regeneration, it is regarded as the first modern nationalist organization.

"Building the World Anew." Title of President Sukarno's speech to the U.N. General Assembly, September 30, 1960.

Bung Karno. A fraternal way of speaking to or of President Sukarno.

bupati. Regent, administrative head of a *kabupaten* or regency.

Darmawangsa. An East Javanese king (c. 985–c. 1006).

Darul Islam. Literally, Land of Islam, the name of the rebellion led by S. M. Kartosuwirjo in West Java. Started in 1948, it drew close to an end with Kartosuwirjo's capture in May 1962 and closer with the shooting of Kahar Muzakar in South Sulawesi in February 1965. The term is used in its technical theological sense in Ve to refer to territory ruled according to Islamic law.

Dekon. Deklarasi Ekonomi or Economic Declaration; a declaration of economic policy issued by President Sukarno in March 1963.

Demak. A sixteenth-century Muslim kingdom of north-coast Central Java which became the most powerful realm in Java after the decline of Madjapahit.

Dewan Perwakilan Rakjat. DPR, the People's Representative Council, parliament.

Dewan Perwakilan Rakjat-Gotong Rojong or DPR-GR. Mutual Cooperation Parliament, the nominated parliament installed in 1960.

Diponegoro. Prince of the royal house of Jogjakarta, an opponent of European influence and a mystic who led an Islamic holy war against the Dutch, 1825–1830.

Djakarta Charter. A Document, issued on June 22, 1945, by Sukarno, Hatta, and seven other members of the Investigating Committee for the Preparation of Independence. Otherwise similar to the Preamble to the 1945 Constitution, it also incorporates "the requirement that adherents of Islam shall carry out their obligations under *sjariat* [Islamic law]."

Djarek. Djalan Revolusi Kita or "The March of Our Revolution," the title of President Sukarno's speech of August 17, 1960.

Erlangga. Eleventh-century East Javanese king.

FDR. Front Demokrasi Rakjat or People's Democratic Front, formed in February 1948 under the leadership of Amir Sjarifuddin; a coalition of parties opposed to the government of Vice-President Hatta. The constituent parties had begun a program of fusion with the PKI when the PKI-led Madiun revolt occurred in September 1948.

Gadjah Mada. Chief minister of Madjapahit from 1330 to 1364. Under his leadership Madjapahit achieved what was probably the greatest power of any precolonial Indonesian state.

gamelan. Javanese orchestra.

gotong rojong. Mutual cooperation, mutual assistance.

Gotong Rojong Cabinet. One of the formulations of President Sukarno's *Konsepsi* (Concept), of February 1957). A cabinet which would contain men of all major parties, including the PKI.

Gotong Rojong Parliament. See Dewan Perwakilan Rakjat-Gotong Rojong.

Hajam Wuruk. King of Madjapahit between 1350 and 1389.

Harian Rakjat. People's Daily, official Djakarta daily newspaper of the PKI between 1951 and 1965.

Hasanuddin. A seventeenth-century South Sulawesi sultan and now a nationalist hero.

Imam Bondjol. A Minangkabau (West Sumatra) Muslim leader who led a war against the Dutch in the 1830's.

Indische Partij. An early nationalist organization formed in 1912 with a platform of Eurasian-Indonesian cooperation. In 1913 it was renamed Partij Insulinde and in 1919 Nationaal Indische Partij. It was dissolved in 1924.

kabupaten. Administrative division headed by a *bupati*; equivalent to the prewar regency.

Karya Cabinet. Literally, "Working Cabinet," the name given to the non-party cabinet headed by Ir. Djuanda, April 1957–July 1959.

kawulo-gusti. Literally, slave and master.

Kediri. East Javanese kingdom of the eleventh to thirteenth centuries.

Linggadjati Agreement. An agreement between the Indonesian Republic and the Netherlands, initialed November 1946, signed March 1947.

lurah. Village head.

Madjapahit. East Javanese kingdom of the fourteenth and fifteenth centuries. Under the leadership of its chief minister, Gadjah Mada, the kingdom achieved probably the greatest power of any pre-colonial Indonesian state, although there is disagreement about the scope and intensity of this power.

Madjelis Permusjawaratan Rakjat (MPR). The People's Consultative Assembly, the highest organ of state, and the body to which the President is responsible under the 1945 Constitution.

Mahabharata. Hindu epic which with the other Hindu epic, *Ramayana*, provides the mythological basis for many Javanese and Balinese art forms, especially the *wajang* or puppet plays.

Manipol-USDEK. Manipol stands for Manifesto Politik, the Political Manifesto based on President Sukarno's speech of August 17, 1959; *USDEK*, an acronym intended to sum up the principal themes of *Manipol*, stands for Undang-Undang Dasar 1945 (1945 Constitution); Sosialisme Indonesia (Indonesia Socialism); Demokrasi Terpimpin (Guided Democracy); Ekonomi Terpimpin (Guided Economy); Kepribadian Indonesia (Indonesian Personality). *Manipol-USDEK* was proclaimed the Republic's central ideological formula in 1960.

Marhaenism. Indonesian proletarianism; see IVa, IVe.

Masjumi. Madjelis Sjuro Muslimin Indonesia or Council of Indonesian Muslim Associations; an Islamic political party first established under the Japanese in 1943. Established in a new form in November 1945 as a federation of many Muslim associations. Banned in August 1960; see VIc, VId.

Mataram. The name of two different Central Javanese kingdoms. The first Mataram, a Hindu state, arose in the eighth century, was temporarily eclipsed, and re-emerged late in the ninth century. The second Mataram, an Islamic kingdom, arose late in the sixteenth century. Sultan Agung, who ruled from 1613 to 1645, saw it as a continuation of Madjapahit. Mataram was gradually reduced in power by the Dutch and in 1755 was split into the small sultanates of Jogjakarta and Surakarta.

Melaju. Sumatran kingdom of the late thirteenth century, probably centered in what is now Djambi.

Mendut. Buddhist *tjandi* or temple built in the late eighth or early ninth century close to the Borobudur in Central Java.

Merdeka. Independent, free; a revolutionary greeting.

Minahasan Federation. A political association of Minahasa (North Sulawesi) during the 1930's.

Mook, Hubertus J. van. Lieutenant Governor General of the Netherlands Indies and head of the Dutch administration there from 1945 to 1948, and a principal architect of the strategy of building a federal state in Indonesia.

MPRS. Madjelis Permusjawaratan Rakjat Sementara or Provisional People's Consultative Assembly; the interim body appointed in 1960 to function as highest organ of state pending the formation of an elected MPR.

mufakat. Consensus, unanimous agreement arising out of deliberation.

Murba party. National-communist political party formed in 1948 by followers of Tan Malaka and banned in 1965.

musjawarah. Meeting, discussion, deliberation.

Nahdatul Ulama. The conservative Muslim organization established in 1926 to oppose the reformist Muhammadijah movement; cooperated with Muhammadijah in Masjumi 1943–1952, then seceded from Masjumi and functioned as a political party. See VIa.

Nasakom. Nasionalisme, Agama, Komunisme; the cooperation of national-ists, religious people, and Communists which President Sukarno frequently advocated, especially after 1960.

Nationaal Indische Partij. National Indies Party; see Indische Partij.

NICA. Netherlands Indies Civil Administration.

NU. See Nahdatul Ulama.

"Overall Development Planning" or *Pembangunan Semesta Berentjana.* The title of a speech given by President Sukarno to the National Plan-ning Council on August 28, 1959.

Padjadjaran. Sixteen-century Sundanese (West Java) kingdom. Its port was the harbor of Sunda Kelapa, the site of modern Djakarta.

Padjang. Sixteenth-century Central Javanese sultanate on the site of the present Solo (Surakarta)

pamong pradja. The territorial administrative corps (from governors to sub-district heads) functioning under the Minister of the Interior.

Panataran. Thirteenth-century Hindu-Javanese *tjandi* or temple in East Java.

Pandawa. The five Pandawa brothers are central figures in the stories of the Mahabharata and much of the Javanese *wajang* literature.

Pantja Sila. The Five Principles enunciated by Sukarno in June 1945 as the basis for the Indonesian state. They are The One Deity, Nationality, Humanity, Democracy, and Social Justice; see Ic.

Parkindo. Partai Kristen Indonesia, the Protestant political party established November 1945.

Partindo. Partai Indonesia or Indonesia Party, established in 1931 after the imprisonment of Sukarno and the banning of his PNI; strove for complete independence by a strategy of noncooperation with the Dutch. A new Partindo was formed in 1958 by left-wing seceders from the PNI.

pemuda. Youth.

Pendidikan Nasional Indonesia. National Educational Association or "New PNI" established in 1932 by Sjahrir and Hatta.

Permesta. Perdjuangan Semesta, literally, over-all struggle, the name used by the North Sulawesi arm of the 1958 regional rebellion PRRI.

permusjawaratan. Consultation, deliberation, conference.

Persatuan Indonesia Raya (PIR). Greater Indonesian Union, a conservative party established in December 1948 by supporters of Prime Minister Hatta's policy of negotiation with the Dutch.

perwakilan. Representation.

PIR. See Persatuan Indonesia Raya.

PKI. Partai Komunis Indonesia or Indonesian Communist Party, estab-lished May 1920, suppressed after the 1927 revolts, re-established Oc-tober 1945 and banned March 1966. See Section VIII.

PNI. Partai Nasional Indonesia or Indonesian Nationalist Party, established under the leadership of Sukarno in June 1927, then banned in 1930. A successor PNI, of which Sukarno has not been a member, was formed in late 1945. See IVa, IVb.

Prambanan. A complex of Hindu temples or monuments in Central Java near Jogjakarta, built probably at the beginning of the tenth century.

PRRI. Pemerintah Revolusioner Republik Indonesia or Revolutionary Government of the Republic of Indonesia. Proclaimed February 15, 1958 in West Sumatra, its Prime Minister was Sjafruddin Prawiranegara (see Biographical Notes). The rebellion came to an end in 1961 when most of its leaders "returned to the fold" of the Republic of Indonesia.

PSI. Partai Sosialis Indonesia or Indonesian Socialist Party, established in February 1948 by Sjahrir when he left the increasingly Communist-influenced Partai Sosialis (Socialist Party). The PSI was banned in August 1960. See Section VII.

PSII. Partai Sarikat Islam Indonesia or Indonesian Islamic Association Party, the new name (adopted 1929) of Sarikat Islam. Refounded in July 1947 but remained a minor party.

Raden Widjaja. Founder of the kingdom of Madjapahit.

Ratu Adil. Just king, messiah.

Renville Agreement. An agreement of January 1948 between the Indonesian Republic and the Dutch.

Resopim. Revolusi, Sosialisme Indonesia, Pimpinan Nasional or Revolution, Indonesian Socialism, National Leadership; the title given to President Sukarno's independence day speech of August 17, 1961.

Retooling. Generally, changing the political climate; specifically the process of transferring officials in government departments and agencies and replacing them by others who are ideologically better attuned. A key term under Guided Democracy.

Round Table Conference. The conference of August–November 1949 in The Hague at which delegations of the Netherlands, the Indonesian Republic, and the Dutch-built federal states agreed on the terms of Dutch withdrawal from Indonesia.

RPI. Republik Persatuan Indonesia or Republic of Indonesian Unity. A federal "state" established in 1960 by a loose association between the PRRI rebels and those of Darul Islam.

sama rasa sama rata. Literally, equality in feeling, equality in position; generally, equality.

Sandjaja. Eighth-century king of Mataram in Central Java.

Sarikat Islam. Literally, Islamic Association; Indonesia's first mass-based party under the leadership of Oemar Said Tjokroaminoto. It changed its name in 1929 to Partai Sarikat Islam Indonesia (PSII).

Serikat Islam. See Sarikat Islam.

SI. See Sarikat Islam.

Sindok. Tenth-century king of the first Central Javanese kingdom of Mataram, who moved the capital to East Java.

Singasari. East Javanese kingdom powerful in the thirteenth century.

Sriwidjaja. South Sumatra–centered empire from seventh to thirteenth century. It was a Buddhist kingdom and its power mainly maritime.

suku or *sukubangsa*. Ethnolinguistic group.

Sultan Agung. Greatest ruler of the sixteenth- to eighteenth-century kingdom of Mataram. Ruled 1613–1645.

Sundanese. A large ethnic group in West Java.

Tavip. Tahun Vivere Pericoloso or "The Year of Living Dangerously"; the title of President Sukarno's speech of August 17, 1964.

Teungku Tjik Di Tiro. An Atjehnese prince who led resistance to the Dutch attack on Atjeh in the late nineteenth century.

Tjirebon. Town of north coast of West Java, formerly a Muslim kingdom.

Tjokroaminoto, Oemar Said. Surabaja businessman under whose chairmanship Sarikat Islam was transformed from a trade association into a mass-based political party.

TNI. Tentara Nasional Indonesia or Indonesian National Army.

Ulama. Muslim religious scholar.

USDEK. See *Manipol-USDEK*.

Volksraad. The People's Council; council with colegislative powers established in Indonesia by the Dutch in 1918.

wajang. Javanese puppet theater.

wajang kulit. A type of *wajang* in which the puppets are cut from flat pieces of leather and cast shadows on a screen.

wali. A semilegendary apostle of Islam in Java; title given to religious leaders.

wedana. District Head.

"Year of Victory" or *Tahun Kemenangan*. The title of President Sukarno's speech of August 17, 1962; refers to victory in West Irian.

zakat. Religious tax or tithe in Islam, obligatory alms.

Appendix III
Chronological Table

Year	Cabinet heads and dates	Important events
1945		
		Japanese set up Investigating Committee to prepare for independence (March).
		Proclamation of Independence (Aug. 17).
	Sukarno Aug.–Nov. 1945	Indonesians fight British in Surabaja (Nov.).
1946	Sjahrir Nov. 1945–July 1947	"Social Revolution" in E. Sumatra (March). Attempted coup by Tan Malaka group ("July 3 Affair").
1947		Linggadjati Agreement with Dutch (March), recognizing the de facto authority of the Republic in Java and Sumatra. Dutch occupy large areas of the Republic in "First Attack" ("First Police Action") (July).
1948	Amir Sjarifuddin July 1947–Jan. 1948	Renville Agreement (Jan.) in which the Republic accepts its truncated territorial control.
	Hatta Jan. 1948–Aug. 1950	Communist Revolt, "Madiun Affair" (Sept.). Dutch invade Republic again in "Second Attack" ("Second Police Action") (Dec.).
1949		Vigorous Republican guerrilla activity (Jan.–July). Cease-fire (Aug.). Round Table Conference (Aug.–Nov.). Establishment of Republic of United States of Indonesia (Dec.).

Year	Cabinet heads and dates	Important events
1950		Dissolution of Dutch-sponsored federal states.
	Natsir	Unitary Republic of Indonesia proclaimed
	Sept. 1950–March 1951	(Aug.).
1951		Crisis over West Irian (Dec.).
	Sukiman	
	April 1951–Feb. 1952	"August Raids" (arrest of many Communists).
1952		
	Wilopo	Nahdatul Ulama established as a separate
	April 1952–June 1953	party (April).
		"October 17 Affair" (abortive army action against parliament).
1953		
		Tandjung Morawa incident, agrarian conflict in N. Sumatra (March).
	Ali Sastroamidjojo	Revolt in Atjeh (Sept.).
1954	July 1953–July 1955	
		Controversial economic policies favoring indigenous businessmen. Increasing interparty conflict as elections approach.
1955		Jogjakarta Conference restores army unity (Feb.).
		Afro-Asian Conference, Bandung (April).
		"June 27 Affair" (dispute between army and government).
	Burhanuddin Harahap	Parliamentary Elections (Sept.).
		Constituent Assembly Elections (Dec.).
1956	Aug. 1955–March 1956	Anti-Chinese "Assaat Movement" (March–May).
	Ali Sastroamidjojo	Army crisis: attempted coup by Zulkifli Lubis
	March 1956–March 1957	(Nov.).
		Resignation of Vice-President Hatta (Dec.).
		First regional councils established in Sumatra (Dec.).
1957		Martial law proclaimed (March).
	Djuanda	
	April 1957–July 1959	Regional movements control much of Sumatra and East Indonesia.
		"Take-overs" of Dutch property (Dec.).

Year	Cabinet heads and dates	Important events
1958		
		Rebel government (PRRI) proclaimed in Sumatra (Feb.).
		Rebels lose their last town (June).
1959		
	———— Sukarno July 1959*	Return to the 1945 Constitution (July). Political Manifesto (*Manipol*) (Aug.).
1960		Expulsion of Chinese traders from rural areas (from Jan.).
		Dissolution of elected parliament (Feb.).
		Masjumi and Socialist parties banned (Aug.).
1961		Launching of Eight-Year Over-all Development Plan (Jan.).
		End of PRRI revolt; the rebels return to the fold (June–Oct.).
		West Irian crisis mounting from December.
1962		Arrest of Sjahrir and other opposition leaders (Jan.).
		Yani replaces Nasution as Army Chief of Staff (June).
		Agreement reached to transfer W. Irian to Indonesia (Aug.).
		Beginnings of "confrontation" against Malaysia (Dec.).
1963		
		Martial Law lifted throughout Indonesia (May).
		Effort at economic stabilization (May).
		Maphilindo established (July).
		British embassy burned; "confrontation" of Malaysia stepped up (Sept.).
1964		
		Critical food situation (Feb.).
		BPS Movement (Body for the Promotion of Sukarnoism) (Sept.–Dec.).
1965		Suspension of Murba party (Jan.).
		Abortive Untung coup ("September 30 Movement").
		Massacre of Communists (Oct.–March).
1966		
		Gen. Suharto acquires emergency powers (March) and arrests Dr. Subandrio.

* De facto leadership of the Cabinet passed to Suharto in March 1966.

Index